The novels of Tobias Smollett

The novels of Tobias Smollett

Paul-Gabriel Boucé
*Translated by Antonia White
in collaboration with the author*

Longman
London and New York

Longman Group Limited London

*Associated companies, branches and representatives
throughout the world*

*Published in the United States of America
by Longman Inc., New York*

English translation © Longman Group Limited 1976

Les Romans de Smollett first published by Librairie Marcel Didier, 1971
English edition first published 1976

Library of Congress Cataloging in Publication Data

Boucé, Paul Gabriel.
　　The novels of Tobias Smollett.

　　Translation of Les romans de Smollett, which was originally presented as
the author's thesis, Sorbonne, 1971.
　　Bibliography: p.
　　Includes index
　　1. Smollett, Tobias George, 1721–1771.　I. Title
PR3696.B613　823'.6　75–31687
ISBN 0 582 50023 0

Set in IBM Baskerville 11 on 12pt
and printed in Great Britain by
Lowe and Brydone (Printers) Ltd, Thetford, Norfolk

Contents

Preface

Authors of critical studies should probably bear in mind the often quoted — but somewhat neglected — advice of *Punch* about marriage, when they set out to write a few pages of prefatory remarks. In spite of Samuel Johnson's remarkably optimistic confidence that he could write 'very well' either introductions or conclusions, a preface — which in fact nearly always turns out to be a *post*face — is a perilous exercise. It will either be skipped over by the harassed reviewer, or taken as some bona fide statement of critical purpose, and hence a convenient short cut through a detailed study.

To begin with, it is only fair to inform the reader that this book is a translation of a Sorbonne doctoral thesis, *Les Romans de Smollett*, published by Didier (Paris) in 1971. The genre of the mammoth French doctoral thesis is a fashionable target for some English and American critics[1]. Even in France, thesis-writing is considered, perhaps not unjustifiably, by a few academics as a mind-drying, jejune and wholly soulless activity. Fortunately exceptions do confirm the rule, and I can aver that I have had as much fun and literary pleasure in discovering Smollett's complex personality and his teeming fictional world as if I had been engaged in writing a novel of my own. I hope that some of this pleasurable experience will be communicated to the reader. The English version of my book presents, in somewhat abridged form, the gist of my long critical acquaintance with Smollett. Two chapters have been completely omitted: the characterological analysis of Smollett's personality — 'La personnalité de Smollett: essai d'analyse' (pp. 69–93), and the chapter on style — 'Aspects stylistiques' (pp. 392–431). Characterology and its psychological concepts have remained practically unknown in the English-speaking world, where any systematised study of human personality usually meets with raised eyebrows and diffident scepticism. The chapter on Smollett's style was written with foreigners rather than native-speakers in mind. In this English version of my book, the notes and bibliography have been updated, some slips have been corrected, and many passages rewritten rather than translated. At this point, it would be discourteous not to thank most warmly my friend Antonia White, who did most of the translating. Her thorough experience as a translator, and as a novelist — I earnestly hope that her fiction will at long last receive the critical attention and acclaim it deserves — has buoyed us up in our gloomiest moments of sheer linguistic despair.

Although I am obviously fond of Smollett's personality and works, no 'lues Smollettiana', I hope, will be detected in this study. In the chapters devoted to biography and the autobiographical elements in Smollett's novels, my purpose is not to sum up Lewis M. Knapp's scrupulously scholarly *Tobias Smollett Doctor of Men and Manners* (1949), but rather to trace what Roland Barthes in his *Sade Fourier Loyola* (1971) has called 'biographemes', that is, dominant biographical traits. Young Smollett's coming to London, like many another hunger-driven 'Sawney Agonistes' in the eighteenth century, the body-and-soul searing expedition to Cartagena (1740—41), the Knowles affair (1758—60) and the political failure of *The Briton* (1762—63) appear as the factual pivots in Smollett's life. This synthetic sketch has enabled me to detect, define, and, I hope, lay a pernicious ghost of Smollettian criticism which I have named 'inverted autobiography' — the totally unwarranted tendency to assimilate Smollett's actual personality with his most profligate or cantankerous fictional characters. In spite of A. B. Strauss's smugly supercilious assertions[2], and even after Wayne Booth, some critics in recent years have been tempted to identify Smollett, the chronic invalid, with Matthew Bramble, the ailing and no less grumbling Welsh squire in *Humphry Clinker*. Some apparently dead horses are still very much alive and kicking. Likewise, in spite of the growing mass of scholarship and criticism devoted to this no less elusive literary maverick, the so-called 'picaresque genre'[3], Smollett's novels are yet too often erroneously dubbed 'picaresque', whereas his apparently most 'picaresque' characters, such as the notorious Ferdinand Count Fathom, are but thin and bloodless '*picaros manqués*'. Finally, against a long tradition of critical detractors, I have striven to show the deep structure which, beneath the apparent factual discontinuity of Smollett's plots, underpins each novel. In spite of his (largely undeserved) reputation as a careless, slapdash and even somewhat coarsely licentious novelist, Smollett, a Scot more or less consciously marked by his Presbyterian upbringing and, even more importantly, by his own innate puritanical trends, never loses sight of the moral purpose, in true Augustan fashion, of literature.

Again, it is fashionable, but rather idle, to scoff at any systematic study in depth of an author who, first and foremost, wrote for a living. With the possible exception of Johnson, Smollett turned his hand to more literary activities than any other eighteenth-century English author. In spite of the wearisome bulk of journalistic, geographical and historical hackwriting, — which, because of its blatant didacticism, was also a way of contributing to his fellow-men's moral edification — it is obvious from his letters and the fond recollections of such staunch friends as 'Jupiter' Carlyle, that Smollett was highly conscious of his moral responsibilities as an author.

But although the novels of Smollett are more serious than a casual glance will reveal, their most secure title to literary fame rests in their wide gamut of sparkling comedy, ranging from the most traditional slap-stick to the most delicate protean web of symplectic humour, as evidenced in Win Jenkins's and her mistress Tabitha Bramble's creative murdering of the English language in *Humphry Clinker*, Smollett's last and undoubtedly best novel. It matters little, at this point, whether Fielding should be rated a better writer than Smollett. This irritating but all too frequent reflex of hard-dying literary docimology — the critic assuming the presumptuous role of an omnipotent, if not omniscient, headmaster at a prize-giving — is not only totally irrelevant but damagingly misleading. Why can't Fielding *and* Smollett be enjoyed in their own right? The subtle structural architectonics of *Joseph Andrews*, and even more so of *Tom Jones*, are as pleasurable as the quintuple prismatic vision in *Humphry Clinker*, but neither more nor less so. In fact, Fielding and Smollett, who are so often lumped together, very much to the critical disadvantage of the latter, are complementary. Fielding's wellbred and courageously optimistic (at least on the surface) view of contemporary society should be balanced by Smollett's more down-to-earth and dour conception of life.

More than ever the plucky and verdant optimism of the Smollett family motto, *Viresco*, is justified, at least on the critical plane. The amount of attention devoted to Smollett and his novels in recent years, the courageous scholarly venture of the Iowa Smollett edition, bid fair to restore Smollett, *le mal aimé* of eighteenth-century English literature, to the enjoyment of an increasing public. If my book may contribute, how-ever little, towards this aim, then I will deem my time and labours not totally wasted.

Sorbonne Nouvelle   *Paul-Gabriel Boucé*
December 1974

Part I
From Smollett to his novels

I
Biographical sketch

Twenty-five years after Smollett's death, the *Scots Magazine*[1] of November 1796 was already complaining of a certain obscurity which enveloped Smollett's life: 'Of the personal history of Smollett, less is known than his rank in English literature might give reason to expect.' Thanks to the labours of nineteenth-century biographers, and most of all to those of Knapp in the twentieth century, the areas of shadow in Smollett's life have been reduced, but nevertheless they still persist. Thus his early years in Scotland are veiled in an obscurity which biographers have often tried to dissipate by the wavering and deceptive light of an arbitrary autobiographical interpretation. In the absence of precise documentation, the chapters in his novels dealing with childhood, particularly those in *Roderick Random*, are used to supply the deficiency. Or again, a romantic and probably romanticised description of the places where he spent his childhood furnishes biographers with material to fill some pages with padding which conveniently serves to disguise the lack of accurate knowledge. Finally, it is all too usual to find these biographers indulging in learned genealogical dissertations, thus showing that they have forgotten Fielding's ironical warning at the beginning of *Jonathan Wild*: 'I have conjectured that the design of the biographer hath been no more than to shew his great learning and knowledge of antiquity'[2].

Before tracing the outline of Smollett's life, what geological folds is it possible to discern in the jagged landscape of those fifty years so crested with successes, yet so deeply furrowed with failures and calamities? From 1721 to 1746–47, the date of his first known literary publications (*The Tears of Scotland*, 1746; *Advice*, 1746; *Reproof*, 1747), Smollett knew his *Lehrjahre* and also his *Wanderjahre*. The story of those years, had it not been for Smollett's exceptional personality, would have been almost commonplace for an eighteenth-century Scot. Like so many others, he is struggling to make his way and that way lies down the road from Scotland to London. He is the typical example of that Scotsman 'on the make', scorned, detested and vilified by eighteenth-century Englishmen who resented the frequently successful intrusion of their northern neighbours, as famished as they were clever and enterprising. The young Smollett is seething with ambition; literary, social and perhaps medical as well. But, without being as isolated and deprived of financial means as his first biographers have said, he must have relied mainly on himself in that London jungle where man — *Homo homini lupus* as Smollett likes to reiterate in his novels — has constantly to maintain a fierce struggle for survival. So, from 1721—47 it is possible to see Smollett as a 'Sawney Agonistes'.

This arduous uphill period is followed by a dozen years (1748—60) of such intense and prodigious literary — or paraliterary — activity that it makes Smollett, along with Johnson, one of the most hard-working, not to say hard-up, authors in England in the eighteenth century. In five years Smollett writes and publishes three of his five novels: *Roderick Random* (1748), *Peregrine Pickle* (1751) and *Ferdinand Count Fathom* (1753). To the production of these works of fiction must be added, perhaps the better to emphasise the contrast, his medical, critical, theatrical and historical publications. It was a painfully ambiguous activity, devoted on the one hand to imaginative creation, but on the other to that more practical and less inspiring form of literature known as pot-boiling. This second period is one of literary successes and literary slavery.

Finally, the last ten years (1761—71) are far from constituting the serene apotheosis of a life too often rendered difficult by a chronic short-age of money. On the contrary, these years are racked with cruel mis-fortunes. The failure of *The Briton* (1762—63), the death of his daughter (1763), and the premature erosion of a constitution exhausted by Herculean labours as a galley-slave of letters, give them a tormented, even tragic character. The two years (1763—65) spent in the south of France allowed a remission in Smollett's physical decline. In fact he seems not to have been so weak, in the evening of his life, as nearly all the biographers before Knapp have liked to say.

But there was nothing — at least to all appearance — to forecast the last novel (1771), published three months before his death. The eight volumes of *Present State* (1768—69) are only a compilation. *Travels through France and Italy* (1766) is like a commemorative tablet, too long forgotten by the public and the critics; Smollett, while preserving the anonymous mask of the splenetic traveller also carved on it his own hopes of health, his fears and his anguish as well as his comments, often more mischievous than spiteful, on the spontaneous genius, sometimes irritating in its levity, of the Latin nations. Finally, in *The History and Adventures of an Atom* (presuming that he really wrote that ferocious satire) his indignation, his political, social and human bitterness blaze up at white heat and perhaps his long-repressed obsessions also explode. If one day biographical and bibliographical research proves that Smollett is *not* the author of *The History and Adventures of an Atom*, it must nevertheless be admitted that his passionate nature might very well have vented itself in a similar volcanic eruption. It was not in the flat, sunlit calm of his Italian retreat that Smollett found peace at last, but in the achievement of his masterpiece, *Humphry Clinker*, the peak which dominates the whole of his literary creation. So this last period might be called 'the difficult years'.

The exact date of Smollett's birth is not known. Only Smeaton[3] gives it as March 16th 1721, but without producing any verifiable proof. On the other hand, it is certain that Tobias was baptised on Sunday, March 19th, in the parish church of Cardross, Dumbartonshire[4]. He was born on the estate of Dalquhurn, near Bonhill, where his grandfather, James Smollett (1648?–1731), lived in the old family mansion.

Smollett's family, without being an exceptionally old one, had been settled in Dumbarton and in the little neighbouring villages from the beginning of the sixteenth century[5]. They belonged to the thrifty, hard-headed Scottish squirearchy, which included lawyers as well as merchants and soldiers among its members. Smollett's grandfather played an important role in the religious and political affairs of his time. He adopted the principles of the Revolution of 1688 and, in spite of the opposition of his fellow-citizens, participated actively in the drawing-up of the Act of Union in 1707. Thus Smollett was brought up in a Whig family. Tobias's father, Archibald, who was delicate and unable to lead an active life, married Barbara Cunningham without his own father's consent. The similarity of this situation to the one described by Smollett in the opening chapter of *Roderick Random* has caused James Smollett to be identified with the irascible old judge of the novel, but the assumption that he is writing autobiographically is for the most part unwarranted.

Smollett was the last of three children. His elder brother James, a captain in the army, died in a shipwreck on the way to being posted to America. His sister Jane survived her two brothers and it is from her that the present representatives of the family are descended. The Telfer-Smolletts still live in the magnificent ancestral home on the shores of Loch Lomond, Cameron House, of which Smollett speaks with so much aesthetic and patriotic fervour in *Humphry Clinker*. Smollett's father, Archibald, died soon after the birth of Tobias, who was thus too young to suffer an emotional shock, though it is probable that this absence of paternal authority had a permanent psychological effect on him. It is disquieting to note that the fathers of his heroes either vanish early from the scene or, worse still, are conspicuous for their total intellectual and emotional vacuity, as in the case of the apathetic Gamaliel Pickle. It is undeniable that Smollett always had a deep affection for his mother who lived until 1770. According to his own evidence, he seems to have felt the loss of his brother very keenly, for, in a letter to Alexander Carlyle about the death of a friend's brother, he writes: 'I once sustained the same Calamity, in the Death of a Brother whom I loved and honoured'[6].

More important than genealogical details is the pride in his ancestry which Smollett retained all his life. Only Walter Scott stresses from the outset this essential element in his personality:

> Our author was descended from an ancient and honourable family; an advantage, to which, from various passages in his writings, he seems to have attached considerable weight, and the consciousness of which seems to have contributed its share in forming some of the peculiarities of his character[7].

Smollett's preoccupation with his family tree is ingenuously displayed in one of his letters to a cousin: 'I begin to think we were originally Malet or Molet and came from Normandy with the Conqueror'[8]. So Smollett was not immune from the snobbery of Norman descent, a snobbery which has far from disappeared in the England of our own day. In this same letter he expresses his desire to collect all the anecdotes concerning his family, some of whom were 'freeholders in Dumbarton four hundred years ago'. Another proof of his attachment to the name and fame of the Smolletts: Matthew Bramble in *Humphry Clinker* recalls that in one of the bays of the Isle of Mull 'the Florida, a ship of the Spanish armada was blown up by one of Mr Smollett's ancestors'[9]. This piece of genealogical bragging had already featured in the now completely forgotten pages of *The Present State* (1768–69): 'The Florida, one of the largest ships of the Spanish armada, was blown up by one Smollet of Dunbarton'[10].

Nearly all the biographers attribute a formative importance to the places where Smollett spent his childhood. The adjective they most frequently use to describe the banks of Loch Lomond and the green valley of the Leven is 'romantic'. One wonders how far that is a pious reconstruction *a posteriori* of sentiments which never troubled young Smollett. Smollett's early years were bathed in a light far more earthly than celestial if one accepts the fact that the descriptions of Roderick and Peregrine in the opening chapters of the novels are not literally autobiographical but represent experiences he had lived through. The awakening of Smollett's sensibility to the charms of his native land is a much later and mainly literary manifestation of nostalgia. It would be dangerous to accept unreservedly the ironic, not to say, brutal allegations of George Orwell on the subject of the poetry, or absence of poetry, of boyhood:

> A boy isn't interested in meadows, groves and so forth. He never looks at a landscape, doesn't give a damn for flowers, and unless they affect him in some way, such as being good to eat, he doesn't know

one plant from another. Killing things — that's about as near to poetry as a boy gets[11].

Wordsworth and his 'Intimations of Immortality' get short shrift from Orwell! But this unromantic view of the psychology of boyhood is remarkably well borne out by the unedifying exploits of those young scoundrels Roderick and Peregrine. Roderick, as no doubt did Tobias, delights in fierce hand-to-hand fights in which teeth, legs and heads are broken and bruised with true Celtic vigour. The local schoolmaster makes liberal use of the whip and, if necessary, the dogs are set on Roderick. It is surprising to note, too, how readily the grown-ups — Bowling in *Roderick Random*, Hatchway and Pipes in *Peregrine Pickle* — join the children on punitive expeditions or to play crude practical jokes in more than dubious taste, euphemistically described by Smollett (*Peregrine Pickle*, Ch. xi) as 'little childish satire'.

Young Tobias entered the school of Dumbarton about 1727 or 1728. His headmaster was the celebrated grammarian John Love (1695–1750), whom Smollett denied having ridiculed in the character of the loathsome schoolmaster in *Roderick Random*. Greek and Latin formed the basis of his education. Smollett and his Scottish heroes, proud of the acknowledged superiority of their native land in academic learning, do not fail to make frequent quotations from Greek or Latin authors, particularly from Horace[12]. It may be safely assumed that Roderick's progress at school mirrors that of Smollett himself when he writes in *Roderick Random*: 'I became a good proficient in the Latin tongue'[13], or again: 'I made a surprising progress in the classics, writing and arithmetic'[14].

In November 1735 Smollett is working in a dispensary in Glasgow. His choice of the medical profession — or, to be precise, his apprenticeship as a surgeon — was perhaps, according to Moore and Anderson, more influenced by his friendly relations with a group of medical students than by a genuine vocation. No trace of Smollett's enrolment at Glasgow University has been discovered, but in those days fourteen was not an unusual age for entering the university. Alexander Carlyle became an undergraduate at Edinburgh University, also in November 1735, at the age of thirteen. It is curious to note that Carlyle nearly took up medicine himself under the influence of two friends. But the horror of dissecting the corpse of a child (bought for six shillings from its father, a poor tailor who wanted sixpence more for it) dissuaded him for ever from pursuing such studies[15]. In April 1736 Smollett began to serve his apprenticeship — theoretically five years — to two famous Glasgow surgeons, William Stirling and John Gordon whom Smollett was accused, perhaps wrongly, of grotesquely caricaturing as Potion in *Roderick Random*.

Those four years (1735–39) spent in Glasgow contributed in two important ways to his formation as a novelist. On the one hand, his apprenticeship to surgery with Gordon familiarised him with the systematic observation of physical, physiological and even pathological facts. The spectacle of misery and disease accustomed the lad to facing the most shattering realities without flinching. Nevertheless, in spite of this professional callousness at the daily sight of human decay, young Smollett's sensitivity was only dormant, not dead. The description of the appalling sanitary conditions of the sick and wounded on board the ship during the expedition to Cartagena sounds like a long cry of impotent rage and disgust. In anachronistic terms, it reads also like a reporter's thorough coverage, marked by apparent professional detachment and, in fact, instinct with deep personal commitment. It was thus an apprenticeship to life as well as to surgery that he was serving during those years.

On the other hand, Smollett continued his literary studies at the university, and there exists a tradition, reported by Moore, that during that time he exercised his natural bent for satire and loosed the first shafts of his barbed wit. His targets in those lost poems (still according to Moore) were not only young beaus and affected coquettes, but also worthy Glasgow merchants, stuffed with self-importance and good jingling guineas, sharp practitioners in business but pillars of propriety in the Kirk. It is obvious that Smollett already possessed that infallible talent for making enemies. These satirical efforts 'gave offence to the more serious part of the citizens' says Moore[16] with discreet brevity. Already Smollett was seized with satirical and literary ambition.

The exact reasons for his departure to London about the middle of the year 1739 remain obscure. He had not finished his five years of apprenticeship. He knew, since the death of his cousin James Smollett in 1738, that he could no longer count on much in the way of financial help. But the prospect of an approaching war with Spain (hence the need for ships' surgeons) and above all the idea of making his fortune in the theatre, thanks to the tragedy *The Regicide* which he had in his pocket, must have contributed to the young Scottish Rastignac's decision.

In London Smollett had two aims: to secure a means of livelihood as soon as possible and to try to get his *Regicide* performed. He suffered the first, but not the last, setback to his theatrical ambitions. By way of compensation, he received his surgeon's mate's warrant on March 10th 1740 and embarked on the *Chichester*, a large ship carrying eighty guns and 600 men. It was on board the *Chichester* that he sailed for Jamaica on October 26th 1740 with the rest of Sir Chaloner Ogle's fleet. His home life in Scotland and his medical training had been the prelude to an experience which was to leave a permanent imprint on his life and work, the experience of life at sea.

It was undoubtedly Thomas Carlyle who saw better than anyone how profoundly important the Cartagena expedition was to Smollett. If Carlyle's florid rhetorical style seems slightly ridiculous to a modern reader, the vigour of his thought and, in this case, the accuracy of his judgment can still be admired:

Excellent Tobias; he has, little as he hopes it, something considerable by way of mission in this Expedition, and in this Universe generally. Mission to take Portraiture of English Seamanhood with due grimness, due fidelity; and convey the same to remote generations before it vanish[17].

The expedition was a combined naval and military operation against Cartagena, then in the possession of the Spanish and now the capital of the province of Bolivar in Columbia. The fleet — a considerable force of some 125 vessels of which twenty were heavily armed ships of the line carrying seventy or eighty guns — was under the command of Admiral Vernon, and the embarked troops were under General Wentworth. The expedition began by winning some partial successes by capturing, on March 9th 1741, the forts which defended the outer harbour, known as Boca-chica. But it remained to reduce the fort of Saint-Lazar, which dominated the town of Cartagena. It was here that the lack of cooperation between Vernon and Wentworth became most disastrously apparent.

The admiral, haughty, choleric and full of contempt for the general — an irresolute man who was probably less up to his task than Lord Cathcart, who had originally commanded the land forces, but who had died on his arrival in Jamaica — refused to bombard Cartagena. Without artillery support, Wentworth's troops, badly guided by a deserter, were massacred outside the fort of Saint-Lazar in a heroic but vain attempt to storm it. The troops suffered less from this defeat than from the tropical diseases that ravaged them. It was the rainy season, more than the resistance of the Spaniards, that surprised and vanquished the assailants. Vernon, who, as a good sailor, did not wish to risk losing his ships, wanted to prove, with the help of a captured Spanish vessel the *Galicia*, that it was impossible to approach near enough to the town to bombard it effectively. This ship, anchored in shallow water, was moored too far from the walls to cause any real damage to the town and, during the retreat, it finally ran aground on a sandbank. It needed no more, according to Admiral Vernon, to prove that the town was unassailable from the sea. It is on this point that Smollett, in his fictional account (*Roderick Random*), in his 'Account of the Expedition against Carthagene' (published in 1756 in *The Compendium of Voyages*) and in his *Complete History of England*, vigorously attacks Vernon, after having insisted all through the account on the disastrous disagreement between the two commanders and particularly on Vernon's constant refusal to cooperate:

but a little farther to the left, he might have stationed four or five of his largest ships abreast, within pistol shot of the walls; and if this step had been taken, when the land forces marched to the attack of St Lazar, in all probability the town would have been surrendered[18].

What were the consequences for Smollett of this expedition to Cartagena? First of all, from these two years spent in the Navy he conceived, on the one hand, a profound disgust for the strategic ineptitude of military commanders and, on the other, a permanent horror of the appalling sanitary conditions in which the sick and wounded were cared for — or rather left to their fate — on board the ships. One reads the same indignation, often in identical terms, in *Roderick Random* and in the 'Account' published fifteen years after the events. Even though, as Martz justly points out, there has been a change between the youthful novel boiling with satirical indignation and the historical account intended to be professional and impartial from 'wanton scorn to rational judgement'[19], it is the medical passages which have been the least altered. It is undeniable that those passages in *Roderick Random* had the merit of arousing the indignation of the public, which had hitherto cared little about the conditions of life at sea, and led the Admiralty to take some hygienic and humanitarian measures. No commentator seems to have stressed the fact that the hell of Cartagena left such a permanent scar on Smollett that in *The Present State*, which appeared in 1768—69, more than twenty-five years after the expedition, he devotes a page to describing the debilitating climate of Cartagena and the diseases it engendered, in particular yellow fever, which killed more than half the 16,000 soldiers and sailors of the expedition: 'The climate of Carthagena is excessive hot. . . . The diseases that make the greatest havock here, especially among the Europeans, are a species of the vomito prieto, or black vomit, called chapoteado, and the leprosy'[20]. This repeated condemnation of the command of the Cartagena expedition earned Smollett the resentment of the Navy in general, all the more so because a detailed analysis of the 'Account' shows that it is finally more on Vernon's shoulders than on Wentworth's that he lays the blame: 'In a word, the admiral was a man of weak understanding, strong prejudices, boundless arrogance, and overboiling passions; and the general, *though he had some parts*, was wholly defective in point of experience, confidence, and resolution'[21]. A second time Smollett implicitly lays the responsibility for the defeat on Vernon, who forced Wentworth to attack Saint-Lazar by his arrogant, jeering letters to the general whose main reason for launching the attack 'seems to have been the importunity of the admiral who . . . vehemently pressed him to the attack saying that it was scarce possible to miscarry'[22]. Finally Smollett repeatedly stresses[23] Vernon's refusal to cooperate, and advances nothing in his defence, whereas at the end of the 'Account' he draws attention to the courage of General Wentworth who 'in person brought up the rear'[24] and, as a man careful of his equipment, ordered five tents and some tools left behind by the American regiment to be loaded on to the ship.

Finally, before ending this synthetic survey of the consequences of the Cartagena expedition in Smollett's life, it is impossible not to mention the remote origin of the hostility of Admiral Knowles — a rancour which broke out in the libel action he brought against the *Critical Review* for the damaging article of May 1758. During the expedition to Cartagena, Knowles was in command of the *Weymouth* and no documents exist to prove that Smollett had any direct contact with him then. It is tempting to suppose that he did but it would be very difficult to support the hypothesis. Like the expedition to Rochefort in 1757, the expedition to Cartagena was a battle fought twice: first on the actual terrain and subsequently in London, where the defeat of the English provoked a veritable war of pamphlets. Among these, Knowles composed *An Account of the Expedition to Carthagena*[25] which must not be confused with Smollett's 'Account'. This pamphlet is a vigorous, but highly partial defence of the Navy at the expense of the Army, whose officers Knowles describes as 'abandoned wretches of the town whose prostitution had made them useful on some dirty occasion, and by way of Reward were provided for in the Army' (p. 55). The American officers of the expedition excited Knowles's contempt equally:

> . . . blacksmiths, taylors, shoemakers and all the banditti that country affords, insomuch that the other parts of the army held them in scorn. And as for engineers, bombardiers, and gunners, worse never bore the name, or could be picked out of all Europe (p. 58).

Each having received his reprimand, Knowles nevertheless achnowledges that the privates 'though they were raw and undisciplined, they wanted not for courage and resolution becoming Englishmen' (p. 58). Such verbal courtesies could only provoke a reply defending the land forces: this reply was *A Journal of the Expedition to Carthagena*[26] attributed in the British Museum catalogue (with considerable circumspection) to Smollett. In this little work the author sticks to refuting systematically, point by point and item by item, the accusations levied by Knowles against the land forces. Knowles's 'Account' is stigmatised as a 'pamphlet made up of glaring falsehoods, facts misrepresented, and mean personal reflections' (p. 48). The responsibility for the defeat is directly attributed to the Navy and Admiral Vernon:

> It may not be difficult to make appear that our great ships lying inactive at a time when they might have been usefully employ'd, was the principal occasion of our not possessing ourselves of the city of Carthagena, and not the miscarriage of the attack of St Lazar (p. 41).

However, the controversy did not end there[27]. Admiral Vernon, in his turn, published *Original Papers Relating to the Expedition of Carthagena* (1744), and a certain L. Raymond, in the same year, wrote *Authentic Papers Relating to the Expedition of Carthagena*.

If Smollett really did compose the *Journal* of 1744 which retorted to Knowles's *Account*, this would better explain Knowles's animosity in the libel action of 1758 which ended in 1760 by Smollett's being found guilty and sent to prison. In fact, it is difficult to recognise Smollett's style in this dry report which counters Knowles's arguments on technical grounds. As Martz says, this *Journal* is 'patently written by a member of the land-forces who witnessed all the operations ashore'[28]. But Martz shows that, in composing his 'Account', published in 1756, Smollett drew largely on the *Journal*.

After her return to Britain in September 1741, the name of Smollett remained on the payroll of the *Chichester* till February 1742[29]. After that all trace of his life is lost until May 1744. But meanwhile, in order to forget the horrors of Mars, he had succumbed to the charms of Venus. It was probably in 1743, during another visit to Jamaica, that Smollett married Anne Lassells[30], the heiress of a well-to-do family of planters. It seems that his young wife did not join him in London before 1747, but, owing to the complete lack of documents, his biographers are reduced to conjecture.

After the war, love and his first literary efforts — patriotic and satirical poetry, drama — mark the difficult beginnings of the career of the young 'Sawney Agonistes' in London up to 1747. Although *The Regicide* was not published till 1749, it is more logical to examine that unfortunate tragedy now, because from 1745 to 1747, Smollett redoubled the efforts he had been making since 1742 to get his play performed.

When the news of the battle of Culloden (April 16th 1746) reached London, 'the nation was transported with joy, and extolled the duke of Cumberland as a hero and deliverer'[31]. It is unlikely, on the evidence of Alexander Carlyle in his *Autobiography*, that Smollett shared in this public rejoicing. The horrors of the expedition to Cartagena were still too fresh in his memory, and Smollett, although no Jacobite, was too attached to his native land not to be grieved and indignant at the fate that lay in store for the vanquished Highlanders. In modern history, these mopping-up operations are discreetly described as 'repression'. Herbert sums up the situation with admirable terseness: '1746 was a busy year for judges, juries, hangmen, headsmen, and Smollett'[32]. The poem composed by Smollett 'The Tears of Scotland'[33] is that of a sincere patriot, aroused equally to pity and indignation by his country's wrongs and, in spite of certain conventional expressions, it represents together with the 'Ode to Independence' (1766), his best poetical work. No critic has drawn a parallel between the poem and the account of Cumberland's atrocities in the *Complete History of England*[34] published by Smollett ten years later. The paragraph in the history describing the ravages and devastation wrought by the troops of 'Butcher Cumberland' closely reproduces the poetical description of them in 'The Tears of Scotland', though it shows a systematic adaptation of style to suit the more sober requirements of historical narrative.

This *saeva indignatio* takes a more social, moral and personal form in

Advice: a Satire (1746)[35] and the complementary poem *Reproof: a Satire* which appeared in the following year. These two juvenile poems, which have all the pungency of Greek satirical verse, add nothing to Smollett's literary reputation. Inspired in turn by Juvenal, Pope[36] and Swift, the violence of the social satire is all the better maintained by Smollett's using the convenient device of dialogue, in which the friend of the poet feigns to vindicate vice, or the amoral conduct which facilitates social advancement, in order the better to allow the poet (mainly Smollett himself) to express his disgust and indignation at the corruption of sexual, political and literary morals. It was an 'angry young man' of the eighteenth century who composed these two satires. One is aware, behind 'that petulance of stile' [*sic*] [37], of Smollett's inflexible morality. It is stamped on this fine line, whose complete sincerity it would be hard to doubt: 'Two things I dread, my conscience and the law'; or again in this cruelly lucid diagnosis of the poet by his friend:

Friend.   'Too coy to flatter, and too proud to serve,
             Thine be the joyless dignity to starve.

Poet.   No; thanks to discord, war shall be my friend'[38].

On the threshold of his career, Smollett already knew himself destined to a hard fight. The lines quoted above might serve equally well as the epitaph or the epigraph to his battler's life. What do these two short poems — less than 300 lines — contribute to our knowledge of Smollett's character? First, they display a curious faculty that one might call 'lucid double vision'. The poet's friend foresees all the difficulties which Smollett's lofty morality is going to encounter in a world of dishonourable compromises. The poet cares not a whit for them and forcefully, indeed violently, affirms his determination to fight for his ideals. This tendency even goes so far as an implicit self-criticism in *Reproof*:

        Thy flowers of poetry that smell so strong,
        The keenest appetites have loath'd the song;[39].

But however rationally he analyses these future difficulties, it is the passionate and aggressive element that dominates these poems. The last words of *Reproof* are 'pity and defy'. Next, these two poems, which Knapp (p. 63) has described as 'a representative rogues' gallery of the time', already demonstrate Smollett's talent for caricature. In a series of satirical vignettes, the homosexual, the cowardly general, the miser, the coquette, are sketched with deadly precision in a few sharp strokes. The sometimes misogynous author of *Roderick Random* is already discernible in this vivid sketch from the life in *Reproof* (lines 17—18):

        While the vain fop, with apish grin, regards
        The gig'ling minx half choked behind her cards.

Lastly, it is also possible to discern that alternation of extreme contrasts which characterises all Smollett's work. Immediately after the patriotic and poetic flights of 'The Tears of Scotland', he plunges into the occasionally brutal satirising of a corrupt world. The lyrical emotionalism of the first poem is followed by the coarse realism of *Advice* and *Reproof*. But, as Buck observes, these three poems have also something in common: 'Smollett's characteristic "wrathiness" is the very breath of their being'[40].

This irascible temperament was submitted to a tough ordeal in the vicissitudes of his tragedy, *The Regicide*, composed when he was eighteen but not published — and then only by subscription — till ten years later, in 1749. The chronology of the tribulations of this unfortunate play, which patrons, actors and theatrical managers (Fleetwood, Quin, Lacy, Chesterfield, Rich and Garrick) tried to pass on to each other like a bad guinea between 1742 and 1747, has been established by Buck and repeated by Knapp with too much precision of detail to need reproducing here[41]. Few critics have found anything whatever to praise in it. On the contrary, it was severely criticised and viciously attacked even in Smollett's own lifetime[42]. The use of the grossest physical insults is rarely absent from the criticism — or rather the satirical lambasting — of the eighteenth century. Charles Churchill, the friend and collaborator of John Wilkes, in *The Apology Addressed to the Critical Reviewers* (1761) is more subtle and refined when he proclaims (lines 156—9):

> Whoever read the Regicide, but swore
> The author wrote as man ne'er wrote before?
> Others for plots and under-plots may call,
> Here's the right method — have no plot at all.

Even Alexander Carlyle, in spite of his friendship with the author, shows no enthusiasm for this tragedy which Smollett 'never could bring on the stage. For this the managers could not be blamed, though it soured him against them, and he appealed to the public by printing it; but the public seemed to take part with the managers'[43]. The preface to *The Regicide* written in 1749, equally earned severe rebukes. Herbert (p. 17) calls it 'puling' and Hannay[44], although the only one to make an impartial analysis of the tragedy, does not hesitate to condemn it as 'lamentable reading' (p. 23). Both criticisms are exaggerated. When he revised this preface in 1749, on the one hand Smollett displayed his usual stubborn pugnacity, on the other he could not conceal his almost visceral attachment to this work. Smollett used obstetrical terms, speaking of 'the miscarriage of all [his] efforts', and again of this 'miserable abortion'[45] condemned to oblivion for two years until his 'paternal sense' should once more be awakened. These words are not mere medical clichés, but express, perhaps unconsciously, all the long drama of this painful childbirth. With children of the mind, as with those of the flesh, it is those produced after a difficult labour that are the object of the tenderest love and solicitude.

Without wanting to prove at all costs that this tragedy is an unrecognised masterpiece — which, of course, would be impossible — it does seem that it has often been condemned without fair trial. The prime cause of its failure lies less in the clumsiness, occasionally ludicrous, of its bombastic style than in the profound antagonism between a violent, sombre, bloody subject worthy of Elizabethan or Jacobean tragedy and the classical form of a 'regular tragedy, confined within the unities of the drama'[46]. The murder[47] of the Scottish poet-king James I at Perth in 1437 was a subject worthy of Shakespeare. Smollett must have felt so, for *The Regicide* is not without echoes of *Macbeth*, though his mechanical blank verse was incapable of creating the atmosphere of blood and horror that broods over *Macbeth*. The characters who bear such picturesque names as Grime and Cattan are mere puppets, manipulated with a total lack of artistry. Angus is the faithful servant, Dunbar is the impetuous warrior, even in love, which partly explains the preference of Eleonora, Angus's daughter, for the young rebel Stuart. Hannay describes Eleonora as 'shadowy' (p. 25). Nevertheless she is the most tragic character in the play. Eleonora *might* have been a great classic heroine, torn between her family's honour and her guilty passion for Stuart. It is a theme worthy of Corneille: indeed Eleonora's apparent marble inflexibility occasionally gives her a faint, crude resemblance to Chimène, but she is also a potential Phèdre or Hermione in her transports of jealousy. As opposed to this classic heroine and the classic theme of conflict between reason and passion, we have the Elizabethan barbarism of the rebel chieftain Athol, of young Stuart and of Grime (who bears some resemblance to Iago). Here are the words in which Stuart welcomes the plan of murdering the king (Act IV, scene 2)[48]:

> O wond'rous plan
> Of unrestrained barbarity! — It suits
> The horrors of my bosom! All! What, all!
> In slaughtered heaps — the progeny and the sire!
> To sluice them in th'unguarded hour of rest!

Smollett — at least in the definitive version we possess, for, in ten years the play was frequently revised — is not embarrassed by the classical unities. But all the good characters (Angus and the king and queen) are cardboard. Dunbar is pathetic in his youthful clumsiness. When he tries to conquer Eleonora, he seems to be mounting to the assault of a stronghold. Among the bad ones, Stuart is too frenzied a fanatic to be tragic. Finally, the innumerable exclamations of rage, the final duet between Dunbar and Eleonora who die declaiming interminable tirades containing such lines as 'O crocodile! — Curse on these faithless drops' (IV, 3), or again such expressions as 'grimly smiling Grime' (IV, 5) have contributed to relegating this tragedy, whose subject[49] deserved to be treated by Kyd or Tourneur, to total oblivion. This was a wound to Smollett's self-esteem

15

which his literary successes in other fields never completely healed.

Thus until 1747 Smollett's life was dominated by frustration. Frustration of his professional, social and literary ambitions — the last in the one nearest his heart, the theatre — even though his first three poems had earned him a certain esteem. The success of *Roderick Random* was to be the beginning of a luckier period for him. From 1748 to 1760, Smollett is gradually building up his literary and social success. But, some two-thirds through those twelve years, 1756 marks a change of direction. From 1748 to 1755 intense literary activity, and also the persistence of his money troubles and of his theatrical and medical ambitions sum up Smollett's life; from 1756 to 1760, if his laborious activity is at its highest point, it is less a question of purely literary creation than of a gigantic task of organisation, research and compilation. These labours, though they gave him more financial stability, especially after the publication of *The Complete History of England* in 1757—58, undermined Smollett's health. At the same time editorship of the *Critical Review*, founded in 1756, plunged him into a series of fierce critical and even legal controversies, guerrilla warfare in which literary grievances were merely a flimsy pretext for the expression of personal rancours and hatreds.

Perhaps the arrival of his wife from Jamaica about 1747 and the birth of his only daughter Elizabeth in the same year, or in 1748, stimulated Smollett's creative genius. The fact remains that *Roderick Random* was written quickly. With the complaisance of a self-satisfied young author, he tells his friend Carlyle how rapidly he wrote it:

> I am tempted to discover that the whole was begun and finished in the Compass of Eight Months, during which time several Intervals happened of one, two, three & four Weeks, wherein I did not set pen to paper, so that a little Incorrectness may be excused[50].

The novel appeared in January 1748 and its success was 'immediate, impressive and prolonged'[51].

As Knapp has shown in two articles[52], *Roderick Random* reached its fourth edition in January 1750; William Strahan printed some 6,500 copies between January 1748 and November 1749. This success may be slight in comparison with that of *Joseph Andrews*, of which the same number of copies was sold within a year after publication, or the 10,000 copies of *Tom Jones* sold less than a year after it appeared. But the situation of the two novelists can hardly be compared. In 1742 Fielding already had an established literary reputation behind him, whereas in 1748 Smollett was still only the obscure author of two satires, *Advice* and *Reproof* and a patriotic poem, 'The Tears of Scotland'. Even the blue-stocking, Miss Talbot, who had just somewhat regretfully left the peace and solitude of Canterbury for the turmoil of London, hastened to ask her friend, Mrs Carter:

Have you read that Strange book Roderic [*sic*] Random! It is a very strange and a very low one, though not without some characters in it, and I believe some very just, though very wretched descriptions. Among others there is the history of a poor tragedy author, ill used by actors and managers, that I think one cannot but be touched with, when one considers how many such kinds of scenes there are every day in real life[53].

Obviously, the story of Melopoyn had moved Miss Talbot. The novel did not bear the name of the author, and many readers thought it was the work of Fielding. Lady Mary Wortley Montagu, having read *Roderick Random* when she was abroad in 1752, after confessing in a letter to her daughter, the Countess of Bute, 'I was such an old fool as to weep over Clarissa Harlowe like any milk maid of sixteen', goes on to say, 'There is something Humourous in R. Random, that makes me beleive the Author is H. Fielding'[54].

Three years after *Roderick Random*, *Peregrine Pickle* was published in February 1751. The inclusion of the 'Memoirs of a Lady of Quality', relating the escapades of the frivolous Lady Vane, earned this novel more of a *succès de scandale* than a success with the booksellers. Smollett had attacked his contemporaries even more ruthlessly and specifically than in *Roderick Random*[55]. Quin, Chesterfield, Garrick, Akenside, Lyttelton and Fielding were the principal victims of his virulent and often unjust satire. Lyttelton and Fielding had incurred Smollett's satirical wrath on account of the negative role — or considered such by the angry author — they had played during the long, fruitless negotiations to get *The Regicide* produced in the theatre. Garrick, already lampooned in *Roderick Random* under the simian pseudonym of 'Marmozet', is attacked in *Peregrine Pickle*, with a burlesque verve sustained through several pages, for his gesticulations on the stage. Akenside, for having spoken ill of Scotland, is outrageously, at times ferociously, caricatured as the pedantic republican doctor. Lyttelton, Fielding's patron, saw his elegy on his wife, 'To the Memory of a Lady Lately Deceased, A Monody', which had appeared in October 1747, parodied in the cruellest but most comic way in what Henley (XII, 26—7) has entitled 'Burlesque Ode'. The attack on Fielding, 'Mr. Spondy', is a good example of that personal satire which in the eighteenth century seemed to care not a straw for the most elementary intellectual and moral decency. Fielding is attacked for his second marriage, to his first wife's maid, and his probity as a judge is questioned. It must be stated here and now, in Smollett's defence, that these inexcusable passages on Lyttelton and Fielding disappeared from the revised second edition of *Peregrine Pickle* (1758).

Finally, the last novel of this trilogy, *Ferdinand Count Fathom*, appeared two years after *Peregrine Pickle*, in 1753. The shortest of the three, it was also the one which had least immediate success. Details of its sales are lacking, but there is nothing to indicate that it had anything like the success of *Roderick Random* or *Peregrine Pickle*. It is highly unlikely that *Ferdinand Count Fathom* was a best-seller, for, three months after its publication Smollett was forced to borrow money from his friend Dr George Macaulay. According to the British Museum catalogue, the second edition of *Ferdinand Count Fathom* did not appear until 1771, some eighteen years after the first.

But these three novels represent only part of Smollett's literary activity between 1748 and 1755. The translations of French and Spanish works, accomplished unaided, or more likely with the help of a team of 'amanuenses', especially for *Don Quixote*, prove his determination to exploit his success with the booksellers and the public, and thus consolidate his finances, an endless task during that period. His translation of *Gil Blas* was put on sale in October 1748. It is probable that he also translated Lesage's *Le Diable Boiteux*, which appeared about February 1750 under the title *The Devil Upon Crutches*[56]. In February 1755 appeared the highly controversial translation of *Don Quixote*[57]. The prospectus aroused an attack by a certain William Windham (1717–61), *Remarks on the Proposals lately published for a New Translation of Don Quixote* (1755), in which forty pages are devoted to denouncing Smollett's insufficient knowledge of Spanish and the Spanish people. Windham has the merit of having realised that a translation, if it is to be faithful, involves more than a *verbatim* transcription. For him the language of a nation and its civilisation are one, and his demands are exceptionally strict for the eighteenth century, when translations generally tended to be more elegant than accurate. Nevertheless, Smollett's translation went into several editions in his lifetime and was often republished later.

Lady Mary Wortley Montagu sums up Smollett's literary situation in 1755 rather well: 'I am sorry that my Freind Smallet loses his time in Translations. He has certainly a Talent for Invention, thô I think it flags a little in his last work [*Ferdinand Count Fathom*]' [58]. Nevertheless Lady Mary is unjust. Smollett had not really wasted his time, since from the obscure surgeon he was in 1747, he had become, in the space of seven years, a famous novelist, known best for *Roderick Random* and *Peregrine Pickle*, and a successful translator, judging from the series of reprints of *Gil Blas* and *Don Quixote*[59]. In addition, he had made two journeys to the continent to improve his education, not having had the benefit of the Grand Tour deemed necessary for the intellectual, aesthetic and social formation of young men of good family. In a letter to Carlyle he alludes to a first brief trip in 1749: 'I am but a week returned from having made a Tour thro' part of France, Flanders and Holland, which has only served to Endear my own Country to me the more'[60]. Without being a xenophobe, Smollett was never an enthusiastic cosmopolitan. All we know of his visit to Paris during the summer of 1750 is based on the vague evidence of Moore, with whom he visited Saint-Cloud and Versailles. But it is highly unlikely that Smollett enjoyed the society of the Parisians whose language he ill understood. His portrait of Parisian life in *Peregrine Pickle* is characterised by a gallophobia which is little diminished in his other works.

Finally, in spite of having sacrificed to the gods of the novel, Smollett had neglected neither Melpomene, Thalia nor Aesculapius. The publication of *The Regicide* in June 1749 was not his only attempt to satisfy his theatrical ambition, exacerbated by the repeated frustrations of his efforts to get that tragedy staged. In a letter to Carlyle of February 14th 1749, he alludes to 'a sort of Tragedy on the Story of Alceste, which will (without fail) be acted at Covent Garden next Season'[61]. But this 'extraordinary combination of opera, tragedy and masque'[62] never saw the light of day: Smollett must have quarrelled with Rich whom he had already severely trounced in *Reproof* and *Roderick Random*. The play has disappeared, but certain fragments have been exhumed from the 'vast cemetery of literature buried in music'[63]. Again, in Smollett's letters[64], we find traces of a lost comedy, *The Absent Man*, composed about 1749–50. It is his third theatrical disappointment. 'I have been frustrated in all my attempts to succeed on the Stage', he wrote gloomily in 1750 (Knapp, letter 8, p. 13).

The success of his novels had not induced Smollett to abandon his medical career completely. In 1748 he observed an abnormal obstetrical case and described it to his friend Dr William Smellie, whose three-volume work he later revised. Since the first volume, *A Treatise on the Theory and Practice of Midwifery*, was revised by Smollett in 1751 (which did not prevent him from writing a flattering article on it in the *Monthly Review* of December 1751), it is therefore not surprising that this case of 'Separation of the Pubic Joint in Pregnancy'[65] features in Smellie's second volume, *A Collection of Cases and Observations in Midwifery* (1754)[66]. Moreover in June 1750, for the sum of twenty-eight Scottish pounds, Smollett obtained the degree of M.D. from Marischal College, Aberdeen[67]. This was current practice in the eighteenth century, and the fact that Scottish medical degrees could be bought increased the contempt of the English for the Scots.

Apart from the reviews which can be attributed, though not with absolute certainty, to Smollett when he edited *The Critical Review* from 1756 onwards, his only known medical publication is a pamphlet, *An Essay on the External Use of Water* (1752). Smollett begins with a eulogy of pure water. Afterwards he fulminates with his usual violence, still more unbridled when he is dealing with questions of public hygiene, against the abominable sanitary conditions that prevailed in the public baths at Bath: 'The great hospital of the nation — frequented by almost all the valetudinarians whose lives are of any consequence to the commonwealth.' With a concern for hygiene still rare at that time, Smollett deplored that the sick 'of all ages, sexes and conditions, are promiscuously admitted into an open Bath, which affords little or no shelter'[68]. Already, in his first two novels, he had raged against the filthiness of Bath, and in his last one he returned to the attack with a vigour that neither exile nor illness had diminished. Smollett always retained his faith in cold baths, to which he had had successful recourse (*Travels through France and Italy*). Matthew Bramble, too, makes a positive cult of *aqua simplex* and hydrotherapy in *Humphry Clinker*. Lastly, besides the vigorous defence of an enlightened colleague, Archibald Cleland, who had been castigated by the obscurantist medical authorities of Bath[69], there are some remarks in the *Essay* which suggest that Smollett had grasped the importance of psychosomatics in the cure of certain affections such as tumours and scrofula. Thus:

> The cure of wens by the application of the hand of a person who hath been hanged can be accounted for no other way but from the coldness of the cadaver, the friction of the member, and the power of imagination (p. 58).

Even though success dominates the years between 1748 and 1755, Smollett also had financial, literary and legal troubles. During that period he is forced to do an immense amount of hack-work. In 1753, he translates the *Journal Oeconomique*, undertakes to produce a travel anthology the following year (the seven volumes of the *Compendium* will not appear until April 1756), revises Alexander Drummond's *Travels* (1754) and collaborates in a gigantic enterprise of historical compilation, the *Universal History*[70], which was to number forty volumes. In the midst of these feverish activities, it is not surprising that he felt the need to go and relax in Scotland, where, after an absence of fifteen years, he spent the summer of 1753. The beginning of a letter to his brother-in-law, Alexander Telfer, in December 1753 sums up his obsessive money worries: 'incredible Vexation and Disturbance of Mind'. The situation appears to be no better in 1754. Smollett despises himself for having translated that *Journal Oeconomique* — 'a paultry Bookseller's Jobb' (Knapp, *Letters*, p. 32) — and in this same letter to Moore he confesses all his weariness: 'I am so jaded that I now write with infinite Reluctance' (ibid.).

A violent assault on an ungrateful debtor, Peter Gordon[71], in November 1752, resulted, four months later, in his being sentenced to a fine of twenty pounds, a large sum in the chronically precarious state of his finances. This first painful contact with lawyers — he had dealings with them over unfortunate loans twice again in 1754 and 1756 before the Knowles affair — did not help to make them loved by Smollett, who caricatures them with redoubled vigour in *Launcelot Greaves* and *Humphry Clinker*.

Finally, in 1751 war was declared between him and his literary confrères. Thus the celebrated charlatan and unabashed polygraph, John

Hill, imagining a court where the works of contemporary writers would be judged, describes Smollett, come to plead the cause of *Peregrine Pickle* as 'a grave Gentleman, who, with great Confidence of his Abilities, told the Court his Name was Smallhead'[72]. *Peregrine Pickle* is sentenced until Smollett understands 'more of Human Nature, and could distinguish better between Satire and Scurrility'.

If Smollett really wrote *Habbakuk Hilding*, the anonymous pamphlet that appeared on January 15th 1752, he lacerates Fielding and Lyttelton with a frenzied violence comparable to the worst excesses of *The History and Adventures of an Atom*. Perhaps it is a reply to Fielding's jeers in his *Covent Garden Journal* (No. 2 of January 7th 1752) where Smollett, under the nickname 'Peeragrin Puckle' is put to flight in the course of his skirmishes in Grub Street, by 'a young brother of General Thomas Jones'[73]. This systematic distortion of the names of his characters and of his own surname was something Smollett often had to suffer. His enemies baptise him in turn 'Smallhead', 'Smallwit' or 'Small Hutt'. It is not impossible that — like the distorted names he used later in *The History and Adventures of an Atom* and *Humphry Clinker* — 'Habbakuk Hilding' may be charged with satirical meanings. To begin with, the succession of aspirates and hard consonants suggests the hiccuping of a drunkard. Fielding is depicted as such, with a wealth of repulsive physiological details, in the pamphlet. 'Hilding', besides its general consonance with 'Fielding' means 'a good-for-nothing (man or woman)' (*OED*). In Shakespeare it designates a 'sorry, paltry, cowardly fellow . . . used likewise for a mean woman' as Johnson recalls in his dictionary. Finally, in spite of the phonetic difference, the syllable 'Kuk' might well represent 'cook' if one remembers that, in the first edition of *Peregrine Pickle*, Smollett jeers at Spondy (Fielding) who is 'inclined to marry his own cook-wench'[74], a treacherous allusion to Fielding's marriage in 1747 to Mary Daniel. Apart from the physiological character of the satire, which depicts Fielding in an advanced state of senile incontinence, it is curious to note that, throughout this pamphlet, Smollett has no hesitation in using religious expressions — 'christian' and 'unchristian' recur several times. In it, Fielding is accused of having plagiarised *Roderick Random* and *Peregrine Pickle* by borrowing the characters of Strap and Miss Williams to turn them into Partridge and Miss Matthews. Without going as far as Buck, who declares that after reading certain disgusting passages in the pamphlet he was 'inclined to question, almost seriously, the mental balance of the writer'[75], it is certain that *Habbakuk Hilding* expresses the intolerable tensions of an irascibility so exacerbated as to seem pathological.

But from 1756 to 1760 Smollett himself was to be the butt of critics who can hardly be accused of mincing their words. Two events constitute, as it were, the magnetic poles of this period. The foundation of the *Critical Review* in 1756 was to involve Smollett first in a series of literary quarrels and then in a libel action brought by Admiral Knowles. The *Critical Review* is the negative pole of this period, while the publication of the four volumes of *A Complete History of England* in 1757–58, which at last provided a certain financial security, represents the positive pole. Up to 1757 he was perpetually harassed by money worries, with the inevitable corollary of having to work at the arduous and ungrateful task of compiler. During that time there was a final revival of his theatrical ambitions, and for once they were satisfied. In 1757 his farce *The Reprisal* was produced on the stage.

The *Critical Review*, launched by Smollett in March 1756, was henceforth to be the great rival of the *Monthly Review*[76] founded by Ralph Griffiths in 1749. The production of the *Critical Review* was originally connected with a plan for creating an Academy of Belles Lettres which Smollett seems to have had much at heart. In August 1756, he confides to his friend Moore that the *Critical Review*

> is a small Branch of an extensive Plan which I last year projected for a sort of Academy of the belles Lettres: a Scheme which will one day, I hope be put in Execution to its utmost Extent. In the meantime the Critical Review is conducted by four Gentlemen of approved abilities, and meets with a very favourable Reception (Knapp, *Letters*, p. 46).

In his pamphlet, *A Sop in the Pan* (1759), Joseph Reed sneers at his project 'for initiating and perfecting the Male-Inhabitants of this Island, in the Use and Management of the *linguary Weapon*, by the Erection of a *Scolding Amphitheatre*' (p. 5). The four collaborators to whom Smollett alludes are probably Francklin, Armstrong, Derrick and himself. However great the initial success of the *Critical Review*, it seems that Smollett was too optimistic. Six years later, in 1762, he admits to Moore that the *Critical Review* is at last making a profit:

> Your Conjecture is right in supposing I still write some articles in the Critical Review. As I am Proprietor of that work I should be a fool to give it up at a Time when it begins to indemnify me for all the Vexation and Loss I have sustained by it; but the Laborious Part of Authorship I have long resigned (Knapp, *Letters*, p. 108).

It would take too long to examine here the many attacks[77] directed against the *Critical Review* and its editor, whom the offended authors always considered the main person responsible for unfavourable reviews. But to give some idea of this 'vexation' to which Smollett alludes, here are a few of the attacks that are most typical in their cantankerous virulence. John Shebbeare[78], in *The Occasional Critic; or the Decrees of the Scotch Tribunal in the Critical Review Rejudged* (1757), a pamphlet of more than 150 pages, exploits the Scottish origins of Smollett and some of his collaborators for satirical ends, as well as the more than rudimentary sanitary arrangements in Edinburgh in the eighteenth century. He compares the *Critical Review* to a certain 'Littlehouse, the Odour is very offensive to all Gentlemen who unhappily have not been educated to the Use of the "Wha wants me"' (p. 2), that is to say the mobile privies which 'continually travel the City of *Edinburgh* for the public Commodity of easing the good Subjects of Scotland in the open Streets'. Smollett by no means possesses sole rights in scatological satire in the eighteenth century. The hatred of Scotland and of her sons who come to seek their fortune in London is one of the dominant notes in all these attacks. In another pamphlet, *An Appendix to the Occasional Critic*, published about December 1757, Shebbeare returns to the charge and attacks Smollett directly in an ironic advertisement:

> An empty Author. He is equally qualified to write tragedy, comedy, farce, history, novels, voyages, treatises on midwifery, in physic, and all kinds of polite letters. . . . He undertakes to fit up books by the yard on all subjects, at the best hand, and with the greatest expedition, for those who cannot write themselves, with great allowance in favour of his countrymen; having much improved the new way of composing new treaties by means of a pair of scissars [*sic*], brown paper, a brush, paste and old authors (p. 25).

All Smollett's activities come under review, but Shebbeare dwells most on his compilations, in particular the *Complete History of England*, which he accuses of being a plagiarism. William Kenrick, another indignant author, displays less violence than Shebbeare in his pamphlet, *A Scrutiny; or the Criticks criticis'd* (1759), but he accuses the critics of not having read or understood his *Epistles Philosophical and Moral* (1759) and refutes point by point the censures of the *Critical Review*. James Grainger, in *A Letter to Tobias Smollett M.D.* (1759), defending his translation of Tibullus, roughly treated by the *Critical Review*, deals with Smollett thus: 'next to *Zoilus*, you Dr. Smollett are allowed to be the greatest of Critics' (p. 1). Grainger advises Smollett to consult 'that noble work the English Dictionary' (p. 14). Throughout the twenty-five pages of his letter, he harps on the Christian name 'Tobias', which Smollett detested. His medical title becomes in turn 'good Dr. Tobias' (p. 5), 'Dr. Toby' (p. 15), and 'Mr. Hypercritical Dr.' (p. 22). Finally Grainger contemptuously adjures Smollett: 'Be a Romance or farce-writer, raise contributions by another Regicide, translate from the French or si Dis placet, murder the Spanish. But henceforth, if you have any shame left, drop the rod of Aristarchus' (p. 25). In 1760 (?) the anonymous author of *The Battle of the Reviews* depicts the conflict between the *Monthly* and the *Critical* in mock-heroic terms. He awards the final victory to the *Critical* but, in spite of granting Smollett certain merits, he censures him, for 'his Prejudice and Passion have often made these abilities, together with his professed Candour, suspected. Yes, this is *Sawney's* Peccadillo, . . . his Merit, such as it is, is quite tarnished by his Vanity; a Vanity, always fulsome and always odious' (pp. 112–13). Lastly, Charles Churchill, in his *Apology addressed to the Critical Reviewers* (1761), paints a satanical picture of Smollett as a critic (which, in view of Churchill's own notorious character, is a case of the pot calling the kettle black):

> Alien from God, and foe to all mankind;
> Who spares no character; whose every word,
> Bitter as gall, and sharper than the sword,
> Cuts to the quick; whose thoughts with rancour swell;
> Whose tongue on earth performs the works of hell.
>
> (lines 301–5).

Nevertheless, these attacks did not prevent Smollett from bringing off a double success in 1757. First, the blow to his self-esteem over *The Regicide* was avenged at long last when, after a reconciliation (perhaps no more than superficial) with Garrick, his mock-heroic and patriotic farce *The Reprisal; or the Tars of Old England* was produced on January 22nd 1757. Second, the publication of the first three volumes of the *Complete History of England* in April 1757 (the fourth and last appeared in January 1758) was to bring him, at last, some financial security. But it was at the cost of his own health and probably, of his premature death, that Smollett thus earned his living.

The Reprisal is, above all, a piece of propaganda destined to raise the morale of the English after the tragic naval and military reverses of 1756. In the prologue, Smollett states that the farce (which in fact he pompously calls 'a comedy in two acts') is a 'sea-ragout . . . Replete with a variety of flavours'. As the basic ingredient among these spices he uses all the crudest clichés about the characteristics and, above all, the short-comings of the Scots, the Irish and, first and foremost, the French. The French commander, M. de Champignon, who has treacherously seized an English yacht in time of peace, is a compendium of all the vices most often ridiculed in the Frenchman as the Englishman saw him all through the eighteenth century and the Napoleonic wars. Vain, cowardly, stupid, a lady-killer, a coxcomb, without an ounce of dignity, he is a grotesque puppet shown as fuel to feed the patriotic fire of an English public exasperated by a series of defeats. By contrast, the English sailors, Block, Haulyard and above all Lyon are hearts of oak. Lyon, the English officer who frees his captive compatriots, shows magnanimity to Champignon, but the last lines of the play sound like a positive ultimatum: 'While France uses us as friends, we will return her civilities. When she breaks her treaties and grows insolent, we will drub her over to her good be-haviour'[79]. The only literary interest of this play, which had a certain success in spite of the very harsh criticisms of contemporaries, is the doggedness of the sailor characters and the constant linguistic jokes about the peculiarities of Scottish and Irish speech, not to mention the 'Frenglish' Smollett puts into the mouth of Champignon.

The publication of the *Complete History of England*, from Julius Caesar to the Treaty of Aix-la-Chapelle (1748), is an astonishing *tour de force*. According to Moore, the some 2600 pages (in quarto) of this history were written in fourteen months. One understands Smollett's weariness when he writes in June 1757 to Moore: 'I am so fatigued with the unremitting Labour of the Pen that I begin to loathe the sight of Paper' (Knapp, *Letters*, p. 58). A year later, another letter to Moore expresses this disgust with the whole business of being a writer: 'I am equally averse to the Praise and Censure that belong to other men. Indeed, I am sick of both, and wish to God my circumstances would allow me to consign my Pen to oblivion' (Knapp, *Letters*, p. 73). If the *Complete History of England* is not of much interest today, at least it had the merit in 1757 of being more readable than the indigestible compilations of Oldmixon, Carte and Rapin. Smollett seems to have been at great pains, at least so he repeatedly asserts, to be historically impartial. In a letter to William Huggins[80] in July 1758, writing of his *Complete History of England*, he forcibly affirms this:

> I can safely say I had no other view in the Execution of that work than historical Truth which I have displayed on all occasions to the best of my Knowledge without Fear or affection. I have kept myself independent of all Connexions which might have affected the Candour of my Intention. I have flattered no Individual; I have cultivated no Party. . . . I pique myself upon being the only Historian of this Country, who has had Honesty, Temper and Courage enough to be wholly impartial and disinterested (Knapp, *Letters*, p. 69).

In spite of these assertions, Smollett was the target of vigorous attacks. His critics rebuked him for a certain partiality for the Tories, his hatred of the Whigs and his Jacobite tendencies. Thomas Comber, in *A Vindication of the Great Revolution of England* (1758), a pamphlet of some 150 pages, rebukes Smollett in particular for having slandered the historical reputation of King William III and his wife Mary, but, above all, for giving a biased version of the repression which followed the Jacobite rebellions of 1715 and 1745. Comber accuses Smollett of religious as well as political fanaticism – poor Smollett who detested popery in all its forms! 'Dr. Smollett appears from *strong* & express passages . . . to be a *determined partisan* of the House of Stuarts, and on numerous occasions to give vent to their malevolent spirit in the most furious expressions' (p. 134). In fact, Smollett's sympathies were less with the Stuarts than with the unfortunate Highlanders persecuted and massacred by the English. The events of the Rebellion and its ruthless suppression were still too near not to be painful subjects of passionate controversy. Twenty years after Culloden, Andrew Henderson, in his *Life of William Augustus*

Duke of Cumberland (1766) again rebuked Smollett for his version of the facts: 'The whole account given of it by Tobias Smollett is one continued misrepresentation . . . [Smollett] when a friend, is far from being bad, but, if an enemy, his very tender mercies are cruel' (p. 260). These partisan attacks in no way detracted from the success of the *History*, which was republished in 1758 (after being revised and corrected), in the form of sixpenny weekly parts, and then in eleven octavo volumes. With legitimate pride Smollett wrote to Moore in September 1758: 'You will not be sorry to hear that the weekly Sale of the History has increased to above Ten thousand. A french Gentleman[81] of Talent and Erudition has undertaken to translate it into the Language' (Knapp, *Letters*, pp. 73–4). One understands better why Smollett then undertook to produce a *Continuation* (1760–65). According to Anderson, he earned about £2,000 by his historical works. But the income earned by the sweat of his brow cost Smollett his health and several years of his life.

In March 1758 Smollett published the second, and expurgated edition of *Peregrine Pickle*, in which the satire on Garrick had been cut out. Was this a desire to live in peace and renounce old quarrels? Or was it that a reconciliation with Garrick might favour his theatrical ambitions, as it had done in the case of *The Reprisal*? In any case, Smollett's critical impetuosity was about to involve him in a new controversy whose material consequences were far more serious than the annoying but superficial skirmishes with his confrères or the critics. By 1757 Britain's military reputation in Europe was notable only for its eclipse. But the hardest blow dealt to England's international prestige was undoubtedly the failure of the expedition against Rochefort in September 1757. Carefully prepared in the greatest secrecy, this manoeuvre, intended to divert the enemy, ended in a total and extremely costly failure. The English fleet, under the command of Admirals Hawke, Knowles and Broderick and General Mordaunt, took possession of the island of Aix on September 23rd. This was a partial success, achieved without much trouble, and gave the troops confidence. Instead of exploiting their tactical advantage, the English, just as at Cartagena fifteen years earlier, launched no attack on Fort Fouras which defended the approaches to Rochefort. The tergiversations of the commanders — another exact parallel with the Cartagena expedition — meant that on September 29th no attempt at landing had yet been made. Stormy weather now intervened and on October 1st the fleet raised anchor; five days later it was back in Spithead. This little sea trip had cost no less than £1 million.

Just as after the defeat at Cartagena, the war of the pamphlets promptly began to rage. The Navy, thinking attack the best form of defence, fired the first broadside — another resemblance to the Cartagena affair. It was Hawke who sparked off the gunpowder with his pamphlet, *Genuine Account of the Late Grand Expedition*. If the attribution to Hawke (British Museum Catalogue) is correct, Hawke must have had his pamphlet published immediately, since a review of it appeared in the *Critical Review* of October 1757 (iv, 371–6). The *Critical Review*'s analysis is very moderate in tone. It is mainly restricted to making an accurate summary of it and to affirming, quite rightly, that it is

> chiefly made up of orders, which contain nothing for the reader's amusement or information. All that can contribute to either, might have been comprehended in one page and that would have been sufficient to excite very melancholy ideas in the mind of every man who retains the least affection for his country (p. 371).

On November 1st 1757 the King ordered a commission of enquiry. A court martial sat to judge the conduct of Sir John Mordaunt, the commander-in-chief of the expedition. The session lasted from December 14th to 20th 1757. At the end of it Mordaunt was unanimously acquitted. Public opinion demanded a scapegoat. Byng had been shot on his quarterdeck on March 16th 1757 and perhaps some Englishmen already shared Voltaire's celebrated opinion in *Candide: 'Dans ce pays-ci il est bon de tuer de temps en temps un amiral pour encourager les autres.'* The pamphlets continued to appear, with such typical titles as *Candid Reflections on the Report of the General Officers* or *The Expedition against Rochefort, fully stated and considered in a letter to the Author of the Candid Reflections.* The *Critical Review* examined four of them in January 1758, and five in April. The tone is in general severe for those who try to justify the conduct of the military, but moderate. Thus the pamphlet *A Vindication of Mr. Pitt* is criticiséd mercilessly, but in comparatively controlled language: 'Nothing but inflated periods, darkened with absurd transpositions and improprieties of expression that a foreigner could hardly be guilty of' (April 1758, v, 354). Considering the verbal violence of the period, these criticisms were quite mild.

The same cannot be said of the article in which Smollett deals with Knowles's pamphlet, *The Conduct of Admiral Knowles on the Late Expedition Set in a True Light* (1758), (May 1758, v, 438–9). In this thirty-page tract, Knowles begins by rejecting *en bloc* all the other pamphlets. It is not a speech for the defence, it is a broadside attack: 'To take Notice of all the Anonymous Pamphlets published on this Occasion would be endless; and almost all agree in some false Accusation' (p. 3). The incensed admiral then proceeds to refute the arguments of the detractors of the Navy and tries to prove, with the aid of technical details (soundings, ballistic data) that 'it is clear that Fort Fouras was not attackable or accessible by sea, and therefore the not attacking it by sea, was not one of the causes of the failure of the expedition' (p. 23) — another exact parallel with Cartagena. Finally, the admiral sheds some tears over his own fate:

> Hard, indeed, is my fate, to stand exculpated in the opinion of my superior officer, who saw my conduct, and under whose command I

acted, and yet to be singled out as the only flag on that expedition left unemployed in a time of war: and this after forty one years constant and faithful Service in the Navy (p. 30).

This last sentence must certainly have aroused Smollett's critical fire. Since Cartagena he had had scant respect or liking for Knowles and he had recently ridiculed him in a caustic paragraph in the *Account* which had appeared in 1756 in the *Compendium of Voyages*. Smollett's article in the *Critical Review* is a discharge of verbal canister-shot which demolishes the arguments, the character and reputation of Knowles, whom he calls 'an admiral without conduct, an engineer without knowledge, an officer without resolution, and a man without veracity' (p. 438). As if these compliments were not enough, he adds that Knowles is 'an ignorant, assuming, officious, fribbling pretender; conceited as a peacock, obstinate as a mule, and mischievous as a monkey' (ibid.). Smollett even gibes at the last words of Knowles's pamphlet: 'If the service can be thus influenced by caprice, admiral K-----s needs not be surprised at his being laid aside after forty years constant and faithful service' (p. 439).

Knowles's reply was not long in coming. He immediately launched a counterattack in the form of a libel action. Hamilton, responsible as the printer of the *Critical Review*, was tried on June 2nd 1759 and acquitted, for Smollett admitted in court that he was the author of the article. Seventeen months later, on November 24th 1760, Smollett himself was tried. He was found guilty of libel and sentenced to a fine of £100 and three months' imprisonment in the King's Bench Prison. Furthermore, he was 'obliged to give security for his good behaviour for seven years, himself in five hundred pounds with two sufficient sureties of two hundred and fifty pounds each'[82]. He came out of prison in February 1761.

Before ending the survey of this middle period (1748–60) of Smollett's life, it is necessary to dwell on certain other important features and facts, such as his increasing fatigue and anxieties about his health, the publication of a new review, *The British Magazine*, in which his fourth novel, *Launcelot Greaves*, appeared as well as a certain number of poems, and lastly the publication, in the form of weekly parts, of the *Continuation of the Complete History of England*, completed in 1765.

Smollett was well aware of the deterioration in his health due to his self-imposed sentence of literary hard labour. In a very friendly letter to John Wilkes (April 20th 1759, Knapp, *Letters*, pp. 79–80), he declines a tempting invitation to a restful country holiday in Aylesbury: 'Were I not restrained by a sore Throat and consciousness of a very capricious Constitution, I should certainly avail myself of your kind Invitation. The Truth is, I love the Country, especially at this Season', and further on he complains of 'reading dull books and writing dull Commentaries *invitā Minerva*'. It is not surprising that as early as 1759 he had tried to obtain a diplomatic post in a Mediterranean country – the consulate of Madrid –

where the mildness of a sunny climate would have been better for his lungs, no doubt already attacked by the tuberculosis which was to kill him. At the end of 1759, Smollett shows that he realises he must accept the fact that he is a very sick man when he writes to John Harvie:

> To tell you a secret, my constitution is quite broken. Since last May, I have hardly enjoyed one day of health: I am so subject to colds and rheums that I dare hardly stir from my own house; and shall be obliged to give up all the pleasures of society, at least those of tavern society, to which you know I have always been addicted (Knapp, *Letters*, p. 87).

Without being a tavern-prop — where would he have found the time anyhow? — Smollett thus shows that he was no surly, unsociable recluse, but greatly enjoyed the company of his chosen friends. It is natural that he should have tried to get away from his many worries by making a brief visit to the Continent, probably between June and October 1759, and the following summer to Scotland. Little is known about these two visits.

But this weariness did not prevent him in January 1760 from launching the *British Magazine*, in which *Launcelot Greaves* ran as a monthly serial up to December 1761. Although this was not the first novel by a great author to appear in this way, as literary critics for a long time wrongly asserted[83], this mode of publication, perfected by Smollett's innovations, certainly contributed to the success of the periodical. The collaboration of Goldsmith was another great asset in the enterprise. The *British Magazine* ran until 1767. It was a much more practical and technical periodical than the *Critical Review*. Among its contents one finds geographical descriptions, such as that of the island of Juan-Fernandez (*British Magazine*, April 1760, pp. 193–7), or articles on such varied subjects as 'An Error practised by Mothers & Nurses in correcting the Deformity of Children' (May 1760, p. 136), and 'A new method of sweetening sea-water' (February 1760, pp. 86–8). In the numbers of January and February 1760, there appears the description of a recently invented plough. These examples show how much the English were animated by encyclopaedic curiosity thirty years before the beginning of what is conventionally called the Industrial Revolution.

It is probable that certain articles and poems of Smollett's[84] are buried in the *British Magazine*, but, in the absence of a copy annotated by his own hand or that of a collaborator or close friend, it is difficult to identify them with certainty. Some poems attributed to Smollett in 1777 by the anonymous editor of *Plays and Poems* were published in the *British Magazine*: 'Ode to Blue Ey'd Ann', 'Ode to Sleep', 'Ode to Mirth'. Their conventional and artificial prettiness adds nothing to his literary fame. However, it is important to note that, after seven years' silence (since *Ferdinand Count Fathom*, 1753), Smollett resumed his activities as a novelist.

Finally, Smollett wished to exploit the success of the *Complete History of England*. The five volumes of his *Continuation of the Complete History of England* appeared between 1760 and 1765[85]. The fifth volume is very rare. According to Anderson (1820; p. 74n), a paragraph alluding to the mental illness of George III provoked government action: the whole edition was bought up and probably destroyed. Although, as with the *Complete History of England*, the *Continuation* has largely lost its interest, the analysis of the years from 1748 onwards preserve the value of a record written by a man who had lived through the events, as does that of the last ten years dealt with in the *Complete History*. These historical works received highly laudatory notices in the *Critical Review*. Already, in January 1758 a review of volume IV had described the *Complete History of England* as a 'work which we may imagine will be better relished by posterity, than by the present age, in as much as it breathes throughout a spirit of impartiality and moderation' (*Critical Review*, January 1758, v, 2). It is not surprising that the same note of admiration recurs three years later about the first two volumes of the *Continuation of the Complete History of England* which the *Critical Review* praises for 'the spirit, candour, and good sense, with which this performance is executed'. The reviewer rejects in advance — a wise precaution when one remembers the attacks launched against the *Critical Review* — 'all suspicion of partiality, on account of our supposed connections with the author' (November 1761, xii, 347).

The publication of the *Continuation of the Complete History of England* did not prevent Smollett from continuing his work on the *Universal History*. This was a collection compiled by several authors, as is evident from his correspondence with Richardson who printed the volumes from 1759–60 (Knapp, *Letters*, Nos 61, 68, 70, 71, 73). Forty-four volumes appeared from 1759 to 1766, and, according to Anderson, Smollett provided the history of France, Italy, Germany, Norway, Sweden and Holland. Whatever else Smollett may be reproached for, at least he can never be accused of laziness. One also better understands his bitterness and anger with the 'booksellers' (at that time publishers as well) whom he describes in a letter to Richardson (October 1760) as a 'set of contemptible Reptiles, who have enriched themselves by works which have scarce afforded their Authors the necessaries of Life' (Knapp, *Letters*, p. 92).

If the middle period (1748–60) of Smollett's life began with a success (*Roderick Random*) and ended with a calamity (three months in prison following the Knowles affair), the pattern of the final period (1761–71) is exactly the opposite. Up to 1763 his life was scarred by his arduous and painful political controversy with John Wilkes and by his profound grief over the loss of his daughter. As a result he exiled himself for two years to the South of France and Italy. On his return to England, his state of health forced him, until 1768, to be one of those pathetic rootless persons who haunt watering-places in quest of a doubtful cure.

Such are the years from 1761 to 1768: difficult years rife with bitterness, pain and anxiety, accompanied by increasing deterioration in his health. From 1768 till his death Smollett experienced a kind of temporary physical regeneration, due to the mildness of the Italian climate. But above all, after ten years of going underground, his genius as a novelist burst out afresh in *Humphry Clinker*, that final resurgence like the last play of a fountain, whose spray shimmers with the rainbow colours of a many-faceted art.

For the next seven years, from 1761 to 1768, Smollett experienced a series of disappointments, vexations and anguished apprehensions aroused by his tottering and often alarming state of health. These are the terrible years of his life. From the beginning of that period, its dominant theme is of physical and psychological exhaustion. It is a disillusioned man, weary of the eternal quarrels with Grub Street who writes to Garrick in April 1761:

> I am old enough to have seen and observed that we are all playthings of fortune, and that it depends upon something as insignificant and precarious as the tossing up of a halfpenny whether a man rises to affluence and honours, or continues to his dying day struggling with the difficulties and disgraces of life. I desire to live quietly with all mankind (Knapp, *Letters*, p. 98).

The biting satirist who wrote *Advice* and *Reproof* seems very far away, yet only fifteen years have elapsed. Discouragement did not prevent Smollett from continuing to lead his laborious life. In May 1761 he deplores being unable to visit his friend William Huggins, seriously ill on account of his 'slavish Engagements' (Knapp, *Letters*, p. 100). His low spirits provoked him to morbid melancholy: 'I have a Presentiment that I shall never see Scotland again' he writes to Moore in June 1762 (Knapp, *Letters*, p. 106), and in the same letter he tells his friend that he is 'extremely emaciated'. By the middle of 1762 Smollett has no illusions about his condition: 'My Constitution will no longer allow me to toil as formerly. I am now so thin you would hardly know me. My face is shrivelled up by the asthma like an ill-dried Pippin, and my Legs are as thick at the Ancle as at the Calf' (to Moore, August 1762: Knapp, *Letters*, p. 108). As early as the end of 1762 Smollett knows that his only chance of recovery is to leave the fog and damp of London for sunnier places: 'My Flesh continues to waste, and I begin to think the best chance I have for Recovering, will be a Removal into a warmer climate' (to John Home, December 1762: Knapp, *Letters*, p. 110). In this letter he also alludes to his efforts to obtain a post as consul in the South of France, at Nice or Marseilles. One after the other, Pitt, Bute and Shelburne disappointed him, which undoubtedly contributed to exciting his satirical violence against both political parties in *The History and Adventures of an Atom* (assuming that he *did* write the book).

In spite of his recent misadventure in the Knowles affair and his precarious state of health, Smollett flung himself with all his polemical might into the struggle between Lord Bute and Pitt. At Bute's request he started a weekly, *The Briton*, which from May 29th 1762, undertook the defence of the government. The *Briton*'s declaration of principles lacked neither nobility nor rhetorical rhythm: its intention was 'not to alarm, but appease; not to puzzle but explain; not to inflame but to allay', and its aim 'to detect the falsehood of malice; to expose and refute the insinuations of calumny; to pluck the mask of patriotism from the front of faction, and the torch of discord from the hand of sedition' (*Briton*, No. 1, May 29th 1762, p. 1). The *Briton* had, as its superscription, the royal arms and the motto *Dieu et mon droit*. Unfortunately for Smollett his efforts went dead against public opinion, which detested Bute, the Scottish favourite who was suspected of delivering England over to the rapacity of his compatriots. Smollett, who had already had to suffer on account of his Scottish origin was perfectly aware of this widespread attitude of mind. This is how he defines the word 'Scotchman': 'This is a term which implies everything that is vile and detestable' (*Briton*, No. 4, June 19th 1762, p. 20). He adds on the next page that this term 'includes *reprobation*'. As Raymond Postgate remarks: 'The *Briton* was driven into the unpopular position of having to praise the valour and virtues of the Scots'[86].

Moreover Smollett found himself confronted with a formidable adversary in the person of his friend John Wilkes, to whom he had appealed several times during the Knowles affair to try and appease the wrathful admiral, and whose aid he had solicited, again in November 1761, for Robert Love, the son of his old schoolmaster at Dumbarton. Wilkes, financed by Temple, launched his rival periodical in the week following the appearance of the *Briton*. The choice of the *Briton* as the title of Smollett's was a blunder, and Wilkes hastened to take an ironic advantage of his opponent by naming his own periodical the *North Briton*. In his opening number, Wilkes too declared his principles: from the first to the forty-fifth and famous number, the same insistence is made on the freedom of expression. '*The Liberty of the press* is the birth-right of a BRITON', so began the first number of the *North Briton* (June 5th 1762), and the last ended with the quotation of a line of Dryden's: 'Freedom is the *English Subject's* Prerogative.'

From the first passage of arms between Smollett and Wilkes, now become his closest enemy, the struggle appeared unequal. Smollett tried to defend himself with the rapier of the stylist; Wilkes bombarded his adversary with stinking balls of filth and with lampoons, especially on the Scots, which delighted the populace. Wilkes, a better polemist than Smollett, turned his opponent's statements to ridicule with the facile skill of a juggler with words. Thus, the first number of the *North Briton* declares that its purpose is 'to detect the *malice of falsehood*'. Any weapon is good enough for Wilkes; even the language of the *Briton* is used as a stick to beat it with. He pretends to be a Scot and endeavours 'to write *plain English* and to avoid the numerous *Scotticisms* the *Briton* abounds with' (No. 1, p. 3). Smollett defended monarchic authority and in general showed himself in favour of a very strict social and political hierarchy, aiming to muzzle the populace, 'the mob', whom he so greatly despises in *The History and Adventures of an Atom* and *Humphry Clinker*. Wilkes did not really present any worked out political pro-gramme. He mainly attacked Bute's foreign policy and, most of all, his alleged favouritism for the Scots. Wilkes's polemical genius consists in his having invented brain-washing by mud-slinging as a method of political propaganda. Charles C. Trench rightly emphasises this point: ' "Give me a grain of truth" he [Wilkes] said, "and I will mix it up with a great mass of falsehood so that no chemist will ever be able to separate them." It is the classic recipe for a gutter-press campaign: Wilkes was a pioneer'[87]. Wilkes went so far as to reproduce in No. 13 of the *North Briton* (August 28th 1762) the *Perfect Description of the People and Country of Scotland* written a century earlier (1649) by James Howell, a tissue of sarcasms and gross insults rebuking the Scots for their dirtiness and their corrupt sexual morals. One sentence on Scotland will suffice to give the tone of this attack: 'The air might be wholesome, but for the stinking people that inhabit it; the ground might be fruitful, had they the wit to manure it' (p. 38).

Smollett, perhaps ill-supported by Bute, who remained stoical under the deluge of calumnies, soon had to admit himself beaten, and on February 13th 1763, the thirty-eighth and last number of the *Briton* appeared. Seven years later, in one of his last letters (May 1770) Smollett bluntly criticises 'the absurd Stoicism of Lord Bute, who set himself up as a Pillory, to be pelted by all the Blackguards of England, upon the sup-position that they would grow tired and leave off' (Knapp, *Letters*, p. 137). Moreover, he admitted defeat in *The History and Adventures of an Atom*. After having assured themselves of the services of polemists, Taycho (Pitt) and Yak-Strot (Bute) confront each other: 'a sharp contest and pelting match ensued: but the dispute was soon terminated. Yak-Strot's versifiers turned out no great conjurers on the trial . . . their balls were inferior in point of composition to those of Jan-Ki-dtzin (Wilkes)'[88]. Smollett's *Briton* had never exceeded a printing of 250 copies, compared with the 2,000 copies of the *North Briton*, a number which one might well multiply by twenty if one takes into account its popularity in the coffee-houses and the habit of the English in the eighteenth century of circulating their periodicals among their friends.

This political defeat was soon to be followed by the sorrow of losing his only daughter Elizabeth, at the age of fifteen (April 3rd 1763). This was not the final blow, but a wound from which Smollett never recovered. The inveterate fighter that Smollett had been all his life was to admit himself vanquished by fate. In a letter to an American admirer, Richard Smith (May 1763), he writes that any happiness for him is henceforth impossible 'having lost my only child, a fine Girl of Fifteen, whose Death has overwhelmed myself and my wife with unutterable Sorrow' (Knapp, *Letters*, pp. 113–14). In another letter (August 1763) he wishes that his correspondent may never 'feel the Pangs of that unspeakable grief which the Loss of a beloved child inspires' (Knapp, *Letters*, p. 118). Smollett does not exaggerate his situation when he describes his departure from England in the first letter of *Travels through France and Italy*, 'traduced by malice, persecuted by faction, abandoned by false patrons, and overwhelmed by the sense of a domestic calamity, which it was not in the power of fortune to repair'. Later, when he described his symptoms (*Travels through France and Italy*, Letter xi) to Doctor Fizès of Montpellier, he reverts again to the terrible blow that his daughter's death was to him: 'Vere novo casus atrox diras procellas animo immisit; toto corpore, tota mente tumultuatur.'

Against these tempests of fate, Smollett sought a haven of peace, rest and forgetfulness during two years spent in France and Italy (Nice at that time was part of Piedmont). He left England about mid-June 1763 and did not return till July 1765. This first exile, described in the *Travels through France and Italy* (published after his return in May 1766) was intended to be a psychological and phthisical cure. In spite of the conclusions of Martz[89] proving that the letters of *Travels in France and Italy* are not a genuine personal correspondence and demonstrating that Smollett's historical and archaeological erudition is mainly borrowed from specialised works, the theme on which Smollett exercises his occasionally caustic verbal virtuosity is one of his most characteristic ones: the hatred of lying in all its forms. Whether he is writing of rapacious innkeepers, unworthy priests, a pretentious and ignorant aristocracy, an impoverished but lazy peasantry, or of travellers prepared to admire any and every work of art to order, Smollett refuses to compromise with his rationalist and puritanical conscience which is rigid in its demands for truth. It is easy to observe that the words 'to impose', 'imposition' and 'extortion' are those that recur most often when Smollett writes of his wrangles, often stormy and invariably disagreeable, with the predators, great and small, who lie in wait for the innocent tourist in their lairs called 'inns'.

It is more difficult to discern behind these acrid criticisms and incessant complaints a deep sense of political, social and religious injustice. Fifteen years before Arthur Young, Smollett is already making a clinical examination of the *ancien régime*. His criticisms are not solely negative. A generous indignation makes him pity the galley-slaves of Villefranche (Letter xiv), condemn the stupid practice of duelling as a 'gigantic evil' (Letter xv) and ridicule the ignorance, superstition and fanaticism of the clergy (Letter xix). There is nothing, even to the climate of Nice, that he does not criticise with his customary lucidity (Letters xxiii and xxiv).

After Sterne, a whole string of ill-disposed critics have reproached Smollett for his philistine views on the masterpieces of Florence and Rome. It is an unjust reproach. In Letter xxv, in less than two pages, Smollett uses the following expressions which show his deep love of art when he is planning to visit Florence and Rome: 'a most eager curiosity', 'I longed impatiently', 'enthusiastic ardour' and finally 'I could not bear the thoughts of returning to England from the very skirts of Italy without having penetrated to the capital of that renowned country'. And yet he had foreseen how he would be scoffed at by the contemporary pundits in aesthetic matters. There is a positive conspiracy of silence on the part of the critics. Have they not read the *Travels through France and Italy*, these severe critics gloating over the sarcasms of Sterne, who baptises him 'Smelfungus' in the *Sentimental Journey*, or of Thicknesse who, in his *Useful Hints to those who make the Tour of France* (1768) suggests an alternative title for *Travels through France and Italy*: 'Quarrels through France and Italy for the cure of a pulmonic disorder'? Why have they attributed so much importance to the unflattering remarks about the Venus de Medici, yet carefully omitted to mention Smollett's reiterated warnings, in which he almost seems to be excusing himself in advance for speaking frankly?

> I do not set up for a judge in these matters, and very likely I may incur the ridicule of the virtuosi for the remarks I have made. But I am used to speak my mind freely on all subjects that fall under the cognizance of my senses; though I must as freely own, there is something more than common sense required to discover and distinguish the more delicate beauties of painting.

(It is a question here of the paintings in the Pitti palace.) The end of this Letter xxviii is echoed again in the following one where, talking of Rome, he announces his intention of giving his opinion 'without ceremony or affectation . . . without any pretence, however, to the character of a connoisseur'. Does not Smollett give evidence of modesty and moderation?

The physical benefit of the sojourn in France and Italy was only ephemeral. On his return to London in July 1765 Smollett complains to Moore of being 'no more than the skeleton of what I was, but with proper care that skeleton may hang for some few years together' (Knapp, *Letters*, p. 124). Towards the end of 1765 (November) he does not show himself more optimistic: 'I am not above half as big as I was when you saw me last. To tell you the Truth, I look upon my being alive as a sort of Resuscitation, for, last year I thought myself in the last stages of a Consumption' (Knapp, *Letters*, p. 126). From now till his final departure from England in the autumn of 1768, Smollett was to be nothing but a pitiable *déraciné*, condemned to exile in his own country, going from watering-place to watering-place in search of his lost health. Whereas he spent thirteen years

(1750—63) at Monmouth House, Chelsea, from 1765 to 1768 he now led a wandering life, living by turns in London, Bath and Hot Wells (Bristol). He visited Scotland one last time from May to August 1766, and lived in Bath again in 1767 and 1768. It is concerning the period when he made his farewell journey to Scotland that Smollett claims to have been plunged from April to November into a kind of 'Coma Vigil' and he begs Moore to be good enough to make excuses for him to his wife: 'With regard to me she has as yet seen nothing but the wrong side of the Tapestry' (Knapp, *Letters*, p. 131). Up to the last he was never to lose that cruel clear-sightedness about himself and other people.

Nevertheless, he had not stopped working as a translator, historian and compiler. In March and April 1761 there had appeared the first two volumes of a translation of Voltaire which in 1765 numbered thirty-nine volumes. Although Smollett only wrote the notes, this undertaking involved a considerable amount of work. The *Critical Review* (May 1761, xi, 377—81) had reviewed the first volume of this translation of the works of Voltaire very favourably — there is nothing surprising in that! — describing him as 'the most original, spirited, pleasing, and popular writer of his age and country' (p. 377). The fifth and last volume of the *Continuation of the Complete History of England* appeared in October 1765, the *Travels through France and Italy* in May 1766 (the year in which he probably composed his 'Ode to Independence') and from June 1768 the *Present State* appeared in the form of weekly numbers before being published in eight volumes (1768—69). This long-forgotten compilation has been analysed by Martz[90], who has emphasised the importance of the parts devoted to Scotland and England in the genesis of *Humphry Clinker*. The work was a mode of satisfying the encyclopedic thirst for geographic, economic and technical information displayed by eighteenth-century readers.

Is it necessary to add that, tired, prematurely worn out and aged as Smollett was, the attacks against him did not cease? Cuthbert Shaw (1738—71) a satirical poetaster, recalled in *The Race* (1765) the failure of *The Regicide* and Smollett's activities on the *Critical Review*, although he had long ceased to contribute to it. Such stings coming from 'Grub Street' kept Smollett alive, or so he claimed with sick humour in a disillusioned and pathetic letter to William Hunter in February 1767. Although for a long time he has had only 'negative Enjoyments' and has almost forgotten 'what positive Pleasure is', Smollett, 'almost stupified with ill Health, Loss of Memory, Confinement and Solitude', claims that his circulation would long ago have stopped but for the goad-pricks of Grub Street: 'Sometimes I am baited as a Dunce, then a ministerial Hireling, then a Jacobite, then a rancorous Knave, then a Liar, Quack & assassin' (Knapp, *Letters*, p. 133).

In spite of the friendly intervention of the rival historian David Hume, Smollett was unable to obtain the post of consul in Nice or

Leghorn. In his letter of farewell and thanks to Hume (August 1768), it is as a man resigned to his fate that he writes that he is going 'into perpetual exile' (Knapp, *Letters*, p. 136). He had made himself too many enemies to be entitled to his country's gratitude. Moreover, his aggressively indepen-dent character had precluded him, in spite of the slanderous accusations of his detractors, from being a toady of the government. 'Dr Smollett had never spaniell'd ministers' is the excellent way Moore puts it in his biography (1872 ed., p. 142).

Before leaving England Smollett had, perhaps, sharpened his Parthian arrow. He entrusted (if he was really the author) the manuscript of *The History and Adventures of an Atom* to the printer during the summer of 1768, and this sociopolitical satire was published in April 1769, after his departure. Was that a precautionary measure? The first words of the preface reinforce this supposition. The author mistrusts these 'ticklish times' and the 'plague of prosecution' and takes the trouble, as two years later for *Humphry Clinker*, to present it as a chance discovery of the original barely legible manuscript. The transmigrations of an atom are described with a great many physiological details and the Japanese fiction is only, as Herbert amusingly puts it (p. 89), 'thin japan'. No one could be deceived and the *Critical Review* (May 1769, xxvii, 362–9), does not hesitate to declare, after a few hasty and prudent reservations, that 'the island of Japan, where the chief scene of the atom's adventures lies, is no other than that of Great Britain' (p. 363). If today one needs keys[91] to identify the political personages behind the mask of their pseudo-Japanese names, it was easy for their contemporaries to identify Pitt as the dema-gogic orator Taycho or Newcastle as the scatological puppet Fika-Kaka. The emphasis on the excremental, especially anal, functions might suggest, just as in *Habbakuk Hilding*, a psychopathological fixation. In fact Smollett, in his largely justified rancour against the thorough corruption of political morals employs the whole arsenal of satire from stinging wit to acrid irony. Nor does he omit to emphasise the grotesque aspects of physiological functions. As the *Critical Review* (xxvii, 362) observes: 'This satire unites the happy extravagance of Rabelais to the splendid humour of Swift.' The responsibility for these epithets, especially those concerning Swift, had better be left to the critic! The influence of Rabelais is undeniable. Smollett shows that he knows the passage about the various arse-wipers tried by Gargantua. He enumerates them and quotes in French the 'volupté merifique au trou de cul' [*sic*]. Whatever the actions Smollett describes, such as the ritual application of the royal foot to the behind of the Prime Minister or the anal osculation to which the Prime Minister in his turn submits the courtiers and clergy, there is at no moment any dubious or pornographic intention. Smollett's concern is to transcribe — at their most repulsive on the physiological plane — the corruption, stupidity and malice of the great of this world and their institutions.

But there is more in *The History and Adventures of an Atom* than a scatological satire on the régime. For Smollett it is a genuine psychological catharsis which relieves him of the accumulated tensions of seven years of misfortune (1761–68). It is a vent for his social as well as his political spleen. In this novel there is a protean character which, even more than Pitt and Newcastle, dominates the whole book: it is the crowd, 'the mob'. Smollett stigmatises in turn its sheeplike submissiveness to the verbal magic of a demagogic Pitt, its dirtiness and its cruelty. The bestial metaphor is a recurring *leitmotiv* in the description of this populace, whose bloodthirsty frenzy Smollett, as the upholder of a rigid hierarchy, dreaded. 'Blatant beast' is the expression which springs most often to his pen. What could be more striking than this infernal vision of a crowd manipulated by Pitt? 'The hydra, rolling itself in the dust, turned up its huge unwieldy paunch, and wagged its forky tail; then licked the feet of Taycho, and through all its hoarse discordant throats began to bray applause'[92]. Finally, it would be wrong to think that Smollett is blinded by personal resentment. Here again, he is able to keep his clear-sightedness, and in his analysis of the English character, of the hatred for the Scots, of the character of Bute and of his own failure with the *Briton* he shows no lack of critical shrewdness.

About the last two years of Smollett's life documentary evidence is sparser. In turn he is in Pisa, in Florence, in Leghorn, then again in Pisa and, in the spring of 1770, he is installed in his villa 'Il Giardino', Leghorn, on the slopes of Monte Nero. In spite of his physical sufferings, his aesthetic sense is far from being blunted. In May 1770 he delights in describing his retreat: 'I am at present rusticated on the side of a mountain that overlooks the sea in the neighbourhood of Leghorne, a most romantic & salutary Situation' (Knapp, *Letters*, p. 138). It was in these places that, according to biographical tradition, he wrote, or more likely finished writing, *Humphry Clinker*. This last novel, announced in the press in January 1771, was published in June. The critics, with a few rare exceptions, received it on the whole very favourably. The *Critical Review* of August 1771 (vol. xxxii, 81–8) emphatically commends it for 'a variety of scenes and characters almost unanticipated' (p. 81), and concludes thus: 'We may venture to affirm it will be ranked among the most entertaining performances of the Kind' (p. 88). The *Town and Country Magazine* (June 1771, iii, 317–21) is also enthusiastic, so too are the *Court & City Magazine* (July and August 1771, iii, 310–12, 357–63). The only reservations concern the author's partiality for his native land and the want of delicacy in certain descriptions. Thus *Everyman's Magazine* addresses the following rebukes to Smollett: 'His descriptions are partial, exaggerated, and ill-natured particularly with respect to the city of London. Of the capital of his native country, the reader will find, he gives a more favourable account, than any that has yet appeared' (July 1771, i, 33). The *Gentleman's Magazine* shows itself reserved as to the literary and moral merit of *Humphry Clinker*. It reproaches Smollett for having been so parsimonious of his invention, that he has twice overturned a coach, and twice introduced a fire, to exhibit a scene of ridiculous distress, by setting women on their heads, and making some of his dramatic characters descend from a window by a ladder, as they rose out of bed (July 1771, xli, 317).

In spite of these few discordant notes, *Humphry Clinker* had a lasting success, as is proved by the many reissues of it after Smollett's death and all through the nineteenth century. It is likely that Smollett did not know of this immediate success. He spent the summer of 1771 at the baths of Lucca and a letter from his friend Armstrong in June 1770 proves that he was either unaware of his weakness or that, parallel with that resurgence of his literary power in *Humphry Clinker*, he experienced a revival of physical strength. Armstrong, in his letter[93], alludes to a plan for an excursion: 'As you talked of a ramble to the South of France, I shall be extremely happy to attend you.' Like a ship long buffeted by the storms of life, 'but still seaworthy, he was swept down by an unexpected and overwhelming blast. The primary cause of his death appears to have been an acute intestinal affection'[94]. Smollett died on September 17th 1771, and one may wish that the last words[95] of the old fighter to his wife are authentic. At the close of 'this strange eventful history' they sum up the stoical courage of that final appeasement: 'All is well, my dear.'

2
Autobiography and the novels

Smollett frequently felt an imperative need to draw his own portrait in his works. This is, as it were, the very hallmark of his psychological and literary personality. Critical assessments of Smollett's novels have not failed to exploit, sometimes *ad nauseam*, this tendency of his. It is rare for a critic not to use the word 'autobiography' when writing of *Roderick Random* or *Humphry Clinker* in particular. The gap between self-portrait and autobiography seems reduced and the critics blithely leap over it. Nevertheless, before examining to what extent it is possible to speak of autobiography in discussing Smollett's novels, it is essential to bear in mind some characteristics of this recognised literary form. This will make it easier to trace the sometimes devious boundary between self-portrait and autobiography.

It seems, in the first place, that the autobiographer feels an irresistible need to unbosom himself; not only to describe the major events of his life but to retrace his psychological, intellectual or moral evolution. In general, it is a middle-aged or old man who is trying to recapture the charm of his childhood and youth. Even if those periods of his life were troubled by grave difficulties, he views them in retrospect with a certain nostalgia. So, straight away, a difficulty presents itself: when Smollett wrote *Roderick Random*, his first novel, he was only twenty-seven and the early chapters dealing with Roderick's boyhood, are devoid of the least trace of this usual sentimental regret for times past. The same applies to *Peregrine Pickle*, published when Smollett was thirty.

The often idealised reconstruction of the author's salad days is a frequent but, in the last analysis, only minor characteristic of auto-biography. When Smollett inserts his physical or psychological self-

40

portrait into his work, he remains faithful to the avid tendencies of his passionate temperament. ('Avid' is used here in the particular meaning of the psychological school of thought known as 'characterology', 'avidity' being defined as 'the will to be, the will to be as fully possible and to persevere in being'[1].)

He tries in this way to grasp his own physical and psychological reality through the momentarily arrested flux of time. The self-portrait is therefore a total apprehension of the lived moment, the disturbing confrontation of the man with his image. This confrontation is accompanied by an anguished fascination like that of Narcissus, or that of Rembrandt watching himself through his various self-portraits. There is such a thing as a genuine autobiographical *angst*, capable of assuming many forms according to the life led by the individual. An autobiography can be either a vindication of, say, a political career or a writer's life, or the apologia of a spiritual journey. Cardinal de Retz, Rousseau and Goethe, Newman and St Augustine, are so many instances of this multiformity. Hence there are two fundamental differences between the self-portrait and the autobiography. Whereas the self-portrait represents the particular moment, the ambiguous and permanent vanishing-point at the shifting intersection of the past and the future, the autobiography is an attempt to re-create the writers' experience of duration, that is to say, the *whole* of his past life. 'The historian of himself wishes to draw his own portrait, but whereas the painter fixes only a moment of his outward appearance, the autobiographer strives for a total and coherent expression of his whole destiny'[2]. This is how George Gusdorf sums up the contrast between self-portrait and autobiography. Even the most inveterate upholder of the autobiographical interpretation of Smollett's novels would be hard put to it to find in *Roderick Random* or *Humphry Clinker* that sometimes heroic determination, often tinged with a proud humility, the autobiographer shows in wanting to re-create the unity of his life over the lapse of years.

Finally, an autobiography is not only a work of re-creation, it is also a creation which enriches the individual's knowledge of himself. 'To remake but also to make oneself', might be the motto of the genuine autobiographer. The deciphering of past experience is a difficult task which the autobiographer has to accomplish without falling into the insidious snares of false humility, pride, or smug self-satisfaction. The great problem for a sincere autobiographer is how to distinguish the mirror from the mirage. To what extent are Smollett's novels the mirror of his life?

Before tackling the central problem of the relationship between personal experience and autobiography, it is necessary to pose it more precisely in the particular case of Smollett. The general correspondences between his life and certain of his novels — *Roderick Random*, written at the beginning of his literary career, *Humphry Clinker* at the end — are such that the critics have succumbed to the 'autobiographical temptation'.

By this expression must be understood the total or partial reduction of Smollett's novels to a more or less direct or disguised narrative of the events of his own life. It is easy — and for two centuries critics and biographers have done so with the utmost zest — to trace a series of parallels between the Scottish origin of Roderick and that of Smollett; between his seafaring activities, the expedition to Cartagena and the part played in it by the author himself as surgeon's mate on board the *Chichester*; between the literary disappointments of Melopoyn and those of the young Smollett subjecting himself to a long round of theatrical door-to-door canvassing in order to get his unfortunate *Regicide* produced at all costs. There is a series of undeniable coincidences. Thus, in order to obtain his surgeon's-mate's warrant, Smollett had to undergo the examination at Surgeons' Hall which he describes with so much satirical verve in Chapter xvii of *Roderick Random* and which might be entitled 'The apprentice-surgeon before his jury'. Smollett himself fell ill during the expedition to Cartagena, as a rather high bill for treatment attests. In Chapter xxxiv of *Roderick Random* he is probably describing his own brushes with yellow fever.

But even more than these cross-checks between Smollett's life and his novels, the very mode of narration in *Roderick Random* invites autobiographical interpretation, for it is a novel written in the first person. The distance between fictional autobiography and autobiographical novel is easily bridged by a critic in search of a magic key, or rather master-key, capable of opening the secret doors of literary creation. Has not Smollett, in the preface to *Roderick Random*, declared his intention of representing 'modest merit struggling with every difficulty to which a friendless orphan is exposed, from his want of experience, as well as from the selfishness, envy, malice, and base indifference of mankind'[3]? This was certainly a noble and pathetic resolve, capable of touching the tenderhearted; moreover it had the advantage of being ambiguous. It was obvious that Smollett was putting himself on the scene with commendable modesty. This, from the very outset, gave his story a character of authenticity for which eighteenth-century readers were as avid as the twentieth-century ones who buy and eagerly devour the memoirs, reminiscences, anecdotes or witticisms of statesmen, filmstars and master criminals. Moreover the canvas Smollett proposes to cover in the preface to *Roderick Random* is wide enough for every reader to identify himself with the hero of the autobiographical story, whose courageous pugnacity cannot fail to gratify the wishful-thinking of armchair heroism. The marvellous ambiguity of the autobiographical, or reputedly autobiographical, novel is therefore triple: the 'I' of *Roderick Random* represents at once Roderick, Smollett and the reader. The autobiographical temptation is not only one to which the critic easily yields, it also appeals to a profound instinct of the reader's. This is the need to identify himself with the hero and to participate in imagination in his adventures, and, in addition, the fascination of the unknown, mysterious connections between the author and his novels. Charles Le Chevalier talks of a 'Jonah complex':

> The desire, 'to know what someone has in his belly' as G. Bachelard amusingly says (*La Terre et les Rêveries du Repos*) is explained by this mystique of the unknown and that hold every veiled form has on our stimulated imagination; but above all by that inalienable hope for the triumph of Jonah and Prometheus, explorers of mysteries, revealers of unknown knowledge[4].

Poor 'Jonah' Smollett! His readers and his critics have all too often imprisoned him in a whale as fabulous as the Leviathan.

Peregrine Pickle lends itself less to an autobiographical interpretation. Young Peregrine is English and not Scottish. He goes to Winchester and Oxford, which Smollett did not. In *Ferdinand Count Fathom* and *Launcelot Greaves* the autobiographical elements seem at first sight non-existent. Even the most cantankerous critics have not dared to liken Smollett to Ferdinand Count Fathom or Launcelot Greaves. But, with the publication of *Humphry Clinker*, the autobiographical delirium returns more violently. Once again, it was tempting to see in Matthew Bramble, the peevish misanthropist and churlish benefactor in search of elusive health, a Smollett worn out by literary forced labour, embittered by his personal misfortunes and the political failure of the *Briton* and rendered still more acid by a body emaciated and undermined by consumption. Just as in *Roderick Random*, the literary technique adopted here by Smollett favoured an autobiographical interpretation. In perusing this series of letters, does not the reader have the delicious feeling of committing an indiscretion of reading over a neighbour's shoulder a letter not addressed to him? There is another ambiguity intended by the author. These letters are written by and for the five letter-writers, by and for Smollett himself and finally by and for the reader himself who has to re-create the answers of the correspondents and who, in addition, connects and compares the various letters with each other. Thus the reader is at once the letter-writer and the recipient. Each letter is therefore a subtle game between Smollett, the fictitious author of the letter and the reader.

Such are the powerful mainsprings of this autobiographical temptation. And for two centuries their mechanism has operated with enough force and regularity to have produced a solid autobiographical tradition in Smollettian criticism. This tradition appeared very early, even in Smollett's own lifetime. When, on February 26th 1763, the American Richard Smith of Burlington, New Jersey, writes to Smollett what nowadays would be called a 'fan letter', he undoubtedly acts as spokesman for an autobiographical tradition already very widespread in England and America. After having apologised, with simple and charming courtesy, for having troubled Smollett, he avers his pleasure in reading his novels and also the curiosity they arouse both in himself and in several of his friends:

> Of the circumstances of your life, we at this distance know little, but should be glad to be informed whether Roderick Random or Peregrine Pickle contain any traces of your real adventures, and at what age of life, and under what circumstances they were written?[5]

The *Annual Register* for the year 1775 puts forward an opinion which was adopted by nearly all the biographers and critics up to the last decades of the nineteenth century. This is what the anonymous critic writes about *Roderick Random*:

> All the first volume, and the beginning of the second, appears to consist of real incident and character, though certainly a good deal heightened and disguised. The Judge, his grandfather; Crab and Potion, the two apothecaries; and Squire Gawkey [*sic*] were characters well-known in that part of the Kingdom where the scene was laid. Captains Oakhum [*sic*] and Whiffle, Doctors Mackshane and Morgan, were also said to be real personages; but their names we have either never learnt, or have now forgotten. A bookbinder and barber long eagerly contended for being shadowed under the name of Strap[6].

A little further on in this same article (p. 47), the author emphasises the literary and psychological affinity between Roderick, Peregrine and Matthew Bramble. Hence he arrives at the obvious conclusion: through these three personages 'the Doctor seems to have described his own character at the different stages and situations of his life'.

From the outset the autobiographical interpretation presents a double aspect. It is Smollett who puts himself on the scene and describes himself through the principal characters of his three great novels. The other highly-coloured characters with whom he peoples his often satirical narratives are not imaginary literary creations but real people whom he knew and detested. Caricature and revenge thus become the unpleasant corollary of autobiography.

This autobiographical interpretation reappears in the sketch of his life which serves as introduction to *Plays and Poems written by T. Smollett* published in London in 1777. 'It is said, and probably with some truth, that the chief incidents in the early part of his life were given to the public in one of the first and best of his productions, the novel of *Roderick Random*' (p. 11). One must not be surprised to rediscover in all these biographies a determinedly autobiographical interpretation of Smollett's works. They pillage and paraphrase each other without the slightest literary shame. It would take too long to quote here all the biographies published in the eighteenth and nineteenth centuries[7]. Anderson does not hesitate to declare that *Roderick Random* 'contained the real history of the chief incidents of the early part of his life'[8].

Moore was the first to make some reservations about the identification of Roderick with Smollett:

> *Roderick Random* unquestionably is sometimes placed in situations similar to those in which Smollett had been; but it is equally certain that other circumstances in Random's story are so different from those which belonged to the Doctor himself, that he believed the application would never have been made[9].

Still very slight reservations which would not have been of much interest had not Moore been the only biographer who knew Smollett well personally. In the life of Smollett written by Walter Scott, the critical mind of this novelist with firsthand experience of literary creation, makes him express certain doubts as to the validity of the autobiographical interpretation:

> It was generally believed that Smollett painted some of his own early adventures under the veil of fiction; but the public carried the spirit of applying the characters of a work of fiction to living personages much farther perhaps than the author intended[10].

And Scott then hastens to recall the identifications generally suggested for Gawky, Crab, Potion, Oakum and Whiffle. The American Smollett scholars are in some sort the direct heirs of this autobiographical tradition. One has only to read the works of H. S. Buck, in particular *A Study in Smollett*, to see how much space is given to the research of the real persons Smollett lampooned in *Roderick Random* and *Peregrine Pickle*[11].

It is only from the end of the nineteenth century that a reaction becomes quite clearly discernible among critics and biographers who protest — at last — against the abuses of the autobiographical assimilation, pure and simple, of Smollett to his principal characters. Herbert takes advantage of it to condemn a certain type of criticism which sees in autobiography and the discovery of contemporary models the hallmark of genuine realism. '*Roderick Random* being written as if by himself, its autobiographic style provoked a sturdy endeavour to identify the originals of the characters — a notable outcome of the fallen spirit of realism'[12]. Hannay, Smeaton and Saintsbury reject in their turn what has become one of the most wornout clichés of Smollettian pseudocriticism. It is undoubtedly Smeaton who raises the most vigorous protest against the identification of the old judge in *Roderick Random* as Smollett's own grandfather. He almost apologises for the passion with which he defends the memory of Sir James against 'an undeserved slur that has been cast on it by some biographers, who have been smitten with the mania for reading the facts of a man's life into his works'[13]. Modern studies in general show the greatest circumspection with regard to autobiographical interpretation. Thus Kahrl says of *Humphry Clinker*: 'With all the parade and array of dates, stages, topography, and only thinly veiled description of personal experience and contemporary events, *Humphry Clinker* remains, nevertheless, almost as unsatisfactory a source for biography as *Roderick Random*'[14]. There is the same warning in Gassman's excellent thesis, 'The Background of Tobias Smollett's *The Expedition of Humphry Clinker*': 'It would be dangerous to read *Humphry Clinker* as a disguised autobiography'[15]. Nevertheless this autobiographical tradition was too firmly established to vanish all at once without leaving traces. It is surprising to read this judgment in *Augustans and Romantics* by H. V. D. Dyson and John Butt:

> Smollett never recovered from a kind of angry perversity that fills his novels like an unholy odour. The naval expedition to Cartagena in which he took part may have made him an artist, but it also enslaved him. His work is curative, like that of a surgeon with unwashed hands, who at times reminds us of a hangman (third revised edition, 1961, p. 49).

It would be easy to multiply examples of this autobiographical bee in the bonnet, and it is probable that such a set critical habit will not be dropped as quickly as the progress of modern criticism might lead one to hope[16]. But, after having examined the sources of the autobiographical temptation and the autobiographical tradition, it is something of a relief to read the evidence of Smollett himself, in his letters as much as in his novels.

It is perhaps because Smollett's letter to his friend Alexander Carlyle of June 7th 1748 (Knapp, *Letters*, pp. 7—9) was not known in its entirety before the middle of the nineteenth century that critics have so often fallen into the autobiographical error. Nevertheless the important passage which reveals, with all the young Smollett's fiery vigour, his opinion on the autobiographical interpretation (already) of *Roderick Random* had been published by H. G. Graham in *Scottish Men of Letters in the Eighteenth Century* as early as 1901. Why has this clearcut evidence been neglected? Why has anyone doubted the ring of almost exasperated sincerity which characterises Smollett's letter? The young novelist, flattered by Carlyle's approbation, admits to him nonetheless that an insidious shadow has darkened the sunshine of literary success. Certain persons believe themselves to be aimed at in the caricatures which abound in *Roderick Random*, in particular John Love, his schoolmaster at Dumbarton. The latter thinks he recognises himself in Chapter v of *Roderick Random*, where the tyrannical pedagogue for once makes acquaintance with his own stinging whip. Smollett is obviously uneasy, for John Love, as a good Scot, is quick at rejoinder and, to revenge himself, has taken pains to spread a certain number of calumnies about him. Already Smollett has well understood the mechanism of autobiographical interpretation. Certain persons think themselves insulted in *Roderick*

Random 'on the Supposition that I myself am the Hero of the Book, and they, of consequence, concerned in the History' (p. 7). In the following clarification, he adopts a solemnity of tone which is all the more noticeable since the rest of the letter is written in a familiar, informal style:

> I shall take this Opportunity therefore of declaring to you, in all the sincerity of the most unreserved Friendship that no Person living is aimed at in all the first part of the Book; that is, while the scene lies in Scotland and that (the account of the Expedition to Carthagene excepted) the *whole* is not so much a Representation of my Life as that of many other needy Scotch Surgeons whom I have known either personaly or by Report. The Character of Strap (who I find, is a favourite among the Ladies everywhere) is partly taken from the Life; but the circumstances of his Attachment to Random entirely feigned (p. 8).

Fifteen years later, Smollett's position has not changed. In the reply to Richard Smith he shows less indignant heat than in the letter of June 1748 to Carlyle, but there too, the tone is categorical:

> The only Similitude between the Circumstances of my own Fortune and those I have attributed to Roderick Random consists in my being born of a reputable Family in Scotland, in my being bred a Surgeon, and having served as a Surgeon's mate on board a man of war during the Expedition to Carthagene. The low Situations in which I have exhibited Roderick I never experienced in my own Person (Knapp, *Letters*, p. 112).

Thus Smollett willingly admitted the existence of certain personal elements in his novels but disclaimed, with a touch of annoyance, his identification with Roderick. Even in his letter of 1748 to Carlyle, Smollett does not deny that in *Roderick Random* he has avenged himself on the theatrical managers who have had the effrontery to refuse his *Regicide*. But the extrapolation of these obvious personal elements into autobiography is more than unwarranted.

Seven years later Smollett redoubled his precautions in writing the fable which prefaces the fourth edition of *Roderick Random* (1755). In these few briskly written pages, Smollett shows that he is on his guard not only against an autobiographical interpretation but also a biographical one, namely the identification of his characters with contemporary models who were still very much alive. It is probable that this fable, like the foreword to *The History and Adventures of an Atom* and the preface in letter form to *Humphry Clinker*, was primarily a kind of legal precaution. Smollett is being prudent for fear that a bailiff will come and serve him with a writ for libel. (He would have done well to observe the same laudable prudence when he analysed Knowles's pamphlet in May 1758.) Moreover, these pages, in spite of their character of a burlesque fable, show a sound psychological knowledge of the public. Smollett was intuitively aware of this tendency which impels the reader to read between the lines and discover living contemporaries behind the fictional characters. But his position is sometimes ambiguous. He admits that he has lampooned the theatrical managers in *Roderick Random*, and yet he had taken pains to state in its preface: 'Every intelligent reader will, at first sight, perceive I have not deviated from nature in the facts, which are all true in the main, although the circumstances are altered and disguised, to avoid personal satire'[17]. A certain bad faith is, in this case, obvious. But Smollett's exhortation to the reader in the fable remains a stroke of intellectual and professional perspicacity:

> Seek not to appropriate to thyself that which equally belongs to five hundred different people. If thou shouldst meet with a character that reflects thee in some ungracious particular, keep thy own counsel; consider that one feature makes not a face[18].

The examination of the autobiographical tradition, however revealing of the mentality of critics and of the public, does not tackle the central problem of the relations between personal experience and the so-called 'autobiographical novel'. It would take too long, and probably be a waste of time, to examine *all* the points of contact between Smollett's life and his novels. For Smollett, as for any other novelist, it is obvious that literary creation is rooted in personal experience. In that sense, and at the risk of stretching the meaning of 'personal' almost to bursting-point, every work is 'autobiographical'! But that is more a facile juggling with words than an honest analysis of the relations between the real personal experience and the fictional account. Only definite examples can help to determine these relations. Now, in the two letters of 1748 and 1763 quoted above, Smollett, who rejects the autobiographical interpretation, makes an exception in the case of his account of the Cartagena expedition. Moreover he reverted twice to this subject, which he treated again in 1756 in the *Compendium of Authentic and Entertaining Voyages* under the title of 'An Account of the Expedition against Carthagena' and subsequently in his *Complete History of England*, published in 1757–58. By comparing the fifteen pages the expedition occupies in *Roderick Random* in Chapters xxxi and xxxii with the twenty pages Smollett takes in the 'Account' to describe and analyse this expedition, it is possible to determine a series of variations between the novel and the historical narrative which comes nearer reality.

In the *Complete History of England* Smollett devotes only a few pages to the operation of Cartagena, but these may be considered as the final quintessence of his historical judgment. Moreover, the discovery[19] of two journals kept by Lieutenant Robert Watkins, one of the officers of the *Chichester*, provides another means of comparison, although Watkins's notes mainly have a typical military terseness. This comparison of the various versions of the Cartagena expedition has already been systematically made by Louis L. Martz in his article 'Smollett and the expedition to Carthagena'[20]. From the line by line comparison of the first two versions of the expedition, it emerges that in *Roderick Random* the historical details are used mainly 'as a string on which to hang the largely fictitious adventures of Smollett's hero; and even the slender descriptions of naval and military manoeuvres are warped by Smollett's satirical tone and purpose in the novel as a whole'[21]. So, since it is thus proved that the historical value of Chapters xxxi and xxxii of *Roderick Random* is slight (with the exception of the observations on the appalling sanitary conditions in the sick-bays), it is legitimate to doubt the autobiographical value of these passages.

Smollett, in his capacity as novelist, takes liberties with historical fact. It is a pity that in his article, which is remarkable for factual accuracy, Louis L. Martz makes no comment on the narrative technique adopted in *Roderick Random* to describe the naval and military operations at Cartagena. Roderick (who must not, as we have just seen, be confused with Smollett) adopts the role all through the expedition of a detached onlooker and ironic commentator. Roderick displays a constant determination to mitigate and, as it were, muffle his opinions in order to emphasise their disillusioned irony. The tone is given at the outset, from the meeting of the two fleets at Port-Royal where they wait for a month for the order to put to sea again: '*something* of consequence was *certainly* transacted; notwithstanding the *insinuation* of *some* who affirmed we had no business at all in that place'[22]. It is obvious that the four words in italic are deliberately put there in order to imply the opposite of what they apparently mean. On the following page (I, 257) the use of verbal mutes has the result of making the irony all the more strident: 'as was said', 'supposed to be lying near that place', 'seemed to consult', 'certain malicious people'; 'But if I might be allowed to give my opinion of the matter, I would ascribe this delay to the generosity of our chiefs, who scorned to take any advantage that fortune might give them, even over an enemy'. This last sentence is a diamond of irony; no rough diamond but one whose facets have been cut with perfidious care. The use of 'I believe', and 'I presume' in the space of two lines in the final paragraph is a pedal-point in this ironical rhapsody. The stylistic analysis of the pages that follow could only multiply examples of this linguistic and psychological duplicity. Now this fixed determination to give a satirical twist to the story is the opposite of that total sincerity at which the genuine auto-biographer should endeavour to aim. At the end of a very searching examination of the factual concordances between Watkins's journals and the two chapters of *Roderick Random*, George Kahrl concluded that 'Smollett selected secondary events, not necessarily autobiographic, and made them the basis for realistic pictures of daily life aboard a man-of-war'[23]. It is advisable, therefore, to treat the exception made by Smollett himself in the case of the Cartagena expedition with the utmost wariness.

If autobiography in its pure state, as it were, a revised and corrected sketch of a destiny, is not to be found in Smollett's novels, it is nevertheless certain that many personal elements are. What is to be understood by 'personal elements'? Not the recounting of events which stood out as landmarks in Smollett's life but the lasting psychological imprints left by certain painful confrontations with reality. If some passages in the novels have an autobiographical tinge, the colouring is more psychological than factual. But such a working hypothesis can be dangerous if its limits are not carefully defined. Pushed to extremes, every character, every opinion expressed in the novels can be attributed to Smollett and then criticism relapses into the unwarranted autobiographical interpretation denounced earlier. This method of work is defensible only in so far as it relies, on the one hand, on Smollett's life history and, on the other, on an analytical knowledge of his personality. Now it seems that there had been three poles of emotional tension in Smollett's life corresponding to three frustrations: medicine (with its naval interlude), the theatre, and politics. His passionate character subjected him to a constant, but not uniform tension. Modern psychology would, no doubt, speak of 'traumatic experiences'.

Smollett, undoubtedly, never forgave himself for not having made the brilliant medical career that would have enabled him to rise far more quickly, socially and financially, than the profession of writer. Is it necessary to recall that in 1750, in spite of the success of *Roderick Random*, Smollett had not yet abandoned all idea of practising as a doctor and received his M.D. from Aberdeen? And it was in 1752 that he published his only medical work, the *Essay on the External Use of Water*. Smollett's personal opinion on medicine is reflected in his novels in three quite distinct ways. It is not, to be sure, a matter of a regular straightforward evolution, clearly determined chronologically, but rather of successive attitudes adopted by stages as Smollett lost all hope of establishing himself as a doctor. First of all, in *Roderick Random*, it is experience of ship's doctors and indignation at their culpable inefficiency that characterise his opinion of naval medicine. When Roderick, thanks to the intervention of a kindly colleague, is promoted to the rank of surgeon's mate, he goes down to the crew's quarters where Thomson and Morgan live. The first impression that strikes him is wholly olfactory: 'my nose was saluted with an intolerable stench of putrified cheese and rancid butter'[24]. That is an authentic personal experience, not a sign of exaggerated sensitivity. Watkins's journals[25] confirm the deplorable state of the ship's provisions. The visit to the sick-bay where the patients are crammed together without air, without light and in an advanced state of physical misery, forces Roderick to the conclusion that Smollett himself must have reached: 'I was much less surprised that people should die on board, than that any sick person should recover'[26].

In *Peregrine Pickle* Smollett considers medicine and its practitioners with a humour often so caustic that it verges on satire. A trace of the interest he took all his life in hydrotherapy reappears when the young hero's mother insists on plunging her baby every day in cold water, according to a method dear to John Locke. The opinion of Dr Comfit Colocynth[27] — this therapeutic oxymoron which serves him for name is already a satirical warning — is a little masterpiece of medical casuistry, dedicated, no doubt, to those of his colleagues who do not share his enthusiasm for the virtues of cold water. Smollett also remembers that he has been a medical student, a lover of physiological practical jokes and remarks made to shock delicate sensibilities. This propensity reappears in the dirty joke played by Peregrine on Jolter and Pallet. Peregrine makes his friends believe that the fricassée of rabbit with which they are regaling themselves is made of cat. The doctor[28] takes advantage of the gastric dismay of the tutor and the painter to launch into a dissertation on the comparative dietetic merits of cat, dog, bear and even of human flesh. This evinces an almost schoolboyish desire to shock the respectable reader. The same desire is responsible for the pages so often decried in *Humphry Clinker* where another eccentric doctor makes a medical defence of stench. This stercoraceous passage does not even have the savour of rumbustious Rabelaisian comedy. What, at a pinch, was pardonable in *Peregrine Pickle*, written when he was thirty, is no longer so in *Humphry Clinker*, completed when he was fifty. It is undoubtedly an error of taste, even though the eighteenth century was not remarkable for its fastidious sense of smell either in ordinary life or in literature. Moreover the critics who have fulminated against this passage[29] always omit to point out that these observations of the doctor's eventually lead to his discomfiture which permit one to think that henceforth Smollett condemned that kind of talk.

Smollett also makes use of reminiscences of *The Present State*, published in 1768—69. The allusions to the preferences of the Greenlanders, the Hottentots and the Senegalese for rotten meat and strong smells are indubitable echoes of *The Present State*. Thus in *The Present State* the reader learns that the Greenlanders 'devour rotten flesh with the utmost avidity'[30]. It is perhaps not so much the medico as the compiler that we detect in these pages. Finally, in *Peregrine Pickle*, Smollett does not spare his colleagues, in particular those who are established in Bath, a town where certain biographers affirm he did not succeed in setting up as a doctor. Peregrine describes the sons of Aesculapius installed in Bath as 'a class of animals who live in this place, like so many ravens hovering about a carcase, and even ply for employment, like scullers at Hungerford-stairs'[31]. Smollett's satirical technique is already sure. Animal similes and the heaping up of disparaging metaphors are its hallmark.

Satire gives place to rancour and regrets in *Ferdinand Count Fathom* and *Launcelot Greaves*. It is in *Ferdinand Count Fathom* that Smollett is bitterest about doctors. His criticisms are acrid. He inveighs against the habit doctors have of making their patients swallow 'a whole dispensary of bolusses, draughts and apozems'[32]. Such medication has the effect of making Ferdinand, who was merely counterfeiting illness, really ill. Interest in hydrotherapy reappears in *Ferdinand Count Fathom* where Smollet explains how Ferdinand, transformed into a medical charlatan, gains an easy victory over a learned but confused old doctor. Might this be a veiled allusion to the little success his medical pamphlet had had in the previous year? In any case, he analyses with a cruel lucidity the popular tendency, so widespread in the twentieth century, to believe a quack rather than a specialist: 'The judgment of the multitude is apt to be biassed by that surprize which is the effect of seeing an artist foiled at his own weapons, by one who engages him only for amusement'[33]. Another trace of Smollett's rancour: the ease with which Ferdinand passes for a genuine doctor. Ferdinand possesses all the ingratiating wiles and obsequiousness which Smollett totally lacked to satisfy the whims of a hypochondriacal and mainly feminine clientèle. Smollett consoles himself by making Ferdinand fail too and being soon 'as much overlooked as any other physician unsupported by interest or cabal'[34].

A last trace of personal preoccupation transpires in *Ferdinand Count Fathom*: the rather painful problem for Smollett of medical degrees. At Tunbridge, Dr Looby, a genuine practitioner duly armed with an Oxford or Cambridge degree, refuses to examine a patient in collaboration with Ferdinand who pretends he has a diploma from the University of Padua. Ferdinand defends himself and Smollett takes advantage of this to criticise English universities where

> there is no opportunity of studying the art; no, not so much as a lecture given on the subject: nor is there one physician of note, in this kingdom, who has not derived the greatest part of his medical knowledge, from the instructions of foreigners[35].

Smollett is not defending foreign universities so much as those of his native land, so often criticised by the English for the ease with which (provided the money was forthcoming) they conferred medical degrees.

Rancour gives way to a certain note of regret, apparent in *Launcelot Greaves*. Thus, in the first pages of this novel, Smollett sketches, with obvious sympathy, the portrait of Dr Fillet, who is not wholly unlike the author himself. This doctor, besides his good qualities of heart and mind 'had practised on board a man of war in his youth'[36]. Finally, when Sir Launcelot tries to move the doctor in charge of him in his lunatic asylum to pity, he makes a plea which is not only eloquent but a very noble profession of medical faith. The aim of medicine is 'to preserve the being, and confirm the health of our fellow-creatures; of consequence, to sustain the blessings of society, and crown life with fruition'[37]. Alas, this almost too flattering appeal has no effect on the doctor.

Thus the insertion of personal elements — in the first place his failure as a doctor — if it does not, properly speaking, constitute an autobiographical background, reveals in Smollett's case a certain anguished disquiet at the passage of time. 'Have I done right to renounce a medical career for that of a writer? Is it in vain?' Such are the personal preoccupations which can be discerned behind the many allusions to medicine with which Smollett scatters his novels.

The second pole of emotional tension, the theatre, is better known. Buck and Knapp[38] have analysed the chronological vicissitudes of the *Regicide* and identified the characters who figure in Chapters lxii and lxiii of *Roderick Random*. The autobiographical value of these passages is undeniable but is never autobiography in its pure state. One must, as it were, neutralise the acidity of the satire against Marmozet—Garrick before being able to deduce the probable relations between the actor and Smollett, to take only the case of Garrick. It is surprising to note that critics and biographers, fascinated no doubt by the possible parallels between the story of Melopoyn and young Smollett's theatrical disappointments have not emphasised how in *Peregrine Pickle* Smollett twice refers back to his own misfortune. First, Cadwallader, disguised as a fortune-teller, invites a penniless young poet into his prophetic lair. The young author has just submitted the manuscript of a play to a 'certain great man, at the head of taste, who had not only read and approved the performance, but also undertaken to introduce and support it on the stage'[39]. But the pseudopatron, in spite of his assurances, has probably not even shown the manuscript to a manager. The young poet suspects he is being tricked and wants to know who is lying and whether his play eventually has a chance of being produced. Cadwallader's exasperated reaction is, in fact, Smollett's. The seer who 'had, in his younger days, sported among the theatrical muses, began to lose his temper at this question, which recalled the remembrance of his own disappointments' (p. 568). Cadwallader's reply has all the savagery of a man whose hopes have been blighted. The theatre is 'intirely regulated by the daemons of dissimulation, ignorance and caprice' (ibid.). The second passage[40] elaborates the sketch quoted above and defines to some extent the part played by Sheerwit—Chesterfield, already attacked in the story of Melopoyn. The verbal violence with which Smollett caricatures Garrick, Quin, Lyttelton and Fielding in the first edition of *Peregrine Pickle*[41] is proof enough of the depth of a wound which still had to wait six long years (*The Reprisal*, 1757) to be healed, at least on the surface. The second expurgated edition published in 1758 and the homage paid to Garrick in the *Continuation of the Complete History of England* are well-known *amendes honorables*. Another favourable allusion to Garrick, dating from the same period (1760) seems less so. In Chapter iii of

Launcelot Greaves Tom Clarke thus describes the first appearance of Sir Launcelot in public: 'There was just such a humming and clapping of hands as you may hear when the celebrated Garrick comes upon the stage in King Lear, or King Richard, or any other top character' (p. 26).

But whereas the theatrical wound was probably well on the way to being healed in about 1760–61, the publication of the *Briton* from May 1762 to February 1763, to defend Bute's ministry, scarred Smollett grievously. Politics is thus the third and last emotional magnetic pole round which it is possible to regroup certain personal tensions that manifest themselves in *Humphry Clinker*. If one excepts the poem *The Tears of Scotland* written in 1746 after Culloden, and more a cry of anguish than the adoption of a political stance, politics make a belated appearance in Smollett's life and work. In a letter to Moore in 1756, he even declares his lack of interest in political affairs: 'I never dabble in Politics' (Knapp, *Letters*, p. 46). All the same, he goes on, in the same sentence, to criticise Admiral Byng severely for his supposed cowardice. It was through history that Smollett came to politics. The publication of the *Complete History of England* in 1757–58 had aroused many bitter accusations of partiality for the Tories. This was a break with the Whig tradition of his family. Smollett, while protesting his desire to be impartial, frankly admits his original intention

> to write with a warm side to those principles in which I was educated. But in the Course of my Inquiries, the whig ministers and their abettors turned out such a Set of sordid Knaves that I could not help stigmatizing some of them for their want of Integrity and Sentiment (letter to Moore, January 2nd 1758: Knapp, *Letters*, p. 65).

His quarrels with Admiral Knowles also have a political implication. But his conservatism was to find its most coherent expression in the issues of the *Briton* and the painful confrontation with Wilkes.

Before examining the traces of personal political opinions in *Humphry Clinker* and the way they were influenced by Smollett's involvement with the *Briton*, it is right to observe first that *Launcelot Greaves* already touches on political problems. At the beginning of the novel the misanthropist Ferret makes a violent attack on the government and rebukes it for its military expenditure and its corruption. Sir Launcelot wastes no time in replying. He denounces with alarming vehemence the damage to their country done by defeatist traitors whose one idea is to sow discord and sedition. The main argument Sir Launcelot uses against Ferret is developed over and over again in the *Briton* and *Humphry Clinker*. It is a moral and intellectual argument. The detractors of the government pervert the Truth 'in defiance of common honesty and common sense'[42]. This expression 'common sense' is especially dear to Smollett and covers the idea of a judicious balance of power between a patriot king and a nation where moral order, based on a rigid social hierarchy, prevails. These political principles imply on the one hand a mistrust of all extremists, and on the other a hearty hatred of the crowd — 'the mob' — which is one of the most detestable main characters in *The History and Adventures of an Atom*.

Smollet offers his readers a practical illustration of this philosophy in *Launcelot Greaves* when he describes the electoral campaign (worthy of Hogarth) between the Tory Sir Valentine Quickset and his Whig opponent, Dr Isaac Vanderpelft. The names of the candidates are revealing in themselves. On the one hand the country squire, uneducated and boorish but attached to the land and the old traditional ways, a worthy hunting and drinking companion of Squire Western; on the other the capitalist big-business man, of Jewish origin, crafty, corrupt and ready to stoop to any kind of prostitution. The postures and speeches of these candidates, who are more extreme types than individuals, emphasise the danger of such diametrically opposed positions. Fortified by his quixotic courage, Sir Launcelot bluntly criticises the two parties and endeavours to make them listen to reason. Though seemingly impartial, he none the less shows greater hatred of the Whig than of the Tory. The end of his peroration betrays Smollett's deep attachment to this moderate notion of 'common sense'. Sir Launcelot implores his fellow-citizens to avoid 'the opposite extremes of the ignorant clown and the designing courtier' and to choose 'a man of honesty, intelligence and moderation'[43]. The expression 'doctrine of moderation' is used on the following page. Is it necessary to say that Sir Launcelot's appeal is not listened to and that this knight errant astray in the eighteenth century only saves his skin by judicious manipulation of his lance? Is this a coincidence? A few months later Smollett will describe himself as 'a political knight errant' and set out Sir Launcelot's noble plan of action, almost *verbatim*, in the sixth number of the *Briton* (July 3rd 1762, p. 31).

But if one excepts *The History and Adventures of an Atom* — political satire in its pure (or impure!) state, already analysed in Chapter 1 — it is in *Humphry Clinker* that Smollett's personal political opinions emerge most clearly. Recent studies have demonstrated the influence of *Present State* on *Humphry Clinker* and in particular on the conception of the characters of Lismahago and Bramble. After a detailed comparison of analogous passages Louis L. Martz concludes that 'Smollett, through both Bramble and Lismahago [in *Humphry Clinker*], gives vent to feelings which he has either suppressed or carefully modified in *Present State*'[44]. Among these opinions, praise of Scotland has pride of place. By a play of paradoxes and successive approximations between Lismahago and Bramble, Smollett manages to present a picture of Scotland, not without shadows, but, as a whole, mainly very flattering. Martz insists on the didactic role of spokesman, not to say propagandist, that Smollett assigns to Lismahago. Another, more recent, study by Byron Gassman analyses in detail the influence of the *Briton* on the political opinions expressed in *Humphry Clinker*. The observations made by Bramble on the liberty, not to say licence, of the press, the defence of peace and of the Treaty of Paris, the hatred of the masses and the faith in an enlightened monarchy, with a 'patriot-king' on the throne — such are the political themes dear to Smollett which the reader can find again in *Humphry Clinker* (where the idea of the patriot-king is not expressly formulated); but Gassman concludes that 'the ideas and experiences of the *Briton* are a strong undercurrent in the thought of *Humphry Clinker*'[45]. Certainly Smollett's opinion, especially on the freedom of the press, takes on all the more vivid a personal tinge when he thinks of the failure of the *Briton* and the success of his ex-friend Wilkes, the editor of the *North Briton*. Without any doubt, it is Wilkes whom Smollett is addressing, when he makes Matthew Bramble write:

> The public papers are become the infamous vehicles of the most cruel and perfidious defamation: every rancorous knave — every desperate incendiary, that can afford to spend half a crown or three shillings, may skulk behind the press of a newsmonger, and have a stab at the first character in the kingdom, without running the least hazard of detection or punishment[46].

In this same letter of Matthew Bramble's, there is a definite textual allusion to the *North Briton*. Smollett deplores the misuse of the expression which he quotes, 'The liberty of the press'. It was no coincidence that Wilkes had begun the first sentence of his first number of the *North Briton* (June 5th 1762) with these words: 'The *liberty of the press* is the birthright of a Briton.' Thus, in spite of the years that had passed, in spite of the personal misfortunes which had just overwhelmed him, in spite of his being far away, the author of *Humphry Clinker* had not forgotten the political struggle between the *Briton* and the *North Briton*.

Events he had lived through, such as the Cartagena expedition, and personal elements grouped under the three headings — medicine, theatre, politics — cannot wholly account for the particular imprint Smollett stamped on his novels. There is also a hallmark, more diffuse, yet unmistakably recognisable. Smollett had too strong a personality for his novels not to be to some extent impregnated with it. Here again, the search for autobiographical traces is not without dangers. But such a search is legitimate if it is based on a knowledge of Smollett's life and works and on analysis of the texts. His most obvious personal characteristic is found mainly in *Roderick Random* and *Humphry Clinker*: his Scottish origin. It would be pointless to dwell at length on this characteristic of his first and last novels. His nationality is responsible for at least two elements in his psychological make-up: pride and resentment. These two factors are the dynamic principle which breathes life into Roderick, and also to some extent into Peregrine, though the latter is theoretically

English. When Roderick defends himself against the lures of Miss Lavement, he perceives that his heart is armoured 'against her charms by pride
and resentment, which were two chief ingredients in my disposition'[47].
Smollett himself might have spoken these words. All the struggle to get
the *Regicide* published (in default of getting it produced) might well be
subtitled 'Pride and resentment'. Moreover, Smollett was conscious of this
Scottish hypersensitiveness. In *Humphry Clinker* he mentions his
apothecary 'who is a proud Scotchman, very thin-skinned' and, a few lines
further on, he adds this general statement: 'A right Scotchman has always
two strings to his bow and is *in utrumque paratus*'[48]. In his own case,
Smollett had not only two strings to his bow, but a Parthian arrow in his
quiver.

Finally, both *Roderick Random* and *Humphry Clinker* end with a
pilgrimage to Scotland. The return of Roderick and his rediscovered father
is not very descriptive but Smollett stresses the attachment and fidelity of
the Scottish peasants to their master. Pride and resentment give the
psychological keynote. Pride at regaining possession of the family
property and resentment towards those who have maltreated or injured
Roderick in his youth. As to the description of Scotland and Smollett's
love of his native land in *Humphry Clinker*, these subjects have been
treated by Louis L. Martz in Chapters v and vi of his book. After having
analysed the influence of *Present State* on the Scottish passages in
Humphry Clinker, Martz concludes that the material borrowed from
Present State is transformed and endowed with literary vitality, thanks to
the task of imaginative synthesis to which Smollett applied himself. In this
synthesis, the catalytic which assured the success of the operation was his
profound love of Scotland.

Violence is another imprint of Smollett's personality shown in his
novels. It is not merely a question of physical violence, described over and
over again in the course of the sometimes reprehensible adventures of his
heroes, but above all of a capacity for violent verbal expression of moral,
social and intellectual indignation. He has given a certain number of
samples of this in his letters, especially those written during the Admiral
Knowles affair. Often sanitary conditions unleash his wrath, whether he is
writing of the sick-bays on board men-of-war, the welcome which awaits
invalids in watering-places (in particular Bath whose dirtiness at once
horrifies and fascinates him), or finally the alimentary hygiene (or rather
lack of it) in a great city like London. Even if criticism of what is eaten
and drunk in London is part of a wider theme — the virtues of rustic
primitivism as opposed to the vitiating effects of progress — even if as
early as 1757—58 pamphlets (reviewed in the *Critical Review*) denounced
the wretched quality of the bread, the fact remains that Smollett's indignation has an undeniable note of personal sincerity. Matthew Bramble
draws up, not without irony, 'a catalogue of London dainties'[49]. He
reviews in turn water, wine, meat (in particular veal bled white), poultry,

vegetables, fish and fruit (Smollett concedes that there is fine fruit at Covent Garden but only the rich can afford it; as to the fruit sold in the street, its dirtiness disgusts him). Finally, watered-down milk makes a counterpart to adulterated wine. To milk Smollett devotes a sentence fifteen lines long in which he piles up its adulterations and contaminations with a ferocious stylistic zeal which is no mere rhetorical exercise. Already, in *Travels through France and Italy* he rages wrathfully against the repulsive dirtiness of inns (French and Italian mainly but English ones too) and the bad quality of food served in them. This dietetic passage is only one particularly clear example. There are other outbursts of indignation in his novels, which will be analysed later. Already, his denunciation of 'such uncleanness as my soul abhors'[50] sums up the almost puritanical vehemence of his virtuous indignation. Smollett's violence sometimes makes one think of the words of the Bible: 'the kingdom of heaven suffereth violence, and the violent take it by force' (Matt. 11:12).

This violence is not gratuitous. On the contrary, it only underlines a fundamental element in his personality as expressed in his novels: the passion for justice. Now Smollett, who on several occasions (particularly in the Gordon affair and the Knowles affair examined in Chapter 1) had had a bone to pick with the representatives of British justice, seems not to have retained a very pleasant memory of these legal skirmishes. It is in *Ferdinand Count Fathom* that his contempt for lawyers breaks out most forcibly. In Chapter xxii, he begins by drawing a decidedly unflattering comparison between French priests and the Templars. This first swift attack is nothing in comparison with Chapter xxxvii (as well as, to a certain extent, the two following chapters). Ferdinand, in spite of his artfulness, has let himself be involved in a case of adultery and has to stand trial. His lawyers are men without conscience, prepared to go to the length of suborning witnesses. They care more about their fees than about honour. They undertake his defence, which is described thus:

> His council behaved like men of consummate abilities in their profession; they exerted themselves with equal industry, eloquence, and erudition, in their endeavours to perplex the truth, browbeat the evidence, puzzle the judge, and mislead the jury[51].

This sentence assumes all its personal significance when Smollett reproduces it *verbatim* in his epistolary diatribe against Alexander Hume Campbell, a lawyer who had taken part in the Gordon—Smollett trial as Gordon's defence counsel. In the course of this long letter of February 23rd 1753 (about a week after the publication of *Ferdinand Count Fathom*) Smollett claims to discover the source of the animosity of Campbell, who had made a sarcastic allusion to *Ferdinand Count Fathom*. The reason for this attack *ad hominem* in court 'is no other than the history of a law-suit inserted in that performance, where the author takes occasion to observe, that the Counsel . . .' And here follows the whole sentence quoted above (Knapp, *Letters*, p. 25). Some years later Smollett, who had bad luck with lawyers, was to come up against Campbell again during the Knowles affair. No doubt this fresh clash with the law inspired his extraordinarily violent attacks on corrupt and uneducated magistrates in *Launcelot Greaves*. The portrait of Judge Gobble — this is not a name, but an act of indictment! — is not unlike Shakespeare's Justice Shallow. But the highly personal tone of a man in love with justice and disgusted at finding only puppets instead of genuine magistrates is predominant in these pages of Chapter xi, entitled 'Description of a modern Magistrate'. Sir Launcelot, denounced by Ferret, falls into the claws of this English Raminagrobis. In prison the quixotic redresser of wrongs learns of all the extortions perpetrated by Gobble. Sir Launcelot, aided by the honest attorney Tom Clarke, decides to nonplus this licensed oppressor of the poor, the widow and the orphan. Nevertheless Smollett, however concerned for justice — and however disillusioned — he may be, does not for all that renounce his social conservatism. When he recounts Gobble's career, he takes great care to insist on the very low birth of this upstart. Gobble owes his position to the venality of a nobleman who acquitted himself of a debt by getting him appointed a judge. Gobble has no legal training, at most he parades a few legal terms he has heard during conversations with hackney writers or attorneys' clerks.

Finally, Smollett attacks individuals rather than institutions. If high offices are entrusted to persons of low birth 'who are thrust into the magistracy without sentiment, education or capacity', then what becomes of 'our admired constitution, the freedom, the security of the subject, the boasted humanity of the British nation'[52]? Nevertheless it must be admitted in Smollett's defence that he explicitly condemns one law for the rich and another for the poor. Gobble's wife points out that her husband has never offended a rich *gentleman* but that, on the contrary he has exercised all the rigour of his authority ('the rigger of authority' says the strident shrew, inventing an ironic portmanteau word worthy of Win Jenkins) against the local small fry. 'In other words (said the knight), he has tyrannised over the poor, and connived at the vices of the rich'[53]. This indictment of Sir Launcelot's is undoubtedly also that of Smollett himself, enraged by a justice available only to the privileged few.

Another kind of injustice against which Smollett campaigned in *Launcelot Greaves* was the arbitrary internment of people in lunatic asylums. There is nothing in his biography which offers a factual counterpart of his interest in the lot of the insane in the eighteenth century. But his humanitarian feelings as a doctor and a writer can largely explain this anxiety for justice to the individual. Again, it is in the name of equity and respect for the human person that he denounces the abuses of private madhouses. Sir Launcelot, the victim of a plot, finds himself shut up in one of these institutions, defined by one of its inmates (Smollett is playing safe) as 'a repository of the most flagrant iniquities', harbouring 'fathers kidnapped by their children, wives confined by their husbands, gentlemen of fortune sequestered by their relations, and innocent persons immured by the malice of their adversaries'[54]. Sir Launcelot, who has never been more sane, is in despair at finding himself thus arbitrarily shut away with no possible recourse to justice. For anyone who knows Smollett's deeprooted gallophobia and his horror of militant clericalism in any form, the thought he attributes to Sir Launcelot assumes a special significance.

> People may inveigh against the Bastile in France, and the Inquisition in Portugal; but I would ask, if either of these be in reality so dangerous or dreadful as a private mad-house in England under the direction of a ruffian[55].

Biographical researches may one day discover whether Smollett was thereby pleading the cause of a relative or friend who was the victim of such wrongful confinement. In any case, Smollett appears as a humanitarian pioneer, just as his description of those floating hells, the ships of the line, no doubt contributed eventually to the softening of the rigours of life on board. The abuses of private asylums were vigorously denounced in the *Gentleman's Magazine* of January 1763 (xxxiii, 25–6). The author of this appeal to Parliament describes a forced internment (with its train of brutalities) and the scandalous, so-called 'medical' treatment designed to debilitate and kill the pseudopatient. The doctor who lends himself to such a heinous crime is sharply stigmatised. All the efforts of friends to discover the whereabouts of the interned person and to see him are systematically thwarted. The article reads like a summary of the desperate situation in which Sir Launcelot finds himself:

> What then must a rational mind suffer, that is treated in this irrational manner? Weakened by physic; emaciated by torture; diseased by confinement; and terrified by the sight of every instrument of cruelty, and the dreadful menaces of an attending ruffian, hardened against the tenderness of human nature (p. 26).

There had already been two legal actions in 1761 and 1762 for forced internments. A Select Committee of the House of Commons was appointed on January 27th 1763[56]. Its eleven-page report on the state of private asylums in Great Britain, was published later in the same year[57]. Its contents are disappointing. The Commission limited itself to two private asylums and to only one patient in each. After having read *Launcelot Greaves* or the appeal in the *Gentleman's Magazine* one finds the conclusion of this official report lacks both force and courage. It contents itself with recommending 'that the Present State of the Private Madhouses in the Kingdom requires the Interposition of the Legislature' (p. 10). Another ten years had to elapse before Parliament consented to pass a law on private asylums. Smollett reverts to this subject, as a historian, in Volume V of the *Continuation of the Complete History of England* (1765). He alludes (p. 210) to one of these sinister institutions in Chelsea. Perhaps he knew of such a house there when he composed *Launcelot Greaves*.

Finally, in spite of his very conservative ideas of a hierarchical society, Smollett shows in *Humphry Clinker* that he hated social injustice. What one knows of his friendly relations with his servants, and also of the irascibility of his character, prompt to be roused to indignation by all abuses, explains the cold, barely restrained anger of Matthew Bramble, who sees in Clinker the pitiable victim of a ridiculous capitalist system. With the smugness of his bourgeois self-righteousness, the innkeeper explains that he sacked Clinker because his rags and his half-starved appearance brought discredit on his inn. The innkeeper defends himself on the grounds that he pays the 'poor's rate'. It needs no more than this to provoke Matthew Bramble's famous reprimand to Clinker: 'Hark ye, Clinker, you are a most notorious offender — you stand convicted of sickness, hunger, wretchedness and want'[58]. Smollett is addressing himself to all bad Samaritans but what he is aiming at most is the injustice of a social system in which the poor are treated as criminals. He has such a passion for justice that he does not hesitate to indict his own era.

Over and above the actual experiences and the personal elements, Smollett's novels bear the whole imprint of his rich and complex character. If autobiography in its pure state is not to be found in them, it is impossible not to discern in them a personal presence, sometimes diffused, but constant and vivifying.

The study of autobiography in Smollett's novels would be incomplete without the analysis of a curious phenomenon one might call 'inverted autobiography'. If autobiography represents a projection of the novelist into his work, inverted autobiography is the total identification of the author with his characters. In the long run the novelist's own personality completely vanishes behind his literary creations. Now, in the case of Smollett, his first three novels related the often none too refined adventures of supposedly 'picaresque' characters. It needed no more for the public, the critics and the biographers to be desperately eager to see in his life and personality the exact counterpart of that of his characters. This interpretation, even more unauthorised than that of the biographer's, was already current in Smollett's lifetime. The best example is reported by Alexander Carlyle in his autobiography. Thanks to Carlyle, the Scottish historian Robertson meets Smollett for the first time in 1753. It is a very enjoyable evening and Smollett displays his gifts as a brilliant talker. And, at the end of this friendly gathering, Robertson admits he is quite surprised to find him such a civilised man. Robertson 'had imagined that a man's manners must bear a likeness to his books, and as Smollett had described so well the characters of ruffians and profligates, that he must, of course, resemble them'[59]. It must be added that Carlyle makes quite a lot of fun of Robertson's naïvety. But this erroneous interpretation unfairly and unpleasantly colours the opinions of a number of critics about the novelist's personality. This absurd bias of the critics is denounced with good reason by Knapp: 'There has usually been a tendency, not justified by what is now known of his character, to attribute to Smollett the vices of the unheroic Roderick, Peregrine and Fathom'[60].

The two most common identifications are those of the young Smollett with Roderick and of the old novelist with Matthew Bramble. Now recent biographical researches have amply shown that these assertions ignore the real facts of Smollett's family, social and financial situation. In Chapter vii Roderick's meagre bundle of clothes is described. A tailor's bill of May 1758[61] proves that, before leaving for London, Smollett had just bought himself clothes costing over £11, a considerable sum for those days and for a young man's pocket. The identification with Bramble is certainly tempting. Character and creator are the same age, both in search of health and both giving evidence of great kindness of heart under a sometimes rugged exterior. But such an identification distorts the psychological and literary truth. If it is likely that Matthew Bramble quite frequently expresses opinions shared by Smollett, one must not forget the subtle play of strongly contrasted juxtapositions which permit Smollett to see the same event, the same landscape, the same institutions as refracted in the eyes of his five letter-writers. Thus Jery neutralises the splenetic acidity of his uncle's observations on Bath or London. Certainly Jery is not sparing of his own criticisms, but since these are proffered with less misanthropic surliness and ill-temper, they enable the reader to form a balanced judgment. And in this prismatic interplay of letters, the enthusiasms, rages and dislikes of the three women must not be neglected either, for these elements contribute to giving light and shade to a picture of the world which results from seeing it simultaneously from widely differing points of view. Even if Smollett implicitly makes fun of Lydia and her girlish enthusiasms, how much did that unsophisticated charm (occasionally a trifle cloying) remind him of his own lost daughter? And Jery, just down from the university, with no apparent material cares, could he not be a projection, not devoid of critical sense, of what Smollett would have liked to be instead of going to seek adventure at Cartagena and elsewhere? Of course these are hypotheses, not assertions. But Smollett's novels (especially *Humphry Clinker*) are too stamped with his personality for it to be legitimate to identify him with any one particular character. Actual experience and creation are so inextricably mingled that it is possible to say with Gusdorf, 'Every novel is autobiography written by a third person'[62]. This is the conclusion Kahrl arrives at about Bramble, in whom he sees 'an idealised portrait into which went some of Smollett's traits, notably without the Scottish inheritance, however, that was fundamental in Smollett's character'[63].

We find ourselves confronted with the problem of the relations between autobiography and fictional creation. To borrow a metaphor from optics, it is possible to distinguish three general aspects of it. To begin with, the reflections, more or less disguised, of actual incidents in Smollett's life woven into the texture of his novels. Next, the looking-glass effects in which Smollett delights; he puts himself on the scene but his reflection is altered by the distorting mirror of his technique. Lastly, there is the inner mirror into which he gazes, and thanks to which he gives human and personal depth to his creation.

A barely disguised reflection is that meeting with the Scottish exiles in Boulogne described in *Peregrine Pickle*. They are the aftermath of Culloden, human wreckage from the Jacobite disaster on whom Peregrine, not without discretion, takes pity. There is a note of commiseration all the more poignant because Smollett has difficulty in concealing his sympathy for his compatriots who go down every day to the quay 'in order to indulge their longing eyes with a prospect of the white cliffs of Albion, which they must never more approach'[64]. Smollett takes his precautions and insists that Peregrine 'differed widely from them in point of political principles' (p. 232). An incident even sets Peregrine against one of the exiles whom drink incites to propose a toast unacceptable to Peregrine's orthodox patriotism. Now among these exiles profoundly affected by the sentence of banishment there was a certain Hunter of Burnsyde on whose behalf Smollett dared to intervene with the government, as his courageous letter of September 28th 1750 proves (Knapp, *Letters*, pp. 14–15). Such a step, taken only four years after Culloden, required considerable audacity and gives all the human resonance to the passage quoted above.

Another example of barely disguised autobiography: Peregrine's debut as a satirist when, out of necessity, he becomes a writer. Driven by ambition and by the leanness of his purse, Peregrine decides to compose 'an imitation of Juvenal, and lashed some conspicuous characters, with equal truth, spirit and severity'[65]. What a fine example of a retrospective 'puff oblique'! As if the allusion were not sufficiently obvious, Smollett also takes pains to point out that this satire was anonymous but that Peregrine arranged that the whole of London should know the name of the author. It is hard not to think that Smollett is describing, not without a touch of complacency, his first success in the realm of satire, namely *Advice*, published in 1746. Finally, in *Humphry Clinker*, he himself appears once more on the scene in the melancholy guise of an old man wounded by human ingratitude, Mr Serle (Jery's letter of May 10th). Paunceford has made his fortune in the East Indies, thanks to the initial help of Serle. On his return to England he shows no gratitude, either psychological or financial, to his benefactor who lives in dignified poverty.

Knapp has analysed this Paunceford incident[66] and identified the original of this ungrateful character with a certain Alexander Campbell whom Smollett had helped, fed and clothed before his departure to India. Such ingratitude must have embittered Smollett, who, besides devoting a whole letter to it in *Humphry Clinker*, had already addressed a few lines to Campbell in his 'Ode to Independence', composed about 1766 but not published till after his death:

> In Fortune's car behold that minion ride,
> With either India's glittering spoils oppress'd.

These reflections, more or less disguised to meet the demands of the novel, cannot wholly explain Smollett's imperative need to introduce himself under a mask at once opaque and transparent. He seems to feel the necessity of a heart-to-heart understanding between the man and the reader. But this intimate knowledge, facilitated by literary creation, he can only attain by assuming the features of one or more of several of his characters. An example of this deliberate dissociation of personality, at once secret and overt, is provided by the two letters which serve as the explanatory foreword to *Humphry Clinker*. Jonathan Dustwich writes to his bookseller in London, Henry Davis, to enquire about the possible publication of the letters which are to follow. It is here a question of respecting the time-honoured fiction of the manuscripts having been discovered by chance and thus avoiding possible legal prosecution. Smollett takes the same precaution in the foreword to *The History and Adventures of an Atom*. But it is more important to note that in this letter Smollett is talking to himself, for his own benefit and that of the public. How can one not be aware of the calculated ambiguity of this sentence: 'I am pleased to find you think they may be printed with a good prospect of success'; or again, 'the letters in question were not written or sent under the seal of secrecy'? And the pretended Jonathan Dustwich will explain that it is a duty to publish them *in usum publicum*[67]. Smollett's cleverness lies in making an accomplice of his reader, whom he allows to penetrate up to a point into his intimate life story, while at the same time keeping himself to himself, thus preserving true literary and personal reticence. Thus Smollett is at the same time subject, virtual object and reflection when he declares, 'the manner in which I got possession of these Letters ... is a circumstance that concerns my own conscience only; sufficeth it to say, I have fully satisfied the parties in whose custody they were'[68]. That expression 'fully satisfied' is worth its weight in ironic duplicity! In the bookseller's reply, Smollett plays the same subtle game. He does not hesitate to mention himself by name and proceeds to a mocking pseudo self-criticism. The bookseller complains of the growing number of travel books recently published' 'what between Smollett's, Sharp's, Derrick's, Thickness's, Baltimore's and Baretti's, together with Shandy's Sentimental Travels, the public seems to be cloyed with that kind of entertainment'[69].

Here is a final example of these many-faceted autobiographical allusions. Henry Davis, in case there is a libel action, exhorts Jonathan Dustwich to appear: 'I hope you will have honesty and wit enough to appear and take your trial. If you should be sentenced to the pillory, your fortune is made'[70]. The reference to Smollett's conduct during the Admiral Knowles case is implicit. But Smollett's courage earned him only troubles, a fine and some weeks in prison. Finally, it is likely that Smollett is thinking, not without bitterness, of all the publicity Wilkes managed to get out of his resounding clashes with the law.

Humour is the inner mirror which gives the autobiographical passages all their human depth. This type of humour is a conscious complicity which Smollett tries to establish with his reader. He makes the public share his private jokes. This tendency is particularly evident in *Humphry Clinker* which, as we have just seen, is full of personal allusions. From its opening lines this humour, which is apt to be grim, emphasises the deliberate ambiguity of Matthew Bramble, at once a fictional literary character and the reflection of its creator. The petulance, not devoid of a touch of bitterness, with which Bramble addresses his doctor is also that of Smollett talking to himself or discussing his case with a colleague like Moore: 'at this time of day, I ought to know something of my own constitution'[71]. The same embittered tone, striking in its biographical and psychological accuracy, is audible when Matthew Bramble declares, 'For my own part, I have had an hospital these fourteen years within myself, and studied my own case with the most painful attention; consequently may be supposed to know something of the matter'[72]. There is no doubt whatever that this fascinated, almost morbid preoccupation with the ravages of disease is that of a doctor, but it is also that of a passionate man watching the day-to-day progress of ageing and illness. The note of autobiographical humour is gayer when Smollett depicts himself in the midst of his literary protégés. Jery is invited to dine 'with S . . ., whom you and I have long known by his writings'[73]. But sadness returns again at the end of *Humphry Clinker*. A little (making all due allowance) like Prospero declaring: 'Deeper than did ever plummet sound I'll drown my book', Matthew Bramble announces his intention 'to renounce all sedentary amusements, particularly that of writing long letters'[74].

An almost prophetic tone is discernible underlying the humour. A final, and not the least curious, aspect of inverted autobiography is what might be called involuntary autobiography, as when Smollett in certain passages describes what is *going* to happen to him some years later. When he wrote *Peregrine Pickle*, he had already had experience of translating: he had translated *Gil Blas* into English and had been working on *Don Quixote* for several years. His translation of *Don Quixote* was announced in the press in 1748 and again in 1749, though it did not appear till 1755. But when he composed *Peregrine Pickle*, Smollett could have had no inkling of the violent criticisms that Windham in 1755 and Shebbeare in 1757 would bring against his work, the major accusation being his lack of familiarity with Spanish. Now, in Chapter cii of *Peregrine Pickle*, Smollett introduces a man of letters who, having undertaken to translate into English 'a certain celebrated author, who had been cruelly mangled by former attempts' finds himself exposed to the calumnies of his enemies who insinuate 'contrary to truth and fair dealing . . . that he did not understand one word of the language he pretended to translate' (p. 645). There is rising anger among this body of writers, all more or less depen-dent on the goodwill of the bookseller-publishers. After having compared the lot of the writer to that of a young whore whom the wily procuress allows to get into her debt in order to exert a still firmer stranglehold on her — a comparison worthy of Hogarth — the learned assembly decide to revenge themselves and reduce their patrons the booksellers to desperate straits by setting up in unfair competition. In January 1758 Smollett himself probably envisaged taking such retaliatory measures with regard to Millar. If Millar refuses him an advance, he confides to another publisher, Strahan, he will be obliged to have recourse to 'certain Measures which, perhaps, he may dislike in the Sequel' (Knapp, *Letters*, p. 67). There it is a vague enough threat but it takes on its full meaning when one reads *Peregrine Pickle*. Moreover, Peregrine becomes so deeply absorbed in his task of translation that soon his health is affected:

> This sudden change from his former way of life agreed so ill with his disposition, that, for the first time, he was troubled with flatulencies and indigestion, which produced anxiety and dejection of spirits, and the nature of his situation began in some measure to discompose his brain[75].

Even if Smollett's physical decline was not so dramatically sudden, he did all the same feel the first ill effects of his intensive work about 1752 or 1753, that is to say a year or two after the publication of *Peregrine Pickle*. There is also a very clear parallel between this passage in *Peregrine Pickle* and the self-diagnosis Smollett will write fifteen years later for Dr Fizès at Montpellier:

> Quibusdam abhinc annis, exercitationibus juvenilibus subito remissis, in vitam sedentariam lapsum. Animo in studia severiora converso, fibrae gradatim laxabantur. Inter legendum et scribendum inclinato corpore in pectus malum ruebat[76].

Five years after *Peregrine Pickle*, in a review written by Smollett himself, the miserable lot of the literary hack is once more referred to. He has to accomplish his daily task, in spite of cramp, colick, vapours or vertigo; in spite of head-ach, heart-ach [*sic*] and Minerva's frowns; otherwise he will lose his character and livelihood, like a taylor [*sic*] who disappoints his customers in a birth-day suit[77].

In *Peregrine Pickle*, Smollett's lucidity confers on these remarks a quality of prophetic autobiography.

But it is in *Humphry Clinker* that occurs the most striking example of this autobiographical projection into the future. It is a curious mixture of harlequinade and Shandean Dance of Death, this farce presented at the end of *Humphry Clinker* when the weddings have been celebrated and the company wants to enjoy itself. 'It was a lively representation of Death in pursuit of Consumption'[78]. Since, when Smollett was writing these pages, he knew that he had not much longer to live, is it possible that he was not thinking of his own case?

Smollett's novels present neither a cryptic fictional version of his own life nor a romanticised life. But they are woven into the fabric of his life even more closely than for Balzac, who declared: 'The great events of my life are my works.' Yet neither is it possible to go as far as Cocteau, who wrote in a letter in 1955: 'I think that every line, blot and wave that escape from us (it little matters what they represent) compose our self-portrait and give us away'[79]. Smollett's novels are rooted in his life. This rooting is also a layering which gives fresh vigour to the author's vitality. In the world of his five novels, Smollett creates not a flat fresco, but a bas-relief. His descriptions and characters have not only a surface significance but a dimension of personal depth. At the risk of shocking the critics who are determined to see in Smollett's novels merely a series of picaresque (in so far as that adjective still retains any meaning) adventures, it is possible to apply to them this affirmation of François Mauriac's: 'I believe that there is no great work of fiction which is not a fictionalised inner life'[80].

Smollett has not so much put himself in his novels as the essence of himself. And in that lies the whole problem of literary alchemy. In the process of transmuting the raw material of personal experience into the gold of imaginative fiction, autobiography cannot serve as the philosopher's stone. If it did, the base metals extracted from life and melted in the crucible of literary creation would be transmuted only into pinchbeck.

Part II
Structure and morality

3
Two sources of inspiration: *Don Quixote* and *Gil Blas*

As a good Scot, proud of a classical education he deems superior to that provided in England, Smollett does not hesitate to parade, with somewhat conceited complacence, the culture which exercised a profound influence on him. Greek and, above all, Latin authors — Horace in particular[1] and Juvenal — are quoted frequently in his novels. Allusions to Elizabethan authors[2] and especially to Shakespeare[3] are numerous. He readily acknowledges his literary debts, and the frankness with which he admits, in the preface to *Roderick Random*, the influence that Cervantes and, above all, Lesage have had on him is certainly a little surprising. It is rare for a young novelist, anxious for literary independence at the outset of his career, to emphasise so clearly what he owes to a predecessor. But it is fair to add that this acknowledgement of a literary debt implies a certain pride. Smollett claims kinship with the famous author of *Gil Blas* while at the same time expressing certain important reservations, too often passed over in silence by the critics. Thus, after having recalled the success of *Gil Blas*, he declares: 'The following sheets I have modelled on his plan, taking the liberty, however, to differ from him in the execution, where I thought his particular situations were uncommon, extravagant, or peculiar to the country in which the scene is laid' (Preface to *Roderick Random*, pp. lxi–lxii).

The knowledge Smollett had of *Don Quixote* and *Gil Blas* is as direct as it is incontestable, at least biographically. It is only necessary to remember that his translation of *Gil Blas* appeared as early as 1748, about nine months after *Roderick Random*, not in 1749 as too many biographers have written. Moreover this was not his only contact with the work of Lesage, since he also translated *Le Diable Boiteux*, published about February 1750. There is no doubt about Smollett's literary enthu-siasm for Cervantes. As early as 1748 he was working on his translation of *Don Quixote*, which was not to be published till seven years later, though, according to Smollett himself, this task had been finished in 1751. A final detail, minor indeed, but whose value is not merely anecdotal, shows his affection for Lesage. When Nathaniel Dance painted Smollett's portrait, probably about 1764, the book he is holding is a copy of *Gil Blas*.

This chapter does not claim to be a systematic study of *all* the literary sources from which Smollett might have drawn his inspiration. Joliat, in his book *Smollett et la France* (1935, pp. 20—31) has tried to show the influence of the French novelists of the sixteenth and seven-teenth centuries known as 'realists' on Smollett. These pages have the merit of showing that, if Joliat has read *Le Baron de Foeneste, Francion, Le Page disgracié, Le Roman comique, Le Roman bourgeois*, nothing in them has proved with any certitude that Smollett himself had. The parallels traced, in particular between Smollett and Scarron, are not without interest, but remain very hypothetical literary speculation. So it seems safer to limit oneself here to the two influences acknowledged by the author and hence undeniable. Moreover this chapter does not constitute an attempt to replace Smollett's novels in a picaresque or Cervantic tradition. Robert Giddings, in his book *The Tradition of Smollett*, has tackled this critical task — a task all the more perilous because it is difficult to speak with absolute certainty of a 'picaresque tradition' — with only partial success.

The limits of the matter proposed to be dealt with in this chapter being thus defined, the first proceeding will be to analyse the influence of *Don Quixote* and *Gil Blas* on the structure, incidents and characters of *Roderick Random* and *Peregrine Pickle*; *Ferdinand Count Fathom* and *Launcelot Greaves* will each be the object of a separate study later on in the chapter. *Ferdinand Count Fathom* is in fact the only principal char-acter in Smollett's novels who really approaches the *picaro*. As to *Launcelot Greaves*, the influence, indeed direct imitation of *Don Quixote*, emphasised by the author himself, is evident and constant throughout this whole novel, which therefore requires a special study.

Although in his novels Smollett alludes more often to Cervantes, in his first two works, *Roderick Random* and *Peregrine Pickle*, it is the influence of *Gil Blas* that is most apparent.

To what extent can the structure of Smollett's novels, with the exception of *Humphry Clinker*, be said to have been marked by the influence of Cervantes or Lesage? It must be admitted that it is far from easy to determine the exact amount of their respective contributions. Nevertheless, it is possible to distinguish certain characteristics which, general as they are, have the merit of synthesising numerous resemblances

scattered throughout Smollett's novels. The first characteristic is movement. Like Lazarillo and Don Quixote, but above all like Gil Blas,
Roderick and Peregrine are always on the move, whether because fate
obliges them to change scene often or because their vagabond temperament impels them to travel. The surname 'Random' and the Christian
name 'Peregrine' symbolise this need for movement. Justifying his choice
of a Scottish hero in the preface to *Roderick Random*, Smollett takes care
to point out that his kinsmen are, by nature, 'addicted to travelling'
(p. lxiii). The initial dream interpreted by the soothsayer in the first lines
of *Roderick Random* only emphasises, at the beginning of a novel which is
anything but static, the basic dynamic tendency of Smollettian heroes.
That violently hit tennis ball in Mrs Random's dream makes the
oneiromancer say that the expected child would be a 'great traveller'
(p. 2). Such a prediction did not go beyond the bounds of sagacious
prudence. Unlike Lazarillo, Don Quixote and Gil Blas, Roderick, Peregrine
and Ferdinand leave their native land in the course of their adventures.
Only Launcelot Greaves and the characters in *Humphry Clinker* are
relatively more stay-at-home, since they never go outside Great Britain. If
Roderick's journeyings are to a large extent forced, Peregrine's are more
comfortable, relaxed and, in a word, respectable. It is here that a first
confusion seems to have crept into the minds of critics from the middle of
the eighteenth century till now. Too many critics forget the complete title
of Smollett's first four novels: *The Adventures of* . . . Now adventure
involves travel as much as journeys attract adventure. Because the *picaro*,
too, is often on the road, the critics thought they could apply the convenient but meaningless label of 'picaresque' to Smollett's novels. This, in
fact, is to confuse 'picaresque' with 'peripatetic', if one takes this adjective
in its etymological sense. The error has already been committed over
Nashe's novel, *The Unfortunate Traveller* which is less picaresque than
peripatetic. The hero, Jack Wilton, has singularly little in common with
Lazarillo who appears like a poor little cramped provincial beside Nashe's
cosmopolitan swindler.

For Smollett's heroes, as for those of Cervantes and Lesage, displace-
ments in space coincide with the chronological lapse of time. With the
exception again, of *Humphry Clinker*, the time of the adventures is a
spatialised linear time. If Don Quixote (like Matthew Bramble) is already
nearer the grave than the cradle, on the other hand, Smollett, like Lesage
in *Gil Blas*, makes his principal characters develop according to an irreversible chronology. He lingers longer over Roderick's childhood than Lesage
does over that of Gil Blas but subsequently he accords less and less importance to this period of life. The childhood of Launcelot Greaves is very
rapidly related by Tom Clarke. In *Humphry Clinker* there is scarcely any
reference to the childhood of the letter-writers. If there is no skilful and
subtle manipulation of time, comparable with Sterne's jugglings in
Tristram Shandy, to be found in Smollett's novels, this is because the

latter keeps very close to his avowed models, Cervantes and Lesage. Since this time is linear, it is therefore divisible. Like Cervantes and Lesage, Smollett does not hesitate to cut the thread of the novel in order to interpolate a narrative which, at least in appearance, has little organic relation to the general structure. Such is the case with the story of Miss Williams (Chapters xxii and xxiii of *Roderick Random*), the tale of Melopoyn's theatrical misadventures (Chapters lx and lxiii of *Roderick Random*) or, again, the famous 'Memoirs of a Lady of Quality' (Chapter lxxxviii of *Peregrine Pickle*), whose brilliant *succès de scandale* achieved in 1751 is much tarnished today. Also in this same category of interpolated narrative must be ranged Chapter cvi in which Smollett recounts the generous life of his friend Daniel Mackercher and his courageous efforts to defend the cause of James Annesley[4]. Fielding himself, in *Joseph Andrews* and *Tom Jones* did not disdain these prolonged digressions imbedded in the mainstream of his novels. Smollett and Fielding were only following the example set by Cervantes and Lesage. The first narrative inserted by Lesage in *Gil Blas*, the story of Doña Mercia of Mosquera, whom the young hero saves from the robbers' cave where he was held captive with her, has only a distant resemblance to the unedifying adventures of Miss Williams, the repentant prostitute. Lesage's and Smollett's heroes manage to save the lives of these unfortunate ladies, but, it must be repeated, in entirely different circumstances. Another possible resemblance – very tenuous: Don Diego de Zelos in *Ferdinand Count Fathom*, during the recital of his misfortunes, reveals how he believes that he has killed his wife with his own hand (Chapter xxvi). In *Gil Blas* there is also a character, who, in a fit of jealous rage, stabs the wife he suspects of unfaithfulness and flees, believing her dead. Like Don Diego de Zelos, Don Anastasio de Rada (*Gil Blas*, Book viii, Chapter viii) has not only not killed his wife but ends up by rediscovering his child in circumstances in which romantic fiction goes far beyond the bounds of probability.

Besides movement and straightforward chronology, the interplay of temperament and chance characterises Smollett's novels, a general trait he may very well have borrowed from Cervantes or Lesage. It is not only the vagabond temperament of the heroes, which has already been mentioned, but their positive and perpetual propensity to adventure helped (or sometimes thwarted) by chance which Smollett's novels has in common with *Don Quixote* and *Gil Blas*. Thus, as a result of chance which determines the encounters (good or more often bad) that Peregrine will make on the roads of life, his satirical nature will land him in many adventures in which he does not always come off best. Smollett takes great care to insist on the innate character of this irrepressible satirical tendency of Peregrine's. It is what he calls 'a certain oddity of disposition, for which he had been remarkable even from his cradle'[5]. Peregrine has the impression, sometimes right but more often wrong, that he has been entrusted with a satirical mission, if not *ab ovo*, at least *ab utero*. The importance of this dominant humour, particularly strong in the case of Peregrine, is far more stressed than in *Don Quixote* or *Gil Blas*.

Apart from these two works, Peregrine puts one in mind most of all of Jack Wilton. In *The Unfortunate Traveller*, Thomas Nashe makes his hero, who is preparing to chastise certain over-refined army quarter-masters in his own way, declare: 'I thinke confidently I was ordained Gods scourge from above for their daintie finicalitie'[6]. Like Jack Wilton and his confederates, Peregrine and his friend Godfrey transform themselves (for once in the name of morality) into 'foole-catchers' when they rid Bath of the gamblers and other tricksters who are battening on the worthy city.

It is also the interplay of humour and chance which often forces Roderick — the only one of Smollett's heroes who is reduced on several occasions to hiring himself out — to leave the temporary financial haven he has managed to find with an employer. Sometimes chance alone takes a hand when Smollett, like Cervantes or Lesage, makes it intervene to bring about the rediscovery of long-lost relatives. But there is a profound connection between humour and chance; the interaction of pride and resentment is as much a psychological constant in Roderick as in Peregrine. Impelled in turn by their pride or by resentment, the three heroes, Gil Blas, Roderick and Peregrine end up by committing grave faults which land them in prison. Gil Blas (arrived at the summit of honour and power, at least so he believes) finds himself, within the space of a few hours, shut up in the tower of Segovia. For Roderick, as for Peregrine, prison plays a symbolic redemptive role. In the penal microcosm they can contemplate simultaneously the intensified interplay of the most eccentric humours and that of the cruellest fate. Prison provides them, as it were, with a concentrated vision of the outside world in which vices and virtues are more clearly defined than in everyday life. But — and here is the point in common with Lesage — prison offers these young men, dazzled by the tinsel of social success and deafened by the clamours of false fame, the saving opportunity to pull themselves together by daring to confront themselves. Finally, Gil Blas, Roderick and Peregrine all three fall ill while they are imprisoned. This illness is for them the key to health and plays the part of a psychological and moral catharsis. This is what Gil Blas, apparently cured of the vanities of the world and the court, declares to his mother: 'Yes, it was my disease and imprisonment that made nature resume all her rights and entirely detached me from court. I now thirst for solitude'[7].

Gil Blas will still have some outbursts of vanity, but prison marks a definite turning-point in his life which from then on will be irretrievably bourgeois. In the same way, Roderick, in the Marshalsea, quickly, almost too quickly, turns into a wretched sloven who goes for two months without changing his clothes, washing or shaving. Roderick's illness — the word 'distemper' is used in the text[8] — is, after all, more psychological than physical, whereas Peregrine suffers in body as much as in mind: 'his health suffered by his sedentary life and austere application; his eyesight failed, his appetite forsook him, his spirits decayed; so that he became melancholy, listless'[9]. During this time, Peregrine cuts himself off from all contact with the world and from the prisoners themselves. He sees himself forced 'to seek for satisfaction within himself' and 'at length secluded himself from all society'[10]. The impulsion to this asceticism is thus two-fold and corresponds to the basic ambivalent motivation of Smollett's young hero, to wit pride and resentment. Thanks to this sojourn in gaol, Peregrine at last becomes aware (with a harshness which would have verged on complete misanthropy had his imprisonment been prolonged) of the vanity of the world and of his own pretensions. He comes to feel 'an equal abhorrence of the world and of himself'[11]. Prison thus puts a final stop to the dangerous interplay of humour and chance.

If the influence of Cervantes and Lesage on the structure of Smollett's novels is undeniable, it is not always easy to determine the full extent of it. On the other hand, the incidents related in Smollett's novels include a certain number of direct borrowings (not really very many) or of more or less clear reminiscences. There is no question here of establishing a complete inventory of *all* the probable borrowings or of all the possible parallels between the works of Cervantes and Lesage and those of Smollett. Such a study of comparative literature goes beyond the scope of this book. Several scholars[12] besides Joliat have taken pains to try and pick out all the points of resemblance between Smollett's novels and *Gil Blas*.

Smollett's borrowings from *Gil Blas* can be summed up under three comprehensive headings: good and bad encounters; the service of successive masters; physiological comedy. Like Gil Blas, Roderick leaves his native land towards the end of his adolescence and is no sooner launched on the roads of life than he finds himself face to face with all sorts of rascals, whether highway robbers or rapacious innkeepers waiting to pounce with delight on their innocent victims. Thus, at the very outset of his adventures, Roderick (Chapter ix) meets a highwayman, just as Gil Blas falls into the hands of thieves, a far more perilous situation than Roderick's. If, in the encounter with the highwayman Rifle, Roderick and Strap escape with no more than a fright, the latinist schoolmaster, disciple of Horace and innkeeper in his spare time, deals as severe a blow to the two young men's vanity as to their purse (Chapter x). Roderick and Strap pay not only a high bill but the price of experience. It is dangerous to trust to appearances and, as well as being a latinist, an innkeeper may very well be also an arrant knave. It is the same philosophy that Gil Blas learns to his financial and, above all, psychological cost at Andrew Corcuelo's inn, where a parasite and sponge gives him his first lesson: 'Henceforth beware of praise, and be upon your guard against everybody you do not know'[13]. Immediately after having (very unwillingly) swallowed this bitter pill, Gil Blas, like Smollett's heroes, feels 'chagrined with these mortifying relections, and inflamed with resentment'[14]. This is the sign that for him, as for Roderick, a long material as well as psychological road remains to be travelled before he has assimilated his lesson. But all the encounters made along the way are not so unpleasant as the preceding ones. Gil Blas rediscovers Fabricius, the son of the village barber and his childhood friend, as early as the end of Book i (Chapter xvii) and Fabricius will reappear many times in Gil Blas's career. It is possible that this fortuitous meeting inspired the coming together again of Roderick and Strap the barber (Chapter viii). But it is difficult to establish any parallel between Strap and Fabricius, the latter having run off with his beloved and some doubloons as well, two audacious acts of which the honest and cowardly Strap would have been quite incapable. Gil Blas also meets another journeyman barber, Diego, in Chapter vi of Book ii.

Roderick is the only one of Smollett's heroes whose misfortunes oblige him to take service with several successive masters. It is possible to draw a parallel between the medical apprenticeship of Gil Blas in the service of Doctor Sangrado — the leech of Valladolid (Book ii, Chapters iii to v) and Roderick's service with Crab (Chapter vii) and later with Lavement (Chapters xviii and xix). But apart from satirising medical humbug — after all a very widespread literary theme — the spirit in which Lesage and Smollett composed these chapters is very different. Whereas for Gil Blas being employed by Sangrado represents a social and financial promotion, Roderick is reduced to working, which never ceases to affront his honour as a gentleman. In spite of his pressing need of money, Roderick dares to ask the irascible Crab 'on what footing'[15] he will be received into his house. It is unthinkable that Gil Blas should have asked such a question. At Lavement's, Roderick is vexed to be considered, at first 'in no other light than that of a menial servant'[16]. Obviously, Smollett was not inspired by the artful speech Fabricius makes to Gil Blas, praising the advantages of domestic service (Book i, Chapter xvii).

Critics often reproach Smollett for certain incidents in doubtful taste in which bodily evacuations play a malodorous part — so-called 'chamber-pot humour'. Lesage, too, does not hesitate to pepper *Gil Blas* with physiological incidents in the robust tradition of Rabelaisian comedy. One of these in particular must have struck Smollett since he reproduces it almost literally, giving the reference to *Gil Blas*. Peregrine, always in search of some dirty joke to play on his travelling companions, decides to make the painter Pallet believe that the excellent fricassee of rabbit he is in the process of guzzling is really stewed tom-cat. As a result, Pallet, and later Jolter, the tutor, suffer from violent stomach upsets. The medico's eloquence of the doctor, helped by the imagination of the two victims, makes the last lines of Chapter xlviii highly emetic. Now, in the course of this incident, Smollett twice alludes to *Gil Blas*: Peregrine 'recollecting the story of Scipio and the muleteer in *Gil Blas*, resolved to perpetrate a joke upon the stomach of Pallet'[17]. On the next page, Peregrine takes care to narrate 'that passage in Gil Blas, which we have hinted at above'. This passage, whose comic and cathartic power Smollett seems to enjoy, is to be found at the end of Book x, Chapter xii. Smollett has, if one may say so, refined the joke which affects not only Pallet but Jolter. Peregrine hastily admits that he only meant to upset Pallet and reveals that it really is a fricassee of rabbit the painter is eating. But Pipes, Peregrine's facetious servant, has sprinkled the dish with some duck's claws, which Jolter takes for feline ones. Lesage himself also seems to enjoy the coarse comedy of this traditional practical joke since he makes another allusion (Book ii, Chapter vii) to innkeepers' transmogrification of cat into rabbit.

Other rather broad incidents retailed in *Roderick Random* are perhaps reminiscent of *Gil Blas*. Diego, the journeyman barber who at night becomes a sighing lover under his lady's window, gets soused 'with the contents of a perfuming-pan, that did not at all delight my sense of smelling'[18]. A similar misadventure, this time in the morning, befalls Strap a little while after his arrival, when he knocks on Cringer's door with ill-timed insistence: 'a window opening in the second story of the next house, a chamber-pot was discharged upon him so successfully, that the poor barber was wet to the skin, while I [Roderick], being luckily at some distance, escaped the unsavoury deluge'[19]. That Smollett is here borrowing from Lesage is highly probable, but it must not be forgotten that picaresque literature, and even *Don Quixote*, offer numerous examples of these purgative, emetic or laxative incidents without being, for all that, scatological.

Direct allusions to Cervantes and *Don Quixote* are numerous in Smollett's novels. Strap, having fallen in love with a buxom wench, declares that his heart 'went knock, knock, knock like a fulling-mill'[20]. The metaphor is unusual enough to suggest a probable reminiscence of the six hammers of a fulling-mill which terrified the good Sancho Panza all one night (Part I, Vol. I, Book iii, Chapter vi). Again, in *Roderick Random*[21], Smollett refers to Don Quixote attacking the windmills. He also uses the word 'quixotism' in *Peregrine Pickle*[22] and *Ferdinand Count Fathom*[23]. He quotes the name of Don Quixote (as well as Guzman d'Alfarache, Gil Blas and Scarron) twice in *Ferdinand Count Fathom*[24]. Lastly, Matthew Bramble is compared to Don Quixote: 'a Don Quixote in generosity'[25] by his nephew Jery. This trope is repeated and distorted with habitual dysorthographic humour by Win Jenkins who applies it this time to Lismahago: 'The young squire called him Dunquickset'[26].

The incident of the love-letter involuntarily destroyed by Pipes, then replaced with the benevolent aid of a pompous quill-driver[27] may have been suggested by the similar expedient to which Sancho has recourse[28] after having forgotten to ask his master for the pocket-book destined for Dulcinea. But this incident is far more elaborated in *Peregrine Pickle*, where it forms part of the plot of the novel. The jokes in doubtful taste which eighteenth-century novelists — and readers — were so fond of are not lacking in *Don Quixote*, especially in the second part. The cats who have had bells tied to their tails[29] are in some sort the ancestors of those who reappear in *Peregrine Pickle* and *Humphry Clinker* shod with nutshells. The monkey fortune-teller exhibited by Master Peter has the same prudent technique in divination as that of Cadwallader in *Peregrine Pickle*: 'This animal gives no response or intelligence concerning what is to come; he is only acquainted with the past and knows something of the present'[30]. Lastly, the physical violence with which Smollett is so often reproached on account of the tavern brawls, street fights, and other affrays described in his novels, perhaps owes its origin and its letters patent of literary nobility to *Don Quixote*. Cervantes also liberally bestows many a blow, beating or cudgelling:

> The barber pummelled Sancho, who returned the compliment; one of the servants presuming to seize Don Lewis by the arm, that he might not run away, the young gentleman gave him such a slap in the face, as bathed all his teeth in blood; the judge exerted himself in his defence. Don Fernando having brought one of the troopers to the ground, kicked his whole carcase to his heart's content[31].

Such a free fight would not be out of place in *Roderick Random* or *Peregrine Pickle*. This delight in the exchange of blows, less sadistic than bestially human, this taste for trickling blood, squashed noses and knocked-out teeth — maybe *Don Quixote* was the source from which Smollett drew them. Even a worthy ecclesiastic displays a brutal joy at the bloody set-to between Don Quixote and the goat-herd:

> The curate and canon were ready to burst with laughing, the troopers capered about with joy and the whole company halloed, according to the practice of the spectators when two dogs are engaged. In fine ... everybody was thus regaled and rejoiced, except the two combatants, who worried each other[32].

Is that not just the behaviour of the idle London onlookers described by Smollett in *Roderick Random* and *Peregrine Pickle*?

Little would be gained by attempting to trace all the other influences which may have affected Smollett's novels. In *Ferdinand Count Fathom* he certainly alludes to Guzman d'Alfarache and Lazarillo de Tormes, but there is nothing to prove, biographically or literarily, that these works, ranged by critical tradition in the picaresque genre, have left important traces in his novels. He perhaps knew that popular Bible of knavery, *The English Rogue* by Richard Head and Francis Kirkman, but, there too, proofs are completely lacking. At most one can cautiously indicate parallels with Nashe's *The Unfortunate Traveller*. And even these observations do not tend to prove that Smollett was inspired by Nashe, but rather that he may be placed in a stream of popular traditional literature, handed down to him as a child through frequently told tales. Nashe displays a Latinophobia as exacerbated as Smollett's a century and a half later. Might not the following passage, if it were transcribed in eighteenth-century language, be an extract from the gallophobic diatribes which abound in Smollett's first three novels and which are repeated with a virulence inflamed by resentment and ill health in *Travels through France and Italy*? 'What is there in *Fraunce* to bee learned more than in *England*, but falshood in fellowship, perfect slovenrie, to love no man but for my pleasure, to sweare *Ah par la mort Dieu* when a mans hammes are scabd'[33]. Italy and Spain are criticised with just as much severity. Jack Wilton, at the end of the book, hastens to quit 'the *Sodom* of *Italy*' (p. 122). Is it a trivial literary coincidence or barbed irony, the use of 'Tabitha' in *Humphry Clinker*? In *The Unfortunate Traveller*, there is an expert procuress so-named: '*Tabitha* the Temptresses, a wench that could put as civil a face on it as chastities first martyr *Lucrecia*' (p. 52). Further on, Tabitha is called 'a Turke and an infidel', an insult Smollett used in his novels. Lastly, Lavement, the French-born apothecary, past-master in the culpable art of adulterating drugs, is a mere apprentice beside the virtuoso of disgusting pharmaceutical *ersatz*, the Jewish doctor Zacharie. 'His snot and spittle a hundred times hee hath put over to his Apothecarie for snow water' (p. 101). Lavement contented himself with transforming oyster shells into crabs' eyes and the muddy water of the Thames into *aqua cinnamoni*.

Before examining the possible influence of *Don Quixote* and *Gil Blas* on Smollett's characters, it is important to define here and now the idea of *picaro*. To begin with, Cervantes does not set out to describe *picaros* in *Don Quixote*. He barely sketches even one in the very episodic character of Ginès de Passamonte who is one of the chaingang of galley-slaves freed by Don Quixote. This rogue does not hesitate to proclaim his literary pretensions in the picaresque genre. He has written the story of his life which is 'so entertaining, that woe be unto Lazarillo de Tormes and all who have written or shall write in that manner'[34]. It is only in 'Rinconete and Cortadillo' and still more in 'The Colloquy of the Dogs' that the picaresque vein will really appear in the work of Cervantes. This fighting shy of the picaresque genre may seem surprising in Cervantes.

> He who had been in closer contact with the picaresque life than any other writer of his time always wished, when he took up his pen, to keep it at a distance, to repel its degrading contagion. The bitter laughter of the picaresque novel is not human enough for him or far too basely human.

Such is Marcel Bataillon's assessment of Cervantes[35]. So here is a first point of confusion eschewed. But it still remains to determine what the *picaro* is. Marcel Bataillon has emphasised in turn three fundamental aspects of the *picaro*. In his introduction to *La Vie de Lazarillo* he defines the *picaro* as 'a beggar, a social outcast, a creature who rubs elbows with ruffians and vagabonds . . . the picaro practises the humblest trades'[36]. This proletarian of the underworld (or demi-underworld) is perpetually spurred on by a visceral necessity: hunger. When Lazarillo serves his second master, the stingy priest, the basic problem for the young *picaro* is less to live than to stay alive. He is involved in a continual struggle against this hunger which twists his guts, and all his tricks, far from being gratuitous like Peregrine's practical jokes, are designed to procure him a meagre subsistence. It is hunger which 'commonly maketh men have ready wittes'[37]. Another characteristic of the *picaro*: far from confining himself to roguery, as soon as he can the *picaro* adopts a regular life and becomes respectable. First the servant of a blind beggar, then water-seller, then town crier, Lazarillo achieves a positive rise in the social scale, modest indeed, and even judged by the author with a certain irony, for Lazarillo has also become a complaisant husband. When Lazarillo, towards the end of his story, becomes a water-seller, he is prompt to acknowledge that 'this was the first staire I climbed up to come to attaine unto good life: for my mouth had then the measure'[38]. Finally, in a series of lectures at the Collège de France on 'L'honneur et la matière picaresque', Marcel Bataillon begins by rejecting the theory according to which the novel known as 'picaresque' is purely and simply a realistic portrayal of the lower classes in which the struggle against hunger is the dominating theme. From then on it is on external and social honour, as conceived by the Spanish, with their solicitude for appearances and of which the literary *picaros* seem to take the opposite point of view towards the end of the sixteenth century, that Marcel Bataillon puts the accent. The *picaro*, in short, is a living symbol, the antithesis of the man of honour obsessed by anxieties about decorum and purity of ancestry; in other words, the tramp as opposed to the comfortably-off. The picaresque implies the oblique or direct denunciation of money and its power as well as the ridiculous halo of respectability its possession confers.

These preliminary ideas having been stated, it will be possible to avoid the irritating vagueness into which the analysis of the picaresque elements in Smollett's novels too often falls[39]. If one examines the Smollettian characters who may have been influenced by the picaresque matter contained in *Don Quixote* and above all in *Gil Blas*, it quickly becomes apparent that there exists a certain number of *false 'picaros'*. The confusion of the critics is also partly due to the arbitrary classification of *Gil Blas* in the Hispano—French picaresque tradition. Now it is erroneous to consider Gil Blas as a *picaro* although the Duke of Lerma, when his future secretary narrates his adventures, says to him: 'Monsieur de Santillane . . . I see you have been in your time, a little upon the Picaro'[40]. The tense ('you *have been*') and the restriction ('a little upon') nevertheless sufficiently mark the difference between Gil Blas and an authentic *picaro*. Maurice Bardon rightly stresses the insufficiencies of Gil Blas who cannot be entitled to the appellation of *'picaro'*:

> Gil Blas has not the *picaro's* delight in misdeeds that is the hallmark of all of them, Lazarillo, Guzman, and Pablo: knave as he is, he does not glory in his knaveries. Neither has he the *picaro's* hatred of the social order which makes Guzman, Pablo and little Lazarillo himself as it were born-enemies of their masters and even of their like. Finally, he has not inherited corruption in his blood, from paternal or maternal infamy, he is not the offspring of a tramp and a prostitute ... Gil Blas's misfortune is that he has to be defined mainly negatively: he is the hero of insufficiency[41].

In short, Gil Blas is a false *picaro*, just like Roderick, Beau Jackson, Melopoyn and Peregrine. There is a picaresque assimilation in Smollettian criticism which is as erroneous as the autobiographical assimilation. It seems difficult, not to say impossible, to subscribe today to that assertion of Joliat's, according to whom Smollett himself was 'a kind of *picaro*'[42]. Recent research into the life and personality of Smollett completely invalidates such an opinion. Neither Roderick nor Peregrine is ever spurred on by hunger. Their origins are extremely honourable and Smollett's first two novels depict not so much a rise in the social scale as the more or less arduous recovery of a material situation impaired either by the caprices of fate or by the follies of these two young men. It has already been seen earlier that only Roderick is obliged to enter domestic service and also that this cruel necessity is felt as a sore affront to his dignity as a Scottish gentleman. Even when Roderick is a lackey in the household of Narcissa's aunt, he haughtily refuses to settle a quarrel with another servant by resorting to fisticuffs: 'I would not descend so far below the dignity of a gentleman as to fight like a porter'[43]. Such conduct promptly earns him a tell-tale nickname: 'Gentleman John'.

Between Gil Blas and Roderick there is all the difference of a social, moral and psychological code of honour of which Gil Blas has not the slightest notion when he is living his few 'picaresque' adventures at the beginning of his life. The gulf between Gil Blas and Peregrine is even wider. While the former is all flexibility, good humour and occasionally even servility, Peregrine is almost an 'anti-*picaro*' in the savagery of his reactions, especially in difficult situations. Peregrine is endowed with a nature 'which was so capricious, that the more his misery increased, the more haughty and inflexible he became'[44]. This was not likely to make his sojourn in prison more tolerable to him. A few pages further on (p. 750) Smollett reverts to this innate characteristic of Peregrine's and speaks of his 'savage obstinacy and pride'. At no moment of his career would it be possible to apply these remarks to Gil Blas. Beau Jackson and Melopoyn, as well as Miss Williams, experience particularly pronounced ups and downs in an adventurous life, but neither is a genuine picaresque character. Equally, it is difficult to see in Bowling a Quixotic character as Herbert Grierson[45], who puts Roderick's uncle in the same category as Parson Adams, does. Bowling is innocent, he is unaware of the deceits and maliciousness of the world, just like Don Quixote. But he belongs above all to the very English tradition of the brave and generous tar who is completely at sea as soon as he sets foot on land!

Nevertheless, there are some *picaros* in Smollett's novels, but they are few and, apart from Cadwallader in *Peregrine Pickle*, they usually make only a very fleeting appearance. Rourk Oregan is more an Irish caricature of a *picaro* than an authentic rival to Lazarillo. He challenges Roderick to a duel on a frivolous pretext and fights with weapons incapable of being fired. His behaviour and his tattered clothes are so bizarre that they excite Roderick's pity. Rourk Oregan tells Roderick his story. Having attained to the rank of lieutenant in the German army, he had had the misfortune to kill his captain in a duel, and since then has been looking for a rich woman to marry. In fact, Rourk Oregan is more of a poor and honest adventurer than a *picaro*. Cadwallader, in his youth, really has been a *picaro*. His many adventures, which frequently land him in prison, his peregrinations and his cynicism make him the only genuine *picaro* in Smollett's work. The following summary of his life is eloquent, but an important reservation must be stated: the disillusioned philosophy it proclaims is less that of the *picaro*, always eager to grasp life with both hands, than that of a soured and blasé misanthrope, the part which he plays in *Peregrine Pickle*:

> I have travelled over the greatest part of Europe, as a beggar, pilgrim, priest, soldier, gamester and quack; and felt the extremes of indigence and opulence, with the inclemency of weather, in all its vicissitudes. I have learned that the characters of mankind are every where the same; that common sense and honesty bear an infinitely small proportion to folly and vice; and that life is at best a paultry province[46].

Another *picaro* is Tim Cropdale, the facetious young author who despoils the fat bookseller Birkin of a new pair of boots, thanks to a trick worthy of Lazarillo. Tim never has a penny to bless himself with, but his mind is as fertile in invention as Panurge's. 'Cropdale literally lives by his wit, which he has exercised upon all his friends in their turns'[47].

And Smollett proceeds to recount some of the outrageous tricks of which Tim has been guilty in order to get himself money. But this amusing sketch of a literary *picaro* full of good humour and *joie-de-vivre*, unembarrassed by scruples, occupies barely three or four pages in Smollett's work. There is another character in *Humphry Clinker* who *might have* been a *picaro*, had not fate and his methodist persuasion prevented it: Clinker himself. In fact Clinker exhibits a certain number of picaresque characteristics. His origin is obscure and, when he meets

Matthew Bramble, illness has just reduced him to near-starvation. More-over, like all *picaros*, Clinker is clever with his hands and capable of exercising several trades. But there all Clinker's possible resemblances to a *picaro* cease. His honesty, his piety, his simplicity and his loyalty place him at the literary antipodes of the picaresque world.

The influence of Lesage on Smollett's characters, for all that *Gil Blas* represents a source of picaresque inspiration, is therefore slight. Neither, apart from *Launcelot Greaves*, whose case will be examined later, is the influence of *Don Quixote* very extensive. But one character, without being a slavish imitation of Don Quixote, bears the imprint of Cervantes and that is Lismahago. Smollett does not conceal the source of his inspira-tion. From the moment Lismahago appears, the image of the Knight of La Mancha is evoked: 'A tall meagre figure, answering with his horse, the description of Don Quixote mounted on Rozinante'[48]. The leanness of his person, his affection for his emaciated steed and the riding accident which marks his ludicrous entrance on the scene of the novel are so many features borrowed from Don Quixote. When Lismahago tries to alight gracefully from his horse, for he has caught sight of Tabitha and Liddy on a balcony, at the very moment when he still has one foot in the stirrup, the girth breaks and he makes a spectacular fall. The same mishap befalls Don Quixote, in the same circumstances, in front of the Duke and Duchess[49]. Like Cervantes, at the beginning of the first and second parts of *Don Quixote*, Smollett stresses the leanness and lankiness of Lismahago. Don Quixote is presented to the reader as being 'of a tough constitution, extremely meagre and hard featured'[50] or again 'so meagre, shrunk and withered, that he looked like an Aegyptian mummy . . .'[51]. Smollett stresses Lismahago's height (over six foot), the narrowness of his shoulders, his preternaturally long thighs, like a grass-hopper's, and his face, as long as a fiddle, baked by the sun and all shrivelled and wrinkled. The mount matches the rider: 'His horse was exactly in the stile of its rider; a resurrection of dry bones'[52] and recalls the skeletal nag, Rozinante. Smollett seems to make a point of Lisma-hago's literary affinity with Don Quixote for he takes care to emphasise it once again when Lismahago, accompanied by Jery's Scottish manservant, Archy Macalpine, goes to bear a challenge to Lord Oxminster: 'Truly, if Macalpine had been mounted upon an ass, this couple might have passed for the knight of La Mancha and his squire Panza'[53]. It is also possible that the scene where Lismahago in his nightshirt gets out of his bedroom window and descends a ladder with extreme haste 'with a quilted night-cap fastened under his chin, and his long lank limbs and posteriors exposed to the wind'[54] is a reminiscence of the chapter where Don Quixote, after his onslaught on the wineskins is described thus:

> He appeared in his shirt, which was too scanty before, to cover his thighs, and still shorter behind, by six inches at least and displayed a

pair of long lank legs, imbrowned with hair, and not extremely clean; his head was covered with a little red, greasy night-cap, belonging to the landlord[55].

Lastly, it is not impossible — but this influence is much less definite than that of Cervantes — that Smollett may also have remembered the valiant Don Hannibal de Chinchilla, that glorious mutilated warrior to whose aid Gil Blas comes and who has lost an eye in Naples, an arm in Lombardy and a leg in the Low Countries. Just like Lismahago, Don Hannibal is poor in hard cash but rich in punctilious honour. Like Don Quixote and Lismahago, Don Hannibal is 'of gigantic stature and extremely meagre'[56].

If, in spite of some reservations as to whether *Gil Blas* really belongs to the picaresque genre, one considers that this book has been, for Smollett, a source of inspiration which has stamped his work, a particular case of a *picaro manqué* remains to be examined, that of Ferdinand Count Fathom. This ambiguous character offers certain undeniable picaresque character- istics, yet it is also possible to wonder whether the spirit in which it was created is comparable to that of the *picaros* who appear in *Gil Blas*.

Ferdinand's first picaresque characteristic is his birth. Even more than Gil Blas, Ferdinand was born in genealogical and moral infamy. In this sense he is nearer to Lazarillo (the son of a swindling miller and a wanton mother) or to a *picaro* like Scipio, Gil Blas's servant and confi- dant. Smollett insists, sometimes with a rather heavy mythological irony, on Ferdinand's confused paternity:

> That he was acknowledged by no mortal sire, solely proceeded from the uncertainty of his mother, whose affections were so dissipated among a number of admirers, that she could never pitch upon the person from whose loins our hero sprung[57].

Moreover, Ferdinand's nationality is a Gordian knot of international law. The son of an unknown father and an English mother, the hero begins to be born on the Dutch frontier but is finally delivered in Flanders. It seems that Smollett has set out from the first to load the odds against his hero with an accumulation of hereditary taints. His mother, a camp-follower, not only administers drink to the soldiers but also repose and even eternal repose. Like Hugo's 'la Thénardier' in *Les Misérables* a century later, Ferdinand's mother roams over the battlefields and finishes off the wounded, friends or enemies, with a dagger, in order to rob their corpses. In the course of one of these expeditions she saves, as a deliberate excep- tion, the life of Count Melvil who later takes Ferdinand under his protec- tion when she has got herself killed during a final bloodthirsty imitation of Atropos. Ferdinand's mother is more than a *picara*: she is a criminal monster who kills as readily as she dispenses her gin to the troops.

Cunning, swindling and grasping, this rival of Thalestris is not immoral; she proves herself, with consistent regularity, to be completely amoral. And as though heredity were not already heavy enough to bear, Smollett gives Ferdinand alcohol as his earliest nourishment. In the form of a rumour he pretends not wholly to believe, he reveals to the reader that, from his tenderest infancy, he imbibed brandy from his mother's keg. His mother's friends did not fail to contribute to this alcoholic regime: 'before he was thirteen months old, [they] taught him to suck brandy impregnated with gunpowder, through the touch-hole of a pistol'[58]. What a diet for a baby! But, far from wasting away, young Ferdinand flourishes; he is as strong and handsome as a young Hercules.

Lesage also does not fail to emphasise these hereditary traits in *Gil Blas*, especially when he tells the story of Scipio. This faithful companion of Gil Blas is the bastard son of a soldier of the Holy Brotherhood (which is not illustrious but neither is it ignominious) and of a gipsy fortune-teller, La Coscolina. Scipio is thus a mongrel. This genetic mixture is extremely important. In recounting his adventures, he repeatedly brings up the 'force of the blood' as an excuse. When he robs the old hermit of his money he explains his action thus:

> I no sooner saw that this was money I could appropriate to myself with impunity than my Aegyptian disposition prevailed. I was seized with desire of stealing it, which can be attributed to nothing but the force of the blood which circulated in my veins[59].

Scipio, like Panurge, has theft in his blood, which Lesage expresses in such phrases as 'my thievish inclinations' (vol. IV, p. 115) or again 'I was naturally inclined to thieving' (vol. IV, p. 87). It is also what Smollett sums up in *Ferdinand Count Fathom* by means of a proverb: 'What's bred in the bone will never come out of the flesh' which he uses as an epigraph to Chapter xliii. Heredity constitutes a picaresque determinism which rules the behaviour of Scipio and Ferdinand.

To heredity should be added the formative influence of childhood years. Ferdinand is adopted by the generous Count Melvil, to begin with as one of his servants: 'The count ... admitted Ferdinand into the number of his domestics, resolving that he should be brought up in attendance upon his own son, who was a boy of the same age'[60]. Later, Ferdinand's position in his benefactor's family becomes more ambiguous. He holds, as it were, 'a middle place between the rank of a relation, and favoured domestic'[61]. This delicate situation involves certain constraints. Young Ferdinand, with precocious sagacity, endeavours to dissimulate (and he succeeds extremely well) the blackness of his nature. He waits for a favourable opportunity to desert Melvil's son, so as to be free in his movements. The thirst for liberty which, in the *picaro*, occasionally borders on instability is another of Scipio's characteristics. The *picaro* has difficulty in staying put in one place and his desire for liberty is so keen that it occasionally seems almost pathological. The *picaro* cannot accept parental, social or professional restraints. He is a creature who proclaims, like Scipio, 'the right of changing the air'[62]. When Scipio escapes from the religious orphanage, at the age of nine, he already feels 'a sensible pleasure in being free, and master of [his] own actions'[63].

Ferdinand not only has the same origins as those of the *picaros*, he also exhibits the same type of character, flexible, astute and, when his interests demand it, servile. Here again, Smollett systematically accumulates the psychological indications. From Ferdinand's childhood, he stresses the flexibility, apparent docility and marvellous adaptability of his young hero. 'Sagacity' is a word Smollett uses over and over again in describing Ferdinand in the first chapters (e.g. pp. 16 and 22), as well as 'pliant' (pp. 19 and 44). Although Ferdinand is devoid of the faintest trace of moral sense, he is so adept at pulling the wool over people's eyes that he deceives the schoolmaster and the entire Melvil family with equal facility 'by means of a large share of ductibility and dissimulation, [so] that, surely, he was calculated by nature, to dupe even the most cautious, and gratify his appetites, by levying contributions on all mankind'[64]. To serve his crafty purposes, Ferdinand employs his marvellous talents as a born actor. They are undeniably useful to him with the women he wishes to seduce (and deceive). Thus, with Wilhelmina, he shows himself an 'excellent actor' (p. 48) and with his accomplice, Teresa, he feigns transports which he does not feel in the least when they meet again: 'and our hero, upon this occasion, performed the part of an exquisite actor' (p. 73).

These are not the only natural assets which Ferdinand possesses. Much more decisively than Lazarillo, Gil Blas or Scipio, he is gifted with artistic and social talents which he does not fail to use in his numerous swindles. While the young (and good) Melvil behaves in a drawing-room like an unlicked cub, Ferdinand charms all around him by the natural grace of his bearing, his polite affability and his agreeable conversation. Even if these qualities are only superficial and deceptive appearances, they very often suffice to dupe fashionable society in London or Bath, the usual scene of his frauds. He is expert at cards, plays draughts and chess, proves himself to be a skilful billiards player and a dancer much in demand by the ladies as a partner. His artistic gifts also enable him to play the flute and violin remarkably well. All these traits already make Ferdinand more of a worldly adventurer than a *picaro* although he possesses certain fundamental qualities of one. Also, unlike the *picaro*, who generally acts on his own, Ferdinand very soon perceives that he needs an accomplice in his many and various frauds. To begin with, he assures himself of the alliance of Teresa, Mademoiselle de Melvil's personal maid, who will be an invaluable help when he tries (in vain) to seduce that young girl. But Teresa only plays a restricted role in *Ferdinand Count Fathom*, where the hero, after having secretly married her during a mock religious ceremony, very quickly abandons her for richer prey. It is in Vienna that Ferdinand finds the ideal confederate, a Tyrolese named Ratchcali (a pseudo-Italian distortion of 'rascal'?), a dice-loader and expert in the science of gaming. Ferdinand and Ratchcali conclude an offensive and defensive alliance: 'thus connected they began to hunt in couples'[65]. The only example of a lasting association between *picaros* in *Gil Blas* is furnished by Don Raphael and Ambrose de Lamela. The partnership of Ferdinand and Ratchcali is not without its drawbacks since these two confederates try to double-cross each other (though only Ratchcali is successful). Practical necessity rather than a basic need drives Ferdinand to gang up with Ratchcali. As soon as he is able, he definitely decides to go it alone. This exaggerated individualism is a characteristic trait of the *picaro*. In Paris he repels the interested advances of scoundrels of his type, for he is 'altogether selfish, and quite solitary in his prospects ... being resolved to trade upon his own bottom only, and to avoid all such connexions with any person or society whatever'[66]. The *picaro*, like the wolf, likes to hunt alone.

Flexibility, social and artistic talents, but also cynicism — such are Ferdinand's principal traits. The hunting simile employed above is suggested by the frequent use Smollett makes of this stylistic device. Ferdinand's philosophy could be summed up by Plautus's adage '*Homo homini lupus*' repeated and illustrated by Bacon and Hobbes. The following passage is a gloss on this expression of human pessimism:

> He had formerly imagined, but was now fully persuaded, that the sons of men preyed upon one another, and such was the end and condition of their being. Among the principal figures of life, he observed few or no characters that did not bear a strong analogy to the savage tyrants of the wood. One resembled a tyger in fury and rapaciousness; a second prowled about like a hungry wolf, seeking whom he might devour; a third acted the part of a jackall, in beating the bush for game to his voracious employer; and a fourth imitated the wily fox, in practising a thousand crafty ambuscades for the destruction of the ignorant and unwary[67].

And it is this last animal — 'Reynard the Fox' is the archetype of the *picaro* — that Ferdinand decides to imitate. This choice explains the Machiavellism of the character whom Smollett frequently describes as a 'subtle politician' (p. 79), or again as an individual 'never deficient in his political capacity' (p. 81). Finally, cynicism and Machiavellism do not prevent Ferdinand from being a hedonist in his leisure hours, yet, however surprising this may seem, he is capable, when reduced to it, of leading an ascetic life. This is a trait common to Lazarillo, Gil Blas, Scipio, Don Raphael and Ambrose de Lamela, who frequently find themselves obliged to make the best of a bad job until fate, aided by their natural roguery, proves kinder. When Ferdinand lets himself be duped in Paris by the archrogue Sir Stentor Stiles, 'he bears his fate like a philosopher' announces the heading of Chapter xxv. He stoically decides 'to accommodate himself to his fate, and profit by the lesson he had so dearly bought' (p. 107). This forced stoicism would have been cold comfort if Ferdinand, transformed into a one-eyed musician and living henceforth under the false name of Fadini, were not capable of living 'with incredible frugality, that he might save a purse for his future operations' (p. 108).

Such are Ferdinand's picaresque traits, but they do not suffice to make him an authentic *picaro*. In fact, Ferdinand completely lacks that insouciance, that *joie de vivre*, which make the ambiguous charm of Gil Blas or Scipio. *Ferdinand Count Fathom* is a sad novel, one from which the comic spirit and good humour are, for the most part, absent. The cynicism of Lazarillo, Gil Blas and Scipio is a cheerful cynicism. They are the first to laugh at their misadventures, even when (especially in Lazarillo's case) they are goaded by hunger. In a word, *Ferdinand Count Fathom* is not really written in the picaresque spirit even though, as will be seen later, this novel is the one in which Smollett handles the picaresque form with the most expertise.

Now the divorce between the form and the picaresque spirit had been foreseeable since 1748, the date when Smollett composed the preface to *Roderick Random*. If he freely admits, as has been seen earlier, that he has imitated Lesage's plan, he promptly proceeds to criticise the comic conception of Gil Blas:

> The disgraces of Gil Blas are, for the most part, such as rather excite mirth than compassion; he himself laughs at them; and his transitions from distress to happiness, or at least ease, are so sudden, that neither the reader has time to pity him, nor himself to be acquainted with affliction. This conduct, in my opinion, not only deviates from probability, but prevents that generous indignation which ought to animate the reader against the sordid and vicious disposition of the world[68].

It is to be feared that Smollett has not properly taken in the preliminary lesson of *Gil Blas*, offered in the advertisement entitled 'Gil Blas to the Reader', and that he has stopped short at appearances without grasping the very substance of the book. Smollett, confined within the narrow frame of a satirical and puritanical preoccupation, so much does the moral element seem to take precedence for him over all others, has not perhaps understood all the full significance of *Gil Blas* beyond the comic adventures of the hero. The criticisms Smollett brings against Lesage make him seem like the scholar who could not pierce the mystery of the epitaph inscribed on the tombstone of the licentiate Pedro Garcias. He ought to have pondered Lesage's solemn warning:

> If thou perusest my adventures, without perceiving the moral instructions they contain, thou wilt reap no harvest from thy labour: but if

thou readest with attention, thou wilt find in them, according to the precept of Horace, profit mingled with pleasure[69].

Very different is the spirit which animates the dedication, or rather the autodedication, of *Ferdinand Count Fathom*. Its dominant literary note is the struggle waged against vice by terror. Smollett dwells repeatedly, with heavy insistence, on the moral value of terror. In *Ferdinand Count Fathom*, he proposes to paint such a realistic picture of evil in all its forms that the reader will no longer dare to succumb to it. The spectacle of vice being utterly rooted ought, according to Smollett, to leave 'a deep impression of terror upon the minds of those who were not confirmed in the pursuit of morality and virtue, and while the balance wavers, enables the right scale to preponderate'[70]. A little further on, he underlines the preventive and curative virtues of fear: 'The impulses of fear which is the most violent and interesting of all the passions, remain longer than any other upon the memory' (ibid.). On the same page two expressions reveal the importance Smollett attaches to the description of vice *in terrorem*: 'an hundred are deterred from the practice of vice, by that infamy and punishment to which it is liable, from the laws and regulation of mankind'. As to those still wavering between good and evil, they 'may be terrified from plunging into that irremeable gulph, by surveying the deplorable fate of FERDINAND COUNT FATHOM'.

Nothing could be further removed from the method and spirit of *Gil Blas*. Where Lesage laughs, Smollett fulminates. Finally, even when Gil Blas and Scipio launch on adventures in which morality is treated somewhat cavalierly, they still do not cease to present a sympathetic side which always guarantees them the amused indulgence of the reader. Between Lesage and his literary creations, there is a constant distance, an objective detachment which is the guarantee of impartiality. Lesage does not hate Gil Blas any more than Scipio, Raphael or Ambrose de Lamela. His art as a story-teller is such that he breathes an autonomous life into them. The writer is effaced behind the literary creation. Exactly the opposite happens with Ferdinand. Smollett is so impassioned by his terrifying moral demonstration that he ends up by raging (in a way that would be pathetic if it were not half-ludicrous because it is so out of place) against the monster he has just created.

> Perfidious wretch! thy crimes turn out so atrocious that I half repent me of having undertaken to record thy memoirs: yet such monsters ought to be exhibited to public view, that mankind may be upon their guard against imposture ... and ... iniquity ... will at last be overtaken by that punishment and disgrace which are its due[71].

This *esprit de sérieux* (in the proper sense and perhaps also in the Sartrian one) in some way crystallises Smollett's moral puritanism. But the art of the novel suffers when these didactic preoccupations take precedence over the demands of literary objectivity.

There is another fundamental trait which forbids Ferdinand to be regarded as an authentic *picaro*: his innate perversity, his instinctive love of evil. Smollett, obsessed by his puritanical idea of evil, has created a metaphysical monster whose final conversion is highly unconvincing. If *Ferdinand Count Fathom* is, on the whole, a mediocre novel, this is because Smollett made a literary wager with himself: to depict a person fundamentally bad, without a single redeeming feature. Two centuries later Steinbeck met with the same literary failure with the character of Kate in *East of Eden*. It is not from the *picaros* created by Lesage in *Gil Blas* that Smollett derived his model. A rapid analysis discovers two very distinct types of *picaro* in *Gil Blas*: those who are reclaimable like Gil Blas himself and his servant Scipio, and the irreclaimable, Don Raphael and Ambrose de Lamela. Above all, Lesage does not commit the grave literary error of saving *in extremis* a *picaro* presented up to then as past saving. Don Raphael and Ambrose de Lamela perish at the stakes of the Inquisition, which causes the worthy Gil Blas some retrospective terrors for having once taken part in the guilty activities of these ruffians. If Gil Blas has been 'a little upon the Picaro', Scipio has been much more of one and does not fail to admit it:

> The son of Coscolina has purged his morals, and . . . virtuous senti-
> ments have succeeded his vicious inclinations . . . if Scipio in his
> childhood was a real *Picaro*, he has corrected his conduct so well
> since that time, that he is now the model of a perfect servant[72].

And this transition is gradual. From the moment Scipio enters Gil Blas's service, he abandons his life of dishonest adventures to aspire, just like his master, to the quiet of a comfortable bourgeois life. Scipio has made his social and moral ascent just like Lazarillo. Ferdinand, on the contrary, has no excuse for his acts of gratuitous wickedness. Evil is rooted in his nature from the cradle: 'a most insidious principle of self-love, that grew up with him from the cradle, and left no room in his heart for the least particle of social virtue'[73].

Smollett insists too much on the innateness of evil in Ferdinand's soul for his final conversion to be acceptable, even if one grants a double significance to the disease which prostrates him at the end of the novel: physical punishment for his sins, symbolic catharsis of repentance. In the long run, it is no longer a living character that Smollett depicts when Ferdinand is lying on his straw pallet, but a clumsy symbol of all his own hatred of evil translated into terms of physical decay. One comment reveals this exaggerated moral intention and sums up all Smollett's failure. It is not a repulsive sick man whom young Melvil contemplates, but a 'melancholy lesson'[74]. Smollett may have been aware of the improbability of such an edifying end. Ferdinand reappears just once again right at

the end of the novel in order to implore the pardon of the Melvil heir. The young man not only behaves magnanimously but even pushes generosity so far as to provide a decent home for Ferdinand and his wife to retire to. Smollett then feels the need to say of Ferdinand: 'all his vice and ambition was now quite mortified within him, and his whole attention engrossed in atoning for his former crimes, by a sober and penitent life'[75].

No doubt this affirmation still seemed inadequate to Smollett, for, eighteen years after *Ferdinand Count Fathom*, in *Humphry Clinker*, he feels the need to make Ferdinand reappear on the scene, now become a country apothecary renowned for miles around for his obligingness, his professional seriousness and the severe dignity of his austere life. To crown this metamorphosis, Ferdinand, who has adopted the symbolic name of 'Grieve', saves the life of Count and Countess Melvil (which Smollett spells 'Melville' in *Humphry Clinker*). It is obvious that Smollett wishes to reconsider the case of Ferdinand. This is the reason why he introduced the Melvilles again in his last novel in order to be able to insist one last time on the sincerity of Ferdinand's conversion. Smollett justifies himself *a posteriori*, perhaps to revenge himself on the numerous critics who had remarked on the laboured improbability of the end of *Ferdinand Count Fathom*. This reverting to the world of an earlier novel proves how constant was Smollett's preoccupation throughout his whole career as a writer with attacking the forces of evil and aiding the moral victory of the good. This anxiety to edify may seem boring, indeed absurd to a twentieth-century reader, but nonetheless Smollett's courageous fidelity to his moral ideal deserves to be respected. It is even touching that in his last novel — and he knew that his end was near — he should have taken pains to revert to the fate of a character created nearly twenty years previously in order to prove to his readers that Ferdinand really was 'a sincere convert to virtue'[76]. But this delayed ending is almost too edifying. Ferdinand remains a *picaro manqué*.

The majority of critics condemn *Launcelot Greaves* as a pale imitation of *Don Quixote*. Here again, it does not seem that Smollett's warning, just as his reservations about the character of *Gil Blas*, has always been appreciated at its true value. The critics are content, as a rule, with quoting the remark of the misanthrope Ferret when Launcelot Greaves appears in the dining-room of the inn armed from head to foot: 'What! [said Ferret] you set up for a modern Don Quixote? — The scheme is rather too stale and extravagant'[77]. And Ferret proceeds to criticise with his customary asperity the ridiculous anachronism such a project involves. But, too often, they forget that this remark is made by an eminently unpleasant character, Ferret, whose judgment is warped by misanthropic prejudice. Moreover, this concession of Smollett's is a rhetorical device, the epitrope, which consists in pretending to agree with something in order promptly to derive an advantage from it, i.e. give more authority to what one really wishes to prove. Now the important assertion is not Ferret's but rather the immediate retort of Launcelot Greaves himself:

> He that from affectation imitates the extravagances recorded of Don Quixote, is an impostor equally wicked and contemptible. . . . I am neither an affected imitator of Don Quixote, nor, as I trust in Heaven, visited by that spirit of lunacy so admirably displayed in the fictitious character exhibited by the inimitable Cervantes[78].

Launcelot Greaves also hastens to add that he has never taken windmills for giants nor this inn for a splendid castle. Thanks to this fierce verbal battle between the knight and Ferret, Smollett achieves a double aim. To begin with, he specifically warns the critics that his intention is not to write a servile imitation of *Don Quixote*. He even defends the credibility of his character from the point of view of English law. Greaves cannot be regarded as a vagrant guilty of causing disorder on the public highway, since every gentleman has the right — and even the moral duty in the eighteenth century — not to travel except duly armed. Ferret does not consider himself beaten and then accuses Greaves of wanting to 'co-operate with the honourable fraternity of thief-takers' (p. 14). This false and spiteful accusation permits the young knight-errant to proclaim his profession of faith: 'I do purpose . . . to act as a coadjutor to the law, and even to remedy evils which the law cannot reach; to detect fraud and treason, abase insolence, mortify pride, discourage slander, disgrace immodesty, and stigmatize ingratitude' (ibid.). This is a noble programme, but less Utopian than it appears at first sight. The great difference between Greaves and Don Quixote is emphasised by Smollett from the very beginning of the novel. Greaves's appearance and behaviour may be eccentric, but the evils he intends to fight against are extremely real. In spite of his anachronistic armour, Greaves is attacking the injustices and social abuses of the years 1750—60, he is rooted in his century and not setting off in pursuit of chivalric fantasies. Thus, in Chapters xi and xii, it is definitely against the corrupt justice of the eighteenth century that he is protesting. All through the novel, Greaves fills the role of redresser of wrongs, whereas Don Quixote, obsessed with his chivalric ideas, causes more damage than he repairs, especially in the first part of the book.

But, whatever the worth of the warning Smollett addresses to the reader, the influence of *Don Quixote* is indisputable. Smollett does not conceal his debt to Cervantes in *Launcelot Greaves*, any more than he does that to Lesage in *Roderick Random*. Towards the end of the novel, Dawdle, Sycamore's facetious parasite, decides to egg on his master to challenge Greaves according to the rules of knight-errantry: 'It would be no difficult matter, in imitation of the batchelor Sampson Carrasco, to go in quest of Greaves as a knight errant' (p. 147). The admission is clear; Smollett proposes to imitate, in burlesque fashion, the efforts of Sampson

Carrasco, in turn Knight of the Mirrors, then Knight of the White Moon, to vanquish Don Quixote in combat and bring him back to his village, cured once and for all of his chivalric madness. Thus, there is from the outset, in *Launcelot Greaves*, a superficial imitation of Don Quixote which might be called the mask of chivalry. The armour is the most obvious element of this imitation. This armour formerly belonged to Greaves's great-grandfather and it has to be cleaned and repaired when young Launcelot decides to set out on the career of knight-errant (p. 43). But once the surprise is over, Smollett does not make a point of describing the armour, any more than he lingers over the ceremonies of dubbing. Tom Clarke, in his discreet legal way, simply refuses to name the knight who performed this ceremony and lets it be known that *perhaps* he was not *compos mentis*. This is a first difference from Don Quixote who is dubbed knight by an innkeeper during a grotesque masquerade. Moreover Launcelot is young and handsome which is certainly not the case with Don Quixote. His wandering life hardens him and brings him a revival of health and vitality. When, for a few moments, he sees his beloved Aurelia again, she remarks that his travels have put 'a glow of health and vivacity on his features' (p. 120). The unfortunate Don Quixote emerges sore and sorry, most of the time, from his adventures. Finally, this much-ridiculed armour does not play a major part in *Launcelot Greaves*. It must not be forgotten that in reply to the sarcasms of Ferret, Launcelot had, from the beginning of the book, justified his wearing armour, declaring that he had donned it, either 'for exercise, in order to accustom myself to fatigue, and strengthen my constitution', or 'for a frolick' (p. 14). Two-thirds through the novel (p. 135) he decides to abandon this armour when he gets near London, and this indeed is what he does some twenty-five pages later (p. 161).

This armour assumes, nevertheless, a double role, symbolic and practical. It represents the defence mechanism of an idealist, bruised by the sordid malice of the real world. When Greaves is once again able to face his own emotional problems in a more rational and conventional way, he will no longer need this symbolic carapace. He will then be able to confront himself as well as pit himself against reality. But perhaps, above all, Greaves's armour fulfils a practical role: it protects the author more than his character. Under cover of these eccentric trappings, Smollett can, with complete immunity, denounce the social and moral failings of his own day with his usual virulence. Launcelot's armour is a rampart against possible lawsuits. In 1760, with the action brought against him by Admiral Knowles hanging over his head like a sword of Justice, Smollett owed it to himself to be cautious. Thanks to the armour and the supposed madness of Launcelot Greaves, Smollett revives the classic device of Cervantes: denouncing the madness of the world through the medium of a person apparently bereft of reason.

The madness of Launcelot Greaves is very different from that of Don

Quixote, both in its causes and its manifestations. Like Don Quixote, he has read too much, not romances of chivalry but Greek and Latin authors, not to mention those in other languages. The love of books, however, is not the principal cause of Launcelot's temporary derangement. The play of circumstances, the traditional hatred between the Greaveses and the Darnels, the imposture of an apocryphal letter, forbid him to marry Aurelia Darnel, who is anything but an imaginary creature like Don Quixote's Dulcinea. But the eccentricities of an unhappy lover cannot entirely account for Launcelot Greaves's strange behaviour. Greaves's madness is all the more ambiguous since, like Don Quixote's, it is intermittent. Cervantes calls Don Quixote 'a party-coloured maniac, full of lucid intervals'[79]. Greaves is at once idealist and realist. His profession of faith has the same nobility as that of Don Quixote who claims to belong to 'the order of knight errantry [which] was first instituted to defend damsels, protect widows, and succour the needy and the fatherless'[80]. Greaves's intentions seem to be directly inspired by Don Quixote. He declares himself

> determined . . . to honour and assert the efforts of virtue; to combat vice in all her forms, redress injuries, chastise oppression, protect the helpless and forlorn, relieve the indigent, exert my best endeavours in the cause of innocence and beauty (p. 12).

These are not idle words. Launcelot is also capable of action. In his activities on his father's estate, and in the neighbouring parishes, he displays what one might call a crazy generosity. Even if this paternalism may seem Utopian, Launcelot Greaves is concerned with the welfare of the poor, he repairs their cottages, feeds them and clothes them. His father's great reproach is that, by thus concerning himself with the indigent, Launcelot is lowering himself and betraying his social caste by mixing with the 'dregs of the people' (p. 23). In spite of his father's opposition, Launcelot succeeds in bringing happiness to all the surrounding countryside: 'one would have thought the golden age was revived in Yorkshire' (p. 24). When, later, Launcelot launches himself on the knight-errant's career of redressing wrongs, his friends cannot prevent themselves from admiring 'the accomplishments of the knight, dashed as they were with a mixture of extravagance and insanity' (p. 104).

It is, above all, the differences between Don Quixote and Launcelot Greaves which require to be emphasised. Launcelot is never really ridiculous, he is never physically maltreated in the course of his adventures. Unlike Don Quixote, in wanting to do good, Launcelot never brings about evil. But a common bond unites them; both are aristocrats, not only by birth, but in heart and soul. Launcelot, like Don Quixote, refuses to soil his lance with plebeian blood. It was therefore necessary that Launcelot should be attended by a man of the people who, like Sancho, would serve as a foil to his master.

Sancho Panza and Timothy Crabshaw, Greaves's squire, belong to the same literary family. As regards the character of Crabshaw, the influence of Cervantes is indisputed. The two servants have the same physique, the same coarseness, and express themselves in the same style. The resemblances are very definite. The two men are ugly, dull-witted clowns. Nevertheless Crabshaw's ugliness is much more heavily caricatured than Sancho's. Smollett devotes much energy to giving Crabshaw a grotesque physical appearance (p. 10), whereas Cervantes skims quickly over the description of Sancho. Both are strong, but cowardly. Nevertheless the characters of the two men are fundamentally different. Sancho is an honest peasant 'but one who had a very small quantity of brains in his skull'[81], whereas Tom Clarke admits he finds Greaves's choice hard to understand, since Timothy 'of all the servants about the house . . . was the least likely either to please his master, or engage in such an undertaking' (p. 45). Greaves's squire is narrow-minded and spiteful, and has a redoubtable tongue. It is probably this natural perversity which makes Timothy have such an extraordinary affection for his draught-horse 'Gilbert', an animal which is not only clumsy but vicious. There too Smollett transforms Sancho's donkey, which is no more stubborn than any other asinine mount. But, by way of compensation he has retained the affection the rider bears his steed.

If Bronzomarte, Greaves's spirited horse, is the equine antithesis of Rozinante, Gilbert and Sancho's Dapple have the right to the same adoration – the word is not too strong – from their respective masters. Crabshaw's despair when he thinks he has lost Gilbert, then the joy of the reunion, are directly inspired by the same incidents treated by Cervantes in a vein of grotesque buffoonery. Crabshaw goes so far in his solicitude for his beloved Gilbert as to ask an astrologer to predict the fate of this old comrade 'who truly did not deserve so much at his hands; but he could not help loving him better than e'er a friend he had in the world' (p. 181). When Sancho rediscovers the donkey, which Ginès de Passamonte had stolen from him, he embraces and kisses it (a demonstration of joy imitated by Crabshaw) and addresses it in these words: 'How hast thou been, my dear Dapple? my trusty companion and joy of my eyes!'[82]. The literary affinity between Sancho and Crabshaw is so obvious that Smollett does not attempt to conceal it. Two (false) officers quarrel with Crabshaw:

> They cursed and abused him, calling him Sancho Panza, and such dog names; and bade him tell his master Don Quicksot, that, if he made any noise, they would confine him to his cage, and lie with his mistress Dulcinea[83].

These false officers (and real disguised draper's apprentices) show, thanks to Smollett, that they are well-read.

Like Sancho, Crabshaw is a coarse fellow who, in the course of his adventures, suffers several physiological debacles. He does not, like Sancho, go so far as to forget himself in front of his master, nevertheless Smollett, with his usual medical realism, dwells heavily on the malodorous scene where Crabshaw is treated by an apothecary who is an advocate of purges, vesicatories and alexipharmics. Sancho and Crabshaw are both of them hearty drinkers and good trenchermen, and their minds are frequently preoccupied with their ravenous stomachs. It is not surprising that these two country bumpkins should talk in the same way. Smollett has imitated, not to say copied, the style of Sancho, whose popular wisdom is often expressed in flights of proverbs and other hackneyed aphorisms. Don Quixote, weary of hearing his squire cheerfully emitting an endless string of these sententious stupidities complains of 'those innumerable shafts of [his] proverbs'[84]. Crabshaw, set in the stocks, consoles himself by reeling off a series of maxims suited to his very limited philosophical education (p. 85). The scatological element is seldom lacking in popular wisdom and, when Crabshaw is discovered in a wretched state by his master, he complains that the latter helps him more by words than deeds to get out of his trying situation: 'Thatch your house with t[ur]d, and you will have more teachers than reachers' (p. 127). The final paronomasia gives the tone of this splendid intellectual effort. But, if the imitation of Cervantes is obvious, Smollett has nevertheless created a character altogether different from Sancho. Timothy Crabshaw displays no affection except for the impossible Gilbert. There are no deep bonds between Launcelot Greaves and himself, comparable to the friendly relationship which develops between Don Quixote and his squire. Crabshaw is never touched by his master's madness, he never shares it for a single instant whereas Sancho's rustic good sense allows itself to be seduced by the promise of an island to govern. Finally, Sancho does not conceal the fact that he follows his master of his own free will, although he knows he is mad:

> Had I been wise, I should have left my master long ago; but this was my fate and my misventure; I cannot do otherwise; but follow him I must; we are of the same town; I have eaten of his bread; I have an affection for him; he returns my love and has given me his colts; but, above all, I am constant and faithful and therefore nothing can possibly part us but the sexton's shovel[85].

One would seek in vain for such an expression of devotion in *Launcelot Greaves*. Crabshaw occasionally needs a stinging rebuke (verbal or physical) to consent to go on being Launcelot Greaves's squire. It would be impossible to apply to Crabshaw and Launcelot Greaves the following words of W. H. Auden on Don Quixote and Sancho:

> The two are eternally related. Don Quixote needs Sancho Panza as the one creature about whom he has no illusions but loves as he is.

Sancho Panza needs Don Quixote as the one constant loyalty in his life which is independent of feeling[86].

The examination of the influence of *Don Quixote* on *Launcelot Greaves* would be incomplete without an analysis of Crowe, the sailor who falls in love with chivalry. This character is not simply a member of the maritime family which includes Bowling and Trunnion. Smollett has transferred to Crowe all the grotesque elements comprised in the adventures and even in the character of Don Quixote. Crowe is the ridiculous double of Launcelot Greaves. Whereas Launcelot never suffers physically in his adventures (which is not the case with Don Quixote), Crowe emerges bruised and battered from his chivalrous feats. With Launcelot Greaves and Crowe, Smollett splits one personality in two. On the one hand, Launcelot embodies the idealism of Don Quixote in all that is noblest and most generous, on the other Crowe bears all the ridicule encountered by Don Quixote. The traditional ignorance of the world of landlubbers is a characteristic shared with sailors such as Bowling and Trunnion, but Crowe's also resembles the innocence of Don Quixote. Crow is 'as little acquainted with the world as a sucking child' (p. 2). Crowe's credulity partly explains the ease with which he becomes fired with a passion for chivalry and offers Smollett a considerable source of comedy. Whereas Launcelot's vigil of arms is dealt with in a few lines, Crowe's is as burlesque as Don Quixote's. On this occasion, Fillet, a facetious doctor met at the inn, recalls that 'Don Quixote was dubbed by his landlord' (p. 52). Crowe's vigil of arms in a neighbouring chapel allows the lovers of coarse practical jokes to give free rein to their playful instincts. Ferret and Tom Clarke disguise themselves as ghosts with phosphorescent foreheads and come to throw terror into the heart of Crowe who has borrowed (without permission) Launcelot's armour for the occasion. In short, Smollett elaborates a whole series of jokes in the taste of the eighteenth century arising from the scene where Don Quixote is dubbed knight by an innkeeper.

Crowe's armour recalls that of Don Quixote. It is made up of bits and pieces — his buckler is a pot-lid and his lance a hop-pole (p. 136). Like Don Quixote, whose morion is fastened on with green ribbons, Crowe cannot remove his warlike headgear after an encounter in which he is trounced by his opponents. The face of the tyro Crowe is so puffy and swollen that the flesh has to be cut into in order to sever the straps of his helmet. Smollett uses Cervantes' idea but, as often, turns a comical situation into a grotesque caricature. Finally, it is possible to wonder whether the name 'Crowe' was not suggested to Smollett by a passage in *Don Quixote*[87] where Cervantes alludes to the legend of King Arthur transformed into a crow and recalls the love affair of Lancelot of the Lake with Queen Guinevere. This is merely a conjecture, not an assertion, for it is more likely that 'Crowe' suggests nautical implications.

Two currents of influence flow through Smollett's novels. *Don Quixote* and *Gil Blas* are their distinct sources. But the contribution of these two streams cannot remain separated. Their waters mingle in the first two novels, the picaresque wells up in *Ferdinand Count Fathom*, whereas, after a long subterranean flow, the Quixotic inspiration wells up again in *Launcelot Greaves* and is still discernible in *Humphry Clinker*, where the picaresque stream, by contrast, has almost dried up. These variations of influences on Smollett's novels correspond to a dialectical process in his moral thought. If Roderick and Peregrine represent the average man, Ferdinand is an evil person pushed to extremes who makes absolute the divorce between picaresque form and picaresque spirit in Smollett's work. The depiction of evil having ended in a literary failure, Smollett wanted, after seven years of silence, to create a character as morally good as Don Quixote. Another extreme, another failure. Between the evil genius of Ferdinand and the good daemon of Launcelot, it was necessary to strike a balance in keeping with the philosophical and human common sense of the author. Thus, *Humphry Clinker* no longer appears as an unhoped-for miracle after two near-failures. In fact the unsuccessfulness of *Ferdinand Count Fathom* and *Launcelot Greaves* was indispensable in order to assure the success of *Humphry Clinker*. This last novel is no longer an adventure but an *expedition* through life. This word implies the conscious search for the physical and moral equilibrium indispensable to the happiness which each of the five letter-writers desires in his or her own way. In the following chapters, the detailed analysis of the novels, in relation to their moral purpose, will make it possible to grasp more fully the extent of this dialectical swing between Good and Evil throughout Smollett's work.

4
The structure of *Roderick Random* **and** *Peregrine Pickle*: **adventure and morality**

Is it legitimate to analyse the structure of *Roderick Random* and *Peregrine Pickle* in one and the same chapter? Though there is no absolute identity between the two books, it is nevertheless possible to draw a general parallel between these novels which tell the story — long become a literary archetype — of a young man launching out on the roads of life. *Roderick Random* and *Peregrine Pickle* are not merely adventure stories, but, above all, stories of apprenticeship to life itself. Their more or less apparent structure, of which Smollett was doubtless more or less conscious, reproduces the same ternary rhythm: loss of innocence, ordeals, final happiness.

First of all, the coupling of two such terms as 'adventure' and 'morality' may seem surprising. Smollett's critics have not failed to reproach him, sometimes with more virulence than literary impartiality, both for his almost total lack of structure (replaced, according to them, by a fortuitous piling-up of adventures with no common connecting link) and for his amorality, if not immorality. After the autobiographical and picaresque myths, this is the third well-worn cliché of Smollettian criticism. Examples abound, as much in the eighteenth century as in the twentieth, and it would be impossible to quote them all here. In 1783 Beattie already took a severe line with Smollett:

> It does not appear that he knew how to contrive a regular fable, by making his events mutually dependent and all co-operating to one and the same final purpose. On the morality of these novels I cannot compliment him at all: He is often inexcusably licentious. Profligates, bullies and misanthropes, are among his favourite characters[1].

At the beginning of the nineteenth century, a clergyman, Edward Mangin, having wished to see the day when *Roderick Random* and *Tom Jones* 'will either not be found at all, or only in the cabinets of the curious and the reprobate', condemns Smollett in these words:

> The author is not satisfied with expatiating on the revelry of the stews, and the vile debaucheries of the bully and the harlot: but thinks it incumbent on him to subjoin nastiness to obscenity; and brings into full view the infirmities by which man is degraded; the ravages of loathsome distemper, and the stench and vermin of the hospital[2].

This extremist judgment has at least the merit of revealing the obsessions of the reverend gentleman! David Herbert, in his biographical introduction to the 1870 edition of the works of Smollett, uncompromisingly declares that 'Smollett was no structuralist. These two novels [*Roderick Random, Peregrine Pickle*] owe nothing to plots and high play in mystery — the whole thing is byplay' (p. 23). Andrew Lang, at the beginning of the twentieth century, shares Herbert's opinion:

> As regards plot, *Roderick Random* is a mere string of picturesque adventures. It is at the opposite pole from *Tom Jones* in the matter of construction. There is no reason why it should ever stop except the convenience of printers and binders[3].

The same condemnation, all the more serious since its author is a fervent admirer of *Peregrine Pickle*, comes from the pen of H. S. Buck (1925): 'in general Smollett shows little or no architectonic sense' (p. 19). Finally, David Daiches in his *Critical History of English Literature* (1960) merely reproduces the opinions of his many predecessors. He furbishes them up according to contemporary taste by using the fashionable critical jargon when he discerns in Smollett's novels

> a masochistic note in this catalogue of beatings, diseases, betrayals, and hoaxes. And the art is a surface one; there is no subtlety or complexity either of moral and psychological patterning or of structure (p. 728).

However formidable this serried cohort of detractors, it luckily does not represent the whole body of critics. Smollett himself perhaps lacks impartiality, being judge of his own case, but his preface to *Roderick Random* and the solemn warning placed at the head of the second edition (1758) of *Peregrine Pickle* at least set out his intentions in regard to the structure and morality of his novels. In the preface to *Roderick Random*, the verb 'improve' occurs twice on the first page ('universally improving' and 'the heart improves by the example'). A little further on (p. lxi), he announces: 'The following sheets I have modelled on his [Lesage's] plan', and he speaks again (p. lxiii) of 'the nature of my plan'. This is the usual purpose of prefaces written in the eighteenth century: to make use of the interest aroused by the story in order to make the implicit or explicit moral teachings more acceptable. As John Tinnon Taylor justly observes: 'the standard preface of the XVIII-century novel contained the dual protestations of fidelity to fact and of moral aim'[4]. In his foreword to the expurgated edition of 1758 Smollett is indignant — after having conceded that *Peregrine Pickle* was not without a few small blemishes — that his novel could have been condemned as 'an immoral piece'. In the *Monthly Review* of March 1751 Cleland — a paradoxical defender of morality! — warmly welcomes those novels (of which *Peregrine Pickle* is one) capable of serving 'as pilot's charts or maps of those parts of the world which every one may chance to travel through; and in this light they are public benefits' (iv, 356). Cleland's enthusiasm for *Peregrine Pickle* does not prevent him — all honour to his impartiality! — from expressing some reservations about certain passages where Smollett may have flouted decorum. But these passages, if not *risqué*, at least highly Rabelaisian, cannot obscure the moral purpose of *Roderick Random* and *Peregrine Pickle*. This is what a modern critic has seen very clearly, when he writes:

> Nashe and Defoe and Smollett deal, in varying degrees, with moral issues, but the germ of their books is never an idea, never an abstract concept. They are not in any sense allegorists. They are less consciously concerned with the moral significance of life than with its surface texture. Their talent is devoted first and foremost to getting life on to the page, to conveying across to their readers the sense of what life as their characters live it really feels like. If any pattern emerges from their books it is not the kind of pattern that is imposed upon the material by the writer's conscious philosophy, but one which somehow or other springs out of the 'sense of life' in the particular book[5].

In the eighteenth century no incompatibility existed, in the minds of authors as well as critics, between adventure and morality. Johnson, who cannot be suspected of undue partiality for the novel, nevertheless willingly acknowledges the moral utility of these works. In the fourth number of *The Rambler* (March 31st 1750), he explains that these books are capable of teaching

> the Means of avoiding the Snares which are laid by Treachery for Innocence, without infusing any Wish for that Superiority with which the Betrayer flatters his Vanity; to give the Power of counteracting Fraud, with the Temptation to practise it; to initiate Youth by mock Encounters in the Art of necessary Defence, and to increase Prudence without impairing Virtue (p. 22).

A little further on Johnson mistrusts the mixture of Good and Evil which certain characters present in the course of their adventures. Vice, for Johnson, if it is necessary to show it, ought to disgust the reader and on no account to be accompanied by such qualities as gaiety and courage. *Rasselas* (1759) reflects this central preoccupation of Johnson and the authors of the eighteenth century: the quest of happiness (that is of the Good) in spite of the omnipresent forces of Evil. In the course of this quest, Rasselas, from the very beginning of the book is engaged in 'experiments upon life'. In the *Dialogues of the Dead*, Lyttelton (or more accurately Mrs Montagu who wrote the last three dialogues) well sums up the profound ambiguity of adventure novels which had at once to attract the interest of the reader and tend to his moral edification: 'Our readers must be amused, flattered, soothed; such adventure must be offered them as they would like to have a share in', exclaims the bookseller. To which the sage, Plutarch, promptly retorts: 'It should be the first object of writers to correct the vices and follies of the age. I will allow as much compliance with the mode of the times as will make truth and good morals agreeable'[6].

Whatever may have been the influence of Johnson and the moralising critics, one must not seek in the novels of the second part of the eighteenth century the unanimous and systematic expression of a moral philosophy which conformed only to the canons of Johnson[7]. Neither is there in Smollett's works a bookish theory of moral life inspired by Hobbes, Shaftesbury or the Scottish school of 'common sense', as Goldberg has vainly tried to demonstrate. What appears in them much more simply is the sometimes banal expression of a moral good sense inseparable from experience of real life as presented by Smollett in the series of adventures which befall his heroes. It is in this sense that it is legitimate to postulate a morality of adventure. Therefore what must be understood by 'structure' is the more or less conscious recurrence of particular moral themes — a central and constant preoccupation in Smollett's work which reflects his passionate, puritanical temperament — of the problem of Good and Evil. This is what Chesterton succinctly expresses in a preface written in 1936 to an edition of *Peregrine Pickle*:

> The novel of Smollett's time was better than the novel of the Victorian time, in so far as it recognized more clearly that good and evil exist and are entangled even in the same man. The novel of Smollett's time was better than the novel of our own time, in so far as it recognized that, even when they are entangled in the same man, they can still be distinguished and are very different, and at war till death[8].

The moral significance of the adventures lived through by Smollett's heroes does not lie at the end of the story; it runs through it, sustains it and underpins it all the time. In other words, it is a question of distinguishing 'some significantly recurring thread which, however deeply hidden in the dense texture and brilliance of local colouring, accounts for our impression of a unique identity in the whole'[9].

However tempting a synthetic analysis of both novels at once might appear, it would, in fact, mutilate literary truth and its vital complexity. A juxtaposed analysis of *Roderick Random* and *Peregrine Pickle* will permit a better assessment, at the end of this chapter, of the resemblances and differences between these two works and enable their complete individuality to be all the more thoroughly grasped.

Three clearly articulated stages mark the narrative in *Roderick Random*. First of all, the failure of the lone fighter (his childhood and adolescence in Scotland, the journey to London and first sojourn there, the interlude in the Navy) occupying perhaps 300 pages; next an uncertain, sometimes confused battle: the lessons of adversity (his apprenticeship to service, the worldly period, the long decline) taking up about 250 pages; lastly the final success, swift and unexpected, an unbalanced appendix to the two other sections. The hero, like the novel, 'comes to an end' very much sooner than his end comes to him.

In the preface, the dominating impression is one of tension and struggle. Smollett makes free use of an accumulation of stylistic devices charged with a negative affectivity, as in this passage: '. . . that generous indignation which ought to animate the reader against the sordid and vicious disposition of the world' (I, lxii) or again in the following one which contains the phrase 'modest merit struggling with every difficulty'. This gives the tone of the whole novel and this tension is not relaxed, except at a few rare static moments in the course of the narrative. Moreover the adoption of the autobiographical technique imposes a linear structure on *Roderick Random*, a simple chronology, with little manipulation of time (except for those pauses in the action required by the included stories and very rapid flashbacks to explain the reunions, for example, with Strap, Bowling and Morgan. Along this temporal and spatial line Smollett has taken care to place not only ample geographical landmarks but well defined chronological milestones. The reader learns that: 'in the space of three years' (I, 27) Roderick has turned the time spent at the university to good account; then 'for the space of two years' (I, 40) he remains without news of his uncle; the only date in the novel, November 1st 1739, is given (I, 44) as that of his momentous departure for London. These indications are not always absolutely precise: after various initial incidents, this journey 'continued six or seven days longer' (I, 88). But, especially in the first half of *Roderick Random*, there is no lack of reference to the duration of time. Roderick spends eight months with Lavement (I, 144) and his participation in the Cartagena expedition (1740–41), or again in the battle of Dettingen (June 27th 1743) makes it possible to establish the linear chronological sequence of the novel.

Roderick's regimental life lasts for seven months (II, 50). During his commercial expedition at the end of the book, he is away from England for eighteen months (II, 288).

This chronological plot must not be confused with the very structure of the novel which the author-narrator endeavours, with naïve clumsiness, to indicate in broad outline on the first page. His mother's premonitory dream answers a double purpose. On the one hand, Smollett means to reassure the reader about the fate of the hero, who, after innumerable violent tribulations, 'would flourish in happiness and reputation' (I, 2), on the other, to emphasise the erratic nature of his adventures, thanks to the image of the tennis-ball disappearing after being struck at full volley . . . by the devil. Thus Smollett had intuitively divined the basic character of dramatic interest held in suspense. This is of an intellectual nature and not purely an emotional thrill. The certainty that the hero's life will be saved, whatever the danger that threatens him, only heightens the dramatic interest. It is curious to note that the dream theme is repeated, but in a mainly ironic way, by Bowling, concerning the eternal damnation of the old judge (I, 18). Without being a repetition of the first dream, there is a very brief reminder of those lucky predictions in the words of Mrs Sagely who, after listening to all Roderick's adventures 'drew a happy presage of my future life from my past sufferings' (I, 308). But these few indications of the hero's happy lot are at the most well-worn conventional pegs inserted into the general framework of the novel.

If the failure of the lone fighter dominates the first half of *Roderick Random*, the latter is subdivided into three clearly distinct periods in the narrative. His childhood and adolescence in Scotland take up the first seven chapters. From his very entry into the world Roderick is doomed to misfortune, and the tone of these pages is very sombre. He speaks of his unfortunate birth (I, 4), the result of a marriage which his paternal grandfather has refused to countenance. On the following page, his mother is dead and his father has disappeared. Already alone and rejected by his grandfather, a few years later Roderick sees his sole support collapse. His uncle Bowling, after a duel with the captain, has had to desert his ship and finds it impossible to go on supplying Roderick's needs (I, 31). Nevertheless Roderick is not unhappy all the time. He experiences, especially early on in his life, some years of respite which, without being the height of felicity, enable him to bear his lot patiently during three years with Crab, then two with Potion.

In addition to, or rather, closely intermingled with misfortune, the blind form of metaphysical evil independent of all human volition, there is physical and psychological violence, a fully human and conscious manifestation of evil. As the physical violence which characterised Roderick's childhood and adolescence has already been mentioned several times, it is enough here to recall a few examples, such as the apparatus invented by the schoolmaster to atrophy the hand of the young letter-writer, the constant maltreatment to which Roderick, who is often savagely beaten (I, 8) is subjected, and also the vengeance of the pupils who, aided by Bowling, seize the tyrannical schoolmaster and give him a taste of his own medicine. But, right from the beginning of *Roderick Random*, it is psychological violence that predominates. Roderick himself, in the midst of his boyish sorrows, admits his arrogant nature (I, 8) and his resentment is promptly transformed into an aggressiveness which he can hardly control. Expressions which imply the powerful sway of the passions, in particular anger, abound in those pages where young Roderick, seething with impotent fury, comes into head-on collision with the compliant apathy of an indifferent or malevolent environment. One day he is 'incensed' (I, 10), another, during a 'transport of rage and sorrow' (I, 10), he obeys the 'dictates' (I, 32) of his fury. It seems that Roderick has need of a centre of hostility in order to canalise all his aggressiveness; the old judge, to begin with, his schoolmaster, his female cousins and, later, Crampley on board the man-of-war.

This psychological violence culminates in a compulsive need for vengeance. 'Revenge' is a key-word, not only in the first half of *Roderick Random* but of the whole novel and also of the others, with the exception of *Humphry Clinker*. When he realises for the first time that one has few friends in adversity — a cruelly commonplace lesson — his immediate reaction is a thirst for vengeance (I, 34). This psychological effervescence is nearly always accompanied by an access of perfectly lucid moral consciousness. Roderick does not hesitate to describe himself as 'vain' (I, 35), an adjective echoed on the following page by such expressions as 'the fumes of my resentment' or 'the vanity of my success'. But this lucidity is ambiguous, for the reader is entitled to wonder whether these are the instantaneous feelings of the hero or the clear judgment of the author-narrator weighing up his own actions after the lapse of time and seeing the whole experience in perspective. It is probable that Smollett plays in turn, and sometimes simultaneously, on these two possibilities. It is certain that Roderick, while he is still very little capable of analysing or controlling himself, nevertheless succeeds in grasping the basic motivation of a creature like Crab, who is more crafty than intelligent. If Crab takes Roderick into his service, it is because he is impelled much more by an implacable resentment against his rival Potion (I, 37) than by any motives of charity.

Finally, injustice is a marked feature of Roderick's youth: the injustice of fate which makes him an orphan so early, the injustice of his grandfather who refuses to have anything to do with him, the injustice of the schoolmaster — 'the injustice and barbarity of his behaviour' (I, 9). The injustice of his grandfather, who had already cut off all relationship with his own son for marrying without his consent — 'his unnatural usage of my father' (I, 19) — culminates in that will in which he leaves his entire possessions to a single heir. Thus, in spite of his tender years, Roderick has already learnt some hard lessons, at least his vanity leads him to think so, just as, later on, it will lead him to forget those same lessons.

But it is important to note, in opposition to the critics who accuse Roderick of not developing, that from his youth onwards he progressively acquires a certain good sense. After being sent to the university, thanks to his uncle's guineas, he starts reflecting on his precarious lot, for henceforth he feels capable of thinking (I, 27). When he has to work for his living, with Crab, he realises that he is no longer 'a pert unthinking coxcomb' (I, 41). His early misfortunes have even taught him a rudimentary skill in observation. He decides, for example, to study 'Crab's temper with all the application, and manage it with all the address in my power' (I, 39). Daring to oppose this choleric man is the best way of dominating him: 'By this conduct, I got the ascendancy over him in a short time' (I, 40). But these are mere tricks and convenient recipes, rather than maxims of genuine wisdom. In a given circumstance − the affair of illegitimate paternity which Crab reckons he can foist off on Roderick − the latter certainly shows some perspicacity, but is this sufficiently developed to put him on his guard against the snares of the journey and his stay in London? Up to the beginning of Chapter xxiv, Smollett will subject his hero to the often cruel interplay of appearances and reality.

When he leaves Scotland and takes the road to London which, twenty-five years later, Johnson defined as 'the noblest prospect which a Scotchman ever sees, the high road that leads him to England', Roderick leaves behind him the known world to launch on the highways of life. These fifty pages present a remarkable thematic unity. At the − often harsh − contact with realities, Roderick's illusions break down and the crumbling of deceptive appearances constitutes a genuine deflowering of the hero's innocence. The journey itself has almost as much symbolic as realistic value; both literally and figuratively, Roderick is 'ignorant of the proper stages' (I, 46). The chance meeting with Strap is more a technical than a moral necessity. It is less monotonous to recount the adventures of two companions than to keep the reader's interest fixed on one character and narrator.

In this part of the novel, Strap plays the subordinate role of comic foil to his comrade and master, Roderick. He is only a ludicrous companion in adventure, with little influence on Roderick's decisions. Whereas Roderick displays a certain practical sagacity, as in the affair of the highwayman, Rifle, Strap is the almost automatic victim of appearances. The series of incidents and encounters which occur on this journey to London is a succession of variations, not devoid of technical ingenuity, on the theme − certainly not an original one but one to which the eighteenth century attributed great didactic value − of the perpetual dialectic of reality and appearance. A cowardly officer simultaneously spurs and reins in his horse which eventually bolts, thus preventing its master from setting off in pursuit of the highwayman Rifle (I, 54). The country vicar, Shuffle, in spite of appearing to be a good sort, is a thorough scoundrel, an expert card-sharper who fleeces the simpletons of their money and decamps without paying for the meal to which he has invited them. In reality, this rascally cleric is a former valet whose noble master has rewarded his services as a pimp by appointing him to a small living in his gift (I, 55—7). This theme of appearance and reality may occupy only a few paragraphs. This is how certain little incidents must be interpreted, such as the recruiting-sergeant's nightmare (I, 62—3) or the fright the tame crow gives Strap and Roderick (I, 86—7).

But the most significant episode is that of the erudite innkeeper with a passion for Horace. While, up to now, Roderick has seen others being duped, it is his turn to experience human deceitfulness. In this context, it is easier to grasp the full ironic import of the verb in this fragment of one sentence: 'the landlord who *seemed* to be a venerable old man' (I, 63). This scene is not gratuitous; on the contrary, it recapitulates with considerable skill the theme of the pages describing the sharp practices of Shuffle. The duplicity of the innkeeper is more subtle and his other occupation of schoolmaster permits him to moralise at Strap's and Roderick's expense. The worthy man had straightway overwhelmed them with good advice, even going so far as to tell them explicitly 'that he was no stranger to the deceits of mankind' (I, 64). This assurance takes on its full ironic value a few pages further on when the schoolmaster-innkeeper reveals his dishonesty. Strap plays the role of ludicrously gullible victim. He has let himself be so taken in by the benevolent appearance of the host 'that he positively believed we should pay nothing' (I, 65). Roderick proves less credulous: 'the experience I had of the world made me suspend my belief till the morning' (ibid.). It is not uninteresting to note that the innkeeper reproaches Roderick precisely for not knowing the world (I, 66). Experience this time proves not too costly, but henceforth such an argument as 'As he had not the appearance of a common publican . . .' (I, 66) will no longer enter Roderick's mind. But it will still be a very long time before he assimilates the lessons of life.

The adventures experienced in the closed world of the waggon must also be allocated to this constant interplay between appearance and reality. Furious cries, 'which both he and I imagined proceeded from the mouth of a giant' (I, 68), proceed in fact from an emaciated ex-valet, promoted to Captain thanks to the good offices of his former master, who, in spite of his blustering, is no better than a coward. The way in which the passengers are first introduced is not lacking in technical skill. As it is dark inside this slow and uncomfortable vehicle, Smollett begins by reporting a series of overheard remarks, without its being possible to identify the speakers. It is only when they arrive at the inn that the truth will be revealed to Roderick's astounded eyes. His innocence is once again recalled in this provisional clause 'had I not been a novice in the world' (I,

71). Already an innkeeper's daughter had judged Strap and Roderick to be nothing but 'raw and ignorant' Scotsmen (I, 49). The vocabulary of appearances is repeatedly used in these pages, in particular that of vanity, affectation and pretentiousness (I, 68, 71).

As a night cannot be spent at an inn without a few ludicrous adventures, Smollett contrasts the totally innocent mistake of Strap, who gets into the wrong bed, with the artfulness masquerading as outraged innocence displayed by the prostitute who has lured the money-lender into her bed and her snare. One last variation on this theme of appearances: the practical joke of the sham highwayman (I, 82–3) allows Roderick to gauge the courage, or rather the cowardice of the passengers, and in particular of Captain Weazel.

As soon as they arrive in London, Roderick and Strap, on account of their appearance, excite the jeers of the London street-loafers who are amused by their clothes, 'a very whimsical appearance' (I, 88). They will have to adopt a more civilised attire and so conform outwardly to social conventions. But from their first skirmishes in London, it is evident that the lessons of the journey have not gone home. Strap, honest paragon of innocence, still trusts to people's looks. According to him, the valet, who is planning to lead them astray in London is 'an honest, friendly man by his countenance' (I, 91). A little later Roderick will be just as incapable of realising that Cringer is staving him off with empty words. The most revealing incident is the one where Roderick is the victim of that clever pickpocket, the 'money-dropper' (I, 98–102), whose principal weapon is flattery. This man and his confederates cheat at cards, certainly, but the most telling ace up their sleeve is Roderick's vanity, which they shamelessly exploit. As with the schoolmaster-innkeeper, the lesson is paid for, but the moral lesson given by the card-sharper is free of charge: 'you are a young man, and your passions too impetuous; you must learn to govern them better. However, there is no experience like that which is bought' (I, 101). This shaft calls to mind the lesson inflicted on Roderick by the schoolmaster-innkeeper, so does the irony of putting him on his guard against all the rogues with which London swarms (I, 98–9). At the end of their first two days in London, Strap and Roderick find themselves in a wretched plight (I, 103). This is only a beginning and however unpleasant it may be, according to Strap's vigorously expressed opinion, the consequences are not yet very serious. These first skirmishes are only the preliminaries of the struggle for life in which Roderick will be engaged in London.

In the capital, although he does learn some patience — especially during the examination at Surgeons' Hall, which Smollett himself had taken and passed on December 4th 1739 — Roderick has still not kept his recent lessons in mind and continues to trust to appearances. Among the candidates for a naval surgeon's mate's warrant, he notes that 'many . . . made no better appearance than myself', and after having examined 'the physionomy of each . . . at last made up to one whose countenance I liked' (I, 111). It turns out that Thomson is an honest fellow, but the case of Beau Jackson, met in the same circumstances, is much more dubious. The latter admits, 'appearances are against me' (I, 116) and lets himself be captivated by the Drury Lane actress whose ill-spelt love-letter is the direct precursor by twenty-two years of the epistolary style adopted by Win Jenkins in *Humphry Clinker*. For once Roderick is not the dupe of these absurd matrimonial projects which enrapture Jackson. But these pages (pp. 116–18) acquire all their ironic savour when, a little later, he himself will embark on equally hazardous projects. Here there is a genuine amorous counterpoint: even Strap thinks, wrongly, that he has just discovered that rare bird, an innocent young girl (I, 120). Smollett uses the adjective 'raw' (ibid.) again to describe Roderick (cf. I, 49), thus summing up the still invincible naïvety of his hero. More delusions again in his introduction to dissipated life, to prostitutes and strong drink! Roderick believes, but mistakenly, that the whore will grant him her favours without being paid for them: 'but she not relishing my appearance, refused to grant my request' (I, 127).

This crazy nocturnal escapade precipitates Roderick towards another perigee, but before this his first clash with a corrupt justice will have taught him that, in the realm of Themis, judgment by appearances may entail awkward consequences. The magistrate, who is hand-in-glove with the procuress, confuses Roderick and his friends with common criminals and is prepared to send them to the gallows. 'Your face discovers it' (I, 131). Such is the irrefutable argument on which the magistrate relies when he takes Roderick for a thief. On emerging from this adventure, Roderick no longer has a shilling in his pocket and he learns that his chances of entering the Navy are slender if he cannot grease the palm of the secretary. As always, Strap experiences similar misadventures, which reproduce in serio-comic miniature the tribulations of his master (I, 134–6). In the last stage of his downfall before the enforced embarkment on the warship, the young 'gentleman' (see Strap's harangue, I, 137) if he does not lose caste, at least loses his self-esteem, for he is momentarily dependent on Strap for money. It is also thanks to Strap, whose material help is for once efficacious, that Roderick finds a job with the apothecary Lavement, where, just as with Crab, he quickly acquires the rudiments of an empirical wisdom, soon dispersed however by his constantly reviving vanity.

Roderick makes progress in that false knowledge, the knowledge of London: 'I every day improved in my knowledge of the town, I shook off my awkward air . . .' (I, 149). He thinks he has climbed some rungs up the social ladder, and so Strap's embarrassing friendship is a burden to him: 'ingratitude is so natural to the heart of man' (I, 155). This is a cynical excuse which cuts little ice. In reality Roderick, having acquired a veneer of worldly sophistication, regards himself once more as a 'gentleman': 'I now began to look upon myself as a gentleman in reality' (I, 156). He is harshly reminded of this reality. Victim of a plot set on foot by his ex-school-fellow Gawky, the eagerly welcomed husband of Miss Lavement, Roderick is accused of stealing medicines which his enemy Gawky has planted in his chest as evidence against him. What can Roderick say in his own defence except: 'Sir, appearances, I own, condemn me' (I, 162)? A new perigee: Roderick's fortune is at its lowest ebb, he has lost his reputation and has caught a venereal disease (I, 164). Moreover, he is absolutely alone: all his former friends desert him, and his faithful Strap is away.

This important articulation of the plot of the novel is emphasised by the insertion of the story of Miss Williams which has the technical merit of occurring when Roderick, confined to his room during his treatment, cannot be involved in any adventure. This pause in the narrative serves as a thematic counterpoint. Once again it is appearances, reinforced by emotional and intellectual vanity, that precipitate Miss Williams's moral and physical downfall. The story in itself is not very original. Flattered, seduced, rejected and abandoned, Miss Williams becomes a prostitute (I, 196—7) without being completely degraded, however low she has fallen. Finally, this interpolated story is a warning to Roderick who starts comparing his lot with that of Miss Williams (I, 195). Her naïvety and the strength of her passions have earned her a real descent into hell, in the Bridewell incident (I, 188). Roderick has not descended to the bottom of the pit of horror but he will soon know the floating horror of a ship of the line.

To sum up this first sojourn in London, Roderick continues his apprenticeship not only to life but to that city's way of life. As in Scotland, he acquires, when he is working for Lavement, a certain practical sense, more akin to cunning than to rationality, and mingled with a psychological near-ferocity, as his dealings with the bully O'Donnell prove. There is still not, strictly speaking, a moral and psychological evolution of the hero but rather a confirmation of his passionate tendencies which dangerously blind him to reality. Nevertheless, this period is not negative. If Roderick is vanquished for the moment, both through his own impetuosity and the deceptiveness of society, he begins to realise that his own lot, however hard it may be, is not exceptional. For the first time, when he himself is in a very bad way, he breaks out of his self-centredness to pity the fate of another human being: 'Such extremity of distress must have awakened the most obdurate heart to sympathy and compassion' (I, 166). If the technical link between Roderick's adventures and those of Miss Williams is very tenuous — again a chance meeting, Miss Williams having recently tried to get herself married by Roderick who had nibbled at the bait of deceptive appearances — the moral similarity is very clear, and deliberately stressed by the author. Finally, in the infernal jungle that London is — Strap thinks the devil has set up his throne in it (I, 105) —

Smollett takes pains to arrange for the presence of decent people, such as the schoolmaster Syntax, Roderick's and Strap's landlord, and the constable who advises Jackson to settle his difference with the procuress amicably. Lavement is not a bad man either, and Strap is the very image of sincere, almost doglike devotion to his master: 'I'll beg for you, steal for you, go through the wide world with you, and starve with you' (I, 104). Even Jackson, who feels the need to make up his face – 'for it gave him the appearance of age, which never fails of attracting respect' (I, 126) – in spite of his frivolity and his being an inveterate cadger, is not fundamentally bad. In desperate situations where human wickedness seems to triumph there often appears a person who is courageous and kind. This is the case with that naval lieutenant who saves Miss Williams the first time from the horrors of Newgate (I, 192).

Just before being pressed into the Navy, Roderick reaches another perigee, the lowest in his life so far. Penniless, his natural pride on the point of yielding to his urgent financial needs, he even thinks of joining the Army – this thought had already occurred to him (I, 114) – or the Navy. Fate, in the shape of a detachment of the press-gang, spares him the trouble of making a difficult decision (I, 199).

The following 100 pages, up to the end of Chapter xxvii, are among the most sombre in Smollett's work. Roderick finds himself not in the realm of Poseidon but rather in that of Hades, peopled, if not with ghosts, at least with living corpses. Contempt of life in all its forms darkens these pages. It is curious to note that this description of infernal scenes begins with a descent as literal as symbolic. Roderick is flung into the bottom of a hold (I, 199); on board, he has to go down several ladders in order to reach his berth (I, 205); just as on his arrival in London he had already had to go down into a cellar where there was a squalid cheap eating-house which he described as an 'infernal ordinary' (I, 93). Whether the symbolism is deliberate or not, these descents give a structural indication of the author's intentions.

The theme of appearances does not disappear in these pages; on the contrary it is diversified still more, assuming a crueller and often more dangerous aspect for the hero. Plunged into the unknown world of a warship, Roderick begins by being 'exceedingly depressed by the appearance of everything' (I, 206). His first encounter with the explosive Welshman, Morgan, is no more favourable (I, 208–10). But these are trivial details compared to such serious incidents as the ill-timed setting free (at the Captain's orders) of a dangerous madman. Morgan, who knows that this patient alternates between outbreaks of violence and periods of calm, argues in vain that 'there was no trusting to appearances' (I, 228). The justice the captain of the *Thunder* claims to render is, in fact, only an 'appearance of justice' (I, 244). He relies on false testimony or on an interpretation, systematically unfavourable to the accused, of alleged proofs of guilt, such as Roderick's private diary written in Greek characters.

Appearances have become an absurd nightmare in which the hero struggles in vain, only to plunge into a gulf of stupidity, malice and triumphant ignorance. Words are suddenly emptied of their real meaning and become monstrously inflated with grotesque and dangerous significance. A quarrel between false witnesses saves Roderick in the nick of time from swinging at the end of the yard-arm. Occasionally appearances not only coincide with reality but impudently proclaim it. The new Captain, Whiffle, is an elegant fop, quite out of place on a ship's quarterdeck. The minute description of his effeminate dainty costume (I, 279—80), prepares for and foretells the discovery, a few pages further on, that this dandy is also homosexual.

Certain traits in the hero's character persist in asserting themselves. Roderick needs more than ever a focus of hostility and finds it ready to hand in the detestable person of Crampley, whose cruelty is obvious at their very first meeting (I, 200) and only confirmed by what follows (I, 204, 221, 278). This hostility is carefully sustained by various incidents such as the boxing match between Roderick and Crampley, which prepares one for the final duel on land. This hostility, which induces a perpetual psychological tension in the hero, is further inflamed by the underhand malice of the surgeon Mackshane (I, 237—8). This atmosphere of perpetual conflicts in which Roderick, placed in a subordinate position, is far from always getting the upper hand, contributes to making this period a hell where passions are unleashed and tear each other to shreds in the claustrophobic world of the ship.

But the specific character of this interlude in the Navy is a constant mixture of gratuitous cruelty and absurdity. Examples abound and constitute a crescendo of horror. To begin with, the review of the sick men on the deck (I, 225—8) gives the degree of absurdity which can be reached by moral cowardice (that of Doctor Mackshane) and the ignorant inhumanity of the captain and the surgeon 'who so wantonly sacrificed the lives of their fellow-creatures' (I, 227). Roderick moves in a world where signs, words and gestures no longer have any meaning yet obey an implacable pseudologic reminiscent of the world of the concentration camp. The life of an individual depends on the convenience of stupid and barbarous despots. After having been the impotent onlooker — which reinforces the impression of nightmare — Roderick is exposed in his turn, at the peril of his life, to the bloody and futile horror of a pointless naval battle. Covered with blood, spattered with brains and entrails, Roderick, in irons on the deck, believes, and feels, that he is going mad. While criticism often reproaches Smollett for paying little heed to establishing a coherent structure in his novels, it is right to point out that this scene of horror on the deck is all the less gratuitous because it reproduces in reality — and with what savage force! — the problems posed *in abstracto* during the examination at Surgeons' Hall (I, 124—5), to wit on intestinal wounds and severed heads. This massacre for a trifle only prepares the reader for the cruel absurdity of the whole Cartagena expedition, whose gratuitous horror is exposed over and over again. Smollett is as enraged as he is sickened by the military stupidity which causes the death of hundreds of men. 'Contempt of life' — the words he uses on p. 267 — prevails everywhere, whether it is a question of dangerous and futile naval actions or the negligence of the military in the matter of provisioning the troops and caring for the wounded. Finally Roderick battles against that physical and metaphysical absurdity, illness, the incarnation of the gratuitous evil that infests the whole world. His vitality and his resolution not to swallow any medicine enable him to survive this attack of yellow fever (I, 272–8). But, at the crisis of his fever, Roderick has suffered 'the pains of hell' (I, 276).

One also encounters again in these pages, steeped as they are in despair, that constant feature of Smollettian morality, the presence of simple and kindly people in the midst of this inferno. Thanks to them, Roderick knows some periods of respite or receives some opportune aid when his situation appears irremediable. Besides Morgan, one must cite an episodic character such as the sailor Rattlin, the only one to show some humaneness to Roderick when he is carried off by the press-gang (I, 200); or again Mackshane's predecessor on board the *Thunder*, who, before leaving the ship, succeeds in getting Roderick appointed to the rank of surgeon's mate (I, 221); finally that sergeant who gives up his hammock to Roderick when he is ill (I, 273).

If one leaves aside the analysis of the structural role played by morality in the story, it is evident that the technical links of the plot are too obviously contrived to be always convincing. The critic who stops short at these arbitrary, not to say artificial, devices is justified in expressing some reserves about the plan of the novel. These dramatic strings are as nakedly visible as the cables of the *Thunder* and are largely borrowed from theatrical tradition. Thus honest Jack Rattlin knows and reveres Uncle Bowling with whom he once served in the *Thunder*. So he is naturally disposed to help his nephew Roderick and, what is more, he informs him that Bowling did not kill his superior officer in a duel, as he believed, but that the latter is well and truly alive and in command of the *Thunder* in which Roderick is about to serve. As if 'by accident' (I, 201), Roderick has his uncle's letter in his pocket and one may also be surprised by this 'accident' which makes the nephew embark on the uncle's former ship. Other rediscoveries[10]: Thomson (I, 204), already met at the Admiralty, driven to extremity by the persecutions of Mackshane, decides to throw himself overboard; but Roderick meets him again, miraculously rescued at sea (by one of his own schoolfellows!) in Jamaica (I, 242). Smollett takes care to recall the existence of Bowling on two other occasions (I, 262, 288) so that he shall not disappear completely from the reader's memory. Finally, in order that the hero's fall should be harder, Smollett arranges a relative apogee for him before precipitating him down to an absolute perigee.

The meeting with Thomson is the beginning of a lucky period for Roderick: 'this small interval of ten days was by far the most agreeable period of my life' (I, 294). Only one shadow menaces this happiness: the presence of Crampley on board the *Lizard*. Technically, Smollett was concerned with balancing good and bad fortunes. There again, Roderick does not hesitate to describe Crampley's behaviour to him as 'infernal' (I, 295). It seems that not only Roderick's destiny but also his psychology follow a repetitive pattern. As soon as fortune smiles on the hero, the reader can expect two kinds of consequences. Roderick's vanity, in spite of the series of humiliations he has just undergone, will promptly revive. Thus, after having received Thomson's generous gifts, he declares: 'I began to look upon myself as a gentleman of some consequence, and felt my pride dilate apace' (I, 296). But this respite does not last long. On the ship which is bringing him back to England, Crampley becomes captain and pursues Roderick with his vindictiveness. When the ship sinks at the end of the voyage, through Crampley's negligence, Roderick takes a place on the lifeboat in spite of the captain's fierce opposition. As soon as he arrives on shore, Roderick, deaf to everything but his rage, provokes Crampley to a duel and wounds him. But Roderick does not have time to triumph. A treacherous blow stuns him and, while he is unconscious, the crew rob him of his money and nearly all his clothes (I, 303). This duel is more than a mere incident in the course of Roderick's adventures. It represents a microstructure, that is to say a technical reminder which simultaneously summarises and symbolises the motivations and adventures of the unlucky hero. So Roderick finds himself back in England as penniless as at his enforced departure. If he is not at the end of either his troubles or his adventures, the rhythm of his life will be less headlong after this crisis of violence. Can one speak, at the end of these brutal adventures, of a philosophy of adventure? The word is too ambitious to apply to the rudiments of wisdom he may have managed to acquire. He is capable of bearing adversity with a certain patience (I, 231), but he is still far from the simple and noble stoicism of Jack Rattlin (I, 261–2) whom Smollett describes as a 'sea-philosopher'. In the struggle of life against the forces of evil, whether in their metaphysical or human form, Roderick, the lone young fighter, has up to now been defeated.

If it is possible to plot a graph of the first half of *Roderick Random* by a downward slanting segment AB in which A represents Roderick's birth and B the lowest point of his fortunes — that is, his physical, social and psychological shipwreck — the second half (a little over 250 pages) might be symbolised by a peak, whose ascending slope BC would correspond to Roderick's adventures between his shipwreck and his meeting Narcissa again in Bath, and the descending slope CD to the period which ends with his imprisonment in the Marshalsea, B and D being equidistant from C. Two significant features characterise these pages. On the one hand women, who, apart from a few prostitutes, have played hardly any part in

Roderick's life, will introduce a sentimental element, sometimes artificial and clumsy, but none the less important, into the novel. On the other, Roderick is no longer utterly alone. He relies alternately on the judicious advice of Mrs Sagely and the momentarily prosperous finances of Strap, whom he meets again by a chance as lucky as it is technically improbable. There are three articulations in this section of the narrative: the apprenticeship to servitude (domestic, sentimental and military); the lessons of the period in the fashionable world; the long social and moral decline of the hero. Thus, under this triple aspect, Smollett presents the lessons in adversity given to his individualist hero, who has to submit to the constraints of society before deserving to find his definite niche in it.

Smollett arranges two transitions between Roderick's adventures at sea and his apprenticeship to servitude. One, at once ludicrous and dramatic, presents a bitter variation on the theme of human charity, or rather of its absence (I, 304–6). No one wants to be saddled with this wounded man who is trundled from door to door until he is taken in by Mrs Sagely, who, as Smollett points out with some irony, was suspected of witchcraft (I, 307). The other is the story of Mrs Sagely herself who symbolises the moral antithesis of Miss Williams. This woman, rejected by her family as a result of a secret marriage, soon widowed and abandoned by everyone, instead of launching on the path of light love, decides to master her great grief and yield with calm stoicism to the exigences of adversity. She therefore retired with a woman friend to the country (I, 310), where she leads a life of serene dignity. This significantly named woman will play the part of a practical and moral mentor in Roderick's life. It is she who advises him to enter the service of the eccentric bluestocking. Mrs Sagely becomes a centre of equilibrium for Roderick who will not always, however, resort to her.

Besides the not very original physical and psychological portrait of the perfect specimen of female highbrow and Roderick's initiation into his duties as footman (on which Smollett does not dwell long) it is the sentimental element, resulting from his meeting with Narcissa, which dominates these pages. Roderick's menial situation is important only in so far as it constitutes a social obstacle (for the moment insurmountable) to his sentimental aspirations. He falls in love, and the more artificial the symptoms of the malady the easier it is to diagnose. Roderick is the victim of a *coup de foudre* which would be trite if it were not, after many tribulations, to be transformed into a lasting passion. 'My heart was captivated at first sight,' he declares (II, 3) and, on the next page, he is already raving with the verbal delirium of unhappy lovers. He calls Narcissa 'this idol of my adoration' and declares that his soul 'was thrilled with an ecstasy of tumultuous joy'. These onesided transports only serve to emphasise all the more the dilemma in which Roderick has put himself. After having cursed his menial situation (II, 3), he yields to his habitual tendency to vanity and, in spite of his inglorious position, begins to conceive presumptuous ideas concerning Narcissa (II, 8). Love — like friendship in his former adventures — almost automatically implies for the hero a corollary of cantankerous hostility. The object of his hatred is none other than the suitor for Narcissa's hand, a very rich and boorish country squire, for whom Roderick conceives 'a mortal aversion (II, 5). With the illogical inconsequence of lovers, he dares to condemn the presumption of Sir Timothy Thicket! As Roderick is in an inferior social position, his only claim to fame is his learning as a well-educated Scot. Once again he succumbs to the snares of his own vanity by revealing how extremely cultured he is (II, 10—11). Nevertheless this ill-considered action is promptly condemned by its author — 'self-condemnation' is the term employed (II, 9) — with perfect lucidity, but this is powerless against the compulsive force of his vanity.

After a respite, 'this season of love and tranquillity' (II, 9), according to the usual pattern, a series of swift and unforeseeable catastrophes occurs (II, 22) which oblige him to flee from the home of Narcissa (whom he has defended against Sir Timothy's brutality and to whom he has dared to declare his passion). Carried off by smugglers, Roderick is left in Boulogne, where chance, pressed once more into service by Smollett, makes him meet Uncle Bowling again, himself in a very bad way (II, 22). After two antithetical encounters — the worthy Scottish priest and the dissolute, thieving Capuchin — he is reduced to enlisting in the French army. Military service has nothing in common with the period spent in that of Narcissa's aunt. Roderick becomes inured to even more intense physical and psychological hardships than he was subjected to in the Navy. He suffers from hunger and thirst, finds the fatigue of long forced marches hard to bear and 'the mortification of [his] pride' even harder (II, 39). He is humiliated in a duel with a soldier whose appearance is against him. He is vanquished by this walking scarecrow and once again proves 'the folly of judging by appearances' (II, 41). This theme of appearances remains a parameter throughout these pages. Roderick, with revenge in view, takes fencing lessons from an Irish drummer, apparently desirous of helping a compatriot, but in reality seeking to avenge his own matrimonial misfortune through a third person (II, 43). After the battle of Dettingen, his situation is anything but cheerful, for he finds himself 'in the utmost want of everything' (II, 47) but it must be observed that he does not give himself up to despair. The ordeals he has just been through have enabled him to rediscover his old remedy, patience (II, 47), and he adds that he consoles himself 'with the flattering suggestions of a lively imagination that never abandoned me in my distress' (ibid.).

As always, when the action is in danger of languishing in a cul-de-sac (as during the stay in winter quarters in Rheims) Smollett and chance do things in style. Roderick rediscovers his friend Strap, who has pursued the opposite social path from his master and now has all the appearance of a gentleman. The little fortune which Strap has just inherited will enable the action to get going again. With a touching fidelity, not however devoid of perspicacity (II, 49), he decides to put it all at Roderick's disposal. He advises him to try his luck, no longer with Mars, but with Venus. So it is matrimonial adventure that Roderick will pursue in the midst of the social, psychological and moral snares of London. In this heiress-hunting, interrupted by a brief political interlude, Narcissa is almost completely forgotten, in spite of a belated expression of doubtful remorse: 'the remembrance of my charming Narcissa was a continual check upon my conscience, during the whole course of my addresses; and perhaps contributed to the bad success of my scheme, by controuling my raptures, and condemning my design' (II, 111). From Chapter xlv to lx inclusive Roderick moves in an urban milieu, of which he will acquire a far more extensive knowledge than during his first stay in London. The description of social milieus and social types is inextricably interwoven with the vectorial theme of making a rich marriage.

Smollett insists on the suddenness (the adjective 'sudden' is used twice: II, 52, 54) of this reversal of fortune, and plays on the chronological omniscience of the author-narrator. He mingles with a statement concerning the immediate present, moral considerations which suppose a certain recession in time. Such is the implication of this explicit judgment of the still insufficient moral evolution of the hero: 'Here I had time to reflect and congratulate myself upon this sudden transition of fate, which to bear with moderation required some degree of philosophy and self-denial' (II, 54). When Roderick proceeds to describe his clothes, symbolic of his vanity and all the changes in his fortune, it is very evident (though only by implication) that the young hero, now once again back on the footing of a 'gentleman of figure' (II, 55), has *not* yet reached the moral maturity which will enable him to confront both good and bad fortune successfully. His social and psychological behaviour is stigmatised all through these pages, but nowhere more vigorously than at the beginning of Chapter xlv, where, in a few lines, Smollett heaps up condemnations of his hero in such terms as 'vain enough', 'silly conceit', 'intoxicated', 'guilty of a thousand ridiculous coquetries'. The frequency of pejorative or negative expressions gives the tone of these pages right from the start. The pursuit of a rich wife is eminently well suited to the theme of appearances. Roderick's first pseudo-conquest is a courtesan who has assumed the airs of a great lady (II, 58—61). Strap, always a great pedant and ready to display his tags of Latin culture, draws the moral of the story thus: *Fronti nulla fides — nimium ne crede colori* (II, 61).

The result of avoiding this first peril is to make Roderick only the more self-confident. His introduction to coffee-house society brings out the affectation, futility and falsity of this noisy and cruel little world. The names of the characters are so many labels which define their behaviour: Banter, Chatter, Slyboot, Bragwell, Dr Wagtail. The theme of marriage recedes into the background in these pages, without altogether disappearing. Roderick and his ribald accomplices set about tormenting poor Dr Wagtail, with the connivance of a prostitute who pretends she is pregnant by him. This comic and cruel variation is only the thematic prelude to the grotesque matrimonial adventures of Strap (II, 87–9) whom the shrewdness of his master prevents from marrying a pregnant whore. For some thirty pages (II, 89–125) Roderick, in spite of the cynical advice of the young misanthrope Banter, will chase after Melinda Goosetrap, then Miss Gripewell. Before Roderick renounces (for a time) his matrimonial projects, Smollett makes an ingenious inversion of roles. From the hunter, Roderick becomes the hunted. Vanity is the dominant trait of these two rich heiresses (II, 89, 114). Roderick stands no chance of winning with such coquettes. As Banter had foreseen, he wastes his time and his money and loses his illusions. He is still too raw an apprentice to London, for he still preserves the diffidence of honesty, as Banter warns him: 'You are too honest and too ignorant of the town' (II, 95).

Discouraged by his lack of success, Roderick takes to drinking, continues his rather dissipated life and prepares his own downfall: 'I thus posted, in a thoughtless manner, towards poverty' (II, 117). The final matrimonial setback makes an ironic contrast with the two previous attempts, just as the incident with the hot-headed Oregan was a mock-heroic interlude (II, 103–8). Pursued by a series of more than ardent love-letters, Roderick allows his imagination to be fired and his vanity 'soared beyond all reason and description' (II, 121). The fair unknown is, in fact, an old sex-starved governess, who is not without literary kinship with Mrs Slipslop and her craving for love.

This misadventure puts a provisional end to Roderick's matrimonial projects (II, 126), but, if the means are different, the end remains the same. He wants to procure himself financial security, not this time thanks to an heiress's fortune, but thanks to a post obtained through the influence of aristocratic friends who are in favour at Court. This attempt at sociopolitical climbing as a hanger-on of Lord Strutwell is in fact only a variation on the central theme of this second part of the novel. Roderick, instead of relying on himself, constantly seeks to escape from the real world in order to rely on the vagaries of his ever-optimistic imagination. In this there is a genuine psychological failure on the part of the hero, whose Scottish pugnacity allows itself to be muzzled by vain idle dreams, whether of marriage or a career at Court. Thus after having been entertained with fine words by Lord Strutwell, a rapacious homosexual, Roderick gives free rein to hopes as flattering as they are fallacious. He sees himself already as Prime Minister and Strap as First Secretary (II, 134). Banter plays the double role of touchstone and stumbling-block. It is he who reveals the truth to Roderick and who, for the second time, draws the moral of an affair in which his friend has been taken in by Strutwell's prepossessing appearance (II, 127): 'nobody who knew any thing of mankind could have been imposed on by his insinuations' (II, 135).

Roderick has been taken in but he has still not taken in the moral lesson. On the contrary, he has got into the bad habit of shirking facts. He declares himself to be 'so well skilled in procrastinating every troublesome reflection, that the prospect of want seldom affected me very much, let it be never so near' (II, 138). In fact, it is to these expedients that he has recourse to pull himself out of this financial and social impasse. He pawns his sword, gambles with the money and wins 150 guineas, which allows him to revive his matrimonial ambitions. Luck also smiles on Roderick in another domain. Chance − once again − causes him to meet Lavement's daughter, the unhappy wife deserted by Gawky. Before helping her financially, Roderick demands that she should unmask the plot of which he was the victim in her father's home (II, 145). Money is the sinews of war and also of love. Roderick tries once again to embark for Cythera on a galleon but all he finds is a dilapidated old tub in the unattractive person of Miss Snapper. In the coach which is conveying them to Bath, Miss Snapper proves to have a biting wit and a redoubtable gift of the gab: 'I dreaded her unruly tongue, and felt by anticipation the horrors of an eternal clack' (II, 160). As Smollett has had recourse to the already classic device of their meeting taking place under cover of darkness in the microcosm of a coach, it is not till dawn that he sees Miss Snapper's face. He admits his embarrassment: 'my pride and interest maintained a severe conflict' (II, 163). But the attraction of a fortune outweighs Miss Snapper's lack of attractions. Roderick would have succumbed to the financial charms of Miss Snapper, had not Narcissa reappeared in the nick of time, sending him into a verbal and emotional frenzy as vehement as it is unrealistic after having, for so long, almost totally forgotten her (II, 168−9). As if Smollett had not invoked chance enough already, he drives another artificial peg into the framework of his novel by making Miss Williams, the repentant prostitute, Narcissa's personal maid.

This providential meeting with Narcissa in Bath constitutes a peak in Roderick's life where he breathes the intoxicating air of social and amorous success. Narcissa and her fortune are at last within his reach. So, after so many ordeals, one must not be surprised at the sometimes almost hysterical nature of this envisaged bliss which soon becomes a torture of Tantalus for this young hero burning with impetuous ardour. When he learns that Miss Williams is Narcissa's maid, he becomes 'delirious at this piece of intelligence' (II, 172). It is possible to speak of Roderick as being literally 'madly in love'. Smollett constantly resorts to hyperbolical words borrowed from the vocabulary of ecstasy or of madness: 'ecstasy' is used several times (II, 190, 192). Jealousy of an aristocratic rival only increases the frenzy of this verbal delirium. Roderick calls himself in turn 'distracted' (II, 195); 'a frantic bedlamite' (II, 196) and abandons himself to a destructive fury which he describes as 'mad pranks' (II, 197). In this there is more than the old literary convention which likens love to madness.

This uncontrolled emotional outburst implies the immaturity of the hero and prepares the reader for the catastrophe which will snatch Roderick's happiness from him. This new development in the plot is carefully prepared for by Smollett. From the first moment when Roderick sees Narcissa again, Smollett stresses the incorrigible vanity of his hero, who promptly takes to reviewing all the assets he thinks he has 'in all the aggravation of self-conceit' (II, 169). At this point in the story, Roderick's success would be immoral: he does not deserve the happiness of possessing Narcissa and her fortune. He himself has his doubts — 'a very hard matter to make good my pretensions' (II, 176). Miss Williams is more flattering than clearsighted when she tries to reassure him: 'the miseries I had undergone, by improving the faculties both of mind and body, qualified me the more for any dignified station' (ibid.). Strap, who usually shares the rash enthusiasms of his master, cannot believe wholeheartedly in the benevolence of fate: 'he prayed heartily, that no envious devil might, as formerly, dash the cup of blessing from my lip' (II, 193). Roderick's old enemy reappears: pride, the automatic corollary of every rise in the social scale (II, 194). The premonitory signs of catastrophe are clearly indicated by Smollett, such as the presence of Melinda, and the soon open rivalry of Lord Quiverwit who is also a suitor for Narcissa's hand ('unlucky omen' is used: II, 199). Roderick's happiness is therefore menaced by a brewing storm (II, 200).

This storm bursts, because Roderick is still incapable of controlling his vanity and his resentment (II, 203). He is a man ruled by passion and the prospect of losing Narcissa, on his own admission, 'disabled all my philosophy, and tortured my soul into madness' (II, 200). The sole indication that he has made any moral progress is his refusing the secret marriage Narcissa proposes. For once he gives proof of moral, not merely financial generosity by showing he is capable of resisting temptation and overcoming his egocentricity (II, 206). Even on the technical plane Smollett erects a warning signpost — a blatantly obvious one — by announcing the fatal absence (II, 206) his hero is going to endure. The incidents which precipitate Roderick's long social, psychological and moral decline, according to Smollett's usual technique, follow fast on each other's heels, and according to an implacable logic of misfortune. First of all there is the duel with Lord Quiverwit, then the forced departure of Narcissa, carried away by her brother, and the two losses at the gaming-table (II, 209—16). Reduced to the wretched expedient the twentieth century calls 'fraudulent conversion', Roderick is arrested and imprisoned in the Marshalsea (II, 220).

Prison plays an important part, as in *Peregrine Pickle*, but a belated and artificial one. In it Roderick again meets Jackson, whose matrimonial and financial misfortunes are a comic rather than pathetic counterpoint to his own and make the reader think of what might have happened to Roderick himself. It is the interpolated story of Melopoyn (the structural counterpart of Miss Williams's narrative) which, by creating a pause in the novel, allows Roderick to indulge in serious reflections on his conduct and, for a second time, become detached from his imperious passions. On the surface, Chapters lxii and lxiii appear to have nothing to do with the hero's moral development. In fact, for the first time Roderick is sufficiently disinterested to sympathise freely with the lot of another. When he had helped Miss Williams, his conduct, however generous, was also dictated by necessity. His gesture towards the unhappy wife of Gawky was not entirely gratuitous either, since he had demanded a reparation for the insult he had suffered when he was with Lavement. And even his decision not to marry Narcissa clandestinely becomes suspect when the reader remembers that her brother's consent is the testamentary condition without which she cannot come into the fortune she has been left.

The story of Melopoyn has a structural function completely ignored by those Smollettian critics, intent only on distinguishing the technical threads of the web of the plot, whose interest is as restricted as their ability. But a global thematic analysis, centred on the hero's moral evolution (or its beginning), makes it possible to connect this series of adventures, otherwise without much significance, and to integrate these interpolated stories, of which the longest are those of Miss Williams and Melopoyn, into the body of the novel. Technically it is quite apt that Roderick should recede into the background since nothing much can happen to him while he is in prison and waiting for the highly problematical arrival of his Uncle Bowling (see the reminders of this character, II, 217, 218, 222). But it is, above all, the constant thematic parallelism which gives Melopoyn's story its whole interest. To begin with, his simplicity and naïve ignorance of the world recall Roderick's own case (II, 253). The ladder of recommendations up which Melopoyn makes his theatrical ambitions climb is as rickety (II, 244) as those of the worthy Bowling in the seafaring world. This parallelism, the autobiographical element of which has already been examined, does not, however, exclude a certain irony. Melopoyn considers himself extravagant because, in the space of six months, he has spent ten guineas (II, 233). In the same amount of time Roderick has frittered away not only the little fortune inherited by Strap but also his winnings at cards. And what can be said of this severe self-judgment of Melopoyn's when he accuses himself of being addicted to dissipation? It is by juxtaposition and implicit comparison that the irony of these comments makes Roderick's moral levity all the more evident. Melopoyn, too, is destined to experience violent ups and downs because his imagination is too lively to let itself be held in check by his reason. Thus, he constantly finds himself 'precipitated ... from the highest pinnacle of hope to the abyss of despondency' (II, 249) which sums up Roderick's moral and social situation extremely well. A final detail: Melopoyn, too, is arrested on a complaint lodged by his tailor (II, 252). The effect of this story on Roderick is salutary. He forgets his own misfortunes in his indignation at the unpardonable indifference of the world to a case like Melopoyn's (II, 253).

Prison has a triple effect on Roderick. For a while, at first, he rejoices in the forced asceticism which cuts him off from a corrupt world, but almost at once, the memory of Narcissa intrudes itself. He remembers then that his beloved also forms part of this society he abhors (II, 253). Confronted with this ambiguity of life, Roderick is left with no solution. He even gives himself up to melancholy and such is his despair that he neglects to wash and shave or to change his linen. This detail might seem irrelevant if Smollett had not taken care to insist over and over again on his hero's physical and sartorial vanity.

Having reached this other perigee, only an almost miraculous inter-vention can get Roderick out of this right corner. At last Bowling arrives! Smollett feels it necessary to repeat the adjective 'sudden' twice in the same paragraph (II, 256), as if this technical shortcut were not sufficiently obvious already. The moral importance of this conventional ending is that, for the first time, at Bowling's suggestion, Roderick will work of his own free will and not because he is constrained or forced to. Yet he inevitably has agonising qualms about making the decision, for his uncle's offer does violence to his love for Narcissa (II, 258). Once again Smollett uses the vocabulary of madness as well as that of psychological torment (II, 259). Roderick decides to consult Mrs Sagely before setting off on his commer-cial venture. It is curious to note that what almost amounts to an emotional and psychological transference has taken place in his mind. Mrs Sagely plays the part of a mother-substitute for the orphan Roderick (II, 263). A secret meeting with Narcissa revives the dramatic interest of this intermittent love affair. The venture, in itself, is not of much interest. The beginning of the hero's moral evolution does not include the faintest humanitarian feeling for the cargo of slaves.

In these final pages, Smollett draws together and fastens off the scattered threads of the tapestry of his novel. The meeting of Roderick and his father is somewhat clumsily prepared for by a series of remarks on the psychological reactions of Don Rodrigo at the sight of Roderick (II, 274–6). It is this long-lost father found again in Paraguay, thanks to Providence (II, 281), who draws the moral of the adventures Roderick has been through. It is no use searching for any staggering philosophical profundity in it. Don Rodrigo expresses, in simple terms, a morality of good sense, mingled with elements of Christianity and stoicism, accessible to the average carnal man his son is, and thus to all young adventurers who hunted, or tried to hunt, fortune in the middle of the eighteenth century. Adventure therefore has an educative function on the physical, intellectual and moral plane. To sum up, adventure prepares a young man 'for all the duties and enjoyments of life, much better than any education which affluence could bestow' (II, 280).

The last two chapters celebrate the financial and amorous triumph of

Roderick, who finds happiness at the end of this long quest. The search for happiness is a basic theme in Smollett's novels: 'felicity' is the last word of *Roderick Random*. Roderick meets his old friends again: Jackson in Jamaica, Mrs Sagely, Morgan and Banter, and later, in Scotland, he pays his debts to Crab's heirs and refuses to see the Potions. A final unexpected development gives some measure of his moral progress. This time good fortune does not turn his head, as Strap feared (II, 282). He abandons neither his faithful servant, nor Narcissa, whom her brother refuses to give him in marriage. It is a Narcissa *without* a dowry whom Roderick is to marry. His heroism is certainly qualified, since he is now rich, but it is only right to emphasise the evolution of this dowry-hunter into a generous-hearted man. Narcissa's brother's brutal refusal to give his consent, far from vexing Roderick, delights him because it gives him the opportunity of proving his disinterested love (II, 298). Nevertheless, vanity does not entirely disappear from his character. He still remains just as proud of his fine clothes (II, 302) as of his wife's beauty (II, 302). But this vanity is almost legitimate, since, in Smollett's eyes, his hero at last deserves his material prosperity and his marital happiness. He knows *true* happiness at last after having succumbed over and over again to the tinsel of appearances. Even if the reader remains a trifle sceptical about the sudden transformation of the hero, there is no doubt about the consistency of Smollett's moral intentions all through the novel: they give the book a structural unity which the plot in itself could not give it. Smollett makes his hero achieve a certain evolution, somewhat marred by clumsiness and improbability. Roderick is at last able to dominate the impulsiveness of his passions: 'The impetuous transports of my passion are now settled and mellowed into endearing fondness and tranquillity of love, rooted by that intimate connection and interchange of hearts, which nought but virtuous wedlock can produce' (II, 308). This sentence, so pompously Johnsonian in style, might equally well conclude an allegory on happiness.

Although *Peregrine Pickle* is much longer[11] than *Roderick Random*, it is easier to distinguish the structure of this novel whose articulations are more clearly defined than in *Roderick Random*. This task is also facilitated by Rufus Putney's study[12]. Written with much vigour and perceptiveness, it remains, in its broad outline, indispensable for any analysis of *Peregrine Pickle*. It is possible to distinguish five major articulations in the novel. First of all, Smollett devotes fifty pages to introducing the major characters other than Peregrine: this is a kind of prehistory of the story which presents the social and emotional milieu in which young Peregrine will develop. Then, up to Chapter xxxvii inclusive[13], Smollett describes Peregrine's childhood and adolescence, in particular his time at school and university. The adventures experienced during the Grand Tour hold the reader's attention up to Chapter lxx. The serious crime Peregrine commits against Emilia constitutes the fourth articulation. The long social and moral decline of the hero and his rehabilitation *in extremis* occupy the remainder of the book from Chapter lxxxvi onwards, this section of the novel being technically thrown out of balance by the inclusion of the memoirs of a lady of quality and the story of Mackercher.

As in *Roderick Random*, Smollett, especially in the first half of *Peregrine Pickle*, marks out the course of his story with chronological[14] and geographical signposts. The age of the characters, in particular that of Peregrine and of Trunnion and his wife is stated at regular intervals, especially in the case of Peregrine. At the beginning of *Peregrine Pickle*, the reader learns that Trunnion is fifty-five (p. 48), and Peregrine first appears on the scene at the age of three (p. 51). Peregrine spends fifteen months in France (p. 223), Trunnion dies at seventy-nine (p. 422) and his wife at sixty-five (p. 584). As to the geographical indications, they are so numerous and precise that it is impossible to give a list of them here. But Peregrine's financial means, much greater than Roderick's, allow him more freedom of movement, especially on the continent. Peregrine, along with Fathom, is Smollett's most cosmopolitan hero, thus remaining true to his Christian name, which is also a label. This temperamental disposition to travel, which is almost international, differentiates Smollett's heroes from those of Fielding who are more stay-at-home and more typically English.

To introduce the principal characters other than Peregrine, Smollett sometimes uses the omniscient author's direct description of them, sometimes depicts them as seen through the eyes of other characters. Gamaliel Pickle, his sister and his future wife come into the first category. Gamaliel appears right from the first pages as a flabby creature, totally devoid of willpower, whose natural apathy allows his wife to manage his fortune and destiny. The oblique method of presentation has the merit of giving a character like Trunnion a three-dimensional quality lacking in mere conventional 'humours' such as Mrs Grizzle or Mrs Pickle. The tavern-keeper proceeds to build up the picture by successive touches, revealing in turn the naval eccentricity of the Commodore and his friends, the garrison life regulated like that on board a battleship, then his horror of lawyers, his misogyny and his credulity. Smollett does not fail, subsequently, to exploit the peculiar quirks of the Commodore, whom the tavern-keeper describes, not without reason, as a 'very oddish kind of gentleman' (p. 6). Corresponding to this indirect introduction is the entrance on the scene — it would be more appropriate to Trunnion's nautical temperament to speak of the heaving alongside! — of the man himself, who, together with Hatchway and Pipes, indulges in a convincing 'marine pantomime' (pp. 8—12). The long dissertation on Trunnion's character — in which vanity, kindliness and irascibility are blended, and, as with all Smollett's sailors, great ignorance of the world of landlubbers — is intentional on Smollett's part. The author is sedulous to emphasise the part Trunnion is going to play in the novel: 'I have been the more circumstantial in opening the character of Trunnion, because he bears a considerable share in the course of these memoirs' (p. 12).

Smollett thus devotes himself to a preliminary study of the human environment in which Peregrine is going to grow up. It is above all Peregrine's psychological ancestry which seems to interest the author. Although his father's apathy plays no part in his heredity, it is possible that his mother's cravings and fanciful whims when she was carrying him were not without some influence on the character of the child (pp. 20–4). Such seems to be Smollett's not very scientific opinion. The daily immersion in icy water, in spite of his aunt's pessimistic forebodings, hardens and strengthens the baby, but perhaps this barbaric treatment helps to reinforce the child's natural tendency to be unruly and passionate. The false pregnancy of Mrs Trunnion, who in order to get the misogynous Commodore to marry her has played cleverly on 'a large share of that vanity and self-conceit that generally predominate even in the most savage breast' (p. 29), has a double function. Smollett again uses the parallel theme of eccentric cravings (pp. 47–8) enhanced by Mrs Trunnion's ancestral pride. Secondly, this psychological pregnancy is a rude blow to Trunnion's own pride, for he is extremely proud of his virility (p. 48). Trunnion projects this thwarted paternal love on to Peregrine, whose own mother conversely abandons him more and more after the birth of her second son. So, when Peregrine makes his appearance in Chapter xi, the reader knows not only his whole family history, but also the psychological and emotional climate in which he is going to grow up.

Peregrine's childhood and adolescence occupy the next twenty-seven chapters (xi to xxxvii inclusive). The hero's early childhood is remarkable for the formidable precocity of his satirical propensities, in so far as one can apply the word 'satire' to a series of dubious practical jokes of which Trunnion is usually the victim (pp. 52–3). Just as Smollett has made a point of emphasising the eccentricities of his parents and relatives, he insists on what he calls, by turns, in his young hero 'a certain oddity of disposition' (pp. 51–2) or again 'unlucky pranks' and 'vicious inclinations' (p. 53). A tutor who believes in strong-arm methods only stupefies the boy. But, at his first school, Peregrine has the luck to meet an intelligent schoolmaster, Jennings, who reawakens his pupil's competitive spirit (p. 55). Peregrine's success is not without psychological and moral drawbacks. His intellectual prowess and his pugnacity enable him to triumph over all his schoolfellows. From his earliest years, he manifests all the signs of an inveterate arrogance: 'His pride rose in proportion to his power' (p. 56). Unlike Roderick, this pride will never desert Peregrine, even in his darkest hours, which never have the desperate character of the ordeals endured by Roderick. Whereas the latter, bereft of all luck, puts up with his misfortunes, Peregrine does everything he can to create them. He never relinquishes the aggressive corollary to his pride, to wit, insolence.

Smollett's moral intention is declared, right from the beginning of the novel, with a complete clarity which is facilitated by the omniscience of the author, unlike that of the narrator in *Peregrine Pickle*. The author's angle of vision is so wide that it enables him to include his hero's past, present and future at every turn. Smollett no longer proceeds by innuendos, as in *Roderick Random*, but by definitely pronounced judgments which enable the reader to see in what moral direction he is inflecting the story. Smollett intervenes directly like this when he asserts that, from his earliest years, Peregrine 'contracted a large proportion of insolence, which a series of misfortunes that happened to him in the sequel could scarce effectually tame' (p. 57). As this judgment risks rendering his hero too unpleasant in the reader's eyes, Smollett hastens to add, in the next sentence: 'Nevertheless there was a fund of good nature and generosity in his composition'. The data of the moral problem are thus stated with extreme precision: *Peregrine Pickle* is the story of a struggle between the forces of Evil, symbolised by that sin which fascinates puritans, pride, and the forces of Good. This 'dubious battle' is sometimes interior, sometimes it involves the society in which the hero moves.

The interval of about a year spent in the garrison only confirms Peregrine's satirical genius. Smollett insists several times, after giving examples of these jests liable to put the life or the reputation of the victim in danger (pp. 67, 68, 72), on this irrepressible urge which leads Peregrine into his practical and psychological machinations. If the expression 'peculiar turn in Peregrine's imagination' (pp. 64–5) is moderate, Smollett explicitly condemns that joyous rage which impels Peregrine and his two enthusiastic accomplices, Hatchway and Pipes, to torment the Commodore and his wife. 'Howsoever preposterous and unaccountable that passion may be, which prompts persons, otherwise generous and sympathising, to afflict and perplex their fellow-creatures, certain it is our confederates entertained . . . a large proportion of it' (p. 72). Some pages later, the vocabulary of torture is once more employed about the practical jokes of which Trunnion is the victim: 'the unwearied endeavours and inexhausted invention of his tormentors, who harrassed him with such a variety of mischievous pranks' (p. 77). But, whatever Trunnion's defects, he is not lacking in perspicacity and realises that such acts are 'rather the effect of wantonness than malice' (ibid.). This mania of young Peregrine's, if on the one hand it derives from the play instincts of childhood, on the other comprises in embryo the sadistic pleasure of doing harm more or less gratuitously. However these practical jokes are not devoid of a certain punitive merit, especially at the beginning, as in the case of the jalap poured into Mrs Trunnion's brandy (p. 67). It is people's personal oddities and unconscious mannerisms that Peregrine and his friends exploit. But this need to humiliate others denotes, in Peregrine, a feeling of intellectual and physical superiority. The author of the practical jokes assumes for a few moments the role of an omniscient and omnipotent deity who manipulates people and brutally forces them to realise their own inferiority which they were tending to forget. It is thus the role of an arrogant judge that Peregrine plays towards his benefactors and the rest of the novel proves how strong this propensity is in the hero. The only entirely new moral element during this period is the unnatural aversion his mother begins to feel for Peregrine: 'unnatural' (p. 64) reappears almost every time Smollett alludes to this inexplicable vagary of the mother's. As a result, Peregrine, rejected by his mother, becomes almost the adopted child of the Trunnions (p. 79).

The years spent at Winchester permit not only of Peregrine's intellectual development, but above all of the unleashing of his satirical talents which incite him to violence and rebellion. They therefore more than confirm his proclivities, they increase their already virulent intensity (pp. 85–8). But the decisive turn is taken when he is about fourteen. The boy becomes an adolescent who begins to assume the arrogance and the feelings of an adult (p. 92). Peregrine leaves the world of childhood to discover that of women, a new motive for giving free rein to his physical, sartorial and psychological vanity: 'his vanity took the lead of his passions' (p. 93). The meeting with Emilia has the same effect of a *coup-de-foudre* on Peregrine as that with Narcissa had on Roderick. The outward forms of the passion are similar, nevertheless with this difference, that Peregrine's social situation is equal, even superior, to Emilia's, and that he is already 'a most egregious coxcomb' (p. 93, the word being repeated p. 94). But, unlike Narcissa (a pale sentimental convenience of the story), Emilia has her own personality and is by no means devoid of vanity herself (pp. 120–1). The relations between Peregrine and Emilia, sometimes interrupted for long intervals and frequently stormy, form the structural pivot of the novel.

However numerous the accidents which subsequently disturb these relations — misunderstandings, separations, momentary forgettings, Peregrine's serious crime — Smollett takes care to guarantee this passion against the attrition of events. The charms of Emilia 'in a moment rivetted the chains of his slavery beyond the power of accident to unbind' (p. 96). But Emilia's insecure financial situation immediately raises obstacles for Peregrine's pride. Smollett depicts the struggle between his love and his own interests (p. 97). To keep this very long love story true to life, Smollett gives Emilia a perspicacity (p. 99) and a flexibility of character (pp. 105, 107) which are totally lacking in Narcissa. There is never a complete rupture between the lovers. Thus, after the misunderstanding of the reconstituted love-letter (pp. 104–5), there is an interruption of the relations between Emilia and Peregrine but their feelings persist. When Peregrine, by chance, sees Emilia again at Windsor 'that passion which had lain dormant for the space of two years flashed up in a moment, and he was seized with an universal trepidation' (p. 120).

Meanwhile, the years spent at Oxford contribute nothing

fundamentally new about the moral personality of Peregrine, who continues to behave in the same turbulent way as at Winchester (pp. 115–19). However he acquires a certain culture, Smollett being anxious to reassure his reader about Peregrine: 'He enjoyed many lucid intervals' (p. 119). Peregrine experiences his first financial difficulties and momentarily quarrels with Hatchway and Pipes on account of Emilia. The only element which is important for the structure of the novel is the fire at the inn (p. 145). Peregrine rescues his beloved and exchanges a ring with her, which, on the surface, seems to augur well for the future. On the technical plane, the meeting with Emilia's brother Godfrey (p. 148) gives Smollett the opportunity of describing the confrontation of the two characters, which ends in a duel and a reconciliation (pp. 151–2).

Godfrey will henceforth serve as a link between Emilia, Peregrine and the garrison, since Trunnion discovers that Emilia's brother is none other than the son of an old comrade-in-arms (pp. 162–3). Without playing a decisive role in the novel, Godfrey becomes a trusty comrade of Peregrine's, who, when he has the opportunity, shares his amorous and social adventures (in Bath). The two young men have, all the same, a very hierarchic idea of morality. Though Peregrine is not thinking yet of assaulting Emilia, he does not hesitate, in company with Godrey, his future brother-in-law, to tumble a few peasant girls or maidservants (p. 166). This sometimes involves them in misadventures rather reminiscent of Chaucer's 'Miller's Tale' (pp. 168–9). After a scene of extreme psychological violence with his mother, who continues to feel an unnatural hatred for Peregrine (p. 172), the consequences are twofold. Julia, Peregrine's sister, takes refuge in the garrison. Hatchway, Godfrey and Peregrine contrive a faked duel between the Commodore and his old friend Gamaliel. Peregrine substitutes himself for his father, but this last practical joke before his departure for the Grand Tour nearly costs him his life (p. 176). The letter, on his departure, in which Peregrine renews his vows of fidelity to Emilia (p. 181) has a double ironic value if one thinks of Peregrine's recent lecherous escapades and the temptations which are bound to assail him in Paris according to the misogynous Trunnion's vigorous warnings (p. 180).

This journey on the Continent, in company of a tutor with no authority, Jolter, was announced as early as Chapter xxviii (p. 140). The news of his approaching departure in the following chapter has had the immediate effect of gratifying his ambition and his vanity (p. 142). Moreover, foreign travel would furnish Peregrine with ample material for his gifts of observation. Finally, with a possible touch of insincerity, Peregrine opines that his absence will in no way diminish his love for Emilia but, on the contrary, will heighten its value. Between these hopes and the reality is interposed all the complex mass of adventures he experiences, which make him forget his good resolutions and his vows of fidelity.

The thirty-three chapters (xxxviii–lxx), in which Smollett tells the adventures of Peregrine and his chance-met companions, have been described by George M. Kahrl in his book (1945) as 'one great, sustained prose satire on the Grand Tour, every detail of which can be fully substantiated from contemporary books on Continental travel' (p. 40). This realistic and satirical aspect, important though it is, should not make one ignore the structural value and thematic unity of these pages. Far from being merely a satirical commentary on France, the French, the Dutch and other nationalities, these chapters present a recurrence of themes which interweave and overlap, thus reconstructing the social and moral jungle of worldly life in its global complexity.

The first theme of this journey is the constant criticism of France's political regime, her economy, her inhabitants and their morals. His tutor, Jolter, is a convinced Francophile (p. 189) but each of his flattering statements about France and the French is irremediably contradicted by the reality. Such is the significance of the incidents with the ferryman and later with the porters and customs-officers (pp. 190–1). The remarks about agriculture in the north of France (p. 192) already foreshadow the ruthless criticisms of *Travels through France and Italy*. The loquacious politeness of the aristocrats is described entirely in pejorative and negative terms, which indicate how much Peregrine, stunned by so much volubility, resents it (p. 209). Smollett does grudgingly admit the necessity of paying a few rapid words of homage to the taste and culture of certain Frenchmen (p. 210). He promptly hastens to add, with a chauvinism that, there again, *Travels through France and Italy* will not belie, 'the result of all his inquiries was self-congratulation on his title to the privileges of a British subject' (ibid.).

Above all it is against the forms of arbitrary power that Peregrine's haughty nature rebels (Chapter xliv). He declares himself 'a professed enemy to all oppression' (p. 212) and challenges a redoubtable musketeer to a duel after an altercation in a theatre. Other incidents arouse his indignation, such as the behaviour of officers who refuse to pay an innkeeper (p. 268). There is even the beginning of a historical debate on the military strategy of Louis XIV (pp. 291–2), in which Peregrine is coward enough to abandon his position in order not to displease the Francophile lady he is courting.

But it is the tireless and reiterated denunciation of stupidity in all its protean shapes that forms the kernel of this account of a journey. Affectation, vanity, pedantry, pretentious ignorance are so many variations on this one theme. Certain characters, such as Jolter, Pallet and the doctor, seem to have escaped from an allegory in which they symbolise prejudice, ignorance or pretentiousness. Smollett takes advantage of his unflattering description of Jolter to attack tutors in general: 'those animals who lead raw boys about the world, under the denomination of travelling governors' (p. 207). The meeting, in Paris, with those two eccentrics, Pallet and the doctor, is an opportunity for Smollett to burst out against a certain kind of artistic appreciation, as enthusiastic as it is devoid of aesthetic and cultural basis. Pallet's howlers (pp. 224–7) serve as a foil to the pedantic erudition of the doctor, a passionate devotee of the Ancients. His Greek quotations do not dazzle Peregrine who promptly sets down the doctor[15] as 'a mere index-hunter, who held the eel of science by the tail' (p. 226). The antique banquet (pp. 233–41) is only a long practical and gastronomic demonstration during which the systematic insistence on Graeco–Roman customs is turned to ridicule by a series of mechanical, emetic and cathartic disasters. Nothing is missing from this banquet, not even the stale spice of homosexuality (p. 242).

In particular, it is against feigned artistic enthusiasm that Smollett protests with a vigour which anticipates that of *Travels through France and Italy* and which has long, and unjustly, caused Smollett to be regarded as an iconoclastic philistine in the matter of artistic appreciation. The words 'enthusiast' and 'enthusiastic', heavily loaded, in the eighteenth century, with pejorative meaning (literary, artistic and religious), recur regularly in describing the affectations of Pallet and the doctor. Peregrine very quickly sees them for what they are: 'false enthusiasts, without the smallest pretensions to taste and sensibility' (p. 228). The doctor repeats Shaftesbury's moral arguments 'with all the violence of enthusiastic agitation' (p. 232). Pallet's eccentric behaviour in Antwerp is due to his 'enthusiastic admiration' (p. 332) for Rubens, and, on this occasion Smollett describes his character as a 'pseudo-enthusiast' (p. 332). A scene in a stagecoach is transformed into a debate in which Jolter's philological vanity and the doctor's religious intolerance are glaringly apparent. Even the faithful Pipes succumbs to this epidemic of stupidity, by evincing a conceited pig-headedness which causes him to be dismissed from Peregrine's service (pp. 278–9).

Peregrine does not remain an amused spectator of the display of human stupidity. He himself launches into a series of amorous adventures which contribute appreciably to his moral downfall. Two aspects of this subject call for particular attention. At first, the proud Peregrine's conquests are nothing to flatter himself about, either as regards beauty or social prestige, since he seduces a former oyster-seller, Mrs Hornbeck, and keeps a common prostitute who loses no time in being unfaithful to him. Subsequently, his sexual appetites are more often frustrated than satisfied. It seems that an imminent justice, in the form of farcical mishaps instigated by Pallet, is always destined to thwart Peregrine's amorous designs, with the implacable logic of a ludicrous fatality. His first conquest, Mrs Hornbeck, has only the semblance of being well educated: 'so easy is it to acquire that external deportment on which people of condition value themselves so much' (p. 193). Her hearty sensuality, and Peregrine's stratagem of drugging her husband and Jolter, make her an enthusiastic victim. Not for one moment has Peregrine had any scruples about adultery (pp. 199–203). In the same way, he later abducts the lady (pp. 219–20) at the risk of getting into trouble with the authorities. Always on the hunt for easy game, Peregrine misunderstands the plain speech of a traiteur's wife he importunes which results in a scratched nose and a pitched battle with the watch.

Mortified by his lack of success, Peregrine secures himself the paid services of a prostitute (p. 210). This limited sexual prowess hardly raises Peregrine to the rank of a Don Juan or an English Casanova. In fact his illicit love life is far more remarkable for failures than successes. The only time he lays siege to a woman of social standing, he fails, which has the effect of exciting in him 'the utmost turbulence of unruly desire' (p. 286). This setback has also a structural value, for it anticipates the attempt at seduction which he will dare to perpetrate on Emilia. When the beautiful Fleming refuses him, Peregrine flings himself on her 'with intention of seizing that which she had declined to give' (ibid.). In the course of the next chapter (lviii), there is a mounting surge of concupiscence. Peregrine assists as a Peeping Tom at his fair one's undressing, and, in spite of her virtuous protestations, is on the point of storming the fortress when Pallet, for the first time, intervenes to thwart his enterprise (p. 288). Smollett makes his characters dance a quadrille of lechery in which the chosen partners never succeed in completing the figure they have begun. Peregrine is frustrated and the vocabulary of madness appears once again, as well as that of an erotic gastronomy which likens woman to a delicious dish. The unfortunate hero is 'mad with seeing the delicious morsel, snatched (as it were) from his very lip' (p. 290).

The beginning of Chapter lix offers explicit confirmation of a structural unity. In the company of the Flemish lady, Peregrine is present at the execution of two young men, accused of having raped a prostitute. The parallel with Peregrine's attempted seduction is underlined by the presence of a French courtesan with whom Pallet, himself the victim of the interplay of love and chance at the inn, has not succeeded in achieving his aims (p. 291). To avenge himself on a Jewish rival whom the courtesan has succeeded in seducing — a theme already used in *Roderick Random* — Pallet mounts a punitive expedition which fails ludicrously and frustrates Peregrine's designs a second time (p. 296).

A third amorous rendezvous of Peregrine's is also doomed to failure (p. 300): he is 'tantalised upon the brink of bliss' (p. 300), or again 'half frantic with such a series of disappointments' (p. 301). When a fourth attempt fails, as usual because of the wretched Pallet, Peregrine is 'well-nigh deprived of his senses' (p. 303). Once again Smollett uses the vocabulary of madness to describe his hero's impotent rage (pp. 308–9, 310–11). This is not Peregrine's last frustration as a lover and it must be observed that the fair Fleming's final motive is her sense of religious duty (p. 309) reinforced by that capacity for self-denial (p. 310) so conspicuously lacking in Peregrine. So, here again, it is a moral solution in accordance with Christian ethics and sound sense that Smollett adopts in order implicitly to condemn his hero. After having consoled himself very carnally with Mrs Hornbeck, whom the sorely abused chance so frequent in novels has made him meet again (p. 312), he pursues the Fleming again and starts an intrigue with a young girl in a convent (p. 325). He has another moral lesson inflicted on him by the incorruptibility of the portress, whose refusal to be bribed is perhaps less due to her love of virtue than to her lack of the virtue of love: 'for the first time, he found the art of corruption ineffectual' (p. 327). A quarrel between rival nuns once again deprives Peregrine of the fruit of his ingenuity in managing to get into the convent disguised as a woman (pp. 329–31). This story, which might have been drawn from one of La Fontaine's tales, ends with a moral, and a very puritan one.

The entries on the moral balance-sheet of this journey are almost exclusively on the debit side. Smollett's position is unambiguous. In contact with a frivolous world, intent on pleasure, young Peregrine has plunged into a moral degeneration already begun at Winchester and Oxford. He has let himself be seduced by the false wordly values which are current on the Continent, especially in France, a land of moral iniquity in Smollett's puritan eyes. Nevertheless, the author is clever enough not to deprive his hero of *all* moral sense. The object of the following passage is to make this clear:

> No man was more capable of moralizing upon Peregrine's misconduct than himself; his reflections were extremely just and sagacious, and attended with no other disadvantage, but that of occurring too late. He projected a thousand salutary schemes of deportment, but, like other projectors, he never had interest enough with the ministry of his passions to bring any one of them to bear (p. 217).

This impetuosity of his passions has the result of falsifying the whole scale of values he still had when he left England. Seen in this perspective, Emilia is no longer a pure girl whom he loves, but a sex object that he must possess at any price, even that of honour. Emilia, even though absent, remains at the centre of the novel, and Smollett is preparing the psychological and moral climate which will bring the hero to commit his crime against her. Long before the attempted seduction, Peregrine has already degenerated morally:

> These dictates of ridiculous pride had almost effaced the remembrance of his amiable mistress, or at least so far warped his morals and integrity, that he actually began to conceive hopes of her altogether unworthy of his own character and her deserts (p. 218).

Even before his return to England, Peregrine is thinking of seducing Emilia 'on his own terms' (p. 223).

Peregrine's moral deterioration is accompanied by a curious phenomenon. The more corrupted he becomes, the more clearly he sees the stupidity or amorality of others. This produces a moral inversion in Peregrine, who, egged on by his pride, deliberately decides to take justice into his own hands. On several occasions he punishes Pallet (p. 333), and the many quarrels he starts up between the painter and the doctor are explained by this excessive mania for summary justice of which he himself is the sole arbiter. He delights in this self-imposed task and revels with an almost sadistic pleasure in the terrors felt by those two wretched puppets, Pallet and the doctor (p. 351). But nowhere is this inversion more flagrant than in the case of Hornbeck (of the fated name) who is not only cuckolded but thrashed by Peregrine. Peregrine's argument is a fine example of specious sophistry. The cuckold deserves to be punished for his want of courage! Smollett flares up with the verbal vehemence that characterises him every time he denounces that barbarous, unjust and stupid institution, the duel, of which he gives any number of ridiculous examples in his novels. It is symbolic that the Grand Tour should end after a rather sordid incident in a music house in Amsterdam. However Peregrine has not yet finished his journey to the end of moral night.

Peregrine's return to his native land soon makes his moral and psychological transformation apparent. If the thought of Emilia, whom he has neglected during his stay in France, does now and then, for a few moments disturb his self-complacency — 'the proud recollection of his own improvements' (p. 352) — it is obvious that the hero is more 'self-sufficient' (p. 353) than ever. In order to stress his moral purpose, Smollett does not hesitate to intervene directly: 'Sorry am I, that the task I have undertaken, lays me under the necessity of divulging this degeneracy in the sentiments of our imperious youth' (p. 353). The moral intention is further reinforced by the implicit irony of the utterances of Mrs Trunnion who hopes that his morals and his religion have not been corrupted by his sojourn in France (p. 355). The Commodore, in his ignorance of the truth, also contributes the same note of unconscious irony when he congratulates Jolter on the care with which he has supervised his pupil's education and morals (p. 356). It is Trunnion who announces the thematic transition (from travelling to marriage) when he hopes that he will live to see Peregrine's children (p. 355). The prospect of his sister Julia's approaching marriage ought to channel Peregrine's thoughts towards marrying Emilia. But nothing of the kind. Though Peregrine displays his impatience to see Emilia again (p. 360), he expresses somewhat tepid feelings when Trunnion speaks to him of Emilia in glowing terms. The warning of the old Commodore (p. 360), who is anxious to assure himself of Peregrine's honourable intentions towards Emilia, is repeated in a tone of pathetic solemnity on his death-bed: 'if you run her on board in an unlawful way, I leave my curse upon you, and trust you will never prosper in the voyage of life' (p. 393). Nevertheless, Peregrine is far from having a pure heart. When he goes to see Emilia, his sentiments are those 'of a man of pleasure, who sacrifices every consideration to the desire of his ruling appetite' (p. 360). In a word, he has become a libertine (p. 361). Emilia is perfectly aware of this trans- formation, due to the wordly sophistication he has acquired in Paris. Nevertheless, Peregrine has not renounced all kindly feelings. He looks after the Commodore solicitously during an attack of gout (p. 363) and helps Godfrey to obtain an officer's commission (p. 365). When Trunnion dies, he tries in vain to hide his profound grief (pp. 391—2). So it is not possible to classify Peregrine as a cynic or a misanthrope.

His moral evolution accentuates the antithetical character of his behaviour. Although he is harbouring dark designs regarding Emilia, described as 'vicious' (p. 397) and 'unwarrantable' (p. 399), he is equally capable of raging indignantly against the worldly corruption of Bath. With the active assistance of Godfrey, Peregrine again sets himself up as a judge who punishes in turn a gang of crooks in Bath (pp. 366—9), the doctors avid of consulting fees (pp. 373—5) and the worthy bourgeois who rely on the faithful services of their turnspit-dogs for the Sunday roast (pp. 377—8). But, above all, it is the meeting with the misanthrope Cadwal- lader Crabtree which will enable him to give free rein to his punitive imagination. Thanks to his feigned deafness, Cadwallader is able to learn the secret history of families, which he uses, on occasion, to castigate individuals (p. 387). The alliance with Crabtree marks for Peregrine the beginning of contemptuousness. Armed with this veritable ring of Gyges (p. 388), Peregrine, after his failure with Emilia, enjoys the feeling of omniscient superiority conferred on him by the knowledge of intimate secrets. He is also in danger of letting himself be contaminated by the misanthropy of Crabtree, who has discerned in him 'a rooted contempt for the world' (p. 383). For Smollett, the misanthropist is an outsider who cuts himself off from society, in which he refuses to take an active part, but the spectacle of which fascinates, disgusts and also delights him (p. 387). This is a moral and psychological danger, still not yet encountered, to which Peregrine will nearly succumb in prison.

But, however important it is, the first meeting with Crabtree is only a brief indication of the almost fatal slope on which he is about to launch himself. The death of Trunnion and the £30,000 he inherits (p. 395) pave the road of the profligate, which inevitably leads to London, with gold and make it possible for him to indulge in every kind of folly. His acquisi- tion of material wealth only increases his vanity (p. 397) and his social ambition. Far from forgetting Emilia, he is obsessed by the sinful thought of seducing her. And it is here that his previous acquaintance with a corrupt society proves useful. He tries in turn flattering Emilia's uncle (p. 399) then perjury (p. 403), then base physical machinations, isolating his victim (p. 404), and drugging her (p. 405). Although Emilia displays her usual prudence — for, like Pamela, she means to concede nothing without promise of marriage (p. 400) — it should however be noted that, from the young lovers' first meeting, Smollett has been clever enough not to turn his heroine into an impeccable paragon of improbable virtue. Emilia, too, is slightly to blame. In spite of her good sense and sagacity, she lets herself be attracted by the appearances of a marriage flattering to her self-esteem: 'She . . . enjoyed the present flattering appearance of her fate' (p. 403), although her feminine pride forbids her to press Peregrine to the point of making an unambiguous declaration of his intentions.

Peregrine's attempted seduction of Emilia is characterised neither by the erotic violence nor the psychological machiavellism which Lovelace displays in order to possess Clarissa. Nevertheless, Peregrine's frenzied plea for extramarital love (p. 407) and the evident strength of his sexual desires drive him to treat Emilia as a mistress who must be bought. Emilia's dignity and self-control enable her to escape from the trap. Peregrine's reactions are instantaneous. He behaves like a madman (pp. 409, 413, 419, 421) and such is the turbulence of his passions that he is threatened with apoplexy (p. 419). But illness assumes here, for Smollett, the value of a physical and moral catharsis: 'A seasonable fit of illness is an excellent medicine for the turbulence of passion' (p. 421). Peregrine is not proof against all moral sentiments, and remorse promptly assails him (pp. 410, 419). Although, in his physical and psychological exasperation he curses Emilia and her virtue, one part of him cannot help admiring her (p. 409). The opposition between his passions is frequently stressed by Smollett: 'In short, he was torn by conflicting passions; love, shame and remorse contended with vanity, ambition and revenge' (p. 410). So Peregrine tries to be reconciled with Emilia, but she foresees the manoeuvre and thwarts it (p. 411). A letter of apology to Emilia's mother has no more success, but Smollett is clever enough to suggest a possibility of reconciliation, however slight (p. 412 and especially p. 421 in her mother's letter). Following this storm, comes the calm of resignation (p. 421) and, after his attack of fever, he meditates reforming his morals: 'he moralized like an apostle, and projected several prudential schemes for his future conduct' (p. 422). But the social whirlwind will scatter these good resolutions like wisps of straw.

This last section of the novel — the decline of the hero and his final rehabilitation — is the bulkiest. Though it occupies over 350 pages (nearly half the whole book) the 100 pages taken up by the Memoirs of Lady Vane[16] and the forty which narrate the life of MacKercher[17] must be deducted from it. These interpolated stories break the thread of the narrative, in the narrow sense of its dealing only with the adventures of Peregrine. But if, technically, they upset the balance of the novel, they are integrated into its thematic structure. The Memoirs of Lady Vane, however long they are and however much their anecdotal interest has faded after the initial blaze of their *succès de scandale*, harmonise with the moral purpose of the novel. This is what Rufus Putney (op. cit., p. 1064) has seen very clearly: 'Even if Smollett did not intend it, they reinforce his thesis that the life of the upper classes was often vicious and immoral.'

Their role of stasis and thematic counterpoint has remained for long unappreciated, even by a critic on the whole favourable to Smollett like Walter Scott, who defines them in his *Lives of the Novelists* as 'a separate tale, thrust into the work, with which it has no sort of connection, in the manner introduced by Cervantes, and followed by Le Sage and Fielding . . ., now regarded as a tiresome and unnecessary excrescence upon the main story' (Everyman's Library edn, p. 80). In fact, these Memoirs, without being directly connected with Peregrine's moral evolution, are like a monolithic block. They point out the danger incurred by those who more willingly obey the dictates of their passions than the rules of moral good sense, and thus have the value of an admonition.

Even on the technical plane, the Memoirs of Lady Vane, like all the interpolated stories in Smollett's novels, occur at a moment when a momentary pause in the unfolding of the narrative is justified. They avoid the repetition of Peregrine's follies after his return to London where he has once again met Crabtree, ready as usual to play the dangerous role of penetrator of secrets, as Asmodée does for Cléophas in *Le Diable Boiteux*. The Memoirs are one long variation on a central theme: the rule of a woman's passions over the whole of an extremely hectic sensual and emotional life. From the very first lines of Chapter lxxxviii, this theme is clearly announced in antithetical terms: 'candour' is opposed to 'indiscretion', just as 'head' to 'heart', in this extract from the opening sentence: 'howsoever my head may have erred, my heart hath always been uncorrupted' (pp. 432–3). And here an observation is called for. Whatever the respective shares of Smollett and Lady Vane in the composition of these Memoirs, they are full of touches of feminine psychology which are totally lacking in Smollett's heroines. Only a woman, or rather a young bride, can speak of her sexual modesty and her refusal to go to bed with her husband in broad daylight (p. 440). Only Lady Vane could depict her wedding night with her second husband in such strong terms of physical and psychological revulsion as 'the pawings of an imp' (p. 451) to describe his impotent fumblings. Only a woman thinks of dying of grief when her first lover deserts her, but is delighted to learn later that he regrets having left her (p. 473). The rudimentary knowledge of the feminine heart Smollett displays in depicting his heroines did not enable him to invent such subtleties of amorous machiavellism as anticipating the rupture with an adored lover for fear that he should be the first to make the break (p. 489); or again that exquisitely feline remark about ugly women who live in perpetual fear of threats to their chastity: 'I cannot help observing, that an homely woman is always more apt to entertain those fears, than one whose person exposes her to much more imminent danger' (p. 525). Though it is probable that Smollett really wrote these Memoirs himself, it is equally probable that he kept very close to the account Lady Vane gave him of her past.

During this geographical and matrimonial game of snakes and ladders which Lady Vane plays with her second husband, the search for pleasure is her only guide and her only philosophy: 'Love which is pleasure, or pleasure which is love, makes up the whole' (p. 532). Lady Vane is not afraid of admitting her amorous hedonism (pp. 521, 526), and during this frenzied quest for pleasure, which she distinguishes from base sensuality, she discovers the corruption of high society, in England as well as on the Continent. These rich and idle people — 'idle' is a key word (p. 495), though it seldom appears — indulge freely in the sexual promiscuity which deprives women of all emotional dignity (p. 485), whereas Lady Vane wishes to be faithful (p. 487), even though she is given to transferring her fidelity to a series of lovers. Whatever her *faux pas* she always retains the generosity of a great lady and declares that she would rather give herself to a footman than sell herself to a prince (p. 474). Finally, the violence of her passions is accompanied by unusual physical and psychological stamina. No catastrophe can keep her down for long. She endures fatigues and dangers without flinching. Lady Vane is a lady of quality in more senses than one.

The effect of her story on Peregrine is twofold. It neutralises his passion for Emilia, thanks to an incipient, and hopeless, one for Lady Vane. He thus finds himself *'in equilibrio'* (p. 539), a formula of a physical state of emotion repeated and developed on the following page (p. 540). The second consequence is more unexpected: Peregrine takes advantage of being delivered from the torments of his heart to give free rein to that 'practical satire' (ibid.) for which he has felt himself so gifted from his earliest childhood. And, after the long dramatic stasis provided by the Memoirs of Lady Vane, his decline will become more and more evident. At first the descent is almost imperceptible, but the slope grows steeper and steeper as his excesses and follies follow hard on each other's heels at increasingly breakneck speed. Destiny is then indeed, as Giraudoux has said, 'the accelerated form of time'. In the first stage, Peregrine, assisted by Crabtree, inaugurates a reign of satirical practical jokes which have a triple motive: the satisfaction of his ludic (and occasionally lubricious) instincts, the study of a corrupt society, and the fulfilment of that need to set himself up as a punitive judge. A positive anatomy of social corruption is presented by means of thumbnail sketches (the clergyman in search of a richer living, avarice, lust, disappointed literary ambition, pp. 562–8). Thanks to the practice of palmistry, Crabtree reveals to Peregrine the vices of a society stripped naked: 'the whole variety of character undisguised, passed as it were in review before the confederates' (p. 568). Crabtree's clients are doubly punished. On the one hand they are subjected to the tyranny of their passions (p. 564), and, on the other, Peregrine and the fortune-teller contrive to chastise them still more. The vocabulary of punishment recurs frequently and emphatically in the course of these pages (pp. 541, 547, 550, 556, 568). Even when Peregrine becomes an author, he promptly turns into a critical judge whose weapons are ridicule and contempt (p. 576). This orgy of misanthropy does not, however, make him forget the duties of charity and Peregrine is still capable of being generous on occasion (pp. 557, 572, 573). But undoubtedly his judicial role, assumed as much from vanity as from solicitude for moral equity, is not devoid, especially in Crabtree, of a certain morbid relish (p. 564) which is dangerous for Peregrine.

In a second phase, Peregrine launches into a whirlwind of dissipation and follies, punctuated by pranks of varying degrees of outrageousness (pp. 577–81). Debauchery, extravagant spending, the vanity of being the boon companion of a band of young noblemen, all notorious black sheep and spendthrifts, plunge Peregrine into these 'nocturnal riots and revels, among a set of young noblemen, who had denounced war against temperance, œconomy, and common sense' (p. 581). Nevertheless all hope of moral reformation is not lost, for Peregrine, in his heart of hearts, continues to hate these ways of behaviour (p. 582). But it is possible to measure the progress of his moral corruption, whose development takes place 'insensibly', 'imperceptibly' (p. 582), by comparing his activities with his ones in Bath where he chastised the gamblers instead of offering himself to them as a willing victim. Peregrine's excesses are all the more violent for not being continuous, since they are subject to 'intervening checks of reason' (p. 583). The marriage of his friend Godfrey enables him to see Emilia again. She is still as implacable as ever (pp. 587–8) in her haughty refusal to be reconciled with him, in spite of the good offices of her brother, her sister-in-law, and even the clumsy intervention of Pipes, who, for the second time, seriously compromises his master's relations with the Gauntlet family (pp. 593–4). Emilia's hardness is, in fact, dictated more by her inflexible pride (pp. 592, 595) than by her deep resentment, and Pipes's unfortunate stratagem has at least the merit of revealing this (p. 593).

Peregrine, thus punished more rigorously than he deserves, decides to avenge himself on a society whose worldly conventions wound him to the core. He sets out to transform a beggar-girl[18] into a young society lady (pp. 599–601). The partial success of this plan is a vengeful satire on a pseudo-education which is almost entirely superficial. After this relatively calm interlude, Peregrine returns to his follies which cost him more and more dear (pp. 606–8). A swindling, very glib-tongued nobleman turns his mind towards politics, advises him to economise and promptly involves him in a shady business transaction in which Peregrine invests three-quarters of his fortune, already reduced by half (pp. 609–10). At this point, the hero's moral confusion is such that he can no longer clearly distinguish between vice and virtue. He continues to show himself generous in private, but criticises these acts in public (pp. 611–12). Like Matthew Bramble, Peregrine 'did good as other people do evil, that is, by stealth' (p. 611).

After his costly and futile attempt to enter political life, Peregrine's

financial downfall is precipitated. The summary of Chapter xcviii states
that the hero 'descends gradually, in the Condition of Life'. A parallel
social decline begins for him: 'he was obliged to descend another degree'
(p. 622). Crabtree reappears, like a bird of ill omen (p. 630), and Peregrine
quarrels with the old cynic whose almost sadistic morbidity he begins to
suspect. Peregrine, in punishing his former associate, explicitly condemns
his misanthropy (p. 630). After a comic literary interlude of some twenty
pages, highly autobiographical in character, but whose theme is in accordance with Smollett's repeated condemnation of vanity throughout the
book, the news of the almost total loss of his fortune (p. 635) obliges
Peregrine to work as a translator to make a living. Even in this less brilliant
milieu, he retains his feeling of superiority (p. 665). For the first time in
his life, he puts up a fight against a crushing adversity: 'he maintained a
good battle with disappointment' (p. 667). But the news of his total ruin
(ibid.) induces a physical and psychological paroxysm close on madness
(pp. 667–70). A virulent libel on the minister who has duped him leads to
his being sent to prison. There Peregrine draws up the bitter balance-sheet
of a life and fortune frittered away (p. 678). On this occasion, Smollett
outlines a theory of the passions which is closely linked with toxicology.
The poison of grief is soon effectively counteracted by the antidote of
vengeance, which gives him back his taste for life. But this imprisonment
marks most of all for Peregrine the beginning of a forced, but willingly
accepted, asceticism, very much harsher than that endured by Roderick.
Prison also plays the role of a maieutic for him. He realises at last that
happiness is to be found in oneself and not in the hollow shams of a
corrupt society. 'Let me search in my own breast for that peace and
contentment, which I have not been able to find in all the scenes of my
success' (p. 678). This resolution is confirmed by the last sentence of his
examination of conscience: 'After all, a jail is the best tub to which a
cynic philosopher can retire' (ibid.).

But prison is also a social microcosm ('microcosm' is used on p. 682)
where he meets other people who have gone down in the world, mainly as
a result of follies dictated by their vanity. This society in miniature has its
own laws, applied with rigorous equity. Not without irony, Smollett
describes the trial of an attorney charged with theft and of a naval
lieutenant-commander accused of sowing disorder in the prison (pp.
684–5). Peregrine thus enters an inverted world, which, while preserving
contemporary social structures, is not its true image, since the reflection,
especially in the matter of justice, corrects the reality. So he adapts
himself to his new way of life and evinces a philosophical detachment
with regard to the world outside (p. 692).

It is at this point Smollett brings in the edifying story of the unfortunate MacKercher, which occupies a place analogous to that of Melopoyn
in *Roderick Random*. Like the scorned poet, MacKercher is 'one of the
most flagrant instances of neglected virtue which the world can produce'

(p. 692). The story of MacKercher plays a contrasting role in the moral structure of *Peregrine Pickle* to that of Lady Vane. If pleasure dominates the life of Lady Vane, charity, thwarted by human perfidy, is the core of MacKercher's existence. In a sense, Lady Vane and MacKercher are both victims of society. But if the one, in spite of her disappointments, gains much from the worldly advantages due to her rank, the other is ready to sacrifice everything in order to see truth triumph in the Annesley affair. In a word, MacKercher represents for Smollett 'a rare instance of primitive benevolence' (p. 735). MacKercher is possessed by the demon of good.

Even in misfortune, Peregrine retains his inflexible pride. He refuses the generous help of Pipes and Hatchway (pp. 736, 740–1). He even quarrels with his two faithful comrades (pp. 744–5), who do not, for all that, desert him. But he turns in more and more upon himself and cuts himself off from the other prisoners (p. 746), thus shutting himself off in a claustrophobic world in which madness[19] lies in wait for him. Another series of catastrophes befalls him (p. 747) but he remains unshakable. The result is a social, psychological and moral alienation (p. 748) which leads him to wish for death. Having reached this perigee of his life, Peregrine feels as much hatred for himself as for the outside world (ibid.). But from Chapter cix to the end — that is to say in some thirty pages, less artificial than the end of *Roderick Random* — Peregrine sees his fate take a kindlier turn. The *vir bonus ex machina*, Godfrey, playing a part here analogous to Bowling in *Roderick Random*, rediscovers a misanthropic Peregrine who is no more than the ghost of himself (p. 751). Good tidings flow in as fast apace as formerly bad ones did (pp. 752–6). Even Emilia decides to break her cruel silence and at last renounces all appearance of resentment (p. 759). But here a double obstacle intervenes to hinder the swift conclusion of their marriage. Emilia has just become an heiress and her situation as a rich woman forbids the proud Peregrine to marry her when he himself is ruined. Besides this motive of personal pride (p. 760), which Godfrey does not hesitate to criticise, there is a more solid reason which proves the moral development of the hero. For the first time, just like Roderick towards the end of his adventures, Peregrine proves that he is at last capable of self-denial (p. 761). Smollett is careful to make clear that this resolution is not entirely praiseworthy, since a large proportion of haughty obstinacy enters into it which makes him describe his hero as a 'headstrong humorist' (p. 762) in his relations with Emilia. Their roles are reversed, and Peregrine's — momentary — inflexibility leads to a dangerous social and emotional checkmate. It is the very cause of his difficulties, money, which providentially solves them: *Aurum ex machina*. Peregrine's father dies intestate, and his eldest son inherits his entire fortune. Thus money, which had alienated him from Emilia, brings her back to him, just as the sea, which had deprived Roderick of his fortune, procures him another one and restores him to his father, Narcissa and happiness. Although Peregrine inherits a considerable fortune — £80,000 — he has also bought, and at a high price, 'a stock of experience' (p. 766).

Fortified by these costly lessons (p. 770), it is a changed Peregrine, all moderation, who meets Emilia again in London where his frantic impatience to become the husband of his beloved hurries on this long-deferred marriage. A twofold antithetical movement marks the closing lines of the novel. From now on, Peregrine despises the social world of London where he frittered away his first fortune. He not only pays his financial debts, he also pays off his arrears of resentment against those who jeered at him in his misfortunes. But the second movement is even more significant. Just like Roderick, Peregrine abandons the tainted and futile pleasures of the town and retires with his wife to the country, to live on the estate left to him by his father. For Smollett, happiness, far away from the forces of evil described almost exclusively in their manifold urban forms in *Peregrine Pickle*, can only be found in the depths of a rural retreat.

The lack of structure, of which *Roderick Random* and *Peregrine Pickle* are so often accused, is only apparent on the surface. Under the chaos of incidents, anecdotes, adventures and interpolated stories, the very unity of moral life with its alternating peaks and precipices gives these two novels their structure. It is even possible to construct a stylised diagram of these structures. The adventures of *Roderick Random* follow a geometrical pattern like a capital 'W', whose three high points, from left to right would represent Roderick's birth, his meeting Narcissa again in Bath, and his marriage, while the two symmetrical low ones would symbolise his shipwreck and his sojourn in prison. It is obvious that these segments schematise unequal sections of the novel since the shipwreck, for example, occurs about halfway through it. Moreover, each segment is the abstract and idealised figuration of the general direction the hero's life follows, rather than a systematic transposition of *all* the incidents Roderick lives through. In other words, these segments are an abstraction which covers a number of microstructures, as the previous analysis of various articulations has demonstrated. During the first half of *Roderick Random*, Roderick's lot is not uniformly on the decline; the hero has some respites, and even some brief periods of good luck. Finally, although Smollett has paid more attention to the construction of his novels than critics in general have been willing to admit, it would be dangerous to go to the opposite extreme and be determined, at all costs, to see a firmly established intention of creating a global structure. In fact, it is probable that these thematic structures are not organised by a completely conscious process but rather obey an inner compulsion more or less independent of the author's intentions. This is a literary phenomenon which does not

apply solely to Smollett. Paul Fussell has called it 'the pattern of comic —
or ironic — reversal', and he explains it thus:

> This motif — a perennial favourite of conservatives — suggests a
> pitfall concealed at the end of an inviting open road or a sudden
> unmarked precipice which opens at the end of a pleasant mountain
> trail. Whether we encounter it in fiction — Fielding and Smollett
> delight in it — in memoirs, letters, journals, essays, poems or travel-
> books, the pattern is the same. It consists of two elements betoken-
> ing in their way the perpetual dualistic rhythms which introduce a
> kind of moral order into the continuum of human experience. We
> have first a protracted but smooth ascent to some height of felicity
> or optimistic perception; this condition then precipitates a sudden,
> surprising reversal, a rapid descent into perception or comic dis-
> illusion — the two being very much the same thing. One implication
> of this beloved humanist motif is that, although the human capacity
> for self-delusion is infinitely varied, it is yet possible for humanity to
> redeem itself by sudden, last-minute perceptions of its natural limita-
> tions. A similar implication of the motif seems to be this: it renders
> metaphorically the action of the movement towards wisdom. It is as
> if the eighteenth century protagonist were condemned to re-enact
> constantly a sort of wry, psychological, secular version of the action
> of losing a paradise but — '*O felix culpa*' — gaining a firmer
> humanity[20].

The connection between *Roderick Random* and *Peregrine Pickle* is
tacitly admitted by Smollett when he makes Morgan reappear in Chapter
xxxviii of *Peregrine Pickle*, which enables him to give some details about
the fate — a happy one — of the ebullient Welsh apothecary and of
Roderick and his wife (pp. 183–5). This inclusion of former characters is
like the restricted and clumsy beginning of a *comédie humaine*, in which,
as in Balzac's novels, the heroes continue to lead their lives throughout
several works. But there is also a certain parallelism of structure, without
Peregrine Pickle being, for all that, the faithful reproduction of *Roderick
Random*. It would be possible to schematise the structure of *Peregrine
Pickle* (with the reservations stated above) not by a 'W' but by a 'V'. The
top left horizontal edge represents the introduction of the characters, the
descending section Peregrine's moral development from his early childhood to his imprisonment and the ascending one the extraordinarily rapid
recrudescence of his fortune, ending at the top right edge on a plateau of
marital happiness. The technical imbalance is still more evident in
Peregrine Pickle. But, in both the novels, the author's moral preoccupation is the same. Behind pride and the many forms it takes (more cultural
in Roderick, more social in Peregrine), it is the conflict of the forces of
good and evil that fascinates Smollett. Pride, charged as it is with
ambiguous, indeed contrary, affectivity, tending at once towards the life

and the destruction of the individual, is, according to Hatchway's perspicacious conclusion, 'no better than self-murder' (p. 755). According to Pope's formula in *The Essay on Man* (I, ll. 189—90):

> The bliss of man (could pride that blessing find)
> Is not to act or think beyond mankind.

Wishing to upset the established order of their little world is a sin for which Roderick and Peregrine pay dear, whether in suffering or in cash. Smollett condemns the artificiality of pride and, in so doing, implicitly preaches a return to nature, the very core of primitivist morality[21]. But Smollett refuses, for all that, to moralise out of season, and lets fly a passing shot in a stinging paragraph aimed at Fielding's habits in *Tom Jones*: 'I look upon this practice as an impertinent anticipation of the peruser's thoughts' he declares (pp. 682—3). To what extent does he respect his own counsels in *Ferdinand Count Fathom* and *Launcelot Greaves*?

5
Ferdinand Count Fathom **and** *Launcelot Greaves*: **the moral antipodes**

Seven years (1753—60) separate *Ferdinand Count Fathom* and *Launcelot Greaves*, the two of Smollett's novels which the public and the critics admired least. But, apart from this fortuitous link of lack of success, everything seems to make these two works a complete contrast. The psychological, moral and literary distance which separates them is far greater than the time interval might predictably account for. Fathom and Launcelot appear as antithetical characters, the first wholly dedicated to Evil, the second devoting all his physical and moral powers to the accomplishment of Good. On one side, the traitor, the scoundrel, who oscillates between drama and melodrama, only just avoiding tragedy; on the other, a paladin in armour astray on the highroads of eighteenth-century England, a gallant but occasionally mad knight-errant in the service of Good. The contrast extends even to the form of these two novels. *Ferdinand Count Fathom* is nearly twice as long as *Launcelot Greaves*, whose monthly publication necessarily influenced its content by imposing, sometimes indeed artificially, the composition of the story in sections, each of which could stand on its own, whereas such cutting up into instalments would have been far more difficult in *Ferdinand Count Fathom*.

The point of view of the eponymous heroes differs radically, but, in reality, the moral purpose, illuminated from two antipodal sources, remains the same in these novels. In wishing to plumb with Fathom[1] the depths of moral degradation, Smollett is far from forgetting the existence of Good in its providential or human manifestations. But he does not always escape falling into a systematic Manichean dichotomy which is anything but realistic. Whatever the literary value of this contrast, sometimes emphasised with clumsy insistence, this moral preoccupation, more didactic in *Ferdinand Count Fathom*, more fanciful in *Launcelot Greaves*, permeates and underlies these novels and gives them their thematic structures. Even more than in *Roderick Random* or *Peregrine Pickle*, Smollett appears fascinated by the battle, often dubious in its outcome, in which the forces of Good and Evil are engaged on a triple level, individual, social and metaphysical. The moralising intentions of the author are made plain right at the beginning of the auto-dedication of *Ferdinand Count Fathom*, where there is mention of 'remuneration of merit' as well as of 'disgrace and discomfiture of vice' (p. 3). Smollett does not escape the moral mercantilism which stamps the eighteenth-century novel: the reward of virtue is happiness. Griffiths, in the *Monthly Review* of March 1753 (vol. viii), after having expressed some reservations about the plausibility of such a monster of iniquity as Fathom, nevertheless recognised the didactic value of the book:

> The Story of *Melville* [*sic*] and *Monimia* affords as fine a lesson as we remember to have ever met with, against that criminal *credulity* by which the peace of many families hath been destroyed, and the ruin of many innocent and unsuspecting persons effected (p. 205).

Contrary to more recent critics, Griffiths applauds the final conversion of Fathom, always on the ground of its moral value: 'his self-accusation, and retrospective view of his past conduct, is very pathetic, and adapted to answer the moral end which the author professes ... to have had in view' (p. 206). Mrs Delany, in her letters of March and April 1753, makes three allusions to *Ferdinand Count Fathom*, for which she does not feel unmitigated admiration. But she recognises that: 'Though a great deal bad there are some things very interesting, and the whole well-intended.' More explicit is her final commentary, which has the merit of comparing *Ferdinand Count Fathom* with the novels of the day. She writes to her correspondent, Mrs Dewes:

> I agree with you in your opinion of the modern stories; they do not build on a right foundation. Their *heroes* (whatever their heroines are) are never virtuous ... I think 'Count Fathom' (though a bad, affected style) written with a better intention, and Melvin's [*sic*] character a good one, but they none of them are to be named in a day with our good friend Richardson[2].

It is significant that, in order to judge *Ferdinand Count Fathom*, Mrs Delany refers more or less explicitly to the moral and fictional criteria dear to Richardson. Monimia is not without some distant feminine and literary kinship with Pamela and Clarissa.

The analysis of Smollett's borrowings from *Don Quixote* has already made it possible to show that behind the chivalric mask and the mask of madness, Smollett wished to create a redresser of very real wrongs and abuses rampant about the middle of the eighteenth century. In his profession of faith at the beginning of the novel, Launcelot declares that he proposes to act 'as a coadjutor to the law, and even to remedy evils which the law cannot reach' (p. 14). From the quasipathological delin- quent[3], Fathom, to the lover of justice stricken by the madness of Good, Launcelot, moral preoccupation dominates Smollett's fictional creation. The analysis of the thematic structure of these two novels will enable the causes of the partial failure of *Ferdinand Count Fathom* and *Launcelot Greaves* to be more accurately determined. As in the previous chapter, the juxtaposition of the critical proceedings has seemed prefer- able to any artificially synthetic method.

Just as for *Roderick Random*, but in more detail, Smollett clearly indi- cates his conception of the novel as a whole. This conscious aim of general organisation appears in the auto-dedication, where Smollett ventures to give a now-famous definition of the novel. The word 'plan' is used three times in a single page of the auto-dedication (p. 2). Smollett offers a twofold definition of the novel. He distinguishes, in the first place, the background of the canvas 'a large diffused picture, comprehending the characters of life, disposed in different groupes, and exhibited in various attitudes, for the purposes of an uniform plan, and general occurrence, to which every individual figure is subservient' (ibid.). This oft-quoted defini- tion has not always aroused the sympathy and understanding of the critics[4]. It is interesting that Smollett should have used the vocabulary of painting, and, more specifically, that of composition. The author likens the novel to a canvas on which he disposes groups of people, characterised by their actions or their occupations. Against this human background, a central personage stands out who attracts and retains the attention, just as in a picture. Such is the second half of this definition.

Consequently, it is natural to expect an antithetical structure in *Ferdinand Count Fathom*. The rise and fall of Fathom in some ways recall the general plan of *Jonathan Wild*, where the hero is subjected to the caprices of Dame Fortune (Book iv, Chapter 1). But the antithesis is also found in the character. Smollett takes pains to insist (somewhat heavily) on the deliberate contrast between Fathom and Melvil, whereas Fielding avoids this radical opposition of Tom Jones and Blifil. He prides himself on having 'raised up a virtuous character, in opposition to the adventurer, with a view to ... form a striking contrast which might heighten the expression, and give a *Relief* to the moral of the whole' (p. 3). And this poses the fascinating problem of literary teratogeny which has resulted in so many failures for writers who have set out to create a perfect monster. Smollett has felt the necessity of giving a virtuous counterpart to the iniquities of Fathom but he has not always managed to avoid a moral Manicheism which is both artificial and boring. This failure can be all the better assessed by comparing the solutions to this problem proposed by

147

novelists who were Smollett's contemporaries. In creating Mr B. and Lovelace, Richardson was wise enough to allow them just enough goodness to make their designs not uniformly ebony black, but capable of assuming a whole range of moral shades. Fielding returned on several occasions to this problem which lies at the very heart of literary creation, especially for the novelists of the eighteenth century.

At the end of his preface to *Joseph Andrews*, Fielding replies in advance to the criticisms which might be levelled against him for having introduced the description of vices into his novel:

> To which I shall answer: first, that it is very difficult to pursue a series of human actions, and keep clear from them. Secondly, that the vices to be found here are rather the accidental consequences of some human frailty or foible, than causes existing in the mind. Thirdly, that they are never set forth as the object of ridicule, but detestation. Fourthly, that they are never the principal figure at that time on the scene: and, lastly, they never produce the intended evil.

It is a pity that Smollett when he composed *Ferdinand Count Fathom*, did not remember this fourth rule enunciated by Fielding. There is the same rejection of extremes in *Jonathan Wild*: nature

> seldom creates any man so completely great, or completely low, but that some sparks of humanity will glimmer in the former, and some sparks of what the vulgar call evil will dart forth in the latter: utterly to extinguish which will give some pain, and uneasiness to both (Book iv, end of Chapter 4).

Even more explicit is the friendly apostrophe to the reader (Book X, Chapter 1) in *Tom Jones*. After having reminded him that it is unnecessary to condemn a character because he is not a model of perfection, Fielding concludes:

> To say the truth, I a little question whether mere man ever arrived at this consummate degree of excellence, as well as there hath ever existed a monster bad enough to verify that:
>
> — 'nulla virtute redemptum
> A vitiis — '
>
> in Juvenal; nor do I, indeed, conceive that the good purposes served by inserting characters of such angelic perfection, or such diabolical depravity, in any work of invention.

Smollett's technique therefore marks a definite literary and psychological recession in comparison with the tolerance shot with irony which Fielding advocates in his novels. The antithetical structure which Smollett adopts in *Ferdinand Count Fathom* results in a double series of literary phenomena. First of all, it would seem that Smollett had conceived his novel as a fictional Noah's ark in which the characters would meekly embark in opposite couples. Fathom—Melvil, Teresa—Mademoiselle de Melvil and, most notably, Monimia, Madame La Mer—Madame Clement, the good Jew Joshua—the merciless usurers, these are the most important pairs of opposite characters. The second phenomenon, to wit the mixture of genres, without any transition brought about by the unfolding of the story or the evolution of the characters, constitutes the major defect of the novel. Fathom and his nefarious cynicism dominate three-quarters of the novel almost uninterruptedly, then, in the last ten chapters, this story dissolves into a lachrymose melodrama. These floods and torrents of tears which spout from Smollett's pen drown the dramatic interest, already lessened by the obsessive didactic and moral intention of the author.

It is not impossible that Smollett was vaguely aware of the dangers of this antithetical structure. All through the novel, but especially at the beginning and in the first half, he endeavours to maintain a distance between himself and his characters, so as to avoid their becoming mere fictional puppets committed to acting as spokesmen for his ethical, psychological or metaphysical convictions. This attempt to be ironically impartial (which assured the success of *Jonathan Wild*) assumes a double aspect, one historical, the other mythological. It is curious to note how insistently Smollett tries to pass himself off as a historian, or again as a memorialist, in the first pages of *Ferdinand Count Fathom*. As he repeatedly stressed in connection with the *Complete History of England* and the *Continuation of the Complete History of England*, he envisaged the role of the historian as that of an impartial, dispassionate narrator, unprejudiced by any personal bias — a noble ideal which he did not always live up to, far from it!

As if to protect himself from stating a direct opinion (which is the opposite of irony) Smollett takes care to begin his book with some observations on Cardinal de Retz as a famous memorialist. The words 'historians', 'history', 'historical truth', 'memoirs' (pp. 5–6) are driven home in these first pages as if to reinforce the fiction of a narrative *transmitted* (p. 6) by Smollett with all the desirable objective detachment. With a heavy historical irony — doubtless not uninfluenced by *Jonathan Wild*, but Smollett would then be revealed as a paltry imitator of that masterpiece — he compares the eventful arrival of Fathom on the shores of England in turn to the landing of Julius Caesar and to that of Scipio on the coast of Africa (pp. 128–9). More laboured still is the mythological irony. Following the mock-heroic tradition, Smollett likens vulgar, corrupt and inferior characters to gods or goddesses. The more ordinary, not to say trite, the subject, the more elaborately artificial the lexical and syntactical expression becomes. Thus Smollett appeals to mythology (pp. 6–7) to suggest that, in the heroic age, Fathom would undoubtedly have been regarded as an extraordinary being of divine origin. Terms such as 'uncommon', 'promising', 'extraordinary' (ibid.), the use of 'greatness'

(p. 6) betray the conscious imitation of Fielding's irony in *Jonathan Wild* (Book i, Chapter 2) where history and mythology are combined to compose a burlesque genealogy. It is above all Fathom's mother who excites Smollett's historical and mythological irony. This vivandière of death is transformed in turn into an amazon (p. 12), Penthesilea (p. 14), Camilla (p. 15), Atropos, Semiramis, Tomyris, Zenobia and Thalestris (p. 16) which is a good deal for a mere murderous whore. Was mythology, for Smollett, an ironic method of disguising his literary misogyny? The beautiful daughter of the Viennese jeweller, in her ragings as a deceived and deserted mistress, is also compared to Thalestris and Penthesilea (pp. 71–2). 'Enraged Thalestris' is applied a second time to a coarse Wapping landlady whose Billingsgate eloquence arouses a comparison with the verbal contests in which the matrons of Athens engaged during the Eleusinia (p. 131). Smollett had already compared the imprecations of the jeweller's daughter to the hymn of the Spartan women round the altar of Diana (p. 62). Only the unhappy Elenor has the honour to be compared to Helen of Troy (p. 141).

Why has this attempt at ironic detachment, inspired by Fielding[5], failed? The post-mortem on a literary failure is rendered all the more perilous by the fact that two centuries of critical accretions have proliferated on the *corpus depicti*. It is nevertheless possible to suggest that the discontinuous use of this ironic detachment in its historical and mythological form (and also in the form of a more or less explicit commentary contained in the chapter headings) has probably contributed to the architectural heaviness of *Ferdinand Count Fathom*. Moreover, if the adventures of a scoundrel like Fathom lent themselves very readily to being treated with a satirical irony that brings out his basic ambiguity (Fathom's social impostures condemn their author but they equally condemn the corrupt society which more or less directly encourages them), all possibility of irony is quenched in the sentimental and tear-sodden atmosphere which pervades the last quarter of the novel. The sentimentality, not to say mawkishness of Monimia and Melvil at the end of the book prohibits all detachment, all seeing things in perspective, all that critical self-examination which irony implies. Thanks to irony, consciousness frees itself from the emotional weight of the immediate present, wrenches itself out of that sticky morass of tears and becomes capable once more of assuming the responsibilities of its past and its future. Fielding's irony lightens *Jonathan Wild*: the heaviness of Smollett's sinks *Ferdinand Count Fathom*.

These remarks on the plan, the antithetical structure and the attempted distanciation enable the technical skeleton of *Ferdinand Count Fathom*, that is to say the aggregate of (often theatrical) methods used in constructing its framework, to be more clearly distinguished. Kahrl (pp. 52–3), as Pearce[6] did earlier, observes the influence of Congreve's *Double Dealer* (1694) and Otway's *The Orphan* (1680) on *Ferdinand*

Count Fathom. Smollett himself, in the auto-dedication (p. 3) alludes to Richard III and Maskwell as theatrical types of 'villains'. Later (p. 222) he plays on the name of Otway's heroine (Monimia) to remind young Melvil of his amorous torments. The name Monimia, undoubtedly borrowed from Otway, features already in *Roderick Random* (II, 224—5). It is to her that Melopoyn dedicates his elegy, whose three last stanzas create an atmosphere of melancholy where the stock properties of terror (the lonely church, the gloomy castle, ghosts, mildew and tears) already herald, in a much simplified way, the lachrymose and pre-Gothic orgies of *Ferdinand Count Fathom*. In fact, the tragic misunderstanding at the core of Otway's plays is not developed to the full in *Ferdinand Count Fathom* which contains only the rough draft of a tragedy. Neither Polydore nor Castalio is fundamentally a 'villain'. The unhappy love they bear Monimia, the cruel and tragic play of fate, transform a commonplace lovers' rivalry into a series of catastrophes. Mrs Cibber (to whom Smollett alludes in *Peregrine Pickle*) and her interpretation of the part of Monimia probably inspired Smollett more than Otway's character. As to Congreve's play, it presents a similarity with *Ferdinand Count Fathom* much more than a definite source. In Maskwell, just as in Fathom, there is a deep and innate sense of evil. Both being of humble origin, they are forced to seek the favour of their master. Both have strong sexual appetites, characterised by the swift onset of revulsion after the conquest, a frequent symptom in pathological Don Juans. Maskwell tires of possessing Lady Touchwood as Fathom does of his amorous successes. Finally their cupidity is obvious: they are both 'on the make'. Maskwell, however, has a far more fertile malefic imagination. He is able to mobilise all his resources at a moment's notice. He surpasses and outclasses Fathom, whose frauds often fail to succeed and are nearly always petty. Maskwell's technique is far subtler than that of Fathom, who remains at best, or rather at worst, a scruffy, small-time crook, a *picaro raté*. It is not surprising that Maskwell shows no sign of repentance. He keeps silent when he is discovered and displays up to the last that cynicism to which people who wish to be, and think themselves, superior are addicted. There is ambiguity as well in Maskwell's character. How can he not feel superior to the idle rich, such people as Lord and Lady Froth or Sir Paul Plyant who surround him? Maskwell and Fathom both exploit human weaknesses. They bemuse people with the mirages of Truth and Falsehood. Their best mask is often the absence of a mask:

> No mask like open truth to cover lies,
> As to go naked is the best disguise (Act V, sc. 1).

The lesson of this ambiguity is certainly bound to be unpleasant, but it also, in the long run, has some artistic — that is to say didactic and moral — value, as Maskwell stresses in Act V, sc. 3: 'Why, *qui vult decipi, decipiatur* — Tis no fault of mine. I have told 'em; and if they will not

151

hear the serpent's hiss, they must be stung into experience, and future caution.' Monimia and Melvil must have been deaf.

Those tenons and mortises of the framework of a novel, chronological and historical references, are not lacking, especially in the first part of *Ferdinand Count Fathom*, whereas the geographical indications, which are fewer, remain very vague. It is disappointing to find that the most cosmopolitan of Smollett's novels, whose action takes place in turn in Vienna, Paris and London, not to mention Presburg, Belgrade, Prague and Brussels, is almost devoid of local colour. The Bohemia of *Ferdinand Count Fathom* is a featureless Ruritania. On the other hand, there are abundant historical points of reference. There is nothing surprising in this, since Fathom spends his childhood and part of his youth following the campaigns of an army. The first indication of this kind, 'the last year of the renowned Marlborough's command' (p. 7) places the beginning of the action probably in 1711, since the great commander fell into disgrace on the last day of 1711. Ferdinand was in his sixth year when Prince Eugene won the battle against the Turks, on August 5th 1716, at Petervarad on the Danube. Smollett gives the number of the forces engaged: 60,000 Imperial troops against 150,000 Turks. The latter were so completely routed that they left an enormous quantity of booty behind. While she is robbing the dead and wounded, Fathom's mother discovers a wounded officer of her own side and decides to save his life, from self-interest rather than humanitarian motives. Once cured, Count de Melvil becomes the benefactor of young Fathom, whom he brings up with his son of the same age. Smollett sets his novel against a solid historical background. In the *Complete History of England*[7], a few years later, he recalls, in a note, the same number of troops and adds: 'The infidels were totally defeated, with the loss of all their tents, artillery, and baggage; so that the victors obtained an immense booty.' There are other allusions to Prince Eugene's victories: Temiswaer, 1716 (p. 13), Belgrade, 1717 (p. 14). It was at this battle that Fathom's mother died, from when on he was entirely under the protection of Count de Melvil. After the peace of Passarowitz, 1718 (p. 18), the Count retires with his young protégé to the bosom of his family in Presburg. As well as giving these historical landmarks, on several occasions Smollett mentions Fathom's age. At the battle of Belgrade (August 16th 1717), Fathom has just entered his ninth year (p. 16); at twelve (p. 22), he begins to be interested in women; at sixteen (p. 24), he plans to seduce his benefactor's daughter; at eighteen, he accompanies young Melvil to Vienna (p. 40), where he spends two years (p. 73). The only important chronological indication in the second half of the novel is the length of Melvil's and Serafina-Monimia's stay in Great Britain, about eighteen months (p. 339). Melvil has been in London eight months (p. 200) when he meets Fathom again.

Another element in the technical framework is the interplay of chance and Providence, those zealous but overworked servants of the omniscient novelist. Fathom's whole life is placed under the sign of chance, lucky or unlucky. Engendered by the chance copulation of some soldier and a promiscuous camp-follower, the orphan fortuitously becomes the protégé of Count de Melvil. After having made the acquaintance of Ratchcali, his Tyrolese confederate, in Vienna, he meets him again in Philipsburg (p. 75), 'an accidental meeting', then again in London where 'He by accident encounters his old friend' (p. 143). These re-encounters with Ratchcali set the action going again each time. The two accomplices promptly engage in a new series of swindles and other misdeeds. It is likely that Smollett wishes to suggest a parallel between the heroic manner in which young Don Diego de Zelos saves his commander, Don Gonzales Orgullo (p. 112) and the same courageous behaviour of Melvil who, by the greatest chance, arrives just in time to lend a hand to Don Diego when he is fighting with a gang of highwaymen (pp. 309–10). Chance, in the person of Fathom—Fadini, serves to link the love interest (Melvil—Monimia) to the sub-plot of the misadventures of Don Diego. Such is the dramatic function of the story of the noble Castilian and his unfortunate involvements with Fathom—Fadini (Chapters xxv and xxvi). Mercury, god of amorous adventures, ought to have watched over Fathom when he surprises the intentions of the jeweller's fair and flouted daughter: 'but fate ordained, that the design should be defeated, in order to reserve him for more important occasions' (p. 70). But chance does not smile on scoundrels only and, in spite of their ordeals, Melvil and Monimia also benefit from its favours. For example, the doctor who treats Monimia, when she has taken refuge with Madame Clement, is a foreigner who knows Melvil. He can immediately assure Madame Clement that certain allegations of Fathom's are, to his knowledge, false, which naturally reinforces the benefactress's resolution (p. 241). Melvil, in the grip of a morbid melancholy has the luck to run into − 'a fortunate rencounter' (p. 283) − a former comrade-in-arms, Major Farrel, who snaps him out of his gloomy, paralysing daydreams and urges him (cautiously) to take a line of direct or indirect action and put an end to the machinations of Count Trebasi. This last, as a tyrannical stepfather, has promptly sent Mademoiselle de Melvil into a convent in Vienna, where Wilhelmina, seduced and abandoned by Fathom, has just taken the veil (p. 297). Through this repentant sinner, Mademoiselle de Melvil learns of Fathom's baseness and is able at last, not without difficulty, to open her brother's eyes. The fortuitous re-encounter with Ratchcali, now a convict serving a life sentence, allows Smollett to get rid of a character he no longer needs and at the same time to confirm Fathom's crimes to Melvil. The moral intention of such a scene is obviously trite: the wicked always end up by being punished, and Fathom will not escape the justice of God and man. Melvil and retribution are on the march.

But, before this, Fathom has already benefited at least twice from the kindly interventions of Providence. A first time (p. 133, see the heading of Chapter xxix), Fathom is delivered just in time from the clumsy and dangerous clutches of a magistrate, thanks to the intervention of a young nobleman who arrives at the inn where the mockery of a trial is being held. Melvil's discovery of Fathom in prison (p. 196) is announced at the beginning of Chapter xlii as 'an unexpected rencounter, and a happy revolution in the affairs of our adventurer' (ibid.). These meetings, so providential for Fathom, mark a point of contact between the senti-mental sub-plot (the thwarted love of Melvil and Monimia) and the adven-ture story (the impostures of Fathom). But it is, above all, Monimia and Melvil who have a right to the favours of Providence. The last quarter of the novel is even marked by frequent allusions tinged with a sancti-monious sentimental religiosity, which, coming from the pen of Smollett, is both shocking and boring in its extreme artificiality. Already, after the attempt at seduction perpetrated by Fathom on the chaste Monimia, the latter only owes her rescue to the intervention of a charitable widow, Madame Clement, which Smollett describes as 'providential deliverance' (p. 239). One may wonder whether the repetition of this cliché, already used (p. 133, see above), but the first time in connection with Fathom, is stylistic carelessness or whether it reveals a conscious manipulation of irony. In the case of Monimia, Smollett again feels the need to emphasise (perhaps in the vain hope of hiding it) the quasi-miraculous improbability of this intervention, by speaking of 'sudden and unlooked-for transition' (p. 240). It is the Catholic Don Diego who, most of all, readily addresses his prayers or his thanks to Providence, to Heaven or to the Almighty[8]. These pious ejaculations are all the more incongruous since Don Diego is a tough Castilian warrior, more accustomed to wield the sword than the holy-water sprinkler. His religious convictions give place, at the end of the novel, to a latitudinarian tolerance, perhaps œcumenical before its time, but in direct opposition to the views of the Inquisition.

A last manifestation of both chance and Providence is the unforeseen manner in which the Melvils and their attendants suddenly contemplate the spectacle of Fathom at death's door at the beginning of the last chapter. The word 'spectacle' should not shock anyone's sensibility. It is indeed a final tableau to which Smollett invites his readers, a tableau where the barely veiled allegory takes precedence over the novel. The ways of Providence may perhaps be inscrutable but they lead the virtuous to happiness, the supreme moral and material reward, whereas Vice invariably ends by being punished. The moral and religious triteness of this ending is doubled by an almost intolerable display of bourgeois self-righteousness which is comparable, a century in advance, to the pious endings of those 'edifying' books on which good little Victorian children were brought up. The insipid Melvil loses what little sympathy his mis-fortunes may have aroused in the reader's mind when he adopts the biblical style (the use of 'thou', the antitheses, the pious injunctions) to exhort Fathom on his deathbed (p. 359). By wanting to insist overmuch during this emotional crisis, mercifully of short duration, on the immense goodness of Providence, Smollett ends up by sickening his readers with all this mawkish religiosity. Thus, in the course of the narrative, those dangerous Ariadne threads of the novelist, chance and Providence, become crude, mechanically jerked puppet-strings.

Other technical devices used in constructing the plot of the story are the author's direct interventions or, conversely, his omniscient silences, which interrupt the no less omniscient retrospections. Smollett's interventions in *Ferdinand Count Fathom* are of two kinds. At the beginning of the novel, he feels the need to justify himself, not only in the auto-dedication, but also by offering, on at least two subsequent occasions, his literary self-defence. The speech in his own defence, albeit not devoid of eloquence and of sincerity exasperated by the stereotyped reproaches of the critics, only repeats and develops the literary and moral argument adumbrated in the auto-dedication. Smollett anticipates the reader's objections and makes a direct reply to him. He rejects in advance any accusation of vulgarity for daring to describe 'the obscene objects of low life' (p. 7). This adjective 'low', for an eighteenth-century novelist, such as Fielding or Smollett, has a critical and caustic force whose virulence has almost evaporated after the lapse of two centuries. Smollett is indignant that, as a novelist, he is not able to touch on these reputedly 'low' subjects whereas the prestige of venerable antiquity (Petronius and Ovid for example) or of a more recent success (Swift, Pope) allows these authors not to incur the opprobrious epithet. Carried away by his wrath, Smollett foresees that such critical restrictions will end by killing all satirical wit and all vitality in the novel, so that 'the inoffensive pen for ever drops the mild manna of soul-sweetning praise' (p. 8). It is a pity that Smollett did not heed his own warning when he composed the last quarter of *Ferdinand Count Fathom*. The disappearance of the acid satire (implicit or explicit) contained in the adventures of Fathom, to be replaced by the treacly sentimentality of the ending provides a clear example of the alchemical mutation he deplores (ibid.). But however vigorous a defender of satire Smollett might be, he knew very well, even before his troubles with the law, that the handling of such vitriol had its dangers for an author. So he takes care to inform the reader that it is ridiculous *individuals* he attacks rather than *institutions* (p. 92). A wise precaution, after having drawn a series of unflattering parallels between the priests at the French court and the English 'Templars'. In order to forestall any possible legal action by a former 'Templar', or to avoid the accusation of being an anti-papist Gallophobe, he hastens to declare: 'while I laugh at the folly of particular members, I can still honour and revere the institution' (ibid.).

Another kind of intervention is the vigorously expressed moral judgment which is in direct contradiction to the initial intent of historical objectivity analysed above. Smollett's moral preoccupations are revealed for the first time at the end of Chapter vii. Teresa and Fathom have just bound themselves by a mock ceremony of marriage. Smollett inveighs against this absurd practice, which he explains by the survival of religious sentiment even in the most degraded human beings. The only justification of this paragraph would be, at a pinch, the preparation for Fathom's distant final conversion. But as, meanwhile, hardly anything occurs to remind one of this desperate act of faith in humanity, these didactic statements seem gratuitous, not to say pointless. However, the embarrassing pseudoreligious moralism of *Ferdinand Count Fathom* has at least the merit of proving that Smollett was far less impervious to these sentiments than critical tradition has long claimed him to be. Another paragraph of condemnation (p. 199) explicitly stresses Fathom's amoral hardness. But the best-known intervention in the novel is the one in which Smollett directly takes his character to task: 'Perfidious wretch! thy crimes turn out so atrocious, that I half repent me of having undertaken to record thy memoirs' (p. 242). It is paradoxical that, at the beginning of this apostrophe, Smollett resumes the vocabulary of the historian, when he has just violated the rule of objectivity he layed down for himself. Such a proceeding is the opposite of the irony in *Jonathan Wild* and reveals the total failure of the attempt at distanciation. But the pusillanimity of such a diatribe against a fictional personage also shows how much Smollett was caught up in the world of his characters. Finally, the horror inspired by Fathom's monstrosity retains, above all, a didactic and monitory value. Stigmatising vice was not enough to satisfy the public. Smollett is careful to let it be seen that vice defeats its own ends. Whatever the perfidy of Fathom, the virtue of Melvil and Monimia will ultimately triumph. This direct intervention of the author is also a structural artifice. So when vice seems to be triumphing, Smollett allows the reader to hope that all will turn out well for Melvil and that Fathom will be punished, thus preparing him for the final development of the plot.

Smollett's omniscient silences are eloquent preteritions. He has recourse to these devices either to hide the real identity of a character or to delay the unfolding of the plot, or at least defer the knowledge the reader may have of it. Thus, the stranger whom Don Diego welcomes into his family (p. 118) is none other than young Melvil travelling incognito in Spain. It must be said for Smollett that he does not spare his efforts to put the reader on the track. Don Diego suspects that this drawing-master is of noble birth but the latter 'still persisted in declaring himself the son of an obscure mechanic in Bohemia' (p. 119). Conversely, Melvil makes some allusions to his thwarted love (p. 198) and to his travels abroad (without further precision) under a disguise in order to avoid the search of his family who want to marry him against his will (pp. 199–200). All these details will be repeated and explained at the final *cognitio* (it would be more correct to speak of the final *cognitiones*). With the airiness of omniscience, Smollett abandons Elenor (also spelt 'Ellenor' or 'Elinor'), seduced, deserted and driven mad by Fathom, to Bedlam 'where we shall leave her for the present, happily bereft of her reason' (p. 147). A few much shorter indications imply that the mystery is temporary. Smollett decides to call his heroine 'Monimia' 'for the present' (p. 201). These few words must have whetted the curiosity and dramatic appetite of readers eager for sensational genealogical disclosures at the end of a novel.

Twice towards the end of *Ferdinand Count Fathom*, Smollett shame-lessly takes refuge behind his privileged position of author endowed with omniscience as regards his novel. Melvil tells Joshua, the good Jewish moneylender, the state of Don Diego's affairs 'with certain circumstances, which shall, in due time, be revealed' (p. 322). There is the same unskilful resort to this transparently obscure device when Melvil, still on the subject of Don Diego, 'communicated some circumstances, which shall appear in due season' (p. 328). Confronted with the clumsiness of such structural props, one cannot but regret the architect's skill and sureness displayed by Fielding in *Tom Jones*, or, in a different key the chronological and thematic tricks of Sterne in *Tristram Shandy*. The letter which Monimia, apparently deserted by Melvil, is writing after the departure of the faith-less one, will only be made known to the reader 'in due time' (p. 230) i.e. seventy pages later (pp. 300–1).

The retrospections which occur at intervals in the last ten chapters of *Ferdinand Count Fathom* are not unlike the speeches in classical plays which sum up the action that has taken place off-stage. Thus the whole of Chapter lvii, which marks the transition from adventure to melodrama, enables the threads of the love interest, broken off by Melvil's departure, to be picked up and rejoined. Smollett himself speaks of 'Retrospect' (p. 282) in connection with this chapter. It is also the function of Chapter lix, in which Mademoiselle de Melvil reveals Fathom's villainies to her brother. This kind of flashback is much less clumsy than that of Chapter lvii, where Smollett intervenes directly. The author must have realised the technical heavy-handedness of such a method, for the last two retrospec-tions are inserted more naturally in the narrative. Both times it is Melvil who informs the characters of the adventures he has previously been through. First, he gives a brief summary (p. 328) of his journey to Bohemia and his return to Great Britain. Later, in Chapter lxv, he solves the various little mysteries which had remained in suspense. Faithful to his stated definition of the novel, Smollett entitles this chapter: 'A retrospec-tive link, necessary to the concatenation of these memoirs' (p. 335). The novel would not be complete without a retrospective glimpse of the mis-fortunes of Fathom and his wife (pp. 356–8), who turns out to be none other than poor Elenor, cured of her madness and met again and married by Fathom in the debtors' prison of the Marshalsea. Situated elsewhere in the novel, this story of a Hogarthian downfall might well have become an interpolated narrative similar to that of Miss Williams in *Roderick Random* and been entitled 'The story of the fair Elenor'. This retrospec-tion is the most skilful, since it enables the reader to learn not only the fate of a woman who is likeable in spite of (or because of) her downfall, but also the series of catastrophes which have overwhelmed Fathom since his imprisonment, in other words, since his disappearance from the novel.

The technical structure of *Ferdinand Count Fathom*, the only one the critics disdainfully examine, is therefore clumsy; unbalanced by the direct interventions of the author and above all by the incompatibility of the adventure story in the line of Defoe — 'the novel of roguery' — with the unfortunate incursion into the sentimental novel dominated by Richardson. But without wishing, for all that, to make *Ferdinand Count Fathom* out a masterpiece, it is still possible to discern, independently of the clumsy technical framework, a certain thematic structure following a general pattern determined by two closely linked factors, to wit Fathom's social success and his amorality. In a first ascending movement, which is far from being regular and unswerving, up to Chapter xxxv inclusive, Smollett shows the victories of Evil and Fathom's rise in the social scale. Three stages can be distinguished in this 'Rogue's progress'. Childhood, adolescence and the arrival in Vienna, say the first ten chapters, constitute Fathom's first ascent, important, but not reaching any extraordinary height. The sojourn in Vienna marks a temporary culminating point, followed by a fairly rapid decline, leading to Fathom's first nadir in Paris, which it is impossible to separate from the stasis constituted by the interpolated story of Don Diego. The stay in Great Britain, up to the social triumph of Bristol Spring, represents the third phase, the one in which Fathom reaches his apogee. The second movement, symmetrical with the first, retraces the decline of the scoundrel and the final triumph of Good. But, there again, the development is not regular. Fathom's decline to his last nadir is swift and occupies only three chapters (xxxvi to xxxviii). Prison (xxxix to xli) forms a stasis similar to the first one in Paris, followed by a new moderate rise which culminates in Chapter xlix in the attempt at seduction perpetrated on Monimia. After this second stage in Fathom's decline, the final fall (artificially postponed by the sentimentality of the last ten chapters) is also very swift, since Fathom is in prison again at the end of Chapter lvi, this time without any hope of coming out of it. The absolute nadir having been reached, Fathom disappears from the novel, whose last ten chapters cannot appear on the same graph. It would be necessary to draw a supplementary graph of the adventures of Melvil, this time with virtue and happiness as coordinates. But such a task would be rendered difficult by the frequent and long disappearances of this character. The adventures of Melvil are circular, not linear. He returns, after the classic ordeals of the heroic cycle, to his point of departure, to wit happiness and fortune.

Smollett skims rapidly over Fathom's childhood and adolescence, Chapter ii, according to the heading, presents only a 'superficial view of our hero's infancy'. But already he outlines the themes which will subsequently be repeated and amplified. First of all, the major part languages will play in the formation and adventures of Fathom. His mother, a great chatterbox, talks English to him even when they are living in Prague (p. 11). This knowledge of English helps to strengthen the interest Count de Melvil already takes in him, as he is glad to hear the sound of his mother tongue (p. 17). The scraps of French Fathom then knows enable him to frustrate a plot (pp. 17–18). His ability to speak English makes it easier to gain access to Mademoiselle de Melvil (p. 23). Fathom has the linguistic gift of the great international crooks, since, after two years in Vienna, he speaks French and Italian extremely well. Rather oddly, no mention is made of Hungarian or German, but on his arrival in Paris in a cheap cosmopolitan ordinary 'he at once distinguished the high and low Dutch, barbarous French, Italian, and English languages' (p. 90). When, on his arrival in England, he is up against the magistrate and cannot make use of English because he has adopted the device of travelling incognito, he tries to plead his case 'successively in French, High-Dutch, Italian and Hungarian Latin' (p. 136) with no success, very much the reverse! This linguistic gift is closely associated with the flexibility of character and adaptability of Fathom, already analysed in the examination of the picaresque elements in *Ferdinand Count Fathom* (see above, p. 85–92).

The psychological and moral antithesis between Fathom and Melvil's son is strongly emphasised at least twice in these first ten chapters. While young Melvil is only interested in intellectual and athletic prowess, Fathom learns little at school, but already evinces remarkable social talents. Smollett contrasts the uncouthness and shyness of young Melvil, who for the moment despises the simperings dear to feminine society, with Fathom's innate aptitudes for gallantry, politeness and other external rituals of a static hierarchical society. The dialectic of reality and appearance is at the core of *Ferdinand Count Fathom*, as it is of the two previous novels. Fathom's fellow-student willingly allows him his little social successes 'while he himself [Melvil] was conscious of his own superiority in those qualifications which seemed of more real importance than the mere exteriors and forms of life' (p. 19). Behind the mirage of appearances, by which Melvil's father and later the young man himself allow themselves to be deceived, Smollett contrasts the fundamental egotism ('self-love', p. 20) of Fathom with the genuine qualities of heart which make life in society ('social virtue', ibid.) possible[9]. But, just as Smollett implicitly criticises women for their superficial judgment of young Fathom, it is none the less implicit, right from the beginning of the novel, that this society on which Fathom will wreak his ravages is guilty of having encouraged him. So, when Smollett underlines a second time the contrast between Fathom and Melvil, it is clear that society is ready to let itself be duped with a criminal credulity: 'he [Fathom] and the young count formed a remarkable contrast, which, in the eye of the world, redounded to his advantage' (p. 40).

The theme which dominates Fathom's adolescence is the precocious awakening of his sensuality. Probably Smollett wished to suggest that Fathom inherited his sensuality from his highly sexed mother, who married five times in the course of a single campaign (p. 7), not to mention the numerous other men she slept with. At about the age of twelve, Fathom has already spent the night in 'more effeminate amusements' (p. 20) than translating Caesar. In these conditions, it is not surprising that, at the age of sixteen, he tries to seduce Mademoiselle de Melvil, thanks to a carefully devised plan of amorous poliorcetics: 'the method of sap' (p. 24). Smollett often has recourse to the vocabulary of sieges, fortifications and military tactics to describe Fathom's amorous manoeuvres. This first attempt at seduction proves Fathom to be a born strategist in the wars of Venus but it ends at once in a defeat and an unforeseen success. Though Mademoiselle de Melvil remains icy, Teresa catches fire, or rather at last reveals her ardent passion (pp. 27—8). Here again it certainly seems that *Jonathan Wild* was not without influence on the conception of Teresa and Fathom, unless Fielding and Smollett borrow their ideas of sexual criminology from the common fund of Anglo-Saxon puritanism. Jonathan Wild's penchant for women is his only great weakness 'so naturally incident to men of heroic disposition; to say the truth, it might more properly be called a slavery to his own appetite' (Book iii, Chapter iv). Teresa, just like Laetitia in *Jonathan Wild*, 'was furnished by nature with a very amorous complexion' (p. 27), and Smollett calls these young lovers 'real voluptuaries' (p. 31). But whatever nightly revels Fathom and the maid-servant may have indulged in, Smollett describes with a puritanical fascination, not wholly devoid of complaisance, the psychological and physical methods leading up to this curious attempt at seduction. Fathom, the great amorous strategist (the military metaphor recurs again in this passage: ibid.), approaches Mademoiselle de Melvil through the intermediary of his mistress, Teresa. The latter has become his accomplice in the hope of sharing Mademoiselle de Melvil's fortune. In this systematic enterprise of seduction, the first but not the last in the novel, Fathom attacks on three fronts. First of all, he makes use of a limited, but quite effective knowledge of psychology, in this case the dynamic value of contradiction (pp. 32—4). He will use this psychological tool again to manipulate Melvil (p. 43). Next, he tries to play on Mademoiselle de Melvil's passions by exciting her sexual appetites (pp. 34—5) by licentious anecdotes and books. He had noticed beforehand that Mademoiselle de Melvil's temperament showed 'some marks of inflammability' (p. 31). Smollett uses an earthy metaphor — 'the warm luxuriant soil of youth' (ibid.) — which reveals all his puritanical mistrust of the impulses of youth. Lastly, he has recourse, like Peregrine, to aphrodisiac drugs (p. 34) to try, in vain, to seduce Mademoiselle de Melvil.

Right from the beginning of the novel, the problem of Evil, particularly in its sexual aspect, is definitely posed. But, in fact, Smollett does not question himself about the *origins* of Evil (apart from the few details about Fathom's heredity). He merely *states* the existence of amoral monsters, and then goes on to describe the ravages they are capable of causing in a society guilty of always being ready to let itself be hoaxed. Fathom, according to Smollett, who tries to adopt the irony of Fielding, is 'naturally a genius self-taught, in point of sagacity and invention' (p. 28). Behind the transparent ambiguity of the ironic inversion ('genius', 'sagacity', 'invention'), it is the insistence on the innateness of Evil ('naturally', 'self-taught') which is important. It is impossible to speak of a moral decline in Fathom, since, from the beginning of his life, this character is set, with no further explanations, on the level of complete amorality. Thus, in the enterprise of seduction conducted by Fathom and his mistress: 'All principles of morality had been already excluded from their former plan; consequently, he found it an easy task to interest Teresa in any other scheme tending to their mutual advantage, however wicked and perfidious it might be' (p. 35). In adopting an amoral character right from the first, Smollett condemns himself to describing a collection of heinous crimes, without being able to draw any gradation in perversity. Fathom, like the other scoundrels, in particular Ratchcali and Teresa, is a monolithic character, who does not develop, but is shattered at the end of the novel. Conversely, the faultless goodness of Melvil, and later of Monimia, makes them spectral beings, without real fictional consistence. The aseptic perfection of Monimia also kills almost any life in this character.

This antithetical duality involves the absolute necessity of duplicity in the villains of the novel. Without this duplicity all relationship between the 'good' and 'bad' characters would be impossible. *Ferdinand Count Fathom* is the novel of misunderstanding, sometimes spontaneous, more often provoked by Fathom and his acolytes. A stylistic examination of *Ferdinand Count Fathom* would doubtless reveal the frequency of the prefix 'mis'[10], which is, in a way, the indication of the thematic continuity of the novel. The duplicity of Fathom helps or engenders misunderstandings. Thus the systematic inversion of reality is tinged with an irony which ends by becoming wearisome because it is of such a mechanical type. The incident of the copied translation (pp. 20–2) lacks neither psychological credibility nor logical coherence. The schoolmaster's misunderstanding, and above all Melvil's own father's, is only the beginning of a long series of injustices endured in all good faith by the innocent Melvil. When, later, the Count suspects his son of having stolen some jewels from his sister, the irony is triple. Fathom and Teresa are the guilty ones; but this time Fathom has nothing to do with it, the father immediately suspects his son; and, third level of irony, the father proposes Fathom to his son as 'a preceptor and pattern' (p. 39). The logic of this ironic concatenation is almost too rigorous to be acceptable.

The Hobbesian *credo* of the scoundrel with which Chapter x ends is a pedalpoint in these variations on the theme of Evil. The meeting with Ratchcali, the ideal confederate, will enable Fathom to put all these principles into practice in Vienna, a training ground and field of action more worthy of his talents than the closed world of Presburg.

This second stage (up to the beginning of Chapter xxvii, some eighty pages or so) marks a temporary decline in Fathom's social success. In spite of some little financial and amorous success, these sojourns in Vienna, in the Imperial and later the French army, and in Paris are dominated by failure. Fathom learns to his cost the many risks which beset the path of the professional crook. In spite of the mediocre quality of *Ferdinand Count Fathom*, it must be admitted that Smollett takes pains to vary the fortune of his hero, according to an alternation, artificial perhaps, but which at least has the merit of avoiding the equation: 'Evil = Social success', and its inverse.

Venus — and Mercury — rule Chapters xi—xvii inclusive, which provide confirmation of Fathom's greedy sensuality. But though he seduces Wilhelmina and her stepmother, these are paltry conquests and already mark a social setback for Fathom. His obscure birth denies him admittance to the same world as Melvil's, and Fathom has to be content with more middle-class game in a 'humbler sphere' (p. 44), which Smollett also calls 'an inferior path of life' (p. 45). These chapters, and all the manoeuvres of seduction with an eye to the main chance, are based on an antithesis: the hot-bloodedness of the two women and the cold-bloodedness of Fathom. Besides the well analysed animosity which sets the stepmother against the stepdaughter, Smollett takes care to stress[11] their ardent temperament. The stepmother has 'an increased appetite for pleasure' (p. 46), while Wilhelmina can pride herself on a 'complexion . . . very much akin to that of her stepmother: indeed they resembled each other too much to live upon any terms of friendship or even decorum' (p. 46). Fathom thinks above all of making profit out of this double love affair carried on at the same time at the price of a little invention and psychological agility. As he plans this operation with the cold-blooded tactics of a strategist, it is not surprising that the metaphor of besieging a city is continued throughout these pages[12]. Seducing Wilhelmina becomes an exercise in style, or rather in amorous rhetoric, cold, bombastic and artificial. On Fathom's side, there is no fire, no impulsive ardour. He fans the flames, but does not burn. Even in taking the precaution of informing his reader that Wilhelmina is 'an utter stranger to addresses of this kind' (p. 47) Smollett is unconvincing. Besides a feeling of improbability and monotony, this declaration of love gives an impression of disproportion between the verbal battery brought into action and the objective.

These pages (pp. 47—8) are such an accumulation of sentimental clichés, even including those of pseudo-archaic pastoral eclogues, that it is permissible to wonder whether they do not constitute a satire, in the second degree, on the stupidity of Wilhelmina as well as of women in general. The technique of lying, the favourite weapon of his duplicity, remains in almost constant employment by Fathom. Ever since his first attempts with the Melvils, Fathom contrives to make use of the truth as much as possible even though he does not scruple to reverse its meaning and its consequences. Thus he ends by achieving his aim — getting possession of a very valuable gold chain — by making his victim believe he is doing her a favour (pp. 59–61).

Nevertheless, these dubious occupations are not without their risks. These range from the farcical but dangerous incident to terror, including the mortification of being duped. His double amorous intrigue involves Fathom in unpleasant situations, in which the frustration of interrupted love-making is mingled with the fear of being discovered by one or the other mistress[13]. Fathom is afraid, being naturally cowardly, and Smollett delights in describing his emotions in terms which are almost behaviouristic before their time, and indicate only physical or physiological reactions. Subsequently Fathom succeeds in overcoming his cowardice, when he is living in a military environment, and Smollett, on this occasion, adumbrates a psycho-sociological theory of the influence of environment (p. 75). Another untoward incident in Fathom's career: he gets cheated by Ratchcali at the very moment he was thinking of giving the latter the slip. Thus the theme of misunderstanding does not disappear from these pages. Misunderstanding acts sometimes in Fathom's favour, sometimes against him. He succeeds in deceiving, not only the jeweller's wife and daughter, but the worthy Viennese himself. When the latter at last begins to think that the necklace has been stolen by a member of his own family, his suspicions fasten (wrongly) on his own wife (p. 63). Fathom uses the flight of Melvil's valet to cover the theft he has committed himself. Melvil continues to take his companion for 'a mirrour of integrity and attachment; in such an exquisite manner did he plan all his designs, that almost every instance of his fraud furnished matter of triumph to his reputation' (p. 79). But this triumph is shortlived, for Ratchcali takes possession of Fathom's booty (p. 83). Smollett thus makes himself the interpreter of a certain picaresque socialism, in which money circulates by ways as hidden as they are unpredictable. Melvil, his valet, Fathom, Ratchcali and the swindlers on the other side of the Rhine who finally relieve the Tyrolean of his money (p. 144) form an original channel for the redistribution of property, itself considered as theft by Proudhon a century later. Need one add that Smollett observes this furtive circulation of liquid assets with regret rather than approval? Fathom, without being a model of stoical resignation, bears this setback fairly philosophically. Experience has taught him that even he can be the victim of a misunderstanding. This first adumbration of misfortune is repeated and developed in the account of his stay in Paris.

But, previous to this, Fathom endures the ordeal of terror, described in the most celebrated pages of the book, to wit the journey through the forest by night and the meeting with the thieves who rob and murder travellers (pp. 83–9). There are few critics who have not praised the quality of this passage, even if they have not thought much of the rest of the novel. Hazlitt, in his *Lectures on the English Comic Writers*, is harsh about both the subject and the characters of *Ferdinand Count Fathom*, but admits that 'there is more power of writing occasionally shewn in it than in any of his works'[14] and he expresses his wholehearted admiration for the scene of the robbers in the forest. Scott has an equally unfavourable opinion of Fathom's moral depravity. Nevertheless, he is glad to draw attention to the excellence of the passage in question: 'The horrible adventure in the hut of the robbers, is a tale of natural terror which rises into the sublime; and, though often imitated, has never yet been surpassed, or perhaps equalled'[15]. It is difficult to find direct precursors of Smollett in the literary use of terror. Shakespeare uses the unleashed elements in *King Lear* and *Macbeth* to emphasise the human storm, but the terror thus inspired is more a symbol than an end in itself. Perhaps it is possible to draw a parallel with the night in the entrenched camp, described by Defoe in *Captain Singleton* (1720). Besieged by a horde of ferocious animals, the shipwrecked men in the African bush combat the wild beasts and their terror, which is rapidly conjured up: 'The Moon was near the Full, but the Air full of flying Clouds, and a strange Hurricane of Wind to add to the Terror of the Night'[16]. Nearer to *Ferdinand Count Fathom* is the chapter Lord Kames entitles 'Of our Dread of Supernatural Powers in the Dark' in his *Essays on the Principles of Morality and Natural Religion* (1751). This essay (pp. 307–14) starts out from the fact that children and men fear the unknown. This fear works on the imagination which it thus predisposes to exaggeration. Lord Kames stresses that this terror is due 'entirely . . . to the operations of the imagination' (p. 314). He adds, as proof, that, in company, man is not afraid of the dark. Smollett's pages seem like a literary illustration of this theory, but no document proves that Smollett knew this work of Lord Kames's at that time.

A critical analysis relying very closely on the text makes it possible to detect the means employed by Smollett and thus to grasp more clearly the ends he set out to achieve. It matters little that readers nowadays, surfeited with literary, cinematic and, above all, atomic terror, may be inclined to smile at this scene — not to say scenario — which has since become classic. One must try to rediscover the original novelty of this passage. Smollett begins (p. 83) by giving a few rapid indications of the gloom, the silence, the solitude, without neglecting the psychological background, to wit, Fathom's dejection at the loss of the jewels. The fear mounts by degrees ('began', gradually'). Fathom's apprehensions take a more definite shape when the guide tells him of travellers murdered in these woods. Abandoned by the guide, Fathom is aware only of the dying away of the horse's hoofbeats and the rising gusts which announce the coming storm soon to burst in full fury (p. 84). Auditory sensations play nearly the most important part in Fathom's terror. In spite of being over-come with fear, Fathom is still able to think coherently and the intel-lectual vocabulary predominates in the last two paragraphs of this page. The two following ones (pp. 85–6) prove once again that Fathom too can be the victim of misapprehensions. The haven he thinks he has found is a den of thieves. Appearances deceive him, in spite of his almost profes-sional mistrustfulness. The old woman answers him 'with such appearance of truth and simplicity, that he concluded his person was quite secure' (p. 85). The adventure of the strayed traveller might have been quite commonplace but for the discovery of a still warm corpse in an attic from which there is no escape, for the old woman has locked him in from outside. The manipulation of terror is extremely skilful. First, the prelude, in which fear, rather than terror, predominates; then the horror of the macabre discovery, but above all the nightmare feeling of being unable to escape, when Fathom knows that the same fate awaits him. As the great modern purveyor of horrific thrills, Hitchcock, stresses, it is not so much the unknown danger as the known and measured one which terrifies man. Panic gives way to anguish, and, for the first time, Fathom, at the approach of what he deems near and inevitable death, proves that his monstrous mechanism can, for a brief moment, be thrown out of gear when confronted with the monstrous. The comment is crisp, 'his con-science rose up in judgment against him' (p. 86), but it betrays Smollett's moral intention.

This scene of terror is undoubtedly less fortuitous than the critics have claimed. It is advisable, first of all, to relate it to the auto-dedication in which Smollett announces his intention of putting the psychological power of terror to profitable use. Consequently, the terror in this scene should, on a man other than Fathom, have had a cathartic effect. In Smollett's mind this journey through the forest and this night in the hut were a moral ordeal which should have halted Fathom on the path of crime. But the determination to survive soon reawakens all Fathom's ingenuity and he puts the corpse in the place he himself should have occupied in the bed. As he had foreseen, the old woman's assistants come and stab . . . a corpse. It is the turn of the robbers to be deceived by that sigh exhaled by the twice-murdered dead man. There is thus a certain balance of structure. Fathom has just let himself be deceived by Ratchcali. But he, in his turn, thwarts human wickedness in a far more dangerous situation. As he is not troubled with scruples, he robs the corpse, and this money will enable him to cut a better figure in Paris. The end of the scene (pp. 87–9) presents less interest. Fathom, in his turn, terrifies the old woman when he comes downstairs after the murderers have departed on another hunt. Irony resumes its rights. The old woman devoutly puts herself under the protection of all the saints. Fathom, after having got himself conducted, pistol in hand, to the nearest village, rewards his conductress with a little moral sermon. The interplay of ironies keeps events perpetually dovetailing into each other, at a very swift, but unobtrusive tempo. The old woman hastens to betray Fathom by having him accused of murder, but Fathom has prudently deemed it expedient not to linger in the village, and has thus thwarted the old vixen in advance. Smollett returns to the theme of terror (p. 88): noises and Fathom's frenzied imagination play the principal part. Finally, this passage has the merit of clearly expressing, not only the duplicity of the man, but also his duality. Fathom owes his life to his instinct of self-preservation — 'an impulse that seemed supernatural' (p. 86) — but also to the swiftness of his mental reactions, intensified by the stimulus of a situation out of the ordinary. But is not terror the ironical falling back of intelligence on instinct? Smollett, the ironist, plays a double game, between the duality and the duplicity of his hero.

Having escaped from this adventure, Fathom is given a brief respite. Appearances and his own illusions combine to make him fall into the gravest error of his career up to now. He takes a master crook, Sir Stentor Stile, for a rustic fool whom he will be able to fleece. The game of dice (pp. 105–6) proceeds in a way that recalls the one in which Roderick (I, 98–101) is the victim of the same kind of rogue. There again the thematic structure is very balanced. In a first section, Fathom, oversure of himself, is the victim of a sham country bumpkin whom he thought he could cheat. Stripped of everything, Fathom is determined to profit by this dearly bought lesson (p. 107). He survives by getting himself engaged as a violinist at the Opera and is thus transformed, against his will, into an attentive spectator of the fashionable world.

In these circumstances the interpolated story of the noble Castilian plays the part of a necessary stasis before the resumption of adventures in Great Britain. This story has often been condemned by critics[17], but wrongly, for it makes an indispensable pause and serves as a thematic counterpoint of honourable deeds to the sordid adventures of Fathom. Don Diego de Zelos is doubly the victim of his misunderstandings. In Spain, first of all, where he is mistaken about the identity of Orlando-Renaldo, and where he believes he has sacrificed his wife and daughter to his Castilian sense of honour. Later, and in a more commonplace way, he is deceived by Fathom, to whom he entrusts his jewels to sell. Thus, far from being boring and irrelevant, the story is of a new type in Smollett's work because it sets the action going again (Fathom will be able to leave for Great Britain) and serves as a dramatic and thematic link between the adventures of Fathom and the love affair between Serafina-Monimia (Don Diego's daughter) and the young Orlando-Renaldo Melvil.

The sojourn in Paris reveals another literary quality of Fathom's. His duality and his duplicity meet in the ambiguity of his satirical function. He observes this cosmopolitan and French society (Chapters xxii and xxiii) where the corruption of morals does not prevent him from moving freely in it. Fathom, however reprehensible his deeds, judges with the cold lucidity of a man accustomed to take advantage of the weaknesses of others. The nocturnal brawl in a Paris brothel is more than a repetition of incidents already dealt with in *Roderick Random* (I, 127–32). It is an opportunity for Smollett to launch into a virulent satire on the French, their morals and their religion, without, for all that, sparing the national types of the Englishman and the German. The moral intention is so obvious that it threatens to turn the satirical verve into caricatural allegory. The bawd (p. 93) is less an ancient handmaid of Venus than a repulsive description of vice and disease. Smollett sketches, incidentally, a sexual typology. It is, of course, the Italian and the French priest who first decide to visit the brothel, whereas the more phlegmatic Dutchman withdraws from the party (ibid.). The Englishman and the German quarrel for the favours of the same beauty, and their remarks display the sarcastic arrogance of the one and the Teutonic fury of the other. But it is the violent anti-Catholic and Gallophobic satire that is most striking in these pages. The inmates go to Confession before the *concubitus*, and the priest, scolded by the brothel-keeper, kneels down before her to ask forgiveness. The ironic inversion verges occasionally on sacrilege, as the heavy-handed onomastic satire with which the priest is burdened indicates[18].

Fathom's departure for Great Britain was prepared for on the thematic plane almost from the beginning of the novel. The importance of the English language in his adventures has already been evident. This linguistic attachment is reinforced, in Fathom, by a pragmatic patriotism. Great Britain appears to him as 'the Canaan of all able able adventurers' (p. 77). The same biblical metaphor recurs when he contemplates the English coast from Boulogne, 'like another Moses reconnoitring the land of Canaan from the top of Mount Pisgah' (p. 128). The description of the wealthy English (pp. 129–30) and the analysis of the British national temperament (pp. 145–6) are doubly effective satires, since most of the observations are not lacking in perspicacity, and they are made by swindlers (Fathom and Ratchcali). Right from the first the two confederates are sure of making their fortune in a country where opulence, credulity and liberty offer them such lucky prospects (p. 146).

Fathom's great triumph is rapid, but of short duration (Chapters xxvii–xxxv inclusive, some forty pages). His rocket-like rise is almost too rapid, unless the swiftness of his success is not in itself an oblique satire on worldly infatuation, the wilful, social and sophisticated form of misunderstanding. The journey in the coach from Canterbury to London plays a triple role. First, as in *Roderick Random* and *Peregrine Pickle*, this little enclosed world is an opportunity for Smollett to present a satirical microcosm[19]. Secondly, the misunderstanding of which Fathom is the victim (Chapter xxix) will enable him to make the acquaintance of the young nobleman (pp. 136–7) who introduces him to London society (p. 148). Finally, the hasty seduction (Chapter xxx) of the innocent Elenor is relevant to both the thematic structure and the dramatic manipulation of the story.

With the help of Ratchcali (Chapter xxxi), Fathom's social ascent is dazzling, for the adventurer takes care to let the false treasures of his knowledge, his talent and his taste shine with all their deceptive glitter (pp. 148—9). The mirror of appearances ensnares good society like so many scatterbrained larks. Worldly success is heightened by a shameless financial exploitation for which it is rather hard to blame Fathom, since he is only taking advantage (he does not lack descendants today) of the craze for antiques. Now these rare pieces, jewels, Cremona violins, bronzes, medals, pictures, are all fakes. But the fascination and infatuation (p. 151) of his admirers is such that all critical judgment is suspended. Smollett was not the only man about that time to denounce the scandalous traffic in pseudo-antiques. Samuel Foote, a year before *Ferdinand Count Fathom*, had published a comedy in two acts (played without much success at Drury Lane in 1752) *Taste*, in which Carmine the painter and Puff the auctioneer divide the money of their dupes between them. In the prologue Garrick wrote this guilty boast of the auctioneer's:

> My best Antiquities are made at Home.
> I've *Romans, Greeks, Italians* near at hand
> True *Britons* all — and living in the Strand.

As such a success does not fail to arouse the jealousy of the swindlers, Fathom is exposed to their machinations. But, thanks to various stratagems, he succeeds in defending himself against appearances by the very play of appearances. This is the thematic significance of Chapter xxxiii, in which he puts his bullying adversary to flight by having recourse to a gory stratagem.

This social and financial success would not be complete without a conquest flattering to Fathom's demanding and perverse sexuality. The seduction of the unfortunate Celinda in Chapter xxxiv enables one to measure the experience Fathom has acquired since his (somewhat bungled) love affairs in Vienna. As a clearheaded Don Juan, he has quickly divined the hypersensitiveness of this young illegitimate daughter who is persecuted in her father's house. As in the forest, auditory sensations (pp. 160—1) play a major part in the awakening of Celinda's superstitious terror. The ruin of this young girl is complete, for not only does Fathom seduce her but to get rid of her more easily he makes her an alcoholic. Thus, just as Fathom's covetousness achieves its highest satisfaction, his sensuality wins its most complete victory. But it is precisely his taste for women that will be the ruin of Fathom. The sojourn in Bristol, where Fathom 'as usual, formed the nucleus or kernel of the beau monde' (p. 165), marks the fatal apogee of his career as swindler and seducer.

The decline of the scoundrel cannot be symbolised, any more than his ascent, by an unbroken downward line. There again, Smollett arranges a level stage halfway which represents a second nadir before a partial reascent and the final fall.

The causes of this decline are simple. Betrayed by his carnal desires, Fathom, in his turn, is the victim of an adventuress, Mrs Trapwell. The play of appearances and illusions is complicated by a triple irony. Mrs Trapwell has married, thanks to a stratagem. Instead of complaining, her husband gives her to understand that they can both take advantage of an unpleasant situation and, fully agreeing with him she seeks a victim in Bristol. Finally, at a third level of irony, the husband wishes to make some money, but above all to get rid of this burdensome and wanton wife; of this the adventuress is unaware. Caught in the trap — *rem in re* — Fathom leaves some financial plumage in it but wins a fine feather in his Don Juan's cap (p. 171). This vain glory does not last long. The psychological and logical sequence of Chapters xxxvi and xxxvii has an inexorable precision. Pressed for money as a result of the trial, Fathom is imprudent enough to be a little too clever at cards. Ratchcali, too, makes a mistake, and, as a crowning piece of ill-luck, Fathom is recognised by Sir Stentor Stile, who has returned to London. His social decline is as swift as his ascent. He has lost the favour of the fashionable world (p. 173). Bled by the lawyer who defended him, sentenced to a fine of £1,500, abandoned by his friends, betrayed by his confederates, Fathom sinks to the depths in the space of a few hours (p. 181). The three following chapters (xxxix to xli) represent a stasis similar to Chapters xxv and xxvi. In the microcosm of the debtors' prison, Fathom is able to observe the realm of illusions, which file before his eyes like the shadows in Plato's mythical cave. Theodore[20], the dethroned King of Corsica, or the pathetic illusion of power; Mungo Barebones[21], or the theological mirage; Minikin, or the ludicrous demands of the point of honour, are fantastic puppets rather than genuine characters. Yet two of them (Theodore and Mungo Barebones) are people who had really existed. The technique of doubly indirect presentation of these characters (pp. 181—2) and the vigour and variety of the style make these pages one of the best passages in the novel.

The thematic significance of Fathom's providential liberation is twofold. Evil, aided by chance, can come to the help of Evil. Melvil, victim of an age-old confidence trick (p. 199) comes to help a hypothetical female relative confined in this prison. The unexpected result of this visit is the setting free of Fathom, who is recognised and promptly aided by Melvil. A second result of this apparently lucky chance (for Fathom) is that, confronted with Monimia, the adventurer promptly catches fire and forgets 'the prudential maxims he had adopted on his first entrance into life' (p. 201). Evil therefore carries within itself the power of thwarting and destroying itself. Fathom is the slave of a destiny inscribed in his flesh:

In all probability, Heaven mingled the ingredient in his constitution, on purpose to counteract his consummate craft, defeat the villany of his intention, and, at last, expose him to the justice of the law, and the contempt of his fellow-creatures' (ibid.).

Chapters xliv to xlix have as their central theme the momentary triumph of misunderstanding. It is a series of variations, not lacking in psychological truth, on the problems of moral semiology, or rather the deciphering and interpretation of intentions. All the near-diabolic clever-ness of Fathom consists in taking advantage of the financial difficulties against which Melvil is struggling (Chapter xliv) to sow mutual doubt in the minds of the lovers. It is fair to observe that Smollett avoids drawing up a Manichean table of responsibilities. If Fathom is guilty, Melvil and Monimia are partly so too, through the ill-advised pride which impels them to keep silent. The misunderstanding which, in their case, could have proved tragic, is a momentary paralysis of their social and psychological abilities to communicate. Moreover, Smollett implies that there is a purpose in Evil. Melvil, the young aristocrat who has led a coddled life, needs to suffer, to face up to the harassing problems of money. The author observes, not without irony, that Fathom 'was willing to let Melvil be better acquainted with adversity, which is the great school of life' (p. 205). The lesson is the same as in *Roderick Random*, though the adventures are very different.

Doubt soon arouses jealousy. From then on Melvil and Monimia behave like broken-down automata, immured in their silence and bitter-ness. Their actions succeed each other with the paralogical unreality of a nightmare, and their eyes no longer see except through 'the false medium of prejudice and resentment' (p. 214). As thematic counterpoint Smollett invokes professional and racial prejudice. Such is the meaning of the opposition between the heartless Christian usurers and the Jewish money-lender Joshua, who, contrary to all expectation, decides to help Melvil (pp. 224–9). The attempt to rape Monimia (pp. 236–7) had been preceded by a first error on the part of Fathom, who had declared his passion too soon, before Melvil had left England (p. 216). Monimia's haughty coldness only inflames Fathom's desire. Smollett ironically applies to Fathom the theory of contradictory passions which the latter uses to excite Melvil's resentment against the innocent Monimia (p. 217). Fathom's failure is due to Providence, but above all to the point of the sword with which Monimia, the noble daughter of a hidalgo, threatens him.

Taken in and rescued by Madame Clement, Monimia disappears from the novel, while Fathom sees his final downfall fast approaching. From Chapter l onwards, he changes his way of life. The 'zenith of his fortune' (p. 243) is past. He cannot resume the place he occupied in the fashion-able world. After a few reflections, at once prudent and moral, on the passion for gambling which has seized English society (pp. 244–5), he decides to practise the medical profession, in other words to lower himself 'one step in the degrees of life' (p. 245). His sojourn in Tunbridge Wells is not lacking in irony. Whereas in Bristol Fathom had an unlooked-for medical success, in Tunbridge Wells he has to wage a fierce battle against colleagues already installed on the spot. Smollett launches a fresh attack against the infatuations of upper-class society (pp. 247–8), and the medical blindness of the patients as much as that of the doctors (Chapter li).

But, in spite of a few small successes, Fathom begins to pile up mistakes. In courting the daughter, once again, without realising it at first, it is the mother who falls for him (p. 257). In London, there again, the new doctor has great difficulty in establishing a clientèle, in spite of the numerous and picturesque stratagems to which he resorts (pp. 259–60). For once the play of appearances deceives no one but Fathom himself, who has chosen, as his ally, an apothecary as rascally as himself. Fathom's bad luck takes a series of surprising turns which have manifold consequences. The amorous widow dies and the disappointed daughter vows implacable hatred against her ex-suitor (p. 262). A merchant, allured by the damsel's calumnies, and anxious to get rid of his wife, has recourse to Fathom's bad offices. Contrary to the merchant's expectations, as a result of a particularly violent treatment, the wife recovers. The husband promptly claims that Fathom intended to poison his wife, but this extraordinary cure earns Fathom a certain success (pp. 263–4). Another surprising turn: Fathom, impelled as usual by his demon of sensuality, seduces a clergyman's wife, whose liberal and mainly bookish education somewhat reminds one of Miss Williams's in *Roderick Random*. The young woman, overcome with remorse, confesses to her husband, who takes legal action against Fathom.

As a result of this scandal, Fathom's reputation and his clientèle vanish into thin air (p. 267). The three following chapters (liv to lvi) might, indeed, all bear the same title, 'his eclipse and gradual declination' (p. 267). In the previous chapters, it seems that Smollett wished to suggest the tortuous ramifications of Evil, which alternately assume a positive and negative aspect for Fathom. In these last three chapters, it seems that he wishes, above all, to accentuate the rigorous, inescapable concatenation of mischances, the blind but also ambiguous form of Destiny, since Fathom's mischances prepare the way for the defeat of Evil and the final victory of Good. Smollett's recipe for making Fathom founder (definitely) is the same as the one employed for the momentary eclipses of Roderick and Peregrine: the acceleration and concentration of unfortunate incidents (ibid.).

But if this formula is therefore not new, there is nevertheless an appreciable difference in technique, due to the specific case of Fathom. On the one hand, even in this final decline, Smollett arranges a respite one might call a 'microstasis'. This is the story of the old female kleptomaniac hoaxed by Fathom, thus, on the thematic plane, the exploitation of evil by evil (pp. 271–3). Still impelled by his sensuality – the genetic form of transcendental Evil (p. 271) – and his cupidity, Fathom marries an ardent young widow. But he is mistaken about his wife's fortune. A plot between his father-in-law, a lawyer, and fellow charlatan who fears Fathom's rivalry results in having him thrown in prison, this time with no hope of getting out.

Now this ending lacks neither ingenuity nor irony. Fathom has been deceived on all fronts. He loses his wife, his reputation, his liberty and his hopes on a (false) charge of bigamy. The irony of systematic misunderstanding is thus reversed. For the first time, Fathom expresses remorse for his past crimes. But Smollett takes care to stress that from momentary remorse to lasting repentance there is all the long and arduous road of penitence to travel, a journey Fathom is far from inclined to take. It even seems that Smollett does all he can to minimise his hero's remorse in order to reduce it to no more than self-pity. Thus, Fathom's duality, duplicity and ambiguity are checkmated by a double-crossing lawyer (p. 281).

One may regret that Smollett, at the price of a simple imaginary chapter, did not then make Fathom disappear from the scene and wind up the sentimental sub-plot and its corollary, the story of the noble Castilian. But, at that time, the moral standards of the novel demanded the total ruin of the villain and, if he survived, his more or less convincing reformation. At the end of *Tom Jones*, Blifil is converted to Methodism, which, coming from the pen of Fielding, is perhaps as little flattering to Blifil as to Methodism. Technically, the last ten chapters overweight and unbalance *Ferdinand Count Fathom*. But without wishing, at all costs, to salvage this novel whose end founders in a morass of boring sickly-sentimentality, it is possible to discern a certain thematic continuity between the adventures of Fathom and their sentimental appendix. In the first place, the theme of misunderstanding persists. Melvil comes to wish he had kept his illusions about Monimia (pp. 282–3) and when his sister tells him the truth about Fathom's activities, he begins by denying the evidence (p. 295). The hasty remarriage of the Countess de Melvil is yet another variation on the same theme (pp. 284–6). But there are other misunderstandings whose results are less painful. In his supposed coma, Melvil gives the appearance of being dead (p. 303). The illusion of a dream (pp. 305–6) prepares the way for the final reunion with Monimia, who has been hidden and cured by the worthy Madame Clement. There is even a wish, manifested in a way at once antithetical and parallel in both Melvil and Fathom, to cling to the unreal in order to make it easier to deny a reality which seems to them illusory. Such is Melvil's psychological reaction when he meets Monimia again (p. 329) and Fathom's when he is saved through the good offices of Melvil (pp. 358–9). Fathom believes himself the victim of a 'vision so perfect and distinct, as to emulate truth and reality' (p. 360). This morbid interplay of illusion and reality is emphasised on the stylistic and sentimental planes by the repeated use of oxymorons which imply bitter-sweet delights and fantasies of love and death. Expressions such as 'pleasing anguish' and 'gloomy enjoyment' (p. 306) recur several times in these pages[22]. But the most striking and unexpected feature is the suggestion of necrophilia in Melvil's melancholy ravings. Sorrow is described by Smollett in the language of erotic excitement exacerbated by the frustration of sexual desire. As he approaches London 'his impatience became so ardent, that never lover panted more eagerly for the consummation of his wishes, than Melvile for an opportunity of stretching himself upon the grave of the lost Monimia' (p. 315). The references to an erotic pleasure derived from intercourse with the departed are even more explicit in the pages that follow. Melvil considers the first night he spends keeping vigil by the supposed grave of Monimia as a wedding-night (pp. 317–19, 323).

A second persistent theme is the interplay of illusions and prejudices. In this respect, the dénouement of the Castilian story is full of information about Smollett's intentions. Don Diego examines his conscience and deplores the murderous folly which impelled him to poison (at least, so he believes) his wife and daughter. But, above all, he condemns his haste, due to the vengeful demands of Spanish honour: 'I was guided by that savage principle which falsely we call honour: accursed phantome! that assumes the specious title, and misleads our wretched nation!' (p. 329). These declarations of Don Diego's do not however remove all anxiety for the honour of his name a few pages later (p. 341) although, a fresh contradiction, he has renounced the 'vindictive principles of a Spaniard' (p. 342). As to Don Diego's prejudices, the embryonic interpolated story (the frustrated loves of Charlotte and Valentine, pp. 345–50) provides a thematic counterpoint to them in a minor social key. Smollett is quite conscious of the possible parallel with Don Diego's story since Melvil tells his in order to persuade the intractable father. After Joshua, Melvil makes a positive plea, full of common sense, in favour of marrying for love rather than money ('mercenary and compulsive matches', p. 348).

The edifying end of the novel is in conformity with its thematic structure. The banality of this happiness awarded to the good and of the physical punishment (disease) and the moral one (repentance) of the wicked which concludes this story renders any continuation of the analysis pointless. A single feature, also unexpected, mars these last conventional pages to the point of repugnance. This is the lesson of latitudinarian tolerance given by Don Diego, hitherto the most rigid and monolithic of the good characters. In order to be able to marry Madame Clement, the benefactress of his long-lost daughter, he decides to be converted to Protestantism. Besides the haste of this marriage, which cannot fail to come as a dramatic surprise, thematically this decision makes Don Diego once again contradict himself, since the heretical religion of his daughter's suitor was at that time one of the main causes of his parental ire. But is it really a contradiction or a conversion? Don Diego's sincerity compromises with a certain prudent casuistry. He hastens to declare that he will not make his conversion public until *after* his return from Spain, whither he is going to settle his family affairs and his affairs of honour. But, having made this reservation, it is only fair to point out that there is no trace of Protestant proselytism in Smollett. Don Diego condescends to embrace the Protestant faith rather than adopting it with fervent conviction. He is converted not so much for positive reasons as for lack of negative ones or, to quote his own words: 'though I am fully satisfied that real goodness is of no particular persuasion, and that salvation cannot depend upon belief, over which the will has no influence' (p. 363). What is striking about this moderate and tolerant profession of faith, is more the number of reservations and negations, implicit or explicit, than the positive ardour of the neophyte. Hence, though a concern for religion is not absent from *Ferdinand Count Fathom*, it remains subordinate to a level-headed rationalism. The only trace, a very faint one, of metaphysical anguish is Melvil's exasperated cry: 'sacred Heaven! Why did Providence wink at the triumph of such consummate perfidy?' (p. 316). The final happiness of the lovers reunited at last, such is Smollett's moral reply, since, like Richardson, he is a defender of ethical mercantilism. Happiness is *earned* through trials created by God and man. The supreme reward — one is strongly tempted to write 'the bonus' — is the carnal possession of Monimia, 'the well-earned palm of virtue and of constancy' (p. 351). A good sixty years before the conspirators of *Hernani*, Melvil might have murmured: '*Ad augusta per angusta*'.

In spite of the antipodal opposition between Fathom and Launcelot Greaves, it is nevertheless possible to discern certain links and parallels between the two novels. To begin with, Melvil, with his moral zeal, is a character not without Don-Quixotism. He thus constitutes an early first rough sketch of Launcelot, especially when he returns to Bohemia in order to redress the wrongs suffered by his mother and sister[23]. Like Melvil, Launcelot is strong and handsome, but Smollett gives a more detailed description of the knight-errant, which is unusual in his novels, where the hero's physical appearance is generally left very vague. Both are highly educated and both are great readers, in particular Launcelot. Their fundamental kindness is expressed, and even betrayed, by a crazy generosity. This last adjective assumes a more literal meaning in the case of Launcelot. Two events in their lives present a surprising analogy. Both Monimia's mother and Aurelia's, each on her deathbed, entrusts her daughter to the protection respectively of Melvil and Launcelot. In both cases, mother and daughter are separated from the rest of their family, with whom they are on bad terms. A similar incident in both novels is the duel of the young heroes with the unscrupulous guardians, which reproduces the literary and moral archetype of the battle of the just against the forces of Evil. Trebasi and Anthony Darnel are grievously wounded by Melvil and Launcelot, but do not die. Lastly, the amorous distress of Melvil, his melancholy, his torpor, interrupted by paroxysms of excitement, prepare the reader for that series of variations on the theme of madness which lies at the very heart of *Launcelot Greaves*. But, definite though these resemblances are, Launcelot, in spite of his supposed madness, is much less naïve and credulous than Melvil. Launcelot is capable of standing up to Ferret or to a riotous mob. And if argument does not suffice, the whip or the butt of his lance are freely used to implement his rhetoric. Launcelot surveys the world with a keen eye, quite unlike the myopic gaze of the sentimental Melvil, too frequently turned inwards on his own problems.

Apart from *Don Quixote* (see above, pp. 92–8), it is difficult to relate *Launcelot Greaves* to any previous work liable to have inspired or influenced Smollett. The title of Fielding's play, *Don Quixote in England* (1734) raises some hopes, but they are quickly disappointed. To begin with, there is no proof that Smollett knew this mediocre comedy of Fielding's. Next, this play does not bear much likeness to *Launcelot Greaves*, except for being also inspired by Cervantes. Fielding keeps much closer to Cervantes than Smollett does. He imitates, in a quite servile way, the aberrations of Don Quixote, and also the buffooneries, the cowardice, the gluttony and the proverbs of Sancho. The idea of elections in a country town already appears in this play, but Fielding does not exploit it to the full. He limits himself to denouncing the stupidity and corruption of the voters who mean to sell themselves at the best price, but to *two* candidates. A lawyer, Brief, makes great use of legal jargon, just like Tom Clarke in *Launcelot Greaves*. But lawyers and doctors had been favourite targets for satirists long before Fielding and Smollett. It is therefore impossible to conclude that Fielding's play, in spite of its few very slight analogies with *Launcelot Greaves*, can have exercised any influence on this novel[24].

Chronological landmarks are not lacking in *Launcelot Greaves*, but they are less abundant than in *Ferdinand Count Fathom* and are mainly limited to indicating the ages of the characters[25]. Thus we learn that, when the story begins, Launcelot is under thirty (p. 11) and that he saved Aurelia from death when she was about seventeen (p. 27). The geographical background is much simpler than in *Ferdinand Count Fathom*; all the action takes place along the Great North Road between Weston (Nottinghamshire), where the famous Black Lion inn was situated, and London[26]. The publication of this novel as a monthly serial during the first two years of the *British Magazine* might lead one to think that the technical structure of *Launcelot Greaves* has been neglected by Smollett. Though there are indeed signs of haste[27] in the composition of *Launcelot Greaves*, the whole is more homogeneous than the method of publication might allow one to hope. The first five chapters are devoted to the introduction of almost the entire cast of characters. The main love affair between Launcelot and Aurelia, the secondary one between Tom Clarke and Dolly, and the inheritance problems of Crowe — another sailor bullied by his family, just like Trunnion in *Peregrine Pickle* — are all sketched in these introductory chapters. Subsequently, up to Chapter xix inclusive, the story of Launcelot's chivalric adventures on the road and the ludicrous or farcical ones of Crabshaw and Crowe is unfolded. Finally, the last five chapters are set in London, where Launcelot recovers Aurelia, his reason and happiness. A twofold genealogical surprise will enable Tom Clarke to marry Dolly without any social or financial qualms and Crowe to come into the inheritance of which his aunt had defrauded him.

On the technical plane, two characteristics hold the reader's attention straight away. First, the extraordinary density of information conveyed in the opening lines of the novel which set this inn scene, so often imitated, especially by Dickens[28]. If one analyses merely the first sentences, here is the sum of the information the reader can gather from it: where the action takes place, the month, the time of day, the number of travellers, the circumstances that drive them to take refuge in the inn, the size and situation of this inn, its sign and an ironic comment — 'which was said to exhibit' — on the emblematic figure. The following sentences show an equal wealth of more and more precise details. Thus the second sentence described the kitchen, the habitual and only common meeting-room of the inn, its red-tiled floor, its cleanliness, its furniture, its shining copper and pewter, the good coal fire — 'sea-coal' Smollett points out — in the hearth. Faithful to the pictorial technique enounced in the auto-dedication of *Ferdinand Count Fathom*, Smollett arranges his characters in groups. To the 'social triumvirate' (p. 1) composed of Fillet, Crowe and Tom Clarke is opposed the 'solitary guest' (p. 2), the misanthropist Ferret, whose physical isolation, emphasised from the very first page, is symbolic of his cynical breach with the rest of the world. The proprietress and her two daughters make up the third group. It is noticeable that the pictorial background gradually narrows away into the distance like a *trompe l'oeil* perspective. Little luminous points enliven this painting in the manner of the Flemish school of interior painters just as the small mirrors shown in their pictures seem to give more depth and reality to the domestic scenes they depict.

The introduction of the characters (pp. 1–3) is effected either according to the direct technique of the omniscient author or indirectly, i.e. through the eyes of another character, as Tom Clarke introduces Launcelot. Smollett had already used this indirect method of presentation in *Peregrine Pickle*, where Trunnion is described in advance by the inn-keeper. Secondly, Smollett uses linguistic characterisation. Crowe, like Trunnion, is a sailor but his nautical jargon, larded with technical terms, is even harder to understand than the Commodore's. Crowe's spoken chain is rather a series of disconnected links (see pp. 3 and 4–5). Another idiolect is that used by Tom Clarke, the attorney, whose legal language lends itself very well to ribald interpretations. The method is not new. Fielding uses it in *Joseph Andrews* (Book i, Chapter xii) and Sterne, in

Book iv of *Tristram Shandy*, a year after the publication of *Launcelot Greaves*, also revels in displaying the juridical niceties of Kysarcius, Didius and Triptolemus.

The publication of *Launcelot Greaves* in monthly parts[29] meant that Smollett had to use a special technique for the end of his chapters. He had to keep the reader's interest in suspense till the next instalment. So he deliberately addresses himself to his reader, particularly at the beginning of *Launcelot Greaves* (the last lines of the first four chapters). He varies his effects and, for example, to interrupt Tom Clarke's recapitulation, he introduces incidents which have the double merit of avoiding the monotony of the straightforward narrative and whipping up the reader's interest. Thus the break between Chapters iii and iv is well contrived since it leaves Aurelia in danger of death on the edge of a precipice and the reader, literally, in cliff-hanging suspense (pp. 29—31). These remarks addressed to his public certainly do not have the airy lightness of the verbal pirouettes in *Tristram Shandy* and Smollett does not adopt this technique regularly all through his novel. He only uses it for three other chapter-endings (pp. 119, 145, 153). On at least two occasions he also has recourse to the reticence of the omniscient author. At the beginning of Chapter viii, he announces that Crowe and his nephew Tom Clarke will disappear from the novel, but along with the misanthrope Ferret 'will reappear in due season' (p. 63). At the end of this same chapter, Smollett reveals that, without knowing it, Launcelot has just rescued Aurelia. But he remains silent about the circumstances which have caused the fair Aurelia to be considered mad (p. 69). They will be revealed 'in due course'.

The examination of the technical framework would be incomplete without a rapid analysis of the other methods employed by Smollett in *Launcelot Greaves*. As in his previous novels, chance plays an indispensable part in the meetings Smollett arranges between his characters. Thus Tom Clarke, Launcelot's godson, turns up very opportunely at the inn in order to inform the reader about his godfather and his chivalric eccentricities, due to his thwarted love affair with Aurelia. When Launcelot comes to the rescue of a carriage that is being attacked, he has no idea that he is flying to the aid of his Dulcinea (pp. 66—8, 84). In Gobble's prison, Launcelot meets his old nurse again (p. 91) whose long-lost son reappears in the nick of time (p. 99) to overwhelm her with happiness after the nightmare induced by the unworthy magistrate's persecutions. Another opportune arrival is that of Fillet and a lawyer friend (pp. 93, 96) who help Launcelot to extricate himself from the clutches of Gobble. It is not impossible that Smollett imitated Fielding when Launcelot receives Aurelia's pocket-book which has been found by the landlady of an inn. There is one difference however: Tom Jones knows that the object belongs to Sophia (Book ii, Chapter iv) whereas Launcelot does not know the identity of its owner (p. 113). Chance shows itself kinder to Aurelia, when she has the good fortune to win Dolly over to her side with a promptitude that defies probability (p. 117). However chance does not always smile on the hero and heroine for the love affair between Launcelot and Aurelia is marked by a series of missed meetings (pp. 66–7, 111, 191). In this last case, in the madhouse, Launcelot *cannot* set Aurelia free, because he is a prisoner himself.

Three mysteries, two of which hinge on people's real identities, serve to connect the two love affairs and the problem of Crowe's inheritance. The letter breaking off relations which Launcelot receives is the immediate cause of his chivalric eccentricities (pp. 37–8). This letter of Aurelia's reappears several times in the story (pp. 107, 112–13, 122–3, 199). The final explanation of the misunderstanding comes very late and the structural artifice by which Smollett avoids clearing it up sooner is rather improbable. The love affair of Dolly and Tom Clarke occurs very suddenly, but right from the beginning of the novel Smollett had taken the precaution to emphasise Tom's natural propensities. The revelation of Dolly's superior birth is less artificial than the end of the novel might lead one to think. As early as Chapter xv (p. 124), Launcelot 'for the first time, considered her face, and seemed to be struck with her features. He asked her some questions, which she could not answer to his satisfaction.' For an eighteenth-century reader, endowed with average perspicacity, this sudden interest evinced by the hero and the inadequacy of the answers he receives would allow him to foresee a probable genealogical disclosure. Dolly's identity is finally revealed (pp. 207–9), not without an unexpected new development which makes the delicious fear of incest hover momentarily over the loves of Tom Clarke and Dolly. There again, the imitation of Fielding is not improbable. Fanny, too, believes, after the pedlar's revelation, that she is the sister of Joseph Andrews. A second disclosure proves Joseph to be the son of Mr Wilson. Tom Clarke does not change his identity, but the truth about Dolly's parentage is revealed in two stages, which enables Smollett, too, to give his reader the thrill of incest avoided just in time (p. 209). The problems of Crowe's inheritance (pp. 204–5) are also solved by the discovery of an identity. Ferret is Crowe's uncle by marriage since he has secretly married Bridget Maple, Crowe's aunt. As a married woman she can therefore not alienate a family property without Ferret's consent. Therefore any docking of the entail is null and void, which guarantees Crowe the legal possession of his inheritance. This third juridical thread of the plot (a very thin one) above all gives Smollett the means of getting rid at the same time of Crowe and Ferret, both difficult to fit into the customary final tableau of matrimonial and social bliss.

Apart from the final revelations, Smollett is twice obliged to interrupt the flow of his narrative. He gives the reader the information he lacks to reconstruct the plot in its entirety. He intervenes to declare that Miss Meadows is none other than Aurelia (p. 114). The abduction of

Launcelot, after being lured into a trap, is described at the beginning of Chapter xxiii (pp. 184—5), when the other characters are still ignorant of his fate. Smollett thus gives the impression of wanting to take the reader into his confidence. The reader, furnished with particulars communicated in a stage aside, becomes in some sort the accomplice of the omniscient author. Such a technique gives him the feeling of being superior to the other characters, but also of participating in their adventures. This ambiguity of detachment and involvement helps to keep the reader's interest awake. He is alternately the God of this fictional microcosm and the willing slave of a fiction elaborated by a creative will other than his own. When Smollett reverts twice again to Launcelot's disappearance (pp. 193—4), the reader has the advantage over Crowe and Tom Clarke of knowing that Launcelot has indeed been abducted. But he does not know *how* his friends set about finding him again, and so he participates in their search (ibid.). Finally, it also remains to him to discover *why* Launcelot has been thus ill-treated and at whose instigation (p. 201).

Even if *Launcelot Greaves* does not figure, any more than *Ferdinand Count Fathom*, among Smollett's best novels, it is high time to recognise in it certain qualities of technical structure generally passed over in silence. *Launcelot Greaves* has been too long considered as a vaguely absurd and burlesque imitation of *Don Quixote*. In fact, the tutelary shade of Cervantes has been as deadly to it as that of a literary Upas tree.

But if the technical structure, admittedly imperfect, nevertheless deserves more attention than English and American critics have, in general, been willing to grant it, what can be said of the thematic structure? There is a geometrical structure in *Launcelot Greaves* as rigorously drawn as that of *Ferdinand Count Fathom*. And before even tackling this analysis, it is permissible to wonder whether the architectural vigour of Smollett's moral intentions, much more assertive in *Ferdinand Count Fathom* and *Launcelot Greaves* than in *Roderick Random* and *Peregrine Pickle*, is not the very cause of the failure (highly interesting, for all that) of these novels. 'Who proves too much, proves nothing', such was the warning given by a rule of ancient dialectic. Fathom, the diabolical scoundrel and Launcelot the daimon of the Good are exaggerated monsters who no more succeed in making vice detestable than virtue lovable. But one must admit that Smollett spares no effort in order to emphasise, in a series of variations not devoid of thematic subtlety, the folly of extremes. To condemn extremes by extremes, such is the paradox, and also the literary wager, of *Ferdinand Count Fathom* and *Launcelot Greaves*.

The first five chapters constitute the prelude in which all the thematic elements are already assembled and adumbrated. Smollett reveals Launcelot's hereditary antecedents to his readers. His mother, according to one Tom Clarke[30], cautious even in his choice of words, was 'a little upon — the flighty order — a little touched or so' (p. 19). Tom

Clarke also informs us that a great-great-uncle of Launcelot's cut his throat in a fit of madness (p. 43). But these are only passing allusions, whereas the immediate causes of Launcelot's mental troubles are carefully explained. To summarise them, Launcelot's studious and retiring disposition has been unable to bear the cruel disappointment of the rupture signified in Aurelia's letter (pp. 37–8). This crisis is not a rude shock, it is prepared for by Launcelot's exasperated behaviour because Anthony Darnel has forbidden him all communication with his niece (p. 35). Why smile at Launcelot? In our day, his friends would have taken him to a psychoanalyst. Launcelot himself will play out his 'psychodrama' on the highways of chivalric adventures. Smollett was only applying, on the literary plane, the observations of William Battie, who, in his *Treatise on Madness* (London, 1758), ranged in the ninth class of secondary causes of madness: '*unwearied attention to any one subject*, as also *love, grief, and despair*; any of these affections will sometimes be annihilated by the tumultuous but less dangerous and sooner subsiding passions of anger or joy' (p. 85). Smollett knew Battie's work, analysed in the *Critical Review*[31], as well as John Monro's pamphlet, *Remarks on Dr. Battie's Treatise on Madness* (London, 1758). Launcelot's insanity should therefore not have surprised the first readers of the novel too much.

This madness is presented under its triple aspect, physical, psychological and moral. A certain over-excitement can be discerned in Launcelot's eyes or on his face (pp. 12, 16). Tom Clarke describes Launcelot's pitiful physical state (p. 37), undermined by his grief on his return from Italy. This interaction of mind on body and vice versa is a frequent implication in Smollett's novels, and one which finds its most coherent expression in *Humphry Clinker*. Smollett is in agreement with the ideas of his time, such as they are set forth by Jerome Gaub[32] in his essays of 1747 and 1763. Psychologically, Launcelot is subject to sudden changes of mood which do not always exclude physical violence (p. 35). The word 'pranks' recurs twice to describe his odd behaviour (pp. 35, 45). Like Melvil, he is subject to the caprices of his melancholy, which oscillates between morbid lethargy and feverish activity.

But Smollett is principally concerned with the moral consequences of Launcelot's (supposed) madness. After having rejected any imitation of Don Quixote, Launcelot emphasises the rational nature of the war he intends to wage against the enemies of virtue and, on two occasions, (p. 13) he uses the words 'to reason', the rest of his controversy with Ferret being marked by the abundance of intellectual vocabulary. The dialectic of madness and reason is given free play right from these first declarations of Launcelot's. A wise man, with his mind deranged, he wants to make a world, itself a prey to the madness of corruption, venality and debauchery, listen to reason. Launcelot's madness is to be wise, and his wisdom is to be mad. Like Hamlet, to whom there is an allusion right at the beginning of *Launcelot Greaves* (p. 9), Launcelot might say: 'I am but mad north-north-west; when the wind is southerly I know a hawk from a handsaw.' And, again like Hamlet, there is method in his madness. Nevertheless, Smollett suggests that Launcelot cannot be acquitted of all suspicion of insanity. The hero is driven by a (potentially) tragic 'Até', a kind of arrogance of the Good, which leads him to wish to take the law into his own hands (pp. 14, 40). It is thus that the anecdotes told by Tom Clarke of Launcelot's generosity (pp. 21, 21–2, 38–40) should be interpreted. A double irony endows these acts with some glimmer of madness. Launcelot's father is heartbroken to see his son devoting himself body and soul to these charitable tasks among clodhoppers and other humble people (p. 24). Moreover his thirst for justice is only approved by the neighbourhood in so far as Launcelot does not upset the established social conventions. To oblige the son of a rich farmer to marry a cottager's daughter whom he has got with child — what could be a more definite sign of dangerous mental derangement?

It is not only Launcelot's madness which is portrayed in these first chapters. As counterpoint and also as counterpoise — for, if Launcelot is constantly soaring up to the heights of moral generosity, his squire Crabshaw, a wily lout of the coarsest clay, constantly acts as a weight to bring his master down to earth — Crabshaw brings the burlesque touch of a cowardly individual, anything but generous (except to his lunatic horse, Gilbert) and, in spite of (or because of) his sound commonsense, only half resigned to sharing Launcelot's chivalric follies (pp. 10–11, 41–2, 45–6). Beside this comic buffoon there hovers the more sinister shadow of a malevolent mania, that of Aurelia's uncle, Anthony Darnel. This man, of ill-omened name since 'darnel' is a synonym for the tares in the Gospel parable — but then the good and beautiful Aurelia surely gives the lie to her surname, embodies the absurd madness of gratuitous evil. He hates Launcelot and his family, whom he pursues with implacable vindictiveness by using every possible means to thwart his niece's marriage. Smollett does not explain this insuperable animosity. Parliamentary rivalry is more a pretext than a deepseated cause (p. 25). As with Fathom, he merely *states* the existence of this brutal and perverse individual (pp. 25, 34–6) and his hatred of the Greaveses, which suggests the obsessions of madness. Moreover, in these first five chapters, Smollett contributes, by the constant use of adjectives or nouns belonging to the semantic realm of madness, to giving the impression of a world that is mad itself. 'Distracted', for example, is used in contexts ranging from imminent tragedy (p. 36) to the effects of the averted tragedy (p. 32), including the antithetical cliché 'distracted with joy' (p. 23). Ferret, a character largely inspired by one of Smollett's frequent adversaries, the pamphleteer John Shebbeare[33], a rabid enemy of the government, declares that the ministry 'is mad, or worse than mad' (p. 15). This pessimistic opinion is repeated right at the beginning of Chapter vi in Crowe's celebrated statement — it appears in the *Oxford Dictionary of Quotations*: 'I think for my part one half of the nation is mad — and the other half not very sound' (p. 52). The irony of this judgment is all the more biting since its author is himself suspected of madness, or at least of having a bee in his bonnet. In this world, where reason and mental aberration rub elbows or occasionally jostle each other, the characters do not fail to judge one another. Besides the eloquent, circumstantial and circumspect opinion Tom Clarke pronounces on Launcelot, the rector of the parish gives his. With the ambiguity of a hierophant, he predicts that Launcelot 'would turn out either a mirrour [*sic*] of wisdom, or a monument of folly' (p. 20). Crabshaw, himself suspected of not being quite in his right mind, does not hesitate to think his master crazy (p. 46), but wonders, not without cause, whether the madness of the master will not reflect on the servant. Even Gilbert, in the animal world, gives signs of covert and dangerous madness (ibid.). It is therefore not surprising that this Chapter v should end on an unpleasant note of absurd folly with violent consequences. The two incidents — the hunt interrupted by Crabshaw and the skirmish with the soldiers — demonstrate in opposite ways the same innate tendency of mankind to madness and evil. In fact, these two episodes come under the heading of 'folly' rather than 'madness', terms which recur constantly throughout *Launcelot Greaves* and are sometimes synonymous. 'Folly', however, generally designates an impulsive, thoughtless act whose consequences may prove disastrous. 'Madness' is easier to adumbrate in this novel: it implies all the semantic gamut which ranges from incurable mental illness to Launcelot's momentary eccentricities. It is an uncontrollable impulse, 'prompted by his own mischievous disposition', for instance, in Crabshaw's case (p. 47), which causes Crabshaw to get a good drubbing, though not without inflicting physical damage on his adversaries. In the same way, the drummer, at the sight of Launcelot in armour, suddenly feels 'an inclination to divert his company' (pp. 47–8). With the inexorable logic of the absurd, this joke quickly turns into a scene of general brawling. The drummer, mutilated by a kick from Gilbert, will finish his days at Launcelot's expense at Greavesbury-hall (p. 50) because the knight considers compassionately that the man 'had suffered so severely for his folly' (ibid.). And for the first time, Launcelot, who poses as the defender of order, has contributed, by his haughty contempt for the common soldiery, to disturbing the public peace and finds himself being brought before a magistrate.

After these five chapters of thematic prelude, the expository movement can be subdivided into three major sections. First, for seven chapters, a series of variations on the mirages of madness and reality (vi to xii). Next, three chapters on the relations between madness and love (xiii to xv). Lastly, up to Chapter xix inclusive, the final temptations of madness. It is very obvious that *Launcelot Greaves* was not conceived and composed by Smollett according to such a rigid plan as the articulations distinguished above might let it be supposed. Smollett's febrile personality and the method of publication of *Launcelot Greaves*, on which the reactions of the monthly public must have exerted some influence, are not consonant with a composition carefully prepared according to a plan more dependent on an oversimplified and artificial literary algebra than on reality. The intention of these pages is not to prove that Smollett followed a set plan, which is very unlikely, but that his novels, in particular *Launcelot Greaves*, have an internal structural cohesion due to the thematic unity, conscious or unconscious, of the work taken as a whole.

Chapters vi and vii present a burlesque counterpoint to Launcelot's eccentricities, with Crowe's début in the career of 'knight-errantry'. There is not the slightest doubt about the thematic intention. Crowe goes so far as to repeat Launcelot's very expression by declaring that he wishes to 'take to the highway in the way of a frolick' (p. 51; cf. p. 14). But Smollett has another intention, not devoid of irony. Behind this long and laboured series of practical jokes, with ghosts and liquid phosphorus, which remind one of the best (i.e. the worst) of Peregrine's inventions, lies the question: 'Who is the madder, Crowe and his chivalric vagaries or those who make themselves the amused accomplices of this grotesque masquerade?' Those who try to cure Crowe of his madness are not entirely sane themselves. It is not surprising that Smollett chooses Ferret, the disillusioned cynic, to express this opinion. After a rude collision with a pillar in the darkened church, Ferret takes to cursing 'bitterly against his own folly' (p. 56). Another piece of tomfoolery worthy of Gribouille punishes Crabshaw for his scared participation in this nocturnal joke (p. 59). Nevertheless, a note of amused tolerance can be heard at the end of Chapter vii. Launcelot refuses to condemn Crowe; anyhow he plainly has no right to do so: 'madness and honesty are not incompatible — indeed I feel it by experience' (p. 60). In a few words, and not without humour, intentional or not, Launcelot sums up the problem at the core of this dialectic of madness and reason.

Chapter viii marks a pause in the action — of which Launcelot and Crabshaw take advantage, devoting it to some reflections on madness (that of others). The second half is the putting of these observations into practice, an antithetical juxtaposition strongly tinged with irony. Smollett exposes, not without malice, the relativity and arrogant self-complacence of human judgment. After Crowe's mummery, Crabshaw thinks that the sailor is possessed by the devil, and that in any case, being a knight-errant 'becomes him as a sow doth a cart-saddle' (pp. 63—4). Crabshaw's own superiority is more than implied in this rustic aphorism. Launcelot also diagnoses Crowe as mad (p. 64), but throughout this page there develops a battle of wits in which Crabshaw is more like one of Shakespeare's clowns than like Sancho Panza. The calculated impudence of his replies, the insincerity which deceives neither himself nor his master, his pirouettes of ingratiating flattery make this page one of the subtlest in the novel. After a parallel alternately comic and serious drawn between madness and cowardice, the coach attacked by highwaymen gives Launcelot and Crabshaw the opportunity of putting their principles to the test. Launcelot reacts to the stimulus of this situation with mechanical promptness, whereas Crabshaw, as usual, pays the price of the adventure. Smollett tries to demonstrate the madness of blind heroism, when divorced from reality. Launcelot *forgets* to ask the name of the female traveller he has saved. He is punished for this omission, in the sense that he thus misses, for the first time, meeting Aurelia again (p. 69). By a touch of additional irony, the reader learns that this female traveller is not quite in her right mind.

The four following chapters (ix to xii) present, like a diptych, the macrocosm and microcosm of madness. The election in the country town (Chapter ix) allows Smollett to expose with a vigour worthy of Hogarth, who had treated the same political subject in 1755 in 'An Election', the madness of extremes. The thematic structure is simple. On the one side the verbal extravagances and the most stubborn traditionalism in every sphere of the Tory, Sir Valentine Quickset. This red-faced, loud-mouthed character belongs to the same lineage of fox-hunting squires as Squire Western. On the other side the Whig, supple, crafty, ambitious and mercenary, and, to complete the contrast with the Tory, probably Jewish, as his name Isaac Vanderpelft, suggests (pp. 73–6). The reasonable intervention of Launcelot advocates an enlightened parliamentarianism, but does not omit to condemn with equal vigour – or almost, since the Whig gets an even heavier reprimand than the Tory – the excesses of these political candidates. 'Moderation' is the keyword of this harangue, which acquires a doubly ironic flavour. Launcelot, it is not irrelevant to remember here, is *mad*. And his moderation and 'common sense' arouse the general wrath of the populace, without distinction of party. Thus moderation excites and unleashes madness. Launcelot is considered 'like a monster, or chimæra in politics' (p. 78). In other words, he is mad because he is right, but he is right because he is mad.

In the following chapter (x), the eloquence of the quack, Ferret, besides being a piece of admirable stylistic virtuosity, has the merit of constantly mingling alchemical charlatanism with the alchemy of that other charlatanism, politics. Great Britain, panting under the scalpel of her charlatans, is a prey to madness. All these bloodletters 'have intoxicated her brain, until she is become delirious: she can no longer pursue her own interest; or, indeed, rightly distinguish it' (p. 79). Launcelot ought to have passed unnoticed in England. As the gravedigger in *Hamlet* declared: 'Twill not be seen in him there; there the men are as mad as he.' The gleams of irony play through the prism of madness. Ferret, a charlatan and above all a virulent enemy of the government, otherwise the human race, displays a vehemence near to madness. Launcelot listens to him, along with a whole mob of gaping rustics stunned by Ferret's masterly fluency and dazzled by his pseudo-erudition. If Smollett cannot accept personal responsibility for Ferret's seditious arguments, Launcelot (above suspicion since he is mad) admits that he 'had mixed some melancholy truths with his scurrility' (p. 81).

Judge Gobble's prison (Chapters xi and xii) presents in miniature the saddening image of a microcosm in which the madness of one individual wreaks havoc on the community. Here again irony appears right from the beginning. Launcelot has been arrested, on the denunciation of Ferret, because he conceals sinister designs 'under an affected cloak of lunacy' (p. 86). The complaints of the prisoners are such that Launcelot thinks at once of those that will be brought against Gobble on the day of the Last Judgment (ibid.). Inverted irony gives these pages their structure. Never has Launcelot shown so much good sense and moderation as in his investigation of the cases of his fellow-prisoners. His final indictment of Gobble displays the same qualities (pp. 93–4). All these unfortunate people, arbitrarily imprisoned by Gobble, pose the fundamental problem of human injustice: why should such wickedness exist in this conceited puppet of a judge? The social vanity of the parvenu is only a false answer. Smollett reaffirms once again that Man is absurdly possessed of a destructive will and a lust for evil, 'the poisonous issue of a malignant heart, devoid of humanity, inflamed with pride, and rankling with revenge' (p. 97). The worthy mate of such a monster, Mrs Gobble has all the qualities required for playing her satanic role: 'pride and diabolical malice' (p. 98). Launcelot insists several times on the evil such creatures can spread around them (pp. 97, 98, 101). A world inverted by irony but also a world turned upside-down by madness, such is the pessimistic picture Smollett presents to his readers. The madness lies not so much in Launcelot's acts as in the insane situation created by social and metaphysical corruption. The accused Launcelot accuses his judge, draws up a remorselessly lucid indictment and condemns him. But Smollett does not, for all that, forget this theme of madness which recurs like a leitmotif throughout the hovel. If the happpiness of all the prisoners rewards the efforts of Launcelot, the lover of justice, who has crushed the bad judge, Smollett takes care to remind one that his character is still *non compos mentis*. Launcelot once again feels the moral temptation to take the law into his own hands (p. 98) but he is already wise enough to rely on the established laws of his country (ibid.).

On the thematic plane, the beginning of Chapter xiii prolongs the preceding movement. In the eyes of the lawyer, Clarke, madness, even though as generous and beneficent as Launcelot's, remains 'a perversion of sense to the end of the chapter' (p. 104). Irony is given free play when Launcelot, convinced by Clarke's rational arguments, tries in his turn to persuade Crowe to abandon chivalry. And yet the only result of these good intentions is to launch Launcelot off on other adventures in which love comes into its own again (pp. 106–7).

The three following chapters (xiii to xv), in which Smollett brings love and madness into play, are less rich and successful than the subtle variations on madness and reality in the preceding ones. Aurelia is one of those perfect heroines, so much so that this physical and moral perfection gives her the sexless unreality of an angelic being. If Chapter xiii renews their love affair, the other two have the merit of both illuminating and obscuring the situation of Launcelot and Aurelia. To begin with, during Chapter xiv the reader learns of Anthony Darnel's stratagem to make his niece pass as mad. It is frightening to note how easily those about her accept this diagnosis and even go so far as to interpret her most ordinary behaviour in an unfavourable light (pp. 115–16). Can the world of madness be separated from that of reason by such a hair's breadth that the semiology of everyday life can be regarded as equally relevant to either? The meeting between Aurelia and Launcelot bears the stamp of ironic ambiguity. At the very moment when the knight finds his lady again, he uses the vocabulary of madness to describe himself more than he has ever done before (pp. 121–3). Another ironic development: when Launcelot is rejoicing in this 'transition from madness to deliberation, from despair to felicity' (p. 124), he is, in fact, far from being cured. Once again he responds, like a human automaton, to the chivalric stimulus (the cries of a traveller who is being attacked). The comparison Smollett uses – 'The supposition of such distress operated like gunpowder on the disposition of our adventurer' (p. 125; cf. p. 28: 'as hasty as gunpowder') – stresses Launcelot's blind obedience to this impulse which promptly suspends all his rational faculties. Victim of a stratagem to get him away from Aurelia, Launcelot once more becomes 'mad with vexation' (p. 125), and, though the hero raves, his horse, in ironic compensation, proves to be 'inspired with reason' (p. 126) just as in a fairytale. As always, Crabshaw's ludicrous adventures are at once the distorting mirror and the reflection of his master's. Launcelot is therefore not cured, he has to submit to other trials.

These final trials and temptations are presented in Chapters xvi to xix to an antithetical progression not devoid of logic and thematic coherence. The first two offer the misadventures of Crabshaw and Crowe as burlesque counterpoint, but it must be emphasised that this habitual proceeding, the comic duplication of Launcelot's adventures, is always connected with the central theme of madness. Launcelot's rage, when he realises he has been tricked, is quickly appeased. The vocabulary of reflection replaces that of passion (pp. 130–1). The re-encounter with his squire, who is in a bad way, gives Smollett the opportunity of inserting a new variation on the ambiguities of reason and madness. Crabshaw, in his fury against the apothecary and the nurse, is never so right as when he is mad with rage and appears to be raving. An unexpected detail, a somewhat cynical and misanthropic doctor, admits that he is right (pp. 133–4). The irony of Launcelot's decision to abandon armour and chivalry (p. 135) becomes immediately obvious. He renounces one form of madness only to plunge straightaway into another, to wit sweet daydreams of the happiness he will enjoy with Aurelia. Moreover, though he abandons his own follies, those of others, in this case Crowe and Sycamore (xviii), bring him back to himself. The recourse to justice (pp. 140–5) – Judge Elmy is the antithesis of Gobble – provides an unexpected reversal. Crowe gets off very lightly but not his dishonest accuser, the litigious farmer Prickle. This minor character is a concrete example of those fundamentally bad men who are invariably to be found in all ranks of society. But Launcelot's ambivalence still persists, in spite of his progress on the path of reason. A few lines later, Smollett contrasts the knight's personality 'dashed as it was with extravagance' with the charm of his 'sober and rational' conversation (p. 145).

The madness of Sycamore, Launcelot's rival, is the touchstone which puts Launcelot's reason to the test, a confrontation from which it emerges fortified. Like Launcelot, Sycamore has a comic double in the person of his hanger-on Dawdle, an unmitigated scoundrel who leads his master by his purse-strings (pp. 146–7). The reversal of the situation is such that Launcelot, having received his rival's challenge, 'began to reflect, not without mortification, that he was treated as a lunatic' (pp. 148–9). This mental revolution also marks an *evolution* in Launcelot, who condemns these mortal contests with Smollett's habitual vehemence when he denounces the absurdity of duels. Launcelot accepts the reasonable side of chivalry but rejects everything which may violate 'every suggestion of reason, and every precept of humanity' (p. 149). It is therefore in the name of reason that Launcelot refuses this challenge. He refuses to take a decision 'that contradicts my own reason as much as it would outrage the laws of my country' (p. 151).

The encounter between the two knights takes place, nevertheless, at the instigation of Dawdle, always in search of a chance to play someone a dirty trick. If Launcelot shows his characteristic bravery and magnanimity, Dawdle vanquishes Crowe in the course of a ludicrous tourney in which low cunning plays considerably more part than knightly honour. This confrontation appears on the thematic plane as an interplay of distorting mirrors. There is another fight, a third reflection, between Crabshaw and Sycamore's valet, then, as a last refraction, the mêlée becomes general (p. 157). So when Launcelot has just won a chivalric victory (the only time he fights a tourney), he announces his intention of renouncing this way of life but promptly tells Sycamore that he intends to call him to account for his conduct 'not in the character of a lunatic knight-errant, but as a plain English gentleman, jealous of his honour, and resolute in his purpose' (p. 158). Is the return to reason only another form of madness?

If the last five chapters end with the triumph of reason and the usual scenes of marital bliss, Launcelot, although he has begun to be cured, still has to travel a road full of pitfalls, material and above all spiritual. Like the heroes of the cosmogonic cycle, Launcelot begins by descending into the Underworld, as the heading of Chapter xx indicates. This descent takes place in two stages. In the first, the knight is a mere spectator who, in spite of his anguished haste to find Aurelia again, displays an awkward, not to say ill-advised, curiosity about certain unfortunate prisoners (pp. 167–8). In the second Launcelot himself is struggling in the doubly absurd world of a madhouse. The providential chance which enables Launcelot to recover his freedom and Aurelia matters little; these are only tricks of the novelist's trade. But after this final ordeal, in which Launcelot's reason has perhaps never been more menaced, he finally liberates himself from the insidious chains of his madness.

The idyllic description of the King's Bench prison (pp. 163–4) still surprises the modern reader as much as it surprised Smollett's contemporaries[34]. But a more searching reading soon reveals the ironic value of this description when it turns out to be juxtaposed to a series of pitiful life stories. Crabclaw and Tapley present a grotesque caricature of chivalric combat (pp. 166–7). Felton is the victim of an inexorable creditor and the insanity of the judicial system (imprisonment for debt). The story of Clewline (pp. 168–72) in which the physical and moral downfall of a naval officer and his wife stresses the absurdity of family vindictiveness, and perhaps also the absurdity, the metaphysical scandal that the death of a child is. Madness lies in wait for these easy victims (p. 171). The better to emphasise the results of blind misfortune – the story of Mr Coleby (pp. 174–5) – Smollett places just before it the case of the affected, extravagant and irresponsible coquette. Launcelot also has to learn moderation in charity and not automatically put his hand in his pocket (p. 174) to relieve no matter what distress, genuine or feigned. Before penetrating into the absurd world of the madhouse, Smollett lingers in the company of the two buffoons of the novel, Crabshaw and Crowe, and treats their anxious credulity with some irony. Their visit to the astrologer, none other than Ferret in disguise, is not unreminiscent of the palmistry business set up by Cadwallader and Peregrine. The astrologer's technique is the same as Cadwallader's. The only pieces of information Ferret gives the sailor and the squire are those they have already provided him with during the preliminary interview (pp. 180–3). Astrology is also a method of exploiting human folly, just like the charlatanism already practised by Ferret.

The madhouse plays the same maieutic role in *Launcelot Greaves* as prison does in the previous novels. Abducted and wrongfully interned, as a result of a machination of Sycamore's Launcelot, who has never been saner, becomes aware of his past follies. The wails of the madmen in the night (pp. 185–7) and the information furnished by one of the inmates, the satirical poet Dick Distich[35], plunge Launcelot into bitter cogitations: 'he heartily repented of his knight-errantry, as a frolic which might have very serious consequences, with respect to his future life and fortune' (pp. 186–7). 'Frolic' was the very word Launcelot used at the beginning of the book (p. 14). The arbitrary internment is the ironic apogee of this dialectical interplay of madness and reason (p. 190). The irony gives rise to a series of paradoxes which endow these two chapters (xxiii and xxiv) with all their sparkling thematic value. Thus, at the moment when Launcelot finds himself shut up in a madhouse, he has never been more *compos mentis*. It is not because of his chivalric eccentricities that he is interned. It is not even his own madness which has led to his internment, but the madness of evil, in this case that of Sycamore and Dawdle. The use of a copious cognitive vocabulary even attests, on the stylistic plane, Launcelot's rational lucidity (see in particular the paragraph beginning at the bottom of p. 186). Another cruel paradox: that of being treated as a madman by an alienist who retreats behind a torrent of crazy medical jargon (p. 187). Launcelot is never so threatened with losing his reason for good as in this exasperating world of the absurd. Such is the significance of this paroxysm which almost overwhelms him when he hears Aurelia's voice (p. 191). This sojourn in the madhouse represents a complete thematic revolution since the beginning of the novel. Launcelot has wished, more or less consciously, to flout society and to use the mask of madness to chastise men for their follies. Now, in these two chapters, society blindly revenges itself and makes the mask stick to Launcelot's face, at the risk of suffocating him. In the jousts of madness and reason, the knight sees his own weapon turned against him.

The final deliverance, the reunion of Launcelot and Aurelia and their happiness, are part of the moral mythology of the eighteenth-century novel. One metaphor deserves to be noted because it brings out Smollett's moral intentions. He speaks of the happiness 'to which, as to the north pole, the course of these adventures hath been invariably directed' (p. 205). Two thematic reminders can be discerned in the last chapter, which is otherwise not of much interest. Smollett confirms that Launcelot is definitely cured. Instead of pursuing Sycamore and Dawdle to the ends of the earth, Launcelot decides to use a means that is safer, more rational and more in conformity with the customs of his time, to wit the law (p. 202). Subsequently, the satirical Ferret surrenders, but does not die. Glutted with the domestic bliss of Launcelot's home in Yorkshire, he decides to return to London where he can always satisfy 'the ravenous appetite of his spleen' (p. 211). Thus a satirical note of ironic restlessness persists to the end of the novel. Ferret refuses to let himself be snared in the sticky toils of a treacly felicity. Misanthrope and cynic as he is, he also embodies the freedom of the individual who rebels against the insanity of bourgeois society.

If one tries to draw a diagram of the structures of *Ferdinand Count Fathom* and *Launcelot Greaves*, that of *Ferdinand Count Fathom* looks like an inverted capital 'V' flanked by two small inverted 'v's'. The three peaks thus obtained represent the heights reached by Fathom in his social success. These are situated in Presburg and Vienna, the highest in Bristol and the last in London, in Chapter xlix. The two low points, as well as the final fall, occur in Paris and in prison in London. *Launcelot Greaves*, unlike the preceding novels, has a circular structure. The hero returns to his point of departure, topographical (Yorkshire) and mental (sanity). After having passed through the nadir of his arbitrary internment, he finds reason and happiness again in the company of Aurelia. What Launcelot set out on, as in ancient mythology, was a heroic quest in search of his identity and his feminine *alter ego*.

The strength of their moral intentions gives these two novels their internal structure. But this thematic cohesion, too long unrecognised by critics, is also the major cause of the partial failure of these two novels in which the didactic purpose too often takes precedence over the aesthetic demands of literary creation. It is difficult to raise these novels to the first rank, but they deserve to emerge from the darkness and quasi-oblivion to which a hasty and superficial reading has relegated them for two centuries. Without ever attaining the virtuosity of Fielding, Smollett handles irony with a certain dexterity. Often clumsy, over-obvious and therefore tiresome in *Ferdinand Count Fathom*, it becomes much richer and subtler in *Launcelot Greaves*. Irony vivifies the moral themes which Smollett treats. A protean irony, the ludic mainspring of the interplay of madness and reason gives its vital acidity to the implicit or explicit satire of *Ferdinand Count Fathom* and *Launcelot Greaves*. As Vladimir Jankélévitch writes:

> Irony is the disturbing and uncomfortable aspect of life. It presents us with the concave mirror in which we blush to see ourselves distorted and grimacing, it teaches us not to worship ourselves and ensures that our imagination retains all its rights over its intractable progeny[36].

Irony guarantees the satiric freedom of the author, threatened for a moment in *Ferdinand Count Fathom* by an access of sentimentality, of which there still remain a few fairly unimportant traces in *Launcelot Greaves*. But after these two antithetical attempts, which met with mediocre success, Smollett had barely ten years left in which to create the synthesis, and also the masterpiece of his genius as a novelist, with *Humphry Clinker*.

6
Humphry Clinker **or the adventure of morality**

The first problem which compels the attention of the reader of *Humphry Clinker* is: 'Why did Smollett choose the epistolary form?' There are several possible explanations. Smollett had already used this method in *Travels through France and Italy*, but it is certain — as Martz and Kahrl have shown[1] — that he did so mainly in deference to a didactic convention of the period. Before and after *Travels through France and Italy*, travellers' letters (fictitious or real) had a vogue to which Smollett himself does not fail to draw attention at the beginning of *Humphry Clinker*[2]. Already, in 1755, John Shebbeare, under the Jesuitical pseudonym of Batista Angeloni, had painted a picture of English manners, in general a rather gloomy and satirical one, which often bears a resemblance to the pessimistic remarks made by Matthew Bramble about London: the contempt for *belles-lettres* in England, the religious problems and the relations with servants, not to mention minor themes such as the extravagance of women's fashions or the English taste in horticulture. But Batista Angeloni is not really writing impressions of travel; he remains fixed in London except during a journey to Wales described in Letter xxx of Volume II. Closer to *Travels through France and Italy* (chronologically, but certainly not psychologically) Philip Thicknesse's *Observations on the Customs and Manners of the French Nation* (London, 1766) shows a staunch love of France. The author, in marked contrast to Smollett, speaks French fluently and does not hesitate to parade his knowledge of Parisian high society. While agreeing with Smollett about the lack of cleanliness, delicacy and decency of the French, Thicknesse, in a letter dated from St-Germain, August 15th 1766, acknowledges the receipt of *Travels through France and Italy*, which he promptly sets about criticising. He writes to his correspondent 'Did you send them [*Travels through France and Italy*] to me to steal from, *to correct*, or to amuse? If the latter, they have answered your design'[3]. Like so many lesser men, what Thicknesse detested most of all in Smollett was the man of the *Critical Review*. But, in the *Observations*, it must be admitted that Thicknesse shows a certain moderation in his attacks on Smollett and the *Travels through France and Italy*: 'I do not mean to impeach his veracity, but to shew his real incapacity to give an account of people with whom he never eat or conversed' (pp. 104—5). This restraint totally disappears two years later in the *Useful Hints . . .* (1768)[4] in which Thicknesse lets fly with all the venomous virulence of which he was capable against Smollett and the *Critical Review*. Joseph Baretti also published two travel narratives, *An Account of the Manners and Customs of Italy* (1769) and *A Journey from London to Genoa* in 1770. The first work does not adopt the epistolary method, but in it, Baretti, who was of Italian origin, vigorously refutes, chapter by chapter, the erroneous observations published by Sharp in his *Letters from Italy* (1768). On the advice of Johnson, Baretti had kept a diary of his journey (August 14th to November 18th 1760) from London to Genoa via Portugal, Spain and France. This second book is presented in the form of letters, very favourable to the English and their institutions. Nevertheless, Baretti expresses some reserves about the xenophobic behaviour of the London populace, though he hastens to add that in Italy the credulous and fanatical populace is no better. Baretti even admits that Londoners of the lower classes have a spontaneous generosity, as shown for example in the treatment of French prisoners of war or in the help given to Portugal after the earthquake of 1755. Though these letters, which Johnson admired, can still be read with pleasure for their lively style and good-humoured apt observations, it is very obvious that for Baretti the epistolary form was merely a useful literary convention. Finally, in order to make Smollett's technical and literary originality stand out more clearly, even a rapid comparison with Richardson's works enables one to grasp the distance which separates *Pamela* or *Clarissa* from *Humphry Clinker*. Smollett's novel borrows from the various accounts of travels a geographical dynamism which is lacking in Richardson. The absence of replies to the five letter-writers on the move eases the strain on the technique of the author, who, rather like Sterne in *Tristram Shandy*, trusts in the imagination of the reader to recreate, with a deliciously guilty feeling of indiscretion, the possible answers of the correspondents. *Humphry Clinker* therefore also assumes a certain psychological dynamism on the part of the reader.

Round about 1771 there was not only a craze for travel-books — partly explained by favourable socio-economic and international conditions — but also a vogue for the epistolary novel. American scholars[5] have discovered that, out of the 3,000 novels published between 1740 and

1799, 506 are in letter-form. Though, between 1740 and 1749, there were only fourteen epistolary novels, between 1770 and 1774, eighty-one were published, this being the highest figure except for the period between 1785 and 1788, when 108 epistolary novels appeared. In 1771 alone, twenty-seven epistolary novels (including *Humphry Clinker*) were published. These figures serve no purpose other than emphasising both Smollett's participation in the literary current of his day and the vigour of his technical and literary innovations which enabled him to write an enduring masterpiece, while the vast majority of these epistolary novels has sunk into the dusty oblivion of the nether regions of libraries.

What then are Smollett's innovations, or at least the peculiar characteristics of his epistolary technique[6]? This technique is striking in its variety, as is suggested straight away by the diversity of the ways in which the writers head their letters and the formulas they use in signing them. Going only by the mode of address, it would be almost possible to discern the psychological evolution of Matthew Bramble merely from reading the brusque 'Doctor' (p. 5) which softens to 'Dear Doctor' (p. 33) and expands into a warm 'Dear Dick' (p. 244). Jery Melford, too, uses in turn 'Dear Phillips' (p. 8), 'Dear Knight' (p. 20), 'Dear Wat' (p. 110), 'Dear Watkin' (p. 310). This wealth of technical invention is even more apparent in the opening paragraphs of the letters. The furious denial of the first letter written by Matthew Bramble (p. 5) contrasts strongly with the much calmer and politer tone of the second (p. 11). Jery begins his second letter (p. 16) by deploring the rumour a facetious fellow Oxford undergraduate had spread about a quarrel he, Jery, was supposed to have had with a mountebank's buffoon. He replies thus to an hypothetical letter from his correspondent, Sir Watkin Phillips, of which he allows the reader to guess part of the contents. This technique maintains the fictitious, but virtual presence of the correspondent. By the end of a certain number of letters, especially those of Matthew Bramble and Jery, there emerges not only the personality of the letter-writers but also that of the people to whom they are writing, and of whose discreet, but perceptible existence Smollett is careful to remain aware.

Smollett's methods vary in almost every letter and it would take too long to examine them all in detail. Here are the principal ones: interest or curiosity kept keen (p. 20 and p. 118); the repetition of a question asked by the correspondent (p. 64); conversely, the reply (p. 23), or again the beginning *ex abrupto* (p. 86); the account of fulfilling a commission solicited by the correspondent (p. 136); Jery's excuses, admitting that he has launched into a somewhat too prolix description of Lismahago (p. 208); Matthew Bramble's joy when he receives a letter from Dr Lewis after a long interruption of their correspondence, due to the rapid and slightly disorganised return journey southwards (p. 339). But Smollett deploys even more epistolary subtlety in the ever-changing interplay of revelations, flashbacks and echoes which create a pattern in the letters and gives them the shifting fascination of a literary kaleidoscope. If one examines the first six letters of *Humphry Clinker*, as the initial narrative unit, the incident between Jery and Wilson (the strolling player who dares to court Lydia) appears only as a mere allusion in Matthew Bramble's letter (p. 5). Tabitha Bramble's silence on this subject is explained by the injunction of absolute discretion, which the servant, Winifred Jenkins, promptly disobeys. Her version is over-simplified (p. 7) but already throws light on the previous allusion, at the same time whetting the reader's curiosity. Jery's letter, in its turn, brings some further explanations, but obviously incomplete and onesided. Jery lingers over describing his role of defender of virtue and family honour with egocentric self-satisfaction (note the exaggerated frequency of the 'I' in his version of the affair).

The person involved among the five letter-writers remains to be heard. Lydia writes two letters on the same day, no doubt one after the other, and, contrary to rule in *Humphry Clinker*, to two different correspondents: her governess and her friend and confidant Laetitia. These two letters, very different in tone and content, are in fact complementary. In the first, Lydia appears as a contrite little ninny who has nearly fallen head over heels in love and humbly begs her revered governess's pardon. There too, the use of the first person emphasises the childish egotism of this more or less real distress. In spite of her boarding-school miss's innocence, Lydia is not lacking in a certain basic feminine duplicity. The phrase 'at the usual place' (p. 10), for example, to tell Laetitia where she can return the miniature he had given Lydia to Wilson, shows that relations were much better organised than Lydia wishes the governess to think. The sentimental submissiveness of the previous letter gives place to the genuine emotion of a young girl in love, torn between her feelings and the social taboos set up by the family circle, in this case her uncle and brother. Thus, by a series of gradual revelations, ranging from a mere allusion to a near-avowal, Smollett presents with subtlety what might be no more than (yet another!) trite story of thwarted loves such as appears in all his other novels. Seen through the prism of four personalities, this beginning of a sentimental affair loses all its literary banality and becomes animated with sparkling life. It must also be added that Smollett completes the reader's information by giving him a lucid summary of the whole affair written by Matthew Bramble (pp. 12–14) and a piece of evidence attached to his letter – a love-letter of Wilson's intercepted by Jery (pp. 15–16).

Side by side with this gradual discovery of an always relative truth, Smollett uses other technical methods, such as the systematic opposition of opinions on the same subject. When Matthew Bramble and his niece describe Ranelagh and Vauxhall, the reader may well wonder if they are talking of the same places, so antithetical are the descriptions, as also of the growth of London, the buildings, the crowd, the traffic, the bridges and the nightly amusements. But, in fact, the difference between these two letters (pp. 86—90 and 90—5) is not so profound as it seems at first sight. The platitude of Lydia's comments is such that these well-worn adjectives ('stupendous', 'prodigious' and other crude superlatives, pp. 91—2) in some way corroborate Matthew Bramble's pessimistic impressions when confronted with a city suffering from physical, economic and social insanity. Conversely, the opinions of the letter-writers can confirm and perpetuate each other, as in the case of Jery's severe criticism of his friend Barton (pp. 95—6) which is repeated and amplified by Lydia eight days later (p. 135). In the same way, Jery and his uncle agree in noticing the affinities between Wales and Scotland (pp. 240, 247).

Repetitions of incidents and opinions are the very core of this protean technique. Whether it is a question of a minor incident — such as Win Jenkins's mishap when she is dressed up in Parisian (?) fashion at Newcastle, recounted by Jery (pp. 208—9) and then by Win herself (p. 219) — or of a structural leitmotiv — such as the whiteness of Clinker's skin (pp. 81, 208) — Smollett weaves a close web of references and allusions which give the novel its global unity. The multiple echoes add still more to its teeming life. The description of the ladies' bath in Bath, written by Win Jenkins (p. 43) is an echo (attenuated but caricatural) of the one already given by Lydia (p. 40). Conversely, Matthew Bramble's allusion to the dishonesty of servants in Bath (p. 57) is amplified and illustrated by Win Jenkins's quarrels with her fellow-domestics (pp. 70—1). Though there is a direct echo between Tabitha's and Win's letters on the subject of the lack of provisions in Scotland (a stupid belief of Tabitha's enunciated on p. 213 and repeated by Win on p. 220), it is liable to become much fainter and more distant: the habit of dressing a good twenty years out-of-date of which Tabitha is guilty in the eyes of Lady Griskin (p. 94) reappears (increased by one or two lustrums) in Jery's description of her wedding finery (p. 347). These methods, employed all through the novel, enable Smollett to create a very close network of technical links which constitute, in a way, the underlying plot of the novel taken as a whole and not just as a series of isolated letters written by five different people.

In spite of the specific character of the epistolary technique in *Humphry Clinker*, it would be unfair, as well as inaccurate, not to suggest Smollett's probable debt to certain eighteenth-century authors and characters. In the first place, the *New Bath Guide* (1766) by Christopher Anstey (1724—1805) is most often cited[7] for its possible influence on *Humphry Clinker*. This collection of fifteen letters in anapaestic verse had a lively satirical success, confirmed by five editions in the year of publication alone. But these memoirs and mishaps of the Blunderhead family provide general parallels with *Humphry Clinker* rather than a genuine source. Anstey, like Smollett five years later, attacks ignorant, pedantic and rapacious doctors; the lack of hygiene and quiet in these pretended health resorts; the follies of fashion and the guilty passion for Methodism whose zealots are once again accused of taking more carnal than spiritual interest in their charming female converts. Smollett has perhaps borrowed the Blunderheads' maidservant's Christian name 'Tabitha' and also her chlorotic complexion, to baptise Matthew Bramble's sister and to suggest the poor health of Win Jenkins, who is subject to the vapours and fainting fits. Popular good sense believed in those days (and still does) that these virginal ailments would vanish under the vigorous embraces of some lusty young man. Win undoubtedly waits till she is honourably married to Humphry, but poor Tabby Runt has let herself be seduced by the Methodist:

> And, if right I can judge by her Shape and her Face,
> She soon may produce him an Infant of Grace.

Sim Blunderhead writes with evident mischievousness in Letter xv. This same character, in Letter v, irritates the irascible, gouty old Lord Ringbone by practicing music and dance steps in the room overhead. Smollett has perhaps transposed this incident when he recounts the same kind of confrontation between Matthew Bramble and Sir Ulic Mackilligut (pp. 29—30). All these parallels between the *New Bath Guide* and *Humphry Clinker* are presumptions rather than absolute proofs of literary borrowings, and, in general, Anstey's influence on Smollett has been exaggerated.

The character of Matthew Bramble, the surly, but benevolent misanthropist[8] was no literary novelty in 1771. Two of his predecessors deserve notice: Giles Crab in *The Englishman Return'd from Paris* (1756) a farce in two acts by Samuel Foote, and Mr Drybone, 'The Man in Black' in Goldsmith's *Citizen of the World* (1762). Like Matthew Bramble, Giles Crab has the guardianship of the orphan son and daughter of a dead friend (in *Humphry Clinker* it is brother). At the beginning of the first scene, Giles Crab explodes with all his rancour, faced with what he considers an intolerable burden:

> The Conduct of a Boy, bred a Booby at Home and finish'd a Fop abroad; together with the Direction of a marriageable, and, therefore an unmanageable Wench; and all this to an old Fellow of Sixty-six, who heartily hates Bus'ness, is tir'd of the World, and despises every Thing in it. Why how the Devil came I to merit . . .

The tone, rendered more violent by theatrical exaggeration, is nevertheless not unreminiscent of that of Matthew Bramble's first two letters. The resemblance is even clearer between Giles Crab's declaration, when outraged by the duplicity of a tutor who is out to deprive the young man of his fortune: 'Fresh Instances, every Moment, fortify my Abhorrence, my Detestation, of Mankind. This Turn may be term'd Misanthropy'[9] and Matthew Bramble's splenetic outburst: 'Heark ye, Lewis, my misanthropy increases every day — The longer I live, I find the folly and fraud of mankind grow more and more intolerable' (p. 47). A review, on the whole quite favourable and attributed to Smollett[10] appeared in the first number of the *Critical Review*: 'Crab's character is well coloured; but we apprehend, not so correctly designed. Is not his deportment too brutal, and his heart too humane?' (January—February 1756, i, 83). Rather oddly, too, Smollett reproaches Samuel Foote for his Gallophobia: 'Are not such reflections so many sacrifices made to the galleries, at the expence of politeness and common justice?' (ibid.). A year later, the heavy charges against the caricatural Frenchman in *The Reprisal* were to make Smollett, once again, contradict himself.

The link between the 'Man in Black' (Mr Drybone) and Matthew Bramble is such that Goldsmith's character, the friend and London mentor of the Chinese philosopher Lien Chi Altangi, appears like the moral and psychological prototype of the surly Welsh country squire. In Letter xxvi, Goldsmith brings out the inner contradictions of Mr Drybone:

> He may justly be termed an humourist in a nation of humourists. Tho' he is generous even to profusion, he affects to be thought a prodigy of parsimony and prudence; though his conversation be replete with the most sordid and selfish maxims, his heart is dilated with the most unbounded love. I have known him profess himself a man-hater, while his cheek was glowing with compassion; and, while his looks were softened into pity, I have heard him use the language of the most unbounded ill-nature. Some affect humanity and tenderness; others boast of having such dispositions from nature; but he is the only man I ever knew who seemed ashamed of his natural benevolence. He takes as much pains to hide his feelings, as an hypocrite would to conceal his indifference; but on every unguarded moment, the mask drops off, and reveals him to the most superficial observer[11].

With a few alterations, it would be hard to find a better summary of the psychological and moral paradoxes which characterise Matthew Bramble's behaviour, towards the widow he secretly helps, for example (pp. 20–2). Just like the Chinese philosopher, Jery can say of his uncle: 'He affects misanthropy, in order to conceal the sensibility of a heart, which is tender, even to a degree of weakness' (p. 28). Besides this literary kinship between Mr Drybone and Matthew Bramble, there are several other possible connections between *The Citizen of the World* and *Humphry Clinker*. Letters xxix and xxx which describe a meeting of authors, denounce — with an irony a little less biting than Smollett's in *Humphry Clinker* — the pretensions of these needy writers, their vanity, their money worries, their constant struggle with the bailiffs, their ruses to avoid them, their frauds. The wily Tim Cropdale would certainly have felt quite at home with them. The amazement of Lien Chi Altangi at the sight of the Vauxhall illuminations makes one think of Lydia's admiring ecstasies, and the attacks (especially in Letter cxi) on Methodism prepare the way for Matthew Bramble's cantankerous gibes at this doctrine in which inner light obscures the light of reason. Goldsmith's book had a very favourable reception in the *Critical Review* of May 1762 (xiii, 397—400). Another possible parallel with Goldsmith's work is the scene in Clerkenwell prison where Humphry Clinker preaches to the denizens of the underworld. Smollett perhaps derived his inspiration from a similar situation in *The Vicar of Wakefield* (Chapters xxvi and xxvii). But Dr Primrose encounters at first a much rougher, not to say brutal, opposition and nevertheless accomplishes a more effective transformation (at least on the material plane of the economic organisation of the prisoners).

It is traditional (but not convincing) to suggest that a certain Robert Stobo served as the model for Lismahago. The numerous studies[12] of this historical character of almost legendary dimensions have at least had the merit of emphasising Smollett's great originality in comparison with this very hypothetical source of inspiration. Likewise, and with a little more probability, it is possible that the pathetic scene where 'Captain Brown' meets his old father again (pp. 263—4) was inspired by a real incident[13]. Lastly, Smollett perhaps drew a first rough sketch of Win Jenkins in no. xi (August 7th 1762) of the unlucky *Briton*, that weekly pro-government pamphlet in which Smollett had already used fake letters from readers to reply to Wilkes's *North Briton* (or attack it). At the end of this no. xi appears a letter (pp. 65—6) written in fanciful spelling, and also imitating the way the lower classes spoke English. It is signed 'Winifred Bullcalf'. This person writes thus to Mr Brittin:

> Althof my neighbour Firkin says you can't rite English, therefore must be a Scotchman; and being a Scotchman, you have no right to call yourself a Brittin; and as how you are a vagabond people, that come over in shoals with every fair wind, like locusts to devour us; yet I knows what's what.

This is only an indication of stylistic interest in plebeian syntax, bearing no relationship to the subtle linguistic elaboration which gives Win Jenkins's letters their savour.

It remains to determine whether the choice of the epistolary form can be explained by motives inherent in Smollett's fictional work. Tuvia Bloch, in his article 'Smollett's quest for form'[14] puts forward the theory that Smollett's choice was dictated by his failure when he tried, in *Ferdinand Count Fathom* and *Launcelot Greaves*, to imitate Fielding's handling of irony, in particular so as to maintain a constant distance between the author and his characters. However interesting it may be, this hypothesis is not entirely satisfactory and above all repeats wellworn comparisons between Fielding and Smollett, to the advantage, nearly always, of Fielding. Smollett's (partial) failure, as regards *Ferdinand Count Fathom* and *Launcelot Greaves*, lies, as the preceding chapter has tried to show, on the moral plane. The inner dialectic of his work had impelled Smollett to depict, after such average heroes as Roderick and Peregrine, extreme personalities, directed wholly towards Evil (Fathom) or towards Good (Launcelot Greaves). The failure of these antipodal characters was in some sort the condemnation of the simple vision, that of the principal character as conceived in the auto-dedication of *Ferdinand Count Fathom*. Fathom and Greaves, in spite of graduations, much more apparent in *Launcelot Greaves*, remained monolithic characters whose perception of the world was conditioned by the dichotomy of moral Manicheism.

The single point of view, damned by the double failure of *Ferdinand Count Fathom* and *Launcelot Greaves*, is replaced in *Humphry Clinker* by a prismatic vision, that of the five letter-writers who describe and comment on the incidents of their external or internal world. Each character is a prism which breaks up the light derived from the sources of life according to an index of refraction which varies with his or her physical, emotional and moral idiosyncrasies. But, keeping to this optical metaphor, the angle of incidence of each fact varies according to the physical, social or psychological nearness or distance of each letter-writer. These multiple variations, added to a quintuple vision, enable Smollett to emphasise the relativity, conscious or not, of every impression, every judgment, every condemnation, whether within the family group or outside it. *Humphry Clinker* marks the splitting-up of the principal character and its quintuple fragmentation. The relativity of these views, sometimes superimposed, sometimes overlapping, now confirming, now contradicting each other, is better fitted to convey the organic multiplicity of life, physical or mental, which Smollett strove to capture with the avidity of his passionate nature. Relativity and contradiction, such are the dynamic mainsprings of this epistolary form adopted — and adapted — in *Humphry Clinker*. The two prefatory letters, between the bookseller Henry Davis and Jonathan Dustwich, in a way give the keynote of this infinite scale of relative contradictions in *Humphry Clinker*. Too often neglected by the critics (sometimes even omitted, as in Henley's edition), these letters have enabled one critic to call *Humphry Clinker* 'a novel of discrepancy'[15]. Even as regards nomenclature, the characters are not what they seem, and Leon V. Driskell concludes his article thus: 'Apparently included to augment the book's credibility, those early letters raise far more questions than they answer — not least of which is who is Jonathan Dustwich?' In *Humphry Clinker*, five characters are in search of themselves as much as the readers are in search of five characters.

The technical framework of *Humphry Clinker* is at once easier and more complex to grasp than in the other novels. The fragmentation of the principal character, and also of the plot — or rather plots — means that it has to be reconstituted by juxtaposing the pieces of partial information provided in each letter.

There are plenty of chronological landmarks (dates of letters, mentions of intervals of time elapsed) but they are not always reliable. Certain obvious errors of dates pose some thorny bibliographical problems[16]. In what Franklin B. Newman calls Text B of *Humphry Clinker*, the letter of October 26th (Matthew Bramble) is dated (not without reason) October 25th, while the following letter (Jery) of November 8th is dated November 14th. Byron Gassman, in Appendix I of his thesis (pp. 332—48) notices fifteen internal contradictions[17] of chronology in the letters. The problem is to know whether such errors constitute oversights on the part of Smollett, undermined by illness at the end of his life and too tired to verify the concordance of chronological details, or whether the author deliberately inserted them or left them in the text. Though it is not possible wholly to dismiss the first hypothesis, seeing the biographical conditions in which *Humphry Clinker* was composed, the second deserves to be examined with more care than criticism, in general, is prepared to grant it.

In accordance with his passionate temperament — *passionate* being taken in the characterological sense — Smollett tended to be extremely meticulous about precision of details. Martz has shown in *The Later Career of Tobias Smollett* what care the man responsible for historical and geographical compilations devoted to his task. The copy of *Travels through France and Italy* annotated in Smollett's hand (in the British Museum) corroborates this impression of meticulous care. Finally, certain chronological contradictions are too obvious not to be deliberate, for example the date of the three weddings according to Jery (pp. 346—50) and according to Win Jenkins (pp. 352—3). According to Jery, the weddings took place before the 8th of November (or the 14th in Text B), but only on the 19th according to Winifred ('We were yesterday three kiple chained', p. 352). Such a contradiction could not have passed unnoticed, even by an author exhausted by the gnawing anxiety to send off his manuscript as soon as possible so as to have the joy of seeing his novel published. These temporal discrepancies acquire a meaning if the reader remembers that contradiction and relativity are the core of this epistolary novel. By these possibly intentional inexactitudes, Smollett implies the psychological, moral and philosophical doubt that hovers over human testimony and the reliability of memory. Like Sterne in *Tristram Shandy*, but with much less virtuosity, Smollett could be playing with time by flouting the narrow constraints of chronology. Thus, he would mark the difference between the spatialised time of clocks and calendars and time apprehended as a flux, flowing faster or slower according to the acceleration provided by the different interest aroused by the incidents in the characters. Behind these temporal *non sequiturs*, the Eleatic dialectic of the moving and the static can be discerned. Each letter-writer tries to arrest the flux, that is to say to fix the moving stream of the lived sequence in the fluid immobility of memory. Memory, and hence the evidence based on it, appear to Smollett at once as a mirror and a trap. The evidence is not the reflection which is projected *on to* the mirror of five different personalities, it is also registered *in* the mirror so as ultimately to become the mirror itself. The implicit lesson of such chronological games is one of prudent scepticism which, by refusing spontaneous and definitive judgment, arouses tolerance, since human testimonies are not even capable of agreeing on the particulars of a common lived experience as apparently simple as an immutable date.

As in the previous novels, the age of the characters is given or suggested. The flight of time and process of growing old are evoked by Matthew Bramble with the allusive discretion of deep preoccupation. 'There is, however, one disease for which you have found as yet no specific, and that is old age . . .' (pp. 172–3), he writes to his friend and regular correspondent Dr Lewis. Her brother reveals that Lydia is seventeen (p. 8). Matthew Bramble entrenches himself behind his fifty-five years to claim, not without a touch of proud anxiety, that he knows his constitution better than anyone else after fourteen years of illness (p. 23). Jery begins the description, or rather the unkind character sketch, of his Aunt Tabitha by announcing straight away, like an irremediable blemish, that she is a spinster of forty-five (p. 60). It is Jery who gives Clinker's age, twenty (p. 81). This figure, twenty, recurs with some regularity in Matthew Bramble's comments. The reunion with Quin and old friends met again in Bath is, for him, 'the most happy day I have passed these twenty years' (p. 56) and later, in the Dennisons' home, he at last attains 'that pitch of rural felicity, at which I have been aspiring these twenty years in vain' (p. 320). Jery's exact age is not given: evidently he is older than his sister, but has not yet come of age. His father has been dead fifteen years (p. 113). Smollett also gives the age of episodic characters: sixty-five for Sir Ulic Mackilligut (p. 48), about nineteen for Wilson, Lydia's suitor (p. 321). As to Lismahago, his age is not given directly, but numerous indications suggest that he must be about the same age as Matthew Bramble and probably a little older. The unfortunate Lieutenant was scalped by the Indians at Ticonderoga in 1758; he bought his officer's commission thirty years earlier. For his wedding to Tabitha, he wears the same wig 'in which he had made his first appearance as a lawyer above thirty years ago' (p. 347). Whatever Lismahago's exact age, he looks older than Matthew Bramble who describes him as 'an old weather-beaten Scotch lieutenant' (p. 202). This opinion might seem suspect, were it not confirmed by two other allusions. Matthew Bramble deplores that the Lieutenant should be constrained by poverty to end his days (p. 267) among the Indians. Winifred Jenkins in her composite idiolect, declares that Tabitha's future husband is 'as old as Matthewsullin' (p. 306); a corruption of 'Methuselah', but also a possible allusion in the second degree to *Matthew* Bramble, who, in view of his surly character, might be described as *sullen*.

The geographical landmarks are so numerous that they have enabled Knapp and Parreaux to draw up a map of the itinerary followed by the five letter-writers, in the Oxford English Novels edition (1966) and in the Riverside Editions (1968). Here again there is no lack of studies[18] of the topography and the physical and economic geography of *Humphry Clinker*. This very vaguely circular journey has neither beginning nor end. The reader is not present at the departure from Brambleton-hall, which could be situated in the 'Black Mountains' of Wales. The first letters are dated from Gloucester. In the last twenty, all indication of place disappears. The last indication of the writers' whereabouts is given by Matthew Bramble, who intends to visit 'Chatsworth, the Peak and Buxton' (p. 273) as well as by Tabitha who, three days later, announces that she has seen 'the *Devil's Harse a-pike*, and *Hoyden's Hole*' (p. 274). All these places in Derbyshire are described by Smollett in the *Present State* (II, 390–5). 'Hoyden's Hole' might well be a capricious verbal corruption of Tabitha's, who does not hesitate, for example, to transform 'Hamlet' into 'Gimlet'. Smollett (ibid., p. 392) mentions a certain 'Elden-hole'[19], the third wonder of the region: 'It is a dreadful chasm in the side of a mountain, of an unfathomable depth; so that a line and plummet of near nine hundred yards, has been let down without reaching the bottom.' This remark agrees with Tabitha's 'Hoyden's Hole, which hath got no bottom'. The linguistic distortion may also be explained by a bawdy double meaning, such as Tabitha's letters abound in.

The absence of precise geographical details in these last twenty letters is doubtless to be related to the apparent lack of respect for chronology. So as not to incur the reproach of partiality, even in geography, Smollett lets the places where Matthew Bramble and his travelling companions at last find their physical, psychological and moral equilibrium remain vague. The rural paradise found again at the Dennisons', is also a paradise lost. All topographical or economic description of the countryside disappears almost completely in these last letters, to give place to the solution of the personal and family problems of the group. There is, however, a piece of information about the distance between Gloucester (where Lydia's correspondent Laetitia Willis lives) and the Dennisons' home, where the travellers are staying. Lydia, in order to persuade her friend to come to her wedding, writes: 'The distance from hence to Gloucester, does not exceed one hundred miles, and the roads are good' (p. 335). In two stages, Laetitia could be with Lydia. It is therefore probable that the Dennisons do indeed live in Derbyshire. On the second, more abstract level, it is permissible to wonder whether this absence of beginning and end does not imply the perpetually recommenced and perpetually unfinished cycle of human development. The examination of the thematic structure of *Humphry Clinker* will enable this hypothesis to be invalidated or confirmed.

But first it remains to unravel, briefly, the threads of the plot, or rather plots, in so far as they exist with sufficient clarity and strength to be discerned. The eighty-two letters of *Humphry Clinker* are divided up between the five writers: twenty-eight for Jery; twenty-seven for Matthew Bramble; eleven for Lydia; ten for Winifred Jenkins; six for Tabitha; in all, a little more than two-thirds for the men. With three exceptions[20] and one interpolated letter, they always write to the same correspondent, from whom they receive no reply. The Welsh origin of the travellers and their correspondents is not the result of pure literary chance. Smollett could not choose French people, who were still too often hated, in spite of the recent peace. Being themselves objects of ridicule in English public opinion, Frenchmen could not have allowed themselves to criticise or satirise the English. Moreover the French were suspected of psychological and political partiality for their traditional allies, the Scots. These latter, the object of a virulent renewal of loathing since the Bute ministry, were just as unacceptable as the French. Conversely, the Welsh, geographically close to the English, did not lack, as Jery and his uncle hasten to point out, ethnic and linguistic affinities with the Scots. Nor is the choice of the silent correspondents a random one. Matthew Bramble, a more or less chronic invalid, writes to Dr Lewis, his personal physician and old friend. Tabitha, with her petty-bourgeois obsession for cheese-paring and her determination to get the best possible price for any saleable home produce, overwhelms Mrs Gwyllim, the housekeeper at Brambleton-hall, charged with keeping an eye on the bills and the servants, with her advice on domestic economy. Jery, just down from Jesus College, Oxford, keeps up a friendly and socially flattering correspondence with Sir Watkin Phillips who is still at their Alma Mater. Lydia exchanges girlish letters, palpitating with romantic friendship, with a boarding-school friend, Laetitia Willis. Winifred Jenkins imparts her amazing discoveries and her misadventures to another Welsh servant at Brambleton-hall, Mrs Mary Jones. This correspondence therefore offers a whole gamut of social and intellectual variations.

The plot can be reduced to two major trends. On the one hand, Matthew Bramble is searching for the physical health which will also bring him psychological and moral equilibrium. On the other, the three women are in search of a husband. For Tabitha it is the desperate search, not of a faded nymphomaniac, but of an old maid clinging to the last straw of hope, for forty-five in those days corresponded physically and physiologically more to fifty-five nowadays; for Lydia, the palpitating search for the romance of which she has been frustrated; for Winifred Jenkins, attempts to get married dictated by chance encounters and her own vanity. This double quest is in fact, reduced to one, that of happiness, as in Smollett's other four novels, which would seem to exclude any originality. The discovery of the true identity of Wilson and Clinker enables him to knot the two principal threads of the plot. Moreover, the meeting with Lismahago and his marriage to Tabitha relieve Matthew Bramble of a domestic tyranny which for years had been almost unbearable.

It is, above all, the therapeutic function of this journey which has engaged the attention of critics[21]. Smollett does not spare the comments on his health which crop up at regular intervals during the itinerary of that perpetual invalid, Matthew Bramble. Thus, in spite of his virulent diatribes against Bath and London, his lamentations over the vexations his wards and his sister cause him, Matthew admits, almost with regret, that 'the exercise of travelling has been of service to my health; a circumstance, which encourages me to proceed in my projected expedition to the North' (p. 90). In spite of his abnormal irritability, Matthew Bramble is clear-sighted enough to realise that there is a basic and reciprocal connection between his physical health and his psychological state. Fresh troubles plunge him 'again in a sea of vexation, and the complaints in my stomach and bowels are returned' (p. 141). On the contrary, a piece of good news — the release of Clinker — leads him to make the following statement:

> I find my spirits and my health affect each other reciprocally — that is to say, every thing that discomposes my mind produces a corre-spondent disorder in my body; and my bodily complaints are remarkably mitigated by those considerations that dissipate the clouds of mental chagrin (p. 154).

It is also noticeable that Matthew Bramble feels better the nearer the travellers get to Scotland. In his first letter from Edinburgh, he has the pleasure of informing Dr Lewis: 'I now begin to feel the good effects of exercise — I eat like a farmer, sleep from mid-night till eight in the morning without interruption, and enjoy a constant tide of spirits, equally distant from inanition and excess' (p. 219). And, after his stay in Scotland, he declares to Dr Lewis: 'You will find me much better in flesh than I was at our parting' (p. 273).

The technical plot, whose warp and woof have just been indicated, can hardly be admired either for its originality or its convincingness, especially as regards the love affair between Wilson and Lydia. In the last analysis, all the mystery which obscures Wilson's true identity is due to a trifling and highly improbable cause. In her confusion, the feather-brained Win Jenkins has been unable to remember the information Wilson gave her when he was disguised as a Jewish pedlar (p. 26). The device is so thin that Smollett feels it necessary to remind the reader twice of this disastrous lapse of memory (pp. 42, 259). Moreover, the meeting of father and long-lost child, thanks to a revelation of identity, have been part of the mythology of literature since Sophocles. From Shakespeare to Fielding this device has been worn threadbare to its last shred of probability.

Smollett himself had already used it at the end of *Roderick Random* and *Launcelot Greaves*. In short, the long-lost child reappears everywhere.

It remains to determine the role of Jery. It is difficult to maintain, following the example of certain critics like Scott Garrow, that the evolution of Jery constitutes in itself alone one of the minor plots of *Humphry Clinker*. The reason is simple: Jery does not change at all. At the very most, he loses a little (but not all) of his social, intellectual and psychological snobbery. But, in reality, Jery does not *want* to get involved in the problems of the group. The only time he makes an exception to this rule of conduct is when he yields to a blind impulse of social and personal hatred for Wilson, who, though in the despicable status of a strolling player, has the effrontery to dare to stand up to him. It is therefore a matter of a passionate, uncontrollable reaction. Jery's vocation — and mission — is to hold himself aloof from events and human problems in order the better to *observe* them. This is definitely a keyword to the understanding of Jery's function in *Humphry Clinker*. From the very outset of the journey, he is delighted to have enough time 'to observe the singularities in my uncle's character' (p. 17). During a fire alarm in the middle of the night at the inn, he boasts of having had 'a pretty good observation' (p. 176) of the scantily attired ladies torn from their slumbers. The 'nocturnal spectator', as Restif de la Bretonne calls himself in *Les Nuits de Paris* might, at a stretch, be accused of certain voyeurism, not only when he surprises his uncle in conversation with the widow (pp. 20–2) but most of all the zeal (it is almost an obsession) with which he keeps watch on his sister, and his readiness to suspect her. The tender-hearted Lydia ends by becoming aware of it and complains to her friend: 'all day long Jery acted the part of an indefatigable spy upon my conduct. . . . This may be owing to his regard for my honour, if it is not the effect of his own pride . . . and really it will not be in my power to afford him any share of my affection, if he persists in persecuting me at this rate' (p. 309). All this passage is dominated by the vocabulary of suspicious observation. But it would be unjust and completely inaccurate to see in Jery a potential sexual pervert, the victim of a morbid fixation on his sister[22]. Jery *describes* (p. 8) and analyses the character of his uncle, aunt, and sister. He has a natural aversion to committing himself, tinged with the slightly cynical and amused scepticism of a wit who is still under age. Whilst his uncle fulminates his splenetic diatribes against the follies of Bath, Jery decides to laugh at them (p. 49). After meeting his old friend Barton, now launched on a political career at Court, Jery declares himself to be 'happily of no party' and, a little further on, 'still uninfected and unbiassed' (p. 95). On another level, but without the charming unselfconsciousness of Watteau, Jery is indifferent. Apart from some probable sexual experiences at Oxford, admitted to his correspondent — 'all my other connexions of that nature' (p. 27) — Jery, to his sister's great regret, does not show himself at all susceptible to the charms of the fair sex. The bright eyes of Miss Renton in Edinburgh do flutter his heart a little (p. 224). But a month later, there is no longer any sign of it: 'he no sooner left the place than he relapsed into his former insensibility' laments Lydia, who hastens to state: 'I feel, however, that this indifference is not the family-constitution' (p. 258). Obviously this is not so much a defence of the family as a plea in her own cause.

Humphry Clinker therefore presents a plot worn threadbare from over-use. It comprises all the elements of a bad comedy of manners, ending with the conventional triple marriage. But it is in the thematic structure that all the wealth of psychological imagination and literary virtuosity with which Smollett treats this adventure of morality is revealed.

There are three major articulations in *Humphry Clinker*, and, within the movements thus determined, a triple dialectic, socio-economic psychological and moral is developed.

In a first period, up to Matthew Bramble's letter written on July 4th from Scarborough (p. 179), Smollett presents a rather gloomy picture of urban civilisation in England and the various human aspects of progress. Subsequently, a series of letters about Scotland occupies a little less than 100 pages, up to Matthew Bramble's letter of September 20th (p. 275). These articulations are not purely geographical. The first two letters of this group are written from England (Newcastle and Morpeth) but already belong to the Scottish sequence by their subject, namely Lismahago, his adventures and his pronounced taste for systematic and paradoxical disputation. The two last are also written from England, with no other detail of place, but still remain Scottish in content, especially Matthew Bramble's, the intellectual calibre of Tabitha's remarks being rather poor, not to say nil. In these pages Smollett paints a much less sombre, more variegated and optimistic picture. It is the rediscovery of a land of more unspoilt natural beauty and a simpler way of life. Finally, in the last eighteen letters, the problem of a moral choice is posed, the choice, not between two countries (England and Scotland) as too many critics have wrongly said, but between two ways of life. Smollett opts for neither the one nor the other, but proposes a synthetic personal solution, capable of reconciling, up to a certain point, the best aspects of England and Scotland. This plan for a new life can only be implemented after the solution of all the individual problems.

Without wishing to go into all Martz's conclusions here, it is certain that his previous labours in the field of translation (of the *Journal Oeconomique* in February 1754), and of historical composition and compilation had led Smollett to take an interest other than literary in economic facts. But in *Humphry Clinker* he has not written a treatise on the Great Britain of his day. His literary and satirical temperament transforms the data which he may have been able to collect in the *Present State*, for example. Moreover, these various didactic movements discerned by analysis do not follow each other in *Humphry Clinker*, but they coexist, are combined, or even occasionally run counter to each other. If they are studied separately in this chapter, it is for sake of clarity in the analytical approach.

In a first movement of this socio-economic dialectic, Smollett devotes himself (but not exclusively) through the medium of Matthew Bramble, to an often acrid criticism of urban life. There was nothing new about the debate between the partisans of the town and those of the country[23] and it is even one of the most hackneyed themes of the eighteenth century, treated in turn by Pope, Thomson, Fielding, Goldsmith, Johnson, Cowper and Crabbe, to cite only a few great names. But Smollett brings a systematic virulence to this criticism of urban life which is peculiar to him alone. Matthew has hardly arrived in Bath before he is complaining of the drawbacks of the town, and in particular of the noise. Jery describes this cacophony which assails and offends his uncle's ears: dogs, town musicians, dancing-masters, bells and French horns combine to drive the irascible Matthew to fury (pp. 28–33). The same impression prevails when the Welsh country squire revisits London after a long absence. The noise and the confused bustle of the crowd promptly suggest the idea of a world gone demented: 'All is tumult and hurry; one would imagine they were impelled by some disorder of the brain, that will not suffer them to be at rest' (p. 88). Smollett does not lack predecessors, from Juvenal to Boileau, nor even presentday successors in the person of sociologists and town-planners who are campaigning against noise. He pushes his criticisms further and once again appears in a very modern light when he deplores the pollution of air and water, in Bath as well as in London. Whether it is a question of the dust on the roads (p. 64) or the pestilential stinks of a ballroom (p. 65), or again of the smoke of London (p. 119), Matthew Bramble suffocates in these towns.

The symbolic value of this affirmation is reinforced by the pollution of another vital element, water. It is difficult to award the palm of nauseating horror and to choose between the description of the contaminated water in Bath (pp. 45–7) and that of the Thames (p. 120) drunk (with delectation) by the Londoners. However, a common trait characterises Smollett's remarks about the quality of water, a subject he had at heart even from the medical point of view, as is proved by the publication of his *Essay on the External Use of Water* in 1752. He displays an almost Swiftian obsession with pathological human excretions (pus, sanies decomposing matter, etc.). His criticism, however, is not limited to a nauseating list of the elements which sully the water. He implies that the town-dweller is the victim of the negligence of the authorities as well as of the stupidity of the populace, who never hesitate to throw filth into the reservoirs (p. 47). The most serious consequence is that man becomes incapable of realising that he is drinking an appalling concoction. The inhabitants of Bath use the water from a nitrous well although there are numerous springs in the neighbourhood (p. 46). The Londoners' taste is so vitiated that they dare to proclaim their Thames water 'as the finest water in the universe' (p. 120). This reversal of criteria of appreciation of the elements is carried to extremes when Matthew Bramble records the astonishment of Londoners after ten days of fine weather. This phenomenon (too rare, it is true, in London) seems to them 'portentous' (p. 154). Thus air, water and sunlight, the three vital elements are transformed into hidden agents of death.

If air and water do not kill the town-dweller, his adulterated food will undertake the task. The 'catalogue of London dainties' (p. 122) enables Matthew Bramble to expose, with the verbal violence of impotent indignation, the scandalous practices which denature such basic foods as bread, meat, vegetables, fish and fruit. Two constant features appear in the analysis of this dietetic diatribe. In the same way as for the elements, the town-dweller's taste has been perverted by the false values of urban society on the verge of being geared to capitalist industrialism. It is unnecessary to stress that this nourishment, as described by Bramble, contravenes the most elementary rules of hygiene. But in Smollett's eyes it involves something even more serious. This perversion of nature is not so much endured by mankind as *willed*. The Londoners *know* that their bread is a mixture of more or less toxic ingredients (p. 120), but, far from being angry about it, they demand this artificial whiteness. There is no doubt that in this Smollett sometimes shows prophetic intuitions. He stigmatises a monstrous inversion of nature, a kind of ritual destruction of its products, behind which looms the threat of conscious and collective suicide of the masses. Besides this perversion of natural food, the second characteristic is the obsession — there again reminiscent of Swift — with the glutinous, with sticky human and animal secretions, not to mention oral and nasal mucus (pp. 121—2). Matthew Bramble lets himself go and gives free rein to a positive stylistic paroxysm. The interplay of morbid fascination and physiological repulsion gives this passage some of the vengeful vigour which reappears in the work of Céline, a writer obsessed with the Heraclitean flux of the universe, involving the clean and the unclean. Smollett does not, however, reject all possibility of living healthily in town. In Edinburgh, Matthew Bramble draws up the antithesis of his London catalogue. The water and food are of excellent quality (p. 217) and are not denatured by the unenlightened treatment of man.

Added to this criticism of urban life is a multiple attack on luxury and its social consequences. There again, the theme, ever since *The Fable of the Bees* (1714), was not a new one: Bernard de Mandeville had started a controversy which raged all through the eighteenth century[24].

It is the mania for spending, on all levels of society, that most upsets Matthew Bramble in Bath and London. It is thirty years since he has seen Bath and he finds this town has now become 'the very center of racket and dissipation' (p. 34). The cost of living incessantly rockets in Bath and families of moderate means have had to move out of it. Smollett generally used diluvian images to describe this tidal wave of luxury: 'the flood of luxury' (p. 57) would be a monotonous cliché in Matthew Bramble's writing, had not Smollett taken care to revitalise this washed-out metaphor by giving it new vividness and force. Thus, for people in humble circumstances, 'the flood of luxury and extravagance . . . will drive them from place to place to the very Land's End; and there, I suppose, they will be obliged to ship themselves to some other country' (ibid.). The pheno-menon attains the dimensions of a national disaster. The fact that the prices charged in Bath alarm Matthew Bramble is less remarkable than his insistence on denouncing the connivance of those who get themselves robbed:

> Every article of house-keeping is raised to an enormous price; a circumstance no longer to be wondered at, when we know that every petty retainer of fortune piques himself upon keeping a table, and thinks 'tis for the honour of his character to wink at the knavery of his servants, who are in a confederacy with the market-people; and, of consequence pay whatever they demand (ibid.).

Winifred Jenkins's lively and somewhat vulgar brawls with the local servants provide direct confirmation of Matthew Bramble's indictments (pp. 70—1). Another (indirect) confirmation of her uncle's incessant complaints is furnished by the letter in which Lydia described how she spends her time in Bath (pp. 39—42). The emptiest futility is the order of these days in which one only kills time in order to murder it more effec-tively between the round of the bookshops and the dressmakers and the ritual cake at Gill's the pastry-cook's. Matthew Bramble displays the same indignation in London at the spectacle of this 'grand source of luxury and corruption' (p. 87). Smollett notes the changes in the way of life that have taken place in twenty-five years, particularly in eating habits and dress (pp. 87—8). The influence of women, always ready to sacrifice the solid and sensible for the gimcrack and showy, recurs as a constant misogynous theme in Matthew Bramble's letters. Added to the social vanity of women, which Plato was already denouncing in the *Republic*, is the English taste for eccentricity. Matthew Bramble claims that the Harrogate waters owe their success to the caprice and affectation of the patients taking the cure who pretend to like the stench, 'so strikingly offensive' (p. 163), of this mineral spring. Such a remark of Matthew Bramble's is an echo, not devoid of irony, of the long dissertation on stench delivered by Dr Linden and reported *in extenso* by Jery (pp. 17—18). But what matters the liquid, provided the patients are crazy enough to spend their money without rhyme or reason?

The ease with which money circulates in these places of wildly extravagant spending provokes a social upheaval which produces very different reactions, according to the letter-writers. As one might expect,

Matthew Bramble cannot contain his bitter resentment at the destruction of a hierarchic order which he wanted to believe firmly established for all time. The Welsh country squire has a static vision of society and any element of disorder drives him into a paroxysm of impotent rage. Wealth newly acquired in India, the West Indies or the plantations of America, enables a whole class of social parvenus to parade themselves in Bath and crush the less fortunate with their noisy ostentation (pp. 36–7). Matthew Bramble detests just as much the common people – or rather 'the mob', the rabble – whom he condemns with a verbal and psychological violence approaching that which dominates *The History and Adventures of an Atom*. The following sentence vigorously sums up a conviction, repeated over and over again, especially when he is writing from London:

> the mob is a monster I never could abide, either in its head, tail, midriff, or members: I detest the whole of it, as a mass of ignorance, presumption, malice, and brutality; and, in this term of reprobation, I include, without respect of rank, station, or quality, all those of both sexes, who affects its manners, and court its society (p. 37).

Matthew Bramble's great reproach against London society is the disappearance of social ranks and a stable hierarchical structure. 'In short, there is no distinction or subordination left – The different departments of life are jumbled together' (p. 88). But it would be wrong to interpret Matthew Bramble's exaggerated opinions as being those of Smollett. Two other letter-writers express (with less force and conviction it is true) ideas radically opposed to those of their conservative uncle. Jery is well aware of Matthew Bramble's hatred of this social medley, at once temporary and permanent, which is becoming a feature of Bath. But the young man takes the opposite view from the older one and finds 'a source of infinite amusement' in this chaos (p. 49). Taking this attitude of optimism, or of amused cynicism, might be no more than a pose of social and psychological rebellion. But other remarks of Jery's prove that he is not always such a conceited fool as in his stormy relations with Wilson. The social and human melting-pot of Bath gives him the opportunity of seeing men as they are, without the more or less illusory protection of their social mask. It is possible to observe people 'in their natural attitudes and true colours, descended from their pedestals, and divested of their formal draperies, undisguised by art and affectation' (p. 48). Jery inclines to be paradoxical. In Bath, where affectation is the rule, the masks end by sticking so closely to the face that they reveal it in all its nakedness. Lydia does not really express a decisive opinion. She contents herself with recording the extraordinary social medley of Bath, and, after the first shock, becomes accustomed to it and does not suffer from it unduly (p. 39).

As a final general corollary of the influx of wealth, professional corruption is rife at all levels and especially among those whose spiritual or judicial office should put them above this deplorable rat-race. Twice in the same letter (Bath, May 17th) Jery attacks those ecclesiastics swollen with self-importance and pendulous guts, 'great over-grown dignitaries and rectors, with rubicund noses and gouty ancles, or broad bloated faces, dragging along great swag bellies; the emblems of sloth and indigestion' (p. 72). In the latter part of this letter, it is less at individuals than at the system of ecclesiastical preferment that Jery aims his barbed satirical remarks. Such is the thematic function of the incident in which the astute Tom Eastgate, in search of a good living, confronts the haughty, but cowardly squire George Prankley (pp. 73–5). Smollett is clever enough not openly to condemn this practice of the right of presentation. But Jery's remarks on the manner in which Tom Eastgate obtains his benefice at pistol point, in a duel which Prankley cried off from cowardice, leaves no doubt about Smollett's opinion of the scandal of such abuses, already denounced in *Launcelot Greaves*. Jery shows himself just as anticlerical in London, when he notices the almost total absence of members of the higher clergy at the Duke of Newcastle's levée. Although the latter, when he was in power, had nominated nearly all the bishops sitting in the House of Lords, these Anglican prelates have not the slightest scruple in adopting the Jesuitical practice of omission and relegating their benefactor to the oblivion of ingratitude (p. 110). The confrontations of the unfortunate Clinker with the law, when he is arrested, by mistake, as a dangerous high-wayman, give a glimpse of the thorough corruption which reigns at all levels of the legal world, from the common turnkey to the judge himself. The constable who accompanies Clinker to prison knows very well that the latter is innocent. It is a matter of a game of judicial blindman's buff in which Justice cheats and sees through her bandage, but chooses to harass the innocent man, perhaps even to execute him, in order the better to catch the real culprit, Martin, later on (pp. 147–9). The contempt for human life displayed by all these minions of the law assumes the dimension of a nightmare, one that is not restless but has the terrifying calm and tranquillity of administrative routine. If Judge Buzzard (of the evocative name) shows himself so severe when Clinker, whom he knows to be innocent, is brought before him, it is because he hopes for a present from his master 'as an acknowledgement of his candour and humanity' (p. 152). These two qualities ascribed to Buzzard certainly do not lack a dose of vitriolic irony.

The presentation of rural life and its various aspects in this opposition between progress (predominantly urban) and the state of nature, is far from occupying the same place in *Humphry Clinker* as the reiterated attacks on town civilisation. It finds its expression, first of all, in Matthew Bramble's regrets, steeped with a nostalgia that is all the more painfully acute because the lord of the manor has left his Welsh countryside of his own accord and is writing his letters in the midst of the hurlyburly of a town. These remarks, usually put at the end of his letters, all have the characteristic of stressing the double joy it will be to return to his country

\

211

home: 'double relish' (p. 90), 'redoubled velocity' (p. 107), and again 'double relish' (p. 123). More precise than these vague regrets is the page in which Matthew Bramble sets out his 'country comforts' as opposed to his 'town grievances' (p. 118). After having outlined the fundamental opposition between the adulterated pleasures of the town and the genuine joys of country life (ibid.), he describes a kind of rural autarchy. In these pages (118–19), a stylistic examination makes its easier to grasp the almost obsessional character of this static and withdrawn life. Words such as 'home', and the repetition of 'own', 'I', 'my', give the description of his verdant Thebaïd a tinge of unpleasant egotism. Another semantic sequence in the same pages reveals the importance for Matthew Bramble of the natural purity of his food, the air he breathes and the water he drinks. Words such as 'virgin', 'pure', 'crystalline', 'native', 'natural', 'fresh', contribute to this impression of nostalgia for the impeccable purity of a paradisal golden age, a theme already touched on in *Launcelot Greaves*. Matthew Bramble does not remain inactive on his estate; he spends his time looking after his property and tenant-farmers and leads the apparently idyllic life already hymned by Virgil.

But if Matthew Bramble's existence appears as a success, Smollett takes care to bring out very clearly the failures which country life can involve. Such is the thematic significance of the visits to hosts as different as Burdock, Oxmington, Baynard and Bullford. The first portrait is that of the conservative squire, a great fox-hunting man, proud of his hospitality which transforms his house into the semblance of an inn, where the table is always spread. Burdock is of the same family as Western, and Sir Valentine Quickset in *Launcelot Greaves*. In fact, this material hospitality, without warmth or courtesy, ill conceals the state of brute bestiality in which Burdock wallows in the name of a narrow-minded, stupid traditionalism (pp. 164–5). The arrogance of his wife and the insolent rapacity of the servants complete this indictment of bogus hospitality. Matthew Bramble's phrase deserves to be quoted for its infuriated terseness: 'I would rather dine upon filberts with a hermit, than feed upon venison with a hog' (p. 165).

The presence of the Melvilles — spelt 'Melvil' or 'Melvile' in *Ferdinand Count Fathom*, but Smollett is often vague about the spelling of proper names[25] — is rather surprising in the house of such a boor, and the pretext of an acquaintance with the son (the perfect type of the execrable dilettante on his return from Italy) remains extremely thin. Lord Oxmington does not live in the depths of the country, but near a small town (p. 281). Nevertheless it is obvious that his hospitality, described this time by Jery, is designed to form the thematic counterpart of Burdock's. It is a matter of a 'fashionable meal served up with much ostentation to a company of about a dozen persons' (ibid.). The frigid elegance of this entertainment is soon followed by an abrupt dismissal of the guests which offends the choleric Matthew Bramble (p. 282).

The case of Baynard is dissected at length by his old friend Bramble (pp. 285–97) who proceeds to hold a *post mortem* on a failure. A heavy responsibility for it is laid on this woman, Mrs Baynard, whose intellectual and emotional nullity is offset by a frenzied vanity, obsessed with the hollow outward show of a social life where futile extravagance is the only thing reckoned important. Baynard, like so many others, has made the mistake of thinking he could mould his wife and make her share his taste for a simple life in the country, away from the expensive vortex of the follies of the town. But far from changing her vacuous nature, he is caught in its toils. This man, of weak character, but not devoid of intelligence and clear-sightedness, is his own worst enemy (p. 288). His wife, aided and abetted by an inseparable and pernicious aunt, has divined this weakness of her husband's with the sure instinct of a malevolent, carnivorous animal and shamelessly exploits it to lure him into a series of costly extravagances. The vanity of this puppet is such that she cannot bear that her neighbours, even though they are richer, should have a few more servants than herself. And all this enormous expense does not, for all that, ensure any hospitable amenities for the visitor. Matthew Bramble speaks of Baynard's house as 'a temple of cold reception' (p. 290), and the cooking (French of course) provides nothing substantial and revolts the palate of the honest Welshman: 'faded fruit and iced froth, a good emblem of our landlady's character' (p. 295), such is the sweet served after an uneatable meal. Winifred Jenkins confirms, in very direct fashion, the badness of the food in this house, even in the servants' hall: 'there was nothing kimfittable to eat, being as how they live upon board, and having nothing but a piss of could cuddling tart and some blamangey' (p. 307). But these whims of a stupid and pretentious woman would not have been of much consequence, had she not set about destroying the patient work of Baynard's ancestors. She transforms their manor-house and a large adjacent farm according to the dictates of the latest architectural and horticultural fashion (p. 292). In these pages, the stupidity of a woman is raised to the level of a malevolent power which ordains a systematic inversion of nature. The trout river is deflected from its course (incidentally putting two mills out of action) in order to feed an ornamental basin, but the permeable bottom of the latter turns the whole park into a swamp. Water, the symbol of life, stagnates and grows foul, and henceforth becomes the symbol of corruption and death (ibid.). Baynard knows that he is heading for financial disaster, for he is spending double his income.

It would be wrong to suspect Smollett of a shameless misogyny. Even if the case of Mrs Baynard is farfetched, he takes care to observe that two other women in the neighbourhood are driving their husbands to ruin by rivalling each other in idiotic ostentation (p. 293). Recent sociological research (see pp. xxv–xxvi in Parreaux's introduction to the Riverside edition of *HC*) proves that the psychological and social structure analysed by Smollett in these pages is not lacking in rigorous exactness of observation. It is necessary to add that if, by chance, the Baynards' landed property and fortune were not completely swallowed up, the education — or rather non-education — of the young son, insidiously corrupted by his mother and aunt, could not fail to produce a perfect specimen of a conceited puppy, intolerable, puny and vicious, who would promptly set about frittering away the last guineas of his inheritance for good and all? Thus Providence has always practised an implicit form of socialism in the redistribution of wealth. But thanks to the vigilant friendship of Matthew Bramble and the opportune death of his wife, Baynard will not be ruined. For the first time, Matthew Bramble is not only moved to tears (p. 293) but displays a passionate and lasting interest in the misfortunes of another: 'the subject interested the warmest passions of my heart' (p. 297) he declares to his correspondent to apologise for having written him so long a letter. For the first time too, the bitter misanthrope whose favourite adjective, in his splenetic paroxysms, is 'intolerable', evinces a clear-sighted flexibility when he is brought to realise that inexplicable contradictions can exist in the human mind, such as those which attach Baynard to his wife (p. 294). Neither does the whole passage lack a certain irony. Matthew Bramble exhorts his old friend Baynard not to submit to his wife's absurd tyranny (p. 293). But what does the same Matthew Bramble do after years of being faced with his redoubtable sister Tabitha? At the beginning of the journey (Bath, May 19th) he indeed swears to himself: 'O! I shall never presume to despise or censure any poor man, for suffering himself to be henpecked; conscious how I myself am obliged to truckle to a domestic dæmon' (p. 77). When he invites Baynard to free himself from these 'shameful trammels' (p. 296) it is probable that Matthew Bramble is also envisaging his own psychological revenge, belated but all the sweeter for having waited so long for it, on the evil fate which inflicted such a sister on him.

Jery takes over from his uncle to describe Bullford, announced as being the antithesis of Baynard (p. 297). In the case of this gouty and facetious squire, the failure is less financial than intellectual. Bullford represents the cheerful stupidity of the great addict of practical jokes. No artistic or psychological sensitiveness (p. 298) hampers Bullford in his boorish pranks, in which physiological functions play a major part. If poor Judge Frogmore escapes with a fright of having been poisoned, Lismahago does not disdain to pay the impenitent joker back in his own coin (p. 305). Thus life in the country does not imply for Smollett that its inhabitants automatically know how to profit by it. It is curious to note that the letter-writers present three different types of maladjustment (Oxmington, Baynard and Bullford) in the space of some twenty odd consecutive pages (pp. 281–305).

But if Smollett does not commit himself to an unqualified eulogy of country life, neither does he absolutely condemn town life. In spite of its stench and dirt, Edinburgh is the great exception Matthew Bramble admits, sometimes with a certain enthusiasm. He will be very sorry to leave this town, after having confided to Dr Lewis: 'if I was obliged to lead a town life, Edinburgh would certainly be the headquarters of ... Matt. Bramble' (p. 235). But the reasons for this preference will appear more clearly in the course of the thematic analysis of the pages devoted to Scotland. Finally, contrary to Matthew Bramble, Lydia and Winifred, who at the beginning of the journey were writing of their amazed excitement at the novelties of the town life, declare themselves tired of this wandering life. Winifred says she is 'quite jaded with rambling' (p. 306), whilst Lydia, a very different young woman from the scatterbrained little ninny of Bath, admits her nostalgia for rural peace: 'I long for repose and solitude, where I can enjoy that disinterested friendship which is not to be found among crouds, and indulge those pleasing reveries that shun the hurry and tumult of fashionable society' (p. 308).

A second general aspect of this socio-economic dialectic: the description of Scotland, its inhabitants and its resources, constitutes an important thematic modulation for Smollett's relativistic purpose. Martz's book (1942) has had the merit of drawing attention to the close links between *Humphry Clinker* and the description of Scotland and the Hebrides at the end of the first volume and beginning of the second of the *Present State* (I, 430—510, II, 1—150). These pages are, in fact, indispensable for grasping the full extent of the literary transmutation wrought in *Humphry Clinker* out of the geographical, economic and historical material of the *Present State* (see the whole of Martz's Chapter vi, 'Imaginative Synthesis' pp. 147—62). Smollett proceeds to a genuine thematic integration of all these observations on Scotland, which has to be reincorporated in the movement of socio-economic dialectic that animates *Humphry Clinker*.

It is a Scotland at the crossroads, between a traditional past and a commercial and industrial future, straining to discover its destiny in the modern age, that Smollett presents, with a wealth of shades of opinion, not to say contradictions, which are not always apparent at a first analysis. Ravaged by two unsuccessful rebellions, Scotland, after the battle of Culloden (April 16th 1746), was forced to break definitely, with no hope of return, with her Jacobite traditions and her links with France. This defeat at Culloden was also to mark the beginning of a bloody or insidious repression, forcibly denounced by Smollett, as has already been seen, in his poem 'The Tears of Scotland' and his *Complete History of England*. Although, as early as 1740[26], Scotland had already begun to develop rapidly after a long period of lethargy, the conservative and static forces (predominantly rural) and the dynamic impetus of towns like Edinburgh and Glasgow had still to wage a fierce battle before this country, apparently with few natural resources, would launch definitely on the path of massive industrialisation. Far from painting a uniformly flattering picture of Scotland, skilfully composed to contrast with the urban civilisation of England, Smollett stresses the internal contradictions of this country; whether to be a reservoir of doctors, sailors, American colonists, pedlars and gardeners who all take the road to London, or to adapt itself to modern requirements in the realms of agriculture, commerce and industry. In the pages of *Humphry Clinker* where Smollett describes this native land he loves — 'I shall ever retain for it a Regard which is truly filial' he wrote to his friend Dr John Moore in June 1762 (Knapp, *Letters*, p. 106) — the attentive reader can discern the first tremors of the human and economic shock produced by that prolonged earthquake with no well-defined epicentre: the Industrial Revolution. Already, in the *Present State*, Smollett had been very conscious of this development in Scotland:

> A remarkable spirit of industry has of late years appeared very visibly in many parts of Scotland. We have already observed how much agriculture has been improved in the Lothians, and on all the eastern coast: nor have the Scots been more remiss in the article of manufacture (II, 23).

On the following page, he thus sums up his socio-economic observations:

> In a word, this Kingdom, though branded with the reproach of poverty and barrenness, might prove an inexhaustible source of wealth to the natives. The inhabitants seem at length acquainted with their own interest: they understand the nature of commerce: they see the happy effects of industry: they take example by their southern neighbours and fellow subjects, and pursue their steps with such emulation, as hath already opened a fair prospect of opulence and importance (II, 24—5).

This mercantilist philosophy is at the opposite pole from the enlightened, but conservative economic planning advocated by the indomitable Lismahago. Finally, it would be wrong to think that Smollett's socio-economic preoccupations on the subject of Scotland were anything new. Already, in the *Complete History of England*, among the reflections on the disaster of Culloden, he puts forward the theory that the economic neglect of which the Highlanders had long been the victims is partly responsible for their attachment to the traditional structures unfavourable to their integration into the national life: 'Had manufactures and fisheries been established in different parts of their country, they would have seen and felt the happy consequences of industry, and in a little time been effectually detached from all their slavish connexions' (1827 edn, III, 182). The problem of the fisheries — their establishment and development on the coasts of Scotland had already been advocated by James Thomson in *Autumn*, ll. 920—3 — receives Smollett's attention several times in the first volume (1760) of the *Continuation of the Complete History of England* (pp. 29—31, 70—3, 444—6). His personal knowledge of Scotland, matured by long absences, and his historical and geographical labours therefore prepared him better than anyone for this perceptive analysis. Even the danger of partiality is removed, if not wholly, at least to a great extent, thanks to the dynamic relativity of the five different points of view of the travelling letter-writers.

Throughout a little less than 100 pages (pp. 188–281) dealing mainly with Scotland and its inhabitants, it is possible to distinguish three principal aspects in the description given by Smollett: the traditional Scotland, attached to an often barren soil; the Scotland in full economic development, a phenomenon mainly noticeable in towns like Edinburgh and Glasgow; finally, and perhaps the one Smollett loved most since, for him, it existed only in his feelings, an Arcadian Scotland which appears briefly in the pages written from Cameron House.

As soon as they enter Scotland, Jery and his uncle do not spare their criticisms of an agriculture which, in general, seems to them poorer and less developed than that in England. Jery is struck at once by the difference between the robust peasants of Northumberland and the puny farm labourers on the other side of the Tweed (p. 214). The cattle, too, suffer by comparison, but Smollett hastens to make Matthew Bramble say that men and cattle in Scotland are still in better condition (of course!) than in France or Italy. Nevertheless the same Matthew Bramble, agreeably surprised by the fine quality of Scottish wheat, is forced to admit that agriculture 'in this country is not yet brought to that perfection which it has attained in England' (pp. 215–16). The poverty of certain regions where nothing grows but oats and barley, Bramble attributes mainly to the lack of enclosures. This poverty, partly due also to the natural sterility of the soil, cannot, for all that, explain the hydrophobic dirtiness of the Scots in spite of their having plentiful natural supplies of pure water (ibid., p. 245). Another reason for poverty is the smallness of the farms cultivated and the shortness of the exorbitantly expensive leases (ibid.), evils still well known to many European peasants. Matthew Bramble comments later (p. 268) on the frugal but sufficient diet of these peasants (see Parreaux's note, Riverside edition, p. 343) as well as on their clothing and housing.

As to the specific problems of the Highlanders, Bramble presents in five pages (pp. 252–6) a synoptic view of their economic, human and, most of all, political ones. If the solitude and wildness of this desolate region impress the traveller – 'All is sublimity, silence, and solitude' (p. 252) – he can, on occasion, admit the failings of its inhabitants (in particular a certain idleness which, in this cattle-breeding district, often encourages drunkenness), but also their fantastic courage. Matthew Bramble (and no doubt Smollett himself) cannot help admiring these rough men, who, when they reached Derby on December 4th 1745, caused London to tremble. At the same time he feels the necessity of destroying the clans (p. 255) if this part of Scotland is ever to achieve an economic growth comparable to that of the Lowlands. The lack of infrastructure does not seem to trouble the government, whose measures of redistribution of property therefore lose almost all their efficiency.

Finally, every criticism expressed by Matthew Bramble is contested, in its turn, by Lismahago, the king of paradoxical polemics. This poverty is allied to a certain simplicity of manners, and, even to Matthew Bramble, there is nothing disgraceful in it. Lismahago pushes the argument further and claims that poverty is no reproach, supporting himself with examples drawn from Antiquity. Riches, on the contrary, are a source of moral corruption. And his conclusion (pp. 275–6) is a rhetorical pirouette. Scotland is not poor, for her riches are *natural*: 'such a kingdom can never be called poor, in any sense of the word, though there may be many others more powerful and opulent' (p. 276).

In spite of this optimism, though he rather agrees with Lismahago, Smollett does not hesitate to show the defects which are, in some sort, the corollary of insufficient economic development, in particular dirt and superstition. Jery, too, in his remarks on the Highlanders (pp. 239–41) insists on their primitive dwellings ('wretched cabins', p. 239), and Matthew Bramble does not spare his criticisms of the inhabitants of Edinburgh, who, at ten o'clock every night shamelessly empty their ordure into the street (p. 218). Winifred Jenkins indignantly refers again to this nauseating subject (p. 220). All visitors, whether hostile to Scotland like Johnson, or on the contrary favourable (which is much rarer) like the young Edward Topham, have complained of the stench of this city, its lack of water and its execrable inns. In his *Letters from Edinburgh* (written in 1774 and 1775), Edward Topham, then aged twenty-three, is animated by a laudable passion for impartiality about the Scots, so often calumniated and vilified by their English contemporaries. But, in spite of a sincere enthusiasm for Edinburgh and the hospitality of its inhabitants, he, neither, can stomach this contempt for the most elementary hygiene. Even if some progress has been made,

> the dirt is sometimes suffered to remain two or three days without removal, and becomes offensive to more senses than one. The magistrates by imposing fines and other punishments, have long put a stop to the throwing of anything from the windows into the open street: but as these allies are unlighted, narrow, and removed from public view, they still continue these practices with impunity. Many an elegant suit of clothes has been spoiled; many a powdered, well-dressed maccaroni sent home for the evening: and to conclude this period in Dr. Johnson's own simple words 'Many a full-flowing perriwig moistened into flaccidity'[27].

It would be unseemly to dwell on such a subject, if the eighteenth century had not so constantly reproached Scotland for its offensive smells. A second quotation from Edward Topham corroborates Winifred Jenkins's indignant disgust at such practices:

But I cannot help observing the intolerable stench that is produced at this season of the night, on the moving the tub of nastiness from each floor: such a concatenation of smells I never before was sensible of: it has sometimes been so powerful as to wake me, and prevented my sleeping till it was somewhat pacified.

Smollett himself, in the *Present State* had drawn readers' attention to this lack of cleanliness and the fetid stench of the Athens of the North. After having described the 'nocturnal discharge' every night at a fixed time, he concludes:

The truth is, however strangers may be disgusted with these filthy customs, the natives of Edinburgh are, by use, become insensible to the annoyance; and when they perceive new comers giving marks of loathing and abhorrence, generally impute them to false delicacy and affectation. Their neighbours of England, it must be owned, have some reason to twit them in the teeth with these and other unsavoury practices (II, 116).

On the thematic plane, Dr Linden's stercoraceous discourse at Bristol (pp. 17—18) acquires a retrospective ironic value after Matthew Bramble's disillusioned remarks on this tolerance of (in theory) civilised men of the most disgusting filth.

Smollett had already been indignant, in the *Present State*, to see that superstitions of all kinds still flourished in Scotland. In the first volume, writing about the Isle of St Kilda, he devotes four pages (I, 460—3) — inspired by the works of Martin Martin, *A Late Voyage to St Kilda* (1698), and *A Description of the Western Islands of Scotland* (1703) — to the second sight with which certain inhabitants of the island are gifted. Though he gives some examples of it for the pleasure and edification of the reader, Smollett displays an amused scepticism and speaks of their 'ridiculous singularity' (I, 461). In the second volume, he returns to this subject, which seems to stick in his gullet. After having observed that the Scots in general were inclined to superstition and still believed in witches, he describes one of them: 'a poor, old, lone woman, who lives in a solitary hut, and appears with wrinkled face, hollow eyes, and a red petticoat, ever incurs the suspicion of sorcery' (II, 19). It is impossible not to think that Smollett remembered his own description when he makes Winifred Jenkins tell of her meeting with 'an ould vitch, called Elspath Ringavey, with a red petticoat, bleared eyes, and a mould of grey bristles on her sin' (p. 261). But if the servant is a credulous victim of old wives' tales, it is more surprising to see these same beliefs investigated with the utmost seriousness at the table of a nobleman, the Duke of Queensberry (pp. 270—2). Only Matthew Bramble puts forward some rational objections, but he is very conscious that the guests, though ready to ridicule these telepathic or parapsychological phenomena, nevertheless grant them a mysterious credence. The second example (pp. 272–3) is quite simply explained by a punitive action of Lismahago's on meeting a nephew who had turned the ancestral home into a spinning-mill. But such a mis-apprehension had already been carefully prepared for. Here is Jery's description of Lismahago when they meet him again in Carlisle:

> Mrs Bramble was the first that perceived him, and screamed as if she had seen a ghost; and, truly, at a proper time and place, he might very well have passed for an inhabitant of another world; for he was more meagre and grim than before (p. 266).

Thus Smollett combines, not without epistolary skill, the thematic plot and the characterisation of the protagonists.

One last observation must be made about this traditional Scotland. Whether its inhabitants are rich or poor, urban or rural, they offer the warmest hospitality to the stranger. Even the poorest Highlanders enthusiastically welcome strangers into their homes (p. 253). As to the gentry, they show themselves 'so loving to strangers, that a man runs some risque of his life from their hospitality' (p. 239). Jery's description of the gargantuan hunting-breakfast confirms this impression. But this hospitality itself suffers from the immutable weight of tradition. Mr Campbell, a sophisticated and cultured Scot and a musician into the bargain, is not permitted to dispense with his clan piper and has to let his ears be tormented by the sounds he detests (p. 241). As to the funeral of the old lady, the whisky flows so freely that all the relatives and friends are halfseas-over. And in the euphoria of this scene, which might serve as the starting point of a Spike Milligan sketch, the corpse of the deceased old lady is, by pure oversight, left behind (p. 242).

In *Humphry Clinker* there is no complete and systematic picture of Scotland in the course of evolution. Rather there are rapid sketches, opinions that vary according to the letter-writers. Matthew Bramble passes in swift review, but not without appreciative comments, the Scottish legal system, the University of Edinburgh, the hospital and the workhouse. Even the redoubtable Kirk shows signs of change and is becoming more flexible and less fanatical (pp. 231–2). There exists a nucleus of intel-lectuals and scholars which is restoring some lustre to the humanities in Edinburgh after a long eclipse. But it is Glasgow that enchants Matthew Bramble by its spirit of enterprise. If Edinburgh is 'a hot-bed of genius' (p. 233), Glasgow excites such enthusiasm in the uncle that the nephew says, 'My uncle is in raptures with Glasgow' (p. 237). Already, in the *Present State*, Smollett was writing of Glasgow: 'The people of the city are remarkable for their industry, their commercial spirit, their punctual observance of the presbyterian discipline, and their steady attachment to the reigning family' (II, 106). After a eulogistic description, Smollett concludes 'in a word Glasgow is the most beautiful town of Great Britain' (II, 104).

These eulogies reappear in a more literary form in Matthew Bramble's letter (pp. 245—7). The latter is a little less positive than Smollett in the *Present State* since he only sees in Glasgow 'one of the prettiest towns in Europe; and without all doubt, it is one of the most flourishing in Great Britain. In short, it is a perfect beehive in point of industry' (pp. 245—6). What Smollett called 'commercial spirit' in the *Present State* becomes 'a noble spirit of enterprise' (ibid.). It is only with reluctance that Matthew Bramble still finds something to criticise here, the defective water-supply and the shallowness of the estuary of the Clyde. Smollett allows himself to be divined, not without ironic complaisance, under the mask of Matthew Bramble when he reminds Lewis: 'You must know I have a sort of national attachment to this part of Scotland' (p. 247). It is therefore activity that Matthew Bramble admires almost unreservedly in Glasgow as in Dumfries, a commercial and industrial town which is inspired by the example furnished by Glasgow.

Such admiration, new in Matthew Bramble's letters, cannot escape the reactionary censure of Lismahago, who, far from acting as Smollett's mouthpiece — a role contrary to the relativism of the quintuple vision — generally produces arguments not devoid of moral or psychological good sense, but dangerously ill-suited to the times. Sixty years after the union with England, Lismahago is still doubting the benefit of that historic event (pp. 276—8). He is fighting a rearguard action, marked by the emotional bitterness of those who have been cut off from the world for many years. Lismahago suffers from that 'prisoner's complex' which develops in a man for whom the world has stood still during his captivity (among the Red Indians). On his release, he finds everything difficult to understand and takes refuge in an emotional and occasionally cantankerous addiction to the past. It is significant that Lismahago cannot settle down in Scotland to spend his declining years. A Scotland in full evolution cannot conform to the static vision which Lismahago cherishes of his native land. The incident which makes Lismahago renounce Scotland for ever must be interpreted symbolically. His nephew, like the merchants in the temple, has profaned the ancestral home by installing a spinning-mill in it. The tone and the condemnation are biblical, as is proved by the allusion to the prophets (p. 272) and the expression of wrath: 'You have made my father's house a den of thieves' (ibid.; cf. Matthew, 21:13). Thus two generations, two conceptions of Scotland confront each other. After having given free rein to his violent resentment, Lismahago, the ghost of Scotland of the past, thinks of retiring among the Red Indians (p. 273). But in the cyclic development of humanity, past, present and future are only repetitions of non-eternity.

Not all of Lismahago's observations are valueless. His conception of a commerce subjected to state control, 'restrained within its proper channels' (p. 280) does not seem at all feasible. On the contrary, the vigorous denunciation of a society entirely geared to trade and profit, in the name of an insane economic liberalism, enables one to foresee the material and moral follies of the consumer society of the capitalist world: 'a glut of wealth brings along with it a glut of evils' (ibid.). But Lismahago's objection is not solely moral. Opulence seems to him pernicious, just as it does to Matthew Bramble, because it brings in its wake the destruction of the static social hierarchy to which all types of conservative cling.

Quite the opposite of Lismahago is Captain Brown, who, having returned to his native land a rich man, decides to set up in it a manufacture 'to give employment and bread to the industrious' (p. 265). Between the sterile and futile anathema of Lismahago and the positive activity of Captain Brown, it seems that Smollett, or his reader, cannot hesitate which to choose. Nevertheless, it is certain that this economic progress takes place to the detriment of the political independence of Scotland, for the moment subjugated by the superior economic potential of England.

These problems of political economy vanish before the Arcadian vision of Scotland. At Cameron House on the banks of Loch Lomond, not far from where Smollett was born and spent his childhood, the travellers reach an oasis of revivifying freshness and purity. Matthew Bramble sounds the keynote at once: Every thing here is romantic beyond imagination. This country is justly stiled the Arcadia of Scotland; and I don't doubt but it may vie with Arcadia in every thing but climate' (p. 248). The 'Ode to Leven Water' also contains an allusion to the plains of Arcadia (p. 249). Matthew Bramble's prose and Smollett's poetry reveal the same obsession with the symbolic purity of the calm waters of the loch or the rippling ones of the Leven, under the guise of an archaic pastoralism. This insistence on the transparency of the waves is part of the archetypal nostalgia for a paradisal Golden Age. Apart from a reservation about the climate, hastily minimised, Matthew Bramble declares that the country 'would be a perfect paradise' (p. 250), an expression which recurs in the same letter as 'Scottish Paradise' (p. 252) and 'Scotch Arcadia' (p. 257).

Another stylistic repetition characterises these pages: that of the adjective 'romantic' applied to the description of nature, and purified of all the pejorative meanings, so current in the eighteenth century that Johnson's *Dictionary* begins by giving them: (i) 'Resembling the tales of romance; wild', (ii) 'Improbable, false' while the meaning applicable to Nature only appears as the last: 'Fanciful; full of wild scenery'. This adjective recurs with exceptional frequency[28] in the pages devoted to Scotland and to the region of Loch Lomond in particular. With the exception of Tabitha and Winifred, who were too occupied with their own little affairs to be sensitive to the charms of natural scenery, whether wild or cultivated, all the other letter-writers use the word 'romantic'[29]. Matthew Bramble's enthusiasm is such that he does not hesitate twice to use 'sublime' (p. 248) and 'sublimity' (p. 252). To confirm this impression of idyllic bliss, Smollett introduces an old couple (pp. 251–2), not unlike the mythical Philemon and Baucis, although the appellation of 'venerable druid' and the allusion to the oaks (p. 251) also make one think of the Celtic cult. The old man and his wife are a perfect example of this simple life in contact with nature, the rewards of which are health and vigour of body and happiness content with little.

The last phase of this socio-economic dialectic, adumbrated rather than achieved, is the happiness of going back to the land. This is the solution found and put into practice by the Dennisons. Matthew Bramble analyses their success and the quality of their happiness in two consecutive letters (October 8th and 11th). The success of the Dennisons is prepared for on the thematic plane by the lamentable failure of the Baynards.

The Dennisons are at opposite poles, morally and psychologically, from the Baynard couple. The resolution and courage of the husband who decides to quit the sterile life of the town and settle in the country in difficult material conditions contrast with the indecision and weakness of Baynard. The contrast between their wives is even sharper. Mrs Dennison shows herself worthy in every way of her husband (p. 321). The Dennisons are strong-minded enough to leave town even though it seeks to tempt them back. It is interesting to note that all the objections raised by Dennison's city friends before he carries out his plan of living in the country, are based on a series of erroneous social assumptions. They could be summed up thus: a *gentleman* cannot live all the year round in the country without spending even more than in London. Smollett draws the reader's attention to this socio-economic fallacy by means of a triple and conspicuous repitition of the word 'gentleman' in nine lines (ibid.). Dennison's good sense enables him to perceive the falseness of such statements. But his wisdom goes further; he has decided to cut off connections with the elegant society of the neighbourhood, without, for all that, depriving himself of the intelligent company he likes (p. 327). The Dennisons are not unsociable hermits, turned in upon themselves. Activity and friendship are the very mainspring of their happiness. There is the activity of country labours and recreations which enables Dennison to say: 'I am persuaded, that in a raw, moist climate, like this of England, continual exercise is as necessary as food to the preservation of the individual' (ibid.). But friendship plays no slight part in this success, and in very varied forms: the spontaneous friendliness of the Vicar, and, above all, of Wilson — 'There are characters which, like similar particles of matter, strongly attract each other' (p. 325) — the less demonstrative, but frank and generous friendliness of Bland, the farmer, and lastly the friendship between Dennison's wife and Wilson's.

In the portrait of Wilson Smollett sketches, in broad strokes, a cheerful picture of a country gentleman, certainly better with his hands

223

than his head, a concept consistent with the (understandable) mistrust of the English of people who are more cerebral than physical (pp. 326–7). It is therefore not a question of an idle retreat in order to waste all the more time in the social futilities so dear to women (p. 322) and disastrous for family fortunes, but of a return to the land which has been considered and thought out in all its practical (p. 325) and theoretical (p. 327) details. Such happiness, not immune from the bereavements of life (p. 328), is not *given* to the Dennisons; they *build* it together and with the help of their friends. To sum up, for Matthew Bramble, Dennison 'has really attained to that pitch of rural felicity, at which I have been aspiring these twenty years in vain' (p. 320).

Before Matthew Bramble and his travelling companions can know similar happiness, they have all, for even Tabitha and her servant Winifred are capable of changing a good deal, to get rid of their many prejudices. This second great impulse which animates *Humphry Clinker* consists of the psychological dialectic revolving round the central problem of judgment and prejudice. These problems are posed on three levels: family, social (the political and religious realm is included in this term), and national.

In the initial interplay of reciprocal judgments, family relationships are marked by hostility, and spontaneous judgments, most of them unfavourable, are passed in plenty all through the first month of the journey. Jery opens fire in his very first letter. If he is not too hard on a sister whom he nevertheless regards with the faint contempt of an elder brother, he does not spare his acid criticisms of his uncle and aunt (p. 8). But in spite of the harsh, even shattering nature of these first hastily formed opinions of his relatives, Jery leaves himself room for a certain amount of psychological manoeuvre. To begin with, he admits that there may be extenuating circumstances for his uncle, given his state of health, and he freely acknowledges that the squire is well liked by his servants and his neighbours. The 'perhaps, I may like him better on further acquaintance' (ibid.) will not long remain unechoed. On his side, Matthew Bramble passes a series of irate judgments on his two wards (p. 12) and his own sister, Tabitha, on the subject of whom he uses for the first time [30] the adjective 'intolerable' (p. 12), a positive semantic danger signal glowing red with his epistolary wrath.

Lydia makes an exception to this initial atmosphere of hostility. She is well aware of her uncle's irascible nature but promptly excuses him, with some medical naïvety, on account of his gout, hastening to add:

> When he is free from pain, he is the best-tempered man upon earth; so gentle, so generous, so charitable, that every body loves him; and so good to me, in particular, that I shall never be able to shew the deep sense I have of his tenderness and affection (p. 40).

These affectionate feelings of Lydia's for her uncle are not diminished in the course of the novel, but rather reinforced. Though in her extreme innocence, she cannot understand her uncle's hostility to Lady Griskin, she submits to his refusal to let her spend the winter with this very worldly woman, and loses no opportunity of praising her uncle's generosity (p. 94). Jery's final opinion of his sister, 'she is really an amiable creature' (p. 230), does no more than justice to this heroine, not outstandingly intelligent, but not devoid of the charm of emotional freshness.

Jery's opinion of his uncle changes very soon, and rapidly improves. As early as his second letter, he realises that his uncle is not a cynic: his extreme irritability (and touchiness) are as much psychological as physical in origin. He implicitly admits that he has been mistaken about his uncle, and uses a picturesque culinary metaphor, perhaps partly to hide his embarrassment: 'The truth is, his disposition and mine, which, like oil and vinegar, repelled one another at first, have now begun to mix by dint of being beaten up together' (p. 17). The incident in Bristol, where Matthew Bramble is surprised giving money, out of charity, to a widow, at once increases Jery's respect for his uncle and his contempt for the dirty-minded stupidity, squalid avarice and appalling vanity of his aunt (p. 22). In his fourth letter, Jery devotes himself to a positive psychological and moral analysis of his uncle: 'Mr Bramble's character ... opens and improves upon me every day' (p. 28). And, as Jery comes to understand this mask of misanthropy, more protective than aggressive, better, his sincere esteem is mingled with a touch of amused criticism (ibid.). On the contrary, Jery's (ill) opinion of his aunt will never change, and his ruthless remarks about every detail of her physical appearance are matched by an equally ruthless dissection of her character (pp. 60–1). He has no more illusions about the servant than about her mistress. But his analysis of Winifred is not devoid of sympathy for the weaknesses of this maid who is all too ready to ape the dress, language and religion of her employer (p. 208). What redeems Winifred in Jery's eyes is firstly her youth and secondly her kind-heartedness, a quality in which Tabitha is notoriously lacking. Lydia, more aware than her brother of Winifred's emotional fickleness, is a little harder on her, but nevertheless regards her with indulgence: 'As for Mrs Jenkins, she herself is really an object of compassion' (p. 259).

In spite of hasty judgments based on spontaneous prejudices, it would be wrong not to grant Matthew Bramble a certain clear-sightedness about himself and his own weaknesses. He judges his own judgments, and, in particular, his perpetual lamentations and his atrabilious and splenetic humours. He puts a (very human) touch of complaisance into it but this does not wipe out the merit of this cognitive reflection on his behaviour (p. 33). Again it is resigned clear-sightedness which characterises Matthew Bramble's opinion of his sister and also, in the second degree, the opinion he has of this opinion. At first, he admits, without any pleasure, that Tabitha, in spite of her many faults 'has found means to interest my affection; or, rather she is beholden to the force of prejudice, commonly called the ties of blood' (p. 48). Prejudices therefore include, in certain cases, a kind of positive substratum on the level of deep-seated, almost visceral emotions. Later on, Matthew Bramble supplies a corrective to what is too categorical in Jery's judgments, due to his lack of lived experience. The uncle puts the presumptuous youth in his place and tries to make him realise the contradictions in human feelings: 'This precious aunt of yours is become insensibly a part of my constitution — Damn her! She's a *noli me tangere* in my flesh, which I cannot bear to be touched or tampered with' (pp. 61–2). Jery finds it hard to understand this irrational attachment — 'in defiance of commonsense' (p. 62) — to such a creature. He manages, however, to see the bond which unites the brother and sister in spite of everything. He even divines the affection, however frustrated and inverted in its manifestations, that Tabitha has for her brother. His analysis of Tabitha's vigilant and exclusive fondness for her horrible dog makes Jery an astute (modest) precursor of modern psychoanalysts. Thus the interplay of reciprocal judgments produced by the letter-writers is also a judgment on the interplay of their human relationships. Judgments on other people judge the one who judges.

This family interplay is duplicated by the very dense and diffuse network of social, religious and political opinions and prejudices. Mingled together inextricably, they form a lush undergrowth of diverse, often contradictory, views from which the novel draws part of its vigorous sap.

Jery's indignation and, to a lesser degree, Matthew Bramble's when they learn of the budding romance between Lydia and Wilson is due above all to the strength of social prejudices. Wilson (and this is the ineffaceable stigma) is not a gentleman but, to all appearance, a dowry-hunter ill disguised as a play-actor. Jery therefore considers it his *duty* to protect his sister — and the family fortune — from the schemes of an adventurer. It is with some embarrassment that he admits Wilson's humble birth to his aristocratic correspondent. And yet he almost awards himself a moral good mark for his broad-mindedness: he has 'admitted him to the privilege of a gentleman' (p. 8). But the duel will not take place. Matthew Bramble feels the same shame when he relates the whole incident to Dr Lewis (p. 13). The reaction of the magistrate instructed to stop the duel is typical of a hierarchical view of justice, or rather injustice. He rebukes Wilson for his presumption in daring to fight with a gentleman! And Wilson, in his turn, asserts that he does indeed possess this magical social qualification (ibid.). On the same page, Matthew Bramble is aiming at an ironic effect when he writes, 'the young gentleman was on his high ropes', but the end of the novel destroys this cheap irony and invests the phrase with a reversed irony in the second degree, in some sort the irony of irony. Every time Wilson reappears, the problem of his social origin promptly crops up again. In Bristol, he had Lydia told 'that he was a gentleman of a good family' (p. 144). Jery is almost obsessed by this danger of a social mésalliance, and, without other proofs, considers that Wilson is a 'rascal' (pp. 224, 312). When Wilson's true identity is at last revealed, Jery's joy is, first and foremost, the triumphant satisfaction of a deep-rooted social prejudice. He can at last sleep in peace, for his sister, 'instead of debasing her sentiments and views to a wretched stroller . . . had really captivated the heart of a gentleman, her equal in rank and superior in fortune' (p. 332). So all is settled in the most satisfactory way, for, in the pastoral Eden dear to Smollett, it is obligatory that there should be plenty in the bank accounts.

Clinker's case is a more moving one. Thrown out by his master because he is ill, having neither friends nor family, he is forced to bear the stigmata of a down-and-out, even though Smollett chooses, with a certain brutal irony, to attach these stigmata to the ragged breeches which reveal the bare buttocks of the unfortunate postilion (pp. 81–3). Once again Tabitha's virulent stupidity is given free rein, repeated in a different, but equally cruel way by the social indifference of the innkeeper, smugly conscious of being within his rights, since he pays the poor rate. However, thanks to the influence of Methodism, Tabitha ends by ridding herself of her prejudices about Clinker, whereas at their first meeting she had been 'fortified against him with prejudice and resentment' (p. 100).

If Clinker, the ragged proletarian, is preserved, albeit only by the transformation of his clothes, from social reprobation, it is not so for that heterogeneous mass which Matthew Bramble repeatedly condemns. Hatred of the mob is a psychological constant in *Humphry Clinker* and all Smollett's works, which reaches its climax in *The History and Adventures of an Atom*, if this book was really written by him. Bramble re-employs his favourite word, 'monster', to describe the growth of Bath and, later on, of London (p. 37). It would be untrue to think that Matthew Bramble hates only the common rabble. The crowd which is supposed to be well-bred does not escape his censure either and Jery is forced to agree with it after the experiment (the word used on p. 52) conducted by Jack Holder. The vulgarity of a pseudo-fashionable gathering furnishes Smollett with the pretext for one of his most stylistically brilliant pages, but one that, in the last analysis, is profoundly sad. This crowd is alienated, it has no real existence for the author except as an *object* of observation. The decision of Quin and his friend Bramble further emphasises Smollett's intentional distanciation. The two eccentrics, along with Jery, take refuge from the tumult and retire to a gallery where they can look down on it so as better to observe this appalling scuffle. It transforms the patients taking the waters of Bath into greedy Yahoos fighting each other for cakes and nosegays at a given signal (p. 52). However Smollett is less pessimistic than Swift: this crowd has not gone completely mad since the auditory stimulus applied by Jack Holder and his hunting-horns has the contrary effect of what he intended. The scuffle, which was degenerating into a free fight, stops: 'They were ashamed of their absurd deportment, and suddenly desisted' (ibid.). So there exists, in spite of the impulses of collective insanity, a remnant of conscience which restrains the individual on the brink of relapsing into savagery. Finally, this incident proves that Matthew Bramble is not a cynical misanthropist 'without the vortex of the tumult' (ibid.). He does not consider himself delivered of all responsibility towards his fellow man, he does not wish to cut himself off from a world for which he is still capable of feeling a certain rueful pity: 'He hung his head in manifest chagrin, and seemed to repine at the triumph of his judgment' (ibid.). The protective mask of his misanthropy does not succeed in hiding the agonising conflict between heart and head in this lacerated man.

But Smollett is much less categorical than criticism, past or recent, has been willing to admit. Matthew Bramble is not, any more than Jery or Lismahago, his exclusive and monolithic mouthpiece. Bramble judges his fellow men pessimistically but he does not fail to question his own powers of judgment. And this perpetual recurrence of critical reflections on their own behaviour gives these characters their dynamic relativity in the very image of the fluctuations of human life itself. Bramble is fully conscious of the possible distortions of his own judgment, or that of his friends, who see 'imperfectly through the mist of prejudice' (p. 77). It is therefore as well to accept his pessimistic statements with a discretion warranted by his own observations: 'for I have perceived that my opinion of mankind, like mercury in the thermometer, rises and falls according to the variations of the weather' (ibid.). And, for Bramble, the barometer seldom stands at 'set fair'.

It is difficult to separate the religious prejudices, especially as regards Methodism, from their social substratum. In fact this religious revival, as presented by Smollett in *Humphry Clinker* through the character of Clinker, cannot be understood without the existence, towards the middle of the eighteenth century, of a whole lower class of artisans, domestic servants and tradesmen uncertain of their future to whom the Good Tidings preached by Wesley at last brought a little human warmth and divine consolation. Inevitably a certain type of narrow-minded religious fervour had gone to absurd extremes. No one has described this fanaticism better than James Lackington, converted at the age of sixteen, in his *Memoirs*, in which he also related his progressive detachment from all the Methodist excesses. His analysis of Methodism, however coloured it may be by the insidious desire to justify himself, offers many parallels with the way Smollett depicts it in *Humphry Clinker*. Lackington denounces, in particular, the theological and psychological terrorism employed by the Methodists:

> They work on the fears of the most virtuous; youth and innocence fall victims daily before their threats of hell and damnation, and the poor feebleminded, instead of being comforted and encouraged are

often by them sunk into an irrecoverable state of gloomy despondence and horrible despair[31].

If despair does not take possession to this extent of Tabitha, Winifred or Lydia, it is nevertheless certain that the Methodist influence of Clinker disturbs these women's minds, especially Winifred's, whose head is already none too strong. Now Lackington vigorously denounces this effect of Methodism on a feminine audience, by definition credulous, and largely without much education: 'I believe that by far the greatest part of his people are females; and not a few of them sour, disappointed old maids, with some others of a less prudish disposition.' It would be difficult to find a better commentary on Tabitha's ambiguous search, on the indefinite but perilous borderline between flesh and the spirit. The numerous sexual insinuations with which Smollett scatters Tabitha's and Winifred's letters on the subject of the carnal activities of Methodist preachers are no novelty. In 1760 Samuel Foote published his comedy *The Minor*, in which George Whitefield is satirised under the name of Dr Squintum. An old procuress, Mrs Cole, cheerfully and ingeniously combines the demands of her venerean profession with the salvational teachings of Methodism. In Act III, Mrs Cole thus exhorts a young virgin whom she is about to offer to a client: 'Don't you remember what Mr Squintum said? A woman's not worth saving, that won't be guilty of a swinging sin; for then they have matter to repent upon.' What casuistry to mask the *felix culpa*! Smollett himself had not concealed his hostility to Methodism in the *Continuation of the Complete History of England* (IV, 121–2) and was already laying stress on the social aspect of Methodist conversions:

> Many thousands in the lower rank of life were infected with this species of enthusiasm, by the unwearied efforts of a few obscure preachers; such as Wh[itefield], and the two W[esley]s, who propagated their doctrines to the most remote corners of the British dominions, and found means to lay the whole kingdom under contribution (ibid.).

At the price of grave injustice to Whitefield and the Wesley brothers, Smollett considers that in the case of Methodism it is a matter less of conversion than contagion. In *Humphry Clinker*, Matthew Bramble's social prejudice remains inveterate, although he is not devoid of sympathy for Clinker's proselytising. The first time Bramble becomes aware of his servant's religious activities, he makes fun of them, and does not emerge from this brisk theological passage of arms without some personal scratches (p. 100). But his fury breaks out when he discovers his sister and niece at a meeting at which Clinker is preaching. He is shocked by the social incongruity of the situation. A lackey is daring to concern himself with the spiritual direction of his social superiors: 'I don't think my servant is a proper ghostly director, for a devotee of your sex and character' (p. 137), he says to Lydia. The beginning of the debate that ensues between Clinker, threatened with dismissal, and his angry master is important on the thematic plane. For the first time, someone opposes Bramble in the realm of ideas and raises doubts about the moral value of reason alone (p. 138). But Bramble crushes Clinker with his social and intellectual superiority and the poor Methodist, after a very violent attack on his faith, is forced to submit. This submission of Clinker's is threefold: emotional ('I'm bound to love and obey your honour'); social, and intellectual ('It becometh not such a poor ignorant fellow as me, to hold dispute with gentlemen of rank and learning') (p. 139).

It must not be concluded that Bramble is impervious to all religious feeling. His opinion of Clinker — and of Methodism — develops into a clear-sighted tolerance after the release of his servant who, even in prison, has not given up proselytising for Methodism (p. 151). Bramble freely admits Clinker's *sincerity* and *simplicity*, qualities largely lacking in his sister, whose sudden and noisy religious fervour serves, above all, as an imperfect mask for her ardent search for a husband. Tabitha, in her pseudo-spiritual activities, is like a caricature of a stage Methodist, whereas Clinker earns Bramble's respect and no doubt Smollett's (p. 153). But, in spite of this changed attitude[32], Bramble remains sceptical on the subject of religion. It is paradoxical that this rational scepticism is based on the very existence of ineradicable prejudice in the human mind. Writing about the superstitious beliefs of the Scots, he reveals his lack of confidence in the ability of human beings to correct their errors and use their better judgment:

> The longer I live, I see more reason to believe that prejudices of education are never wholly eradicated even when they are discovered to be erroneous and absurd. Such habits of thinking as interest the grand passions, cleave to the human heart in such a manner, that though an effort of reason may force them from their hold for a moment, this violence no sooner ceases, than they resume their grasp with an increased elasticity and adhesion (p. 270).

This adoption of a rationalist standpoint proves ambiguous for it condemns superstition as much as religious beliefs themselves. Smollett shows, not without irony, as regards Winifred and Clinker, that the two are not mutually exclusive. The devout Clinker, who is nevertheless inclined to 'natural superstition', thinks he sees a ghostly apparition when he happens to meet the old 'Druid' in the forest (p. 251). Winifred, too, lets herself be terrorised by the Scottish legends and defines this country in a richly evocative portmanteau word: 'this is the land of congyration' (p. 261). Finally, Lydia regrets that she does not feel the Methodist emotions aroused in her aunt. Although she is disturbed by a sermon heard at the 'Tabernacle', the Methodist signs of grace do not manifest themselves in her (pp. 135–6). Smollett thus implies that a sentimental and romantic nature does not necessarily predispose one to religiosity.

The existence of political prejudices appears most of all in Jery's tenth letter (London, June 2nd). Barton, the friend he has met again, is a man transformed by his political choice. Jery's analysis is not wholly unfavourable to Barton, whose sincerity and lack of malice he willingly admits. Nevertheless, in the opinion of Jery, who prides himself on being an impartial spectator, Barton 'sees every thing through such an exaggerating medium, as to me . . . is altogether incomprehensible – Without all doubt, the fumes of faction not only disturb the faculty of reason, but also pervert the organs of sense' (p. 95). The description, now ironical, now caricatural, of the king, his entourage, and above all of Newcastle acts as a demonstration of these initial comments on Barton. The humour verges on the farcical when Barton, after a series of mistakes over people's names by the muddle-headed Newcastle, sees fit to go into raptures over the fallen politician's wonderful memory (p. 98). Bramble's opinion confirms his nephew's. For him, too, Barton is 'a good sort of a man, though most ridiculously warped in his political principles' (p. 102). But Bramble does not reject all Barton's political ideas wholesale. His views on the liberty of the press – or its licence to be defamatory, of which Smollett must have had bitter experience during the confrontation of his *Briton* with Wilkes's *North Briton* – accord well with the control Bramble advocates in other realms (pp. 103–4).

Smollett seems to concur, without any direct reference in *Humphry Clinker*, with the theories put forward by Bolingbroke in *The Idea of a Patriot King*, a treatise written as early as 1738, though the authorised version was not published till 1749. Bolingbroke developed the theory of an enlightened and democratic conservatism based on the protective role of the 'patriot king', the guardian of the constitution, set above all factions, and the fatherly defender of his people's happiness[33]. There is a continuity of conservative political vision between the *Complete History of England*, the *Briton*, the *Continuation of the Complete History of England*, the *Travels through France and Italy*, the *Present State* and *Humphry Clinker*. Smollett, like his character Matthew Bramble, is full of mistrust of democracy, in which he sees a perpetual danger of social and political anarchy. For him, the safest bulwark of English liberties is the authority of the 'patriot king' in a well-administered society whose economy is controlled by regulative laws aimed at avoiding the proliferation of luxury and the cancerous growth of wealth too suddenly acquired to benefit the nation as a whole. In the *Continuation of the Complete History of England*, he writes: 'after all, the liberties of the nation could never be so firmly established, as by the power, generosity, and virtue of a patriot king' (III, 339). The analysis of the British Constitution, in the *Present State*, though flattering on the whole, nevertheless brings out the same weaknesses denounced three years later in the bitter comments of

Lismahago, retailed by Bramble (pp. 205—6). Smollett benefits from this liberty which he would like to see restrained when he criticises the British Constitution in these terms:

> though said to be as perfect as human wisdom could suggest, and human frailty permit, yet, nevertheless, contains in itself the seeds of its own dissolution. While individuals are corruptible, and the means of corruption so copiously abound, it will always be in the power of an artful and ambitious prince to sap the foundations of English liberty (*Present State*, II, 165).

Lismahago is only repeating these pessimistic themes when he attacks the corruption of Parliament and the abuses of the freedom of the press.

It rightly devolved on Jery, the official observer in *Humphry Clinker*, and also the defender of an obsessive class prejudice, to draw a conclusion from this flaw in human nature, whose extent and danger he has at last measured when the journey ends. After the discovery of the real situation of Wilson—Dennison, Jery confesses his sins: 'I am, however, mortified to reflect what flagrant injustice we every day commit, and what absurd judgment we form, in viewing objects through the falsifying medium of prejudice and passion' (p. 332). A noble admission, certainly. But the dominant concept in *Humphry Clinker* never appears in clear contrasted tones. The black and white of *Ferdinant Count Fathom* is no longer anything but a distant (and bad) literary memory. Smollett's verbal and intellectual palette is so rich and subtle that it endows any judgment with the lifelike and animated relief of indirect lighting. The complex and labyrinthine motions of the human soul cannot adapt themselves to a dogmatic fixity, the spiritual symptom of *rigor mortis*. Through the letters of his characters, Smollett has been able to convey the internal contradictions of all motivation. Jery's contrite declarations are in flagrant opposition to his obvious lack of enthusiasm, on the very next page (p. 333), for Clinker's matrimonial project: 'I told him I thought he might do better, as there was no engagement nor promise subsisting.' The momentarily overcome prejudice reappears, with nearly all its former strength. Moreover, it is camouflaged by a hypocritical legalism. Matthew Bramble is not brimming over with enthusiasm either at the idea of his bastard son — who, after all, is a gentleman's bastard — marrying the servant-girl with the big heart and the empty head: 'I would have wished that Mr. Clinker had kept out of this scrape' (p. 345). But, more human, and rich in experience of life, Bramble takes Winifred's feelings into account, something which does not even remotely occur to Jery. So his resigned father gives Clinker permission 'to play the fool, in imitation of his betters' (ibid.). The bar sinister will always prevent Clinker from climbing to the top of the social ladder.

It would take too long even to sketch the historical origin of the tenacious hostility between the English and the Scots since 1707. But the dates of the two failed rebellions, 1715 and 1745, can serve as convenient landmarks to indicate two new flare-ups of latent antagonism, long after the cessation of hostilities. The administration of Lord Bute, from May 1762 to April 1763, rekindled the brands of this ill-extinguished fire. Already, for many years, the English had had a grievance against the Scots for their social and financial success when they came and settled in the south of Great Britain, particularly in London. Smollett himself gives a sadly lucid analysis of this animosity which Wilkes and Churchill did their utmost to inflame throughout the country. The success of the Scottish immigrants, the haughty and thick-skinned tactlessness of Bute, living in London in the midst of an entourage composed almost exclusively of Scotsmen, and the first campaign of psychological intoxication by means of the press, worthy to be compared with modern vicious methods of propaganda, aroused a virulent revival of unbridled hatred for Smollett's unfortunate compatriots.

In the *Continuation of the Complete History of England*, Smollett can only deplore these inflammatory manoeuvres which shamelessly stirred up the basest, but also the most inveterate, prejudices — such as the stinginess and avarice of the Scots — 'till at length the populace were incensed and impelled even to the verge of insurrection' (V, 118). These lines were written in 1765, barely three years after the Bute ministry. But Smollett had already acquired the ability to see things in sufficient psychological and political perspective to condemn outright, and from a *national* point of view, these fruitless and dangerous quarrels: 'England and Scotland are now too intimately connected in point of interest and communication, to be disjoined without such violent convulsions as would endanger the safety of either, and even the existence of both' (V, 120). In these little-known lines in the rare Volume V of the *Continuation of the Complete History of England*, Smollett appears as a realistic historian, for whom any retrograde step would be a national disaster. But the public lets itself be dangerously manipulated, something as true in 1762–63 as in our own day. It is not by chance that the portrait of Charles Churchill faces the p. 118 already quoted. His incendiary poem of 562 lines, published in 1763, had an immediate and lasting success with the, then numerous, detractors of Scotland. *The Prophecy of Famine* is a little masterpiece of heinous unfairness, in which no insult is too vulgar to appear. The author sees the Scots as 'Nature's bastards' or again 'the refuse of mankind'. And it is with the ferocious pleasure of a necrophilous sadist that he makes the Scottish shepherd, Jockey, lament:

> Five brothers there I lost, in manhood's pride,
> Two in the field, and three on gibbets died.

This brief glimpse of the atmosphere of hostility to the Scots during and after the Bute ministry makes it easier to appreciate the defensive and didactic audacity Smollett shows in his favourable comments on Scotland and in his presentation of the paradoxical Lismahago. To begin with,

Smollett emphasises the ignorance and stupidity of the current prejudices against Scotland. Matthew Bramble blames himself for his lack of curiosity about his northern neighbours (p. 66). But the best examples of idiotic prejudices are provided, as might be expected, by Tabitha and Winifred. The mistress believes that food is scarce in Scotland and is so ignorant of geography that she is quite amazed to find herself in Scotland without having had to cross the sea. Though there is no sea barrier between Scotland and England, an invisible, but formidable wall of stupidity, rancour, ignorance and prejudice has been built up to divide them. And Matthew Bramble cannot prevent himself from observing pessimistically: 'What, between want of curiosity, and traditional sarcasms, the effect of ancient animosity, the people at the other end of the island know as little of Scotland as of Japan' (p. 214). Winifred hastens to repeat the asinine opinions of her mistress, not however without correcting them somewhat (p. 220). This animosity is revealed, at the lowest level, by a proliferation of scurrilous *graffiti* (already!) on the window-panes of inns all along the road to the North[34]. Lismahago refuses to take any notice of these insulting remarks about Scotland and the Scots. Breaking the windows would only make the satire more cutting − and the bill heavier, he argues with common sense and not without humour. On a slightly higher level, Jery begins by seeing Lismahago, at their first meeting, through the prejudiced eyes of one who shares the current resentment of the day of the Scots' cultural pretensions: 'this Caledonian is a self-conceited pedant, aukward, rude, and disputacious' (p. 190). This last adjective, as well as the verb 'to dispute' (p. 191) draws the reader's attention to the double psychological and rhetorical function of Lismahago. Much better armed than Clinker, Lismahago is able to stand up to Matthew Bramble's dogmatic statements with astuteness and tenacity. As Jery remarks, the two men act as a check on each other when the argument threatens to degenerate into a mere wrangle (p. 191). Bramble and Lismahago go in for 'disputation' in the rhetorical sense of the word, and manipulate paradox in the course of this exercise with the skill and vigour (Lismahago in particular) of experts trained in the reconciliation of contradictions (p. 197).

Nevertheless, Smollett, in his barely camouflaged propaganda for Scotland, surrounds himself with precautions. He proceeds first of all to a systematic inversion of roles. Bramble, the non-Scot, defends Scotland more that Lismahago. Moreover, a physiological note on Lismahago's skull passes almost unnoticed but constitutes a subtle safeguard. Lismahago, scalped by the Indians and left for dead with his skull split open by a tomahawk, survives all the same 'though the loss of substance could not be repaired' (p. 189). Smollett does not, in all probability, imply that there was any great loss of brain cells but that Lismahago's pate remains cracked literally, and perhaps metaphorically. As in *Launcelot Greaves*, Smollett provides a possible alibi for himself in the more likely mental derangement of Lismahago. Thus Lismahago is partially excused in advance when he maintains with great fervour and philological erudition that the Scots speak better English than the English themselves (pp. 199–200). This linguistic issue played a large part in the reproaches levelled at Smollett and other Scottish writers, who were accused of using regional dialect by the enemies of the *Critical Review* and Scotland. In spite of Lismahago's learned arguments to prove his theory, it must be added that neither Jery nor his uncle appear to be convinced, and Bramble even goes so far as to claim that 'the Scotch dialect . . . certainly gives a clownish air even to sentiments of the greatest dignity and decorum' (p. 231). A few years later, Topham, in spite of all his liking for the Scots, admits that their pronunciation 'is far from being agreeable: it gives an air of gravity, sedateness and importance to their words; which, though of use sometimes in an harangue or public discourse, in common conversation seems dull, heavy, stupid and unharmonious' (*Letters from Edinburgh*, p. 54). Stimulated by the paradoxical dialectic of Lismahago, Jery and his uncle are soon priding themselves on their enthusiasm for Scotland and its inhabitants, not without some reservations, already mentioned, concerning the lack of cleanliness, the poverty of certain regions and the natural indolence of the Highlanders. Jery begins one of his letters like this: 'If I stay much longer at Edinburgh, I shall be changed into a downright Caledonian' (p. 221). He even comes, unlike his uncle, to like the Scottish accent (ibid.), and admires the impartiality of the Scots who do not indulge in perpetual and malicious criticisms of their English neighbours (p. 222). Even the beauty of the Scottish women has been disparaged, wrongly Jery thinks, by the English (p. 224). In his enthusiasm for Scotland, Bramble forestalls any accusation of partiality by being clearly aware of his former prejudices: 'If I am partial, there is, at least, some merit in my conversion from illiberal prejudices which had grown up with my constitution' (p. 231). And the next lines are devoted to a rational explanation of the origin of these anti-Scottish prejudices (the word 'prejudices' is repeated) which the English cherish. Smollett remarks, and with good reason, on the linguistic and phonetic sensitivity of the English, who are always quick to laugh at a foreign or provincial accent (ibid.).

Without falling into the invidious snare of biographical interpretation, it is permissible to think that here Smollett is indirectly expressing his bitterness about the constant gibes provoked by his own Caledonian solecisms. But, as in the *Continuation of the Complete History of England*, the wish to conciliate triumphs over personal resentments. In this connection, the banquet of the 'caddies' — or 'cadies' or 'cawdies', a Scottish distortion of the French 'cadet' — those astute mischievous and professionally honest errand-boys (who include pimping among the services they provide) amusingly symbolises the desire for harmony between the English and the Scots. The veteran of this respectable corporation proposes the following toast: 'Mester Malford, . . . may a' unkindness cease between John Bull and his sister Moggy' (p. 227). Twenty years after Culloden, such a wish shows good sense. But the disappearance of anti-Scottish prejudice does not, for all that, imply unqualified admiration. Bramble criticises the Scots for a certain tendency to ostentation in their hospitality and does not at all admire their gardens and parks (p. 234).

The third great impulse animating *Humphry Clinker* is the moral dialectic, that is to say the aggregate of all the efforts by which the individual tries to transcend his internal contradictions in the midst of a generally hostile society. Smollett begins by presenting a rather gloomy picture of the moral alienation which characterises the isolation of his letter-writers at the outset of their journey. In his first letter, Bramble uses a solidly negative vocabulary, and the jerky, cantankerous sentences give the impression of a kind of egocentric interior monologue. But it must be emphasised straight away that Bramble is not turned in upon himself to such a degree as to suggest a schizophrenic autism. His personal problems about his health and his family preoccupy him, certainly, but he also displays a frequent, even regular, concern for the wellbeing of his servants, neighbours and tenant-farmers (see, for example, pp. 5, 14–15, 38). Although, as Jery very soon observes, 'nothing but the necessity of his occasions could compel him to get within the pale of society' (p. 17), Bramble is not, however, cut off from the outside world. Lydia's narrow sentimental self-centredness is revealed in her first letter by the irritating quantity of first-person pronouns and possessive adjectives.

More important still is the moral degeneration which insidiously attacks even people mindful of the ills of others. In spite of his genuine kindness and generosity, Bramble experiences a feeling of false shame, of over-prudish discomfiture, when he makes a charitable gift to the Bristol widow. His voice — 'a croaking tone of voice' (p. 21) — betrays his embarrassment, and, as the scene develops into a disconcertingly emotional one, it becomes 'still more and more discordant' (ibid.), no doubt reflecting the internal conflict which rends Bramble, torn between his charitable inclinations and fear of his intentions being maliciously misunderstood. The inopportune irruption of Tabitha unfortunately confirms his worst apprehensions. It is significant that Jery owns to the same false modesty about charitable deeds. Fear of social censure prevents him from following his uncle's example (p. 23). The paralysis of the moral sentiment and its final atrophy may equally well strike the receiver as the giver. This is the moral (or immoral) basis of the quarrel — with autobiographical connotations — between Serle and Paunceford. The ingratitude of the parvenu finds an easy excuse in the sorrowful but dignified silence of his unfortunate benefactor (pp. 67–8).

Money and urban society therefore help to corrupt the minds and hearts of those who let themselves be caught up in the frenzied pursuit of them. Bramble cannot recognise, in the social and moral sense, any of his old friends again, so much has London life changed them. Even intelligent authors are victims of a narrow dogmatism which isolates them behind their wall of arrogant intolerance (pp. 105—6). The result is a rupture of communication between individuals: 'Those originals are not fit for conversation' (p. 106). Men no longer know how to hold dialogue with each other, since their utterances have turned into a hopeless monologue in the void of their moral unconsciousness. As always (or nearly always, for Bramble's errors of judgment only make him more human) Bramble mistrusts his pessimistic opinion, and when he wonders, not without anxiety, 'if the morals of mankind have not contracted an extraordinary degree of depravity, within these thirty years' (p. 106), he takes care to remind himself that he has aged, physically and psychologically, with a quotation from Horace:'*difficilis, querulus, laudator temporis acti*'. Jery confirms the impression of hostile isolation in which the authors wish to keep themselves 'in a state of mutual repulsion, like so many particles of vapour, each surrounded by its own electrified atmosphere' (p. 116). As to the half-starved quill-drivers observed in Smollett's own home, they shut themselves up behind a double wall of petty stupidity and ridiculous eccentricity (pp. 126—7). However, the thematic contrast between the likeable and sociable Scottish authors met in Edinburgh (p. 233) provides a note of antithetical optimism, but a very brief one in comparison with the number of pessimistic pages devoted to literary life in London.

There is the same feeling of nightmarish absurdity about the Court where dehumanised marionettes frenziedly jig and gesticulate. 'Captain C', adventurer, spy and double agent, plays Asmodeus to the Court and reveals to Jery and his uncle the threadbare intellectual and psychological strings which give a semblance of life to that puppet, Newcastle. Smollett, like Montesquieu in his *Lettres Persanes* (1721), has recourse to the old literary stratagem of the innocent Oriental traveller astray in this Court where the stupidity and absurdity of false pretences reign supreme. Amazed by Newcastle's behaviour, the Algerian ambassador finds a Mahomedan explanation: 'Holy prophet! I don't wonder that this nation prospers, seeing it is governed by the counsel of ideots; a series of men, whom all good mussulmen revere as the organs of immediate inspiration!' (p. 112). How can one be English? From the pitiable minister to the foppish valet Dutton, the antithesis of the worthy Clinker (p. 153), society empties men of their moral substance, as a stinking beast sucks an egg. Nothing is left but frail shells of mannerisms of speech and dress and other affected imitations of the French (p. 158). But these dead souls can also spread their own corruption. Smollett treats this theme in a ludicrous manner by harping on Winifred's feminine vanity which only too readily succumbs to flattery (pp. 208—9). The contrast between Clinker and Dutton is emphasised by a culinary simile of Jery's: 'Humphry may be compared to an English pudding, composed of good wholesome flour and suet, and Dutton to a syllabub or iced froth, which, though agreeable to

237

the taste, has nothing solid or substantial' (p. 208). The confrontation between Winifred's two suitors was inevitable and ends up, as morality necessitates, entirely to the honour and advantage of Clinker.

The destruction of personal morality can be almost total, and be exemplified in two minor characters as different as Pimpernel and Mickle-whimmen. The first is akin on the thematic plane to Judge Gobble in *Launcelot Greaves*. A pettifogging lawyer stooping to the lowest form of chicanery, a shameful husband and father, this character, sketched in half a page, is a reminder of the ontological absurdity of this omnipresence of Evil. Not a single pleasing trait lightens this gloomy picture of a dead soul, if indeed it ever existed. However, unlike Gobble, Pimpernel possesses a wife (the verb assumes a cruel significance when Smollett informs his readers that this man has actually *bought* his wife from a drayman) who is not fundamentally bad, but has no authority in her home (p. 172). The character of the whining and facetious Scots lawyer, Micklewhimmen, is more complex[35]. This morally unscrupulous advocate pretends to be a helpless cripple in order the better to exploit feminine compassion, ever liable to be misdirected. Tabitha, that eternal Hecate in pursuit of possible prey, is not the last to make a great fuss of the sham invalid. A trivial incident at the inn — a fire alarm — unmasks the brutal selfishness of this genuine cynic with cruel clarity. In spite of a specious plea in defence of his conduct based, like Falstaff's, but in very different spirit, on the strength of the instinct of self-preservation, the advocate loses his case with his formerly devoted nurses: 'The selfish brutality of his behaviour on the stairs had steeled their hearts against all his arts and address' (p. 176). In spite of his Scottish nationality, Smollett condemns Mickle-whimmen's amoral trickery. But he grants him some extenuating circumstances, for the incident concludes with the culprit dancing a wild Highland jig.

In such an atmosphere of moral derangement, it is not surprising that even the kind-hearted Lydia should lapse into her uncle's pessimism. On two occasions, in spite of the innocent tolerance of her youth, she allows herself to pass severe judgments on her aunt's conduct, and soon on that of the entire female sex — except herself, of course. Lydia analyses the matrimonial manoeuvres of her aunt, who even uses religion 'as a decoy' (p. 259). This is what Winifred also expresses, in terms of disturbing ambiguity, when she talks of the 'private exaltations of the reverend Mr. Macrocodile' (p. 260) which have had the effect of sweetening Tabitha's execrable temper. In conclusion, Lydia declares: 'I am truly ashamed of my own sex . . . In point of constancy, they certainly have nothing to reproach the male part of the creation' (p. 259). There is the same disgust with life, passing, no doubt, but proving a certain mental development in Lydia, when she says she is tired of this perpetual travelling. The childish, uncritically enthusiastic young girl of Bath would certainly not have been capable of writing: 'when Vice quits the stage for a moment, her place is immediately occupied by Folly, which is often too serious to excite any thing but compassion' (p. 308). There follows a second condemnation of her aunt's avid desire to get married. Matthew Bramble lets himself be carried away by a burst of unexpected social vanity during a dinner at Lord Oxmington's. His challenge to the peer of the realm is a thematic reminder of the identical situation in which the strolling player Wilson found himself as regards the 'gentleman', Jery. Lord Oxmington is furious at such an assault on his personal prerogatives (p. 283). Once the incident is over, Bramble realises the sad absurdity of such an uncontrolled reaction. With a passion characterised by uncompromising lucidity, he unbosoms himself thus to Dr Lewis: 'At what time of life may a man think himself exempted from the necessity of sacrificing his repose to the punctilios of a contemptible world?' (p. 285). The question is not rhetorical but reveals that Bramble is painfully and pessimistically aware of his own inner contradictions.

Smollett does not only present victims of this moral pessimism. Also to be found in *Humphry Clinker* are attempts at individual solutions embodied in rebels against society or those whose primitive way of life sets them apart from it. The big-hearted 'gentleman highwayman' is part of popular English mythology, and in the *Beggar's Opera* (1728), Gay had already exploited this admiration of the English for the charming and chivalrous highway robber. At the same period, César de Saussure notes the courteous affability of certain highwaymen:

> Some of them were found to practise their trade with politeness and generosity, apologising to those whom they held up for what they had been obliged to take from them and always leaving something for their travelling expenses[36].

It would certainly be dangerous to adumbrate a social criminology based on literary characters who originate on the borderline between legend and reality, but the fact remains none the less that Martin in *Humphry Clinker* belongs to this tradition of the amiable brigand. Martin is not without a grievance against society. An inflexible father-in-law, whose daughter he has secretly married, turns his wife out of doors and she soon dies. Unlucky as a fortune-hunter, Martin soon takes to the road (p. 149). His courage, his skill, his intelligence and the delicacy (!) of his methods make him a famous and successful highwayman. Martin defies society in the person of Judge Buzzard, with whom he engages in an exciting battle of wits, but which, being a sensible man, he knows he is bound to lose in the end (ibid.). So when Martin, the paradoxical advocate of justice during Clinker's wrongful imprisonment, meets Bramble, he grasps the opportunity of abandoning the road for a less glorious but safer life. The rebel aspires to the peace of an honest profession and he dares to apply to Bramble: 'I don't look upon you as a person that thinks in the ordinary stile' (p. 160). Thus, with the assistance of Bramble, who is himself flouting social conventions by trusting a repentant thief, Martin will go off to carve out a new honest career for himself in the East Indies.

If this rebel turns out to be reclaimable, the eccentric and stoical Colonel Hewett maintains his defiance to the end and commits suicide in the manner of an ancient Roman. A convinced agnostic, Hewett defends the Christian religion to some Turks in a decidedly unorthodox manner which earns him the nickname of 'Demonstrator' and allows Smollett to conceal a sly ribaldry under the phrase: 'he was stimulated to shew his parts' (p. 182). The sexual prowess of this vigorous specimen of manhood seems to have convinced the Turks[37]. Smollett also praises the anti-conformism of this great traveller who always refused to yield to the demands of foreign manners and customs. Smollett's note on Hewett's suicide by starving himself to death, like Pomponius Atticus, barely disguises a touch of admiration for this eccentric who put an end to his days 'with such ease and serenity, as would have done honour to the firmest Stoic of antiquity' (p. 183).

Less cruel, on the surface, is that forced return to the state of nature which Lismahago experiences during his long captivity among the Indians. Evidently, Smollett does not share Rousseau's enthusiasm for the 'Noble Savage'. The ritual mutilations described by Lismahago are on the shaky borderline between sadism and buffoonery (p. 193). Smollett had already recounted, in the *Continuation of the Complete History of England*, the visit of three Cherokee chiefs to London in 1762, whose apathetic lack of curiosity disgusted him:

> They seemed to be in a state of brutal insensibility, which indeed seems to be the character of the North-American tribes in general, notwithstanding all the encomiums which some writers have lavished on the natural good sense and sagacity of that people (V, 25).

In the *Present State*, Smollett, assuming that he wrote those pages dealing with the various American Indian tribes, shows no more enthusiasm for these primitive people. The name of the Miamis appears in a list of the Canadian tribes, but with no specific details. Only a general judgment contests their right to be called human beings: these savages are in general 'so stupid, so cruel, so barbarous, or shy, that they scarcely deserve that denomination' (VIII, 26). Far from describing an idyllic state of nature, Smollett persists in drawing a satirical picture of these Red Indians and their customs[38]. Lismahago's squaw Squinkinacoosta is a crude, gaudily coloured caricature but Smollett's cosmetic and sartorial satire is not directed solely against the barbarous way the Indians bedizen themselves. Tabitha's stupidity impels her to ask a question about the fashion the squaw followed in her dress and *coiffure*, and this is an excellent opportunity for implicitly condemning the frivolities of an English fashion often imported from France. The simplicity of Indian manners, in spite of their grotesque aspects, still seems, in Lismahago's eyes, preferable to the excesses of a society straining after futile and corrupting luxury. The account, well integrated into Lismahago's adventures, of the martyrdom of the missionaries, who have the two grave defects of being Frenchmen and Catholics, gives Smollett an excuse for touching on the problem of natural religion. The word 'simplicity' is repeated (p. 196) for the second time in two pages (see p. 194). Instead of being divided into more or less hostile sects, the Indians, according to Lismahago, are Manicheans and Monotheists. This faith in the Supreme Being[39] is that of 'sensible men', whereas 'the common people there, as in other countries, run into the absurdities of superstition' (p. 196). Lismahago gibes at the obtuse Tabitha's Methodist beliefs far too lightly for her to realise it, but there again Smollett's satire is double-edged. The antipapist satire concealed in the martyrdom of the fanatical missionaries, repeats the usual attacks on the incarnation, trans-substantiation and miracles. Smollett protects himself against all religious censure by stressing that Lismahago is a free-thinker, a characteristic already indirectly announced in the preliminary letter of the Reverend Jonathan Dustwich: 'he has never been once seen *intra templi parietes*' (p. 1). It is probable that this hatred of missionaries was not purely atheistic, but largely political and nationalist, as certain remarks in the *Present State* on the influence of the French Jesuits after converting the Indians suggest[40].

How can this moral alienation be broken? Northrop Frye, in his book *Anatomy of Criticism* observes that before their dénouement, many comedies approach a 'point of ritual death', something which also occurs in *Humphry Clinker*:

> The main characters are nearly drowned in an accident with an upset carriage; they are taken to a nearby house to dry off, and a cognitio takes place, in the course of which their family relationships are regrouped, secrets of birth brought to light, and names changed[41].

However correct Northrop Frye's analysis may be in summing up the incident recounted by Jery (pp. 312–19), it takes little account of the thematic skill Smollett deploys all through *Humphry Clinker* to prepare for this final *cognitio*. Here is the condescending explanatory interpolated clause associated with the above quotation: 'I select this because no one will suspect Smollett of deliberate mythopoeia but only of following convention, at least as far as his plot is concerned' (ibid.). And why must Smollett be denied the deliberate (or even unconscious) building up of a moral architectural structure which underpins the entire novel? The connected themes of identity and paternity are at the core of this quest of five individuals, more or less alienated according to the level of their moral consciousness, in search of happiness and their true selves. And this self-awareness is promoted by the search for and discovery of paternity. Such is the second phase of the moral dialectic.

In *Humphry Clinker*, the theme of mistaken identities, analysed in

Ferdinand Count Fathom, reappears in a more schematic and also more complex form. The case of Wilson, already partly dealt with in the study of the plot of the story, is the clearest example. Wilson is not what he is (apparently a strolling player) but just what he seems not to be (a gentleman)[42]. Smollett complicates at will this mirage of identity which vanishes before the factual reality. On two occasions a double or a man of the same name adds to the confusion over Wilson's true identity. In Edinburgh Lydia faints when she meets a certain Gordon 'who strongly resembles the said Wilson' (p. 235), or, to quote Lydia herself: 'the very image of Wilson stood before me, dressed exactly as he was in the character of Aimwell' (p. 258). The reference to Farquhar's character in the *Beaux' Stratagem* (1707) serves a double purpose: a reminder of Wilson's theatrical activities and, in the second degree, an allusion to a usurped identity, since the younger Aimwell passes himself off as his elder brother. Jery, in his revengeful fury, believes he has challenged the sham Wilson to a duel and finds himself confronted with the father of the real Wilson (p. 311). The Wilsons (the father, Jack, and the son Charles, a fellow undergraduate of young Dennison's at Cambridge) are friends of the Dennison family, which gave Lydia's unfortunate lover the idea of borrowing their name when he ran away (p. 332). Thus Jery's meeting with Jack Wilson is an indirect preparation for the secondary *cognitio* which reveals the true identity of the sham Wilson.

Bramble, Jery and Clinker are also the victims of mistakes about their identity. For the first two characters, these are of little importance and consist of mere misnomers due to the treacherous and muddled memory of Newcastle (pp. 98, 112–13). But these confusions nevertheless imply the frail nature of identity, which also rests on the social function of individual and collective memory. The mistake (although a deliberate one) over Clinker's identity, when he is accused of being a highwayman, comes within an inch of costing him his life (p. 146). The alienating power of (false) testimony is such that Clinker's true character is momentarily destroyed by it in the eyes of the law. The accused Clinker is no longer what he is but what he has never been. This is a revival of the theme of appearances which Smollett handles with such virtuosity in *Roderick Random* and *Peregrine Pickle*. The crowd of spectators assumes the annihilating role of the Sartrian hell. The irony of the following remark dissolves into an acid bath in which Clinker could well vanish without trace: 'The spectators, who assembled to see this highwayman, were sagacious enough to discern something very villainous in his aspect' (pp. 145–6). In a few moments, Clinker's identity, rendered suspect by the religious ambiguity of his answers, is crushed by the pressure of a repressive society.

To have an identity is to have a recognisable place not only in the eyes of society but also within the family groups, both past and present. This explains the genealogical allusions Tabitha is fond of making[43] as also Lismahago (pp. 191–2). A discussion about Christian names leads Bramble – who, like Smollett, hates his – to refuse to admit his identity. Tabitha, as soon as Clinker is recognised as her brother's bastard, feels the need of discovering flattering family likenesses in him (p. 319). Not only the Welsh and the Scots are prone to this genealogical vanity, but also the Irish – can it be a Celtic peculiarity? – in the lowly person of a tailor. His name is Master Macloughlin 'but it should be Leighlin Oneale, for I am come from Ter-Owen the Great; and so I am as good a gentleman as any in Ireland', he claims (p. 211).

Finally, mistaken identity can take a more pathetic turn, as in the incident where the widow of a recently dead blacksmith, whose grief has deranged her mind, thinks that her husband has come back to her when Clinker makes the deserted anvil ring again (p. 186). Besides the emotional significance of the passage – the adjective 'pathetic' is used – this mis-understanding presents a retrospective thematic interest. The epistolary form of *Humphry Clinker* also allows it to be read, in a somewhat un-orthodox way, backwards. In fact this reading is indispensable in order to replace all the structural elements in their global perspective. The meeting between Clinker and the blacksmith's widow only acquires its full value after the final *cognitio*. The weeping woman's reproachful exclamation to Clinker: 'Ah, Jacob . . . how could you leave me in such a condition?' is one that Clinker's own mother, deserted in very different cirumstances by Bramble, might well have uttered about the man who had seduced her.

All through *Humphry Clinker* relations between parents and children assume varied and even occasionally contradictory aspects. There is no lack of violent or latent oppositions. Burdock's son, a fastidious dilet-tante, despises his coarse brute of a father (p. 165). In the course of a conversation with Burdock's wife, Bramble learns that his own father 'had disobliged her family by making a poor match in Wales' (p. 167). The family history thus repeats itself, but Bramble does not seem to have taken the lesson to heart and Lydia's happiness is menaced by social considerations. In the Baynard household, the spoilt son is protected by the wife. After a remonstrance from the father, the mother excuses her offspring, saying, 'Your father cannot abide you' (p. 296). This method of setting a son against his father works to perfection. Dennison, too, has come into conflict with his father for having wanted to marry for love (p. 321). There again the father's difficulties have left no trace on his emotional memory for he is in process of making the same mistake with his own son George. The result of these thwarted loves is 'unspeakable disquiet' (p. 328). This word, which occurs quite frequently in *Humphry Clinker*, betrays the moral and psychological uneasiness of the letter-writers.

Smollett does not only show sons rebelling against their fathers and fathers forgetful of their own past. The return of the prodigal son grown rich brings a sentimental and positive touch to an otherwise rather gloomy picture of filial relations (pp. 263–4). As in the final *cognitio* between

Clinker and Bramble, it is the son who recognises the father. This vignette has the merit of revealing Bramble's extraordinary sensibility. He manifests his joy at beholding such a scene — 'this pathetic recognition' (p. 264) — with an alarming exuberance: 'He sobbed, and wept, and clapped his hands, and hollowed, and finally ran down into the street' (ibid.). One may legitimately wonder whether Smollett did not mean to imply in this way that Matthew Bramble felt a confused psychic need of fatherhood. This would explain, by a quite simple transference of emotions — Bramble putting himself in the place of the rediscovered father — this outburst of uninhibited joy. Contrary, however, to the final *cognitio*, it is the son who brings help, fortune and protection to the ruined father. Another return, this time of the father to the son, is adumbrated when Lismahago thinks of returning to the Miamis in order to devote himself to the education of his half-breed son. But, thanks to the amorous vigilance of Tabitha, this plan is not carried out. Lismahago's attachment to his own father, and, more extensively, to the ancestral domain, was revealed in another project, the angry and eventful visit to the *'paternus lar,* or *patria domus'* (p. 207). For a moment, Lismahago assumes the aspect of a grotesque and pathetic Christ when he chastises the nephew who has dared to profane his father's house (p. 272).

Also to be found in *Humphry Clinker* is an adoptive paternity, of which the clearest case is Bramble's relationship with Lydia. Moreover it is the latter who regards Bramble as a father much more than Bramble regards her as a daughter, though his behaviour to his niece and ward is that of a gruff, but loving and generous father. In her emotion after Bramble's rescue from drowning, Lydia cries: 'Are you indeed my uncle — My dear uncle! — My best friend! My father!' (pp. 314–15). She herself repeats those words reported by Jery, in her own letter where she declares to her friend that, had things gone ill, she would have lost 'my best friend, my father and protector' (p. 334). Lismahago is assimilated into the Miami tribe as the adopted son of the *sachem* (p. 193). Conversely, Smollett analyses the psycho-sociology of the clans and finds, in the last resort, that the system of obedience to the Chief is patriarchal and not feudal:

> The clan consider the chief as their father, they bear his name, they believe themselves descended from his family, and they obey him as their lord, with all the ardour of filial love and veneration; while he, on his part, exerts a paternal authority, commanding, chastising, rewarding, protecting, and maintaining them as his own children (p. 255).

If the ways of spiritual paternity are mysterious, those of the flesh are no less so. Identity and procreation are themes which are entangled and intertwined, and they are unravelled in the *cognitio* without, for all that, deviating from the protean complexity at the very core of the mystery of all life. The problem of bastardy arises on the most carnal level and the one most reprehensible to traditional bourgeois morality. Smollett touches on it on several occasions before the discovery of Bramble's fatherhood. English legislation in force in the eighteenth century, although it varied somewhat from parish to parish, allowed a woman to get rid of her bastard by paying a round sum to the authorities. The abuses are well known. Certain officials ('parish-officers') cared more about getting hold of the money and keeping it for themselves than for assuring the survival of the child. But there was also the blackmail by ladies of easy virtue who denounced (or threatened to denounce) a man to the magistrate as the putative father, even though he had sometimes never ever seen the woman who accused him. The simplest way of avoiding a lawsuit, always a costly business and one whose outcome was uncertain, was to pay the woman a sum of money which varied according to the resources of the pseudo-father.

This was the misadventure which happened to Jery (pp. 27–8). On this occasion, the reader learns that Bramble himself had also had to suffer from this prolific but entirely potential virility: 'betwixt the age of twenty and forty, he had been obliged to provide for nine bastards, sworn to him by women whom he never saw' (p. 28). Here again, the retrospective irony acquires all its cruel force after the belated discovery of the only *real* bastard Bramble had ever engendered. As a corollary to this bastardy, Smollett discreetly alludes to Bramble's possible escapades, although his sexual activities now seem reduced. To the offers of a cure for a problematic venereal disease, Bramble replies to Dr Linden who suggests some miraculous pills: 'Sir . . . I have no reason to flatter myself that my disorder comes within the efficacy of your nostrum' (p. 19). But apparently Bramble is not above all suspicion in the eyes of his nephew and sister. The former thinks, for a moment, that he has surprised him 'in such a state of frailty, as would but ill become his years and character' (p. 20). But, though Jery quickly realises the absurdity of his doubts, this is not so with Tabitha, who persists, perhaps with the obstinacy of dirty minds, in believing her brother guilty of lecherous designs on the widow whom he succours in Bristol. She accuses Bramble, in her more or less consciously obscene idiolect, of 'concupissins' and does not hesitate to censure, in front of Jery, the 'back-slidings of so near a relation; a man of his years and infirmities' (p. 22). Thus Tabitha blames her brother for a misdeed of which he is innocent, but the retrospective irony adds an almost tragic dimension to this farcical scene: who has ever accused Bramble of the sin he really has committed? Jery escapes from his undeserved paternity (p. 59), but another allusion tends to prove that Smollett was conscious of the importance of this theme. In a post-script to his letter of April 23rd, Bramble confides his hesitations before sending a handsome wench to be a maid in the home of a friend who has an amorous penchant for servant-girls. Bramble's moral scruple is admirable, no doubt, but it inevitably loses a little of its exemplary value when the reader learns that Clinker's mother was also a servant in an inn.

The direct relations between Bramble and Clinker constitute a network of signs and indications whose full ironic and structural value is only revealed after the *cognitio*. But the exceptional quality of their relations is evident to the reader right from the start. Clinker's entry into the group of travellers provokes a near-rupture between the brother and sister. Bramble, for the first time, has the courage to shake off the tyranny of this domestic yoke. Clinker, overcome by Bramble's generosity, has decided to serve him and makes a vow of fidelity to him similar to a chivalric oath (p. 83). Moved in his turn by Clinker's behaviour, Bramble makes a pronouncement which the end of the novel confirms with a retrospective irony: 'I have a good mind to take thee into my family' (p. 84). During the confrontation between Bramble and Tabitha, the latter orders him to get rid of Clinker, otherwise she will abandon this ungrateful brother 'and the world shall see whether you have more regard for your own flesh and blood, or for a beggarly foundling, taken from the dunghill' (p. 85). There again, the ironic ambiguity of this ultimatum will be removed by the revelation of Bramble's fatherhood. Clinker makes his submission to Bramble in filial terms: 'I'm bound to love and obey your honour', and he renews his oath of fidelity (p. 139). Like a son, with the aid of Martin (a little additional dramatic irony), Clinker protects Bramble against the highwaymen (p. 158). Lastly, on the thematic plane, the comic false rescue in Scarborough (pp. 183–4) foreshadows the final genuine one. Conversely, Bramble has played the part of a father, first by rescuing him from his wretched and poverty-stricken state, then by exerting himself to get him out of prison.

The scene in which Clinker's true identity is revealed as well as Bramble's paternity is therefore prepared right from the arrival of the ragged postilion. It is even possible to maintain that this recognition of paternity is the answer to Bramble's angry protests (too categorical not to be suspect) against being burdened with his wards. Bramble's rhetorical question: 'what business have people to get children to plague their neighbours?' or again his exasperated assertion: 'I am conscious of no sins that ought to entail such family-plagues upon me' (p. 12) provoke Nemesis (a very clement one), who forces him to expiate, or at least to acknowledge his sins. Bramble admits to his friends: 'You see, gentlemen, how the sins of my youth rise up in judgment against me' (p. 318). From the initial rejection of adoptive paternity to the awareness of his own transgressions – 'I am really shocked at the consequence of my own folly' (ibid.) – Bramble has travelled a long psychological and moral road, at the end of which he will (perhaps) find the equilibrium of happiness. Blood plays a symbolic role in this reunion of father and son. In order to bring Bramble back to life, Clinker has bled him. These few drops and the salt Jery puts under his uncle's head acquire a mythical importance and recall the union, at once carnal and mystical, which gives life and preserves it. Bramble alludes to this mysterious impulse which drove Clinker to him, and falls perhaps into those superstitious beliefs he formerly denounced. What he calls 'the force of blood' (p. 320) becomes, in the letter written by Lydia, who also defends herself against being thought superstitious, 'a stronger impulse than common fidelity', or again, 'the voice of nature' (p. 334).

Alienation of the individual, identity and paternity, and finally coming to terms with life complete the movement of the moral dialectic. Bramble has never been really cut off from the outside world, and on his estate, in Bath and in London, he gladly seeks the company of old friends, even if, as particularly in London, these have somewhat forgotten the ties of the past. But his nostalgic attempt to return to the vanished world of youth is not a true solution of his problems. Bramble is haunted by his painful consciousness of the irreversible process of ageing (p. 173). The meetings with his friends of former days are marred by this distressing contemplation of the ravages of time which has transformed vigorous men into pitiful, barely human objects, fit only for the rubbish-heap of that great court of non-miracles — Bath (pp. 55–6). Their cheerfulness rings false, even though, in a first burst of enthusiasm, Bramble writes: 'It was a renovation of youth; a kind of resuscitation of the dead, that realized those interesting dreams, in which we sometimes retrieve our antient friends from the grave' (p. 56). But this sketch of a Signorelli-like dream cannot hide the truth from Bramble, who very quickly observes 'that they were not without their moments, and even hours of disquiet . . . and they were all malcontents at bottom' (ibid.). Quin's solution to this evil of living (or dying) is only provided by a constant flow of claret and amusing chit-chat (pp. 59–60). Under his mask of a hearty epicurean, Quin's face is already set in a bitter grimace of Swiftian pessimism (p. 51). Even though Bramble is sorry to leave his rediscovered friends, this timorous retreat into the past is only a false solution.

Before Bramble finds his way to establishing equilibrium in his life, Smollett recounts, in a few pages, the solution which Grieve the apothecary, the ex-Fathom, has arrived at after years of patience and humble, charitable dedication. Besides the thematic interest of this minor *cognitio*, Smollett suggests an answer akin to a species of Christian stoicism. The Vicar of the parish declares that, for years, Grieve has behaved like 'a primitive Christian' (p. 170). But it should be emphasised that Grieve has only discovered the solution to his human metaphysical problems thanks to constant activity (ibid.). Moreover, Bramble's liberation, when he finally gets rid of his grievances against life, only occurs after a symbolic preparation, comparable to a series of physical, psychological and moral ordeals. Water plays a major part in this symbolic cure. Smollett contrasts the contaminated water of Bath and the stygian stench of Harrogate with the invigorating effect of sea-bathing. Jery expresses this belief which must be interpreted both on a physical and an ontological level: 'You

247

cannot conceive what a flow of spirits it gives, and how it braces every sinew of the human frame' (p. 179). The absurd incident in Scarborough where Clinker exerts all his might to rescue his master who is not drowning, promptly assumes a structural importance. The moral fault which Clinker embodies prevents Bramble from profiting from this Siloam. The genuine rescue prefigures Bramble's salvation as much as it prepares for it on the factual plane. The son, recognised at last, arouses a liberating awareness in his father. Henceforth Bramble decides to devote himself to an active life of physical exercise and of psychological, moral and material help to other people, above all in the person of the unfortunate Baynard. But before this, Smollett sets out, through the medium of Bramble, if not his philosophical concept of life (these words would be too strong and inaccurate) at least a method of active resistance to the destructive forces of ageing. Man must gamble and even cheat:

> I begin to think I have put myself on the superannuated list too soon, and absurdly sought for health in the retreats of laziness — I am persuaded that all valetudinarians are too sedentary, too regular, and too cautious — We should sometimes increase the motion of the machine, to *unclog the wheels of life*; and now and then take a plunge amidst the waves of excess, in order to case-harden the constitution. I have even found a change of company as necessary as a change of air, to promote a vigorous circulation of the spirits, which is the very essence and criterion of good health (p. 339).

The garbled quotation from John Armstrong ('unloads' and not 'unclogs' appears in *The Art of Preserving Health* (1744) II, l. 261) may also remind one of the famous definition of Shandeism given by Sterne on the last page of Book iv of *Tristram Shandy*.

> True *Shandeism*, think what you will against it, opens the heart and lungs, and like all those affections which partake of its nature, it forces the blood and other vital fluids of the body to run freely through its channels, makes the wheel of life run long and chearfully round.

But though the dynamic value of energetic living is insisted on in both these passages, Sterne's leaps and twirls cannot be compared with Smollett's slower, and also steadier gait. It would be difficult to equate the art of living with a rejection, however courageous, of an encroaching premature death. After this declaration, there is no lack of signs of returning health and vital energy. Joyously, Bramble envisages going shooting with Dr Lewis and, reversing their roles, informs him: 'I intend to work you on the side of exercise' (p. 351). He displays tremendous activity — 'a great deal of exercise' (p. 340) — in order to fly to the aid of his friend Baynard, who is prostrated by the death, although a blessing in disguise, of his wife (pp. 340–3). In spite of this enormous and voluntary task,

Bramble also finds time to occupy himself with the welfare of his son. For the first time, he writes the words 'my son Loyd' (p. 350), and he is busy finding a situation for him on his estate (ibid.).

Similarly, the social group round him is transformed. Winifred speaks of 'a family of love' (p. 338), an impression confirmed by Bramble's declaration: 'I really believe it would not be an easy task to find such a number of individuals assembled under one roof, more happy than we are at present' (p. 343). Even Lismahago is transformed (p. 347), and the pair he makes with Tabitha is compared, not without humour, to that of Saturn and Cybele (p. 348). According to an American critic, William Park:

> By the time the expedition of Humphry Clinker has been success-fully completed, the gentry and the low, the past and the present, the regions of Britain, friends and lovers, the mind and the body, all have joined in a vision of harmony and joy. Once more does Saturn, father of the Gods, reign peacefully with his bride, Cybele, mother of all the earth[44].

Only now is it possible to grasp the meaning — or meanings — of the title *The Expedition of Humphry Clinker*. On the most obvious semantic level, *expedition* is an apt description of the excursion tour of the five letter-writers. The idea of a voyage of discovery suggested by the word is conveyed in the novel by the physical, moral and emotional quest on which the travellers are launched for several months. A second level of meaning, complementary to the first, is equally evident. One must go back to the liberatory meaning of the verb 'to expedite', that is 'to help for-ward, hasten the progress of', still close to the obsolete meaning 'to clear of difficulties' (*OED*). Clinker is delivered from the chains of poverty and also from that extreme alienation, loss of identity, since 'Humphry Clinker' is in fact the name of the farrier to whom Bramble's illegitimate son was apprenticed (p. 317). In this second case, 'of' would have a genitive meaning. But it is also possible to attribute an instrumental significance to it, that is to say, by paraphrasing the title as 'the liberation *worked by* Humphry Clinker'. This hypothesis brings out the role of moral catalyst that Clinker, in spite of his belated appearance on the scene, plays in the evolution of the characters, Matthew Bramble in par-ticular, but not exclusively, for Clinker also affects the behaviour of Tabitha and Winifred and, to a lesser degree that of Lydia, thanks to his religious influence. It is in this sense that there is an *adventure* of morality, strewn with negative or positive episodes, at the core of this *expedition*.

There remains the name of Humphry Clinker. Goldberg and Sheridan Baker, as well as William Park do not fail to pounce with psycho-analytical rapture on a possible slang and faecal meaning of 'clinker'[45]. The more probable significance of this word is onomatopoeic, suggesting either the clinking of the anvil in the farrier's forge or of the prisoner's fetters worn by Humphry in Clerkenwell, a meaning already indicated by Grose. Still reverting to Clinker's former trade, 'clinker' can also mean the slag produced from red-hot iron. Finally, two other meanings cannot be ruled out, if one considers the linguistic virtuosity of the allusions suggested by the Smollettian verbal creations in the letters of Tabitha and Winifred. In accordance with the instrumental value attributed to 'of' examined above, 'clinker' could be interpreted as 'he who or that which clinches' (*OED*). Clinker would then also be the person who consolidates an initially alienated group, he who welds together the diverse personalities, or, to keep the still current maritime meaning of this word (in 'clinker-built', for example) he who clinches together the members of the Bramble family. Lastly, and this possible meaning would not lack irony, 'clinker' can also, according to Partridge, designate 'a crafty, designing fellow'. As to the aristocratic Christian name, 'Humphry' — deliberately mutilated, Sheridan Baker thinks, in order the better to emphasise the incongruity of 'Humphrey' with the vulgar and proletarian connotations of 'Clinker' — the allusion to the picturesque expression for going hungry 'to dine with Duke Humphrey' is highly plausible.

The ambiguity of the title foreshadows and reflects that of the whole novel. The final version, like Smollett's personality, is torn between the multiple perspectives of a predominantly urban precapitalism whose trend is progressive and the static conservatism of a somewhat idealised rural life. The end of *Humphry Clinker* does not offer a true permanent solution[46] to the problems of the letter-writers. The anxiety persists under the apparent and conventional felicity. There remain too many question-marks, vaguenesses and doubts. How long will this physical and psychic recovery of Bramble's last? Before she is even married to Lismahago, Tabitha, within a few days of her wedding, casts a prehensile glance at the newly widowed Baynard (p. 343). Lismahago, after the wedding night, plays the blissfully satisfied lover 'and, no doubt, laughs internally at her folly in believing him sincere' (p. 349). Jery is still as indifferent as ever to the fair sex and thinks of spending the Christmas holidays in Bath before executing 'that scheme of peregrination' (p. 350) with his friend, no doubt in Europe. Tabitha and Winifred have learnt nothing on the social plane, and have forgotten nothing either of the negative aspects of their travels in Scotland. In her penultimate letter (September 18th), Tabitha shows that she has particularly remembered the economical, not to say parsimonious, diet of Scottish servants.

Social vanity breaks out in Winifred's last letter, now that she has raised herself, by dint of her charms, to the rank of Bramble's daughter-in-law (p. 353). Even though Bramble consents to look after his son, it would be an exaggeration to say that his paternal love is gushingly effusive. The nuptial bliss with which the novel concludes is heavily smeared with bourgeois vulgarity, and threatens at one moment to sink into the convention of the drinking-bout, without entirely avoiding that of the practical joke, which social hierarchy demands should only be allowed to disturb the raptures of Winifred and Clinker. The last word rightly belongs to Winifred when she declares: 'Our satiety is to suppurate' (p. 352). There still remain too many humours which the comic catharsis has not succeeded in purging. They will readily become inflamed and then the abscesses will swell and burst and the pus will flow.

This malaise, different from that which affected the travellers at the outset of their expedition, but very real, is partly due to the clear perception of the structural incompatibility between the urban world of progress and rural conservatism. The tentative solution provided by the Dennisons is no doubt viable but it is based on a form of cheating. Dennison, like Bramble, has benefited in his youth and all his life from the advantages inherent in pre-industrial urban civilisation: education, travel, legal activities for Dennison, political ones for Bramble. In spite of their aspiration to an active retirement, far from the unproductive turmoil of towns, they are the inheritors of this world they despise. Thanks to his education, Dennison can profit by the theoretic teachings of Lyle, Tull, Harte and Duhamel du Monceau (p. 327). It is as a result of the experience (negative *and* positive) acquired in the heart of this urban society that Dennison, and Bramble likewise, is capable of adapting himself to a rural way of life and of breaking down the countryman's opposition to progress. The solution adumbrated by Dennison and Bramble is based on landed property, which in turn relies on the possession of considerable capital, as the saving of Baynard's estate amply proves.

It is therefore impossible to escape from one's past and also from one's future. The plan of life outlined by Bramble indicates a short-range imagination of the future, but, without such a dynamic projection, there is hardly any future for the imagination. Yet, in spite of these reservations, *Humphry Clinker* is *not* a pessimistic novel. From it there emerges a lesson of courage, not heroic, but ordinary, almost commonplace, in the trials of everyday life. The threat of disquiet is also dynamic and healthy: it is the guarantee of liberty, or rather of successive liberations, of the *expeditions* on which every man must launch in order to live the adventure of morality.

Part III
Literary devices

7
The representation of the real

Right from the beginning of his literary career, Smollett was aware of the problems posed by the representation of the real in the novel. His preface to *Roderick Random* expresses in very clear terms this prime concern of the author confronted with the choice between a fantastic and fictitious version of life and, at the opposite extreme, a deliberate concentration on everyday existence at its most commonplace, not to say vulgarest. In the first phase, Smollett contemptuously rejects this fallacious vision of humanity and hails with joy the liberating work of Cervantes, whose satirical attacks on it permitted literature to return to the paths of reality and ordinary life (I, lxi). In the second part of this preface, he adopts a tone at once aggressive and defensive. Fortified by the example set by Lesage, Smollett is going to dare to describe scenes which will undoubtedly shock certain readers. The adjectives 'mean' and 'low' (I, lxii) formed part of the critical arsenal of those who were roused to indignation by the liberties taken by Fielding, and even by Richardson, who had the literary courage to be interested in the tribulations of heroes of slender means and humble birth. In his desire to represent reality, the *whole* reality, without omitting the least pleasant aspects of a too often corrupt society, or the physiological necessities of mankind, Smollett declares, in the tone of defiance which is typical of his character: 'Every intelligent reader will, at first sight, perceive I have not deviated from nature in the facts, which are all true in the main, although the circumstances are altered and disguised, to avoid personal satire' (I, lxiii).

Two features are noteworthy in this rough outline, still crude and incomplete, of a literary theory. For Smollett, the representation of the real cannot be dissociated from satire and his moralising purpose. This is why, in the course of this chapter, there will be many references to the satirical vision of the novelist without, however, systematically repeating the observations on the same subject in the previous analyses. Already, Smollett comes up against this problem which, in the nineteenth century, obfuscates all critical discussions on realism. The 'realist' writer, in his overwhelming passion for total objectivity, is led to treat subjects which the aristocratic or bourgeois tradition of aesthetic criticism, based on the taste of the ruling class, regards with contempt or even horror. Louis XIV detested the humble domestic subjects treated by Flemish painters. Did he not, according to Voltaire, say 'Remove those monstrosities', one day when a Teniers had been hung in one of his apartments?

Smollett's adoption of a literary standpoint in favour of describing far from elevated persons and milieux without repugnance, and his refusal to transform man romantically into pure spirit without imperious and sometimes sordid physical needs, arise, as often in his work, more from a spontaneous and instinctive practice than from a deliberate critical intention elaborated into a rigid theory. In *Peregrine Pickle* he almost contradicts his preliminary statements in *Roderick Random* when he derides this obsession with repulsive pictorial detail of that Dutch painter who has taken great trouble to reproduce an enormous flea on a beggar's shoulder. By taking a satirical line over Pallet's absurd enthusiasm for this picture in which flies are battening on a piece of carrion, he implicitly condemns this meticulous insistence of the artist on a mimicry reduced to the most disgusting detail. In fact, the contradiction is only apparent. Smollett, in this brief passage[1], has foreseen the dangers of a slavish reproduction of reality, in which the search for an unusual detail takes the place of genuine inspiration. More important on the theoretical plane is the furious reaffirmation, in *Ferdinand Count Fathom*, of his adherence to a concept — free of social or aesthetic constraints and inhibitions — of the novelist faced with contemporary reality. The auto-dedication of *Ferdinand Count Fathom* presents the same mixture as the preface to *Roderick Random*. Its defensive aggressiveness gives a somewhat strident tone to this personal apologia. Smollett replies straightaway in advance to possible (and probable) detractors, that their indignant objections to the 'obscene objects of low life' (p. 7) or to the 'lowest scenes of life' (p. 8) tend to turn literature into an insipid dish. A certain cantankerous unfairness with regard to illustrious foreign predecessors (from Petronius to Lesage via Rabelais and Cervantes) and English ones (Swift and Pope) gives an unpleasantly polemical tone to this satirical, although courageous, defence of the novelist's aesthetic freedom. Smollett reaffirms his liking for characters of humble origin, in spite of the disapproving snobbery of readers who thoroughly enjoy, in foreign works, what they so strongly condemn in the writings of their English contemporaries. He shows himself fiercely resentful of the criticisms made of his *Peregrine Pickle* and speaks of them with bitterness in his preface to the second edition (1758).

In the *Critical Review*, this concern for authenticity and fidelity to real life which must be reconciled with the aesthetic demands of literary creation also appears on several occasions. In a review of a now totally forgotten novel, the critic — Smollett, according to the conclusions of P. J. Klukoff[2] — insists on the apparent facilities which novelists enjoy for depicting the contemporary world. In fact, these facilities conceal difficulties which are the cause of many failures. After having remarked that the author of *Jeremiah Grant* has not been completely successful in the scenes where the hero experiences the horrors of poverty, he stresses that it requires 'the art of a master to exhibit a character in the lowest scenes of indigence, still an object of attention and esteem' (*Critical Review*, January 1763, xv, 16). Supposing that Smollett really did write these lines, could this be an example of a retrospective and personal 'puff oblique'? Earlier on, the critic touches on the problem of the representation of the real in its most unsavoury aspects.

> A man may paint a hogstye, or a dunghill very naturally, without giving pleasure to the spectator; and describe with scrupulous exactness many scenes and incidents that produce nothing but yawnings or disgust. It is the happy faculty of genius to strike off glowing images; to seize the ridicule of character, to contrive incidents that shall engage the passions and affections of the reader, to support the spirit of the dialogue and animate the whole. It is the province of taste to regulate the morals of the piece, to conduct the thread of the story, to make choice of airs and attitudes, to avoid impropriety, to reject every thing that is extravagant, unnatural, mean and disagreeable (ibid., p. 14).

Even if the terms 'genius' and 'taste' are shrouded in irritating vagueness, this passage has at least the merit of clearly stating the selective and creative role of the novelist. This literary transmutation of crude detail into an aesthetically acceptable element had already been emphasised by Lord Kames in his *Elements of Criticism* (1762). At the end of Chapter xxi, 'Narration and description', Lord Kames asks himself the following question: 'An object, however ugly to the sight, is far from being so when represented by colours or by words. What is the cause of this difference?' In the case of pictorial representation, Kames explains that the spectator derives pleasure from the artist's imitation of the reality. As to the literary description of a hideous object, Kames brings out the importance of language, not only on the plane of social communication but also on the aesthetic plane:

> But nature hath not been satisfied to recommend language by its utility merely: independent of utility, it is made susceptible of many beauties, which are directly felt without the intervention of any reflection. And this unfolds the mystery; for the pleasure of language

is so great, as in a lively description to overbalance the disagreeable-
ness of the image raised by it. This however is no encouragement to
deal in disagreeable subjects; for the pleasure is incomparably greater
where the subject and the description are both of them agreeable
(4th edition, 1769, II, 361–2).

As Kames's book was very favourably received by the *Critical
Review*, in which several long articles were devoted to it in the March,
April and May numbers of 1762, one is justified in thinking that Kames
exercised a critical influence on the opinions Smollett expressed in the
review, already quoted, of January 1763.

For a quick assessment of Smollett's position in relation to his great
contemporaries, Fielding and Johnson, it is enough to remember that this
problem of reality in the novel was one which frequently preoccupied the
novelist and the moralist. Both insist on the importance, for the author, of
an enriching close contact with the reality of everyday life. In *Tom Jones*,
(Book ix, Chapter i), Fielding recommends the assiduous study of the
'vast authentic doomsday-book of nature' as well as the knowledge, not
bookish but human, which an author ought to possess thanks to living in
the social world:

> So necessary is this to the understanding the characters of men, that
> none are more ignorant of them than those learned pedants, whose
> lives have been entirely consumed in colleges, and among books: for
> however exquisitely human nature may have been described by
> writers, the true practical system can be learnt only in the world.

The caricatural characters of the tutor, Jolter, and the Doctor in
Peregrine Pickle in some sort confirm the observations of Fielding, who
reverts again to the necessity of a thorough knowledge of *all* ranks of
society:

> Now this conversation in our historian must be universal, that is,
> with all ranks and degrees of men: for the knowledge of what is
> called high life will not instruct him in low; nor *è converso*, will his
> being acquainted with the inferior part of mankind, teach him the
> manners of the superior.

Fielding's idea is that society forms a whole, whose various follies are
set off against each other. There again, the satirical intention is never far
removed, it underlies the representation of the real. Fielding's warning
about the insufficient knowledge too many authors have of high society is
repeated in Chapter i of Book xiv of *Tom Jones*: 'One reason why many
English writers have totally failed in describing the manners of upper life,
may possibly be, that in reality they know nothing of it.' Smollett might
(and even should) have profited by this warning, this incitement to
caution, from a novelist whose origins and official duties put him in

contact with the greatest as well as the humblest. Could it be an echo of Fielding when Johnson, too, in the fourth number of the *Rambler* (March 31st 1750) insists, in addition to the importance of erudite knowledge, on 'that Experience which can never be attained by solitary Diligence, but must arise from general Converse and accurate Observation of the living World'? He, too, finds that the task of contemporary authors is more difficult than that of the Ancients, for they are 'engaged in Portraits of which every one knows the Original, and can therefore detect any Deviation from Exactness of Resemblance' (p. 20). But this representation of the real is subject to a kind of moral selectivity:

> If the World be promiscuously described, I cannot see of what Use it can be to read the Account; or why it may not be as safe to turn the Eye immediately upon Mankind, as upon a Mirrour which shows all that presents itself without Discrimination (p. 22).

At about the same date, *An Essay on the New Species of Writing Founded by Mr. Fielding* (1751) protests against those who decry the novels of Fielding and Smollett as being 'cursed low, intolerably vulgar', and, on the contrary, congratulates Fielding on 'his thorough Insight into Low-Life' (p. 29). The anonymous author contrasts Fielding's novels with those of his predecessors and never tires of praising the 'exact Picture of human Life' and 'beautiful Plainness, and exact Similitude' which characterise *Joseph Andrews* and *Tom Jones*.

About the middle of the eighteenth century, there is a confrontation between the partisans and detractors of this fidelity to reality which implies (theoretically) the description of the whole of lived experience. This is a protean problem which, moreover, includes moral (amoral, or immoral) life, flat commonplace everyday life endured rather than controlled, as well as exceptional moments of passionate exaltation or physical decline. Smollett had to endure the assaults of those who were hidebound by a traditional criticism based on the intellectual, aesthetic and social canons of the still dominant aristocracy. Not least of the paradoxes in Smollett's life was that he ranked himself among the conservatives in politics, but among the innovators in literature. So, when his last novel appeared, the *Critical Review* of August 1771 was highly laudatory and rightly appreciated this passionate attention Smollett paid to reality:

> Instead of visionary scenes and persons, the usual subjects of romance, we are frequently presented with many uncommon anedotes, and curious exhibitions of real life, described in such a manner as to afford a pleasure even superior to what arises from the portraits of fancy. We are everywhere entertained with the narration or description of something interesting and extraordinary, calculated at once to amuse the imagination, *and release the understanding from prejudice* (xxxii, 88).

On the contrary, the *Monthly Review* of the same month saw in *Humphry Clinker* only the risqué and unpleasant aspects (at least reputed such) of this novel:

> Some modern wits appear to have entertained a notion that there is but one kind of *indecency* in writing; and that, provided they exhibit nothing of a lascivious nature, they may freely paint, with their pencils dipt in the most odious materials that can possibly be raked together for the most filthy and disgustful colouring. These nasty geniuses seem to follow their great leader Swift, only in his obscene and dirty walks. The present writer, nevertheless, has humour and wit, as well as grossness and ill-nature (xlv, 152).

All through the nineteenth century and even the twentieth, critics have attacked, with the wearisome monotony of inveterate literary spleen, the picture given by Smollett in his novels of a violent world, in which mischievous deeds, gratuitous brutality, debauchery and scatological coarseness appear as so many caustic caricatures of deliberately travestied reality. Smollett, accused of distorting reality by his satirical bias, is rebuked, in the same breath, for the vulgarity, or indecency, of incidents or characters he does not hesitate to include in his novels. The moral aim of his satirical representation of reality is compromised by the literary methods he adopts in the choice and description of subjects banned, at least in theory, by good taste and decency, according to the aesthetic and literary standards of that time.

Any examination of the representation of the real in an eighteenth-century novelist comes up against a problem of literary terminology. How can one speak of the representation of the real without using the word 'realism', that paltry critical counter which is almost entirely worthless when applied to the eighteenth century? Used for the first time at the beginning of the nineteenth century in France (1826) and about the middle in England[3], this term cannot account for the satirical and moral purpose inherent in all representation of the real by Smollett and the other eighteenth-century novelists. A few critics have had the courage to denounce the illicit and noxious use of 'realism'. C. E. Jones, in his *Smollett Studies* (1942), puts modern readers of *Roderick Random* or other novels on their guard. He emphasises that 'realism' is 'not only a modern term, but represents a distinction neither considered by the creative artist nor accepted by the critic in the eighteenth century' (p. 74). The same critical prudence is displayed all through the first chapter ('Realism and the novel form') of Ian Watt's book, *The Rise of the Novel*,[4] in which the author denounces the almost automatic implication of social and verbal vulgarity which removes a great part of this term's critical utility: 'the novel's realism does not reside in the kind of life it presents, but in the way it presents it' (p. 11). As a general rule, 'realism' will appear little in this study. After the example of Barbara

Hardy in her work *The Appropriate Form* [5], who substitutes 'truthfulness' for 'realism', the terms 'faithfulness to reality', 'authenticity' and even 'veracity' will be used. If perchance 'realism' (or the adjective 'realist') slip into these pages, what must be understood, according to René Wellek's definition, and with the reserves indicated above, is: 'the objective representation of contemporary social reality' [6]. It is necessary to recall that Smollett's objectivity varies according to the degree of satire, more or less visible and virulent, but hardly ever absent in his representation of reality? For this reason — the indissociability of the satirical and 'realistic' elements — it has seemed artificial to conduct two separate studies. On the one hand, many (and indispensable) references have already been made to Smollett's satirical methods in the particular study of each novel. On the other, satire, either in general or in the work of Smollett, has for some years been the subject of a vast number of works. Conversely, there exists no attempt at a synthetic appreciation of the relationship of Smollett's work to the reality of the eighteenth century [7].

Finally, by 'representation', one must beware of understanding a photographic reproduction of reality in its smallest details. This notion, often implicit in the popular concept of 'realism', in the end confines the role of the author to the passivity of a sensitive plate on to which the external world is projected. Now all representation of reality can only be partial and incomplete. This is what Joyce Cary expresses, with the vehemence of an author who had himself to endure, *mutatis mutandis*, somewhat the same accusations as Smollett:

> It is not valid to charge a writer with falsification because he emphasises one truth rather than another. As for saying that he does not give the whole, that is absurd because the whole truth cannot be known. It would have to include not only events which are happening all the time and changing the phenomenal world while I speak, but the valuation of events. The most important part of truth is what humanity is suffering, is feeling and thinking at any moment, and this cannot be known, as a totality to any person [8].

Lukács also emphasises this resigned modesty when confronted with the shifting complexity of the real in his attempt to define the novel as

> a form of mature virility, as opposed to the normal infantility of the epic — that means that the closed character of his world is, on the objective plane, imperfection, and on the subjective plane of the lived, resignation [9].

The representation is not a simple (!) *transcription* but well and truly a *construction*, indeed creation, according to a critic like Robbe-Grillet:

> Fictional writing does not aim at giving information as does the chronicle, the eye-witness account or the scientific report, but it

261

constitutes reality. It never knows what it is looking for, it has no idea what it has to say. It is invention, invention of the world and of man, constant and perpetually inconclusive invention[10].

But this modern view, however intellectually attractive, cannot give a satisfactory vision of Smollett's novels in which, very definitely, the part played by social testimony, conscious or unconscious, cannot be neglected. Robbe-Grillet's theory has the merit of suggesting that reality is not an amorphous *datum* pre-existent to all literary creation. On the contrary, the novelist, by the creative magic of his word *gives* life to reality. The hellish world of English warships had existed for several centuries, but Smollett was the first who gave it solid dimensions, in a word, the vitality which made it known to the public. Literature and reality are not entities strange to one another and mutually exclusive because of a negative relationship of exteriority. On the contrary, it is necessary to place them on the plane of equivalence, identification or superposition. For Raymond Jean, literature, and the novel in particular, is not mediation but contact, the points of contact between literature and the real being the same as those of our senses with the real:

> There is not the written thing on one side and the real thing on the other: there is a constant dialectical transcendence of this opposition in the act of reading as in the act of writing and this transcendence is a continual creation which enriches life and culture, but also modifies reality and makes it 'advance'[11].

These critical prolegomena will make it easier to grasp what must be understood by 'representation of the real'. If Smollett has left us, consciously or not, a testimony (whose veracity it is the critic's business to assess) regarding the English world about the middle of the eighteenth century, he was also able to create a fictional universe which by very reason of its exaggerations and its satirical distortions seems more real and *is* more real than a flat, didactic type of description. In Volume III of the *Present State*, Smollett (or an amanuensis) gives a description of Bath and London. But these are dead towns beside those which appear, swarming with life, in *Humphry Clinker*. So, in a first critical survey, the testimony of Smollett on his age will be examined, and in a second complementary one, the limits, characteristics, strengths and weaknesses of the Smollettian universe.

The terms 'witness' and 'testimony' also leave something to be desired: nothing in Smollett's work or in his letters really warrants the supposition that he was conscious of his role of 'witness'. But Smollett, whose manifold activities brought him into contact with the most diverse specimens of humanity, even when he was occupied in the historical examination of civilisation and events, nevertheless fulfilled the role of 'witness' by the richness of his observations, even fleeting, on everyday life in the eighteenth century. In a way, the first thing with which Smollett provides his modern readers is an involuntary testimony, that is to say a whole series of particulars which retrospectively acquire a historical or socio-logical value as 'facts of civilisation'. Often these are hidden details which only a slow, thorough reading, backed by an indispensable knowledge of the civilisation, will cause to emerge from the literary text. Of no par-ticular importance for Smollett's contemporary readers, except as proof of his knowledge of the life of that day, these details constitute for the modern reader, whether English or foreign, a very dense network of historical, sociological, not to mention economic, indications of which it is impossible to analyse more than a few samples.

Thus, when Roderick Random is carried off by the press-gang, he is, according to the heading of Chapter xiv, on Tower Hill. The specification of place is not without historical interest, for this spot, dangerous for the solitary pedestrian without social protection or official pass, was the oldest and most popular rallying point of the men whose job was to impress men for the fleet. Moreover in that vicinity there were always plenty of disembarked sailors − the favourite prey of the press-gang − who had just collected their back pay from the Navy Office, situated quite nearby[12]. To stay in the nautical realm, Smollett, at the end of *Roderick Random* (Chapter lxvii), makes Morgan, the Welsh ex-surgeon's mate on board the *Thunder*, settle down as an apothecary in Canterbury. This professional transformation is not just a fanciful idea of the novelist's but corresponds to the fact that it was legally possible for naval surgeons, once they were back on land, to obtain an apothecary's licence.

If one leaves the brutal world of the Navy for the more gracious one of women, Smollett draws attention, at least twice in his novels, to the absence, apart from a few rare exceptions, of Latin and Greek in feminine education. In the library of that muddle-headed bluestocking, Narcissa's aunt, Roderick notices that there is not a single Latin or Greek book (II, 6). Similarly Lismahago, after a long quotation from Ovid, promptly hastens to translate it 'in deference to the ladies' (p. 192). Mrs Trunnion's false pregnancy (pp. 47−50), at once absurd and pathetic, is a gynaeco-logical phenomenon exactly described in popular manuals such as *The Complete Midwife's Practice Enlarged* (fifth edition, 1698). First of all, Mrs Trunnion's breasts harden and her belly swells up (p. 47), then these apparent signs of pregnancy disappear during three fruitless attempts at parturition so that, after three weeks of false hopes, cunningly maintained by an interested midwife, the unhappy aspirant to motherhood becomes 'as lank as a greyhound' (p. 50). The author of the treatise quoted above had already described the same symptoms:

> The face is ordinarily puffed up; the breasts, that at the first were swollen, afterwards become everyday more than other, softer and

lanker, and without milk. In fine, the face, the breasts, the arms, the thighs and groyns grow lank and meager; the belly waxes hard, as happens to those who are troubled with the Dropsie (p. 60).

A few pages further on (p. 64) this same treatise studies the uncontrollable cravings to which pregnant women are subject, and which, allowing for Smollett's satirical intentions, are not unreminiscent of the abnormal cravings of Mrs Pickle (*Peregrine Pickle*, pp. 21—7).

This involuntary testimony cannot be regarded as an absolutely faithful copy of historical events. Smollett transposes, rather than transcribes. The rebellion led by Peregrine at Winchester (pp. 87—92) does not seem, according to the chroniclers of that respectable public school, to have a factual counterpart, at least at the time when *Peregrine Pickle* was written, though, about 1750, this school was going through a difficult period[14]. On the contrary, Eton had six revolts between 1728 and 1832[15]. So it is not impossible that Smollett attributed the sins of Eton to Winchester, unless the agitation fomented by the real models of Peregrine and his band of mutineers was too usual and commonplace an occurrence at Winchester to merit the name of 'rebellion'. But it is quite natural for Peregrine to go up to Oxford from Winchester (p. 113), in view of their historical and administrative links[16], Wykeham having founded New College in 1379 and Winchester School in 1394. But Smollett does not say whether Peregrine went to New College. The reader of *Humphry Clinker* knows from Jery's very first letter that the latter went to Jesus College, Oxford. There again, the choice is not arbitrary, for this college was founded by a Welshman for Welsh students, as John Macky recalls in the second edition (1722) of his *Journey Thro' England*:

> Jesus College for the Welsh, was first founded by Hugh Price, but enlarged by great Benefactions from the *Counties* of Wales since. This college is pretty large, considering the vast number of *Welsh* that come to it, and the President is always a Welshman (II, 69).

Even if this academic detail ought not to escape a cultured Englishman, it is more doubtful whether the British or foreign 'common reader' would grasp the link between Jesus College and Wales at first sight. If the same Macky is to be believed, it is probable that in *Ferdinand Count Fathom* Smollett has reversed the historical connection between the Melvils and Hungary. In his *Journey through Scotland* (1723), Macky observes:

> This family, by the Name, seems to be French; but they say they are *Hungarian*, and came in with Queen *Margaret*, Wife to King *Malcom Kenmore*: However, they are pretty ancient in this Country; for we find Sir *John de Melvil*, of the County of *Fife*, one of the Barons that swore Fealty to King *Edward* the First of *England*, in the Year 1296 (p. 161).

When Macky gives the arms of this noble family (p. 246) he too hesitates over the spelling and writes 'Melvill'. Now Smollett states that the old Count de Melvil, Renaldo's father, 'was originally of Scotland' (p. 13). Would this be a question of a return to his Hungarian genealogical origin for this noble personage? In any case, it is likely that Smollett remembered the historical link between the real Melvil family and Hungary when he created his characters of the same name. Another example of adaptation: at the beginning of *Launcelot Greaves* (p. 14) Launcelot defends himself against the slanderous insinuations of Ferret, who accuses him of being a vagrant. He repeats the very words of the Vagrant Act of 1744[17], proving that his affirmation, 'I am not so ignorant of the laws of my country, but that I know the description of those who fall within the legal meaning of this odious term' (pp. 13–14), was not an idle boast.

Smollett's testimony, even accidental, does not always bear the stamp of absolute originality; on the contrary it sometimes belongs to a socio-literary tradition both anterior and posterior to his work. At the beginning of his stay in London, Roderick is the victim of a 'money-dropper', who, with the complicity of his confederates, fleeces him of all his money (I, 98–101). Now this dirty trick, the character of the swindler, and even his technique, were no novelty to eighteenth-century readers. Gay (to go back no further) already writes in Book iii of his *Trivia* (1716):

> Who now the Guinea-dropper's bait regards,
> Tricked by the sharpers dice, or juggler's cards?

Is Gay being unduly optimistic or is he taking refuge in rhetorical irony? A year before *Roderick Random* there appeared a pamphlet, *The Tricks of the Town Laid Open: or a Companion for Country Gentlemen*, whose seventeen letters were a scarcely altered repetition of another pamphlet entitled *The Country Gentleman's Vade-Mecum; or his Companion for the Town*, published in 1699[18]. Letter xiii (pp. 75–8) is summarised thus in the table of contents: 'The Villany of MONEY-DROPPERS is expos'd, and the Roguish Methods they take to impose on Countrymen'. In less than four pages, the anonymous author retraces the history of this swindle which had been practised for sixty years, its favourite places, and its technique, which, with a few slight variations, corresponds with the one used to fleece Roderick. Smollett thus invents nothing new, he is content to adapt a well-known trick and to insert it, without much difficulty, into the plot of his novel, Roderick, as an innocent young Scot newly arrived from his distant homeland, being a readymade victim. But the career of the 'money-dropper' (or 'guinea-dropper') does not end with *Roderick Random*. This booby-trap of urban warfare turns up again in the *Extracts from such of the Penal Laws as particularly relate to the Peace and Good Order of the Metropolis* (1768) by John Fielding, the blind magistrate and half-brother of the novelist, who sums it up in a few succinct lines (p. 256). It reappears in a highly instructive pamphlet dedicated to John Fielding, *Thieving Detected* (1777). The author devoted ten pages (pp. 28—38) to the subtleties of the operation he calls 'The Drop' in thieves' slang. The three confederates are called the 'Picker-up', the 'Kid' and the 'Cap', the victim being referred to as 'a Flat'. No doubt about the same date[19] Richard King wrote *The Frauds of London Detected*, which also gives an exact description of the 'money-droppers' (pp. 53—5) and their malpractices. Smollett's testimony therefore links up with a series of writings, of very unequal merit, which enable one to appreciate his fidelity to contemporary social reality. He did not write of this form of swindling from any morbid taste for low life or in order to decry his era, but simply because such fraudulent practices were still common in 1748, and long after.

These few examples of an involuntary testimony which can be drawn from Smollett's work raise the more general problem of the novelist's objectivity. In other words, what part is to be attributed to the observation of real life and what part to satirical distortion? To attempt to solve this problem it was necessary to find a collection of scenes in these novels, sufficiently concrete in detail to provide firm ground for analysis and for which there might also exist irrefutable proofs, warranted by the author's actual participation in the events he describes. It was also necessary to be fairly amply documented on the period in order to compare Smollett's version with that of his contemporaries. Only the chapters in *Roderick Random*, where Smollett, through the medium of Roderick, describes life on board the *Thunder* comply with all these critical imperatives. The purpose of the following pages is not to make yet another systematic study of the British Navy as it appears in *Roderick Random*. It would be futile to repeat the labours of Robinson, Watson, Knapp, Martz, Jones and Kahrl[20] to mention only the most important. The aim of this study is more limited: to analyse the picture Smollett gives of life on board in Chapters xxiv—xxxvii inclusive (over 100 pages) of *Roderick Random*. According to the degree of concordance with contemporary documents it will then be possible to appreciate the discrepancy due to satirical distortion on the triple plane of discipline, living conditions and medical treatment.

Roderick's first contact with naval discipline is characterised by the brutality and gross injustice of Crampley the midshipman (I, 200, 204) who spits on him, belabours him with blows and has him put in irons. But Crampley himself soon replaces Roderick in the same decidedly uncomfortable situation, which at least testifies to a rudimentary justice, when the master-at-arms deigns to exercise it (I, 204—5). Smollett emphasises straight away the difference between the naval officer risen from the ranks, like his uncle Bowling, and those who owe their rapid promotion to high-placed and influential patrons. The honest tar Jack

Rattlin says of Bowling: 'None of your Guinea pigs, nor your fresh-water, wishy washy, fair weather fowls' (I, 200). It is not certain to which of the two categories Captain Oakum belongs. Rumour has it that he is the brother of a nobleman (I, 202), but there is nothing to prove that he owes his rank to favouritism. Although he shows himself an ignorant and cantankerously vindictive tyrant when Roderick and Morgan are put on trial, he behaves courageously during the murderous and futile engagement with the French ships. Bowling — and in *Peregrine Pickle*, Trunnion, another officer who has risen to his rank 'by creeping up through the hawse-hole' as eighteenth-century English sailors used to say — is the moral and social antithesis of the effeminate Captain Whiffle who replaces Oakum. Bowling and Trunnion belong sociologically to that generation of about 1755, described by a naval officer in his *Sailor's Letters*, published in 1766: 'The last war, a chaw of tobacco, a ratan, and a rope of oaths, were sufficient *qualifications* to constitute a lieutenant' (second edition, 1767, p. 144). There must also be added, no doubt, for Bowling, Trunnion and Crowe (although the two latter appear only on land) the technical competence of these men for whom ships and the sea constituted their sole horizon, sometimes from the age of twelve or thirteen.

That Whiffle, with his sartorial elegance and his homosexual tendencies, represents a type current in the Navy of that time is highly unlikely, and, after all, difficult to verify. On the other hand, this character belongs to a dramatic and satirical tradition: the predecessor and perhaps the original of Whiffle, is the sea-dandy Mizen, created by Charles Shadwell in 1710 in the play *The Fair Quaker of Deal*. Edward Thompson altered this play which was acted at Drury Lane on November 11th 1773[21]. More than half a century after Shadwell, he only emphasised the fundamental difference between 'Commodore Flip', an officer of the old school, a coarse, heavy-drinking but worthy man, and one of his officers 'Beau Mizen'. Flip loathes Mizen with all his might and maintains — but he is the only one among the group of officers to hold this opinion — that the sailor's profession is incompatible with the status of a gentleman. Dissolute, cowardly and incompetent, the worst thing about these foppish officers, in Flip's eyes, is their wanting to live on board in the same luxurious comfort as on shore:

> I hate a fop; it is impossible a fop can be a good sailor, and therefore I hate my lieutenant; the fellow boasts that he does not know the name of one rope in the ship; the puppy too, lies in chicken-skin gloves to make his hands white, and washes them in almond-paste (1773 edn, p. 5).

Mizen defends himself and it is certain that his arguments met with more sympathy in 1773 than the satirical accumulation of sartorial, cosmetic and olfactory details with which Smollett loads the caricature that Whiffle is (I, 279—86). Here is how he replies to his commanding officer's accusations: 'Why, commodore, won't you permit a man to be clean! will nothing please you, but what stinks of tar and tobacco!' (I, 6). Finally Worthy, the officer who embodies common sense, condemns the opponents: 'Mizen is as great an extreme of absurdity as the commodore' (I, 8). A dated fact will make one realise how slowly the British Navy developed in the direction Mizen desired: soap did not make its official appearance on board warships until 1795. In their excessive refinement, Mizen and Whiffle were the distant literary precursors of an indispensable hygienic measure.

The tyranny of Oakum, absolute master on board, especially at sea when he had to render no account to any higher authority, was not a new feature, either in literature or in the pamphlets of those who had been complaining from the beginning of the eighteenth century of the flagrant abuses of this autocratic discipline. The satirist Edward Ward (1667–1731) does not spare ship's captains, either in his *London Spy* (1698–1709) or, above all, in his virulent and burlesque pamphlet *The Wooden World Dissected* (1707), in which all ranks, from captain to seaman, are ruthlessly lampooned. Ned Ward insists on this tyrannical absolutism of the Captain: 'He is a *Leviathan*, or rather a Kind of Sea-God, whom the poor Tars worship as the *Indians* do the Devil, more through Fear than Affection; nay, some will have it, that he is more a Devil than the Devil himself'[22]. More caustic still is the accusation of one Barnaby Slush, the probable and appropriate pseudonym of a cook whose indignation impelled him to write *The Navy Royal: or a Sea-Cook turn'd Projector* (1709). Slush attacks pell-mell the incompetent officers, the system of bounties for voluntary enlistment, the unfair sharing-out of prize money, the conditions of life on board, and most of all the intolerable reign of terror established on board by certain authoritarian skippers

> who debauch their Power and use it so Tyranically; Tyranically, I call it, since no Slavery is greater than impositions upon the Mind and Temper of a Gentleman. To be ty'd up to a Servile compliance with any Fantastick, Hare-brained injunction, which Pride, or Liquor, shall kindle in the Noddle of a Haughty Blunderbuss, is worse than shackles (p. 9).

After Smollett, Fielding, in his *Voyage to Lisbon* (1755) does not display any tenderness for the various officers he meets and the words 'tyrant' and 'bashaw' recur with indignant regularity to describe their conduct as soon as they feel themselves absolute masters on board. But, unlike Smollett in the *Travels through France and Italy*, Fielding never fulminates, and despite his desperate state of health does not collapse into morbid erethism. His portrait of Captain Veal, a petty tyrant terrified, just like Trunnion in *Peregrine Pickle*, at the thought of having a bone to pick with the lawyers, does not want a certain indulgent sympathy which is lacking in Smollett.

It is obvious that Smollett has condensed the defects both of the system of recruitment and of the various officers he may have met during his time in the Navy. Satire cannot have any impact unless the faults it condemns are concentrated in a limited number of characters, who consequently lose most of their specific individuality and become types. So it is fatal that Smollett's implicit judgment of superior officers such as Oakum and Whiffle should have been guided by his satirical purpose. The appreciation of his objectivity is rendered all the more difficult because the testimonies of his contemporaries on ship's captains by no means agree with each other. A specialist in British naval history arrives at this balanced conclusion: 'Some ships were lax in their discipline, others taut, some officers were humane and considerate, others were sadists and capricious tyrants'[23]. Thus, apart from the punishment of the cat-o'-nine-tails inflicted by command of the Captain (I, 226–7) and which was never officially abolished in the British Navy, there were informal corporal punishments on board which could make life hellish for the members of the crew if a choleric boatswain or midshipman let themselves go in raining blows with a rattan cane. This is what happens to Roderick (I, 204), who gets several stinging slashes from Crampley. This punishment was called 'starting' and was the subject of one of the most usual complaints of ill-treated crews. This practice was only abolished in 1806 but it continued long after[24]. In the case of shipwreck, this brutal discipline completely broke down. Watson (pp. 166–8) and, after him, Kahrl (pp. 15–16) have noticed the similarities between the shipwreck of the *Wager* one of the ships in Anson's expedition, and that of the *Lizard* (I, 300–2). Kahrl suggests (p. 16) that Smollett, without being directly inspired by the account given by Bulkeley and Cummins in their *Voyage to the South Seas* (1743) may well have heard the circumstances from the lips of Captain Cheap, the commander of the *Wager*. John Bulkeley, the gunner, and John Cummins, the carpenter, condemn the looters, who, as soon as the ship runs aground, fling themselves on the ship's provisions and the officers' chests:

> we had several in the ship so thoughtless of their Danger, so stupid and insensible of their misery, that upon the principal officers leaving her they fell into the most violent outrage and disorder; They began with broaching the wine in the lazaretto: then to breaking open Cabbins and Chests, arming themselves with swords and pistols, threatning to murder those who should oppose or question them: Being drunk and mad with liquor, they plunder'd Chests and Cabbins for money and other things of value, cloath'd themselves in the richest apparel they could find, and imagined themselves lords paramount (pp. 14–15).

It is difficult not to compare this passage with the pages in which

269

Smollett describes the same incident on board the *Lizard* (I, 300–31). As Smollett remarks, this was a customary proceeding, which John Byron, 'Foul-weather Jack', the grandfather of Lord Byron, mentions in his own account of the events which took place on May 14th 1741. This immediate breakdown of discipline in the case of shipwreck is explained not only by obvious psychological causes, but most of all by the following maritime regulation: as soon as a ship is wrecked, the crew's pay is immediately stopped, and, at the same stroke, the authority of the officers and the captain vanishes. In his *Narrative of the Honourable John Byron* published in London in 1768, which furnished Lord Byron with the factual sources for the shipwreck described in *Don Juan*, the author confirms the statements of Bulkeley and Cummins about the behaviour of the crew and lays particular stress on the drunkenness which caused some of them to be drowned in the flooded holds and 'tween-decks[25]. Even before the belated testimony of John Byron, another midshipman in the *Wager*, Alexander Campbell, had published, as early as 1747, a pamphlet less well known than the other two, *The Sequel to Bulkeley and Cummins's Voyage to the South Seas* which also confirms[26] the observations of his predecessors on the behaviour of the crew. Campbell complains of the injustice of Captain Cheap, a choleric man who shot dead another midshipman, Cozens, for insubordination when those who had escaped were trying to survive after running aground on a hostile shore. Cheap, who had arrived in Britain a few weeks before Campbell accused the latter (wrongly) of having defected to the service of the Spaniards, when all he had done was to embark on a Spanish ship. Like the gunner who saved the abandoned *Lizard*, Campbell received neither reward for his loyalty to his Captain nor promotion and even lost his position in the Navy. Confronted with so many concordant accounts, one is forced to conclude that Smollett's description of the scene of the shipwreck of the *Lizard* is in no way exaggerated.

As to the living conditions, right from Roderick's first rude contact with them in the tender which served as a floating headquarters of the press-gang, they are characterised by a persistent impression of vile stench which greets the unlucky Roderick wherever he goes (I, 200, 214–15, 216, 273). Tainted provisions, in particular rotten cheese, are the main basic olfactory ingredients of life on board ship. L. M. Knapp's discovery of the diary kept on board the *Chichester* by Lieutenant Robert Watkins states on December 22nd 1740, this officer 'condemnd Eighteen Hundred and Ninety five pounds of cheese' (Knapp, p. 32). But this might be just an isolated incident. Such does not seem to be the case, if one is to believe William Thompson's pamphlet *An Appeal to the Public in Vindication of Truth and Matters of Fact* (1761). This former cooper and inspector of the Pickle-Yard, dismissed for the abuses which he indignantly denounced, tried to draw the public's attention to the deplorable quality of the victuals destined for the British war fleet. He reveals in particular that seamen in the King's fleet have made *buttons* for their *Jackets* and Trowses, with the *Cheese* they were served with, having preferred it by reason of its *tough* and *durable* quality, to buttons made of *common metal*; and that Carpenters in the Navy-service have made *Trucks* to their Ship's flagstaffs with whole *Cheeses*, which have *stood* the *Weather equally with any timber* (p. 18).

On the following page he denounces the ship's biscuit, swarming with black-headed maggots, and the beer which stinks like foul water, which does not surprise the reader of *Roderick Random* (I, 266—7). As early as 1757 the same author had vigorously denounced, in *The Royal Navy — Men's Advocate*, a sixty-page pamphlet respectfully dedicated to William Beckford, the rottenness of the meat (beef and pork) destined for the sailors, the bad quality of the pickling, the dirtiness of the casks and the corruption of those responsible who ordered the workmen to salt down even stinking carrion. The film director Bunuel could find in William Thompson's pamphlet those horrifying gory details for which he has such a passion, like the piglets escaping from the disembowelled sow in the slaughterhouse, reared by hand and then bled to death in their turn. Another film director, Eisenstein, in *The Cruiser Potemkin*, nearly two centuries after *Roderick Random*, managed to recreate this medley of filth and violence with his shots of meat swarming with maggots, his depiction of the men huddled together in the crew's quarters, and the gratuitous brutality of the leading seaman. There is a direct line of continuity from Smollett to Eisenstein, running through Melville, the reformer Melville of *White Jacket* (1850).

Faecal stenches are added to the odours of putrefaction. It is easy to accuse Smollett of enjoying displaying his olfactory and scatological obsessions, for example in the incident in the sickberth (I, 214—15). But once again he is faithful to reality, even in its most malodorous details. This soil-tub, unluckily overturned, is a necessity anticipated in the regulations as early as 1731 and appears in the third section of *Rules for the Cure of Sick or Hurt Seamen on board their Own Ships*:

> The Cooper may, by the Captain's Direction, make out of any old Staves and Hoops, Buckets with Covers, for the necessary Occasions of the sick Men; and if any of them have fractured Bones, or such Ailments as requite their lying in Cradles, the Carpenter may make such a number as shall be necessary (2nd edn, 1734, p. 55).

This mixture of prudent economy and solicitous foresight did not, however, take into account such possible accidents as a sudden heavy roll. It is very difficult to know whether Captain John Blake had ever read *Roderick Random* but, in his very serious *Plan for Regulating the Marine System of Great Britain* (1758), he does not disdain, unlike Smollett's disgusted but futile and narrow-minded detractors, to touch on this problem of general hygiene. Stopping one's nose in the name of a pseudo-aesthetic criticism is no doubt a very refined reaction, but it is not of the slightest practical use. Blake, as a man of experience, knew living conditions on board really well, and proposed the following improvements for the sick:

> That the hospital-room be provided with one or more strong-armed chairs, which may be lashed to the deck, each having in its bottom a close stool-pan made of metal, which may be more easily emptied and washed clean than the wooden buckets directed by the present regulation of the navy to be used, which always retain a smell, though washed ever so clean, and are very inconvenient for a sick man to sit on, frequently overset with him, by the sudden rolling of the ship, and produce very offensive and unwholesome consequences; and on such occasions fill the ship with a stench, which not only annoys the whole company, but retards the cure of the sick, and even contributes to infect those who are well (p. 53).

Captain John Blake's pamphlet was very well received in the *Critical Review* of May 1758 (v, 437–8). In view of such a document which explicitly confirms *all* the details of the scene in the sick-bay of the *Thunder*, can one still talk of satirical exaggeration or excremental obsession? Only the insincerity (or smug ignorance) of a criticism full of contempt for the facts of civilisation can explain such opinions, though not justify them.

The bad ventilation in these ships with superimposed decks and no air shafts constituted a problem all the graver because the health of the crew suffered in these appalling living conditions, especially in tropical zones. When Roderick realises that he has caught the fever, his first care is to find a berth where he can benefit from a little air, for the cockpit where the surgeons lodged was generally situated in the bowels of the ship, often on the orlop deck well below the waterline (I, 273). This problem of proper ventilation attracted the attention of the inventor Stephen Hales, who in 1743 published *A Description of Ventilators*, to wit enormous bellows which would permit the air to be changed in prisons, hospitals and ships of the fleet and the merchant navy. Like many scientists and doctors of the time, Hales was convinced that breathing noxious air was one cause of contagion. In his *Treatise on Ventilators* (1758), he summarises the experiments made on ships in which his cumbrous apparatus had been installed; as early as 1748, on the *Captain*, of seventy guns, the *Blandford*, a slavetrader of twenty guns, the *Laura*, and in 1749 on five Nova-Scotian ships. Another inventor, Samuel Sutton, criticises Hales's bellows in his *Historical Account of a New Method for Extracting the Foul Air out of Ships* (1757). He had got in touch with the Admiralty as early as 1739:

In the Year 1739, I was informed that the sailors on board the fleet at Spithead were so dangerously ill, for want of fresh air, that they were put ashore to recover their health; and the ships to which they belonged, stunk to such a degree, that they infected one another[27].

Sutton's system was a collection of pipes which went right down to the hold where a fire was lit to make the air circulate. Sutton received the support of Dr Richard Mead right from the beginning, but, as always, the resistance due to the inertia of ship's captains and officers was hard to overcome. A letter from Rear-Admiral Boscawen to Corbett, dated April 9th 1748, nevertheless shows that, at the very moment when *Roderick Random* came out (January 1748), reforms were already afoot in the British Navy: 'I cannot help thinking, the air-pipes fixed in the men of war have been of great service in this particular [i.e. of preserving the health of seamen], by purifying the air between decks, and thereby preventing the scurvy.'

Even if the conclusion, which conformed with the medical theories of the day, is erroneous, the effects of this invention, soon followed by other improvements[28] were beneficial, but obviously it was not installed in Smollett's *Chichester*. So Smollett, far from distorting reality in the interests of satire, appears as the literary pioneer of a technological reform vital for the health of thousands of men on board ship.

The details given by Smollett on the food (I, 201, 206, 212), abundant but monotonous and ill-balanced, are confirmed by modern scientific studies by such specialists as Lloyd and Coulter, and D. A. Baugh[29]. The rations fixed by the regulations of 1734 provided between 4,000 and 4,500 calories a day, but the purser had the right to reduce them by an eighth to compensate for his losses. Moreover there were a great many pursers who cheated over the quantity and reduced the rations still more, not to mention the custom which allowed the men to sell them back part of their rations in order to make a little money, or to get credit for tobacco or clothes. For bedding space, the fourteen inches which made Roderick so indignant (I, 213) was exactly the width prescribed by the regulations. In such conditions fleas, lice and bedbugs could only increase and multiply, as Roderick quickly learns from bitter experience (I, 216–17). It is strange that Smollett makes no mention of the rats which infested these wooden ships, rich in inaccessible hiding-holes. In 1783, a curious character, Thomas Swaine who entitled himself 'Rat-catcher to his Majesty's Royal Navy' could boast, in his *Universal Directory for Taking Alive or Destroying, Rats and Mice, by a Method hitherto Unattempted*, of having caught (it was his record!) 2,475 rodents on board the *Duke*, thanks to a preparation based on powdered arsenic, sugar and wheat flour.

Before touching on Roderick's medical activities, it should be remembered that, even in his first novel, Smollett did not indulge in a systematic pessimism. However black the general picture of life on board, the author has brightened it here and there with some touches of human warmth and kindness. Opposed to the 'baddies' — Crampley, Oakum and Mackshane — there are the 'goodies' — Jack Rattlin, Morgan, Thomson, and later, on board the *Lizard*, Tomlins, the surgeon who dies as a result of Crampley's sadistic persecution (I, 299). Atkins (I, 223) Mackshane's predecessor, befriends Roderick after his forced arrival on board and helps him to procure a surgeon's mate's warrant. It is therefore incorrect to accuse Smollett of depicting only the darker side of life. In this perpetual strife between the forces of Good and Evil to which Smollett returns in all his novels, he relies on the support of characters who are sound at heart but not devoid of human weaknesses, like Morgan with his choleric arrogance or Thomson with his inability to stand firm under strain.

The cockpit which served as the hospital and whose space was restricted enough in normal times (I, 205–6) became, during a naval battle, a kind of human slaughterhouse 'where legs and arms were hewed down without mercy' (I, 263). Floundering in blood and human debris, the surgeons and their assistants looked more like infernal killers than doctors. Long after Smollett, surgeons like Edward Ives, about 1755, and Robert Young, in 1797[30], described the bloody horror of this naval butchery, with a wealth of details, before which the same scene in *Roderick Random* (I, 261–4) pales. Once again, the analysis of these pages makes one realise how skilfully Smollett blends his factual knowledge of the navy with fictitious elements. Before the bombardment of the forts of Cartagena, Mackshane, the cowardly surgeon 'insisted upon having a platform raised for the convenience of the sick and wounded in the after-hold, where he deemed himself more secure than on the deck above' (I, 260). Oakum, who detests any manifestation of cowardice, refuses. Mackshane then invokes the regulation which authorises such a transfer. He is referring to Article IX of the instructions to surgeons (*Regulations and Instructions Relating to His Majesty's Service at Sea*, 2nd edn, 1734) which provides:

> In an Engagement, he is to keep himself in the Hold, where a Platform is to be prepared for the Reception of the Wounded Men; and himself, and his Mates and Assistants, are to be ready and have every thing at Hand, for stopping their Blood, and dressing their Wounds (p. 133).

Smollett uses a real fact in order to bring out more clearly the cowardly nature of his character, who, in turn, makes the fact seem a more living reality. The exchange between the real and its representation is therefore not a one-way transaction, like the mere reflection of an object in a mirror. This comparison has obsessed critics ever since Stendhal used it, first in his preface to *Armance* and later in *Le Rouge et le Noir* where he wrote: 'A novel is a mirror that one carries along a road', as an epigraph to Chapter xiii. But the mirror is not lifeless: the reflection of the real object illuminates the latter and gives it a new dimension.

Another example will enable one to appreciate Smollett's fidelity to medical facts. During the storm, Jack Rattlin has fallen from the mast and is suffering from an open fracture of the tibia (I, 233). After a consultation with Mackshane, who is in favour of immediate amputation, Morgan and Roderick decide to take the responsibility on themselves and not to proceed with the removal of the wounded limb. This incident reveals the surgeon's ignorance and his lack of compassion for his patients. Moreover, Smollett relies on his medical knowledge for the treatment given to Rattlin, which saves his leg. The treatment (I, 235) follows the advice given by John Atkins in his *Navy Surgeon* (1734, pp. 37–52). In cases of open fracture Atkins prescribes three operations, extraction of foreign bodies, reduction and bandaging, which Morgan and Roderick perform *secundum artem*. Smollett even specifies that they use 'the eighteen-tailed bandage' which Atkins recommends in these words: 'We always chuse that of eighteen Tails, for the Conveniency and Ease of daily dressing the Wound' (p. 42). And, to leave nothing to chance, Atkins gives, on the same page, two ways of obtaining these bandages, of which this is one: 'It is made of three Doubles of strong Linnen sown in the Middle, and divided at each End with two Cuts of your Scissors, a fit Depth.'

But the efficiency of the nursing care lavished on Rattlin cannot hide the scandalous contempt for the life of the sick and wounded. Even the worthy Morgan refuses to go and tend a dying sailor until he has eaten and drunk his fill (I, 208). No doubt the habit of rubbing elbows with death must have hardened the ebullient Welshman, but even he is shocked by the inhuman order (I, 225) given by Oakum, to wit an inspection of the sick on the quarter-deck. This new kind of medical visitation promptly resulted in the death of several of the sick. Smollett denounces 'the inhumanity and ignorance of the captain and surgeon, who so wantonly sacrificed the lives of their fellow-creatures' (I, 227). The same waste of human life before the forts of Cartagena is even worse in the emergency hospital ships which are so understaffed with surgeons and nurses that they soon become floating charnel-houses (I, 268). There again, Smollett used the adjective 'inhuman' and the word 'barbarity' to describe the abominable behaviour of Crampley (I, 268, 299). It is difficult to estimate the number of victims of Cartagena expedition:

> Because of the numbers that were hastily buried at sea, it is impossible to compute the total casualties. Smollett says that 1,500 out of 8,000 survived, but he is evidently speaking of the army only. Another estimate puts the sick at 8,431 out of 12,000[31].

At the beginning of the Seven Years' War, the great naval doctor James Lind could write in his *Essay on the Most Effectual Means of Preserving the Health of Seamen in the Royal Navy* (1757):

The number of seamen in time of war, who died by shipwreck, capture, famine, fire, or sword, are but inconsiderable, in respect of such as are destroyed by the ship diseases, and by the usual maladies of intemperate climates[32].

The following figures published in the *Annual Register* of 1763, can only justify Lind, and, retrospectively, Smollett too: during the Seven Years' War, the British Navy lost 133,708 men through disease or desertion, but only 1,512 in battle. The horrors in *Roderick Random* were less than they were in reality. In view of the statistics, how can one doubt Smollett's veracity?

Nevertheless, it would be unfair not to express some reservations. Smollett's satirical temperament, his youth at the time of the Cartagena expedition, his total lack of contact with the general staff, especially with Admiral Vernon, made him commit errors which his cantankerous spirit soon built up into injustices. Smollett blames Vernon in very harsh terms and makes him responsible, because of his inflexible character, for the death of thousands of men whose loss could have been avoided if the Admiral had consented to put the naval surgeons available in each ship at the disposition of General Wentworth. And he adds, not without satirical malice: 'but, perhaps, the general was too much of a gentleman to ask a favour of this kind from his fellow chief, who, on the other hand, would not derogate so much from his own dignity, as to offer such assistance unasked' (I, 269). Now the publication of the *Vernon Papers* (1958) reveals a very different man:

The general picture that emerges from these documents is that of an efficient administrator, with an eye for the smallest detail, but always looking and planning ahead, and with a full appreciation of the importance of logistics and humane leadership as essential ingredients of success in battle[33].

Vernon himself complained of the lack of surgeon's mates, and asked the 'Navy-Board' to send out a supplementary contingent with all speed (pp. 346–7). Vernon, throughout his letters, orders of the day and other administrative circulars, appears as a man who cared about the health of his men and their food and clothing. Even in instituting the obligatory diluting of their daily half-pint of rum with two pints of water by his famous order of August 21st 1740, Vernon was trying to fight against the endemic vice of his seamen, drunkenness. (Smollett alludes to this measure of Vernon's, but does not seem to realise its anti-alcoholic purpose: I, 232.) Vernon was also very well aware of the defects of his ships and complains, in particular of the *Chichester* and the *Torbay* which are among the crankiest of the ships, which explains the formidable pitching and rolling of the *Thunder*, as also the panic of the crew during the storm described by Smollett (I, 232). Published two years before

Roderick Random, Vernon's long pamphlet (170 pages) entitled *Some Seasonable Advice from an Honest Sailor* (1746) presents a fervent plea in favour of more humane treatment of seamen and an indirect condemnation of the press-gang. Vernon *prescribes* (without immediate success), Smollett *describes*, but, in fact, both were animated by the same humanitarian concern.

Conversely, the total absence of pity for the black slaves bought and resold at the end of *Roderick Random* (II, 270—3) shocks the modern reader of Smollett. Roderick speaks only of an epidemic (typhus no doubt) which breaks out on board his slaver; and consequently, once the slaves are sold at a good price, he says he is glad to see the ship 'freed from the disagreeable lading of negroes' (II, 273). On several occasions Smollett, too, sold slaves to Jamaica, without a single trace of humanitarian feeling appearing in the correspondence (legal documents quoted by Knapp, pp. 326—8). This insensitiveness is all the more inexplicable since other naval surgeons and officers, before and after the publication of *Roderick Random* expressed (sometimes very fleetingly, but showing the beginnings of an awakened consciousness) their disapproval and horror at this treatment of the negroes. This is the case with Atkins, who, in his *Voyage to Guinea* (1735), deplores seeing their masters regarding the slaves 'only as Beasts of Burthen; there is rather Inhumanity in removing them from their Countries and Families' (pp. 61—2). This sentiment is already expressed in *The Sea-Surgeon or the Guinea Man's Vade Mecum* (1729) by Thomas Aubrey who denounced the brutal behaviour of the crew to the cargo of slaves, the bad food, the lack of water, the inhuman cruelty of the captain and the ignorance of the ship's surgeon (pp. 128—30, 132). Finally, Commodore Edward Thompson, who was not yet even a lieutenant at the time, in a letter from Barbados dated December 5th 1756, writes of his indignation at seeing daily examples of this 'cruel tyranny exercised over the slaves . . . shocking to humanity' (*Sailor's Letters*, 1767 edn, II, 29).

At the end of this analysis of naval scenes, one is compelled to admit that Smollett has not exaggerated the blackness of the reality. Specialists in naval medicine and naval history like R. S. Allison, Lloyd and Coulter, and D. A. Baugh[34], with a few slight reservations, confirm this opinion. Smollett is occasionally unjust, as his prejudiced and ill-informed attacks on Vernon prove. But one is seldom able to catch him out, especially in the medical realm, in some flagrant inexactitude. It is even strange that the scenes in which Smollett describes the horrors of the naval battle, the injustice of the Captain and the incredibly harsh living conditions on board are not more conspicuously animated by the spirit of satire. Attention has already been drawn to a certain callousness in Smollett's attitude to slavery. This is certainly an ethical flaw in his passionate but also puritanical character; the generous indignation of satire must not hinder commercial transactions. In Smollett, as in his contemporaries, there is a certain hardness, due to being more accustomed than nowadays to the daily proximity of death, disease, poverty, dirt and corruption. Thus William Cockburn, an extremely rich quack doctor and a friend of Swift's, in his *Account of the Nature, Causes, Symptoms and Cures of the Distempers that are Incident to Seafaring People* (1696) is not unduly outraged by the living conditions on board warships. The food, the beer, and even the crew's quarters seem perfectly all right to him. The great jurist Sir Michael Foster, in *The Case of the King against Alexander Broadfoot* (Oxford, 1758), relates the famous trial in which Broadfoot was sentenced for having killed a press-gang crimp who had boarded his ship in April 1743 without a search warrant. While admitting that there were extenuating circumstances for the accused, Foster nevertheless firmly defends the principle of the press-gang and supports the theory of its being a national necessity in time of war:

> War itself is a great Evil, but it is chosen to avoid a greater. The Practice of Pressing is one of the Mischiefs War brings with it. But it is a Maxim in Law, and good Policy too, that all private Mischiefs must be borne with Patience, for preventing a National Calamity (p. 6).

Foster is only expressing in lofty legal terms the same hardened resignation as Jack Rattlin, when obliged to allow his hand to be amputated. But Foster was *decreeing* and Jack Rattlin *submitting*. Charles Butler, in *An Essay on the Legality of Impressing Seamen* (1777), was still defending Foster's arguments and even backing them on the grounds of the existence of social inequalities which he regards as inevitable, not to say desirable:

> We shall attempt to shew that an inequality of rank is inseparable from society; that in the distribution of the duties of society, those which are offensive and disagreeable public duties (among which we reckon service in the armies and navies of the State), must fall to the lot of that part of mankind which fills the lower ranks of life; that this mode of distribution, however hard or unjust it may appear to the human eye is necessarily incident to society in all it's states (pp. 6–7).

After all, why should the riffraff on board complain if King and Country demanded that it should die in defence of them? Some of the callousness for which one can blame Smollett, if not for the brutality of the details, at least for the absence of shuddering sensitiveness, is also explained *a posteriori* by the progress of medical and surgical science. The instructions to the surgeons of 1731 laid down that, if their instruments were not adequate for amputations, they should have recourse to carpenter's saws (with no anaesthetic, of course). It is possible, in this case, to talk of insensitiveness? What must also be borne in mind is the

278

incredible inertia displayed by the entire British Navy, from the First Sea Lord to the lowest cabin-boy, towards any attempt at reform. Anson, in *A Voyage Round the World* (1748), complains that nothing had been done to improve living conditions on board, in particular the ventilation. But he realises the obstinate prejudices that exist in the navy against any form of progress. He denounces 'an obstinate, and in some degrees superstitious attachment to such practices as have been long established and ... a settled contempt and hatred of all kinds of innovations, especially such as projected by landmen and persons residing on shore' (p. 37).

This illogical obstinacy is the hallmark of closed conservative worlds. Although it may be amusing when it is a matter of affectations of speech or manners, it becomes tragic if the refusal of all innovation involves contempt for (or indifference to) medical discoveries. Such is the tragic history of the fight against scurvy, that scourge which ravaged the navy all through the eighteenth century[35]. As early as 1617, in *The Surgeon's Mate*, John Woodall already empirically recommends, among other and useless remedies, lemon juice: 'the use of the juice of Lemons is a precious medicine and well tried, being sound & good, let it have the chiefe place, for it will deserve it' (p. 185). James Lind's decisive experiment dates from May 1747. Yet the Admiralty did not recognise the antiscorbutic value of lemon juice until 1795, when it ordered regular distributions of it. Smollett seems to have realised the importance of fresh victuals for the soldiers and sailors of the expedition. He even reproaches the commanding officers for not having used the available transport ships to procure provisions from the neighbouring islands (I, 267). His absence of emotion, his apparent callousness in the face of the most painful sights is here again only a mask. Given the psychological and physical induration of the period, the mere fact of daring to describe, even with a few satirical exaggerations, incidents in which men were treated almost like brute beasts, is already a courageous challenge to the system of social oppression and a cry of hope for the future.

The hope is sometimes indirectly expressed by violent accusation, in the form of an almost frenzied denunciation of the material defects of society. Such is the dietetic diatribe launched by Matthew Bramble as soon as he gets to Bath where he fulminates, to begin with, against the adulterated beverages – wine, light ale, cider, perry, 'and all the trashy family of made wines' (*Humphry Clinker*, p. 47) – and later extends his furious disapproval to every item of food and drink consumed by Londoners. That 'catalogue of London dainties' (p. 122), already quoted in the thematic study of *Humphry Clinker*, affords, besides its structural interest and satiric violence, numerous indications of historic interest which make it permissible to suggest that Smollett based his criticisms on his memories of the controversy that broke out in 1757 about the quality of the bread. As always in the eighteenth century, the occasion was too tempting for numerous pamphleteers not to leap to their pens and dip them deep in vitriolic gall, but also, in the case of Markham and Manning, in the ink of good sense outraged by alimentary practices harmful to thousands of people. Smollett had already denounced, in the *Continuation of the Complete History of England*, the manoeuvres of those who, by cornering the market before the abundant harvest of 1757, caused the price of wheat to soar so high that there had been hunger-riots in several counties (II, 32). In the following year, Parliament passed several laws on this wheat problem (*Continuation of the Complete History of England*, II, 203—4). In 1757 an anonymous pamphlet appeared[36], *Poison Detected or Frightful Truths*, throughout whose seventy-five pages the author declares that he is horrified by the adulterated nutrition of Londoners, and does not hesitate to attribute the (mythical) decline in population which obsesses nearly all eighteenth-century writers to the harmful effects of food and drink rendered toxic by the chemical ingredients which were mixed into it. Apart from the style, which the *Critical Review* of October 1757 justly describes as 'bombast' (iv, 296) or 'solemn fustian' (p. 297), the reader of *Humphry Clinker* (pp. 119—22) finds the same accusations of adulteration in the following passage:

> Tea, detrimental alone, is frequently coloured with copperas; wine is purified with drugs of as noxious properties, or roughened with pernicious asperants; veal is whitened with chalk, and puffed up with, perhaps, the unwholsome breath of the distempered butcher; the brazier may poison us with the lethiferous fusion of arsenical metals in tin with which he lines our culinary vessels; our beer, the common beverage of the populace, is perniciated with the baleful properties of vitriol, or unwholsome intoxicants: but above all, our bread, the universal basis of the food of all ranks and ages of people, is mixed with most noxious and morbiferous matters (p. 5).

The author denounces the lime, chalk and alum which are mixed into the Londoners' bread. Alum is singled out for his fiercest vituperation. He attributes to this element a particularly toxic effect on the organism of the sick (those suffering from gout, rheumatism, colic and venereal diseases, not to mention the chronic hypochondria to which the English are so prone). In conclusion, the pamphleteer proposes that a law should be passed forbidding speculation in wheat and flour and the stockpiling of them in times of scarcity. Also in 1757 there appeared another pamphlet *A Modest Apology in Defence of the Bakers* by Sampson Syllogism, which, in an ironic tone sustained throughout its fifty-eight pages, pretends to inveigh against *Poison Detected* and to defend the bakers for their premature Malthusianism. Like Matt Bramble (p. 120), the author stresses this stupid mania for white bread: 'Cleanliness or wholesomeness are but little regarded by the populace ... 'tis whiteness, no matter whence it derives that desirable quality' (pp. 34—5). The analysis of Syllogism's ironic lucubrations in the *Critical Review* of January 1758 (v,

74—5) provides a revealing parallel with the passage in *Humphry Clinker* (pp. 119—22) already quoted. The similarity of the style and ideas in these pages authorises one to think that Smollett may well be the author of this review, whose ending is reproduced here *in extenso*, with the words, expressions and clauses which recur almost verbatim in *Humphry Clinker*, in italics.

> *Sacrifice* every consideration of *health* and appetite, to the *silly gratification of the eye*. They cannot eat *veal* until the natural colour is *bleached* away *by repeated bleedings*, so that hardly a *drop* of red blood, is *left in the body*, and the *animal* is actually diseased. They will rather eat their coleworts raw, than run the risque of seeing their *colour* faded by *boiling*: they will turn their eyes with loathing, from a loaf, that has any resemblance in hue to the grain of which it ought to be composed; and thus lay the *millers* and *bakers* under a necessity of inventing impositions to deceive them. Be it their portion, therefore, and theirs only, to eat *bread* compounded of *allum*, *chalk*, whiting, and human *bones*.

Moreover, the clause in *Humphry Clinker* beginning 'and the miller or the baker is obliged . . .' (bottom of p. 120) repeats the same idea as above, and the last sentence, of a pessimism at once cantankerous and resigned ('Be it their portion . . .') denotes the same spirit of misanthropic irritation which Bramble expresses about Bath (p. 47) and London (p. 122). In 1758 Peter Markham published *Syhoroc: or Considerations on the Ten Ingredients used in the Adulteration of Bread. To which is added A Plan of Redress*, reproduced the same year under the altered title of *A Dissertation on Adulterated Bread and the Great Benefit of Hand-Mills*. Markham, in the same bombastic style as *Poison Detected* discloses the presence in bread of alkali, slaked lime, chalk, whiting, horse beans, acorns, alum and powdered bones. He also finds a little wheat in it. But he refuses to divulge two other formidable ingredients. After having observed the harmful effects of this mixture on the whole of a population growing progressively weaker, Markham recommends the use of small domestic hand-mills, of which there were still many in Normandy farmhouses less than a century ago. James Manning, a doctor in Bath, also published in 1757[37] *The Nature of Bread*, in which he denounces six harmful ingredients in bread, the same which appear in Dr Markham's pamphlets. These vigorous attacks did not remain unanswered by the trade-guilds incriminated. A certain H. Jackson, who calls himself 'chemist', defended the bakers and millers in *An Essay on Bread* (1758) and alleges that he found no trace of the harmful ingredients denounced in the pamphlets analysed above. If the reader of Jackson is slightly reassured retrospectively about the quality of the bread sold in London about 1757, the same cannot be said for the other current articles of food and drink which Jackson passes under review in an appendix of some twenty pages (pp. 34–55). Beer, cider, vinegar, wine and pickled gherkins in turn excite his dietetic wrath: for example, he discovers powdered alabaster and marble, chalk, crushed oyster-shells, crab's eyes and calcined bones mixed into cider. But, as the taste of this beverage is somewhat flat, they add alum (again!) and treacle to induce a new fermentation and at the same time sweeten it. In the long run, the defender of millers and bakers is just as pessimistic as Smollett in *Humphry Clinker*:

> It is a severe Reproach upon our Intellects, and public Œconomy. when we reflect, that in this vast Metropolis, we scarce eat or drink any Thing pure and void of fraudulent Mixture, pernicious to our Health. Hence we account for the rare Instances of Longevity, and the present pigmy Race (p. 34).

Finally, Emmanuel Collins's pamphlet, *Lying Detected* (2nd edn, 1758), is a direct reply to Dr James Manning's *The Nature of Bread*. Collins launches into a refutation, in turn ironic, humorous and burlesque, of Manning's allegations and it must be admitted that he occasionally scores some points, if only thanks to his commonsense, when he declares: 'Why, Doctor, if one Quarter of what you have asserted be true, our modern Loaves would be as fatal every Whit, as the forbidden Fruit was' (p. 31). And what bread do the bakers eat then? Collins, in his turn, accuses that insatiable monster composed on the one hand of the voracious consumption by the distilleries and on the other of the free export of grain. Markham published a last pamphlet, *A Final Warning to the Public to Avoid the Detected Poison* (1758) in which he vigorously counterattacks Jackson's *Essay on Bread*, whose errors and contradictions he underlines. All this agitation ended by driving Parliament to take action and a law was passed (31 Geo. II, c. 29) forbidding the admixture of alum in particular, and imposing fines or prison sentences on all who contravened it.

This brief study of the diet of the English as Smollett describes it in *Humphry Clinker* would be far too incomplete if no reference were made to the testimony of foreign travellers in Great Britain. Though coloured by various national prejudices and inevitable idiosyncrasies, their observations nevertheless constitute a precious source of information, on condition of never being taken at their absolute face value. Faithful to their gastronomic traditions, the French, as a general rule, have a very poor opinion of English food. Spending eighteen months in England from February 1737, Abbé Jean-Bernard Le Blanc, like the good Burgundian he was, displays a smiling indignation on the subject of London tavern-keepers: 'They are the finest Chemists in England. In a word, they counterfeit our Wines in London as they counterfeit our materials; or rather they fabricate the Wines of all the Countries of the World there', and he adds that not a twentieth part of the claret drunk in Great Britain is imported from France, and in the same way the champagne 'is often only a mixture of Cider, Perry, Sugar and some other ingredients'[38]. When Matt Bramble relates the accident of the staved pipe of port (p. 120) he indulges less in the sombre delights of satirical exaggeration than in the denunciation of a state of affairs all too well known ever since the beginning of the eighteenth century. Madame du Boccage is less severe, but she was a rich, upper-middle-class woman whose stay lasted only two months:

> I find it easy to get used to these foreign dishes, and even to the simple English cooking of which we have such a bad opinion; their butcher's meat, their plum pudding, their fish, which is cheaper than in Paris and which is served at every meal, their chickens in butter sauce are excellent. They make wine without grapes, as we make it from cherries, which resembles burgundy. They serve little pieces of bread in wicker or silver baskets — rather as one serves *pain bénit* in church; the portion for six would barely suffice one. I had been told that they rarely entertained travellers to meals; but I find them religious observers of the laws of hospitality. We have not yet spent two days without an engagement for dinner. The morning is long, one does not sit down to table till four o'clock [39].

Madame du Boccage, an already celebrated literary lady, moved mainly in high society, where she was received by Chesterfield and Lady Mary Montagu. As for Pierre-Jean Grosley, he spent only six weeks in London in 1765, but his declared (and respected) intention of being completely impartial, and the richness and precision of his observation caused his *Londres* (Lausanne, 1770) to eclipse Le Blanc's letters. Contrary to Smollett (but the crisis of 1757—58 was no longer more than a bad memory) he finds that 'English bread is good and light, although it contains a great deal of crumb' (I, 118). Like Madame du Boccage, he is surprised at the thinness of the slices, due perhaps to the bad opinion the doctors have of this food which, according to them, is very indigestible (ibid.). Grosley does not profess much admiration for the butcher's meat, in spite of its reputation, which he considers exaggerated; as to the poultry, he finds it 'flabby and moist' (I, 121). He also shows little enthusiasm for the dreary vegetables impregnated with coal-smoke, all observations which corroborate Matt Bramble's diatribe. But it is for English 'wines' that Grosley reserves his strongest criticisms. He too denounces the adulterated wines, fortified with brandy (claret and red burgundy), and the white wines entirely made of decoctions, or concoctions, based on mulberries, morello cherries and wild berries. Here is the analysis he gives:

> The base is a juice made from turnips, boiled till they are completely dissolved. This juice, mixed with that of wild fruits, with beer and with litharge, produces, after a light fermentation, the port drunk in

London taverns and coffee-houses. They add it, *according to art*, in smaller or larger doses, to claret and even to burgundy, which, by the time it has passed through the hands of several agents, is only too often a bad mixture of *râpé* wine from Languedoc and Provence (I, 144).

Grosley has the merit of recommending an original, very French solution to that suicidal melancholy which afflicts the English: the drinking of wine must be encouraged in England by reducing the excise duty on it, which would make the inhabitants 'gayer and less argumentative, fonder of life and less melancholic' (II, 22). In short, this oenophilous remedy is based on the principle *In vino . . . voluptas*. The meticulous Vaudois, César de Saussure, who spent four years in London from 1725 to 1729, had already noted the thoroughness with which the publicans and vintners practised the art of chemical multiplication[40]. Contrary to Smollett, he notices the abundance of running water provided for three hours a day in people's homes, for which they had to pay a yearly subscription, and the cleanness of the houses, washed twice a week from top to bottom in good families, without the English, for all that, being slaves to cleanliness like the Dutch. The most exact and scientifically impartial testimony is undoubtedly that of the Swede, Pehr Kalm, who arrived in London in February 1748. He, too, is struck by the cleanliness of the English housewives, and the predominance of meat (of excellent quality) in the meals they cook. Kalm, even with the restriction implied in the relative clause in the following quotation, must, however, err on the side of optimism when he writes: 'I do not believe that any Englishman, who is his own master, has ever eaten a dinner without meat'[41].

One last problem is worth elucidating, that of the quality of the fish, of which Matt Bramble complains with disgust (p. 121). Swift already mentions in the penultimate line of his poem *Description of a City Shower* (1710) — whose satirical virulence forecasts that of Matt Bramble's view of London amenities — the 'stinking sprats' which are swept along the muddy gutters. In a satirical pamphlet, *Low Life, or One Half of the World knows not how the other Half lives*, of which the first edition dates from 1752, the anonymous author examines one by one the hours between Saturday evening and Monday morning, in the manner of Hogarth (to whom the pamphlet is dedicated) and thus gives a series of realistic snapshots of London life. Between five and six in the morning, he describes: 'The Pump, near *St. Antholin's* Church, in Watling Street, crouded with Fish-Women, who are washing their stinking Mackrell, in order to impose them on the Publick for Fish come up with the Morning's Tide' (3rd edn, 1764, p. 29). On the fishmarket, those who cornered the supplies were in complete control and, in the *Continuation of the Complete History of England*, Smollett twice states that Parliament attacked these illicit monopolies (II, 220–1; III, 326–31, where he gives long extracts from the bill of 1759, which came into force after June 24th 1760). Here again, Matt Bramble's diatribe is not the misanthropic vagary of exacerbated satire but the echo of social and historical matters of concern.

Nevertheless, whatever their inherent documentary value may be, it is impossible to see in Smollett's novels a deliberate sociological chronicle like that of Henry Mayhew in the middle of the nineteenth century. Although the representation of the real is firmly anchored in solid factual knowledge, in spite of the exaggerations of satirical distortion, it is not submerged by it. In other words, Smollett does not copy reality, he has created *his* literary reality, *his* fictional world, which, without having the breadth and depth of Balzac or Dickens, evince a no less lasting validity.

Smollett's origins have some influence on the limitations of his field of social exploration. The peerage and high society make only fleeting, though quite frequent, appearances in his work. His aristocratic characters are lifeless and one-dimensional and resemble flat conventional puppets rather than creatures of flesh and blood. As a general rule, aristocratic society is depicted as a microcosm of moral corruption and psychological futility, but also of insensitiveness and stupidity. As early as *Roderick Random*, Smollett manifests his aversion for the knavery of noblemen, more or less degenerate ones, such as that evocatively named trio, Straddle, Swillpot and Strutwell (II, Ch. li). Straddle, for all his fine words, is only a wretched pimp with a tarnished scutcheon and Strutwell a homosexual, who, unable to achieve his aim, does not hesitate to deprive Roderick of a valuable watch. Lord Quiverwit does not display these symptoms of degeneracy, but he embodies the wounding arrogance of great aristocrats (II, 206–7). Smollett does not, however, transform him into a grotesque caricature like the preceding ones and grants Roderick's noble rival some good qualities: physical courage, courtesy (icy), and a certain sense of honour, since he tells Roderick of his resolution to persevere in wooing Narcissa (II, 212). It is the wives of the aristocracy who are most of all subjected to Smollett's satirical verve in *Peregrine Pickle*, like that duchess on whom Peregrine is meditating designs (pp. 428–9). Besides her invincible class-consciousness, the noble lady displays a remarkable insensitiveness to the misfortunes of a poor woman. Is it necessary to remember too that the 'Memoirs' of Lady Vane (already analysed) produce an irritating, occasionally even sickening, impression of idle futility, in which the passions are deployed all the more virulently because sex and the search for pleasure in general, are the sole preoccupation of these worldly puppets? Smollett sometimes succeeds better in making one realise all the corruption of this debauched society by means of a single rapid sketch than by that whole long fresco painted in the 'Memoirs'. In a few lines (p. 485), he recounts the amorous frenzy of that Scottish noblewoman who flings herself at Lady Vane's feet and implores her to intervene on her behalf with a lover whom Lade Vane does not

285

want herself. In a single paragraph, he depicts the degrading aberrations of guilty love better than in the entire amorous marathon of Lady Vane. Again, one must grant Lady Vane, in her desperate search for pleasure, strength of character and even the courageous honesty of a person who remains true at least to herself. Lady Vane would certainly never have accepted the lecherous bargain to which a great lady stoops to extricate herself from an awkward financial situation brought about by her own follies at the gaming-table (p. 547).

The male aristocrats in *Peregrine Pickle* do not arouse any kindlier feelings in Smollett; very much the reverse. Peregrine allows himself the luxury of giving a lesson to a young nobleman who is too obsessed by his mania for gambling to listen to his judicious advice (pp. 572–3). Two lords play an active and successful part in precipitating Peregrine's financial ruin, for he is initiated into the thrilling — and costly — pleasures of the turf (pp. 606–8) by a member of the aristocracy. Later a titled crook robs him of almost all of his remaining fortune and of his parliamentary hopes (Ch. xcvii). Right from the beginning of his crazy London period, the debauched young aristocrats with whom he delights to associate contribute to the hero's moral and material downfall (p. 581). Finally, the long chapter (cvi) devoted to MacKercher and the Annesley affair brings out only too clearly the corruption and devious hypocrisy of the usurping Lord, determined at all costs to prevent his nephew from entering into the title and possessions which were his rightful inheritance.

This image of the great English aristocracy is stereotyped and monotonous, and, in the end, boring. Numerous are the puppet nobles who jig their shadow-dance in the Smollettian world, and few are the genuine individualities, apart from the very real one of Lady Vane. This part of Smollett's fictional universe lacks the tumultuous vitality which characterises his representation of the real. The aristocracy exists in his novels, but it does not live. An impression of trivial unreality, of a closed world glimpsed rather than observed, hovers over the scenes of fashionable life which he sketches, rather than describes, in *Ferdinand Count Fathom* (Ch. xxxii). The infatuated craze from which Fathom reaps a rich harvest is in itself a satire on this frivolous society, with no culture and no artistic discernment, which is always ready to hurl itself on the latest fashion, the latest success, the latest discovery. This psychological and social infantilism of creatures cocooned in the cottonwool of the conventions of social etiquette earns Fathom a hard lesson on the moral shallowness of these people, alienated by the frantic search for a pleasure which invariably eludes them. Living in a closed world, these members of high society are motivated by a ferocious egotism which soon transforms them, too, into monads, hermetically sealed to any feeling of compassion. Fathom discovers this a little late, to his cost, when he appeals (in vain) to the good offices of two faithless noblemen who leave him to get out of the scrape with the polite nonchalance of hardened cynics (pp. 176–8).

The lesson is hard for Fathom, less because it surprises him than because it confirms his absence of illusions about high society (p. 177).

The petty nobility and country squires arouse no more sympathy in Smollett's novels. He delights in ridiculing the pretensions and sham distinction of foreign fops, often of dubious origin and with uncertain incomes. Smollett's satirical intent is so virulent that the French marquis, the Italian count and the German baron in *Peregrine Pickle* are turned into grotesque caricatures. In the course of the antique banquet, a merciless series of physical or physiological incidents and accidents befall them, which succeed in making them ludicrous in Peregrine's eyes (pp. 234–41). The boorish, narrow-minded squires, great huntsmen and hardened drinkers, are also a target for Smollett's satire. They generally bear names which are, in fact, labels of their dominant vice or defect. Gawky, Narcissa's brother Orson Topehall (whom Smollett nicknames 'the Savage' or 'Bruin'), his friends Sir Timothy Thicket and Squire Bumper in *Roderick Random*, Sir Valentine Quickset in *Launcelot Greaves* (pp. 73–5) belong to a generation already in process of disappearing on the economical and social plane. But they nevertheless contribute to prolonging the legendary and literary existence of the Tory country squire whose entire horizon is limited to the sterns of his pack of hounds and the bottom of the tankards he swills from[42].

Smollett surpasses himself in *Ferdinand Count Fathom*, where he draws the caricature of a caricature in the loud-mouthed rubicund person of Sir Stentor Stile (Ch. xxiv). Hunting in company with Sir Giles Squirrel (pp. 92, 101–3), no longer the fox but the fool, Sir Stentor Stile acts to perfection the narrow-minded, drinking, gambling squire, landed from his faraway English countryside into the Parisian jungle, and the ideal prey for Fathom. The satiric irony of the situation demands that Fathom should not perceive for one moment the exaggerated character of this boorish fellow whom Sir Stentor Stile successfully impersonates. The clothes, the speech in broad dialect, the coarse exuberance and the savage contempt for everything French enable Smollett to produce a satirical character larger than life and twice as natural, thanks to the concentration of ludicrous details and also to the brimming vitality of this burlesque creation. Here there is satire in the second degree and with a double edge. The squire, who is not one, is less stupid than appearances lead one to believe and Fathom, who wrongly thinks himself superior, lets himself be taken in by an exaggerated piece of character-acting.

There are, however, a few noblemen depicted without rancour in Smollett's work. For once, the author of *Peregrine Pickle* abstains from any disparaging comment on the old French aristocrat with whom Peregrine unexpectedly makes friends (pp. 208–9). Moreover, in *Ferdinand Count Fathom*, the Count de Melvil, his son, and Don Diego de Zelos symbolise, in too rigid a manner to be always convincing, not only the nobility of titles, but above all that of the heart. In compensation,

Smollett sedulously creates a corrupt and malicious character, to wit Count Trebasi, who is the moral antithesis of the Melvils. The same antithetical presentation characterises the squires in *Launcelot Greaves*. On the one hand, the Greaveses, father and son, known (Launcelot in particular) for their charity to the poor; on the other Anthony Darnel, Aurelia's obstinate, choleric and tyrannical uncle, as also the eccentric Sycamore, more stupid than wicked, but driven to evil by his toady Dawdle. Although, in *Humphry Clinker*, Jery and his uncle (pp. 266, 270) agree in writing in praise of the third Duke of Queensberry, the fictional characters of the great or lesser aristocracy, like Lord Oxmington (pp. 281–4) or Sir Thomas Bullford (pp. 297–305), are only variations of types fixed as early as *Roderick Random* in 1748. As may be seen in the chapter on *Humphry Clinker*, Smollett shows a preference for Dennison, not so much because he is a gentleman farmer but because he is a genuine countryman. To sum up, Smollett shows little liking, in his novels, for the various ranks of the aristocracy, but it is impossible to say that these characters are among his most convincing fictional creations, no doubt from lack of real knowledge of this world which remained a closed one for the impecunious writer he was nearly all his life.

At the other end of the social scale the townspeople and peasants appear only as vague entities with no specific individuality, or in the guise of stock stage rustics. However there are numerous allusions to the London populace, that dirty, idle, drunken, dissolute riff-raff, only too ready to fight in the street or to insult a stranger, as Roderick and Strap learn to their cost (I, Ch. xiii). A carter insults them, a coachman deliberately splashes them with mud, a third makes such rude jokes about their appearance that Roderick feels obliged to box with him (I, 90). Strap is unluckier than his master, and, during a similar incident with a blacksmith, receives many punishing blows and is robbed of most of his clothes while he is trying to defend Scotland with his bare fists (I, 135–6). Smollett also occasionally depicts an angry mob, especially in *Launcelot Greaves*, during the election scenes, the first time when Launcelot saves the situation for his father by intervening with a brilliant speech (p. 26), the second when his mediation between the Whig and the Tory, full of sound sense as it is, fails to achieve its end (Ch. ix). The cavalcade of Tories has a bone to pick with the populace which replies to whiplashes with a volley of missiles. The crowd makes a noisy background to the electoral speeches and its din is only equalled by its stupid raging against the voice of reason as embodied by Launcelot. The crowd tries to molest him, but the knight vigorously and successfully counterattacks (p. 78). Once again, Smollett graphically and symbolically expresses his hostility to any form of democratic government. He dreads the psychological instability of people he despises, and the political consequences of this manipulation (already!) of crowds. For him, the populace, far from being sovereign, is above all the victim of professionals who exploit its stupidity to their own profit. As to the peasants, these are cardboard figures, the conventional rustics of comic tradition, rather than real characters. Joey, the waggoner who takes Roderick and Strap into his clumsy vehicle (I, Ch. xi), is the typical stage yokel who, in spite of being a simpleton talking broad Mummerset, is not lacking in sly perspicacity and is well able to inform Roderick of the true character of Weazel and his wife (I, 81—2). The bumpkins who discover the wounded Roderick in their barn (I, Ch. xxxviii) are Mummerset-speaking caricatures of Sussex peasants. Ignorant, cowardly and superstitious fellows, only the prospect of having to pay for a burial induces them to act with the promptness of those who have no wish to be burdened with a dying man and charitable scruples (I, 307). In *Launcelot Greaves*, especially at the beginning of the novel, Smollett draws an antithetical picture of the peasant's condition. On the one hand, there is the wretchedness of poor people, with no defence against the tyranny of a bailiff, on the other, the Edenic happiness of a rural life under the protection of a good man like Launcelot (pp. 23—4).

But it is above all the middle classes, in their manifold grades and activities, that Smollett has most vividly brought to life. The petty bourgeoisie of Scotland and London, apothecaries, surgeons and doctors, often richer in hopes than in guineas, the chattering crowd of the coffee-houses, together with emigrants of all nationalities, compose a world seething with life. Without having particularly high aspirations in their everyday life, at the mercy of a demanding creditor, their existence is characterised by its uncertainty of the morrow and its perpetual financial precariousness, a feeling which Dorothy George confirms: 'The domin-ating impression of life in eighteenth-century London, from the stand-point of the individual, is one of uncertainty and insecurity'[43]. Thus the tribulations of Roderick, Peregrine and Fathom acquire more verisimili-tude from being set in an economically unstable world. The milieu in which these heroes move changes its general characteristics according to the novels. Roderick, who starts rather low in the social scale, mainly frequents the middle social layers and has no reason to congratulate himself on his acquaintances in high society. Peregrine, more fortunate from the beginning, moves in far higher spheres than Roderick, but his excesses, also more notable, lead him to similar, though less violent, nadirs. In company with Fathom, the reader explores a cosmopolitan and often shady world. Apart from encounters on highways and in inns, which ensure variety and surprises, *Launcelot Greaves* and *Humphry Clinker*, as opposed to *Ferdinand Count Fathom*, present the most homogeneous social milieu, without being restricted to the social class Smollett knew best. The accidental social falls, like the wrongful internment of Launcelot in a madhouse and the equally wrongful imprisonment of Clinker in Clerkenwell, become rarer. It would seem therefore that towards the end of his literary career Smollett aspired to the same stability in life as in his novels.

But this stability is in fact more a nostalgic desire than a reality. It is always menaced by one of the great characteristics of the Smollettian universe: violence, whose disappearance is only (almost) total in *Humphry Clinker*. As early as *Roderick Random*, Smollett shows a marked predilection for cruel jokes, confused brawls and straight fights, duels, and all kinds of bullyragging. Teeth are knocked out, blood spurts, eyes turn black and noses red, heads are bashed and broken. Those who get most belaboured are lawyers, attorneys, sheriff's officers and bum-bailiffs, who bear the brunt of the wrath and the blows of their involuntary clients. Trunnion detests the whole tribe of them and when, by a double joke, one appears in the garrison, he receives a smarting lesson (pp. 68–74), as does also the exciseman (p. 76). These representatives of the law would, when necessary, provoke the accused to violence, which provides them with an excellent reason for claiming costs and damages. Fathom lets himself be caught by this ruse when he is arrested by a bailiff who is wily and voluble enough to make him lose his temper and incite him to knock him senseless (pp. 180–1). If violence, in accordance with Fathom's crafty character, plays a minor part compared to hypocrisy in *Ferdinand Count Fathom*, it bursts out again in several passages of *Launcelot Greaves*, where the buffoons, Crabshaw and Crowe, are the victims of it (see the analysis of this novel). If one leaves aside Jery's frustrated duels in *Humphry Clinker*, only Lismahago is the victim of physical violence (among the Indians and in Lord Oxmington's house). It is also he who resorts to this expedient to punish his nephew. Minor incidents, like the blow dealt to Clinker by Bramble in Scarborough, the broken pate received at single-sticks by Burdock (pp. 166–7), that other caricature of a narrow-minded Tory squire, and Clinker's chastisement of his rival Dutton, were too much everyday occurrences in eighteenth-century England to be termed 'assaults with violence', but such actions nevertheless maintain in the most peaceable of Smollett's novels an atmosphere, faint as it is in comparison with *Roderick Random* or *Peregrine Pickle*, of spontaneous resort to force.

If the forms of physical violence in Smollett's novels are so well known and never vary, it is more difficult to determine the thematic function of this repeated manifestation. It is, however, possible to suggest that, as a general rule, apart from gratuitous barbarity, as in the case of Crampley, Oakum and Mackshane on board the *Thunder*, the resort to violence is the desperate and exacerbated reaction of an individual driven to this ultimate affirmation of his human personality when it is threatened with annihilation by the intolerable pressures of the society which surrounds him and stifles him. The injustice suffered by young Roderick from the persecution of the infamous schoolmaster, the bullying of Crampley on board the *Thunder*, call for only one reply, violence, so true is it that Roderick is struggling in a nightmare world where it is impossible to break the sense of impotent paralysis otherwise than by a savage release of bellicose and visceral atavism. Such too is the almost chemical reaction of Lismahago when confronted with his nephew. At this stage, violence is therefore also the prerogative of the weak, or of those who momentarily find themselves in a position of inferiority. In this case, Smollett tacitly approves of it, or at least does not condemn it. On the contrary, he stigmatises Peregrine's gratuitous violence during the incident with the gardener (pp. 85—6) although it is a matter of a nasty quarrel in which this disagreeable man begins by bullying the Winchester boys. The condemnation is more definite in *Launcelot Greaves* where, for example, a stupid brawl between Crabshaw and the soldiers ends in an accident which lames a drummer for life (p. 50). Violence, even in so unjust and revolting a form as forced recruitment by the press-gang, can also present an ambiguous character on which the jurist, Sir Michael Foster, already quoted earlier, harps. Smollett denounces the *methods* of the press-gang, but at no point in *Roderick Random* does he raise the issue and express an explicit condemnation of this institution, which, in some sort, establishes violence as a pragmatic necessity.

The second general characteristic of the Smollettian universe does violence to the social rules of propriety and the tacit conventions of the novel. The physical frankness with which Smollett makes his characters live leads him to present, a century and a half before James Joyce's Leopold Bloom, beings no longer ethereal like those in seventeenth-century French novels, but of flesh and blood, who eat, digest, sleep, defæcate, urinate and, on occasion, feel the pangs of cold, hunger, thirst or sexual desire. In this sense, Smollett's 'realism', so often criticised and ill-interpreted, goes much further than Fielding's. He is not afraid to represent the physiological servitudes of man, without, for all that, indulging in that morbid need for organic humiliation which transpires in the work of Swift. Smollett's purpose is quite different. He is bent, in the first place, on noting, with the impassiveness of a clinical observer, the physiological reactions of the whole man to his passions, his dislikes and his illnesses. Moreover, the clinician is also a puritan moralist for whom the body is always suspect, and often ridiculous, in its natural functions. Finally, it is remarkable that the most disgusting physiological manifestations nearly always occur to punish the impudent arrogance of individuals who wished to forget the burden of their too, too solid flesh. The description of such organic functions is therefore not a proof of Smollett's coarse insensitiveness but, on the contrary, of his heightened awareness of the unstable balance between flesh and spirit in man. Thus excretions, especially accidental ones like vomiting and those due to the relaxing of various sphincters, as also farts and belches are so many satirical recalls to a healthy awareness of the fundamental ambiguity of human beings. In these passages, olfactory offences, in particular, abound in plenty. Morgan — who, ironically, is not a paragon of exquisite cleanliness — complains violently of the stench he (wrongly) accuses a steward of exhaling (I, 216). An unlucky belch puts an end to a ludicrous love scene between

Roderick and an ancient Dulcinea avid for fresh young male flesh (II, 124–5). During the Roman banquet, the unfortunate guests, whose palates and stomachs are subjected to a rude ordeal by the doctor's revolting concoctions, are punished for their ridiculous affectations by uncontrollable visceral reactions (pp. 238–41). Though the malodorous details of the stools of the sick Crabshaw are part of a usual satire on medical jargon (p. 133), the physiological mishaps of Judge Frogmore in *Humphry Clinker* are a punishment for his gluttony, his credulous stupidity and also for his past misdeeds. The catharsis, in its brutal realism, is therefore meant to be both physical and moral (p. 303).

As to sexual activities, they mostly take the form of visits to brothels (stormy ones in *Roderick Random* and *Ferdinand Count Fathom*) and casual affairs, when the opportunity occurs, in inns or on journeys. In the Smollettian world, prostitutes exist, with their flashy charm or their physical and moral degeneration. The story of Miss Williams in *Roderick Random* retraces, without any equivocal complaisance, the ineluctable connection between her weaknesses and the ordeals which this young woman undergoes. Her unexpected re-encounter with Roderick, her cure and her fresh start in life certainly do more honour to Smollett's imagination than to his sociological accuracy. Miss Williams, like Cleland's Fanny, is a quasi-miraculous case of cured prostitution, for having succeeded in breaking the infernal and tragic circle of their sexual slavery.

As to conjugal sexual life, it is reduced to a few modest and greedy allusions at the end of the novel when the inevitable marriages take place. Deceived husbands sprout their shaming horns at regular intervals in Smollett's work: Lavement in *Roderick Random*, Hornbeck in *Peregrine Pickle* and the Viennese jeweller in *Ferdinand Count Fathom* are the most ridiculed representatives of this eternal brotherhood.

Violence and frankness, such are the first two characteristics of the Smollettian world. Must one add a third, indecency, as so many critics have done for two centuries? George Saintsbury, in *The Peace of the Augustans* (1916), denounces Smollett as 'the greatest offender, by far, in actual coarseness and from the esthetic point of view' (p. 115). Nevertheless, there is neither obscenity nor pornography in Smollett's novels, nor (alas! for his heroines[44] would have more red blood in their veins!) the least trace of eroticism. Direct allusions to sexual desire are rare, apart from Peregrine's almost invariably frustrated love affairs, in which this factor is only an element of his psychological and moral alienation. Roderick says, after getting drunk with another young man: 'I in particular was so much elevated that nothing would serve me but a wench' (I, 127), which is the beginning of his adventure, in the company of Jackson, in the brothel. Pipes, too, reveals the lusty weaknesses of his flesh with satirical brevity when Emilia asks him if he has ever been in love: 'Yes, forsooth, (replied the valet, without hesitation) sometimes of a morning' (p. 146). The same Pipes is roused to tumultuous re-awakening of youthful sexual vigour by the titillating proximity of a beggar-girl who attracts him in spite of her layer of dirt. But his proposals couched in nautical language displease the fair one, which soon provokes the valet's wrath (pp. 597–8). Smollett is incapable of manipulating the ribald implication as Sterne does so expertly in *Tristram Shandy*. At the most, it is possible to accuse Smollett of a certain lighthearted promiscuity displayed by characters overflowing with vitality, like Peregrine, his future brother-in-law Godfrey, and Fathom, who all, at one point of their adventure, make it their business to establish Bath as a spa whose waters are an effective cure for feminine sterility. On the other hand, the comic dirty double-entendre certainly does appear in Smollett, but under the protective cover of *lapsus linguae*, used as early as *Roderick Random*, and in luxuriant profusion in the letters of Tabitha and Win Jenkins, as will be seen in the next chapter.

Hence there is no cunningly chaste eroticism in Smollett, as in *Fanny Hill*, any more than the reader will find in his novels the sexual cravings to which Boswell, somewhat complaisantly, admits. To those who might be tempted to indignation in the name of outraged morality, the few examples analysed below, deliberately taken from non-literary sources, will perhaps excuse Smollett's indiscretions by reducing them to their just proportion in relation to contemporary documents on sexuality. In his *Remarques sur l'état présent d'Angleterre* (Amsterdam, 1715) Georges-Louis Lesage (who had nothing to do with the author of *Gil Blas*) notes a peculiar trade:

> One sees every day in London, in St. James's Park, women carrying baskets full of dolls and young women of all classes buying them. When one turns up the doll's skirt, one finds, instead of legs, a cylinder covered with some material, about six inches long and an inch in diameter, whose use is not explained (pp. 149–50).

And this traveller, who is not lacking in Gallic wit, delightedly tells the anecdote of the young woman who, finding the cylinder too large, orders a smaller one, but has to pay in advance, because, if she does not come back to collect it, this merchandise will be unsaleable. The cautious saleswoman explains that 'people only want big ones' (p. 150). Compared to such unnatural practices, the sexual promiscuity in which Smollett's heroes indulge as young men seems decidedly healthier. But what can be said of that (anonymous) poem, published the same year as *Roderick Random*, and which, under the title (already bizarre enough!) *Adollizing: or a Lively Picture of Doll-Worship* (1748), recounts in some thirty pages the story of a young debauchee, Clodius, who falls in love with Clarabella, whose coldness is not unreminiscent of the insipid asexuality of Smollett's heroines? Now, this Clarabella remains icy. Clodius suffers on account of this and finds a mechanical solution to his troubles. He decides to have a doll made which is an exact replica of the unattainable Clarabella, down to the smallest intimate anatomical detail. The doll (Claradolla) thus replaces Clarabella, but Venus takes vengeance and ends by disgusting the ingenious debauchee, who repents and returns to a more carnal love life with Clarabella, who consents to marry him.

This simultaneous fascination and repulsion, which characterises the puritan temperament is given free rein in a libidinously prudish pamphlet *Eronania* (London, 1724) followed by *Letters of Advice* (first printed in 1687). For some fifty pages each, these small masterpieces constitute a subtle exercise in semantic and moral casuistry. Everything is said, nothing is named. The 'self-defiler' is destined for all the physical and meta-physical ills in the universe. If masturbation is a crime, *coitus interruptus* is another, and *retentio seminis* a third. The sexual repression of the Victorian age, more mythical than real according to recent studies, would thus have roots reaching as far back as the beginning of the eighteenth century. It is with the impression of at last meeting someone more relaxed and understanding that the reader peruses the poem by Smollett's friend, John Armstrong, who published *The Œconomy of Love* in 1736. Without being a treatise on sex education before its time, this poem, vigorously condemned in the article on Armstrong in the *DNB*, gives wise counsels to young people who discover the strength of their new sexual appetites. As a doctor with no illusions, Armstrong even prescribes astringents and other styptics provided by plants which a young girl who has been deflowered can try to use to repair the irreparable. Armstrong, too, denounces the horrors of masturbation, the abominations of homo-sexuality, advises old men to be continent and proscribes aphrodisiacs which are always injurious to health. Many, too, are the documents on prostitution in the eighteenth century[45] which prove that not only has Smollett not exaggerated the adventures of Miss Williams but, rather, if anything, diminished their bestial and degrading character. One need only consult the annual publication, pragmatic but scarcely at all lewd, *Harris's List of Covent Garden Ladies*[46] to measure the extent of the social scourge that prostitution was in the eighteenth century. The number of prostitutes, the variety of their prices, the details of their physique, their erotic specialities — here are some of its ingredients which (almost) relegate Smollett and his novels to the sexless world of Berquin.

In this Smollettian world of violence and sometimes crude frankness it is not surprising to find that the emotions and the inner life are restricted to a limited gamut of gradations. In this realm, too, violence predominates. Smollett likes depicting paroxysms, whether of bad temper (with all its degrees of intensity from passing irritation to cold anger, rage, fury, not to mention — in the case of Roderick, and, above all of Peregrine — near-insane frenzy) or overwhelming joy. Now the invariable character-istic of these psychological manifestations is their translation into terms of physical or physiological reactions. For Smollett the body betrays, and above all translates the life of the feelings. This is a constant factor in his novels from *Roderick Random* to *Humphry Clinker*, with a particularly definite phase in *Peregrine Pickle* and a quite marked attenuation in *Humphry Clinker*. In the frenzy of his jealous passion for Narcissa, Roderick begins by maltreating poor Strap, who is too disconcerted to protest and is reduced to blubbering like a child (II, 196—7). This scene in *Roderick Random* finds many echoes in *Peregrine Pickle*, where the young hero, whose strong point is certainly not patience, gives free rein to his spectacular rages, especially when an unforeseen obstacle prevents him from satisfying his sexual appetites (pp. 300—1, 310—11 for example). These explosions of fury are not always negative. Roderick frequently gains fresh energy from them when he finds himself in a desperate situation, as during the fight with Crampley or the duel with Quiverwit. Stimulated by rage at finding himself on the verge of defeat, Roderick has a sudden burst of energy and defeats his opponents. In the same way, Launcelot's anger with the misanthrope Ferret (pp. 13, 16) springs more from the 'righteous wrath' of the Bible than from the violence of an overexcited psyche.

Smollett also automatically resorts to physical description to depict violent emotions such as fear, terror or agonised apprehension in the face of mysterious phenomena. The best example of this last is the analysis of Fathom's reactions when he is lost in the forest during the storm, but above all when he discovers the corpse of a traveller among the bales of straw in his refuge (p. 86). Smollett begins by describing the physical symptoms of terror: 'Then his heart began to palpitate, his hair to bristle up, and his knees to totter.' Next he reveals Fathom's chaotic thoughts, and finally the reaction (the chemical connotation of this term is amply justified by the use of such words as 'agitated', 'a state of fermentation', 'produced', ibid.) which stimulates him to take action to protect himself. Smollett had already analysed Fathom's terror in less tragic circumstances, when he was surprised in Wilhelmina's bedroom, by a series of physical indications: 'he trembled at every joint, the sweat trickled down his forehead, his teeth began to chatter, his hair to stand on end' (p. 51). Confronted with Launcelot's wrath, Ferret's reactions are no less spectacular: 'His eyes retired within their sockets: his complection, which was naturally of a copper hue, now shifted to a leaden colour; his teeth began to chatter; and all his limbs were agitated by a sudden palsy' (p. 13).

At the other end of the psychological scale, overwhelming joy is expressed by capers, exclamations, tears and cries, which strike a rude blow at the dubious myth, particularly current among foreigners, of British phlegm. This psychological invention of international folklore may be true of the nineteenth century, but certainly not of the eighteenth, whose exuberance can be compared to the recent explosion of vitality in the British young. Re-encounters are propitious occasions for these emotional outbursts. When Strap meets Roderick again in France, he behaves like a vulgar Latin and not like a dignified Anglo-Saxon: 'he leaped upon me in a transport of joy, hung about my neck, kissed me from ear to ear, and blubbered like a great school-boy who has been whipt' (II, 49). Clinker, too, lets himself go in a frenzied St Vitus's dance when he discovers that Bramble is his father (p. 317). Nevertheless, Smollett seems to mistrust any display of emotion. His description of terror, characterised by exclusive insistence on physical reactions borders on *Grand-Guignol* and, on the other hand, he often deliberately breaks the dramatic intensity of a scene by introducing some ludicrous detail. Smollett shies away from the emotion, which might be intense, of the meeting of son and long-lost father: Clinker drops a coal-scuttle on Lismahago's toe. In the same way, when Bramble rediscovers his old friends in a piteous state in Bath, Smollett contrives to slip in a ridiculous detail, almost a piece of slapstick, which promptly changes the key of the scene (p. 55). Charlie Chaplin too, at the most pathetic moments, loses his buttons on his trousers.

In the course of the thematic analyses of the novels, the love relations between heroes and heroines have already been examined in detail. Love does exist in Smollett's novels, or rather it survives, menaced by the physical and psychological violence of the men and the whimpering passivity (except for Emilia) of the women. The emotional outbursts oscillate perilously between athletic prowess and the most syrupy melodrama. Smollett's heroes are in love with love rather than with their mistress. As to friendship, it is manifested in an intermittent way and liable to chop and change. Such is the case with Roderick and Strap, and with Peregrine, who at one time or other quarrels with Trunnion, Godfrey, Hatchway and Pipes. In the case of the two servants, Strap and, especially, Pipes, it is not quite accurate to talk of friendship, since for Smollett, who belonged to a hierarchic society, the relations between masters and servants should be based on respect rather than cordiality. But, as appears above all in *Humphry Clinker*, friendship can resist time and separation, and Bramble immediately offers his help to Baynard. The friendship between Dr Lewis and Bramble must often have been severely tested by the sudden changes of mood and the paroxysms of gout of the lord of the manor. Finally, friendship between rogues — Fathom and Ratchcali — is subject to the unpredictable fluctuations of their selfish and divergent interests.

In view of the record of physical expression employed by Smollett in his depiction of feelings, it is not surprising that the inner life occupies so little place in his fictional world. If an awakening of conscience, often belated and fleeting, is produced in *Roderick Random* and *Peregrine Pickle* by the maieutic of prisons, Fathom's repentance is too sudden and theatrical to carry conviction. Launcelot at last realises the dangerous extent of his past follies when he is cooling his heels in the private madhouse, but his definite return to sanity cannot be likened to a moral or intellectual crisis. The only novel in which Smollett best conveys the capricious fluctuations of human consciousness is *Humphry Clinker*. The letter, by its very nature, is at once soliloquy and virtual dialogue and tries to convey, first for the letter-writer himself and secondly for the person to whom he is writing (whether one or many) a fragment of inner lived experience. By the indirect means of the epistolary form, Smollett comes somewhere near, without every really achieving it, to a literary exploration of the inner life. Certain passages, especially in Bramble's letters, where rage, indignation, disquiet or lassitude are expressed, could easily be translated into interior monologues. In the same way, the letters of Win Jenkins and Tabitha, whose verbal deformations and psychological and syntactical *non sequiturs*, could, with a few modifications – in particular the suppression of any allusion to the correspondent – be inserted into a novel by Virginia Woolf (for their precursory stream of consciousness technique) or James Joyce (for their jewels of scintillating polysemy).

To sum up, how can one characterise the strengths and weaknesses of the Smollettian universe? A dominant trait of this literary realm is Smollett's predilection for closed worlds: the battleship; watering-places (Bath in particular) which end up by living turned in upon themselves, as well-defined places which pulsate with fashionable life at seasons determined by the migrations of high society; the microcosms which regularly appear in all Smollett's novels: inns, coaches and prisons. These closed worlds are at once reflections and distortions of reality. The actions and emotions which are depicted in them gain in precision and intensity, but, on the other hand, lose some of their verisimilitude, for Smollett is forced to exaggerate his characters in order to turn them into types. Weazel, in spite of his caricatural physical appearance, which makes him a very typical Smollettian character, is also the type of the *miles gloriosus* furbished to the taste of the eighteenth century (I, 79–80).

A second ambiguous characteristic of the Smollettian world is the dislocation of the family group. In *Roderick Random*, the father soon disappears, the mother dies, Uncle Bowling manifests his blusterous contempt for the old judge who showed himself 'an unnatural and inflexible parent' to his own son (I, 3). Roderick's female cousins in Glasgow are not conspicuous for their charity, but, on the contrary try to injure the orphan. The Lavement family is not exactly a model of family harmony; the father is scorned and the mother and daughter are rivals in love. At the end of the novel, Narcissa breaks with her brother and all the rest of her family in order to marry Roderick.

It is in *Peregrine Pickle* that the family picture is darkest. The father, Gamaliel, is an amorphous character, with no outstanding feature; in turn terrorised and tyrannised over first by his sister, then by his wife. All through the novel, he behaves like a non-existent father (p. 107). But his mother's aversion to Peregrine dominates the family relations like a painful obsession which at times erupts into scenes of almost unbearable psychological violence. The adjective 'unnatural' recurs frequently to describe the prejudice of this unworthy mother (pp. 64, 79, 109, 110, 112, 172, 358) who rejects Peregrine and his sister in order to concentrate, with an unhealthy exclusiveness, all her affection on the younger brother. The result of this pathological aversion is twofold. Abandoned by his family, Peregrine's plight arouses all Trunnion's paternal instincts so that he becomes the boy's real father-figure (p. 109); the meetings between Peregrine and his mother are marked by a psychological violence in which the strident note of ill-controlled feminine hysteria is clearly discernible (pp. 171–3, 358–9, 767–8). Trunnion himself has also long broken with his family, which forced him to become a sailor for a mere peccadillo (pp. 72–3), just as Crowe is frustrated of his inheritance by the machinations of a rapacious grandmother and aunt (p. 4). As to the wives – Mrs Trunnion, Mrs Pickle, Mrs Tunley – they exercise a tyranny which makes their uxorious husbands ridiculous, a common state of affairs 'as the disease of being hen-peck'd was epidemic in the parish' (p. 156).

Family relations are no more brilliant in *Ferdinand Count Fathom*, where a misunderstanding drives Don Diego de Zelos to injustice and an (unsuccessful) attempt at murder. For once a man, the Countess de Melvil's second husband, Trebasi, tyrannises over his wife, as does Pimpernel in *Humphry Clinker* (pp. 171–2). Smollett vigorously denounces these abuses of family authority and presents, in the portrait of the Dennisons, the picture of a loving and well-balanced couple.

In spite of Smollett's emotional and literary attachment to Nature, she occupies only a restricted place in his work. Smollett is perhaps the first accurate painter of life on board warships, but his feelings for nature unleashed in storms at sea in no way presage the admiration of the Romantics for the raging elements. On the contrary, he is only impressed by the destructive horror of the wild fury of the winds and waves, whether it is a matter of the tempest the fleet encounters on the way to the West Indies (I, 232), or, more modestly, of the squalls that buffet the ship on which Peregrine is crossing the Channel (pp. 186–7). This horror of the sea also transpires in the *Travels through France and Italy*, where the spectacle of a wave-beaten shore is described: 'The waves dashing against the rocks and caverns, which echo with the sound, make such an awful noise, and, at the same time, occasion such a rough sea, as one cannot hear, and see, and feel, without a secret horror'[47].

It is only in *Humphry Clinker*, during the Scottish part of the journey, that there are indications of a romantic sensibility to the wild aspects of nature. But they need to be interpreted with some caution. Matt Bramble's emotion (letters of August 28th and September 6th written from Cameron House) at the sight of the charms of Loch Lomond, or the wild beauty of the Highlands, is tinged with the more or less conscious and admitted desire or praising this land of Scotland which too many English travellers have despised and decried. On the other hand, Smollett is not lost in admiration of nature in the wild and hostile to man.

On the contrary, he takes care to put some touches into his pastoral pictures which recall the civilising presence of man. Woodlands, *wheat-fields, meadows* and *villas* border the shores of Loch Lomond, the islands are *habitable*, some of them harbour *game*, similarly the waters of the Loch contain a quantity of *edible* fish. Likewise, the 'Ode to Leven Water' is characterised, from the stylistic point of view, by the frequency of words with a negative connotation which imply a rejection of the in-controllable violence of the elements. This idyllic vignette only acquires its full value for Smollett in so far as man and his industry are represented in it, something which the author stresses in the last eight lines. Already, in *Travels through France and Italy*, he had voiced his enthusiasm for a sunny and well-tilled southern landscape such as that of the valley of the Rhône. The vineyards on the slopes of the river's banks and the religious edifices, far from detracting from it for Smollett, 'add greatly to the romantic beauty of the prospect' (XI, 98). When Nature presents an arid, hostile and dangerous aspect, as in high mountains and waterfalls, she arouses in him a feeling of anxiety mingled with physical horror (XI, 365, 367, 374, 395—8 for example). In *Humphry Clinker*, Smollett shows that he is not devoid of poetic sensibility when confronted with the spectacle of Nature, provided she remains subjected to man.

The representation of the real in Smollett's novels has an undoubted value as socio-historic evidence, but cannot be limited only to this function. Like all human evidence, it shares its brittleness, due to the relativity of perception. Thus, while Jery and his uncle are indignant about the state of the roads, a French traveller, Elie de Beaumont writes in 1764:

> The roads of England are beautiful and well-kept. As pedestrians there are considered to be part of the nation, care has been taken to provide a footpath for them, which is usually on the right. . . . Signposts indicate the roads with clearly visible directions[48].

But Elie de Beaumont's admiration is explained, in its turn, by the com-plaints of foreign travellers, and of Smollett in particular in *Travels through France and Italy*, about the deplorable state of most of the roads on the continent. The accuracy of details of civilisation is seldom a basic assumption for the modern reader but has to be reached by a certain amount of archaeological probing. It is not unimportant that young Wilson disguises himself as a Jewish pedlar in order to try and meet Lydia. This humble profession was one of the few open to Jews in the eighteenth century. The vast number of these pedlars — the disguise was therefore a good one — is explained by racism and the socio-economic pressure exerted on this underprivileged, uneducated minority which could not be easily assimilated by the more civilised Sephardim Jews who had been settled in London since the middle of the seventeenth century[49].

Smollett introduces his readers to a world swarming with rogues, crooks, thieves, prostitutes and highwaymen. The critic may be shocked by this display of the more or less sordid sides of the eighteenth century. But Smollett does not show any *complacency* in this description of the underworld, which he surveys in general rather than systematically exploring it. Moreover, he was haunted by the fascinating problem of the interplay of Good and Evil in life and its literary expression. He had already realised that it is impossible to make good literature with good sentiments alone. Conversely, the modern critic who is shocked by Smollett's choice of subjects could (and should) ask himself the following question: in two or three centuries, what idea would these then engaged in research on the twentieth century form after having ransacked the columns of *France-Soir* or the *News of the World* which wallow ambiguously in the depravities of our era? The flat, everyday, commonplace life of Mr So-and-So is a recent literary discovery which Smollett has foreshadowed in *Humphry Clinker* by offering his readers the activities and thoughts of a group of letter-writers who, by their connections and occupations, constitute an analytical cross-section of English society about 1765–70.

He runs no risk, however, of becoming bogged down in the boring morass of what, in the nineteenth century, was called the 'slice of life', cut from some monstrous, highly indigestible cake. The omnipresent leaven of satire contributes to making his literary pastry more digestible without always avoiding an excess of acidity. The moral preoccupations of satire partly explain why the fresco painted by Smollett in his five novels is not complete, and at least as rich as that of Balzac or Dickens. Smollett suffers not only from the almost inevitable but rather fruitless comparison of his work with Fielding's, but also with the massive work of his openly avowed admirer, Dickens. In fact, it would be fairer to place Smollett among the painters, half-way between Hogarth and Rowlandson. Satire of a personal character (literary and political) belongs henceforth to the abstruse world of erudition. It has lost its brilliance and most of its interest (first and foremost in *The History and Adventures of an Atom*) and shares the same fate as *Le Canard Enchaîné, Punch*, or *Private Eye* a few weeks after their publication; this kind of satire is a dish which needs to be eaten piping hot: the slightest delay renders it flat and tasteless. On the contrary, satire allied to the representation of the real, thanks to the curative virtues of its acidity, presents the occasionally aggressive, but always very lively éclat of a world where social and economic tensions were at once to disappear and revive in the profound unheaval which precedes the Industrial Revolution. Thanks to this mixture, the representation of the real in Smollett's novels has not aged and occasionally even retains a surprising ring of actuality. Two centuries after Matt Bramble, a French writer on gastronomy is denouncing[50], with many scientific proofs to support him, the shameful (and dangerous) chemical adulterations to which the capitalist consumer society submits the most everyday articles of food. But, whatever the authenticity and vigour Smollett deploys in his novels to represent reality, this study would be incomplete without the analysis of the structures of the comic which give the Smollettian world its specific literary individuality.

8
Structures of the comic

Right from his first novel Smollett places his literary creation under the sign of comedy. The young author proposes to depict 'familiar scenes in an uncommon and amusing point of view' (*Roderick Random* I, lix), and his third novel, *Ferdinand Count Fathom* — albeit the least comic of the five — bears on its title-page a quotation borrowed from the tenth Satire of Juvenal (ll. 47—52):

> Materiam risus, invenit ad omnes
> Occursus hominum . . .
> Ridebat curas, nec non et gaudia vulgi;
> Interdum et lachrymas fundebat.

It is curious to note that the whole of this last line does not appear in Juvenal's satire: Smollett adds *fundebat*; which gives the opposite meaning to that of the original one[1]. The novelist shows straight away that he is conscious of the ambiguity of laughter and tears, as this illicit addition to Juvenal's line has just emphasised. This avowed intention of placing his work under the auspices of the comic Muse, did not then represent for Smollett a literary aim which after all was quite a common one, but, on the contrary, a courageous challenge to English critical opinion. The twentieth-century reader does not generally take into account Smollett's Scottish birth and the lack of humour of which the English accused the Scots all through the eighteenth century. It was therefore unusual, not to say rash, for any Scot, even one who had spent two-thirds of his life away from his native land, to venture into the comic novel. Smollett himself brings up this accusation of congenital lack of humour in *Humphry Clinker*, where it is not surprising to find Lismahago defending his compatriots. For him, the Scots are ill at ease when they are speaking English, a language which is not their natural, spontaneous one. The Scot 'therefore finds himself under a restraint, which is a great enemy to wit and humour', whereas in his own dialectal idiom he is capable of comic invention (p. 199). The same generalisation, no doubt a trifle hasty, is expressed, a few years later, by Edward Topham, who writes: 'Wit and Humour are not known; and it rarely happens that a Scotchman laughs at ridicule'[2]. It is against this notion of deficiency in humour, developed in the *Mirror*[3] of February 22nd 1780, that Smollett's friend, Alexander Carlyle, hotly protests in his autobiography. Such an opinion set forth by Englishmen or their Scottish colleagues in the *Mirror* seems to Carlyle 'a gross mistake'[4] and, not without a touch of chauvinist nationalism, he attributes this decline of humour in Scotland to the linguistic preponderance of English over Scots. At the beginning of the nineteenth century, the *Edinburgh Review* is still repeating this supposition of the inferiority of the Scots, although Smollett and Arbuthnot, according to the critic, suffice to preserve their native land

> from the imputation of wanting talent for pleasantry, though it must be owned, that we are a grave people, happily educated under an austere system of morals; possessing, perhaps some humour, but fearful of taking the liberty of jesting in a foreign language like the English[5].

Thus, nearly fifty years after Lismahago's explanations, the literary legend of the Scots' incapacity for humour was still very much alive.

Smollett's *vis comica* is nevertheless undeniable, and, despite its excesses — in particular the too frequent resort, especially in the first two novels, to the most mechanical comic devices — is one of the reasons why his novels are still read. Doubtless there is no longer, alas!, a doctor who prescribes his patients a daily reading of a few pages of *Peregrine Pickle* (see Knapp, p. 315), but, in the nineteenth century, Hazlitt, Thackeray, Dickens and Meredith, in spite of a few reservations, readily acknowledged Smollett's comic genius. Did not Thackeray write, in his *English Humourists*, that the letters of Win Jenkins and her mistress Tabitha Bramble were 'a perpetual fount of sparkling laughter, as inexhaustible as Bladud's well'? In Thackeray's eulogies of these comic characters in *Humphry Clinker*, it is possible to see the (distant) precursory sign of the sustained critical attention which has been focused for some years on this last of Smollett's novels. The series of perceptive articles devoted by W. Arthur Boggs[6] to the language of Win Jenkins confirms this impression. But this polarisation of Smollettian criticism on *Humphry Clinker* must not make one forget the profusion of comic invention Smollett displays in his other four novels, even if he uses less subtlety and scatters his work with coarser effects than in *Humphry Clinker*.

It is necessary to emphasise that there is no break in comic invention between the first four novels and *Humphry Clinker*, just as the four preceding chapters have been alloted the task of analysing the thematic continuity which is traceable from *Roderick Randon* to *Humphry Clinker*. All the comic structures are already there in embryo in *Roderick Random*, and *Humphry Clinker* rejects none of the methods used in *Roderick Random*, but the proportion of comic effects is quite different. Between 1748 and 1771 the comedy in Smollett's novels has grown more refined, thereby following the general literary trend of the century, as Edward N. Hooker shows in his article 'Humour in the age of Pope'[7].

The analysis of the structures of comedy will follow three main lines of research. First, the synthetic examination of the structures of the traditional type which depend largely on *mechanical methods* (practical jokes and slapstick, comic concatenations of events, caricatures). Next, the *psychological mainsprings* will be subjected to analysis; the obsessions, manias and fads of the characters; the interplay of innocence and vanity; the cases of professional alienation (doctors, lawyers and, above all, sailors) which are manifested by the systematic use of a specialised language in circumstances beyond its normal application. Finally, the transition to the third and last stage of this study of Smollettian comedy will not present major difficulties. This, too, is a specialised language, not to say meta-language, which all these characters, at once great destroyers and creators of words charged with a double or treble meaning, speak and write. From many interferences between these semantic fields springs the *verbal and stylistic interplay*: witticisms, but also the humour of those crazily misspelt or mispronounced words which crop up in Smollett's work as early as *Roderick Random* and in *all* the other novels, to reach their comic apogee in *Humphry Clinker*.

Before severely judging the coarse (and occasionally dirty) jokes with which Smollett peppers his novels, it is as well to remember that these practical jokes in rather dubious taste constituted a tradition firmly anchored in eighteenth-century British society at all its levels. James Lackington, at the beginning of his *Memoirs* (1792), recounts, with malicious and complaisant zest, his real or fictitious exploits as a young rascal; snowballing, snakes surreptitiously introduced into houses, firecrackers, perilously perched lanterns, nailed-up doors, in short a whole series of misdeeds considered more or less comical which raise Lackington to the rank of a rival of Peregrine's. At the other end of the social scale, although the preparation and execution of these practical jokes require more sublety and, above all, the necessary amount of money, the passion for this mechanical jest is just as ardent. Horace Bleackley, in *The Life of John Wilkes* (1917) records how Wilkes succeeded in mystifying the impious and dissolute members of the famous 'Hell-Fire Club'. During an orgiastic scene, Wilkes, with one or two accomplices, arranged for a sweep to come down the chimney, to the great consternation of these rationalists who were firmly convinced they were in the presence of the devil. Another time, Wilkes let loose a baboon dressed up as the devil during one of his friends' sacrilegious ceremonies. These two examples have at least the merit of showing that even for raging anti-puritans the devil securely maintains his importance!

There can be no question of drawing up the systematic catalogue of the practical jokes and slapstick episodes which pullulate in Smollett's novels. Such a method of analysis would be far too long and boring and yield very little in the way of results. The vast number of jokes of this type would risk obscuring the basic mechanisms which are repeated with such regularity that Smollett himself must have wearied of them, since in its second expurgated edition of 1758, *Peregrine Pickle* is shorn of several of such practical jokes. Schematically, these jokes present a single ternary structure. First there has to be a predestined victim, marked out by physical or psychological idiosyncrasies which in some way *invite* the perpetrators of nasty jokes to go into action. Trunnion presents the ideal victim for the plots hatched by Peregrine, Hatchway and Pipes, in view of the abundance, peculiarity and virulence of his prejudices, against his family, women in general and lawyers in particular. There ensues a stage of preparation which involves the fabrication of an object which will provoke terror or rage in the victim. It may be simply a matter of a mechanical or chemical alteration of some article in everyday use or its contents: the chamber-pot perforated by Peregrine (p. 60), or the jalap in Mrs Trunnion's brandy (pp. 66–7). Much use is made on these occasions of liquid phosphorus, whose diabolical glow helps to strike terror into the (apparently) boldest spirits. Peregrine resorts several times to chemistry (pp. 71, 541) and the misanthropic quack Ferret has among his possessions 'a small vial of liquid phosphorus, sufficient . . . to frighten a whole neighbourhood out of their senses' (p. 53). The apparition of two ghosts with phosphorescent foreheads does not fail to terrify the brave Crowe a couple of pages further on (p. 55). The third stage shows, on the one hand the hilarity of the perpetrators of practical jokes — unless turned against them, as in the unenviable case of the exciseman who is at once Peregrine's instrument and victim (pp. 72–6) — and the psychological or physiological effects of the hoax; extreme fright, fainting, various cathartic effects which mark the comic downfall of the victim who is reduced to a mechanical puppet by the machinations of the jokers.

These practical jokes — of which Fielding does not disdain to make use on occasion, as when the unlucky Parson Adams falls into a water-tub (*Joseph Andrews*, Book iii, Chapter 7) — are liable to take different forms according to the means employed, even though the ternary structure remains basically the same. The one of which Dr Wagtail is the victim is mainly psychological when his companions present him with a pregnant whore and try to pin an entirely fictitious paternity on him (II, 80–4).

The laughter of Banter, Bragwell, Slyboot, Roderick and the other accomplices is decidedly cruel. It is the result of an expert psychological torture which ends in an almost sanguinary piece of slapstick, for the prostitute, under pretext of kissing her pretended seducer, bites his cheek 'to the unspeakable diversion of all present' (II, 83). Peregrine's practical jokes, right from his tenderest (?) age are characterised by this same ambiguous delight in creating physical or psychological confusion in someone else.

This *Schadenfreude*, which plays a by no means negligible part in their composition, is also characteristic of the satiric temperament (see *Peregrine Pickle* pp. 52–3, 58–61 where Smollett speaks of *jeu d'esprit*, 68–76). Moreover, Peregrine's jokes are played with most relish on those who have some intellectual or spiritual pretensions. The tutor Jolter is the victim of a plot hatched by Peregrine (pp. 81–2) which reminds his Mentor that the flesh is weak. Peregrine exercises a positive power of collective and comic hypnosis on the members of the political club (pp. 114–16) whom he describes as 'wrong-headed enthusiasts' (p. 114). Even the clergy, in the person of the vicar-accomplice of young Gamaliel, learns to its cost what comes of plotting against Peregrine. It is a double joke, for Peregrine plays on the jealousy of the innkeeper, Tunley, who becomes his instrument of revenge on the vicar. There is even a third comic level, when the innkeeper, only imagining himself a cuckold but in a genuine rage, half stuns himself with his own flail which he mishandles (p. 157). These practical jokes express that irrepressible need to punish the people around him, a tendency already analysed in the structural examination of *Peregrine Pickle*. There is a series of these jokes in this novel (pp. 366–88 and 577–81) in which Peregrine's comic invention, tinged with satirical pragmatism, is given free rein.

After such a profusion of them in *Peregrine Pickle*, it is not impossible that Smollett grew tired of these comic devices, with their unfailing but monotonous results, which appear less frequently in *Ferdinand Count Fathom* and *Launcelot Greaves*, but once again introduce their discordant note of farcical comedy into *Humphry Clinker*. The race between Birkin, the fat bookseller and Tim Cropdale, the author with more tricks up his sleeve than guineas in his pocket (pp. 128–30) belongs to a comic tradition half-way between a practical joke and slapstick which raises a chuckle rather than a belly laugh, whereas the joke played on Micklewhimmen (pp. 173–5) misfires and results in the intestinal and psychosomatic discomfiture of the chief participant, entirely in the comic tradition of *Peregrine Pickle*. But it is obvious that towards the end of *Humphry Clinker*, Smollett feels less and less liking for this rudimentary form of comedy of which he draws a satirical caricature during the stay with Squire Bullford (pp. 297–305), an inveterate practical joker who seems to belong to a generation of boorish landed gentry already vanishing from the social and economic scene. The episode of the false fire-alarm could also, as Philip Mahone Griffith has shown[8] be regarded as a sly parody of the fire scenes in *Clarissa*. But right up to the last pages of *Humphry Clinker*, the traditional practical jokes do not relinquish their comic rights, and a cat shod with walnut shells disturbs the wedding-night pleasures of Clinker and Win (p. 349).

It is sometimes difficult to separate the practical jokes from the episodes of slapstick farce, but in general the latter are shorter and result from the involuntary clash between two series of actions which were originally unconnected. This type of comedy, rediscovered with graphic concision by the pioneers of the silent cinema and still successfully exploited, uses more or less unforeseeable mechanical results, so that surprise and the abandonment of normal behaviour play a preponderant part in these comic vignettes. Here again, Smollett is not the only eighteenth-century novelist who has resorted to this almost visceral type of comedy. In *Joseph Andrews*, Fielding anoints the noble countenance of Adams with a basin of pig's blood, makes him roll in the filth of a pigsty and tumble all the way down a hill. In *Tristram Shandy*, the unfortunate Dr Slop, terrified by Obadiah's mud-splashing speed, falls into the deep mire of the road after a series of false manoeuvres which Sterne pleases to describe in a single sentence crammed to the hyphens with sparkling comedy. And the poultice that Slop and Susannah throw at each other's heads is the distant precursor of those custard pies which fly about in Mack Sennett films. If the practical joke is typical of the unfair behaviour which allows man to satisfy his aggressive instincts under the guise of a spontaneous prank, slapstick appears as the revenge of material things on man, who is assumed to be in control of them. The comedy springs from the revenge of the mechanical on the human, the unpredictable revolt of objects against the man-machine who had organised everything in order to assure his supremacy. Slapstick is therefore a momentary denial of anthropocentric finality.

Smollett is far from disdaining the mechanical effects of this form of comedy. In *Peregrine Pickle* a row of inquisitive people in the corridor of an inn collapses 'like the sequel and dependance of a pack of cards' (p. 298), a piece of slapstick already used in *Roderick Random* (I, 163). In *Launcelot Greaves*, the groom lays the squire Crabshaw senseless during a knockabout turn worthy of Gribouille (p. 59). Waiters, solicited by orders from all quarters of an inn, remain rooted to the spot while repeating 'Coming, sir' (p. 72), while on the following page there appears a half-shaved Crabshaw, his face partly covered in lather and blood. A few pages further on, the Whig candidate falls into the barrel which he was using as a rostrum (p. 75). Nocturnal misunderstandings in inns set customers suffering from the pangs of love or of stomach-ache dancing a lively ballet of ludicrous errors. Strap, as innocent as Adams when he strayed into Slipslop's bed and then Fanny's, finds himself in Mrs Weazel's, which brings down on him her husband's wrath and a torrent of urine. This liquid is the basic element of this diuretic form of slapstick (Fielding also

sprinkles Adams and his adversary with it in Chapter ix of Book iii of
Joseph Andrews), for which Smollett shows a particular liking in *Peregrine
Pickle*. In an episode, half practical joke, half slapstick, Peregrine makes
the worthy doctor believe he has wetted his bed (pp. 263—4). An
untamed shrew empties the flood of her diabetic incontinence on the head
of her cuckold of a spouse (pp. 424—6). As to the Dutch tragedy, its
effects are such 'that Peregrine's nerves were diuretically affected with the
complicated absurdity, and he was compelled to withdraw twenty times
before the catastrophe of the piece' (p. 349). This is no doubt a parodic
catharsis! The amorous Tom Clarke, just like Peregrine, sees all his hopes
collapse when he finds Crabshaw in the bed instead of the seductive Dolly
(*Launcelot Greaves*, pp. 57—8). While affecting to criticise such coarse
humour, Smollett does not always avoid incongruity. The flatulent
mimicry of that Harlequin who provides wind for the Dutch mills proves
it (*Peregrine Pickle*, p. 348), to the great delight of the Dutch spectators
whose refinement, there again, Peregrine does not exactly admire.

A final type of slapstick is peculiar to Smollett. Just as his practical
jokes are apt to be anti-intellectual, his slapstick tends to be anti-senti-
mental. As soon as a scene threatens to become pathetic, a comic incident
disrupts the incipient emotion. The meeting of Roderick and his old
schoolfellow Strap is the first example of this. The smearing of each
other's faces with shaving-soap makes the scene (I, 44—5) collapse into
clowning. In the same way, when Hatchway is rushing joyfully to
welcome Peregrine, who has at last come to his senses, his wooden leg
catches in a hole in the stairs, breaks and, in the same instant, shatters all
the dramatic intensity this reunion might have had. Clinker's false rescue
of Matthew Bramble at Scarborough belongs to this category as does the
slap administered afterwards (p. 184). During the real rescue, there is also
a piece of quasislapstick which puts Winifred's life in danger. Clinker
leaves her right in the middle of the river in order to fly to the aid of
Bramble who is still a prisoner in the waterlogged coach (p. 313).

Nowadays practical jokes and slapstick provoke a smile of amused
pity in the professional or academic critic, who is generally imprisoned in
the distinguished intellectual's aesthetic straitjacket. And yet these structures, rudimentary indeed, but full of an exuberant vitality — sadly absent
from the dismal hypercerebral elucubrations now in fashion — show how
keenly Smollett was aware of the tastes and excesses of his century.
Kenrick, in a satirical play prohibited in 1752, *Fun*, thus sums up, not
without caricatural exaggeration, the exploits required of a young fop if
he is to be looked up to by others of his kind:

> And then to be truly humorous, you must steal Trinkets and Pocket-
> books from the Ladies, which your are to keep for the Jest's sake; —
> then, Sir, you are to bilk Taverns, — tumble the Waiters down Stairs,
> — break all the Glasses in your Way, — sally into the Street, — take

all the young Women you meet for Whores, and kick the old ones into the Kennel, — knock down the Watch, — lie all Night in *Covent-garden Round-house*, — be carried before the Justice, where you have nothing to do but to prove your Father a Gentleman, and the old Dog his Worship will stand by you in abusing all the World. — This, my Boy, is true Humour[9].

This very pragmatical definition agrees with an even more concise and satirical one by Fielding who, in the *Covent-Garden Journal* of January 14th 1752, speaks of contemporary humour as 'Scandalous Lies, Tumbling and Dancing on the Rope'. So Kenrick and Fielding, like Smollett, were conscious of a certain brutality in the jokes of their time. And Smollett, far from approving of these often dubious practical jokes and bouts of slapstick — although he narrates them with complaisant verve, especially in *Peregrine Pickle* — takes refuge in a vague neutrality. The more or less explicit purpose of this mechanical comedy is to make the accomplice reader laugh as much at the expense of the victims as of the perpetrators of these jokes. It would therefore be unjust to see in Smollett only a buffoon indulging in low comedy.

Moreover the technical virtuosity of his comic sequences would be enough to discredit this erroneous notion. Smollett harps on consequences which soon go beyond the original jokes and come very near, after several comic developments, to a more or less tragic ending. The antique banquet in *Peregrine Pickle*, itself made up of a structural sequence of minor practical jokes, forms part of a chain of comic incidents of which the painter Pallet is the principal victim. On leaving the banquet, Peregrine 'rendered frolicksome with the wine he had drank' (p. 243) decides to go to a masked ball in company with Pallet dressed up as a woman. This first idea is not lacking in humour, since Pallet has just been fulminating against the homosexual practices of two of the guests. The comic elements link up with inexorable logic. Pallet, soon lost in the crowd, is tortured by a diuretic need which his feminine attire prohibits from satisfying 'so that he was obliged to suffer the most racking pangs of retention' (p. 244). Driven by this physiological need, Pallet ends by retiring into a place reserved for men, which provokes the scandalised astonishment of the spectators and also some unseemly advances from an impudent nobleman who gets his face furiously slapped by Pallet. This brawl causes Pallet and Peregrine, when they at last come together again, to be arrested by the musketeers when they leave the hall and to find themselves in the Bastille. Though Peregrine takes refuge in the outraged arrogance of an Englishman sure of his rights, Pallet, who is still disguised, is terrified. Peregrine takes advantage of this to make Pallet believe that his release depends on the definite sacrifice of his virility (p. 252). Pallet, though he does not suspect for a moment that Peregrine is teasing him, is clearheaded enough to realise the tragi-comic concatenation of which he is the victim. Nevertheless, the incident has assumed diplomatic proportions. The prisoners are at last set free, but Pallet, in a final comic development, is convinced that it is a matter of escaping and his fears of being recaptured transform him into a grotesque puppet (pp. 254–5).

This example, analysed in detail, enables one to appreciate a fundamental element in these comic concatenations: the extreme condensation of time, not to say its virtual disappearance. Time is so nearly completely abolished that it no longer checks the course of events. The same phenomenon of atemporality can be analysed in another episode in *Peregrine Pickle* (pp. 649–50) where the authors, panic-stricken by a fire alarm, jump out of the window of the inn where they are holding a meeting and, in doing so, one of them knocks over a handsome effeminate youth. In the space of a few lines, the crowd maltreats the ephebe, and Peregrine takes pity on him and escorts him to the house of an apothecary. The latter takes advantage of his patient's being delirious for a fortnight to present him with a very heavy bill when he recovers. In *Launcelot Greaves*, the sailor Crowe's chivalric mania leads to a series of comic episodes already analysed in the study of the sources and the structure of that novel. But in *Launcelot Greaves* the condensation of time is less noticeable, even if only because it was published as a serial. The perfected method reappears in *Humphry Clinker* in two forms. On the one hand, there is the purely mechanical concatenation: Clinker and his series of bungles – 'repeated blunders' (p. 84) – during the first meal when he waits on Tabitha and Matt. Nevertheless, even in this first case, the consequences are not solely mechanical. Clinker's blunders have very nearly provoked a family and psychological rupture between Matt and his virago of a sister. The comedy of this situation borders on the dramatic, but the deep consequence of this explosion is the still timorous beginning of Matt's liberation. On the other hand Smollett uses a comic structure in which material and psychological causes are interwoven. Although, at the beginning, the quarrel at Lord Oxmington's is due to Bramble's obstinate touchiness (p. 282), it subsequently involves a series of physical incidents (with psychological repercussions) at the expense of Lismahago (pp. 283–4). Thus the comic concatenations give the mechanical devices a literary dimension of more subtle complexity than practical jokes and slapstick.

The last mechanical comic device which Smollett employs is that of graphic caricature to delineate certain of his characters. It is a forced grin, almost a grimace, that he provokes from his readers when they are confronted with the merciless distorting mirror of these creatures who are so hideous that they almost exceed the limit of the tolerable in nightmarishness. In the realm of caricature, Smollett's creative genius, instead of becoming more sober and disciplined, remains as savage in *Humphry Clinker* as in *Roderick Random*. His pen does not draw, it slashes into the living flesh, sharp-edged as the scalpel of a surgeon stricken with aesthetic madness. He does not engrave his caricatures with the burin of his humour, he hacks them out with the axe of his episodic misanthropy. The horrible and the monstrous are never far absent from these caricatures, and for this reason it is occasionally permissible, in spite of their author's obvious intentions, to doubt their comic value. Smollett delights in drawing two types of caricature: the curvilinear silhouettes, like those of Crab and Miss Snapper in *Roderick Random*, and the elongated ones like Trunnion and the Quixotesque Lismahago. The caricature of Crab (I, 36–7) evinces a keen sense of graphic composition; the stomach, the face, the nose and its carbuncles, are so many curves which combine to exaggerate the obese rotundities of the Scottish surgeon. As to the unfortunate Miss Snapper, the generous curves of her bosom are counterbalanced by the hump on her back and, as if these deformities were not enough for her, Smollett feels the need to add to them: 'I perceived that Miss had got more twists from nature, than I had before observed, for she was bent sideways in the figure of an S, so that her progression very much resembled that of a crab' (II, 161). Trunnion and Lismahago are of the same caricatural calibre. Tall, but both stooping, lean, with a mutilated face or a skull in a sorry state, these long-legged caricatures are only silhouettes sketched with extreme graphic economy, yet they imprint themselves firmly on the reader's imagination. Their general similarity, after an interval of twenty years, proves the existence of indelible caricatural structures in Smollett's comic art.

Like all caricaturists, Smollett exploits the antithetical nature of this graphic method: caricature implies both the exaggeration of natural features and their reduction to a limited number. He seems to do his utmost to distort the natural and organic significance of the features of the human countenance. His caricatures of old maids, Mrs Grizzle in *Peregrine Pickle* and Tabitha in *Humphry Clinker*, do not have, according to the current expression, which here has a genuine meaning, a 'human face'. Like a demented demiurge, he sets to work on the mouth, eyes and complexion of Mrs Grizzle (p. 2) whose lightning caricature is only the rough preliminary sketch of Tabitha's. Jery draws up a merciless and detailed catalogue of his aunt's physical defects (p. 60). Being herself a scraggy, elongated caricature, she can only marry a similar scarecrow, to wit Lismahago. When Smollett decides to enhance his caricatures he uses a palette daubed with the gaudiest, most violently clashing colours, as in that grotesque description of Lismahago's Red Indian wife (p. 195). With Smollett, the art of caricature embraces every degree from the ludicrous to the grotesque and ventures so far into the horrible that it risks being submerged by it. He has the secret of those caricatural vignettes, dashed off in a few lines, but which stick in the reader's memory. How can one forget Ulic Mackilligut and his one-eyed, lame dancing-master (p. 29), or that portrait of Isaac Rapine, the Jewish moneylender, side by side with the wrinkled baboon face with which Smollett endows Weazel in *Roderick*

Random (I, 70–1)? Even the people who are not wholly caricatures bear the stamp of a deliberate comic exaggeration and reduction. If it is possible to establish a caricatural kinship between Mrs Grizzle and Tabitha, and between Trunnion and Lismahago, it is also possible to discern graphic similarities between Strap, Crabshaw (the least flattered of the three) and Clinker. Smollett's caricatural automatism stresses the same features, in particular the nutcracker chin, of these three servants. But Smollett does not always control his liking for caricatural exaggeration and when he lets it have free rein it tends towards the most repulsive form of ugliness. Human features are erased to give place to shapeless faces, monstrous lumps of swollen flesh like Pallet's hirsute visage smeared with cosmetics (p. 251) or Crowe's face which swelling and bruises have transformed into a 'most hideous caricatura' (p. 138). Or else a caricatural phantom makes a fleeting appearance like that Boulogne cook in *Peregrine Pickle* (pp. 194–5), the emaciated brother of the one painted by Hogarth with his savage and Gallophobic brush in 'The Gate at Calais'.

This graphic vigour of Smollettian caricature largely explains the strengths and weaknesses of this comic device. The modern reader no doubt feels, more than Smollett's contemporaries who were used to laughing at physical deformities and madness, a certain uneasiness at this trituration of human features. Behind these grimacing caricatures of creatures so monstrous that the reader might think they came from another disquieting world, did Smollett wish to hide his arrogant contempt for humanity, which he considers to be as sordid as Swift does? The steadfastness of his moral purpose prevents him from sinking into final misanthropy, but nothing hinders one from thinking that these caricatures crystallise fits of cantankerous despair. However that may be, caricature is not the subtlest element in his novels nor the one most likely to succeed in resisting the critical attrition of time. Exaggerated caricature, amusing or not, is the kind that most quickly becomes outdated. Smollett is no exception to this rule of literary aesthetics. On the one hand, some of his caricatures, like that of the fox-hunting squire Sir Stentor Stile in *Ferdinand Count Fathom*, are less caricatures than caricatures of caricatures, in which the features of an already almost legendary type are exaggerated to the point of passing into the misty realm of literary mythology with no connection with reality. On the other hand the automatism of the comic methods employed by Smollett is so glaring that it invites parody, that form of caricature in the second degree. It is possible that Sterne's anonymous imitator, the author of *The Life and Opinions of Bertram Montfichet* (1761) had the antique banquet in *Peregrine Pickle* in mind when he describes, at the beginning of the second volume, a caricatural and satirical feast of the same kind. William Beckford, in *Azemia* (1797) openly admits that he parodies Smollett's Trunnion in the guise of his Captain Josiah Wappingshot 'a man far advanced in life — old, weather-beaten, and in almost all respects might have sat to any artist employed to make designs for Peregrine Pickle, so nearly did he resemble Commodore Trunnion'[10].

But, whatever the exaggerations of the caricature, they cannot hide the deeper and more complex mainsprings of Smollettian comedy, and, first and foremost, the interplay of innocence and vanity. It is above all in *Roderick Random*, that, in addition to Roderick and Strap in search of themselves and fortune on the highways of life, there appear those penniless innocents, such as Bowling, Melopoyn and the effervescent Irishman, Oregan. The innocence of these characters is comic in so far as it flatters the reader's sense of superiority by allowing him to indulge for a moment in the euphoric intellectual comfort of omniscience. Besides his comic virtues as a sailor lost among landsmen, Bowling embodies the very type of the innocent let loose in a hostile world which he hardly knows, and understands even less. As soon as he appears in *Roderick Random*, Smollett warns his reader that Bowling is 'entirely ignorant not only of the judge's disposition, but also unacquainted with the ways of men in general, to which his education on board had kept him an utter stranger' (I, 11). Hope, based on the shakiest foundations, inspires the serene confidence of the two letters which Bowling writes to Potion and to Roderick after his duel with Oakum (I, 31). Not for one single instant does Bowling doubt that, if his case is laid before the King, the latter 'will not suffer an honest tar to be wronged', any more than that 'Potion will take care of you, for the love he bears to me' (ibid.). Bowling's comic innocence consists in projecting the simple courage of his own good-heartedness on to others. Such a form of innocence is comic because it betrays a profound ignorance of the world of sordid human realities, while assuming the calm assurance of experience. Even when his difficulties become hopelessly complicated, Bowling remains just as confident of his eventual success. The stylistic examination of his optimistic remarks, when Roderick meets him again in Boulogne, reveals a volatile mixture of startling assertions, chimerical suppositions, barely tempered by a few expressions of doubt, and a pseudological arrangement of conjunctions stressing the stages of his argument with all the more force the less convincing they are (II, 25). Even Roderick, who prides himself on an alleged greater knowledge of the world, cannot help smiling at the self-confidence of such innocence.

The same antithetical comic structure is discernible in the words and deeds of Dr Wagtail, Oregan and Melopoyn. The first, in spite of his learning, is the dupe of ignorant practical jokers (II, 76–8) who abuse his simplicity and credulity. Oregan is the enthusiastic victim of his own innocence, laced with a considerable dash of Irish vanity. How could Roderick dare to trespass on his amorous preserves, even though his right to consider the lady already engaged to him boiled down to a few letters to the coquette, Melinda, which she had left unanswered? For Oregan, his matrimonial and financial desires are already a reality which must at all costs be defended, even with ludicrous weapons (II, 103—5). As to Melopoyn, he rests all his hopes of seeing his tragedy at last accepted on a scaffolding of personal contacts as rickety as Bowling's (II, 244). Melopoyn's frustrated innocence is so crystal-clear in the purity of its intentions that it can cheerfully assume some fleeting glints of black humour. Reduced to desperate financial straits by the shillyshallying of his alleged patrons, he finds himself forced to prostitute his literary talent. In the eighteenth century, just as nowadays, the sensational press enabled many a pot to be kept boiling. Thus Melopoyn declares:

> [I] . . . published an apparition, on the substance of which I subsisted very comfortably a whole month: I have made many a good meal upon a monster; a rape has often afforded me great satisfaction; but a murder, well timed, was my never-failing resource (II, 237).

Without counting the principal heroes, who have all more or less to conquer their pride in order to adapt themselves to the humiliations of everyday life, the vain and their pretensions feature largely in Smollett's novels. The phonetic vanity of that Scot, Mr Concordance, who claims to teach English pronounciation in London (I, 95—6), and expresses himself in appalling jargon; the intellectual vanity of those *virtuosi* who invent crazy theories about coinage or natural history under the sardonic eye of Peregrine (pp. 660—5); the genealogical vanity of Mrs Grizzle in *Peregrine Pickle* (p. 3), repeated and amplified in the person of Tabitha, ever ready to boast of the antiquity of her Welsh ancestry; the pathetic aesthetic vanity, in *Peregrine Pickle*, of the painter Pallet, the doctor with a passion for Greek literature, or again of that stupid Dutch collector, bursting with satisfaction over his pitiful lumber-room of miscellaneous junk; finally, the social vanity of those families of parvenus in *Launcelot Greaves* who make lamentably clumsy efforts to ape aristocratic distinction (p. 21). Though vanity is not the exclusive prerogative of women, they are certainly not immune from it, whether aristocrats like Lady Vane, middle-class like Tabitha, or servants like Win Jenkins. Tabitha's vanity is emphasised by her incredible stupidity, the extreme form of innocence. This model housewife — as she, at least, regards herself — is astonished and even indignant that the thunder should have dared to get into her cellar when there was a padlock on the door (p. 45). As for Win, her provincial ignorance and her superstitious beliefs serve as a foil to her aesthetic, sartorial, religious and social vanity. The worthy servant, as the anonymous author of the apocryphal sequel to *Humphry Clinker*, *Brambleton Hall* (1810) well realises, has the makings of a redoubtable snob, as is proved in her last letter, in which she is bursting with satisfaction at seeing herself at last 'removed to a higher spear' (p. 353), an ambiguous exaltation to say the least of it. For these two women, there is no comic catharsis at the end of *Humphry Clinker*, they remain exactly as they are, ludicrous bottle-imps, perpetually bobbing up and down between innocence and vanity.

The second great mainspring of Smollettian comedy is the more or less detailed description, according to the individual case, of the manias, foibles and obsessions which characterise the inappropriate behaviour of eccentrics. This is a large family with many ramifications running from Narcissa's aunt in *Roderick Random* to Matthew Bramble and Lismahago in *Humphry Clinker* and including Trunnion and Crabtree in *Peregrine Pickle* as well as the elegant Minikin in *Launcelot Greaves*, not to mention Launcelot and Crowe. Not only does the importance of these characters vary, but also their degree of eccentricity, which, for example, is strong and permanent in Narcissa's aunt and Trunnion, episodic in Bramble, temporary in Launcelot and Crowe. To describe these characters, Smollett often used the term 'original', but he might just as well describe them as 'humourists' in the meaning Corbyn Morris gives to this word in his work, little known even in the eighteenth century, *An Essay towards Fixing the True Standards of Wit, Humour, Raillery, Satire and Ridicule* (1744). Corbyn Morris defines humour as 'any whimsical Oddity or Foible, appearing in the Temper or Conduct of a Person in real Life', a sketch which he completes some ten pages later:

> For Humour extensively and fully understood, is any remarkable Oddity or Foible belonging to a Person in Real Life; whether this Foible be constitutional, habitual, or only affected; whether partial in one or two Circumstances; or tinging the whole Temper and Conduct of the Person[11].

This is a definition halfway between Jonson's *humours* and the theory of the ruling passion dear to Pope. Corbyn Morris insists on this ambivalent eccentricity characteristic of those 'humourists', who, like Matthew Bramble, conceal a sensitiveness always liable to be touched on the raw under a deliberate rough and gruff exterior. The first eccentric character who appears in Smollett's work is Narcissa's aunt, introduced in advance by Mrs Sagely (I, 311—12). Her erudite, mystical and poetic pre-occupations leave her little leisure to bother about the elegance, or even the cleanliness of her clothes (II, 1—2). Her absent-mindedness, the legendary sign of a profound mind, provides Smollett with the opportunity for traditional, but always effective, comic incidents, as do her pathological foibles (II, 6—7). The comedy of poetic lines, so ferocious that they become burlesque, acquires a subtle humorous value if — as according to H. S. Buck[12] it is permissible to think — Smollett is quoting and parodying his own *Regicide* in these two pages. But, without any possible literary doubt, Trunnion carries off the palm of eccentricity in the whole of Smollett's work. It is not only his nautical language (studied further on) but his behaviour, systematically inappropriate to the most commonplace situations of everyday life, which creates the comic aura of this character. The audacity, and the success, of Smollett lies in his having pushed to the extreme, with a rigorous logic, all the manias of the former Commodore until they collapse into absurdity. The famous scene of the tacking ride on horseback, in which Trunnion goes to church while scrupulously observing the rules of navigation, derives its comic power from a series of overlapping structures. To begin with, these pages of equestrian navigation (pp. 36–41) are prepared for right from the Commodore's first appearance on the scene, fiercely rebuking Lieutenant Hatchway for not having been able to handle the gig in which they have arrived, not without difficulty, at the inn (pp. 7–8). The marriage of two originals like Trunnion and Mrs Grizzle is enough in itself to arouse the reader's comic expectation. Later, the spectacle of Trunnion and his men in the saddle promptly conjures up the ridiculous image of the sailor on horseback, that legendary worst of riders. The application of the rules of navigation to a simple journey on land produces comedy on three levels. Negation of all commonsense, obstinate respecting of rules which have no connection with the real situation, and finally the material consequences of this deliberate blindness: such are the three comic structures of this passage. Later, Smollett, whose comic invention was at the top of its form, adds Trunnion's fantastic ride, in which he is hopelessly at the mercy of his treacherous mount's ardour for hunting. This is, in some sort, the comic revenge of the animal on the man who, in the first instance, regards his horse as an object incapable of taking the least initiative. Lastly, Trunnion, already made a fool of by a brute beast, is the victim of the horse-dealing sharp practice of a huntsman who buys some excellent hunters back from him at the price of broken-winded screws. Finally, it must be emphasised that Trunnion, like nearly all Smollett's eccentrics, is conspicuous for the outlandish way he dresses (pp. 38–9). The eccentricity of Pallet and the Doctor is only partial. Smollett is aiming, through these two characters, at the aesthetic and literary fads of sham enthusiasts. As to Crabtree, his misanthropy drives him to adopt an eccentric *method* (his feigned deafness) in order the better to unmask human imposture. The opposite of Trunnion, who has no control over his passions, Crabtree is not an impulsive eccentric but a deliberate one, who has trained himself to absolute mastery of his reactions, especially of his laugh (p. 545). Minikin, one of the few comic characters in *Ferdinand Count Fathom*, is entirely different. Smollett endows this original with a wealth of physical and sartorial peculiarities (pp. 182–3). This Captain compensates for his small size by the apparent breadth of his culture, for his conversation consists mainly of a 'series of quotations from the English poets, interlarded with French phrases, which he retained for their significance, on the recommendation of his friends, being himself unacquainted with that or any other outlandish tongue' (p. 183).

Smollett excels in producing comic effects from this patchwork of ludicrous erudition. Moreover, in spite of his far from brilliant situation,

Minikin, from the depths of his prison, remains fascinated by the glamour of fashion, of which he considers himself the arbiter (p. 186). Right to the end of his career, Smollett was attracted by this dubious battle between the mechanical and the living: Launcelot's chivalric mania and Crowe's periodic obsession by it, in the name of an anachronistic ideal of courtesy, tend, without succeeding, to reduce these two men to human automatons. But this mechanism run mad also enables them to regain their sanity. Such a hope is denied to the wretched Grub Street hacks to whom Mr S . . . offers hospitality every Sunday in *Humphry Clinker*. These needy quill-drivers are mercilessly jeered at by Smollett, who revels in bringing out the comedy of the systematic contradictions between their personality and their literary works. The atheist is employed in refuting Bolingbroke's metaphysics, the Scotsman — no doubt of the same family as Concord-ance in *Roderick Random* — teaches English pronunciation, the practical joker, Tim Cropdale, has just finished a tragedy (pp. 126–7), to mention only three of this 'assemblage of originals' (p. 124). All are remarkable, not only for the way they dress, but above all for the foibles they deliber-ately affect. One wears spectacles, in spite of his exceptionally keen eye-sight, another uses crutches in spite of being extremely agile, a third affects absent-mindedness. Smollett explains that these affectations soon turn into habits. Comedy and quasitragedy rub elbows and end in be-coming indissolubly mingled; the comedy of these poor starvelings who ape a physical defect and the quasitragedy of their voluntary slavery from which they derive a pathetic vainglory. In their case, eccentricity is the sole creative talent of failures.

The third psychological mainspring of Smollettian comedy is profes-sional alienation. In doctors and lawyers it takes the form of an almost total inability to express themselves except in their technical idiolect, whether it is appropriate to the situation or not. In sailors, who by far outnumber men of other callings in Smollett's novels, it produces not only a linguistic alienation but also a comic inability to see the world from any angle but that of their nautical profession.

Doctors have always been a readymade object of ridicule for the sarcasm of writers. The presumption of these mortals, the last theoretical and professional rampart against death, confers an ambiguous role on them. If medical science is imperfect, it nevertheless constitutes the supreme hope in our despair as mortals. So, on the one hand, the strong-minded (in good health in the majority of cases, but not in Smollett's) are not deceived by the blasphemous pretension of the doctor who has the audacity to fight against death; but — and this is the second and subtler level of comedy — on the other hand, man, conscious of his ontological misery, refuses to his last breath to accept the metaphysical scandal of returning to nothingness. Laughing at doctors, in particular at their language, is to give oneself the double thrill of blasphemy against God and against oneself, since laughter, in this case, implies both the recognition and the denial of our inescapable condition of being doomed to die. Finally, one must remember, in Smollett's particular case, the auto-biographical echoes already discerned in this constant determination, throughout his work, to ridicule his colleagues. Frequent recourse to medical Latin, or to a language rich in words of Latin origin, fulfilled the double antithetical function of facilitating communication between specialists of different nationalities and limiting this knowledge by invest-ing it with a mysterious character, not devoid of suggestions of magic. It is this last aspect of obscurantist linguistic pedantry, often *ad captandum vulgus* which aroused Thomas Brown's attacks in *Amusements Serious and Comical* (1700) and Fielding's in *Joseph Andrews* and *Tom Jones*, to mention only these two authors. With a comic lucidity, which Smollett inherited half a century later, Brown comments on the abuse of medical jargon: 'The language that is spoken here is very learned; but the people that speak it are very ignorant ... it looks as if *Physicians* learnt their *Gibberish* for no other purpose, than to embroil what they do not understand'[13].

There follows a comic description of those grave practitioners who, after having taken their fees to the last and despatched their patient to the other world 'like a rat with a straw in his arse' (p. 89), hasten to declare that anyhow the sick man's constitution was rotten to the core. As to the doctors' accomplices, the apothecaries, Brown is just as hard on their professional conscience as Smollett is on Lavement's:

> Of all our late pretended *alchymists*, recommend me to the *apothe-caries*, as the noblest *operators* and *chemists*; for out of *toads, vipers*, and a *sirreverence* itself, they will fetch ye gold ready minted, which is more than ever *Paracelsus* himself pretended to (p. 90).

The doctor who has examined Joseph Andrews diagnoses a simple contusion in a language that is far from simple, but promptly raises a smile or a laugh (Book i, Chapter xiv). In similar circumstances, the doctor who treats Tom Jones launches into such Latinising gibberish that it does not even have the effect of disturbing the landlady and her materialistic commonsense (Book viii, Chapter iii). The learned language employed by Dr Wagtail (II, 76) produces its comic effect more by its prolixity than its pedantry. This character, whom Smollett does not treat too harshly, is a dupe on two counts: the dupe of his theoretical knowledge without any practical good sense, and the dupe of his confidence in others. The attacks against medicine and medical practitioners in *Peregrine Pickle* and *Ferdinand Count Fathom* belong more to the realm of satire than to the comedy of professional alienation, and the language used plays a minor part. Conversely, Smollett exerts himself to the full in a stylistic feat of astounding comic verbal virtuosity in the tirade of the quack doctor, Ferret. Quackery, by its very nature, involves, when pushed to extremes, the use of a pseudo-medical language whose purpose is not to communicate knowledge but, on the contrary, to conceal the absence of it by a torrent of verbiage which is an end in itself. The comedy of this tirade — a piece of conjurer's patter — lies mainly in the use of vigorous negations and denegations which lead in turn to a series of such rapid enumerations that Ferret can allow himself to skip the logical connections of the argument in spite of deploying very obvious coordinating conjunctions. Repetitions and the accumulation of verbiage help to lull the attention of the audience, whom Ferret openly ridicules, on the one hand by insulting it — 'I shall not pretend to disturb your understandings, which are none of the strongest' — on the other by subjecting it to a verbal bombardment of obscure medical terms (pp. 79—80). Ferret also displays a quack's contempt for the great names of medicine, ancient or more recent: 'that wiseacre Dioscorides', 'that crazy commentator Galen', 'that mad scoundrel Paracelsus', 'that visionary Van Helmont' (ibid.). He thus appeals to the vanity of the most stupid, who feel flattered at being in the presence of a man erudite enough to pulverise theories which had been accepted for centuries. This trick belongs to the level of elementary psychological comedy, but is coupled with a second ludicrous piece of dupery; the presentation of a vague alchemical theory of which not one of the bumpkins present can understand a single word.

Finally, and this aspect has already been touched on, mingled all through the verbal and psychological comedy is a satirical attack on the government and its continental policy. This constant switching from medical charlatanism to the accusation of political charlatanism gives these pages an exceptional, yet unappreciated, comic dimension.

It is fair to point out elsewhere, in *Launcelot Greaves*, the presence of a somewhat churlish doctor whose originality consists in rejecting the abuse of contemporary pharmacopoeia, and whose vocabulary is decidedly unmedical, whereas the apothecary's is larded with technical terms (p. 133). The scepticism of this doctor is summed up in a medic's cacemphaton: 'A f . . . t for your borborygmata' (ibid.). Right up to his last novel, and in spite of (or because of?) his failing health, Smollett continues to exploit the linguistic alienation of doctors. Dr Linden's remarks, reported by Jery, are strewn with English and Latin medical expressions (pp. 18—19), repeated with indignation, and also disquiet, by Bramble (pp. 24—5). His reactions are nevertheless partly comic. The incantatory effects of medical formulas are such that, in spite of his irascible scepticism, Bramble feels worried by Dr Linden's (doubtless erroneous) assertions. He cannot prevent himself from defending, in a half-reassured postscript, his own diagnosis of his illness (p. 25). The surgeon hastily summoned to Burdock's bedside pontificates with enough assurance to persuade the wife and the son that he is right, as opposed to the apothecary Grieve, who uses no learned words, but nevertheless gives a sensible diagnosis (pp. 165—6).

Legal language makes several, but almost always comic, appearances in Smollett's novels. To the sesquipedalian comedy of Latin words and derivatives and the fixed expressions of Anglo-Norman Common Law must be added the deplorable reputation of lawyers in the eighteenth century, in which their proliferation and their pettifogging rapacity rendered them an easy target for authors in search of comic subjects. It is only with a blush, and much against his will, that Tom Clarke admits, at the beginning of *Launcelot Greaves*, that he is an attorney (p. 2). But legal language lends itself, even more than medical, to bawdy or ribald implications as the facetious lawyer's tirade in *Joseph Andrews* proves (Book i, Chapter xii). It is also during a journey in a coach that this legal language capable of several interpretations first appears in *Roderick Random*. Smollett plays on the words 'conveyancer' and the expression 'settlement in tail' (II, 161) whose phallic connotations are made clear on the following page by these words addressed to a gallant Captain who has not been able to capture the fort, from lack of time: 'If he had suffered a *nisi prius* through the obstinacy of the defendant, he might have an opportunity to join issue at the next stage.'

It is in *Launcelot Greaves*, written at a time when Smollett had a bone to pick with the law, that legal language is most frequently met with, if only because of the profession of Tom Clarke, one of the principal, although episodic, characters. This language is not monolithic but, on the contrary, presents different levels, depending on the particular kind of comic effect Smollett seeks to produce. On the most obvious level, the author of *Launcelot Greaves* does his utmost to play on the purely technical meaning of the terms employed and their systematic accumulation. It is a matter of stunning the non-specialist readers with a verbal volley of such intensity that he can no longer follow the thread of the brilliantly conducted argument. Faced with his own incapacity, the reader takes to smiling or laughing at this language he cannot grasp. This reaction is a psychological defence mechanism in which laughter evades the real issue by reducing the paralysing obstacle to nothing. Such is the comic level of that page (p. 5) where Tom Clarke and Ferret exchange their technical opinions about the inheritance of which Crowe has been despoiled. This comic method is akin to the effects created by Edward Lear, Lewis Carroll or, more recently, Ogden Nash, who successfully exploited the more or less cerebral or visceral anti-intellectualism of the Anglo-Saxons, who are hypnotised by the interplay of creation and destruction in passages where nonsense triumphs. Tom Clarke pushes legal virtuosity to the verge of absurdity when, after his arbitrary imprisonment, he argues thus:

> to constitute robbery, there must be something taken; but, here nothing was taken but blows, and they were upon compulsion: even an attempt to rob, without any taking, is not felony but a misdemeanour. To be sure there is a taking in deed, and a taking in

law: but still the robber must be in possession of a thing stolen; and we attempted to steal nothing, but to steal ourselves away (pp. 83—4).

Behind these quibbles looms the spectre of verbal delirium but, above all, this legal logic pushed to the limit of absurdity makes the reader laugh.

However, it would be wrong to think that legal language does not occasionally fulfil its technical function. During their appearance before Judge Gobble, Tom Clarke and a colleague defend themselves with an efficient virtuosity about which there is nothing comic, except perhaps for the impression of speed of the crossfire of repartees with which they daze and overwhelm Gobble (pp. 96—7). But the bawdiness favoured by Tom Clarke's amorous nature is certainly never very far away. The expression 'in tail', already used by Fielding (in the passage referred to above) as well as by Smollett in *Roderick Random*, allows allusions which are shamelessly twice underlined: 'I seize Dolly in *tail* . . . I settle on Dolly in *tail*' (p. 5), remarks which wound the girl's uncomprehending sensitiveness and are repeated a few pages further on by bawdy comments in language both legal and nautical. Tom Clarke, being of a timorous disposition, thinks it prudent to disappear with Dolly when Launcelot Greaves makes his startling and dripping entrance. Crowe exclaims, 'hope in God a-has not bulged to, and gone to bottom'. To which Ferret replies, with his sour scepticism: 'Pish . . . there's no danger; the young Lawyer is only seizing Dolly in tail' (p. 9).

Finally, Smollett excels in reproducing, and parodying, the stylistic mannerisms of lawyers who are prone — from pomposity or prudence? — to rhetorical battology. The beginning of Tom Clarke's story (p. 18) is one of the numerous comic gems, small, but of the purest ray, scattered throughout *Launcelot Greaves*. After an aposiopesis, followed by a hesitation and a cliché, Tom Clarke launches forth thus: 'I shall tell, repeat, and relate a plain story — matters of fact, d'ye see, without rhetoric, oratory, ornament, or embellishment; without repetition, tautology, circumlocution, or going about the bush'. The rhythm and the comic dittology suggest a comparison with the linguistic style of Morgan in *Roderick Random*, minus the Welsh accent. It is almost a pity that Ferret's angry impatience so quickly interrupts this flight of burlesque rhetoric, but Tom Clarke's story no doubt gains thereby in precision and clarity.

The most striking comic idiolect remains that of the sailors who are among the best-known of Smollett's characters: Bowling, Trunnion, Hatchway, Pipes and Crowe. Though there is no sailor in *Ferdinand Count Fathom*, this comic type appears one last time in *Humphry Clinker*, very briefly, in the crippled shape of an old retired admiral (p. 55). Smollett was not the first to find these nautical terms, used to the exclusion of any other vocabulary and hardly comprehensible to uninitiated landsmen, comic. Ned Ward, in his *Wooden World* (1707), already remarks on the comic inability of a ship's captain to express himself without resorting to technical expressions of life on board:

> His language is all *Heathen Greek* to a Cobler; and he cannot have so much as a Tooth drawn ashore, without carrying his Interpreter. It is the aftmost Grinder aloft, on the Starboard Quarter, will he cry to the all-wondering Operator[14].

The high density of technical words does not entirely explain the comic potency of nautical language. One must add the slang of the crew and even, no doubt, of the officers, the traditional pronunciation which seems to have little connection with spelling, and finally the foreign words picked up at random in ports and more or less naturalised[15]. The linguistic habits of seamen were already being criticised in the eighteenth century, as is shown in an article published in *The Connoisseur* in 1755 on the conversation and behaviour of officers on shore: 'A voyage round the world frequently brutalizes the seaman, who comes home so rough and unpolished, that one would imagine he had not visited any nation in the world except the Savages, the *Chinese*, or the *Hottentots*'[16].

Finally, the very technicality of this language was liable to provoke acrid professional criticisms from more seasoned sailors than Smollett, whose fairly short sojourn on board a warship, in a very inferior and despised rank, could not have enabled him to assimilate all the mysteries of a profession which, apart from his special skill, he had never really practised himself. On this subject, William N. Glascock's article in his *Naval Sketch-Book*[17] contributes some important details and reservations on the real extent of Smollett's technical knowledge of manoeuvres and other naval duties. Glascock criticises 'the forced and inconsistent phraseology put into the mouths of his seamen' (p. 124) and reproaches Smollett for making all his sailors talk in the same extravagant metaphorical way, full of technical incongruities, of which he gives examples in *Roderick Random*, and, above all, in *Peregrine Pickle*, where Trunnion's last words are mercilessly scrutinised. It is impossible to ignore the observations of Captain Glascock, who served for many years in the Navy. But he himself realises that his criticisms are those of a specialist and, on the whole, Glascock — a first-rate sailor but a tenth-rate author of novels about sea-life — willingly stresses Smollett's comic talents. Glascock only repeats and develops the observations made in the *Critical Review* of May 1762 about *Launcelot Greaves* and, more particularly, about Crowe:

> Captain Crowe is a tar of as extraordinary a cast as either Bowling, Trunnion, Pipes, or Hatchway. His manners and dialect are purely those of the watry-element; yet both are perfectly original. It has been said that Shakespear has drawn a natural character in Caliban, not to be found in nature. We may with equal reason affirm, that Crowe is a true seaman that never existed, who talks in tropes and

figures borrowed from his profession, but never used before. In a word, the author has invented a language for this amphibious species, so extremely natural that nothing can be better adapted to express the character (xiii, 428—9).

One must pay homage to the literary and linguistic perspicacity of this critic. His analysis, rightly, puts Smollett beyond the reach of all technical stricture.

Smollett's intention in creating his sailor characters was not so much to record their ways of speech and life as to invent a comic idiom with a high density of technical terms. His sailors mainly appear when they have come ashore for good. Apart from the short scenes in *Roderick Random* in which Jack Rattlin, Crampley and Oakum (whose only slightly technical language is anything but comic) figure, or again Ben Block, Midshipman Haulyard and Lieutenant Lyon in *The Reprisal*, Smollett's sailors are as uncomfortable on land as fish out of water. The linguistic ivory tower in which they immure themselves does nothing to facilitate their relations with landsmen, but, on the contrary, increases their eccentric alienation and makes their loss of adaptability to the accepted manners and customs of life on *terra firma* comical. The comedy of these characters lies in the systematic application of nautical language to *all* situations of daily life, whether material, psychological or ethical. The nautical vocabulary of the steering and handling of a ship plays an important part in the remarks of these sailors, as well as the terms of practical metereology. Bowling uses 'to board' and the expression 'to shoot a-head' in the first sentence he utters (*Roderick Random*, I, 12)[18]. In his contentions with the judge, given the spontaneous hostility he encounters in his house, it is not surprising that he resorts to the vocabulary of boarding and chastisement (I, 13—16). During the punitive expedition against the schoolmaster, the jerky rhythm of Bowling's words (I, 24) is repeated and made choppier still to denote the brusque scamped diction of Crowe in *Launcelot Greaves*. The introduction of Trunnion in *Peregrine Pickle* also takes place under the aspect of boarding and in terms of a naval manoeuvre (pp. 4, 7—8) whereas Crowe's is more meteorological, but soon the vocabulary of action resumes its rights with the breathless account of a shipwreck (pp. 3—4). In this passage Crowe is not comic, properly speaking, on account of the technical expressions he uses to describe a naval operation, but on account of the extreme fragmentation of his speech which is a jumble of aposiopeseses, aporias, onomatopoeias and ellipses. Smollett draws attention several times to this defect in his elocution (pp. 2 and 51). Crowe, his most comical sailor, is also the one whose linguistic alienation seems the most complete. Smollett insists on the necessity of an interpreter in order to understand Crowe's highly specific idiolect, which he does not hesitate to describe as 'dialect' (p. 94). Captain Crowe is a novice 'particularly in those dialects of the English language which are used by the terrestrial animals of this kingdom' (p. 137). Just as in *Peregrine Pickle*, Smollett mingles the semantic fields of horsemanship and seamanship. Here is part of the description of an encounter between Crowe and other riders:

> He descried five or six men on horseback, bearing up full in his teeth; upon which he threw his sails a-back, and prepared for action ... when they came along-side, notwithstanding his hail, he ordered them to clew up their corses, and furl their top-sails, otherwise he would be foul of their quarters (p. 139).

The linguistic transposition is just as comic and complete when Crowe launches a chivalric challenge in this form: 'If so be as how you'll bear a hand and rig yourself, and take a short trip with me into the offing, we'll overhaul this here affair in the turning of a capstan' (pp. 150–1). Breaking a lance in the turn of a capstan is typical of Crowe's linguistic antics.

If material life is ill-suited to this constant resort to nautical language, psychological situations produce an even more pronounced comic discrepancy between the signifier and the signified. The sailors' opinions on women and love are characterised by robust practical commonsense coupled with a general but selective misogyny. Hatchway launches into a series of nautical comparisons and metaphors to express his low opinion of the feminine character:

> He said she was like a hurricane that never blows from one quarter, but veers about to all points of the compass: he likened her to a painted galley curiously rigged, with a leak in her hold, which her husband would never be able to stop (p. 15).

Trunnion compares Peregrine's affection for Emilia to a permanent anchorage (pp. 359–60). As for Crowe, his pragmatic conception of love, restricted to affairs on shore leave, is the grotesque antithesis of Launcelot's ethereal feelings for Aurelia. How can chastity be imposed on sailors?: 'that's not to be expected in a sailor just come a-shore, after a long voyage – sure all those poor hearts won't be damned for steering in the wake of nature' (p. 62). But, though Crowe is very willing to put into port with a companion like Bet Mizen, he refuses to be permanently anchored, at least he puts up a vigorous defence against it, just like Trunnion and Hatchway, who also end up by scuttling themselves in the mooring ground of matrimony (p. 182). Finally, Bowling's speech to his crew before an engagement (which does not take place) is a good example of eloquence couched almost entirely in concrete terms; in spite of the gravity of the situation, the reader cannot help smiling at the brave Bowling's effective oratorical skill (*Roderick Random*, II, 270).

Among ethical problems, death occupies an important place in the sailors' thoughts, whereas religion appears only as a vague corollary. Smollett achieves the feat of arousing laughter, the liberating sign of life, on the very threshold of death. The intentional discrepancy between the nautical jargon and the seriousness of the subject does not, at any time, seem cruel and grotesque, for the sailors who are speaking are either kindly fellows or else have the courage to face annihilation while still remaining true to themselves. Bowling's gruff kindliness on the one hand, and the old judge's crafty cruelty on the other, make it easier to excuse the sailor's brutally frank comments on the judge's approaching end. But, beyond any possible doubt, it is Trunnion's tirade on his deathbed that most judiciously allies pathos with a comedy which balances it evenly all through the passage without ever toppling it into gruesome farce. There is a similar exceptional tonality in the ex-Mistress Quickly's account of the death of Falstaff in *Henry V* (II, sc. 3). The technical errors denounced by Glascock matter little: in these pages (*Peregrine Pickle*, pp. 392–3) Smollett has managed to preserve enough metaphorical probability in Trunnion's remarks for the use of this nautical language not to detract from the solemnity of the scene. Conversely, this language created by Smollett retains just enough comic power to prevent the scene from collapsing into maudlin pathos. In spite of the dramatic tension, Hatchway permits himself 'a waggish sneer' which has the merit of making Trunnion smile. The variety of speech rhythms and the central metaphor of the final shipwreck happily counterbalance such comic verbal extravagances as: 'Swab the spray from your bowsprit, my good lad, and coil up your spirits. You must not let the top-lifts of your heart give way' (p. 392). The same subtle balance does not appear in the nautical epitaph Hatchway composes in memory of Trunnion (pp. 422–3). After an acceptable beginning, Hatchway launches into a metaphorical stylisation in dubious taste, all the more so since the sexual interpretation of several expressions and words is highly plausible, if not probable[19].

As to religious problems, Smollett's sailors display more awareness of hell than of heavenly bliss. The devil is a frequent subject of their dreams and hallucinations (*Roderick Random*, I, 18, 20). Crowe's piety is rudimentary, and during his vigil of arms in the church he would much rather sing 'Black-eyed Susan' than psalms (p. 55). Crowe describes Davy Jones, the mariners' version of Satan, and the torments of hell with the superstition of seagoing men (p. 61). The reader is completely convinced by his affirmation: 'Religion, I ha'n't much over-hauled' (p. 62). Quite naturally, he fulminates in meteorological terms when he discovers that the astrologer has not predicted the (supposed) murder of Launcelot: 'Hark ye, brother conjurer . . . you can spy foul weather before it comes, damn your eyes! why didn't you give us warning of this here squall?' (p. 183).

The constant use of nautical language is only a sign of a more profound alienation. From Bowling to Crowe, these men have only a narrow and comic vision of the world around them. Full of contempt for landsmen, they mistrust the whole species, and dread their rapacity and dishonesty. In spite of his apparent aggressiveness, Bowling is always on the alert. Faced with the assembled family, he cries: 'None of your tricks upon travellers' (I, 18), an expression he repeats in Boulogne before he recognises his nephew, Roderick (II, 22). The sailors come on shore with all their accustomed ways of dressing, eating and so on — as the beginning of *Peregrine Pickle* proves — and with their physical or psychological idiosyncrasies. Hatchway displays his gastronomic virtuosity at Trunnion's wedding (p. 43). Trunnion is not only crippled, but his body is deformed by life on board: 'He was in stature at least six feet high, tho' he had contracted an habit of stooping, by living so long on board' (p. 7). Though this deformity has nothing comic about it (at least for the modern reader) Crowe's professional idiosyncrasy can only raise a smile. For Crowe, the *ne plus ultra* in residential comfort and elegance is to be found in Wapping, in the immediate neighbourhood of the docks and their noisy activity: 'the sweet sound of mooring and unmooring ships in the river' (p. 162). Crowe might pass for a poet, had not Smollett taken care also to mention, among other charms of the place, the presence of 200 pigs of a brewery.

Smollett's sailors are eternally homesick for their closed world, misfits whose inability to adapt themselves to the commonplace demands of shore life is more comic than pathetic. From Bowling to Crowe, there is a progressive decline into caricature, if only on the linguistic plane. Whereas Bowling was able to adapt himself, more or less, to the family situation he finds in Scotland and to take steps to remedy it, Trunnion and his comrades are literally, as well as metaphorically, entrenched in their garrison where they recreate the rites and rhythms of life at sea. As for Crowe, it is improbable that he would even be able to make himself understood without the intermediary of his nephew. Nevertheless, the vitality, good nature and generosity of these men earns them the amused affection of the reader. The laughter they provoke is not in the least cruel, but, on the contrary, marks the visceral and ontological will of man to abolish the finality of death. To laugh at a professional or, linguistic alienation is also to deny it and to annihilate the prospect of a deadly mechanisation of the human being. There can only be comedy here, where man walks in the valley of the shadow of death, even the partial death of this paralysis of alienation.

The richest and most original aspect of Smollettian humour is the verbal and stylistic interplay which constitutes the very warp and woof of fictional life in all the novels, from *Roderick Random* to *Humphry Clinker*. In this study, the word 'humour' is taken in its widest sense, with no concern for a restrictive, and, when all is said and done, unenlightening definition. Humour appears as the obstinate affirmation of an individual dynamism which triumphs in spite of the servitude of our human condition and the constraints of society. It enables man to abolish reality for a few moments, by means of a liberating smile or laugh. Its characteristics are so varied and protean that any attempt at definition, however complete, can only mutilate its fluctuating reality. Can one hope to put a fragment of a rainbow in a cage?

The verbal methods employed by Smollett are not, any more than mechanical comedy or psychological mainsprings, completely original. Shakespeare juggles with mutilations due to ignorance and dialectal speech, including foreigners' doubtful pronunciation of English, especially when spoken by a Frenchman like Dr Caius in *The Merry Wives of Windsor*. Bottom the weaver and Quince the carpenter in *A Midsummer Night's Dream* use words of Latin origin in the wrong sense: 'defect' for 'effect', 'disfigure' for 'prefigure' — 'He comes to disfigure, or to present, the person of Moonshine' says Quince in Act III, scene 1 — 'odious' for 'odorous'. Launcelot Gobbo and his father, in *The Merchant of Venice*, also maltreat these same words of Latin etymology: 'affection' becomes 'infection' (II, sc. 2), 'certify' is concealed behind the hapax 'frutify' (ibid.). In *Much Ado about Nothing*, Dogberry does not so much deform words as systematically use them in the wrong sense as soon as they have the least homonymy: 'Dost thou not suspect my place? Does thou not suspect my years?' he cries instead of 'respect' (IV, 2; see also III, 5). But the Shakespearian ancestress of Win Jenkins is Mistress Quickly, the servant in *The Merry Wives of Windsor* who reappears as the hostess of a tavern in *Henry IV*, Part ii. With Hugh Evans, the Welsh parson and Doctor Caius, the French physician whom Falstaff describes as 'One that makes fritters of English' (V, 5), Judge Shallow and his cousin Slender, this play is the richest in verbal and comic inventions. Semantic mistakes — 'Be not so phlegmatic' says Mistress Quickly to her master Dr Caius in Act I, scene 4, when she means the opposite 'choleric' — and also almost complete deformation of words: 'melancholy' in Mistress Quickly's mouth becomes 'allicholy' (I, 4), while Shallow, the judge, calls himself 'Custalorum' instead of 'Custos Rotulorum', a title which Slender transforms into 'Roto-lorum' (I, 1), almost two centuries before Tabitha subjects it to another comic transformation: 'crusty ruttleorum' (p. 192) — these misuses are brilliantly mingled in this play. It is in *Henry IV*, Part ii, that Shakespeare pushes the discrepancy between the real and the intended meaning furthest. Mistress Quickly disguises 'homicidal' under 'honeysuckle' and 'homicide' under 'honey-seed' (II, 1). Smollett's more immediate predecessor, Fielding, makes Mrs Slipslop, in *Joseph Andrews*, murder the English language with her comic mangling of difficult or quite ordinary words. For Fielding, any kind of pretentious affectation (linguistic, social or philosophical) is *the* great source of comedy, and he does not fail to define Slipslop as 'a mighty affecter of hard words' (Book i, Chapter iii). There again, it is particularly words of Latin origin that Mrs Slipslop mutilates: 'necessary' is changed into 'necessitous' and 'insult' into 'result' — 'Do you intend to result my passion?' she asks the innocent Joseph (Book i, Chapter vi) — 'accommodate' into 'incommodate', and 'interfere' into 'hinterfear' (Book iv, Chapter i).

Before analysing the verbal and stylistic interplay in Smollettian comedy, it is necessary to stress that the humour of distortion is not the only kind to be found in the five novels, but must be set in relation to the witticisms with which Smollett enhances certain passages. Moreover this comic interplay derives its effect from the polysemy which he gives to his verbal creations. Finally, it is wrong to think that Smollett's comic invention is suddenly revealed in *Humphry Clinker*. Even as early as *Roderick Random*, there are tentative verbal deformations which have comic merit and the mechanical methods used in this first novel have not disappeared from the last.

Smollett's reputation as a comic author cannot be based on his handling of wit. His witticisms, as much by their quality as their quantity, can only occupy a small place in the structure of his comedy. Very few of the characters are naturally *endowed* with wit, they *manipulate* it either as a means of attack or self-defence, or in the course of organised verbal contests. Miss Snapper compensates for her lack of physical charms by resorting to sharp-tongued witticisms. Her first victim is a bragging soldier whom she reduces to silence in a few swift thrusts of this weapon (*Roderick Random*, II, 150). The dialogue is transformed into a sarcastic stychomythia. One word leads to another with an unpredictable, brilliant capriciousness: 'Quakers' provoke 'the spirit of folly begins to move', 'out with it' leads to 'midwife' which in turn induces 'delivered', 'mouse' and 'fool', not to mention the double kinetic and obstetric meaning of 'to be *far gone with*'. Beau Nash, always in search of a witticism, even at the sacrifice of good taste, gets a retort which leaves him flabbergasted (II, 166). In this case, the insolence of the question is returned with double velocity against the rude jester. Smollett even ventures, through the third person of Lavement, on a witticism in French, when he puns on 'obligée' and 'obligeante' (I, 146). On occasion, too, he does not hesitate to ridicule the pretentious and misplaced wit, which, height of misfortune, falls flat, like that parody of a witty remark retailed by Weazel (I, 80). Crabtree, in *Peregrine Pickle*, protected by his feigned deafness, has no trouble in silencing a conceited young man who is attacking him, convinced that his victim's infirmity will guarantee his own impunity (p. 381). But in this novel, his readers are invited to assist at two almost professional exercises of wit. Spontaneity suffers from this artificial method even though Smollett tries to make it plausible by explaining it by the antagonism of two disappointed authors. Their duel (pp. 641–2), which takes the form of exchanging personal insults, bears more resemblance to a street fight than to elegant fencing with foils tipped with wit. The buttons are off and the hits are scored with the sharp-pointed blades of ribald slander. As in *Tristram Shandy*, the picturesque vocabulary, in particular the French one, of siegeworks, gives them the opportunity for matrimonial or anatomical allusions: 'hornwork', 'covered way', 'assault', 'batter in breach', 'the angle of *la pucelle* bastion', 'to fill up the *fosse*', such is the witty concatenation of this exchange which soon degenerates into a brawl. Later, still in this assembly of authors, Smollett presents 'an exercise of wit, which was generally performed once every fortnight, with a view to promote the expectoration of genius' (p. 648).

The use of this last expression and the disillusioned tone of the presentation allow one to think that, here, he is more interested in witty parody than in wit itself. The assault of wit is used again, with unequal results. 'Wind-bound in ports' summons up 'Wine-bound' and, in turn, 'Hooped with wine! a strange metaphor' (p. 648). It is a pity that J. Clifford, in his edition of *Peregrine Pickle* does not explain this play on words, which is incomprehensible to the reader unacquainted with nautical customs. Smollett is alluding to the expression 'to run the hoop', a practice which consisted in tying four young sailors by their left hands to an iron hoop; at a signal from the boatswain, they set to whipping each other, progressively harder and harder. 'This was anciently practised when a ship was wind-bound' Grose explains in his dictionary. Like the preceding exercise, this one ends in confusion (pp. 648–9).

A certain Billingsgate vulgarity marks the exchange of repartees between the fat Wapping landlady and the no less corpulent Quaker in *Ferdinand Count Fathom* (pp. 130–1), likewise the sarcastic complaints of Crabshaw in *Launcelot Greaves* (p. 134) where the verbal exchange has a trenchant concision at the expense of the apothecary. Nevertheless, the latter is obtuse enough to ask the doctor to examine this recalcitrant patient more closely: 'he has got a rough tongue, and a very foul mouth, I'll assure you' (ibid.). This was a superfluous statement! Conversely, it is not surprising, given the cultural level of Jery Melford and Matt Bramble, that their witticisms should be of a more refined order. The touch of academic pedantry is not absent even from the epitaph on the drowned dog Ponto: 'deerant quoque Littora Ponto' which Jery caps by stating that his friend Mansel's pretext for throwing the unfortunate Ponto in the Isis 'is an excuse that will not hold water' (*Humphry Clinker*, p. 16). Less innocent is the sexual allusion implicit in the readymade expression 'at bottom', which is used first by the uncle (p. 19) then by the nephew, who, to defend himself against the charge of getting a local whore pregnant, suspects his friend Mansel 'to be at the bottom of the whole' (p. 28). Matt Bramble's remark, reported with complete and innocent incomprehension by Lydia (an extra comic touch) is a little gem of sparkling and cruel wit. To a question asked by Tabitha, who is suddenly in a hurry to leave Bath, Bramble replies 'we shall retreat before the Dog-days begin' (p. 59). It is always disagreeable to take the mechanism of a witticism to pieces for, in doing so, the wit evaporates and the critic has nothing left under his scalpel but the *disjecta membra* of a literary creation that only a little while ago was still very much alive. But later the text, if it is good, resumes all its vitality, and may even be enriched by the analysis, if it is good. In eight apparently innocuous words, Bramble brilliantly condenses several levels of meaning. First of all, a contextual allusion to the incident over the dog Chowder which had turned Tabitha against Ulic Mackilligut; next a meteorological and chronological reference; lastly, and principally, a cynical (!) condemnation of Tabitha's passionate temperament, made explicit by the following words: 'with a little temperance and discretion, our constitutions might be kept cool enough all the year, even at Bath' (ibid.). 'The Deucalidonian sea' (p. 236) is a creation of a very witty composite word which ingeniously telescopes 'Deucalion' and 'Caledonian'. The matrimonial context — and the celebrated example in *Hamlet*: 'Do you think I mean country matters?' (III, 2) — incite one to think that Jery is not altogether innocent when he writes, not without a spice of salacity: 'If Mr. Dennison had an agreeable daughter, I believe I should be for making the third couple in this country dance' (p. 333). Simpler and more sarcastic is the pun on the two possible meanings of 'widgeon' (p. 349), denoting at once a species of wild duck — the ornithological sense emphasised by 'note' and 'decoy' — but also a simpleton, the obvious meaning according to the pejorative context. The *OED* is therefore wrong in designating this meaning as obsolete since 1741, since Jery uses it in *Humphry Clinker*.

The verbal distortion which Smollett employs for comic ends assumes two aspects, easier to distinguish in theory than in practice, to wit the reproduction of national or regional phonetic peculiarities and epistolary dysorthography, a category to which the verbal mutilations committed by uneducated or ignorant people must also be assigned. Smollett often resorts to comic pronunciation to characterise national or regional types, and Frenchmen, first and foremost, are the traditional butts of this ridicule. Shakespeare already makes fun of their lack of ear and their legendary incapacity to pronounce *th* for example, or *h* or *w*, as is proved by the jargons, of very unequal charm, spoken by Doctor Caius in *The Merry Wives of Windsor* and Katharine, the daughter of King Charles VI of France, in *Henry V*. Fielding, too, uses this method in *Tom Jones*, where a French lieutenant, who has forgotten his own language but not yet learnt English, expresses himself in an appalling pidgin mixture of both (Book vii, Chapter xii), as also does that king of the gipsies whose sense of justice is more civilised than his pronunciation (Book xii, Chapter xii).

The apothecary Lavement in *Roderick Random* is the very type of the ludicrous foreign speaker. Not content with deforming English, he perpetually interlards his remarks with French words and expressions (I, 139, 145–6, 159, 160–3). In *The Reprisal*, Smollett exploits the same device so insistently that the pidgin English of the lamentable puppet, M. de Champignon, ends by being more boring than amusing (XII, 129–33, 141–5, 147–9, 152–7, 159–61). The presence of the Scotsman Maclaymore and the Irishman Oclabber, both of whom express themselves in a language full of dialectal peculiarities, more or less well rendered, does not help to lighten this impression of heavy phonetic farce. But at least one must be grateful to Smollett for having enough humour to laugh at the faulty pronunciation of his compatriots, like Mr Concordance in *Roderick Random* (I, 96–7, 164–5) who tries to recompose an artificial and grandiloquent English. The Irishmen — Oregan in *Roderick Random* and Sir Ulic Mackilligut in *Humphry Clinker* — are less remarkable for their phonetics than for their legendary 'Irish bulls', their speech rhythm and certain typical interjections, or at least established as such by literary, and especially theatrical tradition. Oregan threatens Roderick thus: 'I will make your tongue confess, after the breath is out of your body' (I, 103); he speaks 'with a true Tipperary cadence' (I, 104), and sprinkles his sentences with 'honey', 'arrah', and 'by Jesus' (I, 104–5). Sir Ulic Mackilligut replies to Jery's remarks 'in a true Hibernian accent', shows a marked preference for rhetorical accumulation, and uses the interjection 'gra', inevitable in any conversation with an Irishman, here again according to Smollett (pp. 29–30). But it is the Welshman, Morgan, in *Roderick Random* — he makes a brief reappearance in *Peregrine Pickle* — who represents the best example of phonetic comedy, combined with an explosive and legendary irascibility, since the ebullient Fluellen in *Henry V*[20]. It is not within the scope of this study to determine whether the reproduction of the Welsh accent would stand up to a scientific examination: W. A. Boggs has already shown in his articles that Win Jenkins's speech lacks dialectical and phonetic homogeneity[21]. The capricious mutation of *b* into *p*, *d* into *t*, the traditional transformation of 'gentleman' into 'shentleman' and the no less traditional expletive interjection 'look you' (I, 208) are not sufficient to make Morgan comic, although these unpredictable consonant changes — 'God' becomes 'Cot' (I, 209) — end by acquiring a comic value by dint of being repeated. The very rhythm of Morgan's speech, now jerky with rage, now balanced by the ternary rhetoric of his oratorical indignation reinforces the comic value of these lines:

> As Got is my judge . . . and my salfation, and my witness, whosoever has pilfered my provisions is a lousy, peggarly, rascally knave! and by the soul of my grandsire! I will impeach, and accuse, and indict him of a roppery, if I did but know who he is! (I, 255).

It is even certain, by comparing the various passages where Morgan is speaking[22], that the phonetic deformations are less and less frequent, but that, conversely, the rhetorical devices, especially dittology and pedantic accumulation constitute the very framework of the comedy. The Sussex yokels who discover the wounded Roderick (I, 306–7) bring the farcical and bitter comedy of their stupidity to this scene — 'an you be a murdered man, speak, that you may have a christom burial' (I, 306) — rather than their phonetic solecisms. Finally, Smollett makes much sport with the anglicised pronunciation of wantonly distorted French words, especially in *Peregrine Pickle* and *Ferdinand Count Fathom*, his two most cosmopolitan novels. Trunnion rechristens his French adversary, the 'Fleur de Lys', the 'Floor de Louse' (*Peregrine Pickle*, p. 9) — a sarcastic choice probably secretly motivated by Smollett's Gallophobia. But he can also laugh, and make others laugh, at the linguistic murders committed by English visitors ignorant of French or Latin. Pallet takes a Swiss Guard's estimate of a picture in the Palais Royal — '*sans prix*' (p. 225) — to refer to a painter called 'Sangpree'. The parodic comedy is pushed to absurdity with the transformation of Horace's line, '*Mutato nomine, de te fabula narratur*' into 'mute aye toe numbing he . . . Deity, fable honour hate her' (ibid.). Pallet, a tenth-rate painter, is an excellent (comic) verbal alchemist: 'Je ne sais quoi' is transmuted into '*ginseekeye*' (p. 230), a linguistic freak which may well conceal a more complex level of comedy, given the context: 'there's a freshness in the English complexion, a *gin-seekeye*'. This word, decomposed into '*gin-seek-eye*' by a most ungrammatical association of ideas, conjures up the image of those haggard gin drinkers, always in search of their favourite poison, depicted by Hogarth. Win Jenkins's predecessor, Pallet, mutilates proper names: 'Plato' becomes 'Playtor', and 'Pindar', 'Pindoor' (pp. 234, 336). In *Ferdinand Count Fathom*, Sir Stentor Stile mangles French: 'frigasee' (fricassée), 'ragooze' (ragoût, p. 101), 'peajohn' (pigeon, p. 102) and 'bully' (bouilli, ibid.) attest preoccupations more gastronomic than linguistic. Although the deformation of 'lansquenet' (the card game) into 'lamb-skin-it' is recognised in the *OED*, Sir Stentor Stile introduces a variation: 'lambskin net'.

As to comic misspelling and other verbal mutilations which create words that are monstrous, but packed with several possible meanings, Smollett did not wait till *Humphry Clinker* to indulge freely in this game of erratic commutation. Fielding, too, tries his hand at it in *Jonathan Wild*, where Jonathan's love-letter to the fair Laetitia, however, shows less invention than a similar letter in *Roderick Random*. Fielding's only lucky find[23] is the ambiguous hapax 'adwhorable', of which he is so proud that he repeats it with 'adwhoration' and 'adwhorer' (Book iii, Chapter vi). The first involuntary mutation, in the Shakespearian style, is made by Bowling, who says 'predicted' instead of 'addicted': 'Neither is he predicted to vice' (I, 15). This deliberate mistake (on Smollett's part but not on Bowling's) is emphasised in advance by the correct use, 'addicted to all manner of vice', a few lines earlier. 'Obstropulous' (I, 51 and also *Launcelot Greaves*, p. 133, in the slightly different form 'obstropolous') instead of 'obstreperous' is used by lower-class women speakers, a maid-servant in an inn in *Roderick Random*, a nurse in *Launcelot Greaves*: the first form is given in Grose's dictionary. Long before the famous letters of Tabitha Bramble and Win Jenkins, Smollett tests his virtuosity in a letter from a beauty who haunts the ill-famed purlieus of Drury Lane (*Roderick Random*, I, 116—17). 'The animable hopjack of my contemplayshins' should be interpreted as 'the amiable object of my contemplations', and, in imitation of the theatrical style, 'Murfy sends his puppies to the heys of slipping mortals' must be deciphered as: 'Morpheus sends his poppies to the eyes of sleeping mortals'. In view of the more than probable peripatetic profession of the letter-writer, the use of 'slipping' instead of 'sleeping' is not lacking in Gallic wit, like 'whorie time' for 'hoary time', or again 'harrows' for Cupid's arrows. In a less pleasant context, the surgeon Mackshane uses 'without asparagement or acception of man, woman, or child' (I, 246) instead of 'disparagement' and 'exception'. A braggart soldier, boastfully recounting his wounds and bruises, speaks of 'confusion on the head' where 'contusion' would be more normal, but less rich in comic implications. This braggart also makes a thorough and ludicrous hash of the words of a fashionable song and turns them into parodic nonsense:

> Would you task the moon-ty'd hair,
> To yon flagrant beau repair;
> Where waving with the popling vow,
> The bantling fine will shelter you (II, 152).

Buck (1927, p. 43) suggests the following translation:

> Would you taste the noontide air
> To yon fragrant bower repair;
> Where waving with the poplar bough
> The mantling vine will shelter you.

Without possessing the mysterious evocative power of Carroll's 'Jabberwocky':

> Twas brillig, and the slithy toves
> Did gyre and gimble in the wabe

these few parodic lines prove that, as early as *Roderick Random*, Smollett had an innate sense of comic verbal manipulation.

This tendency continues to manifest itself in *Peregrine Pickle*, where Tunley, the innkeeper, says about his supposed rival: 'I have cooled his capissens' (p. 158) probably for 'concupiscence', in view of the context. Pallet condemns 'the hippythets of the vulgar' (p. 338). These epithets were to suffer some twenty years later in the mouth of Mrs Malaprop, the virtuoso of verbal transubstantiation in *The Rivals* (1775), who reproves 'a nice derangement of epitaphs' (III, 3). The verb 'to argufy' used by a loquacious innkeeper, has passed into popular parlance (*Peregrine Pickle*, p. 415) but his other verbal creations 'in reverence of' for 'in reference to' or 'in deference to', like 'judgmatical' for a probable 'dogmatical' or its synonym 'pragmatical' have not achieved such semantic success. The nautical terms used by the amorous Pipes in addressing the vagabond beauty are remodelled by her in an extremely bawdy way: 'cable' becomes 'gay balls' and 'compass', 'comepiss' (p. 597). But again it is in a woman's letter, written by the former oyster wench, Mrs Deborah Hornbeck, in *Peregrine Pickle*, a great purveyor of dysorthographic pearls, that Smollett pushes his exercise in comic destruction of the language furthest. Mrs Hornbeck, who has an ardent temperament, gives Peregrine a rendezvous and begins her letter thus: 'Coind Sur, Heaving the playsure of meating with you at the ofspital of anvilheads, I take this lubbertea of latin you know . . .', the beginning of a sentence which must be translated: 'Kind Sir, having the pleasure of meeting you at the hospital of the "Invalides", I take this liberty of letting you know . . .'. Amorous and sexual implications are not wanting. The 'Hôtel de Mai' is transformed into 'hottail de May', and 'six o'clock in the evening' into 'sicks a cloak in the heavening' (p. 219). Peregrine's name suffers a change not devoid of suggestiveness, 'Pickhell', just as, in *Humphry Clinker*, Win Jenkins deforms the name of Lismahago and the Dennisons. In *Ferdinand Count Fathom*, the shopkeeper who no longer trusts Fathom declares herself to be 'in a very great terrification and numbplush' (p. 276) (for 'nonplus') and uses somewhat anglicised Latin legal terms. 'Siserary' (ibid.) is a current popular corruption of '*Certiorari*', but it is more difficult, on the following page, to recognise '*praemunire*' in 'primmineery'.

The rhythm of uneducated speech is rendered with great comic precision, the result of close observation of levels of language, which Smollett most successfully exploits in *Humphry Clinker*. The play on legal terms, ill-assimilated by Judge Gobble and his wife, enables one to predict the involuntary verbal creations of Win Jenkins and Tabitha. Once again, Smollett means to make one laugh at those who have the intellectual and social pretension to appear more than they really are. Gobble prides himself on being a remarkable orator, which he is indeed, but certainly not for the reasons he imagines. His style is composed of barely disguised repetitions, mutilated legal terms: 'delinquems and manefactors', 'divers occasions and importunities', 'the sewerity of justice', this last expression combining, with much comic aptness, 'severity' and 'sewer' to create a hapax suggesting the judicial sink of iniquity, or else learned words used in the wrong sense as did Dogberry and Mrs Quickly before Smollett and the famous Mrs Malaprop some years after *Humphry Clinker*. Gobble speaks of 'contagious nation' (for 'contiguous') and the power of magistrates 'to litigate the sewerity of justice' (for 'mitigate') (p. 93). As for his wife, she is even more directly the linguistic model for Mrs Malaprop than Pallet with his already quoted 'hippythets'. Mrs Gobble is enraged at hearing herself given 'such contemptible epitaphs' (p. 96). This word is perhaps not all that misplaced, since the proceedings instituted against Launcelot will sound the knell of illusions for Judge Gobble and his wife.

Dorothy Cowslip's letter (p. 130) marks a not very interesting return to the phonetic transcription of more or less homogeneous dialectical peculiarities, spelt in a fanciful way. Dorothy achieves only one good verbal invention: 'bareheir' for 'bearer'. But for the development of comic structures in *Humphry Clinker*, it is interesting to note this third letter from a dysorthographic woman, after that of Clarinda ('Clayrender'!) in *Roderick Random* and Mrs Hornbeck in *Peregrine Pickle*. When Smollett composed Win Jenkins's and Tabitha's letters, he had therefore had the idea of exploiting this comic genre ever since his first novel. In *Launcelot Greaves* too, Crowe indulges in some verbal deformations when he reports the words of Macbeth (*Macbeth*, III, 4) quoted by Dawdle (p. 150): the rhinoceros is changed into 'wrynose o'ross', and the Russian bear into 'Persian bear' (p. 151).

It is in *Humphry Clinker* that Smollett's verbal invention transforms a simple comic device into protean humour.

Before analysing the levels of protean humour in the letters of Win and Tabitha, it is necessary to state that the spelling, or rather misspelling, of these two letter-writers is extremely capricious. Tabitha writes quite difficult words like 'articles', 'damask' and 'blunderbuss' correctly, misspells 'blue' ('bloo'), 'petticoat' ('petticot') and 'wine-cellar' ('wind-sellar') in her first letter. Similarly, Win confuses 'heaving' and 'having', spells 'health', 'mischief', 'Christian' and 'misfortune' right, but trips up over 'mayor' ('mare'), 'servants' ('servints') and 'certain' ('sartain'). Smollett does not so much stigmatise the mistakes of two more or less illiterate women as wish, by this means, to characterise them as absurdly pretentious. On the simplest level lie the verbal muddles — 'malapropisms' before their time — the composite words and the almost total deformations of simple or polysyllabic words of Greek or Latin origin. In the majority of cases the comic replacement of one word by another affects more or less learned and abstract ones, but everyday words of Anglo-Saxon etymology may suffer the same fate, though less frequently.

Besides their comic value, Tabitha's and Win's letters provide sociological evidence, biased indeed, of the little attention given to the education of women in general. Tabitha uses 'partake' instead of 'protect' (p. 6), a mistake she commits again (p. 274). 'Jewels' becomes 'jowls', not without caricatural intentions regarding her wilted face and flaccid flesh. Win writes 'importunity' instead of 'opportunity', replaces 'hysterics' by 'asterisks', and 'prescribed a suppository' by 'subscribed a repository' (p. 7). A word as ordinary as 'grace' is systematically transformed into 'grease' (pp. 156, 262); Win, in spite of her sins, believes in the efficacity of Methodist grace and hopes much to find 'grease to be excepted' (p. 155), this last unfortunate word betraying her to the point of making her say the opposite of what she meant, to wit 'accepted'. Even a conventional tautological expression like 'refuse and scum of the earth' acquires a new and unexpected vigour when disguised as 'refuse and skim of the hearth' (p. 78). The same goes for 'devils incarnate' and 'devils in garnet' (p. 70). Here are a few other oddities arising from mistaking one word for another: 'consumption' for 'conception' (p. 109), 'constipation' probably for 'consternation' — 'the whole family have been in such a constipation' (p. 155) — 'exorcised' for 'exercised' (p. 156), 'circumflexion' for 'circumspection' (ibid.). Under the magic wand — conjuror's or conductor's? — of Win, 'magician' is changed into 'musician' (p. 261). These verbal confusions are based on a partial phonetic similarity, obtained thanks to replacing some letters in the real word meant.

More complex still is the structure of composite words produced by the subtle technique of verbal telescoping, whether voluntary or not, a process minutely analysed by Freud in *Jokes and their Relation to the Unconscious*[24]. The composite word is the vector of the laughable effect produced, on the one hand, by the antithetical character of the verbal condensation, and, on the other, by the coexistence of semantic fields attached to the original words. Since the semantic fields cover different, not to say opposed, realities, the comedy springs from these multiple contradictions. Tabitha complains of being 'much troubled with flutterencies' (p. 45). This last word combines 'flutter' — a word descriptive of her general state of nerves — and 'flatulencies', a more specific internal disorder. Win, in turn, after an incident in the street, declares she hardly knew how she got home, she was 'in such a flustration' (p. 109). There is little doubt that the original expression is 'in a fluster', but the general appearance of this hapax hingeing on only one letter, inevitably suggests 'frustration', a word which very aptly describes Win's state of mind, full of resentment at having the end of the evening's outing spoilt by a rude man accosting her. Another time-honoured tautological expression, 'trials and tribulations', regains fresh linguistic vigour when Win writes: 'I have had trials and trembulations' (p. 219), this last word happily suggesting both the trials and the tremblings of the unfortunate servant. It is with the same economy of means that 'congyration' (p. 261) makes one think at once of 'conjuration' and 'gyration', a whirling motion charged with magical connotation.

But Win and Tabitha push verbal alchemy further still. They are capable of total deformations far removed from their real starting-point. Though it is not too difficult to recognise 'padlock' and 'wine-cellar' in 'pad-luck' and 'wind-sellar' (p. 6), words such as 'honymil' (p. 43), 'merry bones' (p. 72), 'phims' (p. 78), 'looker of cain' (p. 155), 'monkey-bank' (p. 352) demand rather more linguistic efforts to rediscover, in this comic disguise, 'animal', 'whims', 'marrow-bones', 'lucre of gain' — an expression which Smollett used in *Roderick Random* (II, 270) — and 'mountebank'. Win's creative virtuosity runs wild as soon as she attempts to transcribe Latin legal terms. The dignified 'corporal oath' is barely recognisable in the ambiguous 'cruperal oaf' (p. 72), 'mittimus' in 'mittamouse' (p. 155), 'habeas corpus' in 'Apias Korkus' — which Win takes for a man 'who lives with the ould bailiff, and is, they say, five hundred years old . . . and a congeror' (ibid.). Words of foreign origin are disguised in strange anglicised clothes. A *valet de chambre* is, for Win, a 'wally de shamble' (p. 219), or again 'valley de shambles' (p. 306)[25]. 'Calamanco', a material much used in the eighteenth century, becomes the strange 'gallow monkey' (p. 337) and the funereal 'bombasine' takes on a callipygous charm as 'bumbeseen' (p. 44). Proper names, whether of persons or places, do not escape this verbal transmutation: 'Sir Yury Micligut' (p. 43) for 'Sir Ulic Mackilligut', 'gustass Busshard' (p. 155) for 'Justice Buzzard', 'painted Issabel' (p. 219) for 'painted Jezebel', 'Addingborough' (p. 221) for 'Edinburgh', while the cities of Stirling and Glasgow are rechristened 'Starling' and 'Grascow' (p. 260). But it is Lismahago who holds the record for fantastic identities: 'Kismycago' (p. 199)[26], 'Lashmeheygo' (p. 338), 'Lashmiheygo' (p. 352). In Win's last letter, Jery is called 'Millfart' and the young married couple (with an erotic allusion in 'dally') 'the Dallisons' (ibid.). The bawdy intent, in the polyglot manner of Shakespeare in *Henry V* (III, 4), where Katharine is indignant at hearing the words 'De *foot* et de *coun*', is even clearer, in view of the fact that he has caught her naked – when Win makes Sir George Colquhoun into 'Sir Gorge Coon' (p. 261). The play on words is more innocuous in the case of the Reverend M'Corkindale (p. 228), or Mackcorkendale (p. 237), whose Methodist hypocrisy Win underlines by calling him 'Macrocodile' (p. 260), or again for Methuselah anglicised into 'Matthewsullin' by Win's illiterate efforts (p. 306).

This constant verbal play in Win's and Tabitha's letters facilitates the expansion of a protean humour with several levels of meaning. It is not unusual for the malapropism to be coupled with contextual humour. When Win writes 'O Molly! you that live in the country have no deception of our doings at Bath' (p. 42), besides the erroneous use of 'deception' for 'conception', this apparently wrongly used word crystallises the impression of the hidden intrigues going on in Matt Bramble's household without his knowledge. The allusion, in the lines immediately following, to the disguise adopted by Wilson gives 'deception' another facet of humorous meaning. Wilson, as a Jewish pedlar, is indeed trying to *deceive* the vigilance of Jery and his uncle. It is not impossible, either, that 'deception' conceals a distant allusion to the fraudulence characteristic of Jews according to popular antisemitic legend. The substitution, already used by Shakespeare, of 'odorous' for 'odious' – 'twenty other odorous falsehoods' (p. 72) – assumes a new humorous aspect if the reader will only imagine the below-stairs slanging match between Win and the cook in Bath, during which malevolent, and undoubtedly malodorous, epithets must have showered on Win. When Win writes of Lydia: 'I doubt her pore art is too tinder' (p. 262) for 'I doubt her poor heart is too tender', the word 'tinder' contains an allusion to the ease with which Lydia's heart has been set on fire by Wilson. There are two levels of meaning, professional and legal, when Win speaks of that old tinker 'that suffered . . . for steeling of kettle' (p. 306), that is to say 'for stealing cattle'. But, as Boggs points out[27]: 'Tinkers are workers in metal who actually do steal (glaze or cover with metal) a kettle.' The interplay of humour may be sparked off by several words. Win quotes Clinker's remarks on Lismahago, whom he sees as 'no better than an impfiddle, continually playing upon the pyebill and the new-burth' (ibid). 'Impfiddle' covers the original meaning 'infidel' but also decomposes into 'imp' and 'fiddle' which give two other possible semantic filiations. 'Imp' and its mocking Satanism refer back to 'profane scuffle' ('scoffer') at the beginning of the sentence. 'Fiddle' is taken up at the end of the sentence by 'to play'. Smollett has thus considerably enriched a commonplace clause: 'no better than an infidel, continually playing upon the Bible and the new birth.' Right up to Win's and Tabitha's last letters, his humorous virtuosity does not flag. Somewhat pompously, Win announces: 'Providinch hath bin pleased to make great halteration in the pasture of our affairs' (p. 352). One must restore 'alteration' and 'posture'. But 'halter' and 'pasture' belong to the same semantic field of rural life. Finally, 'halteration' can well be understood as an oblique allusion to marriage, a transaction which involves putting a rope round one's neck (cf. 'noozed', given by Grose as meaning 'Married, hanged'). This hypothesis is strengthened by the phrase with which Jery begins his last letter: 'The fatal knots are now tied' (p. 346). Win's phrase and her use of the hapax 'halteration' are thus also a humorous repetition of Jery's words.

There is little doubt that salaciousness, unusual in Smollett's other novels, frequently crops up in Win's and Tabitha's letters, at least for the reader who can discover this occasionally scabrous humour lurking under the apparently innocent verbal deformations of Win and her mistress. Salaciousness, of which Freud gives the following analysis, is characterised by barely veiled allusion to the genital organs and the sexual act:

> Smut is like an exposure of the sexually different person to whom it is directed. By the utterance of the obscene words it compels the person who is assailed to imagine the part of the body or the procedure in question and shows her that the assailant himself is imagining it. It cannot be doubted that the desire to see what is sexual exposed is the original motive of smut[28].

Whatever the merit of this analysis, it cannot be applied, without a major reservation, to the letters of Win and Tabitha. Whereas Freud insists on the voluntary aspect of this ludic activity, Smollett's two letter-writers are completely unconscious of the salacious suggestions contained in their letters. Smollett thus adds another level of humour to this type of comedy by assuring himself of the complicity of the reader at the expense of his characters whose innocence and ignorance put them beyond all suspicion. Moreover, the ambiguity of such a technique also puts Smollett out of reach of censure or legal proceedings. The involuntary salacity of Win and Tabitha betrays, through such Freudian slips, which most of these spelling mistakes are, their profound concern to satisfy their sexuality in marriage.

It is unnecessary to revert to Tabitha's desperate search for a husband. At the end of *Humphry Clinker*, Smollett takes care to confirm the reader's impression of Win: 'the wench seems to be as great an enthusiast in love as in religion' (p. 345). The confusion of 'sin' and 'chin' (p. 43) barely masks the allusion to the shameful parts, the cause of sin. Win defies the devil to say that she is a 'tail-carrier' (p. 71), for 'talebearer'. Apart from the probable reference to the devil and his tail, Smollett plays on the sexual meaning of 'tail' which can designate the male or female organs. The salacity is emphasised by the apparently very innocent use of the expression 'to bring into trouble' at the end of the sentence.

The latent sexual obsession is still more obvious in Tabitha's letters. She waxes indignant in these terms: 'Villiams has got my skin; for which he is an impotent rascal' (p. 78) and again: 'Roger gets this, and Roger gets that; but . . . I won't be rogered at this rate by any ragmatical fellow in the kingdom' (ibid.). Now 'Roger' in eighteenth-century slang, is one of many ways of designating the penis, and Grose defines 'to roger: to bull, or lie with a woman; from the name of Roger being frequently given to a bull'. After having once transformed 'account' into 'accunt' — 'you must render accunt, not only to your earthly master, but also to him that is above' (p. 156) — Tabitha writes again 'I hope you keep accunt of Roger's purseeding' (p. 274), and the same Roger is charged to search into and clear out 'the slit holes which the maids have in secret' (ibid.). If the preceding allusions are clear enough, salaciousness can also conceal its games behind the drawn curtains of a four-poster. Does not the slip 'fatherbed' (ibid.), for 'featherbed', betray Tabitha's desire for maternity and her readiness to offer herself to her husband's virility, implied in 'well haired' a few words later? And, if any doubt still persisted, Smollett removes it by making Tabitha's sprightly pen write 'the blissing of haven'. The frustrated old maid is at last to know the ecstasies of marriage and to reach a haven of bliss. Win, not to be left behind, admires the 'hillyfents', 'elephants' (p. 108), transforms 'virgin' into 'firchin', which is not far removed orthographically and phonetically from 'firking' and 'fucking'. This verbal metamorphosis is not without Gallic wit in the context. Poor Clinker is forced to contribute his share by Win and Tabitha who laud the power of his ardour in ambiguous terms. Win invites her friend Mary Jones to prepare herself 'for the operations of this wonderful instrument' (p. 156), that is to say, at least apparently, of grace. As always, Tabitha is more direct: 'and that he may have power given to penetrate and instill his goodness, even into your most inward parts, is the fervent prayer of . . . Tab. Bramble' (p. 275). A fine family programme — or family planning? — of conversion!

Finally, there is a metaphorical continuity in *Humphry Clinker* which forms an integral part of the structure of the novel. When Tabitha once again lets her resentment break out in the following sentence: 'When I go to market to sell, my commodity stinks' (p. 44), Smollett ostensibly places the expression 'my commodity stinks' on the commercial plane. But there is no doubt whatever, in view of the successive use of 'commodity', that it must also be understood in the matrimonial and sexual sense. A first humorous variation occurs when Jery writes about his aunt: 'The Irish Baronet is an old hound, that, finding her carrion, has quitted the scent' (p. 60). Jery thus establishes a link between 'stinks' and 'carrion'. The reference is even more explicit at the end of Bramble's letter of May 19th to Dr Lewis, which he signs off by asking his friend: 'Can't you find some poor gentleman of Wales, to take this precious commodity off the hands of . . .' (p. 78). 'Commodity' is referred to obliquely in the commercial sense in a letter of Bramble's about the possibility of a husband being found for Tabitha through the good offices of Lady Griskin, 'the matchmaker is to have a valuable consideration in the way of brokerage' (p. 154). There is not even Lydia, the innocent Lydia, who does not develop this metaphorical theme: 'My poor aunt . . . has gone to market with her charms in every place' (p. 259). A last allusion belongs to this image of stinking carrion: Win compares Lismahago to a 'carrying-crow' ('carrion-crow', p. 306). Right from the beginning of this metaphorical filiation, it is obvious that Smollett is thinking of the slang and sexual meaning of 'commodity' — often used by Shakespeare, if only in the subtle passage in *King John* (II, 1, 567–98) — and thus defined by Grose in his dictionary: 'the private parts of a modest woman, and the public parts of a prostitute'. There is a similar metaphorical interplay, but less complex though just as salacious, between Bramble's following remark to Clinker: 'Thou ha'st given her [Tabitha] much offence by shewing her thy naked tail' (p. 84), answered by Clinker's promise: 'I shall take care that my tail shall never rise up in judgement against me' (ibid.), and Bramble's final statement about his own past conduct: 'You see, gentlemen, how the sins of my youth rise up in judgement against me' (p. 318). In this last quotation, salaciousness is replaced by a belated, but sincere consciousness of past errors.

Composite words, multiple levels of meaning, and finally flexibility of style are the basic structures of this protean humour which lights up all Smollett's novels. Long before *Humphry Clinker* [29], Smollett knew how to exploit different levels of style which, by their opposition or their incongruity, kindled the comic spark. He used rhetorical extravagances, as has been seen earlier to characterise Morgan in *Roderick Random* and Tom Clarke in *Launcelot Greaves*. But in *Peregrine Pickle* there is also a genuine search, conducted with spirited virtuosity, for stylistic effects which could raise a laugh. Here again, it is not irrelevant, in view of Smollett's final masterpiece, that the young author should have used various types of letter-writing as an instrument of comedy as early as *Peregrine Pickle*. The proposal of marriage written by Gamaliel Pickle borrows its style and conciseness from the business world, and contains — already! — a latent pun on 'commodity':

Understanding you have a parcel of heart, warranted sound, to be disposed of, shall be willing to treat for said commodity, on reasonable terms; doubt not, shall agree for same; shall wait of you for further information, when and where you shall appoint. This the needful from . . . Gam. Pickle (p. 14).

What does the style matter, since Miss Sally Appleby consents to become Mrs Pickle! In contrast to this 'mercantile plainness' (ibid.) the schoolmaster who recomposes Peregrine's destroyed letter to Emilia to get Pipes, who is responsible for this loss, out of his scrape, produces a bombastic rigmarole. Words of Greek or Latin derivation are largely predominant as this rhetorical flight shows: 'If the refulgent flames of your beauty had not evaporated the particles of my transported brain, and scorched my intellects into a cinder of stolidity . . .' (p. 105). After such gibberish – 'this extraordinary fustian of stile' (ibid.) – it is not surprising that Emilia has doubts about Peregrine's sincerity.

In the same realm of stylistic humour one must include the application of the scientific, and more particularly geometric, vocabulary to a demonstration of practical psychology. Jolter meets with only a limited success with his pupil Peregrine, who is not much convinced by his tutor's lemmas and theorems (pp. 133–4). Again, in *Peregrine Pickle*, the burlesque ode, a parody of the monody composed by Lord Lyttelton[30] on the death of his wife, proves, in a rather cruel way, that twenty years before *Humphry Clinker*, Smollett had amazing stylistic versatility (pp. 655–6). Oclabber's melancholy song in *The Reprisal* (*Works*, XII, 127) is a faint echo of this parodic humour. Before *Humphry Clinker*, Smollett had discovered the comic value of stylistic juxtaposition. Launcelot and Crowe indulge in a verbal duel, in which the knight uses noble language, marked by a profusion of learned words, whereas Crowe attacks and defends himself with the only linguistic weapon he possesses, his sailor's vocabulary (pp. 104–7).

It is probable that Smollett parodies the alliterative style of the romantic love-stories and other ephemeral novelettes written for popular consumption which Robert D. Mayo has taken the pains to disinter and catalogue in *The English Novel in the Magazines 1740–1815*. It is difficult to interpret the following sentence and its caricatural style in any other way: 'The lovers were seated: he looked and languished; she flushed and faltered: all was doubt and delirium, fondness and flutter' (*Launcelot Greaves*, p. 123). Conversely, it is less certain that Smollett was not really making a serious attempt at the grandiloquent style by recklessly using the epanalepsis which obliges him to repeat 'He found her . . .' at the beginning of half a dozen sentences (ibid., pp. 205–6). In that case, Smollett's shot would have misfired and his attempt at stylistic humour ricocheted back on himself. But is not the humorist gifted with an acute awareness of his own imperfections?

341

The structures of the comic in Smollett's work form a complex network extending from the simplest mechanical methods to the symplectic ramifications of protean humour which give *Humphry Clinker* its inexhaustible literary vitality. At the end of this study, the comedy in Smollett's novels appears as the most serious, at any rate the most durable, part of a philosophy of living, or, in other words, of that everyday art of dying well. Not only the pragmatic comedy of satire, but comic effects of all kinds, are basically reduced to a desperate attempt to affirm the liberty of man, or rather to reassure oneself of its possibility. To laugh is to escape for a few moments from the perpetual conflict of the forces of good and evil, by abolishing time and space, the better to affirm the supremacy, often attacked but always victorious, of our indestructible ipseity.

Just as Smollett belongs to the comic lineage of Shakespeare and Fielding, he has, in turn, created a tradition; one which includes Sheridan[31], Dickens[32] and Thackeray, to mention only his most direct heirs in the realm of literary humour. Might not Charles James Yellowplush be the grandson of Win Jenkins? The connections between Smollett and Edward Lear, Lewis Carroll and James Joyce are more remote, but all these authors are distinguished by an ambiguous urge to the creative destruction of language which reaches its apogee in *Finnegans Wake*. Yet, without claiming that Smollett had the slightest direct influence on Joyce, one may regard the author of *Humphry Clinker* as the distant precursor of that verbal creation whose humour scintillates like a many-faceted gem.

Smollett's literary career closes with the paradox of *Humphry Clinker*. This novel, if not written, at least published on the threshold of his death, is the richest not in comic episodes, but in comic *inventions*. Anthony Burgess, recounting the love life of Shakespeare in *Nothing like the Sun*[33], makes him say, in one of those privileged moments of literary intuition: 'Tragedy is a goat and comedy a village Priapus and *dying* is the word that links both.' Not only the word, but the deed. In the end, comic situations — which in fact exist only through and for the on-looker but have no life of their own — are dissolved in the tragedy of ritual death. In the same way, verbal humour tends to kill everyday language in order the better to create an idiom in which word and meaning are confused in the same semiology of comedy. And, as Smollett realised in the evening of his life, beyond this dissolution, this confusion, lies nothing but the silence of the void from which laughter momentarily rescues man only to cast him back into the abyss.

General conclusion

Why devote so many pages and so much time and research to Tobias Smollett? Is he not the eternal second fiddle to Fielding, on whom a revival of literary, academic and even cinematographic interest has focused so much more limelight? Has not Smollett been stowed away for years in one of those impregnable niches of critical mythology, classified, labelled and duly relegated to a subordinate rank among the great English eighteenth-century novelists? Why disturb the ashes in this critical niche, which resembles a dusty funereal pigeon-hole in a gigantic columbarium, ashes condemned for ever, in appearance at least, by two and a half centuries of more or less categorical verdicts, according to the times, to a literary fame mitigated by frequent accusations of brutality, indelicacy, grotesque truculence and immorality, not to say amorality? As to Smollett's personality, his pugnacious and vindictive temperament of a rugged Scot 'on the make' does not predispose one to like him at first sight, any more than his sometimes vitriolic acidity or the perpetual tension of a man racked by material anxieties and illness.

Such were the 'good' reasons for leaving Smollett and his novels in the legendary limbo of critical mythology. But it has seemed preferable to the intellectual comfort and 'good conscience' of venerable judgments mellowed and sanctified by ritual repetition, and also more honest, to make an unprejudiced analysis of Smollett's personality and his novels. A perilous task, and not devoid of imprudence, perhaps even of impudence. In fact, this essay is neither a starting point nor a culmination but fits into the line traced by those scholars, mainly American, who for nearly fifty years have devoted themselves with courage and patience to making known the *true* Smollett, his *true* human and literary face. Just as Knapp, in his work, has devoted himself, with scrupulous factual and psychological honesty, to dispersing the distorting shadows of erroneous biographical legend, this study of the novels attempts to demolish the myths — not without having first explained them — which obscure the appreciation of a vigorous human and literary personality.

For the gods, or demigods, of criticism have undoubtedly been mistaken. Smollett's personality and work are of more contemporary relevance than ever. Smollett's personality, pervaded by an independence at times aggressive and tactless in its passionate intransigence, is defined in the last resort by courage, the courage of accepting the daily toils of an often difficult life and of refusing to the last the insidious attrition of carking cares, illness and death. In his letters, his novels, his poetry and even in the *Travels through France and Italy*, Smollett appears with his faults, his verbal and psychological exaggerations, his meanderings of a passionate puritan, fascinated by life and tightly sheathed in his inhibiting moral convictions. Whereas our century tends to become — it is already a commonplace cliché, but the twentieth century is dying of this tragic banality — that of standardised men, expertly dehumanised by the multiple pressures of society, it is comforting for those who can still read a personality or a novel to study a courageous author like Smollett. Courageous to an immoderate degree, to excess, even to injustice. If, in 1760, he was sentenced to three months' imprisonment for the following paragraph which appeared in the *Critical Review* of May 1758 (v, 438–9), would he not deserve to be applauded today for a courage which, cantankerous as it certainly is, is in process of disappearing? Here are the terms in which he attacked Admiral Knowles, whom, rightly or wrongly he deemed responsible for the catastrophic naval fiasco off Rochefort in 1757:

> He has been compared to a cat, which, though thrown from the top of a house in twenty different attitudes, will always land on its feet; and to the arms of the Isle of Man, which are three legs conjoined in ham, inscribed *quocunque scieris stabo*. We have heard of a man, who, without birth, interest or fortune, has raised himself from the lowest paths of life to an eminent rank in the service; and if all his friends were put to the strappado, they could not define the quality or qualities to which he owed his elevation. Nay, it would be found upon enquiry, that he neither has, or ever had any friend at all; (for we make a wide distinction between a patron and a friend); and yet for a series of years, he has been enabled to sacrifice the blood, the treasure and the honour of his country, to his own ridiculous projects. Ask his character of those who know him, [and] they will not scruple to say, he is an admiral without conduct, an engineer without knowledge, an officer without resolution, and a man with-

out veracity. They will tell you he is an ignorant, assuming, officious, fribbling pretender; conceited as a peacock, obstinate as a mule, and mischievous as a monkey; that in every station of life he has played the tyrant with his inferiors, the incendiary among his equals, and commanded a sq . . . n occasionally for twenty years, without having even established his reputation in the article of personal courage.

Often quoted, but never analysed in detail on the psychological and stylistic plane, this vengeful diatribe symbolises the defiance of a courageous personality woven of profound and violent contradictions. But, before even proceeding to the examination of this passage, is it not right in spite of − or because of? − this extraordinary verbal virulence, to applaud, with some nostalgia, the courage to assume this polemical freedom? In a social, political and literary world where spinelessness is more and more the *sine qua non* condition of an insipid material success, those who still have − for how long? − the sense of individual freedom can only savour the vivifying bitterness of such a tirade. The aim of this analysis is not to determine the precise historical value of this attack launched by Smollett against Knowles, but to appreciate the psychological and stylistic mechanisms of the Smollettian challenge in their true proportions. The whole passage is marked by a paradoxical contradiction which is ramified in the various articulations of the attack. While Smollett's statements are aimed at a man's moral and professional reputation, with an acrimony from which all prudent reticence is excluded, at no point does the author of the article fight barefaced. The 'we' which appears twice loses nearly all personal significance, since, in the first case, it is a matter of a rumour ('We have heard'), and in the second, of a parenthesis which provides a generalised explanation ('for we make a wide distinction'). Whatever Smollett's courage, whatever his aggressive lucidity, he needs, as in the auto-dedication of *Ferdinand Count Fathom* and the auto-biographical passage in *Humphry Clinker* where he brings 'Mr. S . . .' on to the scene, several masks, even if these, by dint of clinging to his face, become the face itself. The personal pronouns, the verbs and their mood, reinforce this ambiguous impression of impersonality at once desired and rejected. 'They' represents the friends, or reputed such, of Knowles and the people who know him. Taking still further care to conceal his own opinion, Smollett resorts to the vague and anonymous passive: 'he has been compared', 'it would be found', 'he has been enabled'. There is a certain marked semantic progression in the use of the verbs referring to Knowles's reputation: 'compared', 'heard', 'found', 'know', that is to say an evolution from the more general to the more particular. To these verbs must be added the direct, but rhetorical, invitation contained in the imperative 'Ask', which in fact is tantamount to a hypothetical conditional. Here again, Smollett keeps on the mask, since he implicitly makes the responsibility for the judgments fall back on those who know

Knowles. He, the author of the diatribe, is only the passive interpreter of a scandalous reputation.

Nevertheless, Smollett's style is far from any amorphous neutrality, like the psychological process which infuses its extraordinary dynamism into this miniature libel. It does not require a very thorough examination to discover that the lexical and syntactical dominant is incontestably negative. But this omnipresent negativity assumes several distinct aspects and, first of all, the use of animal comparisons. The initial feline image, though not very flattering, could at a pinch be classified as neutral. But the insulting triad of peacock, mule and monkey derives its force not only from proverbial mythology but also from the strong negative connotations with which man has furnished these unlucky animals. Negative grotesqueness crosses another threshold when Knowles sees himself compared to the arms of the Isle of Man and reduced to an emblem deprived of all human character and, on the contrary, monstrously objectified: 'three legs conjoined in ham'. It would be hard to find a neater way — and also, in view of the Latin quotation, a more erudite one — of reducing a man to nothing. But if, by chance, these images were to pass unnoticed, one can hardly fail to observe the abundance of all kinds of negations in this passage in which 'without', used half-a-dozen times, is undoubtedly the key word, a highly appropriate preposition to indicate this nullity which Smollett is vigorously denouncing. The negations of the verbs — 'could not define', 'neither has, or ever had' — are reinforced by peremptory assertions which, in Smollett's mind at least, admit no exception: '*always* light', '*all* his friends', '*at all*', 'in *every* station of life'. Similarly, the pejorative epithets, nouns and adjectives all imply a lack, an absence or a highly negative fault: 'pretender', 'tyrant', 'incendiary' would be already violent enough but the Smollettian arsenal is well stocked with pulverising adjectives: 'lowest', 'ridiculous', 'ignorant', 'assuming', 'officious', 'fribbling', 'conceited', 'obstinate', 'mischievous'.

The psychological process presents an example of those latent contradictions exaggerated by Smollett's wrath. At first, he reproaches Knowles for his low birth and thus implicitly makes himself the defender of that all-powerful socio-economic trilogy in the eighteenth century: 'birth . . . interest . . . fortune'. But a few lines further on, he is launching a criticism of the powers that be, the 'establishment'. The government, in which corruption and favouritism are rife, has made itself Knowles's accomplice since it has deliberately promoted an incompetent. But it would be untrue to see Smollett as an angry political rebel ahead of his time. He falls back very quickly on the patriotic values of society, 'the blood, the treasure and the honour of his country'. And he closes the sentence with a flourish, after that fine triple drum-roll of which he is fond. Conservative too, is this adoption of a stance which deplores the rise of a man 'from the lowest paths of life to an eminent rank in the service'. Twice again ('raised', 'elevation'), this rise seems to offend his conception of a rigid and hierarchical society. Finally, Smollett, even in the midst of his polemical indignation, does not forget his rhetoric. The 'Nay', introduces an insincere epanorthosis which corrects the previous expression 'all his friends' and reduces their number to nil. This psychological, moral and professional character sketch is a vigorous miniature philippic, in which Smollett lets himself go to the full, while still keeping on the mask. But he courageously dropped it in June 1759, when he admitted before Lord Mansfield that he was indeed the author of this attack. It is not irrelevant that the final reproach addressed to Knowles, after the vitriolic cascade of other accusations, deals with lack of 'personal courage', a quality with which he, Smollett, was endowed, in dangerously plethoric abundance, in spite of the many contradictions it could cover.

Smollett has the contemporaneity of a complex personality kicking against the pricks in his exacerbated determination to protect his individual liberty. But his novels are also contemporary; fortuitously and almost painfully contemporary. How can one not compare the Smollettian world, torn by violence and passions, to our presentday one? The same glaring and blatant discrepancies exist between rich and poor, glutted and starving, privileged and underprivileged. Only the nuances have changed: Humphry Clinker would no longer die of cold, fever, or starvation in the depths of the English countryside. The local authorities would send him to drag out a larval existence as a statistical unit in some anonymous institution of the National Health Service. And, once cured, he would be returned to the faceless mass which works, rests, eats, drinks and fornicates according to the categorical imperatives created by that other faceless monster, the consumer society.

But there still exist — and for some decades more — Roderick Randoms who fight for survival, suffer frustrations, rebuffs and blows, but end up by forcing the parsimonious hand of fate. The black gold of Alaska, the Sahara or the North Sea will replace the traffic in human ebony. Peregrine Pickles will always fritter away their inheritance, but, instead of attempting to rape an Emilia, they will doubtless experiment a little with drugs or indulge in occasional sex orgies. Crooks like Fathom have diminished neither in number nor astuteness, publicity even giving them the opportunity of exercising their talents legally and with complete impunity. A sign of the intolerance of our more 'progressive' (if that word really means much) age? Except in Great Britain, the last frail refuge of eccentrics, Launcelot Greaves would very quickly find himself back in a psychiatric hospital. But it is still and always *Humphry Clinker* that remains the truest and most contemporary of Smollett's novels. This quintuple constellation of perfectly ordinary people (for even Bramble's surly idiosyncracy is perfectly normal) travels from Wales to Scotland only to find itself more firmly established, changes only to remain more identical with itself, a shifting and fixed conglomeration of protean human relationships.

Smollett is contemporary in the social and human world, but also in the academic one, the best and the worst, like the famous tongues of Aesop. It is a lean year when *Dissertation Abstracts* does not list half-a-dozen American PhD theses on Smollett. In them, Smollett's work, often with very unequal success, is dissected, carved up in slices and examined from the latest fashionable critical angle to make it say what it never intended to say. But it would be unjust and incorrect to condemn all these labours *en bloc*: occasionally they emerge from the academic greyness to prove useful and judicious. Articles and books are not lacking either, as the annual bibliographies of the *Philological Quarterly* and of *PMLA* prove, and it is curious to note that recent Smollettian criticism is undergoing a development analogous to the general appreciation of the eighteenth century. At last, one after the other, the labels are coming unstuck and falling off. Neoclassical literature reveals its complex hesitations, its aesthetic uncertainties, its deep rifts. In the same way, beneath the apparent lack of intellectuality in Smollett's novels and their deceptive lack of structure, it is possible, without doing violence to the texts, to discern a much more elaborate moral architecture. After querying the autobiographical and picaresque myths, it is a task to which the present study is mainly devoted. It was not a question of raising Smollett to the rank of a great eighteenth-century thinker, but of rescuing him at last from that pernicious critical legend of an author qualified as comic, farcical, grotesque, picaresque, realistic − these adjectives being the most current and the most irritating for their inexactness and for the slapdash way in which they are applied. Smollett does not propose, and certainly does not impose, a codified morality. In his last novel, the profoundest and richest, he is content to *state* certain failures, certain successes, certain incompatibilities in characters and life. But, as the chapter devoted to this novel has stressed, *Humphry Clinker* ends with a series, not of adamant certainties but of questions, doubts and unresolved problems. Robert Hopkins's study reaches the same conclusion: 'There is no real resolution in *Humphry Clinker*. The happy ending is a surface one; ironically and deliberately so' ('The Function of Grotesque in *Humphry Clinker*, 163−77; quotation from p. 177, *HLQ*, xxii, Feb. 1969).

The bicentenary of Smollett's death in 1971 was marked by the publication of two critical studies and a dozen articles (see the Select Bibliography). Strangely enough, neither book was published in Great Britain, neither author was English. Whereas *The Times Literary Supplement* of March 17th 1921, had a leader celebrating the bicentenary of Smollett's birth, in 1971, the *TLS* was silent about his death. Yet, encouraging signs exist: the publication of *The Letters of T. Smollett* (ed. L. M. Knapp, Clarendon Press, 1970); the scholarly enterprise of the Iowa Edition, still in progress; the publication in 'Oxford English Novels' of two of Smollett's less well-known works, *Ferdinand Count Fathom* (ed. Damian Grant, 1971) and *Launcelot Greaves* (ed. David Evans, 1973).

J. V. Price's excellent introductory study of *Humphry Clinker* (Arnold, 1973) bears witness to the lasting popularity of Smollett's epistolary masterpiece.

Finally, there remains what, for want of a better word, one must call Smollett's 'literary' contemporaneity, the contemporaneity of a Janus facing towards the past and the future. The history of Smollettian criticism is unfortunately dominated by a false problem of pernicious literary hierarchy. Is Fielding a greater novelist than Smollett or vice versa? An almost inevitable false problem, in view of the chronological coincidence of their fictional work. But such a preoccupation of posthumous critical docimology cannot stand up to an impartial and lucid analysis. Why pronounce, with the arrogance of false certitudes, a value judgment which classes Fielding above Smollett or the other way round? Why compare two lives, two human and literary temperaments which are in no way comparable? Nevertheless, the fact that there are points of contact, and of friction, between the work of Smollett and that of Fielding is a literary phenomenon whose analysis is much more fruitful, as this study has endeavoured to show. Between Fielding and Smollett there is a characterological and literary complementarity whose multifarious interplay enables one to recreate an important fragment of daily life in the eighteenth century better than many specialised historical or sociological works can do.

It is impossible to speak of Smollett's literary contemporaneity without mentioning this modern phenomenon which upsets the (seemingly at least) most firmly established critical judgment: the wide circulation of the cheap paperback edition. Both *Roderick Random* and *Humphry Clinker* are included in the collection of 'Signet Classics', *Humphry Clinker* since 1960, and *Roderick Random* since 1964. More recently, *Humphry Clinker* has been published in 'The Penguin English Library' (1967). These are important signs of literary vitality. The postface written by John Barth for *Roderick Random* (pp. 469–79), in spite of the usual comfortable clichés about the absence of intellectuality and structure in *Roderick Random*, nevertheless has the merit of emphasising this (at first sight) disordered dynamic vigour which enables the characters in *Roderick Random* to retain all their literary force: 'They wail and guffaw, curse and sing, make love and foul their breeches: in short they live, at a clip and with a brute *joie de vivre* that our modern spirits can scarcely comprehend' (p. 478). Doubtless it is this exuberance that John Barth is trying to rediscover, with varying success, in his novels, in particular in *The Sot-Weed Factor* (1961). Although cheap editions, printed in large quantities, are a tangible sign of still flourishing popularity, they also present some dangers. In 1962, an abridged version of *Roderick Random* was published in Panther Books. The gaudy eye-catching cover displays an extremely *décolletée* Narcissa surprised (by her brother?) in Roderick's arms, and also an equally alluring and misleading caption: 'The amorous career of a passionate young rogue'. Poor clumsy, bungling Roderick raised, for the requirements of erotic publicity, to the level of a (tenth-rate) Scottish Casanova!

But there is another, perhaps more lasting, literary contemporaneity, for it is rooted in the very genius of the English language. The verbal virtuosity which Smollett displays in the letters of Win Jenkins and Tabitha belongs to a potent tradition of popular comedy already exploited, as has been seen, by Shakespeare. In his work *Told in Letters: epistolary fiction before Richardson* (1966), Robert Adams Day analyses the same device employed by Tom d'Urfey. The story 'The Prudent Husband: or, Cuckoldom Wittily Prevented' included in *Stories Moral and Comical* (1706), adapted from the *Heptameron*, contains a *billet doux* written by a woman (already!) and studded with revealing *lapsus linguae*. And Robert Adams Day concludes:

> D'Urfey's 'billet' contains true 'portmanteau' words; and we may consider it the most remote ancestor in fiction of the wordplay that passed from Smollett to Dickens and Lewis Carroll, and to its culmination in the verbal complexities of *Finnegans Wake* (p. 137).

Joyce's verbal creations, scintillating and dazzling as they are, end by wearying one with their often laborious display (for the non-specialist) of polyglot philological erudition. More akin to Smollett, authors like Anthony Burgess, in *A Clockwork Orange* (1962), and above all the Beatle, John Lennon, in *John Lennon In His Own Write* (London, 1964) and in *A Spaniard In The Works* (1965) have rediscovered and exploited this vein of popular humour which joys and delights in distorting current English so as to condense into a single word several possible meanings from which jovial bawdiness and nonsense are far from being excluded. Might not Win Jenkins have written the beginning of this 'Last Will and Testicle'?:

> I, Barrold Reginald Bunker-Harquart being of sound mind you, limp and bodie, do on this day the 18 of September of 1924th, leave all my belodgings estate and brown suits to my nice neice Elsie. The above afformentioned hereafter to be kept in a large box until she is 21 of age, then to be released amongst a birthdave party given in her honour (*A Spaniard In The Works*, p. 76).

Is not this comic dislocation of the language the ultimate refuge of the individual who feels himself menaced by the pressures of society and attempts, under cover of an idiolect, to stave off his own annihilation and the death of a civilisation? Smollett's work is situated, on the historical and literary planes, at the crossroads of two cultures: that of a still rural society which is dying and that of a preindustrial society which is in process of being born. Burgess and Lennon shatter the language on the threshold of the space age. Smollett's verbal comedy in *Humphry Clinker*, and that of his modern successors, thus appear as a will to destroy, but also to create in order to protect themselves from an inevitable annihilation by one last incantation to the forces of life. And this final resort to the comic in *Humphry Clinker* enables one to place the whole of Smollett's existence and the whole of his fictional work under the ambiguous sign of challenge and supplication to life, a feeling which he expresses with an unexpected, intuitive force in the last two lines of his 'Ode to Mirth':

> Now Mirth hath heard the suppliant Poet's prayer;
> No cloud that rides the blast shall vex the troubled air.

Appendix
Posthumous works attributed to Smollett

'Ode to Independence'

This poem, which has already been mentioned several times in the course of this study, was printed in Glasgow in 1773 by Robert and Andrew Foulis. Anderson (1820) states that the manuscript had been sent to the publishers 'by a person with whom Dr. Smollett was much connected' (i, 106). Buck, in his book *Smollett as Poet* (Yale University Press, 1927), convincingly elucidates the date of its composition: according to all probability the year 1766 (see pp. 70—9). Luella F. Norwood has established the authenticity of this poem in her article: 'The authenticity of Smollett's "Ode to Independence"', *RES*, xvii (1941), 55—64. Critical opinions have been in general very favourable to this poem, considered as Smollett's best. See in particular Moore (1872) pp. 139—40; Abraham Mills, *The Literature and the Literary Men of Great Britain and Ireland* (New York, 1851), II, 517; George Gilfillan, *The Poetical Works of Johnson, Parnell, Gray and Smollett* (Edinburgh, 1855), p. 217; James Hannay, *Quarterly Review*, ciii (January 1858), 107, in which Hannay sees the author of this ode as the precursor of Burns; Knapp, pp. 291—2. This poem is reproduced by W. E. Henley, in *Works*, XII, 32—6.

The Orientalist A Volume of Tales after the Eastern Taste. By the Author of Roderick Random, Sir Launcelot Greaves, etc. And Others. Dublin. Printed by James Hoey, Junior, at the Mercury in Parliament Street, 1773, 281 pages.

A first edition of this work appeared in Dublin in 1764. It is therefore not a matter, strictly speaking, of a posthumous work, but only the second edition of 1773 (Dublin) is listed in the British Museum catalogue (12613.b.28).

It is a collection of thirty-six eastern tales, mainly quite short (from 3 to 24 pages), except for the first 'The History of Omrah' (pp. 1–37). It is no doubt on account of this tale that the publisher banked on the commercial value of an attribution to Smollett. This literary paternity, as much of the first tale as the others, is hard to prove. The only certain link with Smollett is the publication of this first tale in the *British Magazine* of January to March 1760. But this is in no way a proof that Smollett really did write 'The History of Omrah', of which neither the story nor the style (apart from a profusion of Arabic words) present any great originality. R. D. Mayo, in *The English Novel in the Magazines 1740–1815* (1962) gives some details of this collection (pp. 521–2). In his article 'Tobias Smollett and *The Orientalist*', *N & Q*, xv, No. 12 (December 1968), 456–63, J. Harry Wolf examines with much care and erudition the problems posed by a burlesque Greenlandic tale, 'Igluka and Sibbersik' (pp. 267–76), the last but one of the collection. In spite of certain parallels, with the *Present State* in particular, it is for the moment impossible to conclude with certainty that Smollett is really the author of this Eskimo extravaganza.

Translation of *Les Aventures de Télémaque*
Two volumes published in London in 1776 and bearing Smollett's name on the title-page. Anderson (I, 107) alludes to it in two lines. In general, the biographers, apart from Whitridge (1925), p. 16, do not mention this translation in the list of Smollett's works. He himself makes no reference to a translation of Fénelon in his correspondence, at least such of it as we possess at the moment. This lack of information permits Cordasco, *N & Q*, cxciii (1948), 563, to assert (on erroneous proofs) that this translation is not Smollett's but the one by John Hawkesworth published in 1758 and reissued in 1776. Hawkesworth's version and the one attributed to Smollett are clearly different. Knapp, in his article, 'Smollett's translation of Fénelon's *Télémaque*', *PQ*, xliv (July 1965), 405–6, reproduces a previously unpublished document, bearing Smollett's signature. This acknowledges the receipt, on April 1st 1767, of a sum of £70 for the translation rights of *Les Aventures de Télémaque*. Why was it necessary to wait another nine years for the publication of this translation? The mystery remains complete. This spirited and elegant, rather than faithful, translation was reprinted half-a-dozen times before the end of the eighteenth century. Thanks to Knapp's researches, it can henceforth be classified 'as an authentic opus in the canon of Smollett's works' (Knapp, op. cit., p. 407).

The Israelites; or the Pampered Nabob
This farce in two acts was performed only once, on April 1st 1785, at the Covent Garden theatre. But one had to wait until 1935 and H. R. C. Van

der Veen's thesis, *Jewish Characters in Eighteenth Century English Fiction and Drama* (Groningen), for the appearance in print (pp. 270—90) of this play attributed to Smollett by several periodicals of the time: the *Morning Chronicle* of March 31st and April 1st 1785; the *Universal Daily Register* of April 1st 1785; the *European Magazine*, vii (April 1785), in which one can read:

> This month commenced with the performance of a Farce at this Theatre, never performed before, written by the late Dr. Smollett called *The Israelites; or the Pampered Nabob*. It contained many strokes of humour peculiar to the author. Owing to the severity of the weather, it was very ill attended and but indifferently received. It was played for the benefit of Mr. Aickin (p. 284).

Van der Veen reproduces the manuscript which figures in the Larpent collection of the Huntingdon Library. The handwriting, or rather handwritings, for Act I does not appear to have been written by the same person as Act II, do not look like Smollett's, in so far as it is possible to judge from a photocopy.

The story in itself is not very original. A merry widow, Mrs Wrinkle, lives in a perpetual whirl of receptions, card parties and other entertainments dear to the privileged classes of the eighteenth century. Her brother (the nabob), Sir Simon Lollop, has sunk into total apathy and indolence. Mrs Wrinkle's daughter, the pretty Miss Naivette, is, as her name indicates, a silly young chick barely emerged from the nest of the private school where she has acquired a few vague smatterings of culture. But such game, provided with a £30,000 dowry, cannot fail to arouse the male hunting instinct. Her guardian, the honest Jew Mr Israel, intervenes to protect her. He decides to remove her to his own sister's home in Hackney, where she will no longer have the daily example of her mother's dissipation before her eyes. But Israel has a rascal of a son, Enoch, with a taste for women and wine and solid hard cash. To his father's despair, Enoch has just become a Christian, which he proclaims with all the more impudence since the young convert is an arrant hypocrite. Grasping opportunity by the forelock, he abducts Naivette, reckoning to marry her. But his father discovers him, prevents this marriage, decides to put Sir Simon Lollop's finances in order again and even pardons his son. The only literary interest of this farce is the presence of a good Jew on the stage:

> For the first time the Jew in drama is an ordinary human being whose character is composed of good and bad qualities. The good traits predominate, for there are not many things to find fault with in Mr Israel (Van der Veen, p. 202).

Israel is merely impetuous and lets himself go so far as to beat Sir Simon's impudent black servant (Blanchee!). There is a certain kinship between Israel and the good Jew in *Ferdinand Count Fathom*, Joshua Manasseh.

Naivette occasionally reminds one of Lydia and her sentimental palpitations. Van der Veen thought it was difficult to attribute this farce, which he analyses at length (pp. 198–209), to Smollett, but believed that the anonymous author was strongly influenced by Smollett, in particular by *Ferdinand Count Fathom*. Mrs Wrinkle deliberately affects learned words, which she mangles occasionally, but not as frequently as Tabitha or Win Jenkins in *Humphry Clinker*.

In his article 'Smollett and the *Israelites*', *PQ*, xlv (1966), 387–94, Richard W. Bevis suggests a theory which is more attractive and ingenious than sound. According to Bevis, the dichotomy of the title *The Israelites; or the Pampered Nabob* could represent the double origin of this farce. On the one hand, Smollett's original contribution, that is to say his manuscript entrusted to a printer (Millar for example); on the other, a complete revision of the play to make it appeal to the taste of the day and give it an up-to-date character. In that spring of 1785, it is certain that rich nabobs returned from the Indies were a spicy topic of satire and scandal, in view of the commission for trial of Warren Hastings. So Bevis suggests that: 'The character of the nabob is probably a later graft, or at least a complete rewriting of a role in the original' (p. 391). Smollett could have written *The Israelites* about 1750, the period of the philosemitism of *Ferdinand Count Fathom* and of attempts to get one of his theatrical works performed. This theory, however, remains very frail, for lack of facts to support it. At the end of the article, Bevis admits that: 'More definite evidence will be necessary before Smollett can positively be assigned authorship of *The Israelites*' (p. 394).

The references to this farce, whose importance is more sociological than literary, are few enough to deserve attention being drawn to the most important ones: Anderson (I, 107) makes a curious paraphrase of previous articles, in particular *The European Magazine*, vii (1785), 284, next *The European Magazine*, xxxiii (1798), 104, and lastly, Baker's *Biographia Dramatica*, II (1812), 337. See also Walter Scott, op. cit., p. 103; Genest, *Some Account of the English Stage*, VI (1832), 362; Allardyce Nicoll, *A History of Late Eighteenth Drama 1750–1800* (1927), p. 308.

'The Unfortunate Lovers'
This sentimental story, a few pages long, was published for the first time in Smollett's lifetime, but anonymously. It is presented in the form of a letter to the editors of the *British Magazine*, i (May 1760), 121–5, with the title: 'The history of Alcanor and Eudosia'. The introduction to this letter, genuine or sham, deserves to be quoted for its sententious moral tone:

> Gentlemen, give me leave, through the canal of your magazine, to communicate a story, which is not more romantic than true; and may serve as a lesson of prudence and morality to those parents, who

think there is nothing but affluence necessary or essential to the happiness of their children (p. 121).

This story was not attributed to Smollett till twenty-six years later in *The New Novelist's Magazine* (London), i (1786), 24—7.

The story is certainly romantic, but of a maudlin ineptitude even worse than the pages where Smollett involves himself in describing the agitations and emotions of his heroines. Alcanor, the son of a London merchant, falls in love with the beautiful Eudosia. It is a shared passion, approved by Eudosia's father, himself also a rich merchant. Alas! Alcanor finds himself suddenly ruined, and Eudosia's father no longer wants him for a son-in-law. Alcanor, embittered, decides to emigrate, with death in his soul and love in his heart. Eudosia weeps. The cruel father dies without his daughter Eudosia having married. She inherits his wealth, buys herself a remote country house and devotes herself to good works. However Alcanor has made a fortune in the Americas and decides to return to England. On the way, his ship is attacked by a French pirate and Alcanor, wounded in the neck, which makes him blind, is set ashore quite close to Eudosia's dwelling. This coincidence is hardly fortuitous. Eudosia takes in the wounded man without recognising him. Alcanor, feeling himself on the point of death, asks that his will should be read. In it he leaves his entire fortune to Eudosia. She recognises him (at last) weeps and swoons. Under the shock of emotion, Alcanor recovers his sight but dies, soon followed by his beloved who has presented her fortune to the poor of the parish. Thus Alcanor and Eudosia died happy and never had any children.

In the present state of research, it is not possible to affirm that Smollett is or is not the author of this lachrymose tale. But it is hard to believe he could have perpetrated such a flagrant tear-jerker. The turgid style bears no resemblance to his spirited and incisive writing in *Launcelot Greaves*, which dates from the same period. Moreover, it is difficult to understand why Smollett, who was the founder of the *British Magazine* and was already publishing *Launcelot Greaves* in it, should resort to that most threadbare of subterfuges, the letter addressed to the editor. In any case, if 'The Unfortunate Lovers', a title created by *The New Novelist's Magazine* in 1786, is by Smollett, it certainly adds nothing to his literary reputation, very much the reverse. The story is reprinted by C. E. Jones in *Smollett Studies* (1942), pp. 112—16, with some useful bibliographical details.

'Smollett's Dying Prediction'
A letter of three pages reprinted by W. E. Henley, in *Works*, XII, 436—8. It is supposed to have been sent by Smollett to one of his clerical friends a few months before his death (1771). As L. M. Knapp's article, ' "The Prophecy" Attributed to Smollett', *RES*, xvi (May 1965), 177—82, proves, this letter appeared as early as 1794 in a (rare) book entitled *Literary and Critical Remarks* ... and containing a curious medley of

predictions, prophecies and political and religious revelations. It was also published in 1795 in a pamphlet, *A Dissertation on the Existence, Nature and Extent of the Prophetic Powers in the Human Mind*. This is the source given by Henley, who follows Smollett's biographer Robert Chambers.

The letter contains nothing prophetic. At the very most it is a matter of political forecasts within the reach of a shrewd observer like Smollett, but it had a certain success in France as well as England at the end of the eighteenth century. It foresees the revolt of the American colonies, the rising of the slaves in the West Indies, the French Revolution, and finally the general conflict in Europe after the events which had occurred in France In Letter xxxvi of *Travels through France and Italy* Smollett already does not conceal his opinion on the tragic future of the French monarchy. The thoughts on the imminent revolt of the American colonies are in no way surprising for a historian who had always been interested in the future of the Americans. The humanitarian remarks about the black slaves of the West Indies are more unexpected, for Smollett seems not to have been in the least affected by the great wave of anti-slavery compassion which culminated in Lord Mansfield's judgment in 1772 which declared slavery illegal (it needed another sixty years before it was abolished in the British colonies). In *Roderick Random* the hero and his uncle, Bowling, traffic in slaves without the slightest qualm. Smollett owned slaves on his wife's plantation in Jamaica, and sold them without the least humanitarian scruple. Stylistically, it is not impossible that he could have composed this letter, but the language is less characteristic of Smollett himself than of any cultured man of the eighteenth century.

Is it a forgery? The manuscript having disappeared, it is very difficult to express an opinion. Knapp's conclusion is extremely prudent: 'we cannot be certain that it was his, but we are inclined to believe that he wrote it' (op. cit., p. 182).

Brambleton Hall, a Novel, Being a Sequel to the celebrated Expedition of Humphrey [sic] Clinker, by Tobias Smollett, M.D. (London, 1818), pp. xix, 162.

There is *no* possibility that this sequel to *Humphry Clinker* could be the work of Smollett. But this little-known imitation is not without interest, if only to prove the publicity value of Smollett's name and of the title of his novel nearly fifty years after his death. Knapp has pointed out in the *TLS* of October 6th 1932, p. 716, that there exists an earlier edition dating from 1810. Keats knew and much appreciated this sequel to *Humphry Clinker*, see the letter to Woodhouse, September 21st 1819, No. 152 in *The Letters of John Keats*, edited by M. B. Forman (Oxford U.P., 1952); pp. 152–3.

This imitation is quite remarkable. The style is more than a pastiche, it is genuinely impregnated with the stylistic devices of *Humphry Clinker*, including the involuntary verbal creations of Tabitha and of Winifred, née

Jenkins, now Mrs Lloyd. The unknown author brilliantly reproduces Smollett's epistolary technique. The development of the characters is entirely in line with the original creations. Jery is a little more didactic than in *Humphry Clinker* and is interested in the social and political life of Bath, where he lives with his sister and his brother-in-law Dennison. Jery becomes a member of Parliament, Lismahago a magistrate, Clinker 'mare of the Burro' ('Mayor of the Borough' as spelt by his wife, who is as dysorthographic as ever).

Lydia has a son, so has Win (even two). Matthew Bramble continues to fulminate against the corruption of the modern world and dies regretted by all. Win, in accordance with the psychological indications in *Humphry Clinker*, proves herself the proud parvenu she threatened to become at the end of that novel. She just condescends to write to Mary Jones, and when she becomes the mayoress, she is bursting with self-importance, as witness the following sentence, worthy of the real author of *Humphry Clinker*: 'So you will, in future, address my piscriptions to my Lady Mare-arse' (p. 157). Nevertheless, it is on a note of regret and uneasiness that Win concludes this excellent apocryphal sequel to *Humphry Clinker*.

Abbreviations and editions of reference

Abbreviations of Smollett's works are shown in **bold** *type.*

Editions of Smollett's works

Unfortunately no modern complete edition is yet available (December 1974). Only four of Smollett's novels have been published in the Oxford University Press 'Oxford English Novels' series:

PP   *Peregrine Pickle* (1751), edited with an introduction by James L. Clifford, 1964; xxxiv, 805 pp.

HC   *Humphry Clinker* (1771), edited with an introduction by Lewis M. Knapp, 1966; xxii, 375 pp.

FCF   *Ferdinand Count Fathom* (1753), edited with an introduction by Damian Grant, 1971; xxvi, 384 pp.

LG   *Sir Launcelot Greaves* (1760–61), edited with an introduction by David Evans, 1973; xxvii, 234 pp.

The following are cited from *The Works of Tobias Smollett*, edited by W. E. Henley, 12 vols, Westminster and New York, 1899–1901.

RR   *Roderick Random* (1748), vols I and II.
TFI   *Travels Through France and Italy* (1766), vol. XI.
AA   *The History and Adventures of an Atom* (1769), vol. XII.

All references to poems, plays and miscellaneous writings are to *Works*, ed. Henley, vol. XII.

Other works by Smollett, in chronological order:

CR   *The Critical Review*, 1756–1817
CHE *A Complete History of England* (4 vols, 1757–58), Oxford English Classics edn., 5 vols, Oxford, 1827.
BM   *The British Magazine*, 1760–67.
CCHE *Continuation of the Complete History of England*, 5 vols, 1760–65.
PS   *The Present State of All Nations*, 8 vols, 1768.

Editions of Smollett's works containing biographical material are referred to in the notes by editor's name, as follows:

Anderson, 1820: *The Miscellaneous Works of Tobias Smollett*, ed. Robert Anderson, 6 vols, Edinburgh, 1820.
Herbert, 1870: *The Works of Tobias Smollett*, ed. David Herbert, Edinburgh, 1870.
Moore, 1872: This refers, not to Dr John Moore's 1797 edition of Smollett's works, but to Dr James P. Browne's more readily available edition in 8 vols, London, 1872, which reprints Moore's 'Memoirs' of Smollett's life.

Biographical and critical works, in chronological order:

Scott:	Walter Scott, Prefatory Memoir to *The Novels of Tobias Smollett*, first published in 1821; here cited from *The Lives of the Novelists*, Dent, Everyman's Library, 1910.
Chambers:	Robert Chambers, *Smollett, His Life and a Selection from his Writings*, Edinburgh, 1867.
Hannay:	David Hannay, *Life of Tobias George Smollett*, London, 1887.
Smeaton:	Oliphant Smeaton, *Tobias Smollett*, Edinburgh (1897).
Buck:	Howard Swazey Buck, *A Study in Smollett, chiefly 'Peregrine Pickle'*, Yale U.P., 1925.
Buck:	Howard Swazey Buck, *Smollett as Poet*, Yale U.P., 1927.
Martz:	Louis L. Martz, *The Later Career of Tobias Smollett*, Yale U.P., 1942.
Joliat:	Eugène Joliat, *Smollett et la France*, Paris, 1935.
Kahrl:	George M. Kahrl, *Tobias Smollett, Traveler—Novelist*, Univ. of Chicago Press, 1945.
Knapp:	Lewis M. Knapp, *Tobias Smollett, Doctor of Men and Manners*, Princeton U.P., 1949.
Knapp, *Letters*:	*The Letters of Tobias Smollett*, edited by Lewis M. Knapp, Oxford, Clarendon Press, 1970.

Periodicals

AH	*American Heritage*
AL	*American Literature*
BNYPL	*Bulletin of the New York Public Library*
BYUS	*Brigham Young University Studies*
CE	*College English*
DUJ	*Durham University Journal*
EA	*Études Anglaises*
ECS	*Eighteenth-Century Studies*
ELH	*Journal of English Literary History*
ELN	*English Language Notes*
Expl.	*Explicator*
HLB	*Harvard Library Bulletin*
HLQ	*Huntington Library Quarterly*
JAMA	*Journal of the American Medical Association*
JAmS	*Journal of American Studies*
JEGP	*Journal of English and Germanic Philology*
JHI	*Journal of the History of Ideas*
Lan M	*Les Langues Modernes*
MLN	*Modern Language Notes*
MP	*Modern Philology*
N & Q	*Notes and Queries*

PAPS   *Proceedings of the American Philosophical Society*
PBSA   *Papers of the Bibliographical Society of America*
PLL   *Papers on Language and Literature*
PMLA   *Publications of the Modern Language Association of America*
PQ   *Philological Quarterly*
RES   *Review of English Studies*
RLC   *Revue de Littérature Comparée*
PUF   Presses Universitaires de France
SBHT   *Studies in Burke and His Time*
SEL   *Studies in English Literature, 1500–1900*
SNNTS   *Studies in the Novel* (North Texas State University)
SoQ   *The Southern Quarterly*
SP   *Studies in Philology*
SSL   *Studies in Scottish Literature* (University of South Carolina)
TSE   *Tulane Studies in English*
TLS   *The Times Literary Supplement*
TSLL   *Texas Studies in Literature and Language*
VMHB   *Virginia Magazine of History and Biography*
VQR   *Virginia Quarterly Review*
WSt   *Word Study*
YES   *Yearbook of English Studies*
YR   *Yale Review*

Notes and references

Preface

1   See for instance A. B. Strauss, *PQ*, li, no. 3 (1972), 765–6, and C. J. Rawson, *N & Q*, xxi, no. 2 (1974), 71–3. John Traugott, reviewing Henri Fluchère's *Laurence Sterne: from Tristram to Yorick* (Oxford U.P., 1965) in *ELN*, iv (1967), 297–302, indulges in a hearty piece of thesis-bashing when he attacks the French Doctorat-ès-lettres as 'that triumph of the *esprit analytique* which would reduce all the world to a set of clear headings'. *Sancta simplicitas!*: would it were so!

2   See supra.

3   See for instance Ulrich Wicks, 'The nature of picaresque narrative: a modal approach', *PMLA*, lxxxix, no. 2 (1974), 240–9.

Chapter 1
Biographical sketch

1   'Some account of Dr Tobias Smollett', *The Scots Magazine*, lviii (Nov. 1796), 725–7; see p. 725.

2   Fielding, *Jonathan Wild* (1743), Everyman's Library edn (Dent, 1964), p. 6.

3   Smeaton, p. 12.

4   Chambers, p. 6, note.

5   For the genealogical details on Smollett's ancestors see Joseph Irving, *Some Account of the Family of Smollett of Bonhill*, Dumbarton, 1859, pp. 1–4; also the following biographies: Anderson, 1820, pp. 2–4; Moore, 1872, pp. 73–4; Hannay, pp. 11–15; Smeaton, pp. 13–16; Knapp, pp. 3–5.

6   Knapp, *Letters* (April 15th 1754), p. 38.

7   Scott, p. 71.

8   Knapp, *Letters* (March 9th 1756), p. 43.

9   HC, p. 256.

10   **PS** (1768—69), I, 498.

11   George Orwell, *Coming up for Air* (Secker, 1939); Penguin, 1962, pp. 73—4.

12   For a detailed study of the quotations from Horace in the works of Smollett, see Caroline Goad, *Horace in the English Literature of the XVIIIth Century*, Yale U.P., 1918, pp. 224—31, 534—43.

13   **RR**, I, 7.

14   **RR**, I, 9.

15   Alexander Carlyle, *Autobiography*, ed. John Hill Burton, London and Edinburgh, 1910, p. 58.

16   Moore, 1872, p. 85.

17   Thomas Carlyle, *History of Friedrich II of Prussia*, Ashburton edn, 1886, III, 251.

18   Smollett, **CHE**, III, 51.

19   See the excellent article by Louis L. Martz 'Smollett and the expedition to Carthagena', *PMLA*, lvi (June 1941), 428—46, where the Chapters xxviii—xxxiv of **RR** are systematically collated with the 'Account' of 1756 as well as the anonymous contemporary pamphlets. For this comparison Martz too uses the Henley edn. See also on the Cartagena expedition: Jean Bélanger, *EA*, iii (1939), 250—1; Henry R. Viets, M.D. *Medical Library Association Bulletin* (Boston), xxviii (June 1940), 178—81.

20   Smollett, **PS** (1768—69), VIII, 382. See also pp. 380—1 for the description of Cartagena and a brief reminder of the English defeat. The navigable channel of Boca-Chica has been 'filled up by order from the court of Spain, since the unsuccessful attack made upon the town in the year 1741, by admiral Vernon and general Wentworth'.

21   'An Account of the Expedition against Carthagena', *Works*, XII, 211. The italics are not in the text.

22   Ibid., p. 213.

23   Ibid., p. 217, see also 219 (episode of the *Galicia*).

24   Ibid., p. 220.

25   [Charles Knowles], *An Account of the Expedition to Carthagena with Explanatory Notes and Observations*, London, 1743, 58 pp. (BM, T.1694, I).

26   [Anon], *A Journal of the Expedition to Carthagena . . . In answer to a late Pamphlet; entitled 'An Account of the Expedition to Carthagena'*, London, 1744, 59 pp. (BM, T.1694, 3).

27   See in particular the *Gentleman's Magazine*, xi (1741), Feb., p. 110; Apr., p. 223; May, pp. 264—8; June, pp. 314—16; July, pp. 347, 366—72, 382; also xiii (1743), Apr., pp. 207—9; Dec., pp. 636—7; xiv (1744), Jan., pp. 39—41, 56; Feb., pp. 99—100; Apr., pp. 207—12. See also the *London Magazine*, xii (1743), Apr., pp. 208, 187—91; Dec., p. 624; xiii (1744), Jan., p. 52; Feb., p. 104. According to the monthly catalogues of these periodicals the four pamphlets quoted seem to have been published in the order adopted. The bibliography given by C. E. Jones at the end of *Smollett Studies*, 1942, mentions other pamphlets as well (pp. 129—33), *passim*.

28   Martz, op. cit., p. 431, n. 7.

29   Knapp, pp. 35—6.

30   See Knapp's ingenious theory, pp. 38—42.

31   Smollett, **CHE**, III, 160.

32   Herbert, 1870, p. 10.

33   See Buck's analysis, *Smollett as Poet*, pp. 28—32; the article by William Scott: Smollett's *The Tears of Scotland*, *RES*, viii (Feb. 1957), 38—42, gives technical details about the publication of the poem.

34   Smollett, **CHE**, III, 161. The conclusion of this passage does not lack stylistic beauty: 'all was ruin, silence, and desolation'.

35   Knapp, p. 62, writes that *Advice* 'was available to the public in early September 1746'. This poem already figures in the 'Monthly Catalogue for August 1746' of the *London Magazine*, xv (Aug. 1746), 428. *Reproof* figures in the catalogue of the same periodical, xvi (Jan. 1747), 56.

36   See the critical edition of *Advice* and *Reproof* published by Donald M. Korte, 'Tobias Smollett's *Advice* and *Reproof*', *THOTH*, viii, no. 2 (Spring 1967), 45—57. The author indicates several possible parallels with the satirical works of Pope, in particular the *Dunciad*. See also the same author's article 'Smollett's *Advice* and *Reproof*: apprenticeship in satire', *Studies in Scottish Literature*, viii, no. 4 (1971) 239—52.

37   *Advice*, line 205, *Works*, XII, 11.

38   *Advice*, lines 220, 235—8, *Works*, XII, 11, 12.

39   *Reproof*, lines 193—4, *Works*, XII, 20.

40   Buck, 1927, p. 41, see the analysis of these poems pp. 20—33 for 'The Tears of Scotland' and pp. 38—41 for *Advice* and *Reproof*.

41   Buck, 1925, see the whole of Chapter iii, 'Smollett's quarrels', pp. 53—121, and in particular on the chronology pp. 57—62; see also Knapp, pp. 49—57.

42   See *The Letters of David Garrick*, ed. David M. Little and George M. Kahrl, Oxford U.P., 1963, II, 86, letter no. 49, 'To the Reverend John Hoadly', Sept. 14th 1746, where Garrick tells of his embarrassment about *The Regicide*, which has been recommended to him by Lord Chesterfield; ten years later, John Shebbeare is still scoffing, in *The Occasional Critic*, London, 1757, p. 63, at *The Reegeceede* (a caricatured phonetic transcription of Smollett's Scots accent); see finally the virulent attack of Joseph Reed, an author offended by the CR who lets himself loose against Smollett and his unfortunate tragedy in a picturesque pamphlet, *A Sop in the Pan for a Physical Critick in a Letter to Dr. Smxllxt*, 1759.

43   Alexander Carlyle, *Autobiography*, London, 1910, p. 198.

44   Hannay, pp. 21—7 for the examination of *The Regicide*.

45   *Works*, XII, 41.

46   *Works*, XII, 42.

47   For the historical details, see Anderson, 1820, I, 16—17. See also pp. 27—8, 145—8.

48   *Works*, XII, 91.

49   D. G. Rossetti has treated this subject in 'The King's Tragedy', *Sonnets and Ballads*, 1881.

50   Knapp, *Letters* (June 7th 1748), p. 8.

51   Knapp, p. 94.

52   See L. M. Knapp, letter to *TLS*, Jan. 8th 1931, p. 28, and the article 'Smollett's works as printed by William Strahan', *The Library*, xiii (Dec. 1932), p. [282]–91.

53   *A Series of Letters between Mrs. Elizabeth Carter and Miss Catherine Talbot from the year 1741 to 1770*, London, 1808, I, 166, letter of February 15th 1748.

54   *Complete Letters of Lady Mary Wortley Montagu*, ed. R. Halsband, Oxford U.P., 1967, III, 9, letter of March 1st 1752.

55   See the very detailed study of these quarrels in Chapter iii of Buck, 1925, pp. 65–121, and a summary of these attacks in Knapp, pp. 125–31.

56   On these translations see the opinions, sometimes contrary, of Joliat, pp. 58–66; L. M. Knapp, 'Smollett and Lesage's *The Devil Upon Crutches*', *MLN*, xlvii (1932), 91–3; Francesco Cordasco, 'Smollett and the translation of the *Gil Blas*', *MLQ*, x (1949), 68–71. John P. Kent, 'Smollett's translation of the *Gil Blas*; a question of text', *ELN*, v (Sept. 1967), 21–6, where the author shows convincingly that Smollett used the 1732–37 edition of *Gil Blas* and not that of 1747.

57   On this question of comparative literature, see Linsalata's book, *Smollett's Hoax: Don Quixote in English*, Stanford U.P., 1956, which includes a bibliography (pp. 113–14) of the principal articles.

58   Montagu, *Complete Letters*, III, 78, letter of January 1st 1755 to her daughter.

59   According to the collection — formerly in the possession of L. M. Knapp, and now in Cameron House, Alexandria — (*The Works of Tobias Smollett and Related Material*, privately printed at Colorado Springs, 1963), here are some dates of reissue:

      (*a*) of the translation of *Gil Blas* by Smollett: 1750, 1767, 1773, 1778, 1781, 1809, 1826, 1828–29, 1840, *c.* 1850 (Philadelphia), 1908. This translation appeared in 1907 in the collection of the 'World's Classics' in an abridged form. One may consult on this question, rendered more difficult by the confusion between various translators, a letter published by A. L. Mayhew in *The Academy*, xlii (July–Dec. 1892) 313–14, and the article by Cordasco, cited in note 56.

      (*b*) Translation of *Don Quixote*: 1755, 1761, 1765, 1770, 1782. In his article, 'Smollett's translation of *Don Quixote*', *N & Q*, ccxii (Dec. 1957), L. M. Knapp suggests that there were at least fifteen reissues of this translation of Smollett's between 1761 and 1800.

60   Knapp, *Letters*, October 1st 1749, p. 12.

61   Knapp, *Letters*, February 14th 1748/49, pp. 9–10.

62   Knapp, p. 85.

63   Otto Eric Deutsch, 'Poetry preserved in music', *MLN*, lxiii (1948), 73–88; see p. 88.

64 Knapp, *Letters*, June 7th 1748 to Carlyle, p. 8, and also letter 8, May 11th 1750 to Francis Hayman p. 13; see also the article by Alan Dugald McKillop: 'Smollett's first comedy', *MLN*, xlv (1930), 396–7.

There exists in the British Museum a pamphlet of fifteen pages entitled *The Plagues of the Spleen: An Heroic Poem With An Appendix, entitled The Humourist: Or, The Absent Man.* By the inimitable Author of *Telemachus* (11601.K.4. (2)). The first eleven pages describe in mediocre verse the true or false symptoms of that splenetic melancholy fashionable about the middle of the eighteenth century. The four last pages of *The Humourist* (in prose) are devoted to a character who is a comic caricature of a theatrical humour. Malanthus is an eccentric creature who passes with no transition from the most effervescent gaiety to bursts of uncontrollable tears. The date (London, 1752) might make one believe in a vague echo of Smollett's lost comedy. But who is the inimitable author of *Telemachus*? Smollett did indeed translate Fénelon's masterpiece (see the article by L. M. Knapp, 'Smollett's translation of Fénelon's *Télémaque*', *PQ*, xliv (July 1965), 406–7), but its publication was posthumous (1776). Is it a question of a mere literary coincidence? Or could these four pages be a reminiscence or a résumé of the lost comedy or even an extract from it? For the moment, nothing permits us to solve this little mystery.

65 This is the title of an article by C. E. Jones, *Medical Life* (New York), xlv (1934), 302–5. See also by the same author 'Tobias Smollett (1721–1771) – The Doctor as Man of Letters', *Journal of the History of Medicine and Allied Sciences*, xii (1957), 337–48.

66 This second volume is the sequel to the *Treatise*. The case communicated by Smollett figures in vol. II, 4–5. The last volume (III), of which Smollett also revised the text, appeared in 1764, a year after Dr Smellie's death.

67 W. D. Taylor, 'Tobias Smollett, M.D. Aberdeen, 1750', *Aberdeen University Review*, xxvi (1939), 125–35.

68 *Essay*, ed. C. E. Jones. The two quotations are on p. 70 and p. 73 respectively.

69 See Knapp, pp. 146–50 on the whole controversy.

70 See the article by Louis L. Martz, 'Tobias Smollett and the *Universal History*', *MLN*, lvi (1941), 1–12.

71 On this affair, see H. P. Vincent, 'Tobias Smollett's Assault on Gordon and Groom', *RES*, xvi (1940), 183–8; and Alice Parker, 'Tobias Smollett and the Law', *SP*, xxxix (1942), 545–58.

72 John Hill, *The Inspector*, 1751, p. 75.

73 Fielding, *The Covent Garden Journal*, ed. Jensen, Yale U.P., 1915, I, 145.

74 PP, ch. cii, p. 660.

75 Buck, *A Study in Smollett*, p. 121. For the analysis of the whole quarrel with Fielding, see pp. 112–21. *Habbakuk Hilding* is reproduced in *Works*, XII, 165–86.

76 See Benjamin C. Nangle, *Monthly Review . . . Indexes of Contributors and Articles*, Oxford U.P., 1934, p. 42 for Smollett's association with this review from October 1751 to July 1752. Smollett quarrelled with Griffiths.

77 The CR has been the subject of several recent studies. Attention must be drawn first of all to C. E. Jones's analysis in *Smollett Studies*, 1942, pp. 79–102 and bibliography, pp. 107–10; the same author's following articles: 'Poetry and the

Critical Review', *MLQ*, ix (1948), 17—36; *'The Critical Review'*s first thirty years, (1756—1785)', *N & Q*, cci (1956), 78—80; *'The Critical Review* and some major poets', *N & Q*, cci (1956), 114—15. By R. D. Spector, see the following articles: 'Language control in the eighteenth century', *WSt*, xxvii, no. 1 (1951), 1—2; 'Attacks on the *Critical Review'*, *Periodical Post Boy* (1955), pp. 6—7; 'Further attacks on the *Critical Review* 1756—1763', *N & Q*, cci (1956), 425; 'Attacks on the *Critical Review* (1764—1765)', *N & Q*, ccii (1957), 121; 'Attacks on the *Critical Review* in the *Court Magazine* (1761—1762)', *N & Q*, cciii (1958), 308; 'Attacks on the *Critical Review* in the *Literary Magazine'*, *N & Q*, ccv (1960), 300—1; 'The *Monthly* and its rival', *BNYPL*, lxiv (1960), 159—61. See also D. Roper's: 'Smollett's "Four Gentlemen"': the first contributors to the *Critical Review*, *RES*, x (1959), 38—44 and 'The politics of the *Critical Review*, 1756—1817', *DUJ*, liii (new series xxii) (1961), 117—22.

R. D. Mayo, *The English Novel in the Magazines 1740—1815*, Northwestern U.P., 1962, numerous references, *passim*, esp. pp. 207—8, 274. Philip J. Klukoff, 'Smollett and the *Critical Review*: criticism of the novel: 1756—1763', *SSL*, iv, no. 2 (1966), 89—100; 'Two Smollett attributions in the *Critical Review*: *The Reverie* and *Tristram Shandy*', *N & Q*, new series, xiii, no. 12 (1966), 465—6; 'Smollett as the reviewer of *Jeremiah Grant*', ibid., p. 466; 'Smollett's defence of Dr. Smellie in the *Critical Review'*, *Medical History*, xiv (1970), 31—41.

The most detailed study of the CR during the first seven years when Smollett contributed to it is to be found in R. D. Spector's book *English Literary Periodicals and the Climate of Opinion During the Seven Years' War*, Humanities Press, 1966, 408 pp. This work is an indispensable tool for grasping the political and polemical background of the Seven Years' War.

78   On the personality of this pamphleteer and the origin of his quarrel with Smollett, see James R. Foster, 'Smollett's pamphleteering foe Shebbeare', *PMLA*, lvii (1942), 1053—100.

79   *Works*, XII, 161.

80   For Smollett's relations with this translator of Ariosto and Dante, see L. F. Powell, 'William Huggins and Tobias Smollett', *MP*, xxxiv (1936), 179—92, and the same author's 'Tobias Smollett and William Huggins', in W. H. Bond, ed., *Eighteenth-Century Studies* (New York, Grolier Club, 1970), pp. 311—22.

81   See Joliat, *Smollett et la France* (1935), pp. 213—30.

82   Knapp, p. 233. For a detailed study of this trial, see Alice Parker, 'Tobias Smollett and the Law', *SP*, xxxix (1942), 545—58, and L. M. Knapp, *'Rex Versus Smollett*: more data on the Smollett—Knowles libel case', *MP*, xli (1944), 221—7. See also my own letter, 'Smollett's libel', *TLS*, December 30th 1965, on the discovery, for the moment unexplained, of a copy of CR, v (May 1758), 438—9 (*BM* 261. g.5) in which the first paragraph judged libellous does not appear. For a systematic study of the after-effects of the Rochefort expedition in the periodical press, see the excellent work of Robert Spector, *English Literary Periodicals and the Climate of Opinion During the Seven Years' War* (the Hague—Paris Mouton, 1966), 408 pp; on the Rochefort expedition see in particular pp. 49—55. For a more restricted study, limited to Smollett's reactions to this defeat, see my article 'Smollett and the expedition against Rochefort (1757)', in *MP*, lxv, no. 1 (1967), 33—8.

83   For a detailed analysis of the BM up to 1763, the date when Smollett left this periodical, see Mayo, op. cit., pp. 275—87. Thanks to a particularly rich documentation, the author proves that LG was not the first novel to appear as a serial, but that its publication included a certain number of innovations. Spector,

op. cit., pp. 119—20, 158—9, 232—3, analyses the political literary and scientific opinions of this periodical.

84 See in this connection the hypotheses of Buck, 1927, pp. 53—68; and Martz, 1942, pp. 176—80, thinks that Smollett is perhaps the author of a compilation *The History of Canada* published monthly in the BM from January 1760 to March 1763. See also Knapp, p. 222.

85 See L. M. Knapp's article, 'The publication of Smollett's *Complete History . . . and Continuation*', *The Library*, new series, xvi (1935), 295—308.

86 Raymond Postgate, *That Devil Wilkes*, rev. edn, Dobson, 1956, p. 21.

87 Charles Chenevix-Trench, *Portrait of a Patriot: a biography of John Wilkes*, Blackwood, 1962, p. 84.

88 *Works*, XII, 413. For more historical and political details on the *Briton* and its controversy with the *North Briton* see the following studies:
Thomas Wright, *England under the House of Hanover*, London, 1848, I, 383—4; F. G. Stephens, *Catalogues of Prints and Drawings in the British Museum*, London, 1883, IV, *passim*, references to the *Briton* and to the numerous caricatures of Smollett which appeared between May 1762 and May 1763; George Nobbe, *The North Briton: a Study in Political Propaganda*, New York, 1939, *passim*; Robert R. Rea, *The English Press in Politics, 1760—1774*, University of Nebraska Press, 1963, pp. 28—31; Spector, op. cit., pp. 95—9, 143—5, 257—9.

89 Martz, 1942, pp. 67—89. See also the article by John F. Sena, 'Smollett's persona and the Melancholic Traveler', *ECS*, i (1968), 353—69.

90 Martz, 1942, pp. 104—23.

91 See Knapp, 'The keys to Smollett's *Atom*', *ELN*, ii (1964), 100—2. See also my article, ' "The Chinese Pilot" and "Sa-Rouf" in Smollett's *Atom*', *ELN*, iv (June 1967), 273—5, and O. M. Brack Jr's bibliographical note on the publication of the book, *The History and Adventures of an Atom*, 1769, in *PBSA*, lxiv (Third quarter, 1970), 336—8.

92 *Works*, XII, 315.

93 Anderson, 1820, p. 191.

94 Knapp, p. 297.

95 Smeaton, p. 118, produces no documentary evidence in support. But, even if they are apocryphal, these last words deserve to be true.

Chapter 2
Autobiography and the novels

1 Translated from Gaston Berger, *Traité pratique d'Analyse du Caractère*, PUF, 4th edn 1958, p. 78. For further details on the characterological analysis of Smollett's personality see my *Romans de Smollett* (Paris, 1971), Pt I, ch. 2.

2 Translated from Georges Gusdorf, 'Conditions et limites de l'autobiographie' in *Formen der Selbstdarstellung*, Berlin, 1956, p. iii.

3 **RR**, I, lxii.

4 Translated from Charles Le Chevalier, *La Confidence et la Personne humaine*, Aubier, 1960, p. 49.

5   This letter is reproduced in full in L. M. Knapp's article: 'Smollett's admirers in eighteenth-century America', *Williams Alumni Review*, xxii (Dec. 1929), 114—15. Quotation p. 115. This letter has also been reproduced in John Howard Birss's article, 'A letter to Tobias Smollett', *N & Q*, clxiv (May 6th 1933), 315—16.

6   *Annual Register* for the year 1755, 'characters', p. 46.

7   See my article, 'Eighteenth- and nineteenth-century biographies of Smollett', in G. S. Rousseau and P. G. Boucé, eds, *Tobias Smollett*, Oxford U.P., New York, 1971, pp. 201—30.

8   Anderson, 1820, I, 15.

9   Moore, 1872, I, 86.

10 Scott, 1910, p. 77.

11 See in particular pp. 9—10, 55—7; 'Key to Characters in Melopoyn's Story' and all Chapter iii 'Smollett's Quarrels'.

12 Herbert, 1870, p. 23.

13 Smeaton, 1897, p. 17.

14 Kahrl, 1945, p. 120.

15 Byron W. Gassman, 'The background of Tobias Smollett's *The Expedition of Humphry Clinker*', unpublished PhD thesis, University of Chicago, 1960, p. 26; see the whole first chapter 'The personal background'.

16 German academics in particular have written a certain number of theses on auto-biography in Smollett's novels. These works, mainly written at the beginning of the twentieth century, are no longer of any interest, unless for the history of Smollett — criticism. Here are three of them: Max Leuschel, *Autobiographisches in Smolletts Roderick Random*, Leipzig, 1903, p. 74; Albin Fischer, *Autobiographisches in Smolletts Humphry Clinker*, Coburg, 1913, p. 108; Helene Schumacher, *Die Jugendschilderung im Englischen Roman bis zu George Eliot*, Münster, 1923, p. 127. Far from being a 'dead horse', as A. B. Strauss errone-ously suggests in *PQ*, li, no. 3 (1972), 765, the autobiographical interpretation of Smollett's novels is still a critical maverick, very much alive and kicking.

17 RR, I, lxiii.

18 Ibid., p. lxvi. Smollett scholars believed for a long time that the 'Apologue' did not appear till 1760, in the fifth edition of **RR**. O. M. Brack has discovered a fourth edition (1755) which includes this apologue: see his article, 'The bicentennial edition of the Works of Tobias Smollett', *Books at Iowa*, no. 7 (Nov. 1967), pp. 41—2.

19 See L. M. Knapp's article: 'The naval scenes in *Roderick Random*', *PMLA*, xlix (June 1934), 593—8.

20 Louis L. Martz, 'Smollett and the expedition to Carthagena', *PMLA*, lvi (June 1941), 428—46.

21 Martz, 1942, p. 13.

22 RR, I, 256.

23 Kahrl, 1945, p. 21. See Chapter ii, 'A Scottish surgeon's second mate in the Royal Navy', pp. 12—27.

24 RR, I, 205; see also I, 273, 'the heat and unwholesome smell of decayed provision'.

25 Knapp, p. 32.

26 RR, I, 213.

27 PP, pp. 28—9.

28 PP, pp. 259—62.

29 HC, pp. 17—20.

30 PS, I, 41. See also, on the Hottentots, VIII, 126—7; on the stench of the waters in Senegal, VIII, 174.

31 PP, pp. 372—3.

32 FCF, p. 26.

33 FCF, p. 167.

34 FCF, p. 247.

35 FCF, p. 252.

36 LG, p. 3.

37 LG, p. 192.

38 Buck, 1925: see supra, n. 11; Knapp, pp. 52—7.

39 PP, p. 567.

40 PP, pp. 646—8. This passage is quoted by Buck, 1925 (pp. 84—6) about Smollett's quarrel with Chesterfield.

41 PP. See in particular on Garrick and Quin, pp. 273—4; on Garrick, pp. 651—2; on Lyttelton and Fielding, pp. 655—60.

42 LG, p. 15.

43 LG, p. 77.

44 Martz, p. 169.

45 Byron Gassman, 'The *Briton* and *Humphry Clinker*', *SEL*, iii (Summer 1963), 397—414. Quotation p. 414. See also the same author's '*Humphry Clinker* and the Two Kingdoms of George III', *Criticism*, xvi, no. 2 (Spring 1974), 95—108.

46 HC, p. 102.

47 RR, I, 143.

48 HC, p. 118.

49 HC, p. 122.

50 HC, p. 123.

51 FCF, p. 175.

52 LG, p. 98.

53 LG, p. 96.

54 LG, p. 188. On this distressing problem, see W. Ll. Parry-Jones, *The Trade in Lunacy: a Study of Private Madhouses in the Eighteenth and Nineteenth Centuries* (Routledge, 1972), pp. viii, 361.

55 LG, p. 190.

56 See Courtney Dainton, *The Story of England's Hospitals*, Museum Press, 1961, pp. 145–50.

57 British Museum, 522, m.g. 34.

58 HC, p. 82.

59 Carlyle, op. cit., p. 356.

60 Knapp, p. 314.

61 It is reproduced *in extenso* in Knapp, p. 24.

62 Translated from Gusdorf, op. cit. supra, n. 2, p. 121.

63 Kahrl, p. 126; see also L. M. Knapp, 'Smollett's self-portrait in the *Expedition of Humphry Clinker*', in *The Age of Johnson*, Yale U.P., 1949, pp. 149–58.

64 PP, p. 195.

65 PP, p. 637.

66 Knapp, pp. 290–2.

67 HC, p. 1.

68 HC, p. 2.

69 HC, pp. 2–3.

70 HC, p. 3.

71 HC, p. 5.

72 HC, p. 23.

73 HC, p. 124.

74 HC, p. 351.

75 PP, p. 660.

76 *Works*, XI, 120.

77 CR, i (March 1756), 98.

78 HC, p. 347.

79 Translated from Cocteau's letter-preface to *Formen der Selbstdarstellung*, Festgäbe für Fritz Neubert, Berlin, 1956, p. [9].

80 Translated from François Mauriac, *Journal*, Grasset, 1937, II, 138.

Chapter 3
Two sources of inspiration: Don Quixote *and* Gil Blas

1 See Caroline Goad, *Horace in the English Literature of the XVIIIth Century*, Yale U.P., 1918, pp. 224–31, 534–43.

2 See Lee Monroe Ellison, 'Elizabethan drama and the Works of Smollett', *PMLA*, xliv (Sept. 1929), 842–62. This study is of unequal merit and occasionally debatable.

3 See G. M. Kahrl, 'The influence of Shakespeare on Smollett', in Hardin Craig, ed., *Essays in Dramatic Literature: the Parrott presentation volume*, Princeton U.P., 1935, pp. 399–420.

4   See Lewis M. Knapp and Lillian de la Torre, 'Smollett, MacKercher, and the Annesley claimant', *ELN*, i (Sept. 1963), 28–33. See also Lillian de la Torre's two articles, 'New light on Smollett and the Annesley cause', *RES*, xxii (Aug. 1971), 274–81, and 'The Melting Scot: a postscript to *Peregrine Pickle* (1751–1772)', *ELN*, x, no. 1 (Sept. 1972), 20–7.

5   PP, pp. 51–2.

6   Thomas Nashe, *The Unfortunate Traveller*, ed. H. F. B. Brett-Smith, The Percy Reprints, Basil Blackwell, 1927, p. 23.

7   Lesage, *The Adventures of Gil Blas of Santillane, a new translation, by the Author of Roderick Random*, 2nd edn, London, 1750, 4 vols. See IV, Bk x, ch. ii, p. 18. All further references to *Gil Blas* will be to this edition of Smollett's translation.

8   RR, II, 254.

9   PP, p. 747.

10   PP, p. 746 (first quotation), p. 748 (second quotation).

11   PP, p. 748.

12   F. J. Wershoven, *Smollett et Lesage*, Berlin, 1883, 33 pages; Alexander Lawrence, 'L'influence de Lesage sur Smollett', *RLC*, xii (1932), 533–45.

13   *Gil Blas*, I, Bk i, ch. ii, p. 14.

14   *Gil Blas*, I, Bk i, ch. ii, pp. 14–15.

15   RR, I, 38.

16   RR, I, 142.

17   PP, p. 257.

18   *Gil Blas*, I, Bk ii, ch. vii, p. 182.

19   RR, I, 97.

20   RR, I, 120.

21   RR, I, 270.

22   PP, p. 695.

23   FCF, p. 188.

24   FCF, pp. 7, 185.

25   HC, p. 267.

26   HC, p. 306.

27   PP, pp. 103–5.

28   *The History and Adventures of the Renowned Don Quixote, Translated from the Spanish . . . by T. Smollett, M.D.*, 2nd edn, London, 1761, 4 vols: See I, Pt i, Bk iii, ch. xii, pp. 268–9. All further references to *Don Quixote* will be to this edition of Smollett's translation.

29   *Don Quixote*, IV, Pt ii, Bk iii, ch. xiv, p. 69.

30   *Don Quixote*, III, Pt ii, Bk ii, ch. viii, pp. 221–2.

31   *Don Quixote*, II, Pt i, Bk iv, ch. xviii, p. 240.

32   *Don Quixote*, II, Pt i, Bk iv, ch. xxv, p. 302. On the same theme of violence, see Angus Ross, 'The "Show of Violence" in Smollett's Novels', *The Yearbook in English Studies*, ii (1972), 118—29.

33   Nashe, op. cit., p. 95. The spelling 'u' has been replaced by 'v' as also in the following quotations.

34   *Don Quixote*, I, Pt i, Bk iii, ch. viii, p. 210.

35   Translated from Marcel Bataillon, *Le Roman Picaresque*, Paris, 1931, p. 35.

36   Translated from Marcel Bataillon, op. cit., p. 1.

37   *The Pleasant Historie of Lazarillo de Tormes, drawen out of Spanish by David Rouland of Anglesey, 1586*, ed. J. E. V. Crofts, Percy Reprints, Basil Blackwell, 1924, p. 31.

38   Ibid., p. 67.

39   The overall view propounded by F. W. Chandler in *The Literature of Roguery*, (2 vols, Boston and New York, 1907), retains all its general interest, but the analysis devoted to Smollett's novels (II, 309—20) is often warped by a definite adverse bias: see also *Rogue's Progress* (Harvard U.P., 1964) by Robert Alter, who devotes a whole chapter 'The picaroon as fortune's plaything' (pp. 58—79), to **RR**. The assimilation of Roderick to a *picaro* is highly disputable; C. V. Aubrun, 'De la picaresque dans ses rapports avec la réalité ou Don Quichotte et le gentleman', *EA*, xvii, no. 2 (Apr.—June 1964), 159—62. Robert Giddings in *The Tradition of Smollett*, Methuen, 1967, endeavours, with a vigour more obstinate than judicious, to demonstrate the culmination of the picaresque genre in **PP**. The whole of R. D. Spector's book, *Tobias Smollett*, New York, Twayne, 1968, is based on a contestable assimilation of Smollett's novels with a vague and erroneous idea of the picaresque. On this difficult problem of the picaresque in Smollett's novels, see: Alice Green Fredman, 'The picaresque in decline: Smollett's first novel', in J. H. Middendorf, ed., *English Writers of the Eighteenth Century*, Columbia U.P., 1971, pp. 189—207; G. S. Rousseau, 'Smollett and the picaresque: some questions about a label', *Studies in Burke and His Time*, xii (Spring 1971), 1186—1904; and P. G. Boucé, 'Smollett's pseudo-picaresque: a response to Rousseau's Smollett and the picaresque', *Studies in Burke and his Time*, xiv (Fall 1972), 73—9.

40   *Gil Blas*, III, Bk viii, ch. 2, p. 143.

41   *Gil Blas*, Paris, Editions Garnier, 1962; vol. I, translated from Maurice Bardon's preface, p. xv.

42   Joliat, p. 11.

43   **RR**, II, 14.

44   **PP**, p. 747.

45   Herbert Grierson, *The Background of English Literature* (Chatto, 1934), Peregrine Books, 1962, p. 61.

46   **PP**, p. 386.

47   **HC**, p. 129.

48   **HC**, p. 188.

49   *Don Quixote*, III, Pt ii, Bk ii, ch. xiii, p. 264.

50   *Don Quixote*, I, Pt i, Bk i, ch. i, p. 3.

51 *Don Quixote*, III, Pt ii, Bk i, ch. i, p. 2.

52 HC, p. 188.

53 HC, p. 283.

54 HC, pp. 299–301.

55 *Don Quixote*, II, Pt i, Bk iv, ch. viii, p. 115.

56 *Gil Blas*, III, Bk vii, ch. 12, pp. 83–4.

57 FCF, p. 6.

58 FCF, p. 10.

59 *Gil Blas*, IV, Bk x, ch. 10, p. 77.

60 FCF, p. 13.

61 FCF, p. 18.

62 *Gil Blas*, IV, Bk x, ch. 10, p. 79.

63 *Gil Blas*, IV, Bk x, ch. 10, p. 73.

64 FCF, p. 20.

65 FCF, p. 42.

66 FCF, p. 100.

67 FCF, pp. 40–1. Smollett is paraphrasing St Peter, Epistle 1: 5, 8: *quaerens quem devoret.*

68 RR, I, p. lxii.

69 *Gil Blas*, I, p. xii.

70 FCF, p. 3.

71 FCF, p. 242.

72 *Gil Blas*, IV, Bk x, ch. xii, pp. 137–8.

73 FCF, p. 20.

74 FCF, p. 354.

75 FCF, p. 366.

76 HC, p. 170.

77 LG, p. 12.

78 LG, pp. 12–13.

79 *Don Quixote*, III, Pt ii, Bk ii, ch. i, p. 152.

80 *Don Quixote*, I, Pt i, Bk ii, ch. i, p. 86.

81 *Don Quixote*, I, Pt i, Bk i, ch. vii, p. 54.

82 *Don Quixote*, II, Pt i, Bk iv, ch. iii, p. 45.

83 LG, pp. 107–8.

84 *Don Quixote*, III, Pt ii, Bk i, ch. vii, p. 54. See also the string of homely proverbs: I, Pt i, Bk iii, ch. xi, p. 245; also III, Pt ii, Bk iii, ch. i, pp. 296–7; and IV, Pt ii, Bk iii, ch. xi, pp. 40–5.

85   *Don Quixote*, III, Pt ii, Bk iii, ch. i, p. 295.

86   W. H. Auden, 'The ironic hero: some reflections on Don Quixote', *Horizon*, xx (Aug. 1949), p. 93.

87   *Don Quixote*, I, Pt i, Bk ii, ch. v, p. 100. The name Greaves may also be an (inexact) translation of 'Quixote', as the original 'Quijote' is always written in English translations of *Don Quijote*. 'Quijote' in Spanish means *cuisse*, defined in the *OED* as 'armour for protecting the front part of the thighs'. 'Greaves' is defined in the *OED* as 'Armour for the leg below the knee'. There is not a great difference between *cuisse* and greaves.

Chapter 4
The structure of Roderick Random *and* Peregrine Pickle: *adventure and morality*

1   James Beattie, *Dissertations Moral and Critical*, Dublin, 1783, II, 316.

2   The Rev. Edward Mangin, *Essay on Light Reading*, London, 1808, pp. 31, 51.

3   Andrew Lang, *Adventures among Books*, London, 1905, p. 196.

4   John Tinnon Taylor, *Early Opposition to the English Novel*, New York, King's Crown Press, 1943, p. 88.

5   Arnold Kettle, *An Introduction to the English Novel*, 2 vols, Hutchinson, 1951, I, 21. M. A. Goldberg's book, *Smollett and the Scottish School*, 1959, has at least the merit of distinguishing a thematic structure in Smollett's novels, even though the comparison with the Scottish philosophers and moralists who were Smollett's contemporaries is not convincing. Robert Giddings in *The Tradition of Smollett*, Methuen, 1967, after Donald Bruce, also protests against the critical cliché of the absence of structure in Smollett's novels.

6   George Lyttelton, *The Dialogues of the Dead*, Dublin, 1760, dialogue xxviii, p. 316.

7   See in this connection the admirable researches of Mayo, *The English Novel in the Magazines*, in particular, pp. 193, 198, 200; *also* Carey McIntosh, *The Choice of Life*, Yale U.P., 1973, pp. xiv, 229.

8   *The Adventures of Peregrine Pickle*, Oxford, Limited Editions Club, 1936, I, x.

9   David Lodge, *Language of Fiction*, Routledge, 1966, p. 80.

10   **RR**, p. 287: the surgeon of the *Lizard* is also an acquaintance of Roderick's, made in London during the crazy escapade with Jackson. Chance is a very convenient fictional device for Smollett, but such encounters lose some of their improbability if the reader remembers that the mortality during the Cartagena expedition was alarming and the Admiralty sent out as many as possible of the young doctors and surgeons available, without their being always very judiciously used, as Smollett does not fail to point out.

11   **PP** comprises three volumes in the Henley edition, i.e. 946 pages, whereas **RR** (two volumes) has only 720. Moreover, Henley's edition is incomplete since it reproduces the revised and expurgated edition of 1758. **PP** is Smollett's longest novel: 781 pages in the O.E.N. edition used for reference.

12   Rufus Putney, 'The plan of *Peregrine Pickle*', *PMLA*, lx (Dec. 1945), 1051–65.

13   An analysis of the structure of **PP** would be falsified if the edition referred to were still that of Henley, since the O.E.N. edition, up to now, is the only current one which reproduces the complete text of 1751.

14   See also the chronological notations on pp. 54, 57, 63, 78, 92, 113, 153, 165.

15   For the identification of this character, given by Moore for the first time as being Dr Mark Akenside, see Kahrl's work (pp. 42—9) which applies more particularly to the antique banquet, and Giddings, op. cit., pp. 74—80. See also the two articles by Howard S. Buck, 'Smollett and Doctor Akenside', *JEGP*, xxxi (Jan. 1932), 10—26; 'A New Smollett anecdote', *MLN*, xlvii (Feb. 1932), 90—1. The identification of his companion Pallet as a caricature of Hogarth has been suggested by Ronald Paulson in *SEL*, iv (1964), 351—9. The phrase 'held the eel of science by the tail' may be a reminiscence of *A Tale of a Tub*, Section vii ('fishes by the tail'), or a direct allusion to the *Dunciad*, I, ll. 278—9:

> How index-learning turns no student pale,
> Yet holds the eel of science by the tail.

16   For the historical background of these scandalous Memoirs and the problem of their composition, see Knapp, pp. 119—20, 123—5; one may also consult Cleland's review in the *Monthly Review*, iv (1751), 362; the letters of Lady Mary Wortley Montagu, February 16th 1752 and July 19th 1759 in Halsband, ed., *Complete Letters of Lady Mary Wortley Montagu*, III, 2—4, 219; [David Erskine Baker], *The Companion to the Play-House*, London, 1764, vol. II under the heading 'Smollet'. *N & Q*, March 22nd 1862, i, third series, 232; William Thomas Lowndes, *The Bibliographer's Manual of English Literature*, London, 1864, V, 2433 (list of the pamphlets to which the publication of these Memoirs in **PP** gave rise); Buck, 1925, pp. 20—6, 30—1, 35—6, 38—9, 40—7; Lewis Melville, 1926, pp. 53—8; H. W. Streeter, *The XVIIIth century Novel in French Translation*, New York, Publications of the Institute of French Studies, 1936, p. 71; Rufus Putney, 'Smollett and Lady Vane's Memoirs', *PQ*, xxv (April 1946), 120—6; Judd Kline, 'Three doctors and Smollett's Lady of Quality', *PQ*, xxvii (July 1948), 219—28 (in fact the Dr S . . . of the Memoirs seems indeed to be Smellie rather than Peter Shaw). See also G. S. Rousseau, 'Controversy or collusion? The "Lady Vane" Tracts', *N & Q*, xix (Oct. 1972), 375—8.

17   On MacKercher and his role in the famous James Annesley trial, see Knapp, pp. 121—4; Andrew Lang, *The Annesley Case*, Edinburgh and London, 1912; Buck, 1925, pp. 21—6, 33—6; L. M. Knapp, 'Smollett and the Case of James Annesley', *TLS*, December 28th 1935, p. 899; *N & Q*, cxc, May 18th 1946, 213; L. M. Knapp and Lillian de La Torre, 'Smollett, MacKercher and the Annesley Claimant', *ELN*, i (Sept. 1963), 28—33. For Mrs de la Torre's 1971 and 1972 articles on this topic, see the Select Bibliography.

18   The scene where Pipes, in very outspoken terms, declares his passion to this beggar-girl may be considered as a thematic transposition, in a vulgar and farcical style, of Peregrine's attempt to seduce Emilia.

19   See the allusions to the madness of Peregrine or of Crabtree, pp. 741, 742, 749, 756, 763.

20   Paul Fussell, *The Rhetorical World of Augustan Humanism*, Oxford U.P., 1965, pp. 275—6.

21   See Arthur O. Lovejoy, 'Pride in XVIIIth c. thought', *MLN*, xxxvi (Jan. 1921), 31—7.

Chapter 5
Ferdinand Count Fathom *and* Launcelot Greaves: *the moral antipodes*

1   The surname 'Fathom' suggests not only a measure of depth but, above all, breadth of understanding and flexibility of mind, a meaning this word assumes in this line in *Othello* (I, i, 153): 'Another of his fathom have they none', Iago reluctantly admits about Othello.

2   *The Autobiography and Correspondence of Mary Granville, Mrs Delany*, edited
    by the Right Honourable Lady Llanover, London, 1861–62, III, quotations
    pp. 220, 223.

3   See Alexander A. Parker, *Literature and the Delinquent. The picaresque novel in
    Spain and Europe 1599–1753*, Edinburgh U.P., 1967, pp. 126–30. The author's
    observations on RR and FCF are not without interest. They have the merit of
    giving, at last!, a meaning to this adjective, 'picaresque', almost emptied of all
    content by critics with scant regard for literary accuracy. The hereditary
    delinquency of Fathom, revealed right from the start, appears, according to the
    author, as a break with the picaresque tradition (p. 128).

4   See in particular Ronald Paulson, *Satire and the Novel in XVIIIth century
    England*, Yale U.P., 1967, p. 165, where he qualifies this definition as 'so
    conventional it suggests a lack of interest in the subject'. For a richer and more
    subtle appreciation, see William Bowman Piper, 'The large diffused picture of life
    in Smollett's early novels', *SP*, lx (Jan. 1963), 45–56. Also, on the dualistic
    structure of FCF, see T. O. Treadwell, 'The two worlds of *Ferdinand Count
    Fathom*', in G. S. Rousseau and P. G. Boucé, eds, *Tobias Smollett* (Oxford U.P.,
    New York, 1971), pp. 131–53.

5   See Tuvia Bloch, 'Smollett's quest for form', *MP*, lxv, no. 2 (Nov. 1967),
    103–13, which brings out Smollett's debt to Fielding.

6   J. W. Pearce, 'Otway's *Orphan* and Smollett's *Count Fathom*', *MLN*, xvii, no. 7
    (Nov. 1902), 459–60.

7   CHE, 3rd edn, London, 1759, X, 210.

8   See in particular pp. 310, 324–5, 340.

9   On this subject see Goldberg, *Smollett and the Scottish School*, pp. 82–107,
    '*Ferdinand Count Fathom*: a study in art and nature'. See also p. 23, the descrip-
    tion of the talents, superficial but prized in society, which Fathom acquires at as
    early an age as twelve. For another global interpretation of FCF, see Thomas
    Preston, 'Disenchanting the Man of Feeling: Smollett's *Ferdinand Count
    Fathom*', in Larry S. Champion, ed., *Quick Springs of Sense*, Univ. of Georgia
    Press, 1974, pp. 223–39.

10 See in particular, in the first forty pages, p. 22 (four times in one page), 35, 38.

11 See two other indications of this kind: p. 47 (Wilhelmina); p. 53, the step-
    mother, with an explanatory sentence addressed directly to the reader; also
    pp. 67–8.

12 See FCF, p. 45, chapter heading; p. 47, where this flag of surrender hoisted in a
    face constitutes a metaphor, to say the least of it, dubious; p. 59, 'Having thus
    kindled the train', a sapper's metaphor which Smollett uses again, in another
    sphere, p. 81 ('finds himself countermined').

13 See pp. 51–3, 55–6.

14 William Hazlitt, *Lectures on the English Comic Writers*, London, 1819, p. 232;
    see also p. 231.

15 W. Scott, p. 84. There are many other favourable opinions of this scene: for
    example, *European Magazine*, xix (Feb. 1791), 94; Nathan Drake, *Literary
    Hours: or Sketches, Critical Narrative, and Poetical*, 4th edn, London, 1820, I,
    274. On the literary importance of this scene as precursory sign of the Gothic
    novel, see Edith Birkhead, *The Tale of Terror – a study of the Gothic romance*,

London, 1921, p. 25, which stresses the fortuitous use of terror in **FCF**: 'His use of terror ... is merely incidental; he strays inadvertently into the history of Gothic romance'; the same conclusion is reached in Devendra P. Varma's book, *The Gothic Flame*, London, 1957 (repr. New York, Russell, 1966), pp. 38—40, 206—7. Catherine L. Almirall, 'Smollett's Gothic: an illustration', *MLN*, lxviii (June 1953), 408—10, establishes possible parallels between Congreve's *The Mourning Bride* (1697) and Chapters 62 and 63 of FCF. It seems difficult and not very fruitful to compare Smollett's incidental handling of terror in **FCF** with Horace Walpole's in *The Castle of Otranto*, 1764, where the author declares that 'Terror, the author's principal engine, prevents the story from ever languishing; and it is so often contrasted by pity, that the mind is kept up in a constant vicissitude of interesting passions' (Preface to the first edition). Quite different again is the quality of the terror felt by Vathek and Nouronihar as they await the arrival of the Giaour. See on this subject André Parreaux's thesis, *William Beckford*, Paris, 1960, Ch. v, '*Vathek* et le roman gothique terrifiant', pp. 263—99. See finally Maurice Lévy's thesis, *Le Roman "Gothique" anglais*, Toulouse, 1968, pp. 128—30.

16 Daniel Defoe, *Captain Singleton* (1720), Dent, Everyman's Library edn, 1963, p. 123.

17 Saintsbury, for example, who does not at all like **FCF**, declares in his introduction: 'Few, I suppose, are much enamoured of the History of the Noble Castilian', Navarre edn, 1925, VIII, xvi.

18 This priest signs himself 'Pepin Clothaire Charlé Henri Louis Barnabe de Fumier' (p. 99). The litany of Christian names is meant to ridicule the onomastic ostentation of the French (petty) nobility.

19 See Grant T. Webster, 'Smollett's microcosms: a satiric device in the novel', *Satire Newsletter*, v (Fall 1967), 34—7.

20 On Theodore de Neuhoff, see P. Wilding, *Adventurers in the Eighteenth Century*, London, 1937 (repr. New York, Books for Libraries), pp. 117—63.

21 See Earl R. Wasserman, 'Smollett's satire on the Hutchinsonians', *MLN*, lxx (May 1955), 336—7, which identifies Sir Mungo Barebones as a caricature of the theologian John Hutchinson (1674—1737).

22 See in particular pp. 315—16, 'gloomy satisfaction'; p. 316, 'let me enjoy a full banquet of woe'; p. 319, 'woful enjoyment'.

23 See FCF p. 285 (Melvil defender of the widow and the orphan); p. 289 ('Our knight-errant and his squire'); p. 294 (Melvil, redresser of wrongs); p. 346 ('his Quixotism awoke').

24 By contrast, LG has often been imitated. See Anderson, 1820, p. 73 (list of imitators in which Mrs Lennox and Richard Graves figure); Allibone, *Dictionary of English Literature*, Philadelphia, 1870, II, 2166 reproduces the same list as the preceding one; Mayo, op. cit., pp. 286—7, indicates three other possible imitators.

25 Other indications, see p. 4 (Crowe), 16 (allusion to the war), 17 (death of Launcelot's father), 19 (Launcelot finished his university studies at seventeen), 68 (Gilbert is seven), 209 (Dolly, about sixteen).

26 For more topographical details, see Kahrl, 1945, pp. 57—60. Launcelot does however leave Great Britain to make an enforced 'Grand Tour' through Holland, France and Italy, about which Smollett gives no details (pp. 36—7).

27 The dialect used by the squire Crabshaw and Dolly is far from being homogeneous since it oscillates between the broadest Yorkshire and the most refined English (see on this subject Heinz Lücker, *Die Verwendung der Mundart im Englischen Roman des 18ten Jahrhunderts*, Darmstadt, 1915, *passim*. Smollett contradicts himself in the most flagrant manner at least once. At the end of the novel (p. 196), Crabshaw once again puts on his squire's costume which he had, however, left behind in an inn at Bugden (p. 161). Knapp (pp. 228—9) has considerably invalidated Scott's allegations about the hasty composition of the monthly instalment.

28 See Frans Dirk Wierstra, *Smollett and Dickens*, Den Helder, 1928, 117 pp., in particular Ch. iv on LG and *The Pickwick Papers*.

29 See Mayo's indispensable clarification, op. cit., pp. 273—87.

30 Slightness of the evidence or a simple contradiction on Smollett's part? Launcelot's nurse, Mrs Oakley, gives a much more flattering portrait of her former mistress Lady Greaves (p. 102). She makes no allusion to a mental illness.

31 Although Battie's work is dated 1758, its review already appears in CR, iv (Dec. 1757), 509—16. The critic (Smollett?) deplores that Battie does not advocate ice-cold baths in the treatment of the mad (p. 516). See also CR, v (March 1758), 224—8 on John Monro's pamphlet. The author offers a moderate conclusion and takes great care not to decide between the opponents (p. 228). See too the article by Richard A. Hunter and Ida Macalpine, *MLR*, li (July 1956) 409—11. 'Smollett's reading in psychiatry' which emphasises Smollett's indebtedness to Battie's theories, especially in Chapter xxiii of LG. For the literary response to madness in eighteenth-century England, see Max Byrd, *Visits to Bedlam*, Univ. of South Carolina Press, 1974, pp. xv, 200. Unfortunately, Byrd fails to analyse at any length the subtle dialectics of madness and reason in LG.

32 See L. J. Rather, *Mind and Body in Eighteenth Century Medicine: A Study Based on Jerome Gaub's De Regimine Mentis*, London, The Wellcome Historical Medical Library, 1965, pp. xii, 275; see in particular pp. 109 and 150.

33 See James R. Foster's article, 'Smollett's pamphleteering foe Shebbeare', *PMLA*, lvii (Dec. 1942), 1053—100. When Smollett began to serve his sentence on November 28th 1760 in the King's Bench Prison, Shebbeare had already been there two years. Goldberg suggests (p. 136) that Ferret is not without some resemblances to celebrated quacks such as Chevalier Taylor.

34 See Knapp, pp. 233—6. See also the allusion Philip Thicknesse, another intimate enemy of Smollett's, makes to this description in *Observations on the Customs and Manners of the French Nation*, London, 1766, p. 90.

35 See Alan D. McKillop, 'Notes on Smollett', *PQ*, vii (Oct. 1928), 368—74, in which the author thinks that Dick Distich is a caricature of Churchill and Bullock of Lloyd.

36 Translated from Vladimir Jankélévitch, *L'Ironie ou la Bonne Conscience*, Paris, 1950, PUF, 2nd edn, p. 168.

Chapter 6
Humphry Clinker, *or the adventure of morality*

1 Martz, pp. 132—5; Kahrl, pp. 122—5.

2 See HC, pp. 2—3.

3 Philip Thicknesse, *Observations on the Customs and Manners of the French Nation*, London, 1766, p. 42. Other allusions to **TFI**, see pp. 44, 71, 89—91, 104—5.

4 Philip Thicknesse, *Useful Hints to those who Make the Tour of France in a Series of Letters written from that Kingdom*, London, 1768; see in particular pp. 1—17 (all letter I, a systematic attack whose verbal violence sometimes compels admiration), 25, 27, 28, 30—3, 45, 66, 117, 122, 130, 148—50, 162, 188, 203—5, 279. For a study of Thicknesse, see Philip Gosse, *Dr Viper: The Querulous Life of Philip Thicknesse*, Cassell, 1952, in particular pp. 133—4, 139, 204, 317, on the stormy literary quarrels between Smollett and Thicknesse.

5 These figures are taken from F. G. Black, 'The Technique of Letter Fiction in English from 1740 to 1800', *Harvard Studies and Notes in Philology and Literature*, xv (1933), 291—312; see also the book by the same author, *The Epistolary Novel in the Late Eighteenth Century*, Eugene, 1940, pp. iv—184, and that by G. F. Singer, *The Epistolary Novel*, University of Pennsylvania Press, 1933, pp. ix, 266.

6 To compare Smollett's epistolary technique with Richardson's, one may consult Anthony Kearney, '*Clarissa* and the epistolary form', *Essays in Criticism*, xvi (Jan. 1966), 44—56; Alan D. McKillop, 'Epistolary technique in Richardson's novels', *The Rice Institute Pamphlet*, xxxviii (Apr. 1951), 36—54. This last article is reprinted *in extenso* in Richard C. Boys, ed., *Studies in Literature of the Augustan Age*, Gordian Press, 1966.

7 See Martz, pp. 133—4; on Anstey and the influence of the *New Bath Guide* on **HC**, see Walter Maier, *Christopher Anstey und der 'New Bath Guide'*, 'Anglistische Forschungen' (39), Heidelberg, 1914, also William C. Powell, *Christopher Anstey: Bath Laureate*, Philadelphia, 1944, in particular pp. 96—8.

8 See on this subject Thomas R. Preston's article, 'Smollett and the Benevolent Misanthrope Type', *PMLA*, lxxix (March 1964), 51—7.

9 Samuel Foote, *The Englishman Returned from Paris*, London, 1756, p. 18; the first quotation is on p. [9].

10 See Derek Roper, 'Smollett's "Four Gentlemen": the first contributors to the *Critical Review*', *RES*, x (Feb. 1959), 38—44.

11 Oliver Goldsmith, *The Citizen of the World* (1762), ed. A. Friedman, Oxford U.P., 1966, II, 109.

12 See *Memoirs of Stobo of the Virginia Regiment*, Pittsburgh, 1854, pp. xii, 92; the article by G. M. Kahrl, 'Captain Robert Stobo', *VMHB*, xlix (Apr. and July 1941), 141—51, 254—68; also Kahrl, pp. 132—44; Martz, pp. 175—80; Knapp, pp. 274—6; Edward P. Crummer, 'Robert Stobo', *N & Q*, cciii (Apr. 1958), 180, an article which reveals Stobo's suicide; Robert C. Alberts, 'The fantastic adventures of Captain Stobo', *AH*, xiv (Aug. 1963), 65—77, and the book by the same author, *The Most Extraordinary Adventures of Major Robert Stobo*, Houghton Mifflin, 1965. Gilbert Parker's novel, *The Seats of the Mighty*, London, 1896, inspired by Stobo's adventures, transforms him into an elegant adventurer and attractive patriotic spy. See also Michael Rymer, 'Another source for Smollett's Lismahago', *N & Q*, new series, xxi (Feb. 1974), 57—9.

13 See Robert Anderson, *The Works of the British Poets*, Edinburgh, 1795, XI, 415.

14 Tuvia Bloch, 'Smollett's quest for form', *MP*, lxv (Nov. 1967), 103, 13.

15   Leon V. Driskell, 'Looking for Dustwich', *TSLL*, ix (Spring 1967), 85—90;
     second quotation, p. 90.

16   See Franklin B. Newman, 'A consideration of the bibliographical problems
     connected with the first edition of *Humphry Clinker*', *PBSA*, xlix (1950),
     340—71.

17   Here is a quick summary of the principal ones, the names of the letter-writers
     being reduced to their initials: MB April 20th and LM April 21st (date of the
     incident with the Jewish pedlar); MB April 2nd and 17th (sequels to Wilson's
     letter); JM April 24th precedes MB April 23rd; discrepancy between the letters
     of JM May 17th and of MB and TB both written on May 19th, on the subject of
     the departure for London; the confusion is further thickened by the specifica-
     tion in LM May 31st ('about five days ago', p. 91); MB June 12th precedes JM
     June 11th, and moreover the two letters do not agree about Clinker's arrest;
     same problems for Clinker's release and the departure from Scarborough; contra-
     diction between the beginning and end of JM July 13th about Lismahago's
     plans; variable date of departure from Edinburgh; JM and MB August 8th
     contradict JM September 3rd as well as MB August 28th, the order of these two
     letters is also reversed; contradiction about the date of the triple wedding
     between JM November 8th (or 14th in Text B) and WJ November 20th
     ('yesterday', p. 352).

18   See Austin Dobson, 'The topography of *Humphry Clinker*', *Eighteenth-Century
     Vignettes*, 2nd series, London, 1894, pp. 131—60; Martz, pp. 136—46 on the
     description of Scotland in HC; Kahrl, Ch. ix; Byron Gassman, Chs v, vi, vii, of his
     thesis.

19   Details are not wanting about this reputedly unplumbable gulf, one of the
     'Wonders of the Peak': see John Macky's, *Journey Thro' England*, 1722, II,
     185—6. Macky quotes Charles Cotton (1630—87), the poet friend of Walton and
     translator of Montaigne, who, in 1681, published *The Wonders of the Peak*, a
     descriptive poem dedicated to the Countess of Devonshire. A fifth edition of this
     poem appeared in London in 1765 in the *Genuine Poetical Works of Charles
     Cotton*, pp. 299—348. The *DNB* indicates that this poem is an imitation of
     Hobbes's, *De Mirabilibus Pecci*. Smollett in the PS seems to repeat after Macky,
     in a condensed form, the account of an attempted exploration made in the reign
     of Elizabeth. Cotton and Macky provide very precise topographical information
     about Chatsworth and Buxton, as well as the 'Devil's Arse'. It is probable that
     the compiler who wrote the pages on Derbyshire in the PS knew the descriptions
     by Cotton and Macky.

20   First letter from Lydia to her governess (April 6th); letter from Tabitha to Dr
     Lewis (May 19th); second letter from Lydia to her governess (Oct. 14th). The
     letter enclosed is the one from Wilson to Lydia (March 31st), confiscated by
     Jery, and sent to Dr Lewis in Matthew Bramble's letter of April 17th. There is
     also the note from Barton enclosed in Matthew Bramble's letter of June 12th.

21   See B. L. Reid, 'Smollett's healing journey', *VQR*, xli (Autumn 1965), 549—70;
     Scott Garrow, 'A study in the organization of Smollett's *The Expedition of
     Humphry Clinker*', *SoQ*, iv (July 1966), 349—64 and v (Oct. 1966), 23—46. If
     the preceding articles do not always avoid paraphrase, conversely the one by
     G. S. Rousseau contributes a note of highly technical erudition: 'Matt Bramble and
     the sulphur controversy in the XVIIIth century', *JHI*, xxviii (Oct.—Dec. 1967),
     577—89. Must one be a specialist in hydrotherapeutic chemistry in order to read
     HC?

22   For an erroneous psychoanalytical interpretation of HC, see Howard Leon Hannum's unpublished PhD thesis, 'Tobias Smollett: fiction and caricature' (Univ. of Pennsylvania, Philadelphia, 1963), pp. xiii, 267. The caricature is not only in the title.

23   See the article by David L. Evans, '*Humphry Clinker*; Smollett's tempered Augustanism', *Criticism*, ix (Summer 1967), 257–74.

24   See on this subject Lois Whitney's book, *Primitivism and the Idea of Progress in English Popular Literature of the Eighteenth Century*, Baltimore, 1934, pp. xxi, 342; see also M. A. Goldberg, *Smollett and the Scottish School*, Univ. of New Mexico Press, 1959, pp. 147–53.

25   In FCF the young woman seduced by Fathom and whom he ends by marrying in prison is called 'Elenor' or 'Elinor'; the spelling of Ratchcali varies too (Ratchkali). In HC, Wilson addresses himself to 'Lydia Milford' (A4 setting of the misdated 1671 edition reproduced by Parreaux, Riverside edn, p. 16), which is either a misprint or an error to show that Wilson does not know the girl he is courting very well; after the disappearance of his valet Dutton, Jery engages a Scot, Archy M'Alpin (p. 212) who becomes 'M'Alpine' (p. 226). In the same letter of Bramble's (Sept. 30th) the Christian name changes from Sir John (p. 288) to Charles (p. 293) Chickwell.

26   See Henry Grey Graham, *The Social Life of Scotland in the Eighteenth Century*, London, 1906, Ch. xv, 'Progress of the industry and trade', pp. 506–38; Chs iii and iv devoted to the life of Edinburgh and Glasgow can serve as an invaluable supplement to the rapid sketches of it by Smollett in HC.

27   Edward Topham, *Letters from Edinburgh*, London, 1776, p. 15; second quotation p. 152. These letters are a rich source of possible comparisons with the opinions expressed by Smollett a few years earlier. See in particular pp. 9 (the height of houses in Edinburgh); 18 (execrable inns); 48–56 (the Scottish language and its pronunciation); 87 (the 'caddies'); 146–53 on the skin diseases of the Scots; letter xix on Scottish gastronomy, dishes which the travellers in HC also try, in particular haggis; 184, a sympathetic allusion to Smollett; letter xxiii on the Kirk; letter xxix on superstition in Scotland. See a final reference to the 'caddies' p. 358. Topham, emboldened by his youthful enthusiasm for Scotland, virulently attacks Johnson and his *Journey to the Western Islands of Scotland* (1775) (see letter xvii 'On the Reception of Dr. Johnson's Tour at Edinburgh', pp. 137–45). From the lofty eminence of his twenty-four years, Topham does not hesitate to describe Johnson as 'a man totally unacquainted with mankind' (p. 141). This judgment, rash to say the least of it, is fortunately not typical of the keen sense of balanced observation which Topham evinces all through his book.

28   See Gustav Becker, 'Die Bedeutung des Wortes "romantic" bei Fielding und Smollett', *Archiv für Studium der Neueren Sprachen und Litteraturen*, cx (1903), 56–66.

29   Jery, pp. 214, 236, 238; Matthew Bramble, pp. 248, 250; Lydia, p. 258.

30   See also, for example, the use of this adjective, or the corresponding adverb, pp. 14, 33, 47, 146, 162, 172.

31   James Lackington, *Memoirs of the First Forty-Five Years of the Life of James Lackington*, 2nd edn, London, 1792, p. 106; second quotation p. 134; see also the enumeration of professions affected by Methodism (ibid.); on the 'carnal preachers' see p. 243. Lackington had, nevertheless, a great respect for John Wesley, who died in 1791, and whom he considers 'one of the most respectable

enthusiasts that ever lived' (p. 281). Yet he unsparingly condemns his book of popular medicine *Primitive Physic*, 1747, 'which carries with it more the appearance of being the production of an ignorant opinionated old woman, than of the man of science and education' (p. 284). For an analysis of *Primitive Physic*, see G. S. Rousseau, 'John Wesley's *Primitive Physic* (1747)', *HLB*, xvi, no. 3 (July 1968), 242–56. On the commercial success of Lackington and his religious tergiversations, see André Parreaux, *La Vie quotidienne en Angleterre au temps de George III,*, Paris, 1966, pp. 90–102.

32   See the analysis of Matthew Bramble on this subject by T. B. Shepherd, *Methodism and the Literature of the XVIIIth Century*, Epworth Press, 1940, pp. 219–24; Shepherd quotes (p. 128), Wesley's opinion on the condemnation pronounced by Smollett in **CCHE**. Wesley writes in his *Journal*: 'Poor Dr. Smollett! Thus to transmit to all succeeding generations a whole heap of notorious falsehoods! . . . So does this frontless man, blind and bold, stumble on without the least shadow of truth'. Wesley's posthumous retort (1779) displays an acid unctuousness. See too, on the religious background of **HC**, Byron Gassman's thesis (1960) pp. 163–83, also, by the same author, 'Religious Attitudes in the World of *Humphry Clinker*', *BYUS*, vi, no. 2 (1965), 65–72. Still on this subject, see Claude-Jean Bertrand, 'Humphry Clinker, a So-called Methodist', *Bulletin de la Faculté des Lettres de Strasbourg*, no. 4 (Jan. 1969), pp. [189]–202.

33   On the political background of **HC**, see Martz, pp. 167–9; Ch. iii of Gassman's thesis, pp. 92–163; also his articles: '*The Briton* and *Humphry Clinker*', *SEL*, iii, no. 3 (1963), 397–414 and '*Humphry Clinker* and the two kingdoms of George III', *Criticism*, xvi, no. 2 (1974), 95–108.

34   See Mary Claire Randolph, 'Diamond-satires in the eighteenth century', *N & Q*, clxxxv (1943), 62–5.

35   For a comparative study of cowardice in Falstaff and Micklewhimmen, see Robert B. Heilman, 'Falstaff and Smollett's Micklewhimmen', *RES*, xxii (July 1946), 226–8.

36   César de Saussure, *Lettres et Voyages de M. César de Saussure en Allemagne, en Hollande et en Angleterre, 1725–1729*, Lausanne, 1903, p. 135 (quotation translated).

37   See [S. Pegge], *Anonymiana*, London, 1809, p. 289. Hewett proved, during a discussion with some Turks, that Christians were better made than Muslims or Jews to enjoy Houris in Mahomet's paradise. Modestly, Pegge concluded: 'His *Demonstration* may as well be suppressed; but the story adds, the Turks said if that was the case, they would turn Christians too.' In the name of St Priapus, no doubt.

38   It is possible that Smollett also wished to satirise the idealised portrait of Yarico in Shebbeare's novel, *Lydia*, 1755. See James R. Foster, 'Smollett's pamphleteering foe Shebbeare', *PMLA*, lvii (Dec. 1942), 1076; on the possible influence of an anonymous novel, *Memoirs of the Life and Adventures of Tsonnonthouan*, 1763, see another article by Foster: 'A forgotten noble savage, Tsonnonthouan', *MLQ*, xiv (Dec. 1953), 348–59. Foster's hypothesis is repeated and confirmed by R. D. Spector, 'Smollett's use of "Tsonnonthouan"', *N & Q*, cciv (Mar. 1959), 112–13.

39   There is the same remark in the **PS** (VIII, 299) about the Iroquois, a tribe which finds favour with the author, no doubt because they were the sworn enemies of the French: 'They acknowledge a supreme Being, whom they stile the Preserver

of the universe.' There is another possible parallel on the following page: 'They generally put the prisoners they make in war to the most excruciating and lingering deaths.'

40 See **PS**, VIII, 301, where there is mention of 'Popish Indians ... not well affected to the English'; see also p. 345 on the massacre of Indians in Mexico by the Spanish.

41 Northrop Frye, *Anatomy of Criticism* (1957), repr. Atheneum Press, 1967, p. 179.

42 See pp. 9, 15—16, 25—6.

43 In this connection, see K. B. Harder, 'Genealogical Satire in *Humphry Clinker*', *N & Q*, cc (Oct. 1955), 441—3.

44 See William Park, 'Fathers and sons — *Humphry Clinker*', *Literature and Psychology*, XVI, nos 3, 4 (1966), 166—74. This study offers an example, all too rare, of discriminating and sensitive literary criticism based on depth psychology. Without, for all that, accepting all William Park's conclusions, in particular the farfetched analysis of the anal images, it is difficult not to take his researches into account in a critical study of **HC**.

45 Goldberg, p. 171; Sheridan Baker, '*Humphry Clinker* as comic romance', *Papers of the Michigan Academy of Science, Arts, and Letters*, xlvi (1961), 646; Park, op. cit., p. 173. For the scatological meaning of 'clinker' see the slang dictionaries of Farmer and Henley (1890—1904) and Eric Partridge, *Dictionary of Slang*, 5th edn, Routledge, 1961.

46 Here I modify the conclusion of my article 'Les procédés du comique dans *Humphry Clinker*', *Actes du Congrès de Lille*, Paris, 1966, Didier, pp. 53—75.

Chapter 7
Representation of the real

1 **PP**, p. 335.

2 P. J. Klukoff, 'Smollett as the reviewer of *Jeremiah Grant*', *N & Q*, ccxi (Dec. 1966), 466.

3 See René Wellek's study of 'The concept of realism in literary scholarship', in his *Concepts of Criticism*, Yale U.P., paperback edn, 1963, pp. 222—55. For a critical analysis and various attempts to define this term, one may consult G. H. Gerould, *How to Read Fiction* (1937); George J. Becker, 'Realism: an essay in definition', *MLQ*, x (June 1949), 184—97; D. S. Savage, *The Withered Branch*, Eyre & Spottiswoode, 1950, the preface: 'Truth and the art of the novel'; 'A Symposium on Realism', *CL*, iii (Summer 1951), in particular the articles by Harry Levin, 'What is realism?', pp. 193—9, and Robert Gorham Davis, 'The sense of the real in English Fiction', pp. 200—17; K. Lever, *The Novel and the Reader*, Methuen, 1961; C. S. Lewis, *An Experiment in Criticism*, Cambridge U.P., 1961; G. Lukács, *La Théorie du Roman*, Paris, edn, 1963, as also the following studies: *Studies in European Realism*, London, 1950 and *The Meaning of Contemporary Realism*, Merlin Press, 1963. These indications are by no means exhaustive. Eric Auerbach, in *Mimesis*, Doubleday Anchor Books, 1957, touches on the problem of the representation of the real in western literature with an erudite subtlety which does not exclude debatable prejudices; see also Damian Grant, *Realism*, Methuen, 1970.

4   Ian Watt, *The Rise of the Novel*, Chatto, 1957, Peregrine, 1963.

5   Barbara Hardy, *The Appropriate Form*, Athlone Press, 1964.

6   *Concepts of Criticism*, p. 253.

7   For general studies, see the celebrated articles by Louis I. Bredvold, 'A note in defence of satire', *ELH*, vii (Dec. 1940), 2—13 and Maynard Mack, 'The muse of satire', *YR*, xli, no. 1 (1951), 80—92, both reproduced in Boys, ed., *Studies in Literature of the Augustan Age*; the books by Robert C. Elliott, *The Power of Satire*, Princeton U.P., 1960; Gilbert Highet, *The Anatomy of Satire*, Yale U.P., 1962; Alvin B. Kernan, *The Plot of Satire*, Yale U.P., 1965; R. Paulson, *The Fictions of Satire*, 1967. Studies on satire in Smollett's work: Earl R. Wasserman, 'Smollett's satire on the Hutchinsonians', *MLN*, lxx (May 1955), 336—7; Kelsie B. Harder, 'Genealogical Satire in *Humphry Clinker*', *N & Q*, cc (Oct. 1955), 441—3; Mohammed Awad Al-Usaily, 'Satire in the Novels of Smollett', unpublished Edinburgh PhD thesis, 1963, in which the laborious accumulation of details and the barely disguised paraphrase overwhelm any faint attempt at synthesis; Mary Wagoner, 'On the satire in *Humphry Clinker*', *PLL*, ii (1966), 109—16; Grant T. Webster, 'Smollett's microcosms: a satiric device in the novel', *SNL*, v (Fall 1967), 34—7; Ronald Paulson, *Satire and the Novel in XVIIIth Century England*, Yale U.P., 1967, pp. 165—218 (devoted to Smollett repeat in part *verbatim* in a former article by the same author, 'Satire in the early novels of Smollett', *JEGP*, lix, Jan. 1960, 381—402); R. D. Spector, *Tobias Smollett*, Twayne, 1968, *passim*.

8   Joyce Cary, *Art and Reality*, Cambridge U.P., 1958, p. 115.

9   G. Lukács, *La Théorie du Roman*, Paris, 1963, p. 66. The first edition dates back to 1920. Lukács repudiated it and refused any reprinting until 1962 (trans.).

10   Alain Robbe-Grillet, *Pour un Nouveau Roman*, Paris, NRF, 1963, p. 175; see the article 'Du réalisme à la realité' (trans.).

11   Raymond Jean, *La Littérature et le Réel: de Diderot au 'Nouveau Roman'*, Paris, 1965, p. 17 (trans.).

12   See C. Lloyd, *The British Seaman*, Collins, 1968, p. 127.

13   See C. Lloyd and J. L. S. Coulter, *Medicine and the Navy*, 4 vols, E. & S. Livingstone, 1961, iii, *1714—1815*, 49.

14   See Arthur F. Leach, *A History of Winchester College*, London, 1899, the author speaks of rebellions under the reign of Dr Warton in 1770, 1774, 1778, 1793, but reports nothing before 1770.

15   See *Winchester: its history, building and people*, 3rd edn revised, London, 1933, by the Winchester College Archaeological Society.

16   See *The History of the Colleges of Winchester, Eton, and Westminster . . .* published by R. Ackermann, London, 1816, pp. 44—6. The greater part of this history was written by W. Combe.

17   17 Geo. II, c. 5. See Sir Frederic Morton Eden, *The State of the Poor*, London, 1797, I, 307—8, concerning the 'Vagrant Act' of 1744.

18   See Ralph Straus, ed., *Tricks of the Town*, London, 1927, pp. xiv—xvi; this edition will be used for all references to this pamphlet.

19   The British Museum Catalogue gives 1770, with a questionmark. This date is unlikely, as the author alludes on p. 88 to the activities of smugglers in 1778.

20   C. N. Robinson, *The British Tar in Fact and Fiction*, London, 1909, see in particular Ch. xiii 'Smollett and the naval novel', pp. 266—83: this very anecdotal book can still be read with profit, but lacks order and pays no heed to literary accuracy; more serious is H. F. Watson's book, *The Sailor in English Fiction and Drama 1500—1800*, New York, Columbia Univ. Studies in English, 1931, in which pp. 156—7 are devoted to *The Reprisal*, 164—9 to **RR**; see also L. M. Knapp, 'The naval scenes in *Roderick Random*', *PMLA*, xlix (June 1934), 593—8; L. L. Martz, 'Smollett and the Expedition to Carthagena', *PMLA*, lvi (June 1941), 428—46; C. E. Jones, *Smollett Studies*, University of California Press, 1942; 'Smollett and the Navy', pp. 31—75 gives the most complete study; G. M. Kahrl, *Tobias Smollett Traveler—Novelist*, Chicago U.P., 1945, pp. 1—27. The biographies of David Hannay (1887) pp. 29—41, and of Knapp, 1949, pp. 29—38, also contain useful details about life on board an English warship about 1740. See also Nathan Comfort Starr, 'Smollett's Sailors', *American Neptune*, xxxii, no. 2 (1972), 81—99.

21   For a nautical study of *The Fair Quaker of Deal* and the alterations made by Thompson, see Robinson, op. cit., pp. 204—24.

22   Edward Ward, *The Wooden World*, The Society for Nautical Research, 1929 reprint, p. 15.

23   Lloyd, *The British Seaman*, p. 230.

24   See Lloyd, op. cit., pp. 210, 241—2.

25   *Narrative of the Honourable John Byron*, London, 1768, account of the shipwreck, pp. 10—16, the absurd appearance of the sailors decked out in the officers' clothes they had stolen, p. 25. See also Peter Shankland, *Byron of the Wager*, London, Collins, 1975, pp. 42—52.

26   See the account of the shipwreck, p. 12 onwards; the behaviour of the looters and drunks who stayed on board the wreck, pp. 14—16.

27   See vol. II of the *Medical Works of Dr. Richard Mead*, Edinburgh, 1763, in which Sutton's *Historical Account* is reproduced in part; quotations p. 210 and 237.

28   See on this subject Lloyd and Coulter, op. cit., supra, n. 13, pp. 72—7, 'Ventilation and fumigation'.

29   Lloyd and Coulter, op. cit., Ch. 7, 'Victualling', pp. 81—93; Daniel A. Baugh, *British Naval Administration in the Age of Walpole*, Princeton U.P., 1965, an indispensable work for understanding the naval background of **RR**: see in particular Ch. viii, 'Victualling', pp. 373—451.

30   See Lloyd and Coulter, op. cit., n. ii, all Ch. 5, 'The cockpit, the sick-berth and hospital ship', pp. 57—69. The unpublished evidence of Robert Young (pp. 58—60), shows that fifty years after Cartagena the operating conditions had in no way changed on board. The same surgical nightmare resurrected in the midst of the horrors of Biafra: see *Le Monde*, of May 7th 1969, pp. 1, 12.

31   Lloyd and Coulter, op. cit., n. ii, p. 106.

32   See the edition of this work in *The Health of Seamen* (vol. CVII of the Publications of the Navy Records Society, edited by Christopher Lloyd, 1963), p. 27.

33   B. M. Ranft, *The Vernon Papers*, Navy Records Society, 1958, p. 304; information concerning the *Chichester*, p. 348.

34   See R. S. Allison, *Sea-Diseases*, London, J. Bale Medical Publications, 1943, pp. 65, 117—19 on Smollett; Lloyd and Coulter, op. cit., n. ii, pp. 25—8, in par-

ticular p. 28: 'The description of the hospital ships ... rings horribly true'; Baugh, op. cit., n. 27, pp. 225, 396.

35 See Lloyd and Coulter, op. cit., Ch. 18, 'Scurvy', pp. 293—328.

36 It was signed by 'By my Friend, a Physician', a designation which **CR**, iv (Oct. 1757), 296—8, reproduces (p. 296) in its review of the pamphlet. **CR**, v (May 1758), 443—5, in a review of *A Dissertation on Adulterated Bread* (the work of Peter Markham) begins thus: 'Once more, *our friend the physician* enters the lists' (p. 643). The **CR** thus seems to think that the author of *Poison Detected*, 1757, and of *A Dissertation on Adulterated Bread*, 1758, could be none other than Markham. Moreover, in this second pamphlet, whose first edition, also in 1758, bore the title, *Syhoroc*, there are numerous allusions to *Poison Detected*. To complicate these already confused problems of anonymity a little more, **CR**, v (Jan. 1758), 74—5, is surprised, in its favourable review of *A Modest Apology in Defence of the Bakers*, to have been attacked in this pamphlet (p. 55) when it had recommended the reading of *Poison Detected*, and presumes that the two are the work of the same author.

37 Undoubtedly 1757, in spite of the British Museum catalogue, which gives 1758, with a questionmark: *The Nature of Bread*, is analysed in **CR**, v (Jan. 1758), with much sympathy. But an extract was published in *The Universal Magazine of Knowledge and Pleasure*, xxi (Dec. 1757), 274—6, with the title: 'Extract from a pamphlet just published by the learned Dr. Manning'. This extract was reprinted in 1800, under the title of *Public Villainy Exposed*, on the occasion of a similar crisis in Bath.

38 *Lettres d'un Français*, La Haye, 1745. II, 234, 235 (trans.).

39 *Lettres sur l'Angleterre, la Hollande et l'Italie*, Lyon, 1764, p. 45 (trans.).

40 *Lettres et Voyages ... en Allemagne, en Hollande et en Angleterre 1725—1729*, Lausanne, 1903, p. 165. De Saussure returned to London in 1738.

41 *Kalm's Account of his Visit to England on his Way to America in 1748*, London, 1892, p. 15.

42 See Kenneth Chester Slagle, *The English Country Squire in English Prose Fiction from 1700—1800*, Philadelphia, Pennsylvania U.P., 1938, numerous references to Smollett *passim*.

43 Dorothy George, *London Life in the Eighteenth Century*, 2nd edn, London, Kegan Paul, Trench, Trubner & Co., 1930, p. 269; see also the whole of Ch. vi, 'The uncertainties of life', pp. 269—322 of this indispensable work, which provides a copious bibliography.

44 See Edward C. Mack, 'Pamela's stepdaughers: the heroines of Smollett and Fielding', *CE*, viii (1947), 293—301.

45 See the modern study by Fernando Henriques, *Prostitution and Society*, 2 vols, MacGibbon & Kee, 1963, II, *Prostitution in Europe and the New World*. The following publications contemporary with Smollett can be consulted in the British Museum: *Satan's Harvest Home: or the Present State of Whorecraft, Adultery, Fornication, Procuring, Pimping, Sodomy, and the Game at Flatts*, London, 1749 (see pp. 45—62, 'Reasons for the growth of sodomy'); the poems of Edward Thompson, already quoted, such as *The Meretriciad* [1755?], *The Demi-Rep*, 1756; *Nocturnal Revels, or the History of King's Place and Other Modern Nunneries*, 2nd edn, London, 1779, 2 vols; George Alexander Stevens, *The Adventures of a Speculist*, London, 1788, 2 vols, which gives extremely

precise details about the hectic sex life of London about the middle of the eighteenth century. The *Nocturnal Revels* (II, 234) contain an unexpected confirmation of the physical shortcomings of Lord Vane, to which his wife makes sarcastic allusions in the 'Memoirs of a Lady of Quality': 'Whilst Lady V——E is taking a microscopic view of his Lordship's Sensitive Plant, and with the assistance of this visual magnifier can scarcely perceive a protuberance of one digit . . .'

46   It is not without difficulty that the reader can consult this document in the British Museum. It is part of the books relegated to the 'private case', which may raise a smile. The list for the year 1788 (P.C.30.h.2) gives details on seventy-four prostitutes in an often grotesque pseudopoetic style. The lists for the years 1789–93 carry the shelfmark P.C.22 a. 13–15. There are several references to this well-known publication. Cuthbert Shaw, in his poem, *The Race*, 1765, attributes the paternity of the directory to Samuel Derrick; Grosley alludes to it in *Londres*, Lausanne, 1770, I, 96, the title then being *Nouvelles Atalantes*; see also *Nocturnal Revels*, II, 53, where the anonymous author complains of the more and more frequent errors this publication contains year after year.

47   XI, p. 262. Other remarks on the sea in the **TFI**, *Works*, XI, 377, 430. On the sea as a poetic theme in the eighteenth century, see *La Mer et les Poètes Anglais*, Paris, 1912, by Jules Douady, pp. 152–95.

48   *Un Voyageur Français en Angleterre en 1764, Elie de Beaumont*, extracts published in *Revue Britannique*, 71e année, no. 11 (Nov. 1895), p. 139 (trans.).

49   See George, op. cit. supra, n. 43, p. 129.

50   Robert J. Courtine, *L'Assassin est à votre table*, Paris, 1969.

Chapter 8
Structures of the comic

1   See Thomas R. Preston, 'Disenchanting the Man of Feeling: Smollett's FCF', in L. S. Champion, ed., *Quick Springs of Sense*, Univ. of Georgia Press, 1974, p. 228, where the author suggests that the last line is an allusion to Fielding's *An Essay on the Knowledge of the Characters of Men*, 1743.

2   Edward Topham, *Letters from Edinburgh*, London, 1776, p. 83.

3   *The Mirror*, no. lxxxiii (Feb. 1780), pp. 329–32. The author (no doubt a Scot himself since this periodical was published in Edinburgh) suggests three kinds of causes: psycho-economical (necessity for the Scot to expatriate himself or to lead a very hard life in his own country), geographical and social (distance from the Court), linguistic (the Scottish dialect is the spontaneous language of everyday, English the solemn language of state occasions).

4   Alexander Carlyle, *Autobiography*, 1910, p. 232.

5   *Edinburgh Review*, xxv (Oct. 1815), 485.

6   See the list of his articles at the end of the bibliography given by Parreaux in his edition of HC, p. xxxvii. Four other articles by Boggs should be added: 'Hassock of hair', *N & Q*, ccv (Feb. 1960), 72–3; *N & Q*, ccxi (Dec. 1966), 464, on the expressions 'Birthday suit' and 'cheese-toaster'; 'A Win Jenkins' Lexicon', *BNYPL*, lxviii (May 1965), 323–30; 'Win Jenkins' first citations in the OED', *WSt*, xli, no. 5, 5.

7   See *HLQ*, xi (Aug. 1948), 361–85.

8   P. M. Griffith, 'Fire-scenes in Richardson's *Clarissa* and Smollett's *Humphry Clinker*; a study of a literary relationship in the structure of the novel', *TSE*, xi (1962), 39—51.

9   W. Kenrick, *Fun*, London, 1752, pp. 15—16. This quotation is all the more interesting because at the beginning of the play Kenrick parodies the witches' scene in *Macbeth*, and makes them throw **RR** and **PP** into the cauldron. Fielding appears among the characters under the pseudonym of Sir Alexander Draw-cansir. It is possible that Kenrick intended to represent Smollett in the person of Sir Nackadil Trunnion.

10 J. A. Jencks [W. Beckford], *Azemia*, 2nd edn, London, 1798, I, 14. See also on the following page Wappingshot's physical mutilations, and p. 27 an allusion to Smollett's Narcissa in order to describe the beautiful Azemia with a parodic and delirious enthusiasm.

11 See the edition of this essay published by the Augustan Reprint Society, Series I, no. 4, 1947, quotations p. 12 and p. 23. For the sake of simplicity, the typo-graphical diversity has been disregarded.

12 Buck, 1927, pp. 43—4.

13 Thomas Brown, *Amusements Serious and Comical*, London, 1700, III, 88.

14 Ned Ward, *The Wooden World*, Society for Nautical Research, 1929, pp. [49]—50. The equestrian misfortunes of Trunnion have their counterpart in the same book where the boatswain is unhorsed in as comical a manner as Trunnion.

15 See William Matthews, 'Tarpaulin arabick in the days of Pepys', in *Essays Dedicated to L. B. Campbell*, Univ. of California Press, 1950, pp. 111—36.

16 *The Connoisseur*, no. 84 (Sept. 4th 1755), p. 506.

17 William N. Glascock, *Naval Sketch-Book*, 2nd series, London, 1834; analysis of Trunnion's last words, p. 126; see the whole article, 'Strictures on Smollett', pp. 121—40.

18 See also I, 21 and II, 255.

19 See the possible slang meanings in the eighteenth century of words like 'tackle' and 'poop' in Partridge's dictionary. The images 'He kept his guns always loaded', 'his shot being expended', or 'his match burnt out' may well conceal sexual allusions.

20 See for example Act III, sc. 2, where Shakespeare also brings together an Irish-man (Macmorris) and a Scot (Jamy). On the problem of Irish and Welsh types on the stage and their pronunciation see the following articles: J. O. Bartley, 'The development of a stock-character', *MLR*, xxxvii (Oct. 1942), [438]—47 and the sequel xxxviii (1943), [279]—88. The first article deals with the Irish type up to 1800, the second with the Scottish and the Welsh. See also the more technical article, 'Pre-nineteenth century Stage Irish and Welsh pronunciation', by J. O. Bartley and D. L. Sims, *PAPS*, xciii (Nov. 1949), 439—47.

21 See e.g. W. A. Boggs, 'Win Jenkins' Malapropisms', *Jamnu and Kashmir University Review*, iv (Dec. 1961).

22 See **RR**, I, 245—6, 276—7, 280—1.

23 See also in *Tom Jones* Sophia's ex-maid Mrs Honour's letter reproduced, Fielding insists *verbatim et literatim*, an expression he has already used in *Joseph*

Andrews about the indictment written by the lawyer Scout and Thomas Trotter (Book iv, Chapter v). Mrs Honour's letter (Book xv, Chapter x) is more a simple, even simplistic, phonetic transcription than a many-levelled verbal creation.

24   S. Freud, *Jokes and their Relation to the Unconscious*, newly translated from the German and edited by James Strachey, Routledge, 1960, p. 98.

25   Here Smollett perhaps improves on the verbal creation of Anstey who, in Letter v of the *New Bath Guide*, 1766, speaks of a 'French Valee de Sham'.

26   Giorgio Melchiori in his essay, 'Joyce and the tradition of the novel' in *The Tightrope Walkers*, Routledge, 1956, suggests (p. 47) that these transformations, sometimes not devoid of indecent implications, are also a characteristic feature of *Finnegans Wake*.

27   Boggs, op. cit., p. 138.

28   Freud, op. cit., p. 98.

29   A synthetic study of this question can be found in my article, 'Les procédés du comique dans *Humphry Clinker*', *Actes du Congrès de Lille*, Paris, Didier, 1966, pp. 53–75.

30   On this burlesque ode, see Buck, 1925, pp. 107–10.

31   See Sailendra Kumar Sen, 'Sheridan's literary debt: *The Rivals* and *Humphry Clinker*', *MLQ*, xxi (Dec. 1960), 291–300, and Jean Dulck's thesis, *Les Comédies de R. B. Sheridan*, Bordeaux, 1962, pp. 126–9 on the predecessors of Mrs Malaprop.

32   See William W. Huse, 'Pickle and Pickwick', *Washington University Studies*, x (Oct. 1922), 143–54, and Frans Dirk Wierstra's detailed study, *Smollett and Dickens*, Den Helder, 1928. One might also consult Frank Wilson's older thesis, *Dickens in seinen Beziehungen zu den Humoristen Fielding und Smollett*, Leipzig, 1889.

33   Anthony Burgess, *Nothing Like the Sun*, Heinemann, 1964. Penguin edn, 1966, p. 154.

Select bibliography

I General works

A complete critical bibliography of Smollett's novels would fill a whole volume. For the usual sources of bibliographical information, the student of Smollett may turn to: *The New Cambridge Bibliography of English Literature*, vol. II, *1660–1800*, edited by George Watson, Cambridge U.P., 1971, cols 962–70, best completed, for periodical bibliographies, by Richard A. Gray, *Serial Bibliographies in the Humanities and Social Sciences*, Ann Arbor, Michigan, The Pierian Press, 1969. A list of these general works of bibliography will be found in P. G. Boucé, *Les Romans de Smollett*, Paris, 1971, pp. 452–3, to which should be added T. H. Howard-Hill, *Bibliography of British Literary Bibliographies*, Oxford, Clarendon Press, 1969, and L. M. Knapp, 'Smollett', in A. E. Dyson, ed., *The English Novel: select bibliographical guides*, Oxford U.P., 1973, pp. 112–27.

II Bibliographies of Smollett's works

Luella F. Norwood, 'A Descriptive Bibliography with Notes Bibliographical and Biographical of the Creative Works of Tobias Smollett, M.D., 1746–1771 with the posthumous "Ode to Independence", 1773', Yale PhD, 1931, 300 pp. This remains the only attempt at a full descriptive bibliography of Smollett's works. Although unpublished, it may be obtained in Xerox or microfilm: see *Dissertation Abstracts*, xxx, no. 9 (March 1970), 3914 A.

Nearly all the major critical or biographical studies of Smollett contain more or less selective bibliographies. The four novels published in the Oxford U.P. 'Oxford English Novels' series so far (December 1974), viz. *Peregrine Pickle* (1964), *Humphry Clinker* (1966), *Ferdinand Count Fathom* (1971), *Launcelot Greaves* (1973), also present useful (general and more specific) critical bibliographies. Among the more useful, in chronological order, the following may be quoted.
David Hannay, *Life of Tobias Smollett*, London, 1887, pp. i–ix, a bibliography compiled by John P. Anderson.
Eugène Joliat, *Smollett et la France*, Paris, 1935, pp. 255–69: a bibliography of

391

Select bibliography

Smollett's novels translated into French, German, Dutch, Danish, Swedish, Russian, Czechoslovakian, Spanish, Italian; pp. 270–4: a general bibliography.

Claude E. Jones, *Smollett Studies*, Berkeley and Los Angeles, 1942, pp. 129–33 (repr. Phaeton Press, New York, 1970).

Fred. W. Boege, *Smollett's Reputation as a Novelist*, Princeton U.P., 1947, pp. 150–68 (repr. New York, Octagon Books, 1969).

Lewis M. Knapp, *Tobias Smollett Doctor of Men and Manners*, Princeton U.P., 1949 (repr. New York, Russell, 1963, pp. 339–40).

M. A. Goldberg, *Smollett and the Scottish School*, Albuquerque, 1959, pp. 187–91.

R. D. Spector, *Tobias Smollett*, New York, 1968, pp. 161–7.

P. G. Boucé, *Les Romans de Smollett*, Paris, 1971, pp. 452–7.

III Bibliographies of Smollett criticism

Francesco Cordasco, *Smollett Criticism, 1770–1924: a bibliography enumerative and annotative*, Long Island U.P., 1948, pp. iv, 28. Numbers 305 items. Still useful in spite of its numerous errors or omissions. Should be completed by P. G. Boucé, 'Smollett criticism, 1770–1924: Corrections and Additions', *N & Q*, xiv, new series, no. 5 (May 1967), 184–7.

Francesco Cordasco, *Smollett Criticism, 1925–1945: a compilation*, Long Island U.P., 1948, 9 pp. This checklist also has errors and omissions. The most important are:

1926

Add: **Elizabeth Binz-Winiger**, *Erziehungsfragen in den Romanen von Richardson, Fielding, Smollett, Goldsmith und Sterne*, Weida, 1926, 86 pp. On Smollett, pp. 34–61.

Herbert Read, *Reason and Romanticism*, Faber, 1926, 229 pp; article on Smollett: pp. 187–205. The same article is reproduced in Herbert Read's, *Collected Essays in Literary Criticism*, Faber, 1938, 2nd edn, 1951, London.

1928

Add: **Frans Dirk Wiestra**, *Smollett and Dickens*, Den Helder, 1928, 117 pp. The most complete work on the question of literary influence.

1929

Correct p. 2, no. 12: **Charles Knapp**, 'The classical element in Smollett, *Roderick Random*', *The Classical Weekly*, xxiii, no. 2 (Oct. 14th 1929), 9–11, and the continuation: 'General classical allusions and quotations' (Oct. 21st 1929), 17–19.

Add: **Lewis M. Knapp**, 'Smollett's admirers in eighteenth-century America', *Williams Alumni Review*, xxii, no. 3 (Dec. 1929), 114–15.

1930

Add: **Ursula Habel**, *Die Nachwirkung des Picaresken Romans in England*, Breslau & Oppeln, 1930, 77 pp.

1931

Add: **Lewis M. Knapp**: Letter to *TLS* (Jan. 8th 1931), p. 28, in which he corrects E. A. Baker's erroneous views on the success of *Roderick Random* which by January 1750 numbered four editions.

H. F. Watson, *The Sailor in English Fiction and Drama*, New York, Columbia U.P., 1931, 241 pp.; on *The Reprisal*, pp. 156–7; on *Roderick Random*, pp. 164–9.

1932

Add: **Norman Collins**, *The Facts of Fiction*, Gollancz, 1932, 284 pp.; see pp. 56–69.

Constantia Maxwell, *The English Traveller in France 1698–1815*, Routledge, 1932, pp. ix, 301; on Smollett and TFI, see pp. 77–96.

Exchange of letters in *TLS* on Smollett's language. The most important is J. M. Purcell, 'A note on Smollett's language' (April 14th 1932), p. 271; see also letters in *TLS*, April 21st, p. 291, and April 28th, p. 311.

1933

Add: **Godfrey Frank Singer,** *The Epistolary Novel,* Philadelphia, 1933; repr. New York, Russell, 1963, pp. ix, 266. References to **HC,** pp. 101, 107.

1934

Add: **C. E. Jones,** 'Tobias Smollett on the separation of the pubic joint in pregnancy', *Medical Life,* xli (June 1934), 302–5.

Somerset Maugham, 'Tobie Smollett à Nice 1763–1765', an article translated into French by Mrs E. R. Blanchet, in *Les Anglais dans le Comté de Nice et en Provence depuis le XVIII ème siècle,* Nice, 1934, 237 pp. See pp. 13–22.

George Doublet, 'Les consuls de la nation Britannique à Nice, aux XVIIe et XVIIIe siècles' in ibid., pp. 39–60, which gives some details on John Buckland (and his wife), who was the English consul in Nice when Smollett stayed there.

1935

Add: **F. C. Green,** *Minuet,* Dent, 1935, 489 pp. On Smollett, see pp. 348–64, a very spirited study which can still be read with profit.

H. R. S. van der Veen, *Jewish Characters in XVIIIth Century English Fiction and Drama,* Groningen, 1935, 308 pp.; see pp. 37–50.

1936

Add: 'The Modern Library' edition of **HC,** London, 1936, with an introduction by Arthur Machen, pp. v, xii, and notes, pp. 431–3. American edition (New York) in 1929.

E. L. Allhusen, letter in *TLS* (Feb. 29th 1936), p. 188, on a translation in 1753 of **PP.**

1939

Add: **James E. Tobin,** *Eighteenth Century Literature and its Cultural Background,* New York, Fordham U.P., 1939, pp. vii, 190, see pp. 157–8.

1942

Correct p. 7, no. 59: The correct reference is: Alice Parker, 'Tobias Smollett and the Law, *SP,* xxxix (July 1942), no. 3, 545–58.

1944

Add: **L. M. Knapp,** 'Dr John Armstrong, Littérateur and Associate of Smollett, Thomson, Wilkes, and other Celebrities', *PMLA,* lix (Dec. 1944), 1019–58.

1945

Add: **Sir Herbert Richmond,** 'The naval officer in fiction', in *Essays and Studies,* Oxford U.P., 1945, xxx, 7–25; see references to Smollett's tars, pp. 13–15.

James Sutherland, 'Some aspects of eighteenth-century prose', in *Essays on the Eighteenth Century,* presented to David Nichol Smith, Oxford U.P., 1945, pp. 94–110; references to Smollett, *passim.*

The above additions and corrections are by no means exhaustive. It is a great pity and something of a blot on the Smollettian scholarly escutcheon that F. Cordasco's faulty bibliographical compilations should have been reprinted without any serious attempt at revision and correction. The first pamphlet (1770–1924) was reprinted in 1969 by Darby Books, Pa. Both pamphlets are reproduced in Cordasco's *Eighteenth Century Bibliographies,* The Scarecrow Press, Inc., Metuchen, N.J., 1970, pp. iii, 230; see pp. 7–38, 39–53.

Donald M. Korte, *An Annotated Bibliography of Smollett Scholarship 1946–1968,* University of Toronto Press, 1969, pp. vii, 54. This most useful work of reference numbers 241 items. For some additions and corrections to this bibliography, see my review of it, *EA,* xxiii, no. 3, 1970, 343–4.

IV Critical studies since 1925, in chronological order

Howard Swazey Buck, *A Study in Smollett, chiefly Peregrine Pickle,* Yale U.P., 1925, 216 pp.

Select bibliography

Arnold Whitridge, *Tobias Smollett, a Study of His Miscellaneous Works*, published by the author (n.p., n.d. [1925]), repr. Darby Books, 1968, pp. x, 129.

Howard Swazey Buck, *Smollett as Poet*, Yale U.P., 1927, 93 pp.; repr. Folcroft Press, 1969.

Eugène Joliat, *Smollett et la France*, Paris, Champion, 1935, 279 pp.

Claude E. Jones, *Smollett Studies*, Univ. of California Press, 1942, pp. xi, 29–133.

Louis L. Martz, *The Later Career of Tobias Smollett*, Yale U.P., 1942, pp. xi, 213; repr. Archon Books, 1968.

George M. Kahrl, *Tobias Smollett, Traveler–Novelist*, Univ. of Chicago Press, 1945, pp. xxiv, 165; repr. Octagon Books, 1968.

M. A. Goldberg, *Smollett and the Scottish School: Studies in Eighteenth Century Thought*, Univ. of New Mexico Press, 1959, pp. xiv, 192.

Donald Bruce, *Radical Dr Smollett*, London, Gollancz, 1964, 240 pp.

Robert Giddings, *The Tradition of Smollett*, Methuen, 1967, 215 pp.

Robert Donald Spector, *Tobias Smollett*, New York, Twayne, 1968, 175 pp.

Paul-Gabriel Boucé, *Les Romans de Smollett*, Paris, Didier, 1971, 470 pp.

John Vladimir Price, *Tobias Smollett: 'The Expedition of Humphry Clinker'*, London, Arnold, 1973, 63 pp.

V Selected studies 1969–75
Unpublished theses, reprints, and reviews are not included.

1969
Claude-Jean Bertrand, 'Humphry Clinker a "so-called Methodist"', *Bulletin de la Faculté des Lettres de Strasbourg*, xlvii, no. 4 (Jan. 1969), 189–202.

Paul-Gabriel Boucé, 'A note on Smollett's *Continuation of the Complete History of England*', *RES*, new series, xx, no. 77 (Feb. 1969), 57–61.

E. T. Helmick, 'Voltaire and *Humphry Clinker*', *Studies on Voltaire and The Eighteenth Century*, lxvii (Geneva, 1969), 59–64.

Robert Hopkins, 'The function of grotesque in *Humphry Clinker*', *HLQ*, xxxii, no. 2 (Feb. 1969), 163–77.

Wolfgang Iser, 'The generic control of the aesthetic response: an examination of *Humphry Clinker*', *Southern Humanities Review*, iii (1969), 243–57. The more extensive German version of this essay was published as 'Wirklichkeit und Form in Smolletts *Humphry Clinker*', in H. Friedrich and F. Schalk, eds, *Europäische Aufklärung*, Munich, 1967, pp. 87–115.

Arthur Sherbo, 'Win Jenkins' language', *PLL*, v (1969), 199–204. Corrects some errors in W. A. Boggs's various articles on the same subject.

William A. West, 'Matt Bramble's journey to health', *TSLL*, xi, no. 3 (1969), 1197–208.

See also D. M. Korte in Section III.

1970
Sheryl Barlow, 'The deception of Bath: malapropisms in Smollett's *Humphry Clinker*', *Michigan Academician*, ii, no. 4 (1970), 13–24.

Tuvia Bloch, 'A source for Smollett's Sir Mungo Barebones', *N & Q*, new series, xvii, no. 3 (1970), 95–6.

Paul-Gabriel Boucé, '*Humphry Clinker*: esquisse de panorama critique', *EA*, xxiii, no. 4 (1970), 425–35; gives a survey of modern editions and recent criticism.

O. M. Brack, Jr, and James B. Davis, 'Smollett revisions of *Roderick Random*', *PBSA*, lxiv, no. 3 (1970), 295–311.

Andrea Cozza, *Tobias Smollett*, Bari, 1970, 329 pp. (in Italian). A study of Smollett's life and works, often enthusiastic, but at times unreliable.

William B. Dillingham, 'Melville's Long Ghost and Smollett's Count Fathom', *AL*, xlii (May 1970), 232—5.

Philip J. Klukoff, 'Smollett's Defence of Dr. Smellie in the *Critical Review*', *Medical History*, xiv (1970), 31—41.

Lewis M. Knapp, ed., *The Letters of Tobias Smollett*, Oxford, Clarendon Press, 1970, pp. xxiv, 161, with 108 letters, supersedes Noyes's edition of 1926 and Cordasco's *Letters of Tobias George Smollett*, Madrid, 1950, which contained several forgeries.

Donald M. Korte, 'Verse satire and Smollett's *Humphry Clinker*', *SSL*, vii, no. 3 (Jan. 1970), 188—92.

L. F. Powell, 'Tobias Smollett and William Huggins', in *Eighteenth Century Studies*, New York, Grolier Glub, 1970, pp. 311—22. Ten new Smollett letters, now in the Hyde Collection, and included in Knapp's edition listed above.

Scott B. Rice, 'The significance of Smollett's weather register', *N & Q*, new series, xvii, no. 3 (1970), 94—5; concerns **TFI**.

Diane Parkin Speer, 'Heinlein's *The Door into Summer* and *Roderick Random*', *Extrapolation*, xii, 30—4.

Gary N. Underwood, 'Linguistic realism in *Roderick Random*', *JEGP*, lxix, no. 1 (1970), 32—40; an interesting attempt at a phonetic analysis of the various dialects used in **RR**.

1971

Paul-Gabriel Boucé, *Les Romans de Smollett*, Paris, Didier, 1971, 470 pp.

Lillian de la Torre, 'New light on Smollett and the Annesley cause', *RES*, new series, xxii, no. 87 (1971), 274—81; concerns **PP**.

Paul Denizot, 'Une mal aimée; la Lady de Quality de Smollett', *Lan M*, lxv, no. 2 (1971), 57—60; on Lady Vane's 'Memoirs', in **PP**.

David L. Evans, 'Peregrine Pickle: the complete satirist', *SNNTS*, iii, no. 3 (1971), 258—74.

Frank Felsenstein, 'An unrecorded Smollett letter', *ArielE*, ii, no. 4 (1971), 87—9; dated Leghorn, January 9th 1771, to an unknown correspondent (a Scottish medical friend of Smollett's) to recommend a young Scottish surgeon, Mr Cochrane. This letter should be compared with no. 105 in Knapp's edition. Smollett writes he is holding out 'wonderfully', but complains he is 'much troubled with sudden attacks of the *Tussis convulsiva*' (p. 89).

Alice Green Fredman, 'The picaresque in decline: Smollett's first novel', in John H. Middendorf, ed., *English Writers of the Eighteenth Century*, Columbia U.P., 1971, pp. 189—207; a sound appraisal of **RR**, which is definitely *not* a true picaresque novel.

Damian Grant, ed., *The Adventures of Ferdinand Count Fathom*, Oxford U.P., Oxford English Novels, 1971, pp. xxvi, 384.

Lewis M. Knapp, 'Rare and unrecorded publications of Smollett's works', *N & Q*, new series, xviii (Sept. 1971), 338—9.

Donald M. Korte, 'Smollett's *Advice* and *Reproof*: apprenticeship in satire', *SSL*, viii, no. 4 (1971), 239—52.

Frank McCombie, 'The strange distemper of Narcissa's aunt', *N & Q*, new series, xviii (1971), 55—6; deals with the eccentric virtuosa in **RR**.

C. J. Rawson, 'Fielding and Smollett', in Roger Lonsdale, ed., *Dryden to Johnson*, Sphere History of Literature in the English language, IV, London, 1971, 259—301; on Smollett: pp. 287—95. As all too frequent, heavily biased towards Fielding.

Sondra Rosenberg, 'Travel literature and the picaresque novel', *EnlE*, ii, no. 1 (1971), 40—7; considers Fielding's *Journal*, Smollett's **TFI** and Sterne's *A Sentimental Journey*.

George S. Rousseau, 'Tobias Smollett doctor by design, writer by choice', *JAMA*, ccvi (April 5th 1971), 85—9.

Select bibliography

George S. Rousseau, 'Smollett and the picaresque: some questions about a label', *SBHT*, xii, no. 3 (1971), 1186—904.

George S. Rousseau and Paul-Gabriel Boucé, 'Tobias Smollett and Roger Dibon: the case of the elusive translation', *N & Q*, new series, xviii (Feb. 1971), 55.

George S. Rousseau and Paul-Gabriel Boucé, eds, *Tobias Smollett: bicentennial essays presented to Lewis M. Knapp*, Oxford U.P., New York, 1971, 260 pp. For an analysis of the ten essays contained in this Festschrift, see *PQ*, li, no. 3 (1972), 767 and *YWES*, lii (1973), 285—6.

Albert Smith, 'The printing and publication of Smollett's *Peregrine Pickle*', *Library*, 5th series, xxvi, no. 1 (1971), 39—52; suggests that Strahan was the printer.

Robert Uphaus, 'Sentiment and spleen: travels with Sterne and Smollett', *CentR*, xv (1971), 406—21; holds that HC was partly an answer to Sterne's attack in *A Sentimental Journey* against the splenetic 'Smelfungus'.

1972

Paul-Gabriel Boucé 'Archibald Campbell on Smollett's style', *SSL*, ix, no. 4 (1972), 211—17; Campbell was the author of *Lexiphanes* (1767).

Paul-Gabriel Boucé 'Smollett's pseudo-picaresque: a response to Rousseau's 'Smollett and the picaresque', *SBHT*, xiv, no. 1 (1972), 73—9; cf. Rousseau's article listed above (1971).

Donald Bruce, 'Smollett and the sordid knaves', *CR*, ccxx, no. 1274 (1972), 133—8; on Smollett's political views and his admitted anti-Whig bias.

Lillian de la Torre, 'The melting Scot: a postscript to *Peregrine Pickle (1751—1772)*', *ELN*, x, no. 1 (1972), 20—7; cf. L. M. Knapp's and Mrs de la Torre's 1971 article; deals with Daniel MacKercher and his part in the Annesley cause.

Paul Denizot, 'Féminisme et immoralité chez trois personnages de Defoe et Smollett', in Michèle Plaisant, Paul Denizot and Françoise Moreux, eds, *Aspects du Féminisme en Angleterre*, Lille, PUL, 1972, pp. 51—67; a Marxist view of Moll Flanders, Roxana, and Lady Vane in PP.

Wolfgang Franke, '*Humphry Clinker* as a "party novel"', *SSL*, ix, nos 2—3 (1971—72), 97—106; examines Horace Walpole's famous dictum.

Gehrard Graband, Viktor Link, and Peter Nübold, 'Quantitative Methoden zur Stilanalyse von Texten: T. G. Smollett, *Roderick Random* (1748) and *Humphry Clinker* (1771)', *Mitteilungen der Technischen Universität Carolo-Wilhelmina zu Braunschweig*, vii, no. 4 (1972), 6 pp.

James Milton Highsmith, 'Smollett's Nancy Williams: a mirror for Maggie', *English Miscellany*, no. 23, Rome, 1972, pp. 113—23.

T. K. Pratt, 'Linguistics, criticism, and Smollett's *Roderick Random*', *UTQ*, xlii, no. 1 (Fall 1972), 26—39; a forceful (if somewhat needlessly aggressive at times) plea in favour of the application of M. A. K. Halliday's 'system-structure' grammar to literary analysis.

Scott B. Rice, 'Smollett's *Travels* and the genre of Grand Tour literature', *Costerus*, i (1972), 207—20.

Angus Ross, 'The "show of violence" in Smollett's novels', *YES*, ii (1972), 118—29.

George S. Rousseau, 'Smollett and Sterne: a revaluation', *Archiv*, ccviii, nos 4—6 (1972), 286—97.

George S. Rousseau, 'Controversy or collusion? the Lady Vane tracts', *N & Q*, new series, xix (Oct. 1972), 375—8; interesting for the background of the 'Memoirs of a Lady of Quality' in PP.

Beverly Scafidel, 'Smollett's *Humphry Clinker*', *Expl*, xxx (1972), item 54; analyses the paradigmatic role of the dog Chowder.

John F. Sena, 'The satiric persona of Smollett's *Travels*', *SSL*, x, no. 1 (1972), 81—99.

John M. Warner, 'Smollett's development as a novelist', *Novel*, v, no. 2 (1972), 148—61.

1973

Jerry C. Beasley, 'English fiction in the 1740's: some glances at the major and minor novels', *SNNTS*, v, no. 2 (1973), 155—75; not primarily concerned with Smollett, but contains useful background information on contemporary fiction.

Douglas Brooks, *Number and Pattern in the Eighteenth Century Novel*, Routledge, 1973, pp, x, 198; see pp. 123—59 for an attempted numerological analysis of **RR**, **PP**, **FCF** and **HC**; very ingenious, less convincing, but occasionally illuminating.

David Evans, ed., *Sir Launcelot Greaves*, Oxford U.P., Oxford English Novels, 1973, pp. xxvii, 234.

Frank Felsenstein, 'None of your knockers-down': John Fielding and Smollett's watch', *EA*, xxvi, no. 3 (1973), 269—77. A biographical footnote (Smollett was robbed of his watch in December 1754) which serves as an interesting illustration of John Fielding's methods of criminal investigation.

R. M. Ford, 'A verbal echo: *Humphry Clinker* and Johnson's *Journey*', *N & Q*, new series, xx, no. 6 (1973), 221.

Nan Gillespie, 'All that the Riviera is, it owes to Tobias Smollett', *New York Times* (Travel Section), May 20th 1973.

Linda Pannil, 'Some patterns of imagery in *Humphry Clinker*', *Thoth*, Fall (1973), 37—43.

George S. Rousseau, 'No boasted academy of Christendom: Smollett and the Society of Arts', *Journal of the Royal Society of Arts*, Part I (June 1973), 468—75; Part II (July 1973), 532—5; Part III (August 1973), 623—8.

John M. Warner, 'The interpolated narratives in the fiction of Fielding and Smollett: an epistemological view', *SNNTS*, v, no. 3 (1973), 271—83.

See also **A. E. Dyson** in Section I and **J. V. Price** in Section IV.

1974

Edward Copeland, '*Humphry Clinker*: a comic pastoral poem in prose?', *TSLL*, xvi, no. 3 (1974), 493—501.

David Daiches, 'Smollett reconsidered', in *Miscellanea Anglo-Americana* Festschrift für Helmut Viebrock, 1974, pp. 109—36. A vigorous and perceptive reappraisal.

Robin Fabel, 'The patriotic Briton: Tobias Smollett and English politics, 1756—1771', *ECS*, viii, no. 1 (1974), 100—14.

Robert Folkenflik, 'Self and society: comic union in *Humphry Clinker*', *PQ*, liii, no. 2 (1974), 195—204.

Byron Gassman, '*Humphry Clinker* and the Two Kingdoms of George III', *Criticism*, xvi, no. 2 (1974), 95—108.

Wolfgang Iser, *The Implied Reader: Patterns of Communication from Bunyan to Beckett*, Johns Hopkins U.P., 1974, pp. 57—80: 'The generic control of the esthetic response: an examination of Smollett's *Humphry Clinker*'. Reproduces, with some slight modifications the 1969 article listed above.

Thomas R. Preston, 'The "stage passions" and Smollett's characterization', *SP*, lxxi, no. 1 (Jan. 1974), 105—25.

Thomas R. Preston, 'Disenchanting the Man of Feeling: Smollett's *Ferdinand Count Fathom*', in Larry S. Champion, ed., *Quick Springs of Sense*, Univ. of Georgia Press, 1974, pp. 223—39.

[William Rider], *An Historical and Critical Account of the Living Authors of Great-Britain*, London, 1762, The Augustan Reprint Society, no. 163, 1974, pp. v, 34; on Smollett see pp. 11—12. As noted in the introduction by O. M. Brack, Jr, this is probably the earliest biographical and critical account of Smollett, antedating David Erskine Baker's *The Companion to the Play-House* by two years.

Pat Rogers, *The Augustan Vision*, Weidenfeld & Nicolson, 1974, 318 pp.; see pp. 292—8 on Smollett's novels. Occasionally brilliant, but on the whole displays little deep understanding of Smollett's fiction, especially *Humphry Clinker* which Pat Rogers most wilfully misreads.

Michael Rymer, 'Another source for Smollett's Lismahago', *N & Q*, new series, xxi, no. 2 (1974), 57—9.

Donald T. Siebert, 'The role of the senses in *Humphry Clinker*', *SNNTS*, vi, no. 1 (1974), 17—26.

1975 (up to August)

Paul-Gabriel Boucé, 'Smollett et le roman du dix-huitième siècle', *EA*, xxviii, no. 2 (1975), 183—9.

Paul-Gabriel Boucé, 'The Duke of Newcastle's Levee in Smollett's *Humphry Clinker*', *YES*, v (1975), 136—41.

Frank Felsenstein, 'An early abridgement of Smollett's *Peregrine Pickle*', *N & Q*, xxii, no. 1 (1975), 13—14.

Frederick R. Karl, *A Reader's Guide to the Development of the English Novel in the 18th Century*, Thames and Hudson, 1975, 360 pp.; see pp. 183—204: 'Smollett's *Humphry Clinker*: the choleric temper'. A superficial and mostly negative reading of *Humphry Clinker*, replete with the usual hoary critical clichés.

Thomas R. Preston, *Not in Timon's Manner: Feeling, Misanthropy, and Satire in Eighteenth-Century England*, University of Alabama Press, 1975; see pp. 69—120: 'Tobias Smollett — A Risible Misanthrope'. A thorough and stimulating — at times even startling — discussion of Smollett's five novels, which Preston attempts to place in the satirical and artistic tradition of the benevolent misanthrope.

G. S. Rousseau and **Roger A. Hambridge**, 'David Herbert: Victorian editor of Smollett', *Library Review*, xxv, no. 1 (1975), 17—20.

R. D. Spector, 'An attack on the *Critical Review* in *Political Controversy*', *N & Q*, xxii, no. 1 (1975), 14.

Index